Since Julia Child made this remark, *Feasts for All Seasons* has become one of the most talked about and widely used cookbooks of recent years because of its unique and innovative plan. De Groot divides his text into four sections—winter, spring, summer, and fall. For each season he reviews for the prospective cook the special culinary pleasures at that time of year. He then explains how best to shop for ingredients needed in the recipes that follow. The range is wide—from the adventurous to the practical and simple.

In the de Groot household every meal is a delight whether it be hearty peasant fare for a blustery night, a leisurely Sunday breakfast, or a summer supper of fresh crayfish. While the family celebrates some of the principal feast days of different countries with authentic national dishes (and a few of these menus are in each quarter of the book), for the most part the recipes are planned for day-to-day family meals: appetizers and soups, main dishes of meat, birds, game, fish, and shellfish; a surprising variety of vegetables, of substitutes for the usual potato, of salads both cultivated and wild; and desserts with an emphasis on the marriage of seasonal fruits to suitable cheeses. De Groot includes economical recipes that make good use of leftovers, and at the end of each quarter he supplies notes on wines appropriate to the season.

In the words of one reviewer, *Feasts for All Seasons* is "truly a gourmet's delight."

ILLUSTRATIONS BY
Tom Funk

FEASTS FOR ALL SEASONS

by Roy Andries de Groot

McGraw-Hill Book Company

NEW YORK · ST. LOUIS · SAN FRANCISCO
DÜSSELDORF · MEXICO · TORONTO

 Parts of this book appeared originally in *Ladies' Home Journal.*

123456789 KPKP 79876

Typography design by Warren Chappell

Library of Congress Cataloging in Publication Data

de Groot, Roy Andries
Feasts for all seasons.

Includes index.
1. Cookery, International. I. Funk, Tom.
II. Title.
TX725.A1D4 1976 641.5'9 76-179
ISBN 0-07-016271-9
ISBN 0-07-016272-7 pbk.

To The Three Sisters

R., V., and N.

Acknowledgements

THIS BOOK BEGAN as an idea within our family. It became the shared project of many of our friends. We owe the most intense debt of gratitude to Virginia Leon de Vivero who, for three years, concentrated her rare creative skill on the problem of shaping a formless mass of ideas and notes into the ordered plan of this book. Other friends tested and retested our recipes, tasted and retasted our favorite dishes, read and reread each new page, and added a part of themselves to the manuscript. For this service of friendship we thank especially Clare Boulter Baines, Vaughan Barton, Lona Dubilier, Dorothy Dutton, Celia Eisenberg, Lois Heller, Jane Sufian, and Johanna Wright. For help in organizing our notes on aromatic herbs and spices we thank two friends with wide experience in managing herb farms: Emily Gaar and Patricia Winter. Other friends tasted our favorite wines and helped to confirm, or modify, the opinions expressed in the wine notes throughout the book and the wine directory at the end. Among the drinkers, we remember James Barton, Americo Lugo-Romero, Ruedi Trenka, and especially Robert Heller who from his vantage point in London contributed background information and sparkling ideas on European wines. Then there were the young friends who did the hard day-to-day work: Alice Thomas, at the beginning, Marian Hodges, during the writing, and at the end, when words were fixed in print, Linda MacDonald and Frederick Koyle. For the sustaining strength of their enthusiasm, we shall always be grateful.

Roy Andries de Groot

New York City

P.S. Our gratitude also to our dog, Ñusta, for her patience under the desk during long hours of dictation on the tape recorder, and for her willingness, in the kitchen, to taste absolutely anything at any time.

Prologue

ON BECOMING A GOURMET

CAN THIS BOOK, or any book, teach the average person with an average interest in food to be a gourmet? The answer lies in a clear understanding of the meaning of the word "gourmet," which is surely one of the most overworked and ill-understood in our language. Insistent signs in supermarkets invite the shopper into the "gourmet-foods department," where one might almost expect to find magic potions to produce an effortless fine meal. Every day we read and hear the phrases "gourmet cookery," "gourmet recipe," "gourmet kitchen." But the fact is that the word "gourmet" is not just another adjective in the language of salesmanship, like "super," or "fancy," or "special." It is a title that applies only to a person, a title of honor, confirming certain skills which have been learned by study and practice.

Many French historians believe that the word derives from the *gromet* of the court of Louis XIV at Versailles. The noblemen in their châteaux across France were getting restive. The king, fearing that they might conspire against him, ordered them all to Versailles. There, to keep idle hands busy, he created a large number of jobs around the palace. A business manager was appointed to each household department and given the title of *gromet.* (Some *gromets* managed the royal stables and today we still speak of the man who looks after a horse as a "groom.") The duties of the food *gromets* were clearly defined. The royal food supply depended on the French "tithe" system—each producer had to contribute one tenth of his harvest as a tax—but there was serious discontent among the farmers, fishermen, butchers, millers, wine growers, etc., and each tried to hold back the best of the produce from the king. The first order of the day, therefore, for the royal food *gromets* was to ride out and bring in the proper amounts of the best foods. They had to be sharp judges of quality and value.

This was half the battle in getting good meals at Versailles. It is *more* than half the battle for the gourmet of today, in a world where the imitation often looks better than the real thing and where price seems to bear less and less relationship to quality. No amount of cooking skill in the kitchen can produce a fine meal on the table, unless it is preceded by selective skill in the market. Far more is involved than simply finding a "good buy." It is a matter of getting the right grade for the right purpose and often the higher-priced grade can be quite wrong. For example, in certain types of slow-cooked beef stews, the best grades of sirloin steak would be much too soft and would disintegrate long before the full flavor had been achieved. Again, the preparation of a concentrated chicken stock, where the accent is more on the broth than on the chicken, should start inexpensively with a tough old hen, which can be simmered for hours.

Since the problem of getting the right grade of the right food at the right time is crucial to the gourmet, a substantial part of this book is devoted to the basic questions of efficient shopping. Which are the best foods in season at various times of the year? How much bone and fat is in the various cuts of meat? How does one find better blends of coffees and teas? Which wines are consistently good from year to year? These are among the multitude of questions which must be answered by the gourmet in the market.

When the best supplies were safely gathered into the storerooms at Versailles, the skilled food *gromets* moved into the kitchens. The huge fires were tended by semi-skilled peasants who could roast or bake according to a traditional "rule." But often the fires grew too hot, or the flour was coarser than usual, or the age of the mutton was misjudged. Then the fixed rule broke down and the *gromets* had to take control to save the royal supper.

The need for flexible judgment in the kitchen is the same today. It is impossible to guarantee a perfect result simply by telling the cook to put X pounds of meat into an oven at Y degrees for Z minutes. In an effort to make this book a guide toward the standards of a gourmet, its recipes take account of the variable factors and go beyond the mere uniting of fixed amounts of ingredients in a rigid series of 1–2–3 steps. Instead there is a clear definition of the result that is being sought and of the signs of progress. How is the taste developing at the halfway point? How soft should the meat feel when pressed after the first 30 minutes? How should the color change?

The final duties of the skilled food *gromets* at Versailles were those of the *officiers de la bouche*—the last tasting before service to the king. As each course was ready to be carried to the dining hall on the enormous platters, usually borne by four men, there was a last checking of seasonings. Finally, at the table, the *gromet*-of-the-day had to taste once more in the royal presence to assure the king that all was perfection—and, incidentally, not poisoned!

This then is our three-way definition of a gourmet: one who can expertly judge food in the market, who has both skill and flexibility in the kitchen and who shows, at the table, an exquisite sensitivity to the needs and desires of his guests.

To develop these three qualities is the objective of this book.

PREFACE

To The Revised Edition

When I re-read the original text, which has now been in print for almost ten years, in preparation for this new edition, I was happily surprised to find how few changes were really necessary. Almost a decade of opening letters from readers of this book has confirmed that the deep pleasures and satisfactions that we, as a family, have always found in dining on these menus and dishes, is equally discovered by readers who seriously try the recipes, who take the trouble to learn the techniques of shopping for the right ingredients, and who follow the essential rules of menu-planning and preparation.

When the original text was written, the "gastronomic revolution" in the United States was just beginning. Many of the finest imported ingredients were hard to find. The "fancy food" business was still relatively small. One had to search for imported wild mushrooms, for black or white truffles, for Italian *mostarda di frutta,* for Spanish *membrillo,* for Greek *tarama*—even for first-quality Hungarian paprika, or coarse crystal sea salt. This was why, in the first edition, I included an "Index of Marketing and Mail-Order Sources" with the names and addresses of shops and suppliers of rare ingredients across the country. Now, ten years later, there is hardly a city, town, or village that does not have a "gourmet department" in its local supermarkets and major stores. There are specialty cheese shops with dozens of exotic imported types. There are specialized kitchen equipment shops offering everything from Algerian *couscoussières* to Mongolian firepots and Swiss Roesti pans. Today, if I were to try to assemble a directory of every first-class food or equipment shop across the land, it would mean at least doubling the size of this book. So I have decided substantially to rewrite the Index of Sources (see page 699) and make it very much our personal directory of the people from whom we replenish our own store cupboard—people, in the main, who still have an idealistic determination to resist the easy temptations of mass-production and mass-marketing and to find their satisfactions in handling and distributing the finest quality of everything they touch.

There has been one other serious change in the past ten years. It seems to me that modern biochemical research has raised persuasive questions about health dangers in the regular use of MSG (monosodium glutamate) in cooking. Perhaps, originally, when this derivative of vegetable protein was produced by hand in small quantities in China as *mei jing* and in Japan as *aji-nomoto,* it may have been a natural product and an essential part of the cooking techniques when many of the ingredients were dried and not always entirely fresh. But today, in our Western world, where MSG is chemically manufactured by the millions of tons under various trade names, I firmly believe that its use in large quantities may be a potential danger to health and we have eliminated it from our kitchen. I would have liked to have taken out every reference to it in this book, but that would have involved large technical problems in terms of the reprinting. So I suggest that, if you agree with me, you will simply disregard the MSG wherever it appears in any recipe.

Our family, of course, has also changed in the ten years since this book was first published. Our children, who are so much interwoven into the text, because they played such an important part in the original writing, have now left home and my wife Katherine and I are again living as a duet rather than a quartet of cooks. But we still shop in the same way, still control our food budget (now more than ever) by the simple system proposed in the following pages, still have "encores" instead of "leftovers" and still count the recipes of this book as our lifetime favorites. Feasting by the Seasons remains an unchanging and unending joy.

Roy Andries de Groot

New York City
June 12th, 1975

CONTENTS

EPILOGUE

Recipes, Rules, and Menus

Introduction

A Quartet of Cooks

EXPLANATION OF SYMBOLS

A symbol appearing after a word refers the reader to a particular section of the book for further details. Example: olive oil, crystal salt, cocotte, dry white wine, Parmesan cheese, Beaujolais, turtle meat.

- stands for Raw Materials and Staples, pages 10–18
- stands for Aromatics, pages 18–29
- stands for Kitchen Equipment, pages 32–41
- stands for Wine in the Kitchen, pages 41–5
- stands for Cheeses, pages 660–75
- stands for Wines for the Table, pages 676–98
- stands for Marketing and Mail-Order Sources, pages 699–714

THIS BOOK is a record of the gastronomic experiences of our family, set down over many years and now arranged for the gastronomic pleasure of other families. One might say that both the experience and the writing began about forty-five years ago, one hot summer's day on a green and grassy bank of the river Danube about 20 miles south of Budapest, where I as a small boy had been taken by my mother for a picnic with Hungarian friends. The meal consisted of the wonderful cold meats of the region, accompanied by a locally grown green pepper with sweet and luscious outside flesh, but with fiery-hot inside ribs around the seed pod. Each picknicker, after cutting a chunk of the pepper, carefully sliced off the inside ribs. The Hungarian host prepared the first pieces for me, but when I asked for more, he gave me as a joke a piece with the rib left on. Greedily I stuffed it into my mouth and at once wept with the pain. For the rest of the day I could hardly swallow. That evening I noted the incident in my diary and resolved, from then on, to take an interest in the preparation of my food.

Accompanying my mother to various European countries, I began to be aware of the variety of national dishes. A few years later, in the kitchen of the family home in London, I began trying to reproduce some of them. In my teens, I founded my first Gourmet Society among fellow students. I was already a fairly accomplished cook when I found and married my Katherine, a blond girl of Scots-Irish descent, who knew the true meaning of Scottish *haggis,* tipsy laird, and Irish mutton stew, and admitted me to full partnership in her kitchen. In the requisite time there were two daughters, Christina and Fiona, who should perhaps have been born with boxwood spoons in their mouths.

The family developed into a quartet of busy individualists, each pursuing separate work and study interests. I became a journalist and broadcaster and explored many parts of the world. My wife's work as an actress in the theater took her away from home on national and international tours. In time we cooked in kitchens in London, Vienna, Budapest, Amsterdam, Paris, and across the Atlantic in Chicago, San Francisco, New Orleans and, finally, in New York.

Through much travel and separation the family has remained bound together by a passion for good eating. Since no member was ever at home all the time to cook for the others, each learned to plan and prepare a first-class meal. The most vivid memories of thirty years of family life are of the feasts around the dining table—a send-off on an important journey, the celebration of a new contract signed, homecomings, theatrical opening nights, publication days. Every celebration was also the fun of planning and working together.

From the beginning, when the girls were just old enough to be fascinated by turning the handle of the nutmeg grater, we tried to make the preparation of food an amusing game. When they came home from school, the meal was already underway, but they took turns on alternate days at being either P. E. (Pony Express) or K. H. (Kitchen Helper), with their weekly schedule up on the wall. P. E. would dash to the stores for last-minute shopping, while K. H. set the table and helped serve the food. At the same time, there were opportunities for self-expression and the development of individual skills. Each, on her seventh birthday, had been given a first solo assignment to mix and bake a simple filbert soufflé cake, and it was a moment of high excitement when the cake was taken from the oven. As the girls grew up, we developed more dishes for special occasions, and each season of our year had its traditional ceremonies.

Search for Variety

How did we capture the interest and imagination of our young children, in meal planning and preparation? The first rule of our game with food was always to try to achieve variety in the dishes that came to our table. Too many families seem to have too small a repertoire of favorite recipes and repeat them too often. Too many mothers allow themselves to be enslaved by the prejudices of children who, whenever a new dish is suggested, cry "We know what we like!" What they really mean is that they have no intention of liking anything they don't know. Our rule has always been to try anything once. Of course, we also have our favorite recipes to which we return again and again, especially those which celebrate the reappearance of the great seasonal delicacies, but we count any week ill spent if it has not included some gastronomic exploration. Clearly, an entirely new dish, often involving considerable work, is not produced every other day. It is the small daily variations that maintain an attractive suspense. A new sauce or garnish for a favorite vegetable. Different dressings for various salad combinations. Finding new ways to prepare the ubiquitous potato. We refuse to be bound by the standard herb affinities. How dull always to put basil with tomatoes and rosemary with lamb. We vary the blends of our coffees and the combinations of our teas.

For the sake of variety, we refuse to be bound by the concept of an "authentic" or "classic" version of any recipe. Some of our friends are so overawed by the aura of the French high cuisine that they dare not vary a single ingredient, or even the laboriously old-fashioned methods of preparation. Of course we always try to maintain the special character and personality of a regional dish. But many great recipes, like folk songs, travel around the world, adapting to local tastes and traditions, absorbing local ingredients and subtleties of flavor, so that eventually there are many variations, each with its own pleasure. There is a saying in Italy that there are as many ways of preparing the famous fish stew *cacciucco Toscana* as there are cooks in Tuscany.

Feast Days of the World

The second rule of our family gastronomy has been the exploration of the peoples and cultures of foreign nations through foods. When we travel, we always try to eat in small, unpretentious restaurants where local families dine, so that we "experience" a place through its simple but authentic dishes. At home, while our girls were in school, we thought we might add to their studies on world civilization by celebrating some of the foreign feast days at our own table; with traditional menus, the proper wines, serving customs, often the music of the country, and sometimes even a study of the festive costumes. We began with the *Diplomatic List* of the principal national holidays of the world prepared by the State Department and have gradually enlarged and adapted it. Visitors from far-off countries are always delighted when they find that we know something about their native gastronomy and, in turn, they have taught us some of our most exciting dishes.

In working out these foreign recipes, we regard each unknown ingredient as a challenge. In the "foreign" neighborhoods of large cities we have found virtually every kind of unusual food, generally in small family-owned shops—perhaps among the huge stone crocks filled with olives, the trays of pickled fish, the big burlap sacks of dried produce, the tubs of soft cheeses, or sausages and hams hung on the walls. Combing the foreign quarters of a city has always been one of the particular delights of food preparation for us and we often learn new ways of using the exotic foods in talking to the storekeepers and the other customers.

However, even away from the big cities, the extraordinary development of the international mail-order business has made it easier than ever to shop for foreign ingredients. Friends who live on top of the Black Mesa in Arizona have proved that they can stock a store cupboard full of delicacies simply by building up a card file of mail-order supply houses, as we have done over the years (see the "Index of Sources"). In today's smaller world, we can all share some part of every feast of every nation.

High versus Low Cuisine

The third rule that has helped to hold our family's interest in good eating is to avoid making a burden of cooking by spending too much time in the kitchen. Except for very special parties a few times a year, we avoid the classic *haute cuisine* dishes which involve complicated and lengthy preparation. Instead, our stress is on what the French call *bourgeois* dishes, prepared with fresh, rather than packaged or processed foods. In our experience, the people who eat with the greatest gusto and satisfaction day after day are the middle-income families of the rich agricultural lands. They raise and kill their own animals, grow their own fruits, vegetables, and aromatic herbs, and seem to make the most economical use of everything they have to hand.

Every region seems to have its native one-dish meal, brought to table in a huge clay pot, and we have learned to reproduce some of them in an American kitchen, using fresh meats and seasonal vegetables. These casseroles, ollas, toupins, etc., are simple to prepare, improve with keeping and reheating and are much more time-saving, economical, and delicious than the so-called short-cut foods.

The Game of Budget Control

Our fourth rule with food (and the one which is the most unexpected part of the fun) is the "numbers game" that we have made out of cost-saving. Our system involves no formal accounting, yet gives a day-by-day check on expenditures. Let us say, for example, that for one period we set daily costs at $1.50 per person, or $6.00 per day for a family of four. We keep a small diary by the telephone in the kitchen and write in it in red figures the amount that we ought to have spent on any particular day of the month at the $6.00 per day rate. Alongside these red figures, we write in black what we have actually spent to date in the current month. Comparing the red and black figures tells at a glance whether we are above, below, or close to the planned budget. Then, with our recipe cards divided into three separate files, we plan our meals by the following rules:

1. When food expenditures are running close to the average, we choose recipes from the file marked "Regular Family Meals."

2. When we find ourselves spending less than the budget estimate, or when the budget is entirely suspended for a few days in honor of guests, we choose from our file marked "Parties and Feast Days," in which time and cost are subsidiary factors.

3. When the danger signal appears, we turn to the file marked "Budget Pull-Back Meals" and we stay with them until the budget is under control.

Our children have always helped with this budgeting; often they have been more firm than their parents and would forgo a six-pack of Cokes until the budget was back in balance.

The recipes in this book are divided in the same way between "Party and Feast Day Menus," "Day-to-day Regular Family Meals," and "Budget Pull-Back Dishes."

The Best Foods of Every Season

We discovered very early in our family life that for almost every food there was one time of the year when the highest quality was combined with the lowest price. We began to write down on cards, month by month, the best foods we found in the stores and where they were coming from. We headed these cards "Special Pleasures of the Season," and when we came back to them year after year they told us what to expect: when to start looking for the first good local asparagus, when to expect the first shad, the soft-shell crabs, and the arrivals of all the fruits from the first spring rhubarb to the last of the winter apples.

In each season of the year our meal planning begins not with the haphazard question, "What do we feel like eating tomorrow?" but by looking first at our list of the "Foods in Season" (lists which are reproduced in this book), which tells us the foods that are likely to be at peak supply. Planning one's meals by nature's calendar is, after all, the oldest and most fundamental of all rules for good eating.

I
How to Use This Book

ONE DAY, while we were proofreading the finished manuscript of this book, our daughter Fiona said: "Once it's published, we'll be able to throw away all our card files." It is certainly true that this book includes the menus and recipes, basic rules, charts, directories, etc., taken from the many separate card-file boxes we have been stuffing with information for years. To use it most efficiently, start with the beginning of the season at hand. The year is divided into four gastronomic quarters: January and February combined under the "Winter Dog Days"; March, April, May, and June under "Spring"; July, August, and September under "Summer Harvest"; with the last quarter covering the "Fall Holidays" of October, November, and December. Each of these quarters starts with the tabulation of the "Special Pleasures of the Season" and lists of the abundant fish, fruits, salad greens, and vegetables. Here, with a choice of foods that are at their highest quality and lowest price, is where all menu planning should begin.

Each quarter also includes practical notes on shopping for the seasonal foods and a calendar of the season's principal feast days celebrated in various countries. This calendar is followed by a series of complete party menus with authentic national dishes of these feasts. While many of the party recipes are fairly elaborate and expansive, the family dishes, which follow in the next section, are relatively simple and quick. Yet all share one common characteristic: they make use of the seasonal foods at the peak of their abundance.

"Encores" Instead of Left-Overs

Following the day-to-day family recipes in each quarter, there is a section of "Budget Pull-Back" recipes and these include our "Encore" dishes, designed to make use of foods left over from the recipes in the preceding sections.

We dislike the word "left-over" because of its atmosphere of compromise and inefficiency. "Encore," on the other hand, implies a reappearance by eager demand, as at the end of a brilliant concert, when the audience shouts for more. Our definition of an encore is that when it is served no one at table should realize that it was not planned for its own sake. Sometimes, we deliberately prepare more than is needed of the original dish, so that it can be encored in various exciting ways.

A New Kind of Recipe

In writing out our recipes for this book, we have kept in mind the root difference between the average amateur cook and the crack professional. The amateur assembles the ingredients, measures them, mixes them, sets the oven temperature and timer, all by blindly following a set of fixed rules. The reasons behind the steps remain a mystery to him. Often, with no clear idea of the desired flavor, texture, and appearance of the completed dish, success is a matter of accident. The professional, on the other hand, understanding precisely the function of each ingredient, feels free to make substitutions, and uses judgment in varying the amounts, much like a pianist improvising on the keyboard. During the cooking, the professional will turn the temperature of the oven up or down, lengthen or shorten the time, reading the signals of progress in the food itself, toward an end result clearly in mind. Pressing the grilled steak with the finger, the degree of resilience tells him whether the center is still "bloody," or "rare." The recipes in this book try to give the amateur enough information to achieve the results of the professional. We take into account the variable factors and discuss the kinds of utensils used and the varying effects they can achieve.

Our list of ingredients is divided into two parts: one headed "Check Staples," the other "Shopping List." The order of the staples is the same in every recipe; and is based on a quick and routine progression around the kitchen: first, butter, eggs, milk, and other staples which would normally be kept in the refrigerator; second, a checklist for the spice cabinet and the bin with the aromatic herbs and vegetables; third, the flour, sugar and other dry and packaged ingredients from the store cupboard; fourth, the cooking wines, spirits, and other liquids, vinegars, syrups, essences, etc.

The shopping list also is in a planned order for convenience in marketing. The main ingredient comes first with a precise definition of the cut or type, and with alternatives. Then, listed together, the fruits and vegetables, the dairy items, packaged goods, special wines, spirits, etc. There is a practical flexibility in defining amounts: for example, if a recipe calls for 5 lbs. of medium-size chowder clams, we will add that this weight equals 4 qts., or about 36 clams.

The text of all but the simplest recipes is broken up into separate operations, some of which can be completed earlier in the day, others the day before, and a few, two or three days in advance. This simplifies the preparation of even the most complicated recipe and allows for short kitchen sessions to be filled in at convenient times. A heading shows, first, how far in advance the operation can be done and roughly how long it will take.

When the last phase of preparation begins before the dish comes to table, the timing is given in the form of a countdown: "40 Minutes Before Serving . . . ," "25 Minutes Before Serving . . . ," "Just Before Serving. . . ."

The most important aspect of these recipes, however, is that at certain crucial points in the cooking, they take the time to tell the cook what result is being sought and what signals to watch for to judge the progress toward that result: "When the crust is golden-brown and springy to the touch, turn the oven temperature down to 300 degrees . . . ," "Keep adding maple syrup, 1 teaspoon at a time, stirring continually in between each addition, until the sauce is about as thick as heavy cream. . . ." When the cook learns to judge accurately such indications as these, the results will be professional.

II
Shopping for Raw Materials and Staples

GUESTS ARE always polite and will say, "Thank you for a wonderful dinner," even when the meal was only fairly good. It is when a dish stops the conversation at the table and brings rapturous exclamations as it is tasted that we know we have achieved the final perfection. We are convinced that this ultimate success comes, not so much from anything that is done in the kitchen, but from the skillful shopping for the "exactly right" ingredients.

The problem in shopping is that the same word is used equally for the good and the bad products. Take the word "bacon," for example. In many parts of the United States magnificent bacon is still being produced; firm, lean slabs, cut from properly fed porkers, then properly smoked to a dark mahogony. This kind of bacon gives up its magnificent aromatic flavor to any dish to which it is added, and when a slice is pinned across the breast of a roasting squab or turkey, the aroma seeps deep into the flesh. Yet in 99 out of 100 stores we are offered a product in a flat carton (carefully designed to mislead as to the amount of lean and fat), with slices so thin, limp, and fatty that three quarters disappears in the frying pan. It has been mass-produced at high speed; the color is dead-white. Smoking and flavor are notable by their absence. Yet this product is also called "bacon."

In our shopping we not only make sure that we get good dark smoked bacon, but a number of other somewhat unusual basic ingredients and staples, which are normally not available at the local corner grocer or the big supermarket. Over many years of experience, we have come to rely on these basic ingredients because they add some special taste or texture to any dish in which they are used. Of course, almost every one of them can be replaced by a standard product, but then one must expect a noticeable loss of quality in the finished dish. We do not call for these ingredients just to be different. We are as lazy about our shopping as the next family. We think that each of the items in the following list is worth the slight trouble of ordering in advance. Whenever such a special ingredient appears in a recipe, it is followed by ❋, which indicates that there is a mail-order source listed for it at the back of the book. Obviously, the morning of the day when a dish is to be prepared is not the time to be rushing around searching for an unusual ingredient. We try to keep most of these items on hand in our store cupboard or refrigerator, in addition of course to the standard staples of every kitchen.

ARROWROOT, GROUND: See "Flours and Other Ground Starches."

BACON, DARK SMOKED: Some of the best bacon is still being produced in the "Southern ham country" around Smithfield and Richmond, in Virginia,✲ but surely also in other parts of the country. We order it in slabs of from 2 to 7 pounds and slice it to any desired thickness a few minutes before using it. A long, sharp knife and 2 or 3 minutes of practice will enable even the most timid cook to slice a serving of bacon in a few seconds. Then one can experience the joy of thick bacon which does not shrivel up to nothing. We are never without a slab in the meat container of our refrigerator. Tightly wrapped, it keeps in perfect condition for months.

BESAN, INDIAN CHICK-PEA FLOUR: See "Flours and Other Ground Starches."

BOMBAY DUCK: An Indian delicacy, which is not duck, nor is it always from Bombay; it comes packaged from Indian importers✲ and each piece looks and feels like a stone-hard, dark slice of bacon. It is in fact a boned fillet of a small fish caught in the Indian Ocean, which is then dried, pressed, and cured. When a slice is heated, preferably under a broiler but alternatively in a hot oven, an almost instantaneous change takes place. The Bombay duck becomes dry and crumbly, exactly like crisp bacon. It is highly spiced and not to be eaten as a main dish, but is worth keeping on hand as a condiment. About 1 crumbled teaspoonful per person can be sprinkled over rice or over a poached egg, and Bombay duck is an essential side dish of an Indian menu (page 93). It is never cooked in the dish, but served at the table, pre-broiled and crumbled.

BOUILLON CUBES: Although we normally keep a supply of homemade bouillon in our refrigerator, we also usually have on hand, in case of emergency, one of the outstanding imported brands of bouillon cubes.✲ These have a character which is simply not present in the standard products.

BREAD CRUMBS, PACKAGED: Of course it is always easy, if one has stale bread on hand, to roll out, grate, or grind it into bread crumbs. However, again for emergencies, we keep at least one package of the excellent domestic spiced bread crumbs, often called "Herb Stuffing."

BUTTERS FOR THICKENING: The basic principle of thickening sauces, soups, etc., is that of the flour-and-butter paste known to French cooking as a *roux*. The hot fat brings out from each tiny grain of flour the sticky gluten, which then combines with the hot milk or bouillon, until each tiny speck of flour is expanded and suspended in the liquid, like millions of tiny lumps of jelly. The normal method of doing this, by stirring flour into hot butter, then gradually (or sometimes all at once) adding the hot liquid, has serious disadvantages. Sometimes the flour is overcooked in the fat, producing a slightly burned taste. Or the flour can be undercooked, which gives a pasty taste. There is often the danger of lumping, and it is sometimes difficult to control precisely the thickness of the final result. Also, the *roux* can never be added to the soup in a pot; the soup must always be added to the *roux* in a separate pan, and this can be a nuisance. The French have an alternative method of thickening, which they call *beurre manié,* or "kneaded butter," which we prefer to call "floured butter" and generally consider more efficient and flexible.

BASIC RULE FOR THICKENING WITH FLOURED BUTTER (enough to thicken 1 pint of liquid): Allow 4 tablespoons of sweet butter to soften at room temperature in a small mortar or mixing bowl. When quite soft, work into it, with a small wooden spoon, 4 tablespoons of flour. Keep on kneading it vigorously until butter and flour are completely blended. This is the "floured butter," which can now be used immediately or stored, refrigerated, in a screw-top jar. To use, bring liquid to be thickened up to just below boiling (there must be no bubbling), then drop in, one at a time, lumps of the floured butter, each about the size of half a cherry. Each lump must be vigorously stirred to melt and disperse it before the next is added, or the lump will cook itself into a dumpling and the thickening power will be lost. Encourage the lump to break up and melt by squashing it against the side of the pan with the back of the wooden spoon. Keep adding lumps in this way until the exact desired thickness is achieved. The beauty of this method is that there is really no need for any precise measurements. One can make any amount of the floured butter by simply remembering that the quantities of butter and flour must be equal. There is no need to measure the liquid in the pot. Also, infinite variations of flavoring are possible by substituting different types of flour and other fats than butter. We often use chicken, goose, or bacon fat, with the nutty Indian Besan flour (see entry) or with rice flour. Another variation is the use of arrowroot with heavy cream (see page 14). One can keep several types in small jars in the refrigerator as staples for "instant thickening" of almost anything.

CHICK-PEA FLOUR: See "Flours and Other Ground Starches."

CHOCOLATE, MEXICAN: We like to keep a small supply of the round slabs from Mexico,☧ which are a combination of chocolate with sugar, cinnamon, and other spices. It melts in a few seconds in hot milk, and then can be frothed up with a handmade Mexican molinillo.

CHUTNEYS, PICKLES, PRESERVES, AND OTHER PREPARED CONDIMENTS AND SAUCES: We like all the standard pickles, from dill to watermelon, but demand even more variety around the edge of a plate of cold cuts. In the refrigerator or store cupboard we usually keep in stock a jar of the tiny French pickles called CORNICHONS, the Singapore SPICE SAUCE,☧ first-quality Indian SWEET MANGO CHUTNEY, and Indian LEMON PICKLE (whole quarters of lemon, very hot), together with our own homemade SWEET LEMON-LIME PICKLE (page 405) and GREEN-TOMATO CHUTNEY (page 406). Also, almost always, a jar of the marvelous specialty of the Italian city of Cremona, the MOSTARDA DI FRUTTA. This remarkable Italian preserve is a condiment of whole fruits—pears, cherries, figs, plums, and apricots—together with large chunks of pumpkin and watermelon, all preserved in a sweet-sour mustard sauce. It is one of the world's most original condiments and goes wonderfully with ham, tongue, cold roast pork, as well as chicken and turkey, and even, on occasion, with cold salmon, swordfish, crab, or lobster. In Cremona, it is sold loose from large wooden tubs, but in the United States it can be ordered by mail.✠

CLAMS, MINCED, CANNED: We usually keep a few cans on hand ready for our fastest-of-all emergency main dishes, our 5-minute clam stew (page 187).

COCONUT CHIPS, HAWAIIAN SALTED AND TOASTED: Having these chips on hand eliminates the trouble of opening a fresh coconut and they are an essential accompaniment to an Indian menu. ✠

COFFEE, WHOLE BEANS: For a general discussion of coffee and coffee-making, see page 516. We always, of course, buy and store our various coffee blends in the whole bean,✠ grinding them in a small electric machine a minute or two before brewing.

CORN-BELLY SALT PORK: Just as there is bacon and bacon (see entry) there are various grades of that most common of all basic ingredients, salt pork, which our Southern friends call "white bacon." The best grade, well worth the trouble of ordering in advance, seems to be produced in Memphis, Tennessee, and is called "corn belly," which simply means that it is the cut from the belly of the pig put through a corned-beef process. It is much less highly salted than standard salt pork, has a much better flavor, and can be ordered from many fancy butchers.✠ It can, of course, be replaced by ordinary salt pork, but with some loss of flavor.

CORNMEAL, COARSE WHITE WATER-GROUND: There is simply no comparison between the finest grade of coarsely cracked cornmeal and the standard mass-produced, almost pulverized products. Our various corn breads would hardly be the same without good cornmeal.✠

CREAM, HEAVY NATURAL FARM: We are lucky in New York City in having available for home delivery a magnificent quality of untampered-with heavy farm cream. It comes in glass bottles and keeps in the refrigerator for about twice as long as the carton cream. We use it in the best teas because it brings out the flavor; we also use this cream as an alternative form of fat for liquefying arrowroot in thickening processes and for many other cooking uses. In most cities where we have lived for a while, we have been able to find one source or another for a first-grade heavy farm cream, which is one of the basic essentials of good cooking.

FLOURS AND OTHER GROUND STARCHES: One of the most useful improvements of the last few years is the development of the exaggeratedly so-called granulated instantized all-purpose flour, which runs like salt, never needs to be sifted (in fact, cannot be, for it runs right through the mesh), and disperses immediately in contact with cold liquids. The process is known as "agglomeration" and is roughly the same principle as is used for instant coffee, with thousands of very tiny balls that burst on contact with liquid. Thus, this type of flour is easier and faster to use than the old-fashioned kind. We include it in all our recipes, unless another type of flour is specifically indicated.

Our second staple flour, much coarser, but wonderfully nutty, is the Indian BESAN CHICK-PEA FLOUR,※ which is about the equivalent in use of the standard wholewheat flour. Third, roughly in place of the standard light cake flour, we keep on hand a fine grade of Indian RICE FLOUR,※ very fine and fluffy.

However, for almost all the thickening processes, no flour is quite the equal of GROUND ARROWROOT,※ which is a standard staple of most European kitchens, but still not very widely used in the United States. It is a tuberous root, which grows mainly on the British Caribbean island of St. Vincent and, when dried and finely ground, has more than double the thickening power of wheat flour. Also, arrowroot thickens much more quickly, since with ordinary flour the liquid must be heated to almost 200 degrees before thickening takes place, whereas arrowroot thickens at just over 150 degrees. At this lower temperature, for example, there is no danger of egg-yolk curdling, and this is why we use arrowroot in our basic soufflé and in many other ways.

BASIC RULE FOR THICKENING WITH ARROWROOT: For each tablespoon of flour for thickening called for in a recipe, substitute 1¼ teaspoons of ground arrowroot. This means that 2½ teaspoons of arrowroot will thicken 1 cup of liquid, always a little more or less. To blend in arrowroot, first work it into a smooth cream in a mortar or small mixing bowl, with a few dashes of heavy cream (or, if cream does not fit the recipe, an equal amount of cold aromatic bouillon or wine), then spoon into the not-too-hot liquid, preferably off the heat, and stir each spoonful to disperse it thoroughly before adding the next. At this point, add only about 2 teaspoons of the arrowroot mixture for each roughly estimated 1 cup of liquid. Now gently heat it up and, well before it boils, the thickening will take place. The exact thickening required is achieved by adding the last of the arrowroot quite slowly and stirring thoroughly between each addition. Arrowroot also gives an extremely smooth coating and good color when added to a frying batter. For this purpose, blend 2 tablespoons of arrowroot into each ½ cup of flour.

GLACÉ DE VIANDE: See "Meat Glaze."

GRAINS, WHOLE, OR CRACKED: We enjoy oatmeal with cream and maple syrup for our winter and fall breakfasts on cold Sunday mornings, but there is simply no comparison between the "ready-in-a-minute" oatmeal that has been rolled, crushed, mashed, and practically pulverized for the sake of speed, and the finest whole-grain oatmeal that is still being made in and imported from Ireland and Scotland. It takes a little longer to cook, but the final nutty, chewy result is nothing short of magnificent. In its airtight canister the whole-grain oatmeal keeps for many months in the store cupboard. Also, we keep on hand small cloth bags filled with the large-grain types of raw wheat, used as alternative "foundation" to potatoes and rice, with the grains cooked by the Balkan or Russian method, as kasha. There is the WHOLE-GRAIN WHEAT, which is the actual husked grain of wheat; or the CRACKED WHEAT, which is the half-grain (like split peas); or other forms known variously as BUCKWHEAT BULGUR WHEAT, or WHEAT PILAF, and all of them can be shipped by mail.⁂

HERB STUFFING: See "Bread Crumbs."

HONEYS AND OTHER NATURAL SWEET SYRUPS: We object to too much purity in our lives, especially in regard to our sugars. It is the impurities remaining in the natural sugars which give them their attractive characters and flavors. We seldom keep less than three types of HONEY on hand, and for a general discussion of the infinite variety of the world's honeys, see page 521. We use PURE MAPLE SYRUP in many recipes and save cost by ordering it in half-gallon cans direct from Vermont.⁂

MACAROONS: Another of the unique regional specialities from Italy is the tiny, handmade, and individually wrapped almond-vanilla macaroon, a delicacy of the Lombardian town of Saronno, called *amaretti di Saronno.* One particular firm has been making them for more than 200 years. They are increasingly available in fancy-food stores all over the United States, or from Italian mail-order shops.⁂ We use the *amaretti* not only as habit-forming cookies with cups of coffee or tea, or glasses of wine, but also as an essential ingredient in some desserts.

MAPLE SYRUP, PURE: See "Honeys, etc."

MARMALADE, BITTER SEVILLE ORANGE: When we can find some of the winter crop of the bitter Seville oranges, we make our own marmalade (page 183). Breakfast is not breakfast without it. When we cannot get these special oranges, we consider that the best imported British brands of the famous bitter marmalade are a near second-best.⁂

MEAT GLAZE: Many French recipes call for *glace de viande,* which, in its most perfect form, is the red-blooded pan juice from roasting beef, de-fatted, boiled down, and concentrated until it is as thick as whipped cream. A teaspoon or two of such a meat nectar stirred into, say, the sauce for a *coq au vin,* can help to lift the flavor to heights of excellence. However, in these days, when large ovens and huge beef roasts are a thing of the past, true *glace de viande* has also virtually disappeared. In its place, in our recipes, we use (and almost always keep on hand as a staple) a first quality bottled meat extract imported from Britain.⁂

MOSTARDA DI FRUTTA: See "Chutneys, etc."

MONOSODIUM GLUTAMATE (MSG): This universal white powder is not, as is generally supposed, a miraculously modern chemical invention. Nor does it, as is often assumed, under one or the other of its various commercial labels, add any flavor of its own to a dish. It does however bring out and strengthen many of the flavors that are already there. The tiny MSG white crystals are a natural protein, distilled from certain vegetables. It was known to the Chinese 5,000 years ago as *mei jing* and to the Japanese only a few centuries later as *aji-no-*

moto. But see the Preface to the Revised Edition, above.

MUSHROOMS, DRIED WILD: One of the saddest things about cooking in the United States is that we, as a nation, are so afraid of being poisoned by wild mushrooms that we restrict our entire supply to a single mass-produced type, which is one of the blandest of all the species. How different is this from France, where the skilled gathering of wild woodland mushrooms is still a thriving business, so that the corner grocery in even a small town can usually offer five or six different types. There is really only one way that the city cook can improve the mushroom flavor in a dish. We usually keep on hand a few cellophane packages of French or Italian dried wild mushrooms.✵ Before they are used, however, they must be soaked for an hour or so, preferably in a small quantity of dry white wine. Because their flavor is so strong, they should only be added to (never used instead of) the regular mushrooms in the dish.

OATMEAL, WHOLE-GRAIN: See "Grains, etc."

OLIVE OIL, VIRGIN AND OTHER: Cooks who say: "I don't like olive oil because it smokes and smells and becomes gooey and forces its harsh flavor into the food" are simply not using a good enough grade of olive oil. A fine-quality olive oil has none of these faults and is one of the most perfect of all fats for deep and shallow frying; it is used in pastries and salad dressings, and for incorporating into many dishes. As a frying agent, it is generally superior to butter. However, in buying olive oil, one must at least know something about its various grades. When the finest ripe olives are first gently pressed, they produce the best oil, generally a light green in color, which is called "virgin olive oil" and is often extremely expensive. However we do keep a small supply on hand, solely for our salad dressings. We never use it for frying or cooking. Below the virgin quality, the best come from the south of France, Greece, the Lucca district of Italy, and from southern Spain. It is well worth experimenting with several brands; for our personal preference see ✵.

PÂTÉS, TERRINES, APPETIZER SAUSAGES, ETC.: Although, in general, we prefer to prepare our own appetizer "prologues," we are fortunate in New York City in being able to shop at various French-type charcuteries, butcher shops which have kitchens in the back, where the charcutiers, or butchers, prepare on a small scale and with considerable skill certain appetizer delicacies which are then sold in substantial quantities to New York restaurants. Many a *pâté maison* (the *maison* is supposed to mean "homemade"), even in one of the finest French restaurants, can often be traced directly to one of these butchers. Then there are such excellent products as *saucissons à l'ail en croute* (garlic sausage baked in a crust), or *rillettes de Tours* (a pork *pâté* with an interesting chewy texture, a specialty of the town of Tours), as well as *pâtés,* soft enough to be spread, or *terrines* of meat or game, firm enough to be sliced. We often buy small quantities of some of these,✵ either for a short-notice party, or to keep, well-covered, in the refrigerator for a few days. We have also found such sources in other large cities where we have lived and where there is a good restaurant trade. A friendly and well-tipped head waiter can often supply useful leads.

MEATS, FANCY AND FOREIGN: In most large cities where there are substantial "foreign" neighborhoods (and especially in New York City), one can usually find butchers of all the major gastronomic countries, specializing in the unusual meats and cuts of their origin. This does not mean that they import anything from overseas. They have learned how to produce from American meats the foreign-style joints, roasts, specialty meats, sausages, etc., which are regularly demanded by their customers. Many of these butchers do most of their business before 7 o'clock in the morning, filling the day's orders from foreign restaurants. We give on page 701 our own list of the reliable and authentic foreign butchers which we have discovered in New York City. We challenge readers in other cities to produce their own lists. The search is an entertaining and often exciting Saturday afternoon game.

PICKLES AND PRESERVES: See "Chutneys, etc."

PAPPADUMS, INDIAN: Like the preceding Bombay duck, this is a unique imported Indian delicacy.☩ Each pappadum, when first unpacked, is like a thin round piece of light-brown leather, flexible but tough, about the size of a saucer. In this form, it is inedible! However when strong heat is applied to it for only a few seconds in a lightly buttered frypan, the pappadum immediately pops up, large bubbles form in it, and it becomes a beautifully light and crisp, aromatically flavored, thin sheet of bread.

The transformation in a few seconds is magic. About three pappadums per person are served on a dish at table as a dramatic alternative to sliced bread. Or the pappadums can be crumbled and sprinkled over foods. We are seldom without at least one package in our store cupboard.

PORK, SALT: See "Corn-Belly Salt Pork."

RICE IN VARIOUS FORMS: We look for variety in our rice and think that the expert cook should learn to play for dramatic effects with some of the various types. These do not, for us, include any of the partly cooked, so-called "quick" versions. For dry, separate grains there are the DOMESTIC LONG-GRAIN, the affectionately called DIRTY BROWN, the PERSIAN LONG-GRAIN from Iran and the LONG-GRAIN PATNA from India. Each has its own strong character and is included in some of our recipes. Then for Italian *risottos,* where the cooked rice should have more the consistency of a pudding, there is the ITALIAN SHORT-GRAIN RISOTTO, which is imported from Italy in small cotton 1-pound bags.☩

RICE FLOUR: See "Flours and Other Ground Starches."

SAUSAGE MEAT, HOMEMADE: Our freezer is almost never without a supply of our own pure pork sausage meat (page 179). We prepare it very quickly, with no bread or cereal filler whatsoever, but with a carefully balanced assemblage of aromatic herbs.

SUGAR, VANILLA: See p. 28 for BASIC RULE.

SYRUPS, SWEET: See "Honeys, etc."

TOMATO PASTE, ITALIAN CONCENTRATED: We always keep on hand two 6-ounce cans of the best quality imported Italian tomato paste.

TOMATOES, ITALIAN PEELED AND SEEDED PLUM: This surely is one of the great triumphs of the modern canning industry. We always keep on hand at least one 1 pound 1 ounce (No. 2) can and one 2 pound 3 ounce (No. 3) can of the best-quality imported Italian tomatoes, which is so good and reliable that we have virtually given up the troublesome operation of peeling and seeding fresh tomatoes.

VANILLA SUGAR: See p. 28, BASIC RULE.

VINEGARS, WINE: There has been great "progress" in the modern vinegar industry and almost none of it, so far as we can see, has brought any benefit to the consumer. Once, almost every family in Europe used to make its own wine vinegar. At the bottom of a stone crock in the cellar, there rested a fungoid growth looking rather like a piece of raw liver, called *une mère,* "a mother." The crock was filled up with cheap wine and in about a month the mother had converted it into an excellent wine vinegar. Some of it might be bottled with sprigs of basil or tarragon leaves or other aromatic herbs. As the vinegar was drawn off it was replaced by new wine, so there was an unending supply, and the mother never seemed to wear out. Nature's gifts to man are eternal and true.

Now, the cheap mass-produced vinegars have nothing to do with Nature. They are "put together" chemically in an automated factory with industrial ascetic acid made from wood pulp. The result is nothing less than a corrosive poison. To find wine vinegars still made in the true way, we look usually for imports from France and Spain. The finest French vinegars generally bear the name of Joan of Arc's city of Orléans, and one of its famous firms there has been continuously producing vinegars for almost 200 years. We keep on hand a quart bottle of their robust red wine vinegar and another of a delicate tarragon white wine. From Spain we keep a superb sherry vinegar, produced, as are Spanish sherries, in Jerez de la Frontera in southern Spain. This vinegar is too expensive for cooking, but is magnificent in salad dressings.

III

Aromatic Herbs, Spices, and Vegetables

A FRENCH COOK will often use the phrase *les aromates* to describe not only the herbs and spices that will go into her dish but also the aromatic vegetables—carrots, celery, turnips, the various members of the onion family, even the tomatoes, etc.—of which the flavors must all balance and complement each other. We consider this principle so important that we prefer to replace the phrase "herbs and spices" (always a bit muddled by the question as to which is an herb and which a spice) by the one word "aromatics," covering all the leafy and root vegetables that make up the total flavor balance of a dish. Some understanding of this balance is essential to the education of any good cook.

We believe that it is better to have too few aromatics than too many. It is far better to get to know the personality of each, its affinities and incompatibilities, so that eventually one can extemporize with it in different combinations. In our family we experimented with our aromatics on a step-by-step basis. This practical plan is followed in the basic list that follows.

The ideal is, of course, to have one's own herb garden outside the kitchen door and to go out and pick what is needed for the meal at hand. Then, a simple *omelette aux fines herbes* can be a memorable gastronomic experience. However, even in a city apartment, we have proved that it is possible to grown some of the hardier herbs in summer in window boxes or in winter on sunny indoor shelves. (There are excellent mail-order sources for potted herb plants.✲) For the rest, dried herbs and spices of good quality in tightly screw-topped jars kept away from bright light (never bought in cartons or tins, which cannot be properly resealed) are a very fair compromise, provided one remembers that they are expendable as soon as they begin to smell like old hay. Also, the flavor oils of dried herbs will always be brought out more strongly if they are first gently pounded in a little warm butter or cream. Finally, to begin to get to know the qualities of a particular aromatic herb, we use the following two methods.

BASIC METHOD FOR AROMATIC SPREAD FOR SAMPLING

Several tastings for several people

Check Staples:

Sweet butter (2 Tbs.)
Aromatic: the aromatic herb to be tasted (about 2 Tbs. chopped, if fresh, or about 2 tsp., if dried)

Shopping List:

Mild Cheddar cheese⚐ (1/4 lb.)
Cottage cheese (1/4 lb.)
Sour cream (1 Tbs.)
French Calvados brandy⚐ or domestic applejack (about 1 oz.)

The Day Before—Preparation in About 15 Minutes

Set the 2 tablespoons of butter in a very small pan to warm up until just hot to the tip of the finger. Meanwhile put the aromatic herb (finely chopped, if fresh) into a small hand mortar. When butter is warm, pour into mortar, stir around to coat leaves, then pound and rub lightly with pestle to squeeze out oils. Set aside and cover to marinate at room temperature. Grate the 1/4 pound of Cheddar and thoroughly blend in a mixing bowl with the 1/4 pound of cottage cheese, adding just enough of the sour cream to make a stiff, smooth paste. Now thoroughly work in the herb butter, at the same time adding just enough of the Calvados, dash by dash, to make a spread the consistency of softish butter. The alcohol intensifies the herb flavor. When the right consistency has been achieved, spoon the paste into a refrigerator jar with a tight screw-top lid and refrigerate overnight for further development of flavor. Then have an intense love affair with this aromatic *pâté,* first, of course, bringing it back to room temperature, then spreading it on different kinds of breads and crackers, or simply tasting it from the tip of a spatula and savoring it with mouthfuls of all kinds of foods. Make a list of the best combinations.

BASIC METHOD FOR AROMATIC TOMATO JUICE FOR SAMPLING

Tastings for 3 or 4 people

Check Staples:

Aromatic: the herb to be tasted (about 2 Tbs., finely chopped, if fresh, or about 2 tsp., dried)

Shopping List:

Tomato juice (1 pt.)
Italian sweet red onion (enough for about 4 tsp., finely chopped)

A Few Hours Beforehand—Preparation in About 10 Minutes

Using 1/4 cup of warmed tomato juice in place of the butter, add it to the herb and lightly pound, exactly as in the preceding recipe. Pour remaining tomato juice into a jar with a lid tight enough for jar to be shaken without leakage. Finely chop enough of the red onion to fill 4 teaspoons and add to juice in jar. After herb has soaked for about 5 minutes, add contents of mortar to jar, tightly screw on lid, shake thoroughly, then refrigerate for a few hours for flavor to develop. Stir aromatic juice, sipping it at various temperatures and with various foods. Make a list of the best combinations.

The 10 Essential Fresh Aromatics

We try never to be without these:

CARROTS, the medium for cooking; the small and sweet, when available, for nibbling in sticks.

CELERY, and CELERY LEAF, the green Pascal with the stronger flavor for cooking; the white for nibbling in sticks. We *never* allow the greengrocer to cut off the leaves, which are infinitely superior for all forms of flavoring to the dried celery seed.

Fresh CHIVES, preferably growing in a small pot and snipped off with kitchen scissors as needed, or bought in small fresh bundles, or, as a last resort, in frozen packages.

Fresh GARLIC, *never* the processed kind in powder, flake, or salt form, all of which we avoid like the plague. They have nothing to give but a nasty taste, dominated by preservatives. We keep a fresh bulb in a small, tightly covered, ceramic jar in the refrigerator. It is far better to chop garlic finely than to mash it through a press, since mashing encourages the flavor oils to evaporate.

Fresh LEMONS and LIMES, *never* the bottled or plastic-packaged, so-called "reconstituted" juices, which are bitter with preservatives and have no freshness whatsoever.

YELLOW ONIONS, which we think hold their flavor better stored in the vegetable bin of the refrigerator.

Fresh PARSLEY, which should, of course, be thrown out as soon as it begins to smell musty.

GREEN SCALLIONS, or GREEN ONIONS (as they are called on the West Coast).

Fresh SHALLOT is the halfway cousin between the onion and the garlic, divided into cloves like garlic, but with the reddish-brown skin of an onion and without garlic's overpowering dominance. A couple of tablespoons of chopped shallot, added to the general quota of onion in a dish, supplies a fine and subtle additional character. We almost always keep "a handful" of fresh shallots in our refrigerator salad bin. Shallots did not use to be always easily available away from the large city markets. However, they are now widely accessible in most local markets across the country.

WATERCRESS, which, to us, is much more than just a salad ingredient, often giving its delicately sharp aroma to a fine soup, or replacing the dull lettuce as a base or garnish.

Add Salt, Pepper, and Mustard

In almost all of our recipes we use CRYSTAL SALT, or GROS SEL, which is the finest quality of salt, both for cooking and for grinding at table. A friend asked us, "How can there be differences in salt? Salt is salt, isn't it?" Not true. It is the old story of the impurities making the differences in character. When salt is overpurified, overground until it is ultra-fine, and then mixed with cornstarch to make it run easily, it is, in effect, adulterated. There is no comparison between this weak and effeminate stuff and rough salt crystallized out from sea water. The difference between food salted with one or the other is quite startling. If your own market does not carry crystal salt, it is now available at fancy-food stores or quite easily by mail, even from England,⚜ where the best quality is produced.

We cannot overstress the importance of using only the finest quality of WHOLE BLACK PEPPER. In all forms of ready-ground pepper, even in the coarse butcher's grinds, the flavor oils evaporate within a few weeks. We buy the type known as "Tellicherry Black," grown at the southern tip of India and shipped through the port of Tellicherry. Incidentally, WHITE PEPPER is merely black pepper with the outer black skins removed, and this process eliminates most of the flavor. White pepper was developed because effete diners cannot bear to see a few black specks in their white sauces.

We keep several grinders of various degrees of coarseness, and grind the pepper fresh each time we use it. When we need coarsely cracked pepper, for example, to pound into steak, we smash a few peppercorns in our small hand mortar. We also keep on hand a small supply of the very hot RED CAYENNE PEPPER, Cayenne being the port in French Guiana.

MUSTARD can vary enormously in quality. From the time the tiny mustard seeds are dried and ground, to the time they appear as "made mustard" in a glass jar on a supermarket shelf, they seem to have been so mishandled as to have lost all their bite and power. However, good mustard is still available. The primary form for the aromatics cabinet is the fine quality ENGLISH DRY MUSTARD POWDER, which can then be mixed with any liquid from beer to milk to make fresh mustard for each meal. There are many fine imported French versions of MOUTARDE DE DIJON and German DÜSSELDORFER SENF,⚜ which are "made mustards" of strong and interesting character, while there is also an excellent CREOLE MUSTARD,⚜ in which the mustard is mixed with horseradish and spices, available by mail from New Orleans.

When we were teaching our girls the art of aromatics and they were thoroughly familiar with these first thirteen, we introduced them to the next important group.

Add the Big 5 to Make 18

BASIL is, of course, best when the fresh leaf is available in summer, and this is when we make our basil butter. It is one of the simplest to grow in a window box or pot. When we buy it dried, we try (and this rule applies to all leaf aromatics) to get the leaf as coarsely crumbled as possible. The larger the bits, the longer they will hold their flavor oils. We always avoid, for the same reason, all forms of powdered aromatics.

BASIC METHOD FOR FRESH BASIL BUTTER

A basic supply for several days

Check Staples:
Sweet butter (1/2 lb.)
Aromatics: table salt, MSG,ß lemon juice (about 4 tsp.)

Shopping List:
Fresh basil (1 bunch)

Preparation in About 10 Minutes

Let the half pound of butter come to room temperature. Meanwhile finely chop enough of the basil to fill 1/3 cup. Then cream with the butter, adding a small pinch each of salt and MSG, plus just enough lemon juice to give a slight tartness. Excellent spread on bread, melted on top a fried or poached egg, or on hot cooked vegetables, or blended into our port-wine gravy (page 44).

DILL is also infinitely superior fresh and its season seems to be longer than that of basil. Both the green fronds and the stalks are equally strong aromatically. When buying it dried, we prefer the type labeled "dillweed," the dried fronds, rather than the more usually available seed.

SWEET MARJORAM seems seldom to be available fresh, but can be ordered potted from herb gardens.✿ We buy the dried leaf coarsely crumbled.

TARRAGON is available fresh in our local markets for a short summer season. For the rest of the year, the coarsely crumbled dried leaf is a good alternative.

THYME is a hardy plant which can be grown at home. However, it takes to drying better than most of the leaf aromatics and holds its flavor for months.

After the multitudinous uses of these great aromatics have been thoroughly explored, there comes the next step forward.

Add the Next Basic 5 to Make 23

BAY LEAF, always bought in the whole leaf, never crumbled or powdered. Bay is an edible species of the evergreen laurel, the *laurier* of French recipes, and the best quality comes from Turkey. It is difficult to get to know intimately, since the leaf fiber is too tough to eat. Nor can its slightly bitter flavor be easily defined. Yet it is noticeably missed whenever it is left out of one of the innumerable dishes where it belongs.

FENNEL is always best, of course, during the season when the green fronds are available fresh on a head of the fennel plant, which is somewhat like a head of celery with a bulb at the bottom and may be called, according to the neighborhood, *finocchio, fenu-*

cchi, or anise. Some green grocers try to cut off the fronds and throw them away, but not when we are doing the buying. These fronds add their faintly licorice flavor to many dishes, or they can be finely snipped and sprinkled over foods at the table as a bright green garnish. When the fronds are out of season, the best substitute is dried fennel seed.

OREGANO, always used sparingly because of its dominant power, is seldom available fresh. However, instead of buying the crumbled leaf in jars, we can often find in Arab and Middle Eastern stores whole bunches of the dried plant, which hold their flavor longer in storage. The best quality comes from Italy or Mexico.

ROSEMARY is a hardy house plant that can provide an almost year-round supply of the narrow, needle-like leaf. It also dries well.

SAVORY is our "bean herb," almost always added to a simmering pot of dried beans. We also like its aroma with chestnuts. The fresh leaf is seldom available, but the dried, coarsely crumbled, keeps well.

When complete familiarity has been achieved with these 23 aromatics, a great deal of very good and extremely varied cooking can be accomplished. However, when the next large step is to be taken toward some of the more exotic dishes, the following aromatics should be added to the shelf. In fact, the shelf should now become a cabinet with doors to close out the light when the aromatics jars are not in use.

Add the Aromatic Spices

ALLSPICE is the dried berry of a tree that grows in the West Indies. Since it has some of the flavors of cinnamon, clove and nutmeg, it is called the allspice tree. We buy all such berries whole and, when the recipe calls for them to be ground, it is a matter of a few seconds to produce a coarse or a fine powder in a small hand mortar. Allspice has a special affinity with beef and we often load a spare pepper grinder with the whole berries and grind on top of steaks, or work the powder into hamburger meat.

ALMOND EXTRACT is generally best bought from the drugstore, making sure that the liquid essence is 100 per cent pure almond.

CARAWAY SEEDS are always stored whole and ground in the mortar as needed. The best quality comes from Holland.

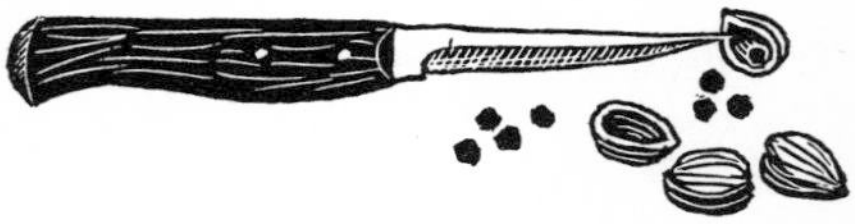

Bleached CARDAMOM PODS, always bought as whole pods, have little black seeds inside. It is the bud of a plant that grows in India and is a staple of Indian cooking. In making curries, the whole pod is thrown into the pan and the dried white petals disintegrate into the sauce. When a recipe calls for the seeds alone, the pod is cut in half with a sharp knife and the tiny black seeds are scraped out.

Whole CHILI PODS come either as the red, dried, or as the green, pickled in cans.✻ The red are extremely hot and must be used with great care. The green are very hot if marked *serrano,* slightly less hot if marked *jalapeño* or *poblano,* and only moderately hot if marked "deseeded *jalapeño.*"

CHILI POWDER is best in the type imported from Mexico, a blend of various dried red peppers with cumin and oregano. American-made chili powders are usually rather heavily salted and loaded with powdered processed garlic, which we consider a disadvantage (see garlic).

CINNAMON, both the whole stick and the ground, is kept in stock, since it is troublesome to grind the stick. However, we prefer to use the stick wherever possible, remembering that it can be re-used again and again. For example, after being boiled in a wine punch, or fried for a few minutes in an Indian curry sauce, it is washed under a strong jet of warm water, then dried and put back in the jar. Cinnamon is the bark of a tree and the best quality comes from Indonesia or Malaysia.

Whole and ground CLOVE are again both kept in stock, since the "nails," as the French call them, are tough to grind. The best quality comes from Indonesia, Madagascar, or the Philippines. We always make sure that the whole clove has the small "bud" in place at the top. If many of the buds have become detached and fallen to the bottom of the jar, this is a sign that the cloves are stale.

CORIANDER SEED is always bought whole and ground as needed. It is the dried berry of a small plant and the best quality comes from Morocco. The seed is a staple of North African and Middle Eastern cooking, including the famous couscous.

NEW ORLEANS CRAB BOIL✻ is a pungent mixture of ground peppers and spices, used to flavor the water in which crab or shrimp are boiled. Naturally, the water becomes highly aromatic and cannot be reused for any other purpose. By adjusting the amount of the crab boil in the water, the shellfish can finally be flavored exactly to one's preference.

CUMIN SEED, the *comino* of Mexican recipes, is always bought whole and ground as needed.

GINGER comes in many forms, but they all originate in the ginger root, which looks like a small potato with other knobby potatoes growing out of it; it is available in Chinese neighborhood groceries.✻ Once the earthy skin is removed, the flesh of the ginger root has the texture and juiciness of a pineapple but of course with the pungent flavor of ginger. It is pale green in the young spring ginger, light brown in the mature winter ginger, and is the finest of all ways to introduce a ginger flavor into a dish. Since it is a fresh vegetable and deteriorates fairly quickly, we have found a way of freezing it and keeping it on hand as a staple.

BASIC RULE FOR FROZEN FRESH GINGER ROOT: First, with a sharp knife, cut away the useless small knobs on the ginger root and any soiled or woody sections. Next, preferably with a sharp potato parer, peel off all skin, exposing the juicy flesh. Wrap tightly in foil and freeze. It will keep perfectly for months. When a small amount is required for a dish, unwrap one end and grate while ginger root is still frozen hard. One teaspoon of these gratings, for example, sprinkled into the butter in a sauté pan in which fish fillets are to be fried, adds a dramatic flavor. The little bits of ginger become crisp and crackly, adding an unusual effect to the sauce.

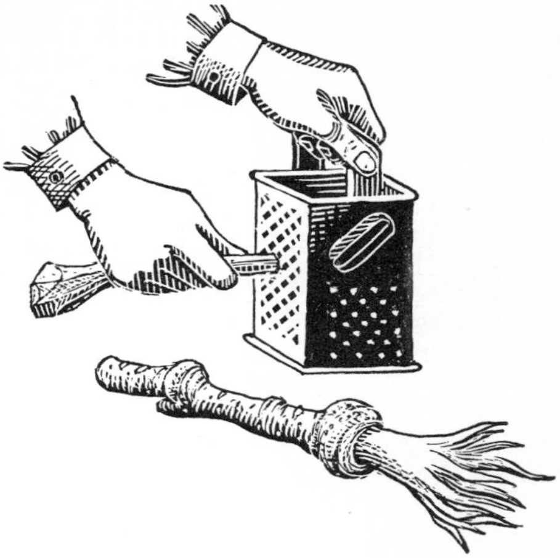

We also keep a staple stock of ginger in other forms: preserved ginger in syrup, crystallized ginger and powdered ginger, the hot type, from Jamaica, the milder from India.

Fresh HORSERADISH is a member of the mustard family and there is simply no comparison between the natural pungency of the fresh root and the mass-produced soggy mash sold in glass jars. The trouble is that one normally has to buy a whole root and much of it may spoil before it is used up. We avoid this by freezing the horseradish, as we do the preceding ginger root. **BASIC RULE** FOR FREEZING FRESH HORSERADISH: As soon as the horseradish root is brought home from the market, while still fresh and juicy, cut away all spoiled and woody parts, then peel off the earthy skin with a sharp potato parer. Tightly wrap the white root in foil and freeze. It will keep perfectly for months. When a small quantity is needed, unwrap one end and grate while still frozen hard. Put back in freezer immediately to avoid defrosting.

JUNIPER BERRIES, which look like dried blueberries, are the fruit of an evergreen bush and are always bought whole. They are quite brittle and can be easily ground in a mortar. When ground and folded into soft butter, they become the famous *beurre de genièvre* of so many classic French recipes.

MACE CHIPS are preferable to the powdered version, because they hold in the flavor and yet can be quickly ground as needed. Mace is very similar in flavor to nutmeg, but there is a subtle difference, so it is essential to keep both in stock. Mace is the outer flesh of the fruit of which the nutmeg is the central stone. The best quality of both comes from the Banda Islands in the East Indies, with other supplies from Java and the West Indies.

NUTMEG is never permitted inside our kitchen in ready-ground form, in which it loses its flavor oils within a few weeks. We keep a small grater hanging near the nutmeg jar and, in fact, the instructions in our recipes usually give the amounts of nutmeg in terms of how many grinds of the grater. Like mace, the best quality of nutmeg comes from the East and West Indies.

The quality of most packaged PAPRIKA is appallingly bad. To make matters worse, it is usually sold in cartons or cans, which cannot be properly resealed, and after a few weeks the paprika has about as much aromatic value as brick dust. The best peppers for sweet red paprika grow in Spain and those for the hot types, in Central Europe. The finest red paprika powder used to come from Hungary, and can still be ordered from Hungarian shops in New York.⚜ They supply samples of several types for tasting so that one can find the exact degree of peppery heat to suit one's personal taste. This paprika must then be stored in airtight tins and will keep in perfect condition for months.

We steer away from all powdered forms of SAFFRON and insist on buying the actual filaments—the dried stigmas, removed by hand, one by one (it takes more than 14,000 to make a single ounce), from the flower of a crocus that grows around the Mediterranean. The Spanish product is usually the best quality. It provides both a brilliant orange-red color and a strong, unique flavor. To bring out the flavor and color of saffron, it should first be soaked, preferably in an alcoholic liquid.

BASIC RULE FOR STEEPING SAFFRON: For each 1 cup of rice to be colored, place 1 teaspoon of saffron in a very small butter-melting pan. Cover with about 1 tablespoon or so of dry white wine or vermouth. Place over a very low flame and bring gently up to just above blood heat, so that liquid feels hot but not stinging to the tip of the finger. Leave at this temperature, stirring occasionally, for at least 5 minutes, but preferably 15. Then stir entire contents of pan into rice, just as it is being brought to a boil. Since a large part of the saffron juice will have coated the inside of the small pan, rinse it out carefully with an extra dash of wine. Saffron should always be soaked in this way before being added into any dish, otherwise a substantial part of its coloring and flavoring power will be wasted.

"Can there be any difference between one SOY SAUCE and another?" There certainly can. There was a news story from Japan about one of the great soy-sauce factories installing automatic machinery. However one of the old-fashioned hand-operated machines was to be kept going especially to make soy sauce for the Emperor. We steer away from the thin and bland Chinese-American and Japanese versions and buy instead the thick and strong authentic Chinese type, imported from Hong Kong.⚜

TABASCO might be said to be merely a liquid form of pepper, but we think it has a certain character and is worth keeping on hand for the occasional use of a drop or two.

Ground TURMERIC can be an alternative to saffron as a coloring agent, the color being a yellowish-brown instead of the orange-red. It is used for Indian rice and Indian curries. Turmeric is the ground root of a plant of the ginger family, although it has no ginger flavor. The best quality is imported from India.⚜

VANILLA BEAN and PURE EXTRACT are both essential for the aromatics cabinet. The extract tends to evaporate when heated, so it is best added at the last moment. The whole bean, however, will stand any amount of cooking and, like the cinnamon stick, can be used over and over again. If one is prepared to sacrifice it, one can greatly increase its flavoring power by cutting it open, as for the vanilla sugar (BASIC RULE follows). A vanilla bean is the sun-dried seed pod of a rare type of tropical orchid. The best beans come from Madagascar and can be ordered by mail.⚜ We keep our beans in a long screw-top test tube, and one of the secret pleasures of the kitchen is to unscrew the top and take a deep sniff of the concentrated aroma.

BASIC RULE FOR VANILLA SUGAR: We use a glass jar with wide ground-glass stopper, large enough to hold 5 pounds of superfine-grind sugar. We cut 2 whole vanilla beans crosswise into 3 equal lengths each—6 pieces in all. Then we cut each piece in half lengthwise. With the point of a small knife, we loosen the central seeds in each half. Then we bury the 12 pieces in the sugar. The jar is kept tightly closed for a week or two and then all the sugar will be permeated with the vanilla flavor. As the sugar is used up, more can be added and, depending

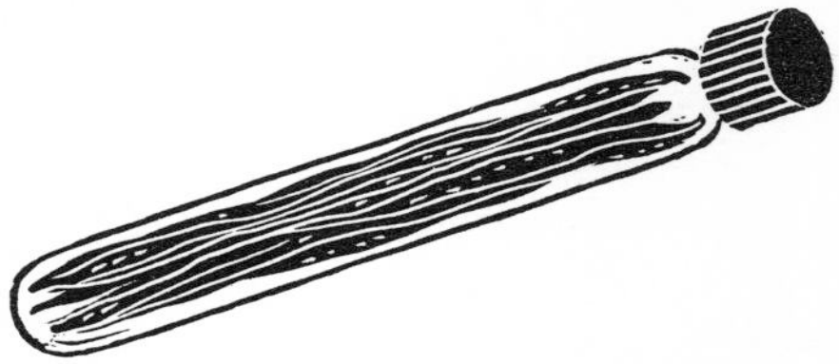

on use, the beans should continue giving off flavor for from six to nine months. When a bean piece is completely dry and brittle, with no more vanilla scent, it is finished and should be replaced. This method of cutting up the beans greatly increases their flavoring power for any use, as for example, when they are added to an egg custard.

WORCESTERSHIRE SAUCE is now manufactured in the United States, allegedly from "the secret British recipe." Unlike many Englishmen, we do not pour it over the steak as a sauce at table, but use it instead as an aromatic ingredient in a number of cooked dishes.

Finally, there is the small group of specialized aromatics which will not be used every day, nor even once a week, but which are essential to the recipes where they belong.

The Final 7

CASSIA BUDS are from the cassia tree, a member of the cinnamon family, from Indonesia and Malaysia. They have a strong cinnamon flavor, but with an added sweetness that gives a special character to hot wine punch.

FENUGREEK is one of the basic ingredients of authentic Indian curries. It is the seed, rather like pale-yellow salt crystals, of an Indian plant. It has a slightly bitter aftertaste when crunched between the teeth, and adds a most attractive and delicate taste of lemon to a curry sauce.*

GUMBO FILÉ is a dark powder ground from the dried leaf of the sassafras bush, a gummy plant that grows in the swamps of Louisiana. The Choctaw Indians gave it to the early French and Spanish settlers in New Orleans. *Gumbo filé* is the essential thickening and coloring agent of an authentic New Orleans gumbo.*

INDIAN MASSALAS are aromatic mixtures of spices and fried ground nuts used by Indian cooks in preparing curries (see the discussion of Indian foods on page 94). Many different *massalas* are used in various parts of India and two of them—a *garam-massala* from the North and a *kala-massala* from the South—are available from Indian importers* and can be used to add a slight touch of curry flavor to many dishes, quite apart from Indian recipes.

INDONESIAN SAMBALS are the famous curry pastes that were adopted by the Dutch settlers and then carried back to Holland. Sambals are now made in Holland from imported Indonesian spices and are shipped to the United States in small jars.* There are many types of sambals that can be used for curry flavoring quite apart from Indonesian or Indian cooking. We find it useful to keep the following on hand: BADJAK is a medium-hot mixture of red peppers, spices and onions; MANIS is a less hot, slightly sweet version; NASI GORENG is a version with mashed fruits added; OELEK is a fiery-hot blend of peppers, to be used with discrimination in very small quantities; OELEK MET TRASSIE is a moderately hot, spiced shrimp paste: PETIS is a medium-hot meat paste, which adds a dark color to any dish in which it participates; RADJA is a basic curry paste; and KERRIE DJAWA is a basic Indonesian curry powder.

Ground SUMAC is a slightly lemon-flavored aromatic spice from Iran, which is usually sprinkled on the meat at the table in an authentic dish of *chellow kebabs,* skewered lamb with rice. Sumac is the ground root of a native Persian flowering bush. It is not an essential ingredient, but we think it adds such an unusual flavor that it is well worth ordering in advance.*

WOODRUFF, or WALDMEISTER, is a plant that grows wild in the Black Forest of Germany. The leaves are an essential ingredient of the German *Maibowle,* the refreshing wine-fruit punch which is always part of the celebration of the spring season. Dried woodruff is imported and available by mail.*

IV
Divide the Kitchen into Efficient Departments *

WE HAVE cooked in large kitchens and small, in the country and the city, on old stoves and new, and we are convinced that good cooking does not depend on any of these physical factors. If the cook will learn to judge the food, in the market and in the kitchen, by sight and smell, by taste and touch, it is perfectly possible to turn out a first-class dinner in a single pot over one burner in a furnished room. Over the past few years, all the recipes in this book have been prepared in the postage-stamp kitchen of a big-city apartment. We agree with the great Anglo-French gastronome André L. Simon, who said that a small kitchen is valuable because it compels efficient organization. This is the key to the saving of effort and time in meal preparation by busy people.

We save more time by using a number of electric gadgets and power-driven appliances. Yet, we cling to many forms of old-fashioned hand operation: the Mexican wooden molinillo for frothing milk; a stone molcajete for hand grinding; a "balloon" wire beater (a design unchanged for hundreds of years), which still beats more air into egg whites than any electric machine. A sharp knife and a cutting board are still the only tools for preparing diced meat, which is something quite different from meat squeezed through an electric grinder. Vegetables passed gently through a food mill are not at all like the same vegetables whipped to a pulp at 15,000 revolutions per minute. We enjoy the amenities of a modern kitchen, but we want the machines to be the servants of our good eating, not its masters.

For the efficient organization of any kitchen, we believe in dividing it into the four departments, surrounding the four basic elements which touch the food: the ice which preserves, the wood which helps to prepare, the fire which cooks, and the water and wine which bring out the flavors.

Ice in the Kitchen

The modern refrigerator has probably revolutionized the kitchen more than anything since the day that fire was first brought indoors. Yet anyone who has read the great narratives of Arctic exploration knows that ice can also be a deadly destroyer. Food improperly stored in the refrigerator may be preserved from going bad, while losing all its pleasurable qualities, and the first casualty is often the flavor. We deplore the modern American habit of dashing to the refrigerator for a fast snack and eating the food immediately at the temperature at which it was stored. One need only sample two pieces of a good soft cheese, side by side, one refrigerator-cold, the other at room temperature, to realize the importance, which we stress in recipes, of allowing enough time for foods to come to room temperature before being prepared and eaten.

Much more serious and irretrievable damage, however, can be done to the taste and texture of food by improper refrigeration and freezing. We are

not concerned here with the fact that frozen foods are "bacteriologically safe" and "good for you." We are quite sure that astronauts can be well nourished by sucking a chicken paste from a toothpaste tube. We *are* concerned with the pleasure of eating. It has been scientifically proved, for example, that certain fish cannot be frozen without almost complete loss of flavor and juiciness. The flesh of the fish contains thousands of tiny tissue sacs, each filled with essential juices. When they freeze the sacs burst, like frozen water pipes, and when the fish is thawed, the juices run out and are lost.

For the same reason that a hot glass dish will crack when placed under running cold water, because of the internal stresses set up by the sudden cooling, so the flesh of a turkey, for instance, can develop similiar internal stresses when quickly frozen and these stresses can sometimes destroy the texture and force out almost all the flavor juices.

Even with cooked foods, usually stored in the refrigerator for only a day or two, serious damage can be done to taste and texture by improper storage in the wrong part of the refrigerator. Our general rules for refrigerator and freezer storage are defined in the diagram text above.

Wood in the Kitchen

We enjoy the feel and texture of wood, especially as it is expressed in our kitchen by the chopping block, the cutting boards, the chopping and mixing bowls, the cheese and carving boards, the light boxwood spoons, the friendly handles of the deadly sharp knives. . . . Even the ultra-modern, streamlined electric meat grinder has to have among its attachments a rough wooden pusher that fits nicely into the hand.

We associate wood with the preparation of the food. (Of course, metal is always there too with glass and rubber; also some plastic has forced its way in, but it is hardly welcome.) Appropriately, our wooden work surface is located next to the ice department (with its basic supply of raw materials) and between the aromatics cabinet and the store cupboard. In front, the wall is covered by a pegboard, on which the most-often-used tools are hung to hand. Thus, everything we need for the fast preparation of the average meal is in a small circle around the work surface.

As to the tools of preparation, we list below those we find especially useful and which are mentioned in many of the recipes. This is not a master list for a young bride setting up her first home. Assuming that the standard tools are already available, we add the following.

BEATING BOWL, COPPER: See "Sabayon."

BLENDER, SLOW-SPEED ELECTRIC: The average fixed-speed blender is much too powerful for its own good. It grabs the food in its twirling teeth, whips it around at 15,000 revolutions per minute, and spews out a soggy baby food. The original texture has vanished. Since all solid matter has been cut up into millions of tiny specks, the flavor oils have been neatly released and have evaporated. Some blender manufacturers have sensed this problem and we now have a machine with a continuously variable speed control from ultra-slow to very high. This gives us the advantages of a blender's ease and speed, without its destructive tendencies. We almost never use the high speeds.

BOARDS AND BLOCKS: There is probably more chopping and cutting in Chinese cooking than in any other and

this means that Chinese kitchen-equipment stores usually offer the widest and most interesting range of boards and blocks at prices often half those in the fancy kitchen shops. The wood is thick and heavy, so that it does not slide around in use. Our cross-section of a tree trunk, about 12 inches across and weighing about 15 pounds, was imported from Hong Kong. Of course, a standard butcher's block will do equally well but is usually much more expensive. We also use Chinese cutting and pastry boards.

BOWL, BEATING: See "Sabayon."

BOXWOOD SPOONS: See "Spoons, Boxwood."

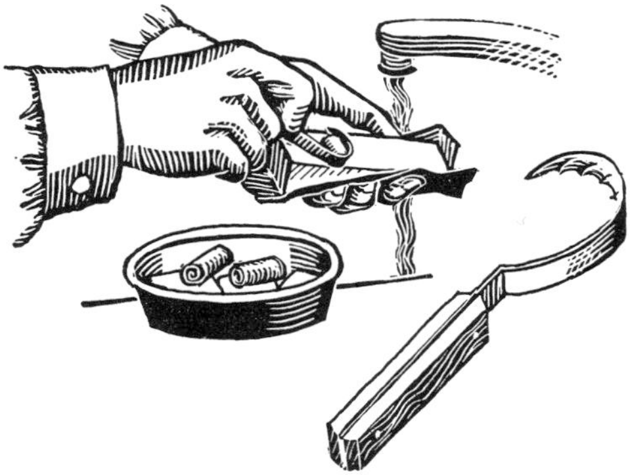

BUTTER CURLER: Serving French-style butter curls at the table in a parsley-garnished bowl of ice is a charming conceit and also very practical, for the curls hold their shape on the ice, yet are thin enough to be easily spreadable.

BASIC RULE FOR BUTTER CURLS: We keep our "butter bowl" always in the refrigerator, to be ready for use at any time. It is oval, about 4 inches long and 1½ inches deep. We fill it with a single layer of ice cubes. Place it on the side of the sink, ready to receive the curls as they fall from the curler. They are very soft when first made, and need to be cooled instantly. Turn on hot water to a gentle thin stream. The curler, which looks like a fluted hook with a wooden handle, has to be repeatedly heated. Take a stick of butter directly from the refrigerator, partly unwrap it so that one long surface is exposed, and hold it in the left hand over the iced butter bowl. Heat the metal hook of the curler in the hot water for a second or two, then, holding it roughly at an angle of 45 degrees to the surface of the butter and pressing down lightly, draw it the full length of the butter. The degree of pressure controls the thickness of the curl. At the end of the stroke, the curl should fall off into the iced bowl. One stick will usually provide enough curls for 4 people. Once the stick gets down to about ⅜ inch thick, it is best to start a new one. All curls should be in contact with ice and should be refrigerated, lightly covered, until needed. Garnish with parsley or watercress before bringing to table.

COFFEE GRINDER, ELECTRIC: Freshly ground coffee from the bean is an absolute essential to the making of good coffee (see the general discussion on page 516). A small electric grinder has stood in one corner of the kitchen counter for fifteen years, with its measuring glass alongside, and in that time has required neither attention nor service, not even a single drop of oil on the motor. Essential features of a good electric coffee grinder are, first, that it should be possible to adjust the coarseness of the grind over a fairly wide range; second, that the container above the grinder should hold a bit more than 1 pound of coffee beans; and, third, that the container shall be easily removable for cleaning.

CORN SCRAPER: We have never seen this simple gadget in any store, but fortunately, the manufacturer accepts mail orders.☆ It consists of a narrow piece of wood, about 18 inches long, with a groove along which the corncob slides. In the center there is a series of blades, which can be raised or lowered. The scraper is placed over a bowl, the husked corncob is pushed along over the blades, which in one position scrape off the whole kernels and in the second position scrape and cut at the same time, producing creamed corn. One stroke takes about one second; six strokes, with the cob turned slightly each time, cleans off one cob.

FOLEY HAND FOOD MILL: This type of sieve, available at almost any hardware store, has a rotary "pusher," turned by hand, which forces the food through the sieve. It produces an excellent consistency of purée, without over-mashing.

GRATERS AND GRINDERS, GENERAL: Two small electric machines dominate these operations. One is a MEAT GRINDER, with alternative coarse and fine cutters, capable of grinding virtually anything from cheese to nuts and vegetables. We keep it continually plugged in on our work counter and find it one of the most generally useful of all electric appliances.

The other is the French ELECTRIC GRATER, using detachable steel drums of varying degrees of coarseness or fineness and capable also of slicing. However, since both of these machines require a certain amount of taking apart and cleaning after use, we still keep a few HAND GRATERS, for quickly dealing with a small quantity of some foods. There is also a ROTARY NUTMEG GRATER, which has other uses as well. Then there are the CRYSTAL-SALT GRINDER and the PEPPER GRINDERS, a larger clear-plastic one for the kitchen and handsome polished wooden ones for the table.

HACKSAW: See "Saw."

HAMMER, MEAT: See "Meat Hammer."

KNIVES: Over a great many years we have had such disappointing experiences with knives which promised well when they were new but failed after a few months of use that we have become obstinately opinionated on this subject. We simply do not believe that there exists any form of so-called "stainless" steel blade which is hard enough to maintain a truly sharp edge. We refuse to buy any so-called "dual metal" knives, with an edge of one type of metal forged onto a stainless blade. We buy only the finest quality of the hardest carbon steel and this, to us, means the products of the French firm which for more than 500 years has supplied French noblemen with dueling swords. Such knives stain in use, need regular cleaning, and the edge must be properly maintained, with daily sharpening on a Sheffield steel, monthly honing on a Carborundum stone, and annual professional regrinding. We keep three chef's knives, with blades of 4 inches, 6 inches, and 10 inches, plus a general-purpose slicing knife with a curved blade, and a long, narrow 12-inch ham slicer, also used for cutting bacon.

LARDING NEEDLE: Ours is 12 inches long and has toothed slots at the blunt end, which firmly hold the "lardoon," a narrow strip, usually about 1/4 inch square and about 6 inches long, of corn-belly salt pork. Often these lardoons are first marinated for several hours in an aromatic liquid such as, for example, spiced brandy. The needle is then "threaded" with a lardoon and carefully pushed through the joint of meat, etc., in the direction of the grain (this is most important—it will not easily go through across the grain), and the lardoon pulled right through until its tip appears on the other side. The needle is detached, leaving the lardoon in the meat. The operation is repeated until the meat is larded with as many lardoons, usually about 1 inch apart, as are called for in the recipe.

MEAT HAMMER: The hammer is double-headed, with blunt metal teeth on one side and grooves on the other. Steadily pounding a steak or strip of meat tenderizes and breaks up the fibers, while at the same time thinning and spreading out the meat. This is an essential operation in all forms of veal *scaloppini*, but we also use it for any slightly tough piece of meat.

MEASURING GLASS: In addition to the usual array of measuring jugs and cups, we find it useful to have a standard 1-ounce medicine glass, graduated in tablespoons, teaspoons, fractions of an ounce, and metric centiliters, the latter useful in converting measurements from French recipes.

MEDICINE GLASS: See "Measuring Glass."

MOLCAJETE: See "Mortar and Pestle."

MORTAR AND PESTLE: We keep one mortar of smooth white heavy stoneware, with a capacity of about 1 cup, plus a small rough-stone MOLCAJETE, used by Mexicans for dried chili peppers and which we use for grinding anything from a clove of garlic to a few juniper berries.

ROLLING PIN, FRENCH: Once one has used one of these narrow pins* and felt the much finer control that is possible over the pastry, all interest is lost in the standard type, which simply does not work as well.

SABAYON COPPER BEATING BOWL: The importance of having at least one copper beating bowl with a round bottom can hardly be overstressed. Any bowl that has a flat base inevitably has corners into which a balloon wire whisk cannot reach. This means, for example, that there will be small amounts of egg white that remain unbeaten, and this can make a noticeable difference in the rising of a soufflé. Virtually every French kitchen has a separate set of round-bottomed copper beating bowls. We prefer a standard French Sabayon bowl, 8½ inches across, and with a brass handle. It can also be used as a double boiler, held over a pan of hot water, in any operation that involves beating eggs while cooking them.

SAW: We keep an 18-inch hacksaw with a narrow blade set on a frame, which is of the type used by plumbers for cutting metal pipes. It cuts quickly and easily through bone and allows us, for example, to cut up a leg of lamb into chops and steaks, etc., within a few minutes.

SPOONS, BOXWOOD: In addition to the usual set of standard wooden spoons, we keep a few small French boxwood spoons and use them mainly for stirring sauces. Because they are so light, they transmit to one's hand the "feel" of the sauce as it thickens. This gives one a very fine control over consistency and texture.

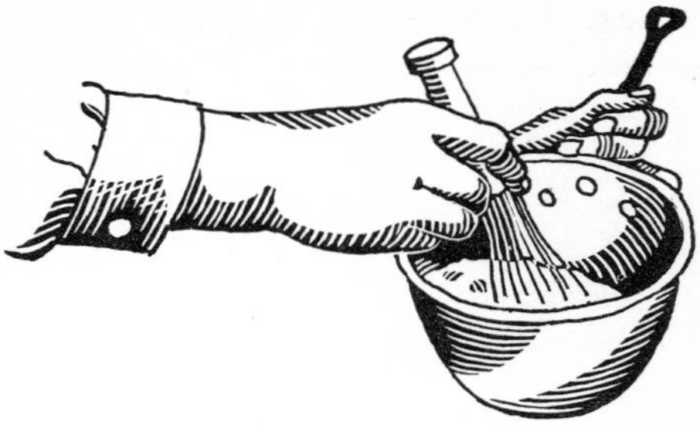

WIRE WHISKS: We keep two whisks, both imported from France, a 12-inch *ballon* (for the larger beating operations in the Sabayon bowl, above) and a small 8-inch one (useful for beating sauces smooth and lumpless).

Fire in the Kitchen

The wall at the back of the stove is covered by a pegboard on which hang the principal tools of the operations connected with heat: the forks, spatulas, spoons, and skimmers; the light sauté and omelette pans; the small pans for sauces; the wooden stirrers and scrapers. . . . On the other side are the shelves with the heavy iron cocottes and baking dishes, all the untidy assemblage which the French call *batterie de cuisine*. Thermometers and other small breakable bits and pieces are in a drawer alongside. Thus, our "fire department" is also a self-contained area of the kitchen, organized within a small circle.

We have cooked over many kinds of heat, from campfires to open coal stoves, from anthracite burners to modern electric and gas ranges. Disregarding for the moment the horrible future prospect of radar cookers, which will do all the work automatically, entirely eliminating human skill, we consider that the most advanced type of gas range, with some automatic controls (many of these developed in connection with space rocketry), is the most flexible and efficient cooking instrument conceived to date. The gas people made a "breakthrough" when they finally admitted to themselves that electricity was not an implacable enemy, but a potential ally, and began to incorporate electrical devices into their gas cookers. For example, our top burners have an electronic "sensing head," a small piece of metal about the size of a half dollar, pushed up by a spring to touch the bottom of the pan and measure its temperature. A thermostat then controls the gas flame to any pre-set degree of heat. The "frying burners" have three rings of flame, which turn themselves off one by one as the heat requirement moves down, from say, fast sautéing, to simmering, to "keeping warm." The infrared broiler makes use of electricity to turn the rotisserie. There is a meat thermometer that can be electrically connected to the oven gas control to turn off the flame when the meat has reached the desired internal temperature. Admittedly, all such gadgets ease the work, yet they do not in any way supersede human judgment.

As to pots and pans, we have used many types, from old battered aluminum to stainless steel and modern heatproof glass. We have reached the firm conclusion that copper and iron, each for its particular use, stand out above other materials. For quick and continuously supervised operations (sautéing, preparing quick sauces, fast boiling and reducing, etc.) a tin-lined copper pan is such an instantaneous conductor of heat that it reaches its working temperature in a few seconds, and then responds in a flash to any changes of that temperature. Since the heat spreads immediately and evenly all over the pan no "hot spots" can ever develop, and the tin coating prevents any interaction between copper and acid foods. When the tin wears out, the pan can be re-tinned. A copper pan over a finely controlled gas flame is an exciting tool to use, and we have noticed again and again that it is virtually the unanimous choice of professional chefs.

For slow simmering and baking operations, we use French cast-iron cocottes, covered on the outside with hard-baked enamel and on the inside with fired ironstone clay, which prevents any interaction with acid foods. These pots heat up gradually and maintain an even temperature for long, slow cooking. The edges of the heavy lids are ground and fit so tightly that sealing with a flour-and-water paste is seldom necessary. Finally, their bright colors make them good-looking enough to be brought to the table.

As to other equipment used on the fire, the following is, again, not a master list for the new bride, but a few notes on some special pieces which we have found to be exceptionally useful and which are mentioned in many of the recipes.

ASPARAGUS BOILER: There are dozens of "special cookers" on the market. In some the asparagus lies in simmering water; in others it stands up in steam. Both methods are completely wrong. Every spear of asparagus presents a dual cooking problem. The tip is so delicate that all it needs is gentle heating in steam. The stalk is tough and needs to be boiled. Our simple solution is a tall, narrow tin-lined copper pot about 9 inches high and about 7 inches across with a tight-fitting lid, which neatly holds a 2-pound bundle of asparagus, standing up. Then enough boiling water is

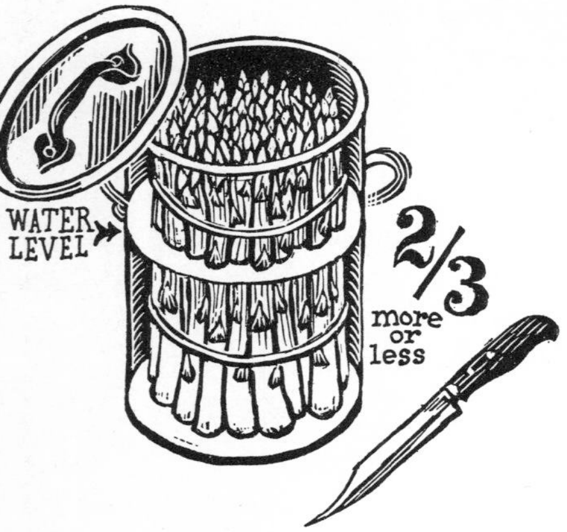

poured in to cover the stalks, leaving the tips above the surface in a steam bath.

BAKING AND AU GRATIN DISHES (see also "Egg Cooking Dishes"): We like the look of earthenware dishes, and our "batterie" includes a large French TOUPIN, for *la garbure* and other one-dish stews; a round, open Mexican BAKING PAN, 8 inches across and 2 inches deep and small INDIVIDUAL CASSEROLES, with many uses. Our open platters are of enameled cast iron, including AU GRATIN dishes of various sizes and the OVAL FISH BAKER, 14 inches long by 10 inches wide.

BELLS, HEATPROOF GLASS: There is no magic about a bell fitted over some food in an au gratin dish. If mushrooms or shad roe can be baked under a bell, they can equally well be baked in a covered casserole. The bell is simply a dramatic serving idea and we like to keep a set of different sizes.

CHINESE WOK: This classic curved frypan of China is such a generally useful instrument that one wonders why it has not been universally adopted in the Western world. It can be found in many sizes and in different shapes and materials, at a wide range of prices, in Chinese hardware and kitchenware stores. It comes in three parts: first, a metal ring, which stands around the gas flame; second, the two-handled metal pan, which looks as if the bottom third had been cut off a large round ball; third, a lid. The pan is placed on the ring over the flame and will rest comfortably in a horizontal position or tilted at any angle. A very small amount of frying fat collects in the bottom nearest the flame, and as the frying of each separate bit of food is completed, it can be slid up the side of the wok and kept warm around the upper circumference.

COCOTTES, FRENCH: A *cocotte* in France is not only a slang expression for a woman of easy virtue but, more importantly, a metal casserole with a tightly fitting lid, available in a multitude of sizes, and having no wood or plastic on the handles so that it can be used equally well on a top burner or in the oven. Some are round, others oval—the better for fitting in a large bird. Each family obviously must choose its own range of sizes. Our cocottes run from the largest, which holds about 3 gallons, to the smallest at 1 quart. They can also be used for light frying or as ordinary saucepans.

COFFEEPOT, TURKISH: See "Imbrik."

EGG COOKING DISHES: When a French cook serves an *oeuf sur le plat,* the *plat* is a very small au gratin dish in which one egg can be baked in various ways. Another fine French way of serving a single egg is *oeuf en cocotte,* the cocotte being a small glazed earthenware pot in which the egg is steamed, then brought to table. Eggs can also be baked, with various meats or fish, in the individual earthenware casseroles mentioned under "baking dishes."

ELECTRIC FRYPAN: See "Frypan, Electric."

FISH BOILER: This is a long, narrow pan to take a whole fish, which rests on a tray on the bottom. A handle at each end of the tray enables the cooked fish to be gently lifted out without any danger of its breaking up.

FRYPAN, ELECTRIC: There is no need to discuss here the general uses of a thermostatically controlled electric frypan. However, we use ours in certain special ways, generally for do-it-yourself cooking in the living room. We also use it as an alternative to a spirit stove or chafing dish, for example, to keep a Swiss cheese fondue hot at the table.

GLASS BELLS: See "Bells, Heatproof Glass."

HAM BOILER: This is a very large, oval tin-lined copper kettle, enough to hold a 20-pound ham. Storing this giant is a problem; our solution is to use the ham boiler, when we are not cooking in it, as a wastebasket alongside the desk.

IMBRIK—TURKISH COFFEEPOT: It seems hardly necessary to describe this universally-known long-handled brass heating pan with the unusual shape, wide at the bottom, narrowing at the top, then opening out with a pouring flange. Apart from its basic purpose for making Turkish coffee, we find it one of the most useful all-purpose pans at the stove. (Incidentally, the shape seems to prevent even milk from boiling over.) We use it for making Mexican hot chocolate, frothing it up with the molinillo.

MOLDS, HOT AND COLD: Apart from standard molds, we have a 2-quart watertight MELON MOLD with a slide-on lid, which is used for our Christmas plum pudding and our fish mousse. It can be used without its lid as an ordinary mold. Another form of mold is a CAST-IRON TERRINE,⚜ a long, narrow covered baking dish, 11 inches long, 3 inches wide, and 3 inches

deep. One mold that cannot be bought but must be constructed by at least an amateur carpenter is the wooden form for the great Russian dessert Paskha. The mold is the shape of a large metronome, open at both ends, made up of four pieces of wood, screwed together in such a way that they can be taken apart when the Paskha is unmolded.

MOLINILLO, MEXICAN: This is a small hand-twirled wooden beater, used for foaming Mexican chocolate. It has paddle-like teeth, and several loose wooden rings, which swirl around. It works best in a narrow pot, and we use it in our Turkish imbrik.

OMELETTE PANS: Exactly as described in the "exposé on omelettes" (page 342), we keep two omelette pans — the larger, for 6 to 8 eggs, is 10½ inches across; the smaller, for 3 to 5 eggs, is 8½ inches across.

PAELLERA, SPANISH: It is a large flat metal platter (sometimes as much as 3 feet across), which is part frypan, part rice boiler, and part baking dish, on which the famous Spanish *paella* is cooked and brought to the table. Neither the exciting taste nor the superbly dramatic appearance of a true *paella* are possible without a paellera. Authentic ones, made of hard hammered steel, are imported from Spain, and there are also American-made types, in stainless steel or aluminum. Some of the American ones provide a lid, but this is useless since the rice for a *paella* must be glazed by being cooked in the open and is quite different when steamed under a lid. Before buying a paellera, the first step is to measure the maximum width of one's oven and then order the largest size to fit. It will first be used on top of the stove, over two, three, or four burners according to size, then will go into a very hot oven (so it cannot have wood or plastic handles) before finally being brought to the table, where a large rough wooden board must be ready to provide a heatproof stand.

DOWN-TO-EARTH NOTE: Some teenage guests once used our paellera to prepare the best pizza that we have ever tasted. They rolled out a large quantity of pizza dough and covered the entire paellera with it, making an edge about ½ inch thick. Then they filled the center with a vast conglomeration of freshly made mozzarella cheese, tomatoes, anchovies, mushrooms, hot peperoni sausage, etc., and baked it all in a fiery-hot oven.

RICE BALL: The rice ball is a simple mechanical device for avoiding the trouble of straining rice after cooking in a large pot of boiling water. The ball is of aluminum, perforated all around with small holes, with two halves that fit together tightly, and can be opened on a hinge to insert the uncooked rice, and later, remove the cooked. There are two sizes of rice ball, one to hold 1 cup of raw rice, the other for 2 cups. See detailed instructions as to use on page 166.

SAUCEPANS, FOR SAUCES AND OTHER USES: A "saucepan" originally meant a pan for making sauce, but now the name means virtually any kind of pan. However, those which we use for sauces and other immediately supervised quick operations are of tin-lined copper, with lids, while those for unsupervised simmering are of enameled cast iron. We try to avoid having ones with wooden or plastic handles, since we often like to finish off the cooking by placing the pan in the oven. We also have some very small saucepans, down to about ¼-cup size, useful for melting butter or soaking saffron in wine, etc. Finally, there is a 5-quart electric saucepan, which doubles as a deep-fat fryer and is also extremely useful for keeping a central main dish hot on a party buffet table. For this, we wrap a clean white cloth around the outside of the saucepan, with the thermostat set at a low keep-warm temperature.

SAUTÉ PANS: One of the essential rules of good sautéing is that the bottom of the pan must be completely covered by the food. If, for instance, just two small lamb chops are being sautéed in a 9½-inch pan, they will absorb heat from the pan at the point where they are touching it, while the rest of the pan is likely to overheat and burn the sauce. For this reason, we keep three tin-lined copper sauté pans, of 9½ inches, 8 inches, and 6½ inches in diameter. Of course a sauté pan is for medium-heat sautéing and not for red-hot searing of steaks. If the sauté pan is made too hot, the tin lining will melt and run into globules. This disaster is not irreparable, since the pan can be sent away to be retinned.

SPATULA FOR OMELETTES: See detailed description on page 343.

STEAMER, MULTIPLE: This is one of the most useful of all cooking pots. It has four tiers: the bottom one contains the boiling water; the next above has holes in its bottom; the next two above have a central chimney so that even foods with runny sauces can be safely heated. The same lid fits all the tiers, so that any number may be used, from two to four (see illustration).

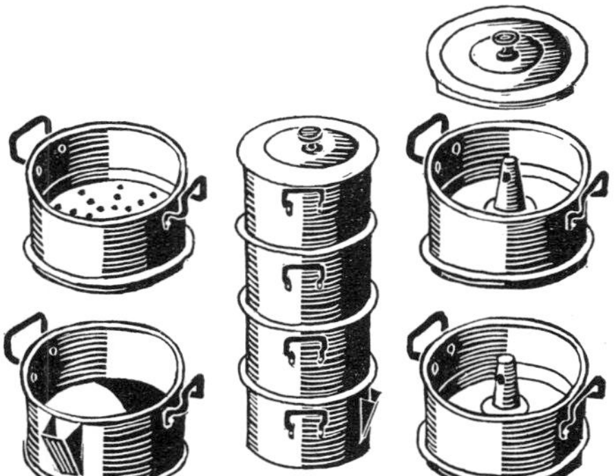

TEAPOTS, ENGLISH: We think that a teapot is for making the best possible tea, not for adding to the interior decoration of the room. Therefore we avoid fancy china or silver pots and concentrate on several sizes of the plain brown earthenware teapots imported from England. See the discussion of teas beginning on page 518.

THERMOMETERS: We keep a CANDY THERMOMETER, an OVEN THERMOMETER, for occasionally checking the oven thermostat (incidentally, also a REFRIGERATOR/FREEZER THERMOMETER), and a MEAT THERMOMETER. The last mentioned should have a scale graduated in degrees Fahrenheit and *not* by the names of the meats and degree of rareness, which at best is indefinite. We use degrees Fahrenheit for our internal meat temperatures in the recipes.

TURKISH COFFEEPOT: See "Imbrik."

WOK: See "Chinese Wok."

Water and Wine in the Kitchen

Water is fine for boiling an egg. It is essential for dissolving out the flavor juices of meat and aromatic herbs and vegetables, to produce the perfect bouillon. Beyond this, however, water adds nothing to a dish. Any recipe that says "thin, if necessary, with a little water" is at once gravely suspect in our kitchen. The right wine, on the other hand, has a character of its own, which it contributes to the food. This has nothing to do with alcohol, which has evaporated and flown after the first minute or two of heating. It has everything to do with the fermented grape juice and the aromatic flavors of the wine.

Some people say that wine is too expensive for cooking, yet they spend many dollars a year on all kinds of commercially bottled artificial flavoring agents, "gravy-makers," "taste teasers," "magic all-purpose sauces," etc. Far better results would follow from spending half the money on a few bottles of the right wine. While it is true that fine cooking is not possible without wine, it is equally true that wine by itself cannot make good cooking out of bad. It is also true that a wine which is too cheap to drink is too cheap for cooking. Yet, obviously, it would be a waste to use a great wine where the delicate subtleties that make it great would be lost in the cooking. (There is at least one exception to this rule, our *coq au vin,* where the wine is featured so dominantly that the better it is, the better the dish.)

We keep a cheap wooden 8-bottle wine rack in the kitchen. The four bottles in the top row are the dry wines for the main dishes; the bottom four are the sweet liqueurs and spirits, mainly for desserts and flaming. The choice of bottles varies from month to month. We may buy a small bottle of something for a special dish, then use up the remainder in other ways. We do more flaming in winter and use more liqueurs for marinating fruits in summer. Here is our master list, from which we choose our kitchen wines.

Basic Dry Red Wines

In general, the wines that cook best are the rich, fruity, powerful "peasant" wines and these, because they are not so much in demand, are usually relatively inexpensive. The requirements are nicely met by a better-quality CALIFORNIA "JUG" WINE of the "Mountain Red Burgundy" type. From France, a good choice would be a moderately priced blended district wine of SAINT-EMILION from the Bordeaux region or a moderately priced blended BEAUJOLAIS from Burgundy. Among Italian reds, we use a wine from Lombardy that lives up to its name, INFERNO, or from Piedmont either a BAROLO or a GATTINARA.

Basic Dry White Wines

The need for robust fruitiness is the same as for the reds and again the choice might be a better-quality CALIFORNIA "JUG" WINE of the "Mountain White Chablis" or "Graves" types (*never* a "Sauternes" type, or any other sweet white wine). A good French wine would be a moderately priced MÂCON BLANC, or among the Italian whites, a dry FRASCATI from the Alban

Hills behind Rome, or a dry ORVIETO from the province of Umbria. (Both Frascati and Orvieto also come in sweet-type and these must be avoided. The dry is usually labeled *secco* and the sweet, *abboccato*.)

Madeira Instead of Sherry or Vermouth

Almost all dry fortified wines are excellent for cooking, because of their strong aromatic base—hence the phrase "cooking sherry," which nowadays simply means cheap and nasty sherry. In a French professional kitchen, however, it means sherry to which enough salt has been added by the *Maître de Cuisine* to ensure that the wine does not go down the throats of the kitchen staff! Even better than sherry, we think, is SERCIAL MADEIRA. (We avoid Madeiras labeled "Boal" or "Malmsey," which are extremely sweet.) When a dish is to be simmered for a long time, it is best to use white wine during the simmering and finally add a small amount of Madeira at the end. It has a special affinity with game birds, mushrooms, and chestnuts. A teaspoon or two may be added at the table to each plate of a rich soup. If SHERRY is used, it must be a dry *fino,* or if VERMOUTH, it must be the driest available.

Imported British Hard Cider

If one can get this strongly alcoholic drink (not to be confused with the domestic sweet stuff), it adds an excellent and slightly unusual flavor to many dishes. It has a special affinity with fish and shellfish. It is extremely good to add to the water in which a whole ham is being boiled and also goes well with pork. Never add hard cider to any dish that is being cooked in an iron pot; the iron tends to turn the cider black.

Port and Marsala

Both of these fortified wines are usually slightly sweet, but, in the better qualities, the sweetness is delicate and the texture never syrupy. They can be excellent in certain main dishes: one uses, of course, a moderately priced RUBY PORT or an authentic MARSALA SUPERIORI from the town of Marsala in western Sicily. Marsala is one of the best wines for deglazing a frypan or sauté pan, by "hissing" a few tablespoons into the hot pan after the meat has been removed, scraping off the "crust," then boiling down the liquid until it glazes and thickens and pouring over the meat as a sauce. Port makes an excellent quick gravy for a roast. . . .

BASIC METHOD FOR QUICK PORT-WINE GRAVY FOR RARE ROAST BEEF, VEAL, OR VENISON

For our family of 4

Check Staples:

Gravy in roasting pan
Beef bouillon about (1½ cups)
Lemon (1)
Aromatics: crystal salt,⁑ freshly ground black pepper,⁑ garlic (1 to 2 cloves, to taste), mace chips
Ground arrowroot (about 2 Tbs.)
Ruby Port (½ to ¾ cup)

Shopping List:

Red-currant jelly (a few Tbs.)

Immediately After the Roast Is Done

Remove meat from roasting pan and keep it warm. Remove all fat from pan, then measure remaining gravy and stir into it enough of the beef bouillon to make 2 cups. Place pan on top burner and slowly bring gravy-bouillon up to gentle simmering. While heating up, stir in: ½ cup of the Port wine, 3 tablespoons of the red-currant jelly, then blend in, a few drops at a time, enough lemon juice to produce a slight tartness. Add a couple of pinches of salt, 2 or 3 grinds of pepper, 1 or 2 cloves of garlic to taste, mashed through a press, plus a pinch or two of freshly ground mace. Now taste and add more of any or all of these ingredients, as needed, to achieve an interesting and slightly sharp sauce. Simmer for 2 or 3 minutes, then turn down heat to below simmering and thicken with about 5 teaspoons of the arrowroot, liquefied with some of the remaining Port (see the BASIC RULE, page 14). When gravy seems exactly right, bring to the table in a hot sauceboat.

Spirits for Flaming

There are two kinds of flaming: the first, solely for flavor, is usually done in the kitchen during cooking; the second, partly for last-minute flavor and partly for dramatic show, is always done as the dish comes into the room, or at table. The rules for success are the same in both cases. . . .

BASIC RULE FOR FLAMING ANYTHING: 1. The spirit used must be 80 proof or more, which means that it must contain at least 40 per cent alcohol. From this minimum point up, the more alcohol the better the fire. The best flaming of all is with the DARK DEMERARA RUM from British Guiana, which is one of the strongest spirits in the world at 151 proof, or three quarters pure alcohol (its flavor, however, is hardly suitable for every dish).

2. If the flaming is to be done in a hot pan in the kitchen, turn up the heat under the pan, pour on about 1/4 cup of the spirit and light. The flames shoot higher and last longer if the dish is held in gloved hands and shaken or firmly stirred with a long-handled spoon.

3. If the flaming is to be done on the serving dish, the 1/4 cup or so of the spirit must be slightly heated, so as to release the alcohol slowly, but must not be made very hot or all the alcohol will evaporate in advance. It is best to put the 1/4 cup of spirit into a very small 1/2-cup pan and heat gently until the liquid is just hot to the tip of the finger. Then pour immediately over the dish and set alight.

As to which spirits we might hold in our kitchen wine rack: there is almost always a small bottle of the 151-proof DARK DEMERARA RUM, mentioned above; also, usually, a moderately priced young and fruity CALIFORNIA BRANDY. There is often a domestic or British DRY GIN, which goes particularly well with dishes containing juniper berries. There is one flaming spirit that has a marvelous effect on lobster and on other rich fish and shellfish dishes, the aniseed-flavored PERNOD, the drink which replaced absinthe when that deadly liquor was banned from commercial sale. For flaming fruits, the best spirit is usually the colorless brandy distilled from wild black cherries, the Swiss or German KIRSCH, or KIRSCHWASSER, but one of the moderately priced labels.

Sweet Liqueurs and Brandies for Dessert

Any remaining spaces in our kitchen wine rack are usually filled with very small bottles of dessert liqueurs and brandies. For a few ideas on the possible marriages of liqueurs with fruits, see page 174. Only a sprinkling of each liqueur is used to heighten the natural flavors rather than dominate them. We usually keep a good APRICOT BRANDY, the best being the Hungarian BARACK PALINKA, or one of the other domestic or imported labels. Also FRAMBOISE, the colorless brandy distilled from raspberries, the best quality imported from Alsace. Then, perhaps, MIRABELLE, the colorless brandy distilled from the small golden plums of Alsace. Finally, almost always a small supply of ORANGE CURAÇAO, made originally by the Dutch from the small green oranges of the island of Curaçao. We buy a medium-priced domestic brand and reserve the nobler versions, the Cointreau, Triple Sec, or Grand Marnier, for sipping at the table after dinner.

THE Winter Dog Days

January and February

EXPLANATION OF SYMBOLS

A symbol appearing after a word refers the reader to a particular section of the book for further details. Example: olive oil, crystal salt, cocotte, dry white wine, Parmesan cheese, Beaujolais, turtle meat.

- stands for Raw Materials and Staples, pages 10–18
- stands for Aromatics, pages 18–29
- stands for Kitchen Equipment, pages 32–41
- stands for Wine in the Kitchen, pages 41–5
- stands for Cheeses, pages 660–75
- stands for Wines for the Table, pages 676–98
- stands for Marketing and Mail-Order Sources, pages 699–714

January-February

WINTER FOODS IN SEASON

GASTRONOMICALLY the year begins at a low ebb and rises toward its spring, harvest, and holiday climaxes. During these dog days there are few local fresh foods in the market. Modern transportation brings fresh delicacies from all over the world, but a journey of thousands of miles is expensive and often dulls the edge of flavor. After the overspending and overeating of the holidays, this is our season for economy and simplicity. Our checklist of the basic winter foods we look for in the markets follows. Obviously it cannot include everything grown in every county of the United States but we have found it accurate over many years of winter shopping on the East, West and Gulf coasts and in Chicago and other Midwestern cities.

The Special Pleasures of the Season

THIS IS a good and slightly less expensive time to experiment with the less well-known cuts of BEEF (page 58).

For an especially good meat value we buy RABBIT, available at this season from many butchers and quite excellent prepared in spiced mustard butter (page 126).

After New Year's, fancy butchers begin to unload their remaining Christmas stocks. Many game farms reduce their flocks and offer "specials" on freshly killed and dressed birds. During cold weather the Chicago mail-order houses✠ ship ready-dressed game birds and oven-ready cuts of the large and small game animals. We always try to avoid frozen birds and meat, but these shipments are not hard frozen; they are refrigerated and sent in insulated packages. We look for bargains in MALLARD DUCK, CANADA GOOSE, white African and pearl GUINEA HEN, RINGNECK PHEASANT and BOBWHITE QUAIL, and SQUAB; also cuts of VENISON (or BROWN BEAR). See shopping notes, page 59.

Our favorite fish of this season, beautiful in appearance and taste, is Gulf of Mexico RED SNAPPER (page 60).

One of the great delicacies of winter is the tiny, sweet, succulent BAY SCALLOP, dredged up, as its name implies, from inshore waters. Conservation laws strictly limit its season, but it is usually in good supply until the beginning of March. See shopping notes, page 62.

For taste and texture variety at a low price few winter fruits can equal the APPLE, but one must know the special qualities of each type. We list the names and seasons of the apples we like, subdivided according to their uses. For one of the best simple winter desserts, we serve coarsely chunked raw apple, with cubes of the winter cheeses (page 173), and freshly shelled walnuts (page 508). Our order of preference for these eating apples; the Northwestern JONATHAN, the New Jersey MCINTOSH and GOLDEN DELICIOUS, and the Northwestern YELLOW NEWTOWN, first of the new crop. For fried apple rings, with which we garnish many main dishes (page 129): the Eastern CORTLAND and the New Jersey WINESAP. For baking apples with a firm texture, to hold their shape in the oven (page 615): the New Jersey ROME BEAUTY, best, and the New England NORTHERN SPY. For general stewing and pies: the Michigan and New York State GREENING, best; the Eastern and Midwestern BALDWIN, and the Eastern and Southern YORK IMPERIAL.

The Freshwater Fish of the Winter Season

These fish have lean flesh and respond generally to similar cooking methods (page 136). Some are sold mainly around Chicago and the Great Lakes:

Lake and river CARP, start of season
LAKE HERRING, fished through ice holes on the Great Lakes, peak season
Great Lakes PICKEREL, start of season
LAKE SMELT, start of season
Great Lakes SAUGER, peak season

And one oily fleshed fish:

Great Lakes CHUB, start of season

The Saltwater Fish of the Winter Season

At this time of year we can often find big fish in smaller 2- to 3-pound sizes, very delicate when baked whole in a buttered casserole (page 136), or oven-poached in foil (page 141). These fish have lean flesh:

Atlantic SEA BASS, start of season
Atlantic YOUNG COD

Other good values in lean-fleshed fish which respond to similar cooking methods:

Atlantic STRIPED BASS, mainly around New York, peak season
Atlantic BLOWFISH, or SEA SQUAB, mainly around New York, start of season
Atlantic and Pacific LARGE COD, cut into steaks
And the various members of the FLOUNDER family, always best prepared with the bone in (page 138)
  Atlantic BLACKBACK, mainly in the Northeast
  New England DAB
  Atlantic FLUKE, start of season
  New England GRAY SOLE
  Pacific REX SOLE, peak season for this West Coast delicacy
Gulf GROUPER, start of season
New England HADDOCK, start of season
Atlantic HAKE, start of season
South Atlantic and Gulf MULLET, good for pan-frying as they do it on the French Riviera (page 137)
New England POLLOCK, peak season
Atlantic PORGY, start of season
Pacific ROCKFISH, the West Coast cousin of the Eastern STRIPED BASS, start of season
New England and Middle Atlantic TILEFISH, which we bake in a nest of potatoes (page 136)
Atlantic and Gulf KING WHITING
New England WOLFFISH, mainly around Boston, start of season

These fish with oily flesh are generally interchangeable:

Atlantic HERRING, peak season
Gulf POMPANO, start of season, excellent baked in foil (page 297)
Fresh SARDINES, which are, of course, small herring

These fish are in short supply at this time of the year and if we find them in the market we make sure that they are not from frozen storage. With oily flesh:

Atlantic BUTTERFISH
The members of the MACKEREL family:
  Atlantic BOSTON MACKEREL
  South Atlantic and Gulf KING MACKEREL and SPANISH MACKEREL
St. Lawrence SMELT, fine deep-fried in our fluffy batter (page 140)

And with lean flesh:

Atlantic and Pacific HALIBUT
Atlantic and Pacific SWORDFISH

The Shellfish of the Winter Season

All have lean flesh:

Atlantic CLAMS, the HARD CHOWDER and the SOFT STEAMER, mainly in the Northeast

Shelled CRAB in refrigerated cans:

- The luxurious *large lumps,* which we flame at table in a sauté pan (page 452)
- The less expensive *small pieces*
- The least expensive *flake bits*

Pacific DUNGENESS CRAB, peak season

Imported South African and West Indian ROCK LOBSTER TAILS, always frozen

Pacific SPINY LOBSTER, start of season

Atlantic MUSSELS, superb in a green sauce (page 195)

Eastern and Western OYSTERS

Atlantic DEEP-SEA SCALLOPS

Florida Gulf and imported SHRIMP, one of the best times of year for fresh supplies, also imported from El Salvador, India, Mexico, Panama, and Venezuela

The Fruits of the Winter Season

We look for the best values in:

Imported South African APRICOTS } both party luxuries
Imported Chilean BING CHERRIES }

Eastern and Western CRANBERRIES

Florida PINK SEEDLESS GRAPEFRUIT

California GRAPES, excellent with Liederkranz cheese, the BLACK RIBIER, the large EMPEROR, the last TOKAY

Imported Belgian hothouse GRAPES, flown over by plane, very luxurious, the BLACK COLMAR and the WHITE MUSCAT

The last Florida KUMQUAT, also imported from Hong Kong and Japan

California and Florida LEMONS

Florida LIMES

Winter varieties of MELON:

- Imported Mexican CANTALOUPE
- Imported Argentine, Chilean, and Sicilian HONEYDEW
- Imported SPANISH MELON, from both Argentina and Spain

Imported Chilean NECTARINES

Winter varieties of the ORANGE:

- Imported Israeli JAFFA, large, seedless
- Florida KING, loose-skinned tangerine type
- California and Florida NAVEL, thick-skinned
- Florida PINEAPPLE JUICE
- Florida and imported Spanish BITTER SEVILLE, for homemade marmalade (page 63)
- Florida TEMPLE, loose-skinned
- California and Florida VALENCIA

Imported Jamaican ORTANIQUES, a cross between an orange and a tangerine. See shopping notes, page 63.

Hawaiian and imported West Indian PAPAYA

Imported Chilean and South African PEACHES: the ELBERTA and the J. H. HALE

Winter varieties of PEAR, excellent poached in wine (page 618)

- California, New York State, and Northwestern ANJOU
- New York State and Northwestern BOSC, ending its season
- New York State and Northwestern COMICE
- Imported British Columbian FLEMISH
- California and Northwestern NELIS

Puerto Rican PINEAPPLE

Imported Chilean SANTA ROSA PLUMS, excellent with Brie and Camembert cheese (page 173)

The first Michigan hothouse RHUBARB

California and Florida WINTER STRAWBERRIES, a party luxury for St. Valentine's Day (page 177)

Florida TANGELOS

Florida TANGERINES

The extraordinary imported Jamaican UGLI, a citrus hybrid that looks like a surrealist grapefruit but has a delightful flavor. See shopping notes, page 64.

The Salads of the Winter Season

We stress the variety of the seasons with different salad combinations and different dressings. To compensate for the lack of delicacy in winter greens we make the dressings more pungent. The BASIC RULES for salads are given on page 73. Winter salad dressings are found on page 169.

California, Florida, and imported West Indian AVOCADO, also sometimes called by such fancy names as CUSTARD APPLE, BUTTER PEAR, or ALLIGATOR PEAR
The young center leaves of CHINESE or CELERY CABBAGE
California and Florida WHITE CELERY
California and Florida CHICORY
Florida and imported West Indian CUCUMBERS
California, Florida, and Texas DANDELION GREENS
Texas fresh DILL
Imported Belgian ENDIVES
California and Florida ESCAROLE
Winter varieties of LETTUCE:
- Florida and Indiana hothouse BIBB
- Florida BOSTON, or HEAD
- Western ICEBERG
- Florida ROMAINE

The Winter salad varieties of the ONION family:
- Frozen packaged GREEN CHIVES
- The socially controversial GARLIC, which should and can be kept under control (page 200)
- New York and imported Chilean and Italian SWEET RED ONIONS
- And the universal GREEN SCALLION

Florida and imported Mexican and West Indian GREEN PEPPER
California, Florida, and local RADISHES
The young leaves of SPINACH
Florida and imported Mexican and West Indian TOMATOES
And the indispensable WATERCRESS

The Vegetables of the Winter Season

We use vigorous sauces and assertive spiced butters to mask the coarser taste and harder texture of the vegetables at this time of the year:

- California ARTICHOKES
- Florida GREEN BEANS
- California and Texas BEETS
- New Jersey hothouse BEET TOPS
- Arizona, California, Texas, and Southern BROCCOLI
- California and the first Texas BRUSSELS SPROUTS, excellent teamed with the last of the imported Italian chestnuts (page 157)
- Winter members of the CABBAGE family:
  - Arizona, New Jersey, New York, and imported Dutch GREEN CABBAGE, excellent prepared by our 7½-minute method (page 310)
  - The widely grown RED CABBAGE, so richly prepared by European cooks (page 646)
  - Arizona, California, and Florida WHITE CABBAGE
- California and Texas CARROTS
- Arizona, California, Florida, and Texas CAULIFLOWER
- Puerto Rican and local CELERIAC, or CELERY ROOT, which converts mashed potatoes into a luxury dish (page 543)
- California and Florida GREEN PASCAL CELERY
- Imported Italian CHESTNUTS, excellent in many ways (pages 157, 531, 562)
- Imported EGGPLANT, or AUBERGINE
- California and Florida FENNEL
- New York and Pennsylvania MUSHROOMS; we cook them as if they were grown in Provence (page 181)
- Florida and imported West Indian OKRA
- The cooking varieties of the ONION, so infinitely variable in accent (page 198):
  - Idaho large SWEET BERMUDA ONIONS
  - The local and indispensable LEEK
  - Fresh or packaged SHALLOTS
  - Idaho and imported SPANISH ONIONS
  - Local WHITE BOILERS
  - Local all-purpose YELLOW ONIONS
- California and Northeastern PARSNIP, which can be prepared like the WHITE TURNIP in a maple-mustard sauce (page 163)

Winter varieties of POTATO:

- The dry IDAHO BAKERS
- Vermont WHITE WINTER and GREEN MOUNTAIN BAKERS
- Maine KATAHDIN BOILERS, fluffy for mashing
- Long Island WHITE BOILERS
- Maine RUSSET BOILERS
- New Jersey and Southern orange and yellow SWEET POTATOES, which we bake in a casserole with sunflower seeds (page 532)

The winter is a good time for Florida, Georgia, and Carolina SOUTHERN GREENS; our favorite of many possible combinations (page 162) consists of:

- COLLARDS
- DANDELION GREENS
- HANOVER SALAD
- KALE
- MUSTARD GREENS
- TURNIP TOPS

New Southern SPINACH; we cook it by the classic method of Brillat-Savarin (page 533)

The Southern and Western members of the WINTER SQUASH family:

- ACORN, superb baked whole with maple butter (page 155)
- BUTTERNUT
- HUBBARD

The winter supply of WHITE TURNIPS, the alternative to PARSNIPS, excellent casserole-baked in a maple-mustard sauce (page 163)

Shopping in Winter

TODAY'S supermarket is a far cry from the seventeenth-century French barns and cellars where the *gromets* of Louis XIV inspected and horse-traded the raw foods for the kitchens of Versailles. The first problem of the modern gourmet remains the same: to judge not only quality and value in the market but also the "character" of the raw foods and their "compatibility" with the recipes in mind. A McIntosh and a Rome Beauty can both be large, high-quality apples, but the list of the season's special pleasures (page 50) shows that the McIntosh has the character for eating raw while the Rome Beauty is compatible with oven heat and will hold its texture and shape in baking. The herring is an oily-fleshed fish that is best when grilled or baked. The list of winter fish (page 51) indicates that the oily-fleshed smelt, but not the lean-fleshed sea bass or whiting, might be substituted in a recipe calling for herring.

We believe that it is shopping skill which makes the difference at the table between the merely good and the memorable dish. For example, it is the greatest mistake to think that a more expensive raw material will automatically bring a better result. We taught a friend how to prepare a *carbonnade flamande,* in which seared cubes of round of beef are simmered in spiced beer. The friend then decided to improve on our method by paying about double the price for a glamorous cut of T-bone steak which, of course, was so delicately tender that it simply disintegrated. We once served a charming newly wedded couple a *waterzooie* of chicken, in which a cheap and tough old laying hen is simmered in an aromatic broth for several hours, until the flesh is butter-tender and the vintage juices of the old bird have brought the broth to a winy peak. A few days later the young wife tried to reproduce the dish with an expensive young roasting chicken which had neither the flavor nor the texture for long, slow simmering, and the meat boiled down to a tasteless white mush.

A general discussion of basic buying problems is in section I of the Introduction. We add here a few shopping notes on some of the winter foods listed in the preceding pages.

Search for Variety and Value in Beef

For every dollar we spend at the butcher's we receive something which is partly edible, partly a semi-useless waste of bones, fat, and gristle. Clearly, we must know how much of each we are getting if we are to judge the value of our purchase. For example, if prime porterhouse steak is about 50 per cent edible lean meat and 50 per cent inedible bone and fat, and if its price is $1.25 per pound, we know that we are actually paying $2.50 per pound for the lean meat.

There is a simple and practical way of making this calculation for the main cuts. Meat animals are now so completely standardized that the industry publishes technical charts showing the average breakdown of lean meat, fat, bone, etc. We have translated these charts, for our own use, into tables typed on cards small enough to be clipped to our shopping lists. Our table for beef follows; the ones for lamb and pork are on pages 223 and 224, and that for veal, on page 369.

In this table the left-hand column lists the principal beef cuts. The middle column shows how to translate the price per pound into the cost of an average serving. It gives an immediate comparison of the relative values of two different cuts. For example: for T-bone steak we divide the price per pound by 2, and if the price is $1.10 per pound the cost per average serving is 55 cents; while for wedge-bone sirloin we divide by 3, and therefore if the price is $1.50 per pound the cost per average serving is 50 cents. In this instance the more expensive meat is the better value.

Finally, the right-hand column of the table shows approximately the amount to order for each person to be served. For example: if we decide on the wedge-bone sirloin steak for 8 people, we need about 7 ounces for each person, or a total of 3½ pounds. This amount allows for the inedible bone and fat.

BEEF

When buying this cut:	To find the approximate cost per serving divide price per pound by:	And buy this amount per person:
Bottom, or heel, of ROUND, lean	3	6 oz.
BRISKET, lean	2	½ lb.
CHUCK, or shoulder, arm, or blade, lean	3	6 oz.
GROUND, best, lean	3	6 oz.
HEART	3	6 oz.
KIDNEY	3	6 oz.
LIVER	4	¼ lb.
RIBS:		
Boneless rolled	3	7 oz.
Short	2	½ lb.
Standing, best cut	1½	10 oz.
STEAKS:		
Club	2	½ lb.
Flank	3	6 oz.
Porterhouse	2	½ lb.
Round, best top, or rump	3	6 oz.
Sirloin:		
Double-bone	2	7 oz.
Hip-bone	2	½ lb.
Round-bone	3	7 oz.
Wedge-bone	3	7 oz.
T-bone	2	½ lb.

Variety and Value in the Neglected Two Thirds

Whether it be a carcass of beef, lamb, pork, or veal, the heavily demanded, high-priced butchers' cuts make up only about one third of the animal. The remaining, neglected two thirds is the happy hunting ground for the adventurous meat shopper. Any cut that is properly cooked according to its character is tender and, if intelligently seasoned, can be exciting to the taste.

For example, few cooks have even begun to explore the wide variety of beef, lamb, and veal cuts for pot-roasting. The first requirement of such a cut is that it be too tough to roast in the oven; then it will become tender without disintegrating in the fragrant steam from the wine, stock, vegetable juice, or fine vinegar in which it is being cooked. Second, the bones should be left in, to conduct heat to the center for even cooking and retention of juices. Here are our favorite cuts, each of which might be prepared in aromatic wine (page 121), either gently simmered on top of the stove or in a 350-degree oven.

TIMETABLE FOR POT-ROASTING

(Braising)

	Average weight of cut	Approximate cooking time, meat starting at room temperature	Final internal temperature
BEEF:			
Chuck, or heel, of round	3 to 5 lbs.	2½ to 4 hours	125°
Shoulder, arm, or blade, bone in	3 to 7 lbs.	3 to 4½ hours	125°
LAMB:			
Shoulder, square-cut with bone	4 to 6 lbs.	2 to 3 hours	130°
VEAL:			
Shoulder, arm, or blade, bone in	5 to 6 lbs.	3 to 3½ hours	155°
Heel of rump, boneless	4 to 8 lbs.	2½ to 4 hours	155°

For the estimated cost per serving and amounts to buy per person, see the Beef Chart (page 58), the Lamb Chart (page 223), or the Veal Chart (page 369). Pork is too tender for pot-roasting. For the preparation of other neglected meat cuts, see the section devoted to "budget pull-back dishes."

Wild Game Is Not So Wild

The idea that game meat is something shot by a hunter is rapidly going out of date. Quite properly, to protect the dwindling numbers of our wild animals, the conservation laws of many states forbid the commercial shipment of wild game across state lines. So more and more of the game in the stores is from animals partly or wholly domesticated and bred on game farms, or in enclosed forest preserves. Perhaps the domesticated animals are better for the table. A wild animal is generally muscular, tough, and thin. The following are points we remember when buying game.

An oven-ready MALLARD DUCK weighs between 1½ and 2½ pounds and usually provides a good meal for 2 people, a skimpy meal for 3. It is truly wild and not to be confused with its fat, lazy Long Island cousin. While the Long Islander is roasted slowly at 325 degrees for about 1¼ hours, to melt off its fat, the slim mallard is rapidly crisped at 475 degrees for not a second more than 30 minutes. No bird in the world can be so dry, tough, and tasteless as an overcooked mallard, nor as magnificent as a perfectly cooked one (page 131).

An oven-ready CANADA GOOSE can weigh up to 8 pounds, though the smaller ones are often more tender and juicy (page 590). The GUINEA HEN, which has an unusual and exciting flavor, is now completely domesticated and can be treated as if it were a small chicken weighing about 1½ to 2 pounds (page 589). The PHEASANT is also largely domesticated, can weigh from 1½ to 4 pounds oven-ready, and while its name is glamorous its taste is mild and un-gamey. We seldom serve it.

In Europe the PARTRIDGE and the QUAIL are two different species of small birds, but in the United States they are the same, regardless of the claims of the game dealer. What is bred as a quail in the North is a partridge in the South. One bird is allowed for each serving (page 129). The SQUAB is a young farm-fattened pigeon, also served one to a person. It has a magnificent affinity for juniper berries and gin (page 444).

A leg of VENISON makes a manageable roast; a haunch can be brought in with trumpets and the cheers of a huge party, or it can provide portion-size steaks and chops. It is one of the finest of all meats when properly marinated in aromatic wine and served with a chocolate sauce (page 540).

Even the butcher has to depend on the free-lance hunter for the BROWN BEAR. For those with large freezers, a hind quarter usually weighs about 60 pounds. We settle for small roasts and steaks, which are also improved by aromatic marination.

Look the Fish Straight in the Eye

In one way the fishing industry is unique. The farmer and the cattleman control what they produce. But the fisherman does not know what he will find in his nets until he hauls them in, and this uncertainty runs right through to the fishmonger's slab. That is why efficient shopping for fish makes special demands on the gourmet.

It is a mistake to go to the fishmonger with only one particular fish in mind. On the day when one demands salmon it may be in short supply and what the fishmonger brings out is a faded and limp specimen, thawed out of a block of ice. It is far better to begin with the question: "What's good today?" realizing that there are very few recipes in which one fish cannot be replaced by another of similar type, as shown in the list of the special pleasures of the season on page 50. We usually leave our menu flexible until the fish is bought, then choose the best cooking method from one of our basic recipes (see "Index").

The first rule in buying fish is to look it straight in the eye. A fresh fish has eyes that are bright and clear, transparent and full. As it becomes stale its eyes become cloudy, turn pink, and collapse into their sockets. Second, look at the skin. If the fish is only a few hours out of the water, the skin is iridescent, the colors shiny and bright; soon they start fading. Third, make sure the fish smells fresh. Fishy odor comes out only when the oil begins to go rancid. If there is still some doubt, press the fish. The flesh of fresh fish is firm and elastic. When buying fish steaks the cut surface should be moist. We always prefer whole fish with the head on and the backbone in, since these conduct the heat to the center of the fish for even cooking and retention of juices. With head and bone included in the weight, we buy ¾ to 1 pound per person to be served. When the fish is beheaded and opened up for grilling, but the backbone still left in, we buy about ½ pound per person. With boneless fillets, all edible, we buy about 6 ounces per person, or about 1 pound to serve 3.

Good Seasons and Good Sizes for Shrimp

Because shrimp is equally available every month of the year, many shoppers believe that it is caught and marketed fresh all the time. This is not true. Huge supplies of shrimp are landed during the fall and winter months and a large part of these catches is put into frozen storage. Then, when the shrimping falls off in the spring, the frozen supplies are brought out to maintain the market. So we think that the winter is a good time to buy fresh shrimp and we generally abstain from eating them during the late spring and summer, coming back to them again in October. We also find it useful to know how many shrimp to expect in a pound of the various sizes. There is an official grading system that is accepted in most parts of the country. When we ask for these sizes, we expect the following number of beheaded shrimp per pound:

"Jumbo"—fewer than 15 per pound, often only 9 or 10
"Large"—16 to 25 per pound
"Medium"—26 to 35 per pound
"Small"—36 or more per pound

Bay Scallops into the New Year

The DEEP-SEA SCALLOP is brought ashore and widely distributed all through the year, but one of the great gastronomic pleasures of living in New York or the Northeast is the BABY BAY SCALLOP, which, as its name implies, is dredged up from shallow coastal waters and is so small, sweet, and tender that it needs only a minute or two of cooking (page 142). The fishing towns on the scallop bays of Long Island and New Jersey used to practice conservation by restricting the season to about eight weeks in the fall and forbidding all near-shore scalloping after midnight on New Year's Eve, but now the beds have multiplied to such an extent that conservation laws have been eased and bay scallops continue to come ashore through January and February and often into March. (But why, oh why, do most American fish dealers sell only the white muscle of the scallop? In Europe, or even in New York's Chinatown, they sell the scallop complete in its half shell, including the red coral, which is a delicacy and greatly improves any scallop dish.) The best-tasting bay scallop is found in the shallow waters of Riverhead and around Shelter Island on Peconic Bay.

Rarest Food in the World?

There is surely no food harder to find than the extraordinary shellfish of New Zealand, the toheroa. If one wants to celebrate New Zealand Day on February 6 with a cream stew of Tikinui toheroa (page 146), one must start an airmail letter on its way to New Zealand in the first week of January. This dish provides one of the world's rarest and finest gastronomic experiences. New Zealand gourmets regard it as a matter of national pride and the New Zealand Embassy in Washington keeps a supply on hand as an instrument of its diplomacy.

The toheroa is a double-shelled bivalve that looks something like a huge clam, but belongs to an entirely different species. It is often more than 6 inches across and is found buried about a foot down in the sand in only one place in the world, the Ironside Beaches of the west coast of New Zealand. When the first settlers came, there were millions of toheroas. Today they are in danger of complete extinction. This is due partly to certain natural changes in the ocean currents, which have taken away much of the toheroas' food, and partly to the fact that the native Maoris taught the English settlers how good toheroas are to eat.

Today every toheroa is a ward of the New Zealand government. The only open season for "toheroaing" is during July and August. One digger may not take more than 20. The police stop and search all cars leaving the beaches. (A black market has developed. Recently, in the dead of night, the police swooped down on a truck with a silencer on its exhaust and found it had 50,000 toheroas aboard. The men involved were arrested and imprisoned.)

The government allows only one canner to pack toheroas for export,❊ but even this trickle is occasionally officially stopped after a bad season.

Rush to Catch the Seville Orange

The fruit with perhaps the shortest season of them all is the BITTER SEVILLE ORANGE, which was once grown only in Spain but now comes also from Florida. It makes the world's finest marmalades, whether one of the famous English brands❊ or a homemade version (page 183). The season for bitter Sevilles usually lasts for not more than ten days in February, so we watch for them or order them in advance by mail from one of the fancy-fruit shops.❊

The West Indian Ortanique and Ugli

The ORTANIQUE is a unique hybrid that was developed by accident by the crossbreeding of an orange and a tangerine. In 1906 an ice storm in Florida froze the citrus crop. To speed up the replacement of young seedling orange and tangerine trees the Florida growers set up nurseries in Jamaica. Years later, after the nurseries had been abandoned, a tree was found in which orange and tangerine had mated. The new fruit, about the size of an orange, was first exported to Britain and is now widely distributed in the United States.

The UGLI is another cross-mating, this time between an orange and a grapefruit. The inside is excellent, but something very strange happened to the skin and the shape which has to be seen to be believed!

THE WINTER FEAST DAYS
An International Calendar

WHEN our children were in school we felt that we could begin to make them aware of the rest of the world by celebrating some of the foreign feast days at our own table. This often involved a shopping expedition in search of extraordinary ingredients, a courageous tasting of strange dishes, and a setting of the table and serving of the meal in an unusual way. It was an adventure which in time eliminated all fear of the gastronomic unknown. Sometimes in preparing for a celebration we also played the music of that country and studied the costumes that might be worn at such a feast. The children are now grown up, but our family pleasure in foreign feasting is as keen as ever.

The shopping is half the fun. In most large cities there are "foreign" neighborhoods with "native" food shops, and in this respect New York City is supreme. But even if one lives a thousand miles from any city, almost all of the stores we know will send virtually anything anywhere by mail. We try to provide the names and addresses of these in our Index of Sources on page 699. During January and February we might celebrate some of the following holidays.

On **January 6** is the Epiphany of the Christian Church, the day on which the Three Kings are said to have visited the newborn Child, bearing their gifts; the "Twelfth Night" of the English, marking the end of their Christmas season; called *El Día de los Tres Reyes Magos* in Spanish-speaking countries; the day that the special feast of *La fête des Rois* is celebrated in France; the day on which we like to make our first obeisance to the French cuisine at the start of our new gastronomic year with a small classic French dinner, including the traditional *galette des Rois.* The complete menu and recipes begin on page 66.

Usually on **January 14** or **15** (the date varies slightly from year to year, as the Hindu calendar has thirteen months), there begins in the South Indian state of Madras the three-day harvest festival of Pongol, when newly harvested rice is ceremonially cooked and then shared by the farm workers and the farm animals (gaily painted and decorated for the occasion) as a symbolic gesture of unity between man and beast. In the evening the cattle walk in the procession to the beat of drums. We might join the celebration in spirit by serving at our table a South Indian home dinner, the menu and recipes beginning on page 398.

Some time between **January 15** and **February 15** (the Chinese calendar is also quite different from ours), we always look forward to joining in the celebration of the Chinese New Year with a classic Chinese feast, served with proper Chinese ceremonial, as described on page 81.

Between **January 9** and **11** in *1967* (the Islamic calendar gains on ours by about 13 days each year), at the end of the great Muslim Fast of Ramadan, which in a way is similar to the Christian Lent, the entire Arab world will break out with the monster feast of *'Id al-Fitr* ("Festival of Fast-breaking"), and we might sample their pleasure at the table with our own Arab buffet supper, including a classic shish kebab or couscous, with menus and recipes beginning on page 256.

On **January 26,** for the national Independence Day of modern India, we almost always serve our favorite North Indian Moglai dinner, with classic dishes that have come down from the courts of the Mogul emperors (page 93).

On **February 6,** the national day of New Zealand, we might (if we have done our difficult shopping well in advance, page 62) enjoy one of the world's most extraordinary and rarest delicacies, a cream stew of Tikinui toheroa (page 146).

On **February 14** we might celebrate St. Valentine's Day with our mallard ducks with cherry hearts (page 131), followed perhaps by a meringue heart filled with red fruits (page 177).

The Winter Party and Feast-Day Menus

Our family feasts are all presented as formal and carefully balanced menus, appropriate to the season and to the feast-day calendar. With the three winter party menus given below we pay our respects, in what we consider to be the order of their importance, to the three greatest classic cuisines of the world: first, the most influential in modern times, the French; second, with a historic tradition going back over thousands of years, the Chinese; third, almost as old and the most regally magnificent, the Indian. Each menu is followed by notes on shopping for the precise ingredients, on planning and timing the preparations, on serving in the appropriate manner, and on the wines.

A French Dinner for Epiphany

MENU

WINES

GREEN TURTLE SOUP AMONTILLADO

A dry Manzanilla Sherry

FILETS DE SOLE BONNE FEMME

A light white wine of the Loire

PIGEONNEAUX VÉNITIENNE

with

PETITS POIS À LA FRANÇAISE

A red Bordeaux from one of the great châteaux

SALADE D'ESCAROLE
AUX FINES HERBES

SOUFFLÉ AU RHUM

A dry Champagne

GALETTE DES ROIS

DEMITASSE

A Cognac, Marc, or Calvados

A Small Classic French Dinner

While it is always exciting to explore dramatic and unusual dishes, there is a deep sense of comfort and joy in returning again and again to the classic simplicity of the great national and regional recipes of France. Everything is familiar, illuminated by memory. We are especially fond of this menu because in March 1949, with many other New York gourmets, we dined for the last time, on its closing night, at the famous Hotel Lafayette, which most of us considered to be among the best French restaurants of New York. This was the menu we chose and afterward when we said goodbye to the three brothers who owned the Lafayette—Raymond, Evariste, and Jean Orteig—we asked, as a remembrance, if they would send us their recipes. In preparing them over and over again and changing them gradually to bring them nearer to perfection we have tried to achieve an almost perfect small dinner.

Shopping for the Ingredients

There are several good brands of ready-made canned turtle soup. (By the way, the French always use the English word *turtle* on their menus, since they give credit to the British for originating the dish. Frenchmen usually refer to it as *le turtle soupe*.) However preparing it at home gives it a body and fineness of flavor that are simply nonexistent in a mass-produced version. If turtle meat is unobtainable fresh, it can be ordered by mail in cans.❋ A *pigeonneau,* of course, is a squab, a fattened domesticated pigeon, available from almost any fancy butcher.❋ Whole dried juniper berries can be ordered by mail.❋ The soufflé is most delicate with a light rum, and a French *rhum* (as they spell it) from the island of Martinique is probably best.

Planning and Timing

This menu can be served by the family, without extra help in the kitchen or at table. When there is a separate wine for each course, the guests never notice a 10-minute break as they sip an extra glass while the gastric juices and the conversation flow. The turtle soup is prepared days ahead. The squabs will be in the oven well before the guests sit down. The sole can be waiting on its baking platter and, just before the soup is served, the squabs can be taken out and kept warm, covered, while the oven is brought up to 400 degrees and the sole put in. When the sole is served the oven temperature is reduced again and the squabs go back in for final heating. By this time the peas will be in the sauté pan ready for their final 5 minutes of steaming. The salad will be ready, except for the dressing, and kept crisp and covered in the refrigerator. The dressing will be mixed, and the salad will be tossed at table. The base of the soufflé will be prepared, with waxed paper pressed on its surface to prevent the formation of skin. The egg whites can be beaten and folded in and the soufflé put into the oven before the service of the salad. The *galette* can be baked the day before.

GREEN TURTLE SOUP AMONTILLADO

For a party of 8 to 10

Escoffier starts his recipe for turtle soup by bringing the live turtle into the kitchen, turning it onto its back, killing it, and sawing open the shell. This operation involves eight men. We haven't tried that adventure yet, but we do believe in honoring a guest with homemade soup.

Check Staples:

Eggs (4 large)
Aromatics: crystal salt, freshly ground black pepper, MSG, whole allspice, basil, whole bay leaf, whole fennel seed, marjoram, dried sage leaf, thyme
Carrots (6 large)
Green Pascal celery (1 head)

Shopping List:

Turtle meat, fresh or canned (2 lbs.)
Lean beef, bottom round, ground (1 lb.)
Veal bones, cut up small by the butcher (about 5 lbs.)
Leeks (5 or 6 medium)
Sherry, medium-dry Amontillado (up to 2 tsp. per person, to taste)

May Be Prepared a Day or More Ahead—4 Hours of Unsupervised Simmering

The veal bones go into a large saucepan and are covered with about 3 quarts of boiling water. We add: 6 carrots, chunked; the celery, chunked, with its leaves coarsely chopped; and the white parts of the leeks, quartered and with the sand carefully washed out under fast-running cold water; plus salt, pepper, and MSG. Skim the liquid carefully as it returns to a boil. Gently simmer for about 3 hours, uncovered, so that the liquid boils down slightly. Separate the 4 eggs and beat the yolks slightly (reserving the white for some other purpose), then mix with 1 pound of ground beef. Spoon this mixture into the simmering stock to flavor and clarify it. Add the aromatics: about 1 dozen whole allspice, 1 teaspoon dried basil, 3 bay leaves, 1/2 teaspoon fennel seed, 1 teaspoon dried marjoram, 1/2 teaspoon ground sage, plus 1 teaspoon thyme. Gently simmer the liquid, covered, 1 hour longer.

Cut the turtle meat into small chunks. Line a colander with cheesecloth and strain soup through it. Pour broth back into clean saucepan, add turtle meat, and simmer for about 15 minutes more. Then it can be cooled and refrigerated, tightly covered.

Serving at Table

To each piping hot bowl of soup add about 1 to 2 teaspoons of the Amontillado Sherry.

FILETS DE SOLE BONNE FEMME

For a party of 8 to 10

Check Staples:

Sweet butter (up to ½ lb.)
Eggs (3 or 4 large)
Aromatics: crystal salt, freshly ground black pepper, MSG, dried tarragon, yellow onions (3 medium), shallots (5 or 6)
Carrots (3 medium)
Green Pascal celery, with leaves (4 stalks)
Parsley (small bunch)
Dry white wine (1 cup)

Shopping List:

Fillets of sole, *see* page 51 (3½ lbs.)
Fish heads and bones (about 2½ lbs.)
Button mushrooms (1 lb.)

The Day Before—the Aromatic Fish Fumet

BASIC RULE FOR A FISH FUMET: A *fumet* is an aromatic fish broth used to magnify the flavor of the edible parts of the fish and for the sauce. It differs from a *court-bouillon* (page 447) in that the latter is a vegetable broth in which fish is poached. For the *fumet* put the washed fish heads and bones in a saucepan with enough boiling water to cover. Add the 3 carrots, the 4 stalks of celery, and the 3 peeled onions, all chunked; the celery leaves, coarsely chopped; the cup of wine; 1 teaspoon tarragon; plus salt, pepper, and MSG to taste. It should boil fairly hard, uncovered, for about 30 minutes to reduce the amount of stock and concentrate its flavor. Finally, we taste it, adjust its seasoning, strain it through muslin, and refrigerate it for tomorrow. There should be about a quart of *fumet.*

An Hour or Two Beforehand—Preparing the Fish in About 15 Minutes

We use our large oval enameled cast-iron fish-baking platter, liberally buttered. Peel and chop fairly fine enough shallots to cover bottom of platter, as a bed for fish to lie on. Coarsely chop a small handful of the parsley and sprinkle it among the shallots. Wipe clean the pound of mushrooms (never wash away flavor oils), pull out and chop stems, leaving caps whole. Wash and dry fish fillets and lay them neatly on platter. Sprinkle them with salt, pepper, MSG, and chopped mushroom stems. Place mushroom caps around fish, cup side up. At this point platter may be covered and held until baking time.

About 30 Minutes Before Serving—Baking the Fish

Preheat the oven to 400 degrees. Take the fish *fumet* from the refrigerator and bring it just to boiling. Separate 3 of the eggs, keeping each yolk in its half shell and storing away whites for some other use. Hold 1 more egg in reserve in case an extra yolk is needed. Mince enough parsley for final decoration. Liberally wet fish and mushrooms with hot *fumet,* until each mushroom cap is partly filled and liquid lies about ¼ inch deep on bottom of platter. Place platter in center of oven, uncovered, then bake for hardly more than 15 minutes, testing with fork until fish flakes. Have ready a hot serving platter and carefully lift fish onto it. Empty any remaining liquid from mushroom caps and neatly place them, still cap side up, around fish. Keep warm while sauce is prepared.

About 10 Minutes Before Serving—the Sauce

Place baking platter, with its hot liquid, over top burner on lowest possible heat—liquid must not even simmer. Blend in first yolk. Melt and blend in 2 or 3 pats of butter. Repeat with next yolk and more butter, continuing until sauce has thickened and is smooth and glistening. An extra yolk may be needed if the sauce is not thick enough. Pour sauce over fish, dribbling some into mushroom caps. Decorate with chopped parsley.

PIGEONNEAUX VÉNITIENNE

For a party of 8 to 10

Check Staples:

Thick-sliced dark smoked bacon (about 16 slices)
Sweet butter (1 lb.)
Fresh limes (4)
Aromatics: crystal salt, freshly ground black pepper, MSG, whole juniper berries (about 7 oz.)

Shopping List:

Young squabs, about 1 lb. each, drawn and trussed (1 per person)
Gin, at least 80 proof (½ cup)

One or More Days Before—the Juniper Butter

Enough juniper berries are finely crushed in a mortar to fill 1 cup. Blend with about ¾ pound of the softened butter, adding salt, pepper, and MSG to taste. This *beurre de genièvre* is then refrigerated, tightly covered, until needed.

About 1¼ Hours Before Serving

The birds are rubbed inside and out with cut sections of lime. Their insides are then lined with the juniper butter—the only efficient way of doing this is with the fingers. Now the outside of each bird is well rubbed with plain butter, and so is the inside of the open earthenware casserole, which will be brought to table. The oven is set at 350 degrees. To begin with, the breasts of the birds are covered by the strips of bacon, skewered into place, and the squabs are placed breast downward in the casserole. After about 15 minutes the birds can be turned over, and after about another 15 minutes the bacon can be removed and crumbled into the sauce. The birds should be turned every 15 minutes and basted with the juniper butter that runs out of them. In 40 to 50 minutes the looseness of the leg joint when waggled, plus the golden brownness of their skins, will be the signs that they are done perfectly. They need no other sauce than the juniper butter. As the casserole is brought to table, the birds are flamed with the ½ cup of gin, slightly heated.

PETITS POIS À LA FRANÇAISE

For a party of 8 to 10

Check Staples:

Sweet butter (about ¼ lb.)
Chicken broth (½ to ¾ cup)
Aromatics: crystal salt,⚘ MSG,▣ dried mint leaf
Fresh parsley (small bunch)
Scallions (1 bunch)
Granulated instantized flour▣ (a few Tbs.)
Granulated white sugar (about 2 Tbs.)

Shopping List:

Green peas, fresh if possible, frozen if necessary (about 2½ lbs. shelled or 3 packages frozen)
Boston lettuce (1 small)

Preparation in About 15 Minutes

Wash and dry the lettuce, discarding any damaged outer leaves, then finely shred and hold. Wash and peel scallions, then finely chop tops and bulbs and add to lettuce. Chop a small handful of parsley and hold. Melt 4 tablespoons of the butter in a sauté pan over medium heat, then add the lettuce and scallions. Stir around until just golden. Add peas and blend into them as they are cooking: about 1 tablespoon of the sugar, the chopped parsley, and 1 teaspoon dried mint. After not more than 2 minutes the heat may be turned off and peas held for final steaming.

About 5 Minutes Before Serving

Add to sauté pan ½ cup of the chicken broth or a little more, according to the size of the pan, then bring rapidly to a boil over high heat. Reduce heat to a gentle bubble, cover and steam peas until just tender, usually about 4 minutes. Finally, add 3 or 4 more tablespoons of the butter and blend in enough flour (about 2 tablespoons) to slightly thicken the sauce.

SALADE D'ESCAROLE AUX FINES HERBES

For a party of 8 to 10

Check Staples:

Aromatics: crystal salt, freshly ground black pepper, MSG, basil, garlic (1 clove), marjoram, tarragon, thyme (fresh herbs replace dried whenever available)
Chives, fresh or frozen (small bunch)
Fresh parsley (small bunch)
Olive oil (4½ Tbs.)
Tarragon white wine vinegar (1½ Tbs.)

Shopping List:

Escarole or alternative, according to the season (2 heads)
French Dijon mustard (½ tsp.)

Not More Than an Hour Before Serving

BASIC RULE FOR ASSEMBLING A SALAD: We use an old, untreated, wooden salad bowl, which over the years has gathered into its grain some of the essence of all the salads it has held. It is first rubbed with the cut side of half a clove of garlic. How many rubs is a matter of trial and error within the taste of each family. We go around five times. The young center leaves of the escarole (or other greens) are washed and dried, and the drying is the most important single trick of salad making. Shaking the leaves or swinging them in a basket is not enough. The least water held in the folds will dilute the dressing. Therefore the leaves must be pressed between absorbent towels. The leaves are torn by hand (never cut) into the bowl, then they are freshened, crisped, and given a chance to absorb the garlic by being lightly covered and refrigerated until serving time.

About 5 Minutes Before Serving—We Do It at Table

BASIC RULE FOR DRESSING A SALAD: We use a small stone mortar and pestle. Cover its bottom with ½ teaspoon crystal salt and ¼ teaspoon MGS. Over this, grind black pepper until the salt is well speckled, perhaps 4 to 6 grinds. Then add all the other dry ingredients—in this case ¼ teaspoon each of dried basil, marjoram, tarragon, and thyme. They are ground a few times with the pestle to bring out the oils and then the wet ingredients are added. We use a 1-ounce graduated medicine glass to measure exactly the amount of the acidulant, in this case 1½ tablespoons of tarragon vinegar. Add it to the dry ingredients and stir it around to dissolve the salt. In the same way, measure exactly 4½ tablespoons of the olive oil and add it to the mixture along with ½ teaspoon of the Dijon mustard. Stir and let it rest for a minute for the flavors to blend. Meanwhile chop finely 2 teaspoons of the chive and 1 tablespoon of the parsley. Add them to the dressing, stir well, and spoon over the salad. Toss for at least 3 minutes. *Une salade, pour être bonne, doit être bien fatiguée.*

SOUFFLÉ AU RHUM

For a party of 8 to 10

After a rich dinner the guests need no more than a tiny portion of this delicately creamy dessert. A 1-quart soufflé is enough, and is the largest size that will rise efficiently. For a bigger party one would prepare and bake two soufflés simultaneously.

Check Staples:

Large eggs, best when about 4 days old (7)
Lemon (½)
Milk (1 pt.)
Aromatic: table salt
Ground arrowroot (2 tsp.)
Superfine-grind sugar (just over ½ cup)

Shopping List:

French Martinique rhum (¼ cup)

Before Attempting a Soufflé

BASIC RULE FOR SPECTACULAR SOUFFLÉS: We use a straight-sided soufflé dish that is one size smaller than the normal and demand that the soufflé shall rise about 2 inches above the top edge. It should almost explode as the spoon breaks it open and the center should be as fluffy as a wisp of cloud. After all a soufflé is not the ideal dish for the presentation of exciting flavors, since no matter how strongly one spices and concentrates the thickening base, or *panada,* as the French call it, it always has to be diluted with masses of bland egg whites so that the flavor remains vague as in a memory. It is the texture and appearance that provide the excitement. Producing the spectacle involves some slight study and practice. . . .

Thickening the Panada

Most soufflé recipes begin with a thickening *roux* of butter and flour. We eliminate them and achieve a lighter texture by thickening with an extra egg yolk and a little ground arrowroot. It is vital that one learn to judge precisely what is the right thickness of the *panada*. If it is too thick it will weigh down the soufflé. If too thin it will not set in the oven and the soufflé will collapse at the table. The perfect consistency is that of an extra-thick cream sauce that drips lazily from the spoon and is heavy to stir when the spoon is held lightly. Adjusting this thickness at the last moment is the first secret of a great soufflé.

Beating the Egg Whites

No rotary, electric, or hand beater can incorporate as much air into the whites as an old-fashioned wire whisk, which literally "traps" the air with each sweeping circular stroke. A round-bottomed bowl ensures that none of the white will escape the beater. We use a copper sabayon bowl.* Most people know that even a single fleck of fatty yolk left in the whites will ruin the beating. Few people seem to realize that even a smear of grease on the bowl or the beater, even the slightest coating from the atmosphere of the kitchen, can largely spoil the beating. We eliminate this danger by first rubbing the bowl and the beater with the cut side of half a lemon and then wiping them dry with a paper towel. The egg whites should be at room temperature, and once the beating begins it should proceed without interruption. One can change hands, but not stop beating for the 4 to 5 minutes that it takes. First, the bowl is held horizontally and the tip of the beater used simply to stir the whites with a vigorous circular motion, until they fill with large bubbles and assume a grayish color. Then the bowl is tilted slightly and the beater lifted out and plunged in again at each stroke. A steady speed of about 4 strokes per second is better than wild enthusiasm at the beginning and limp fatigue at the end. In this way one can watch the gradual change. First there is a dull chalky whiteness. Then the mass begins to glisten and this is the warning that completion is a few seconds away. Remember that if beaten too long the bubbles will get too small and then one ends up with a meringue instead of a soufflé. When the small peak that sticks to the whisk stands up straight without collapsing, the whites are perfectly beaten. The best tool with which to blend them into the *panada* is a rubber spatula or scraper, used in a folding movement with vertical circular strokes. There must be no stirring and the folding must be completed in no more than a minute or air will begin to escape. A few unblended patches of egg white do not matter. We do not butter our soufflé dish because we think that the risen soufflé holds itself up by sticking slightly to the sides. Since we use a smaller dish the mixture, when poured in, fills it to within 1 inch of the top.

Managing the Oven

We place one oven shelf at its lowest setting, perhaps an inch or so above the bottom. We set the soufflé here so that it will form a bottom crust, as a "pad" from which to launch itself upward. Then we set the second oven shelf about 3 inches above the soufflé and place there an inverted 9-inch cake pan, to reflect heat downward on top of the soufflé. Then gently close the oven door and do not open it again for the first 20 minutes. Never, at any time, slam the oven door. The shock may cause a thousand little bubbles to burst and the soufflé to collapse instantly.

Since the efficiency of various ovens varies greatly, it is impossible to set the exact timing for all soufflés. Each cook must first experiment, preferably on a non-party occasion, bearing in mind the following rules:

1. Always bake the soufflé until the top is golden brown, springy to the touch, and probably with a large crack across the top. By this time it should have risen well above the edge of the dish.

2. If when served the soufflé is still too liquid in the center, it has been baked too fast, giving the oven heat insufficient time to penetrate to the center. Next time, without changing any other factor, set the oven temperature 25 degrees lower.

3. If, on the other hand, the first soufflé is overdone at its center, with a texture more like a light cake, the baking was too slow and next time the oven should be set 25 degrees higher. Thus, by changing nothing except the temperature, the perfect soufflé can be achieved by the third or fourth try and can be repeated indefinitely.

Applying the Rules to the Soufflé au Rhum—Preparing the Panada in About 15 Minutes

Carefully separate the 7 eggs, putting 6 of the whites into the beating bowl and reserving the last one for some other use. Put 3 of the yolks together in a 1-quart mixing bowl. Put the remaining 4 yolks each into a separate cup. Pour the pint of milk into a 1-quart saucepan, preferably copper, then heat gently until the liquid is just too hot to the touch. With a small wire whisk beat the following ingredients into the 3 yolks in the mixing bowl: ½ cup sugar, the 2 teaspoons of arrowroot, and ¼ teaspoon salt. Then, still beating continuously, gradually pour in the warm milk. When thoroughly blended, pour mixture back into the saucepan and gently reheat, stirring continuously with a wooden spoon and carefully scraping sides and bottom as *panada* thickens, until it has reached the consistency of a thick cream sauce. Of course, it must never boil. Turn off heat and let it cool until surface can be touched without burning the fingers. Then, one by one, add the 4 remaining yolks, quickly blending in each one before the next is added. Now reheat very gently, stirring continuously, until exactly the right thickness is achieved (see above). Finally, blend in the 1/4 cup of rhum. Now, if required, everything can be held until final preparation is timed to begin. To avoid skin forming on the *panada,* press waxed paper lightly on surface.

About 40 Minutes Before Serving

Preheat oven to 325 degrees and set shelves at proper heights (see above). Beat the egg whites and immediately fold one third of them, with a rubber spatula, into the *panada.* This lightens it and prevents it from crushing the whites. Quickly pour *panada* into center of remaining whites, then immediately start folding with the spatula and complete the operation in about 1 minute. Sprinkle a little sugar on the bottom of the 1-quart soufflé dish, then pour in the soufflé mixture. Set it in the oven and leave it alone for the first 20 minutes, then check every 5 minutes. In our oven the total time is usually 25 to 30 minutes. The diners must be waiting for the soufflé—it cannot wait for them, for as it cools it begins to sink.

GALETTE DES ROIS—CLASSIC THREE KINGS CAKE

For a party of 8 to 10

This traditional Epiphany cake is always served in France perfectly plain. It involves the old game of "Who finds the treasure. . . ." Our "treasure" is a tiny silver crown, used year after year. It can also be a miniature figure of a baby, a single haricot bean, or a bright silver dime. The recipe requires the making of a batch of buttery French flaky pastry, which used to be a difficult and lengthy operation. Nowadays, however, the advent of the new granulated instantized flour, which needs no sifting and runs like salt, makes it fairly quick and simple.

Check Staples:

Sweet butter (6 oz.)
Egg (1 large)
Ice water (1/2 to 3/4 cup)
Aromatic: table salt
Granulated instantized flour,● essential (2 1/4 cups)
Superfine-grind sugar (a few Tbs.)
Haricot bean, or alternative "treasure" (*see* above)

Either the Day Before—or About 2 Hours Before Serving

BASIC RULE FOR OUR QUICK AND SIMPLE FRENCH FLAKY PASTRY: Although this is easy, there are two or three essential tricks. The first is to keep the dough reasonably cool while working it, and as a first step we put the rolling pin (a thin French one is best) into the freezer. Also for coolness, a marble pastry slab is the first choice, but one of enamel or wood is almost as good. The second essential trick is to bring the butter to exactly the right degree of softness. It must not be so hard as to remain lumpy in the dough, nor so soft as to mush, but just hard enough to slice thinly and remain in neat, flat squares. We take the butter straight from the refrigerator, unwrap it, place it on a small cutting board, then leave it at room temperature for not less than 20, nor more than 25 minutes. Finally, the usual rules of pastry making apply: the ice water should be icy and as little as possible of it should be used in the dough.

Dump the 2¼ cups of flour in a heap in the middle of the pastry board and sprinkle over it 1 teaspoon salt. Measure ¾ cup of the ice water. Make a crater in the center of the flour and pour in a good first sprinkle of ice water. Using only the tips of the fingers and scraping the flour with short strokes toward the center, mix the flour with the ice water, adding more water by droplets as needed until no dry flour remains and the dough is just elastic enough to be rolled into a single ball. It must never be soggy. At once wrap tightly in grease-proof paper and cool in refrigerator for 20 minutes. As the dough is put in the refrigerator, the 6 ounces (12 tablespoons) of butter is taken out, unwrapped, and left on a small cutting board.

About 1¼ Hours Before Serving

Clean pastry board and sprinkle it lightly with flour. Take rolling pin out of freezer and also dust with flour. Start rolling out dough, always rolling away from you and never right to the edge, until it is a neat square about ½ inch thick. Quickly cut half the butter into thin squares and place them side by side, but not touching, all over the dough. Put the remaining butter back in the refrigerator. Roll up the buttered dough into a jelly roll and turn it so that one end faces you. Let us call this the first "squeeze." Roll it out again into a ½-inch-thick square, then, without adding any more butter, roll up into a jelly roll and count this as the second "squeeze." Repeat for the third "squeeze." Now lightly wrap it in waxed paper and cool in refrigerator for 15 minutes.

About 50 Minutes Before Serving

Take dough and remaining butter out of the refrigerator. Roll out dough until it is again a neat square, about 1/2 inch thick. Slice the remaining butter and cover the square as before. Roll it up into a jelly roll for the fourth "squeeze." Turn, roll it out again, roll it up into a jelly roll for the fifth "squeeze." This is the finished batch of flaky pastry which French cooks call *pâte feuilletée*. We now tightly wrap this dough in waxed paper and place it in the freezer for exactly the 5 minutes that it takes to turn on the oven and prepare the final operation.

About 40 Minutes Before Serving

Preheat the oven to 425 degrees and have ready a flat baking sheet. Separate the egg and place yolk in a small mixing bowl (saving the white for some other purpose). With a small wire whisk beat 1 teaspoon water into the yolk and hold. Take dough out of freezer and roll out into a neat circle, about 3/4 inch thick. Bury the "treasure" (above) somewhere about an inch from the edge. Gently drape the *galette* over the rolling pin and transfer it to the center of the baking sheet. Smooth and neaten the edge. Then, with a pastry brush, paint the top and side of *galette* with egg yolk. Let dry for a few seconds, then give a second coat. Let dry again, then apply a third coat. Set in oven and bake until golden brown, usually about 20 minutes. Take out and leave on baking sheet to cool slightly. Sprinkle top fairly heavily with superfine sugar, which will partly melt forming a thin crust. Slide *galette* onto a cake rack and cool to room temperature. It may be served, or held, lightly covered, in a cool place (but not refrigerated) until the following day.

Just Before Serving

Sprinkle on as much more sugar as seems right. We do not decorate our *galette* in any way, but this, too, is a matter of personal preference. We serve it with the coffee.

A Chinese New Year Feast
Menu

WINES

PI GWUT

CANAPÉ BARBECUED SPARERIBS

CHOUY-CHOUY TONG

CHICKEN-LIVER SOUP

*Light Black or Jasmine Tea **
or Chinese
yellow rice wine

CHOW BOW

ABALONE WITH VEGETABLES

LOONG HAAH

CLASSIC CANTONESE LOBSTER

VELVET CHICKEN IN SATIN SAUCE

SNOW PEAS WITH WILD RICE

KUMQUATS AND LITCHIS

JASMINE TEA

Ng Ka Py, a sweet cordial
made from tobacco

* It has been our experience, in general, that the special aroma of authentically spiced Chinese food does not blend well with conventional wine. We think that the ideal beverage throughout a Chinese feast is one of these teas (see page 520), served without cream or sugar. However, some of our friends like to serve a rice wine.

A Traditional Chinese Dinner

This menu can be prepared with American ingredients in American pots and pans and served with knives and forks, but we have found over the years that rare and exciting qualities are added, a subtle and delicate ambience to the whole occasion, when one goes to the trouble of incorporating some of the unusual Chinese flavors, magnified by Chinese cooking techniques and dramatized at table by the Chinese ways of serving. Our guests always seem to be surprised and delighted by the gaiety and informality of the classic Chinese dining ceremonial.

The first rule covers the seating arrangements at table. Host and hostess sit side by side, in the positions of least importance, with their backs to the door (the lady always on the man's left). The leading couple among the guests sits opposite. The second guest-couple sits to the right of the first; the third, to the left; and so on, back around to the host and hostess. The soup, in its Chinese tureen with the china serving ladle, is placed on the table and a bowl with a china spoon is set at each place before the guests sit down. The host then invites them to table with the ancient phrase: "The rice is open—please come in." When everyone is seated the gentlemen serve the soup. As soon as it is consumed the ladies rise and help the hostess bring in the remaining dishes of the feast, which are all set on the table at once. It is the historic Chinese contribution to the tradition of dining that servants are not needed around the table because the work can easily be shared by the guests. The tradition that the man carves the roast or the bird is also a throwback to Chinese custom. As the cover is lifted from each main dish, the host takes the first small spoonful and places it in the hostess's bowl. She tastes it and signifies that it is satisfactory for the guests. The leading male guest then expresses the pleasure of all the guests for being allowed to share the food. Then the men begin serving.

Shopping for Chinese Equipment and Ingredients

The Chinese neighborhoods of many of our larger cities are a gold mine for the adventurous gourmet. There are shops where one can buy the delicate table china, the rice bowls, chopsticks, teapots, china spoons and serving dishes, etc., which can also be ordered by mail.⚹ The kitchen shops are filled with low-cost equipment, including laminated cleavers, tree-trunk chopping blocks, steamers, and, above all, the famous Chinese frying "wok," which is described in the kitchen chapter (page 38). Once one masters the trick of tilting the wok to control the tiny amount of hot frying oil at the curved base, one is likely to use it every day of the year for anything from hamburgers to lamb chops. This equipment and the few Chinese aromatic spices mentioned in the following recipes can also be ordered by mail.⁂ We would have fresh ginger root in our freezer. The amount required in any recipe can be grated without first being thawed. If it is absolutely not available, it can be regretfully replaced by ground ginger. Such specialties as the fermented black beans, pea sprouts, bamboo shoots, etc., can all be purchased in any authentic Chinese grocery store or the canned versions are available by mail.⁂ Many supermarkets now carry frozen snow peas, canned water chestnuts, bamboo shoots, and pea sprouts.

Planning and Timing

A Chinese feast as luxurious as this one does, admittedly, involve some complications in final preparation and serving. This is because the brilliant freshness and crispness of authentic Chinese food depends to a large extent on absolutely last-minute quick-frying of the vegetables, which are a part of almost every dish. However, all the preparation up to this final point can be done well in advance. There are three solutions to the last-minute problem. One can arrange for kitchen help during the progress of the meal. Failing that, we sometimes divide our family into two teams of two people each; one team remaining at table to keep the guests entertained during the first course, while the other team tactfully disappears to the kitchen; then the role is reversed for the second course, and so on. Or, one can follow the Chinese custom of accepting the help of the lady guests, but this requires detailed advance planning so that each helper can be given a specific assignment. For this menu, the spareribs and their barbecue sauce are prepared the day before and baked just before the guests arrive. The soup is begun the night before, and since the final boiling takes less than 15 minutes it can be completed while the spareribs are being consumed. As for the main dishes, brought to table together, assuming that all possible preparation is done in advance, the final finishing times are comparatively short: for the abalone, about 7 minutes; for the lobster, 10 minutes; for the chicken, just over 10 minutes; for the snow peas with wild rice, 10 minutes. Thus they can all be brought to completion almost simultaneously, and any of them can be held for a few minutes in a keep-warm oven (150 degrees).

CHINESE PI GWUT—CANAPÉ BARBECUED SPARERIBS

For a party of 8 to 10

We have our spareribs cut small, put shiny foil handles on them, and hand them around to the guests before they come to table.

Check Staples:

Aromatics: crystal salt, freshly ground black pepper, MSG, ground cinnamon, ground clove, fennel seed, garlic (1 or 2 cloves, to taste), Chinese or Indian ground ginger, English dry mustard, Chinese soy sauce (about ¼ cup), Tabasco, Worcestershire sauce

Granulated white sugar (1 to 2 tsp.)

Spanish Sherry vinegar (a few Tbs.)

Shopping List:

Meaty pork spareribs, chopped by butcher into 3-inch lengths (4 to 4½ lbs.)

Pot or cottage cheese, large curd (¼ lb.)

The Day Before—Advance Preparation

Cut spareribs apart and scrape off about ½ inch of the meat from one end of each bone, to provide a handle (keep cut-off bits for some other purpose). Refrigerate overnight, covered. For each sparerib, cut a 1-inch square of aluminum foil and hold, flat, for the following day. Prepare barbecue sauce, putting into mixing bowl: the ¼ pound of cheese, the 1 or 2 cloves of garlic (mashed through a press), 1 teaspoon sugar, 1 teaspoon fennel seed, ¼ teaspoon cinnamon, ¼ teaspoon clove, ½ teaspoon ginger; then begin blending and creaming with a wooden spoon, while adding the ¼ cup of soy sauce, 1 tablespoon Worcestershire sauce, 1 tablespoon of the vinegar, plus about 2 teaspoons salt, a few good grinds of pepper, not more than 2 shakes of Tabasco, and about 1 teaspoon MSG. Now taste and adjust flavors by adding a little more of any or all of the ingredients until taste is strong and the consistency creamy. Refrigerate overnight in a covered jar, to blend and mature the flavors.

On the Day—About 2 Hours Before Serving

Take the spareribs and barbecue sauce out of the refrigerator and let come to room temperature.

About 50 Minutes Before Serving

Preheat oven to 400 degrees. Place spareribs on a flat baking sheet, side by side, touching each other. Stir sauce and spoon thickly over spareribs. Bake until dark brown, usually in about 20 minutes. Then using two large spatulas turn spareribs over, spoon on more sauce, and again bake until dark brown, usually in another 20 minutes. Meanwhile, make 2 or 3 tablespoons of mustard by mixing the dry mustard with vinegar for a sharp tang, and put mixture into small serving bowl. Have foil squares ready, lift each sparerib with tongs, and press foil over bare end of bone. Serve at once on a hot platter with the mustard on the side.

CHINESE CHOUY-CHOUY TONG—CHICKEN-LIVER SOUP

For a party of 8 to 10

Check Staples:

Aromatics: crystal salt, freshly ground black pepper, MSG, Chinese soy sauce (about 2 Tbs.), fresh ginger root (we keep it frozen)
Ground arrowroot (about 2 tsp.)
Olive oil (about 3 Tbs.)
Granulated white sugar (about 1 tsp.)

Shopping List:

Chicken livers (1 lb.)
Chinese cabbage (1 head)

The Day Before—Marinating the Livers

Wash and pat dry the livers, cut into bite-size pieces, and put into covered refrigerator dish. In a mixing bowl assemble the marinade: the 2 tablespoons of soy sauce, 2 tablespoons of the olive oil, the teaspoon of sugar, 2 teaspoons arrowroot, plus a few grinds of pepper. Mix well, pour over livers, stir around gently with a wooden spoon until each piece is moistened, then cover and refrigerate overnight.

About 2 Hours Before Serving

Take chicken livers and marinade from refrigerator and bring to room temperature.

About 25 Minutes Before Serving

Bring 3 quarts of freshly drawn cold water to a boil in a saucepan, while work begins on the soup in a 4-quart soup pot. Remove tough outer leaves of the cabbage, then wash, shake dry, and cut up the heart to bite-size pieces and hold. Skin the fresh ginger root with a potato scraper; we grate about 1 tablespoon of our frozen ginger root and hold. Put about 1 tablespoon of the olive oil into soup pot and bring up to medium frying heat. Drop in grated ginger and sizzle for hardly more than 20 seconds. Stop the frying by pouring in the boiling water. Stir in 4 teaspoons salt. As soon as water returns to boil, drop in cabbage and chicken livers with their marinade. As soon as water boils again, turn down heat to gentle bubbling and continue, uncovered, until cabbage is just done but still crisp, usually in 10 to 15 minutes.

Remember that cabbage will continue softening while soup is being brought to table and served.

CHINESE CHOW BOW—ABALONE WITH VEGETABLES

For a party of 8 to 10

The abalone is a huge barnacle-type shellfish that clings to deep undersea rocks on the Pacific coast. Since Californians discovered how good it is to eat they have practically "loved it to death." So many intrepid divers have plunged down, especially at the mouth of the Golden Gate, that a California conservation law now forbids the shipment of abalone outside the state. However, Mexican divers off the coast of Baja California are much less restricted and their abalone is canned and shipped throughout the United States.✲ Usually a 1-pound can contains a single abalone steak.

Check Staples:

Dark smoked ham,▣ in 1 slice (1/4 lb.)
Aromatics: crystal salt,✲ freshly ground black pepper,✲ MSG,▣ garlic (2 or 3 cloves to taste), Chinese soy sauce▣ (2 Tbs.), fresh ginger root✲ (we keep it frozen)
Ground arrowroot▣ (4 tsp.)
Olive oil▣ (a few Tbs.)
Granulated white sugar (1 tsp.)
Dry Sherry▣ (1/4 cup)

Shopping List:

Abalone meat✲ (1-lb. can)
Chinese bamboo shoots (1/4 lb.)
Chinese cabbage (small head)
White celery (3 or 4 stalks)
Chinese-style snow peas✲ (7- to 8-oz. frozen package)
Fresh mushrooms (1/4 lb.)
Sweet Bermuda or Spanish onion (1 large)

At Any Time Beforehand—Preparing the Ingredients

Defrost the snow peas. In a large mixing bowl assemble: the 1/4 pound of bamboo shoots, thinly sliced; about 8 young, inner leaves of the cabbage, coarsely chopped; the 1/4 pound of mushrooms, wiped clean (never washed), sliced; the sweet onion, peeled and thinly sliced; the 3 or 4 stalks of celery, diced; plus (as soon as defrosted) the snow peas, cut into bite-size pieces. Grate enough ginger root to fill 2 teaspoons and place in a small mortar, add the 2 or 3 cloves garlic, mashed through a press, then pound together. Dice into large pieces the pound of abalone and 1/4 pound of ham. In a smallish mixing bowl prepare the sauce by blending the 1/4 cup of Sherry, the 4 teaspoons of arrowroot, the 2 tablespoons of soy sauce, the 1 teaspoon sugar, plus salt and a few grinds of pepper to taste. Mix and hold covered, to blend and mature flavors. Ingredients may now be held for about 1 hour. If a longer time is needed, they should be refrigerated, but they must then be returned to room temperature before final preparation begins.

About 20 Minutes Before Serving

The ideal frying utensil is a Chinese wok,* but it can also be done in a sauté pan or a large frypan with a fairly tight-fitting lid. Have ready a warm, covered serving dish in the oven at keep-warm temperature (about 150 degrees). Heat up about 2 tablespoons of olive oil to medium-high frying temperature. Then add the assembled vegetables, stir around with a wooden spoon, and sauté hard for not more than ½ minute. Turn down heat to simmer, cover, then let steam for exactly 5 minutes. Turn off heat, lift vegetables with slotted spoon, and put into covered dish in oven to keep warm. Turn on heat under pan to medium-high frying temperature, adding a little more olive oil if necessary, then blend in garlic-ginger paste. Now, working fast because abalone will toughen to leather if overcooked, add the diced abalone and ham and sauté hard for exactly 10 seconds, then put back the vegetables and blend in the Sherry-soy sauce. Turn heat down to simmering and let bubble, stirring gently and continuously, for exactly 3 minutes. Then refill warm covered dish and serve.

CHINESE LOONG HAAH—CLASSIC CANTONESE LOBSTER

For a party of 8 to 10

One of the greatest dishes of the Chinese cuisine. Among many variations, this is the best we know. Although it is not absolutely essential to include the Chinese *Dow See,* fermented black beans,✲ they do bring a perfection of flavor.

Check Staples:

Eggs (4 large)
Aromatics: crystal salt,✱ freshly ground black pepper,✱ MSG,▣ garlic (2 cloves)
Ground arrowroot▣ (2 Tbs.)
Olive oil▣ (several Tbs.)
Granulated white sugar (2 tsp.)

Shopping List:

Live lobsters (2 of about 1½ lbs. each)
Lean pork loin (½ lb.)
Chinese *Dow See*✲ (2 oz.), *see* shopping notes, page 82
Clam juice (slightly more than 1 qt.)

At Any Time Beforehand—Advance Preparation of Ingredients

BASIC RULE FOR HUMANELY KILLING AND CLEANING LOBSTER: The question of cruelty to lobsters has been studied by learned societies and has been the subject of scientific reports. This is the way which we think is best, both for the comfort of the lobster and the perfection of the recipe. Fill a large pot with freshly drawn cold water. Salt it enough so that the lobsters will feel at home. Put them into this cold bath, and immediately place the pot over highest heat. When the temperature reaches 80 degrees, the lobsters gently roll over. When they turn red, they are dead. Remove immediately.

Virtually every recipe calls for cutting up the lobster in different ways, but there is only one right way to clean it. Lay the lobster on its back on a heavy chopping block and, using in turn a small cleaver and a heavy fish knife, open up the underside of the head. Remove the stomach or "lady," the hard sac where its chin would be, if it had a chin. Open up the underside of the tail and scrape out the black intestinal vein. The red stuff inside the head is the coral, the eggs of the female. The green stuff is the tomalley, the liver. Both of these are prized delicacies and should never be discarded. The lobster is now ready for cutting up according to the requirements of the recipe.

Cutting Up Lobster in the Cantonese Way

Chop off the claws and legs, then chop again into manageable pieces. Chop off the front half of the head and throw away. Chop off remainder of head and chop it in half lengthwise. Chop off the tail fin and throw away. Now cut and chop down the center of the body, starting from the underside, until there are two long halves. Chop each crosswise into manageable pieces. Put all pieces into a bowl and hold, covered.

Put the 2 ounces of black fermented beans in a mortar and coarsely grind. Finely mince the 2 cloves of garlic. In a large mixing bowl, assemble: the ½ pound pork, diced; the 2 teaspoons of sugar; 1 tablespoon of the arrowroot, sprinkled over the fermented beans; 2 tablespoons of the olive oil; the minced garlic; plus about 2 teaspoons salt, a few grinds of pepper, and about 1 teaspoon MSG. Mix thoroughly, cover, then hold. Ingredients may now be held at room temperature for about 1 hour. If it will be longer, refrigerate, but return to room temperature before final preparation begins.

About 30 Minutes Before Serving

Put 3½ cups of the clam juice into a saucepan and heat to just below boiling, then keep covered until needed. Break the 4 eggs into a bowl and hold. In a Chinese wok* or a conventional sauté pan with a fairly tight-fitting lid, heat up a couple of tablespoons of the olive oil to medium-high frying temperature. Working fast, add the pork mixture, stir around vigorously, and sauté hard for 15 seconds. Add the pieces of lobster, each still in its shell, and continue sautéing for 30 seconds longer, spreading everything out into an even layer. Now ladle in enough of the hot clam juice to just cover the lobster pieces, turn heat down to simmering, then cook gently, covered, for 10 minutes.

About 10 Minutes Before Serving

Meanwhile set a covered serving dish to warm in the oven at keep-warm temperature (about 150 degrees) ; then start preparing sauce in a 1½-quart saucepan (preferably copper, because it reacts almost instantaneously to heat changes). Liquefy remaining tablespoon of arrowroot in a cup with a little cold clam juice. Put remaining ½ cup of hot clam juice into the saucepan and bring quickly to a boil, then turn down heat to very low. Liquid must not even simmer. Now thicken by carefully blending in the remaining tablespoon of arrowroot, teaspoon by teaspoon, stirring continuously, until mixture is very thick—almost a smooth paste. It may not be necessary to use all the arrowroot. Cover and hold over very low heat. As soon as lobster is done, using slotted spoon and letting liquid drain off, transfer all solids from sauté pan to serving dish in oven. Now start thinning clam sauce with sauté pan liquid, adding it ¼ cup by ¼ cup and carefully blending in enough to thin sauce to the consistency of light cream. Keep hot, but well below simmering. Vigorously beat the eggs with a wire whisk, at the same time spooning in a little of the sauce to warm them slightly. Turn off heat under saucepan and gradually blend in eggs, stirring vigorously and continuously, then turn on heat again and keep stirring until sauce again is very thick and whites cook into spaghetti-like strands. Work in more liquid from sauté pan, plus more unwarmed clam juice if necessary, until sauce finally has the consistency of heavy cream. Taste, adjusting seasoning as required, then pour over lobster and serve.

VELVET CHICKEN IN SATIN SAUCE

For a party of 8 to 10

This dish, prepared in the Chinese manner, is of our own invention. The extraordinary way of cooking the chickens was taught us by a Chinese chef. We know of no other way that can reproduce the velvet smoothness of the flesh, or the concentration of flavor within the chicken. Taste the water afterward. Not a trace of chicken flavor has escaped into it.

Check Staples:

Lemon (1)
Aromatics: crystal salt,⚘ freshly ground black pepper,⚘ MSG,▣ garlic (1 or 2 cloves, to taste), fresh ginger root⚘ (we keep it frozen), Chinese soy sauce▣ (2 to 3 Tbs.)
Yellow onion (1 medium)
Green scallions (1 bunch)
Ground arrowroot▣ (1 to 2 Tbs.)
Granulated white sugar (1 to 2 tsp.)
Olive oil▣ (1 Tbs.)
Dry Sherry♁ (a few Tbs.)

Shopping List:

Young broiler-fryer chickens, whole (2—about 1½ lbs. each)
Fresh mushrooms (¼ lb.)

The Day Before—Cooking the Chickens

The chickens should not be washed, but should be cleaned by being rubbed outside and in with the cut side of half a lemon. Use a large soup kettle or Dutch oven with enough room for both chickens to rest side by side, but do not put them in yet. Fill pot about two thirds full of freshly drawn cold water and bring to a boil. Peel and slice the onion and drop into the water. Grate 2 teaspoons of the ginger root and also add to the water. Inside each chicken put 3 or 4 large silver or stainless-steel serving spoons, to act as heat conductors. This is an essential part of the method. When the water is bubbling hard, lower the chickens into it without dislodging the spoons, adding more hot water, if necessary, to cover. Bring the water back to a boil as quickly as possible and, from the moment it starts bubbling again, count exactly 30 seconds, then turn off the heat, cover the pot tightly, leaving chickens to cool slowly in the water for 4 hours. They will then be perfectly done. Remove chickens from water, take out spoons, drain chickens, wrap them in foil, and refrigerate.

On the Day—2 Hours Beforehand

Remove chickens from refrigerator and cut all meat off them, as much as possible in long, narrow strips. (Put away carcasses for stock.) Let chicken strips come to room temperature.

About 25 Minutes Before Serving—the Sauce and the Reheating

Wipe clean (never wash) the ¼ pound of mushrooms and slice lengthwise into hammer shapes. Grate another teaspoonful of ginger root and hold. Finely mince 1 or 2 cloves of garlic and add to the ginger root. In a sauté pan or frypan with a tightly fitting lid, assemble the sauce: 1 teaspoon of the sugar, the minced garlic and grated ginger, 2 tablespoons of the soy sauce, 2 tablespoons of the Sherry, the sliced mushrooms, the tablespoon of olive oil, plus salt, pepper, and MSG to taste. Stir well, bring to a boil, and bubble gently until mushrooms are cooked, usually in 5 minutes. Now carefully put in chicken strips, making sure that each is coated with sauce, and arrange them in lattice formation so that steam can circulate. Continue bubbling, covered, for 5 minutes. Meanwhile warm a flat serving platter in oven at keep-warm temperature (about 150 degrees). Chop enough green scallion tops to fill ⅔ cup. Liquefy about 3 teaspoons of arrowroot in a cup with a dash or two more Sherry. Lift out chicken strips with tongs, letting sauce drip off, then arrange neatly on serving platter and keep warm in oven. Turn off heat under sauté pan and thicken sauce by spooning in 1 teaspoon at a time the liquefied arrowroot, stirring vigorously. Use only enough arrowroot to achieve the consistency of heavy cream. Blend in chopped scallions, taste, and finally adjust flavors, adding a little more Sherry and sugar if too salty, or a little more soy sauce if too sweet. Then pour over chicken and serve.

CHINESE SNOW PEAS WITH WILD RICE

For a party of 8 to 10

This is not an authentic Chinese dish since wild rice, a form of marsh grass entirely unrelated to rice, is as native American as are corn or squash. However snow peas and water chestnuts are classic Chinese ingredients, and they are now widely available in supermarkets.

Check Staples:

Salt butter (about 7 Tbs.)
Clear chicken broth (7 cups)
Aromatics: crystal salt,* freshly ground black pepper,* MSG
Yellow onions (4 medium)
Green scallions (1 bunch)

Shopping List:

Chinese-style snow peas (1½ lbs. fresh or 2 packages frozen)
Chinese-style water chestnuts (8-oz. can)
Wild rice (2 cups)
Fresh mushrooms (½ lb.)
Almonds (½ lb., in shells, or ¼ lb., shelled and blanched and/or slivered)

An Hour or Two Beforehand—Advance Preparation of Ingredients

If snow peas are frozen, defrost them. Peel and chop the 4 onions moderately fine and hold, covered. In a large mixing bowl assemble the 8 ounces of water chestnuts, sliced; the ½ pound mushrooms, wiped clean (never wash their flavor away under running water) and sliced lengthwise into hammer shapes; the bunch of scallions, the tops cut into 1½-inch lengths, the bulbs peeled and chopped; and the snow peas (at room temperature), cut into bite-size pieces. Pick over the 2 cups of wild rice and wash under running cold water, then hold. As necessary, shell, blanch, sliver, and toast the almonds.

BASIC RULE FOR TOASTING SLIVERED ALMONDS: Preheat oven to 350 degrees. Spread slivered almonds in a single layer over the ungreased bottom of a 9- or 10-inch cake pan. Set in oven. Stir frequently until nuts are a light, even brown, usually in 7 to 10 minutes. Do not let them get too dark or they may blacken and take on a burnt flavor.

About 45 Minutes Before Serving

In a separate saucepan, bring the 7 cups of chicken broth almost to boiling and hold hot, covered. For the main cooking, we use a 4- to 5-quart enameled cast-iron cocotte* with a tightly fitting lid, good-looking enough to be brought to table. Set it over medium frying heat, melt about 3 tablespoons of the butter and just glaze the onions, then add the wild rice and stir around to coat grains with butter, adding, at the same time, salt, pepper, and MSG to taste. Pour in 6 cups of the hot chicken broth and keep gently bubbling, uncovered, until wild rice is tender, usually in 35 to 40 minutes.

About 10 Minutes Before Serving

In a sauté pan, over fairly high frying heat, melt remaining 4 tablespoons of the butter and very quickly sauté the assembled vegetables until mushrooms are just soft, usually in 3 to 4 minutes. At the same time, add salt, pepper, and MSG, remembering that wild rice has already been seasoned. Then turn off heat and hold, uncovered. All liquid should have been absorbed by wild rice at precise moment when it is perfectly done. If it dries out before it is done, add some of the remaining broth. If there is a little excess liquid, evaporate it by boiling hard for a minute or two. With a rubber spatula or a wooden fork, gently incorporate the vegetables from the sauté pan.

Just Before Serving

Liberally sprinkle the toasted slivered almonds on top of the rice and bring to the table.

KUMQUATS AND LITCHIS FOR DESSERT

For a party of 8 to 10

Shopping List:

Fresh kumquats, if available, *see* **page 53, still on the stems and with their leaves (enough to fill a medium-size basket in the center of the table), or kumquats in syrup (two 1-lb. cans)**

Shelled and pitted litchi nuts (two 1-lb. cans)

During January or sometimes even early in February, fresh kumquats are still available from Florida or imported from Hong Kong or Taiwan. The bright yellow miniature oranges, set against their shiny dark-green leaves, make a festive centerpiece for the table throughout the meal. Then at the end of the meal the basket is handed around. If the fresh fruit is not available, candied kumquats may be served on toothpicks. Litchi nuts are like milky-white grapes with a single large stone and a crisp nutlike outer shell. At one time they were only available imported from China, but now small quantities are grown in Florida. In cans they are already shelled and pitted, then preserved in a light syrup. They are also served on toothpicks.

JASMINE TEA

For general notes on the various types of tea, see pages 518–20.

Indian Independence Day Dinner

MENU

Bhujjias—*Savory Canapé Balls*

Tali Machi of Gray Sole in Spiced Batter

with

A dark Würzburger or an India Pale Ale

Indian Fried Tomatoes
Moglai Biriani of Khorrma of Curried
Chicken and Pilau of Rice
Halvah Suji with Alphonse Mangoes
Indian Darjeeling Tea

The essential condiments—

Sweet Mango Chutney
Toasted Coconut Flakes✲
Chopped Crystallized Ginger
Crumbled Bombay Duck✲

Plus, a choice from—

Homemade Green Tomato Chutney (page 406)
Homemade Lemon-Lime Pickle (page 405)
Imported Indian Hot Pickle✲
Chopped Scallion Tops and Green Pepper
Chopped Hard-boiled Eggs
Seedless White Raisins
Grated Orange Peel
Sliced Banana

Also, if available, a choice of Indonesian curry specialties—✲

Ikan Terie (dried baby fish)
Krupuk (crispy spiced wafers)
Serundeng (fried spiced coconut)

Wine: We have never found a wine strong enough to stand up against the dominance of Indian curry spices. With our Indian dinners we prefer to serve beer. Some people prefer to serve Indian tea in little bowls throughout the meal. After the dessert it is perfectly possible to serve Cognac or liqueurs.

A North Indian Moglai Feast

The word "Moglai" on an Indian menu means that the dish originated at the court of the Mogul Emperors. The Moglai *biriani,* a tall, brilliantly decorated pyramid of chicken and rice, is a classic dish of North India. It might equally be served at a diplomatic dinner in New Delhi or at a wedding feast in a Himalayan mountain village. An essential part of the serving of such a feast is the dramatic array of condiments, which we set out as the centerpiece of the table. On a polished wood turntable we arrange sometimes as many as a dozen small bowls of various shapes and colors. After each guest has been served with chicken and rice, he circles his plate with the condiments of his choice. They may be fiery hot, or sweet or sour, or salty, fruity, nutty, crisp, soft, etc.

No curry powder is used in the recipes following. An Indian cook would feel as if he were in a straitjacket if he were forced to use a ready-made curry powder. He uses the aromatic spices separately, employing the characteristics of each to create an infinite variety of flavors, bouquets, textures, and colors. Usually a few minutes before starting to prepare the dish, the Indian cook grinds a basic aromatic mixture, which is called a *massala.* Then he controls the peppery heat of the dish with ginger, the sharpness with fenugreek, the sweetness with coconut, and the color with turmeric. This is the way it is done in the following recipes.

Shopping for Indian Ingredients

Most Indian staples are dried and packed ready for shipment over long distances in hot and damp weather, so it is easy to have them sent by mail from one of the U. S. importers.✻ They will send printed lists of Indian aromatic spices, Indonesian specialties, chutneys and pickles, the pappadums (dried Indian bread), *ikan terie* and Bombay duck (dried fish), etc. The basic ingredient of the Bhujjias canapé balls is Besan, a rich and nutty flour milled from chick peas, which we also use for general purposes and keep among our regular staples.§ The best rice for a pilau is extra long-grain Indian, or Patna,§ but standard long-grain white rice may be used. Indian Alphonse mangoes, quite different from our Hayden mangoes of Florida, come from India in 2-pound cans.✻

Planning and Timing

The basic preparation of Indian food is almost exactly the reverse of the Chinese. While the Chinese way depends on last-second cooking, the culinary pleasures of India require long, slow absorption of the spices. This makes the timing of an Indian menu extremely easy. There is hardly an Indian curry that cannot be kept warm or allowed to cool and be reheated without an actual improvement in the marriage of its flavors. This menu is no exception. The dough for the Bhujjias canapés is best prepared the day before and the balls rolled out, so that the final deep-frying can be done in less than 15 minutes, as the guests are assembling. The batter for the *tali machi* is also best mixed the day before, the fish marinated a few hours ahead of the dinner, and the final deep-frying (in the same oil, as soon as the Bhujjias are finished) takes less than 15 minutes and can be done while the Bhujjias are being served. The pan-fried tomatoes which accompany the fish are prepared at the same time. The Moglai *biriani* is a big production, but the chicken and rice simmer in their separate pots with almost no attention. Building and decorating the tall chicken-and-rice pyramid takes about 15 minutes. The condiments are of course set out in their little bowls well in advance and kept fresh in the refrigerator until it is time to bring them to room temperature. The halvah suji dessert is prepared the day before and served cold. The Alphonse mangoes are ready to serve when the can is opened.

INDIAN BHUJJIAS—SAVORY CANAPÉ BALLS

For a party of 8 to 10

These canapés are the size of large olives and are served hot on toothpicks. However they are quite flexible as to shape and construction. They may be wrapped around pieces of wine-boiled shrimp (page 108) or around bits of savory sausage or single whole nuts or any other central surprise. Generally, however, we serve them plain, relying on the unusual impact of the Indian aromatic combination.

Check Staples:

Aromatics: crystal salt,☆ freshly ground Indian Tellicherry black pepper,☆ whole caraway seed, whole cardamom pods, ground cinnamon, ground clove, whole coriander seed
Yellow onions (3 medium)
Watercress (small bunch)
Indian Besan chick-pea flour§ (2 cups)
Wholewheat flour (2 Tbs.)
Olive oil§ (a few Tbs.)
Oil for deep-frying

Shopping List:

Indian cashew nuts, shelled (½ lb.)
Green peppers (3 medium)

At Any Time Beforehand—Preparing the Dough in About 10 Minutes

We begin by grinding the *massala* (page 400) in a small mortar, putting in: ½ teaspoon whole caraway, 6 whole cardamom pods, ½ teaspoon whole coriander, and 2 teaspoons salt. Now blend in: ½ teaspoon cinnamon, ½ teaspoon clove, plus plenty of freshly ground black pepper. Then hold, covered.

Assemble the vegetables in a mixing bowl: the 3 onions, peeled and finely minced; the ½ pound of cashews, coarsely chopped; the 3 green peppers, diced; and enough of the watercress, finely chopped, to fill 1 cup. Into a larger mixing bowl sift the 2 cups of Besan flour, then sift over it the 2 tablespoons of wheat flour and sprinkle with the *massala*. Lightly toss in the chopped vegetables, then sprinkle over 2 tablespoons of the olive oil and begin working the dough with the fingers. It should eventually be dumpling-firm, and if this is not achieved after thorough working sprinkle on a few more drops of olive oil, but as little as possible. Finally, roll dough into balls, each the size of a large olive. If they are to be held for any length of time layer them between sheets of waxed paper and refrigerate, but return to room temperature before frying.

About 15 Minutes Before Serving

Heat deep-frying oil to 375 degrees. Fry the Bhujjias balls to an even dark brown, usually in 3 to 4 minutes per batch. Serve hot on toothpicks.

INDIAN TALI MACHI OF GRAY SOLE IN SPICED BATTER

For a party of 8 to 10

If gray sole is not easily available it may be replaced by a boneless fillet of some other firm, lean-fleshed fish. The fine Pacific Rex sole is especially good prepared this way. The fish should be deep-fried in the same oil used for the Bhujjias (preceding recipe).

Check Staples:

Aromatics: crystal salt,* freshly ground Indian Tellicherry black pepper,* whole caraway seed, whole cardamom pods, Indian chili powder,* ground cinnamon, ground clove, whole coriander seed
Green scallions (1 bunch)
Watercress (small bunch)
Indian Besan chick-pea flour (about ¼ cup)
Wholewheat flour (about ¼ cup)
Tarragon white wine vinegar (2 Tbs.)
Oil for deep-frying

Shopping List:

Boneless fillets of gray sole or Rex sole or alternative, *see* page 51 (about 2½ lbs.)
Clam juice (8-oz. bottle)

About an Hour Beforehand—Advance Preparation in About 15 Minutes

Wash and dry the fish, cut into approximately 2-inch squares, and set on a platter in a single layer. Prepare a *massala* by grinding into a small mortar: ½ teaspoon whole caraway, 6 whole cardamom pods, 1 teaspoon whole coriander, and 1 teaspoon chili powder. Next blend in: ½ teaspoon ground cinnamon, ½ teaspoon ground clove, and freshly ground black pepper. Then hold and prepare marinade. In a small mixing bowl blend together: 1 teaspoon of the *massala,* 2 teaspoons salt, and the 2 tablespoons of vinegar. Stir well, then sprinkle over each piece of fish. While fish is marinating, prepare batter by mixing in a bowl: the ¼ cup of Besan flour and the ¼ cup of wheat flour, sifted together; the remainder of the *massala,* 1 more teaspoon chili powder, and 2 teaspoons salt. Blend to the consistency of a medium-thick batter, with dash after dash of the clam juice, judging thickness but probably making use of about 6 ounces from the bottle. Finally, chop enough of the green scallion tops to fill 1 cup and blend them into batter. Everything may now be held for the final frying.

About 15 Minutes Before Serving

Heat frying oil to 375 degrees. Check consistency of batter and if it has thickened, blend in a little more of the clam juice. Now beat batter steadily with a wire whisk for about 2 minutes. Dip each piece of fish in batter and fry to golden-brown, usually in about 3 minutes. Drain on paper towels and serve garnished with watercress and accompanied by fried tomatoes.

INDIAN FRIED TOMATOES

For a party of 8 to 10

The trick in preparing this dish, taught us by an Indian chef, is to cut off a thin slice from each end of the tomato, allowing the inside water to escape as steam and thus concentrating the flavor.

Check Staples:

Salt butter (about 5 Tbs.)
Aromatics: crystal salt,⁑ freshly ground Indian Tellicherry black pepper,⁑ dried dillweed,⁑ turmeric
Dry Sherry (about 2 Tbs.)

Shopping List:

Ripe medium tomatoes (1 per person)

About 15 Minutes Before Serving

Cut a thin slice from the top and bottom of each tomato. Over medium-high frying heat, melt the 5 tablespoons of butter in a sauté pan large enough to hold all the tomatoes at once. Make butter very hot but do not let it brown; then put in tomatoes and fry fairly hard, first on one side and then on the other. Sprinkle each side with salt, pepper, dill, and a pinch of turmeric, which gives a rich reddish-brown color. Meanwhile set a serving platter in the oven at keep-warm temperature (about 150 degrees). When tomatoes are slightly brown on each side and beginning to collapse, lift each out with a spatula, place on platter, and keep warm. At once, turn up heat under sauté pan and boil butter sauce hard to reduce amount. Add, dash by dash, stirring around each time, about 2 tablespoons of the Sherry. When the sauce is just beginning to thicken and glaze pour it over the tomatoes and serve.

INDIAN MOGLAI BIRIANI—CURRIED CHICKEN WITH RICE PILAU

Part 1: The Khorrma of Chicken

For a party of 8 to 10

In this party version the chicken and rice are combined. However the recipes are given separately since the chicken is an excellent main dish on its own and the rice pilau is a fine addition to many non-Indian menus.

Check Staples:

Salt butter (about 1/4 lb.)
Lemon (1)
Aromatics: crystal salt, freshly ground Indian Tellicherry black pepper, MSG, whole cardamom pods, ground cinnamon, ground clove, whole coriander seed, garlic (3 cloves), ground turmeric, fresh ginger root (we keep it frozen)
Yellow onions (5 medium)

Shopping List:

Young roasting chickens, cut up (2, about 2 to 2 1/2 lbs. each)
Plain yogurt (1 qt.)
Almonds (1/2 lb., in shells, or 1/4 lb., ready-shelled and blanched)
Whole poppy seed (about 1 Tbs.)
Decorations: any fancy baker who makes wedding cakes will usually sell the multicolored decorations: holly leaves of spun sugar, colored gold, silver, green, and red; sugar balls of various sizes; multicolored sugar-coated almonds; crystallized flowers; bright-green lengths of angelica, etc., etc.

The Day Before—Marinating the Chicken

We begin by toasting 2 tablespoons of the poppy seeds, using the BASIC RULE for toasting slivered almonds (page 91). Prepare the *massala* by grinding in a small mortar: 8 whole cardamom pods, 1 tablespoon whole coriander, 1 tablespoon of the toasted poppy seeds; add 1/2 teaspoon cinnamon and 1/2 teaspoon clove and hold, covered. Peel and finely chop 3 onions and hold, covered. Clean the chickens by rubbing with the cut side of half a lemon. Grate enough of the ginger root to fill 1 tablespoon, then hold, covered. Shell and blanch the almonds if necessary, then grind and hold. In a refrigerator dish (one with a cover) large enough to hold the chickens mix the marinade: the quart of yogurt, the chopped onions, the grated ginger, 2 cloves of the garlic (finely minced), the *massala,* the ground almonds, and several good grinds of pepper. Finally, blend in, ½ teaspoon at a time, the ground turmeric, until a light-brown color is achieved, usually with about 2 teaspoons. Since the turmeric adds flavor as well as color, do not add too much. Now work in chicken pieces, making sure that each is well coated with marinade. Refrigerate overnight, covered.

On the Day—4 Hours Before Serving

Take dish with chicken out of the refrigerator and let stand at room temperature for at least 3 hours, to let flavors absorb into chicken.

About 1 Hour Before Serving—Cooking the Chicken

This is best done in a fairly large Dutch oven with a tightly fitting lid, under which the pieces of chicken will be steamed in their own juices. This is the secret of the concentrated flavor. Peel and chop the remaining 2 onions. Finally mince the remaining clove of garlic. Over medium frying heat melt about 4 tablespoons of the butter in the bottom of the Dutch oven, then sauté onions until just wilted. Add the minced garlic and sauté for a few seconds longer, then add chicken with its marinade. Now add salt to taste. Bring marinade to a merry bubbling, then cover tightly and let chicken steam until tender, usually in 25 to 35 minutes. As soon as steaming begins start preparing the rice pilau (below). When chicken is done it can be kept warm over a low flame on top of the stove or in a keep-warm oven (about 150 degrees), and this enhances the curry flavor.

Part 2: Indian Pilau of Rice

For a party of 8 to 10

Check Staples:

Salt butter (½ lb.)
Aromatics: crystal salt,☧ freshly ground Indian Tellicherry black pepper,☧ MSG,◼ whole allspice, whole cardamom pods, ground cinnamon, ground clove, garlic (1 clove), filaments of Indian saffron
Yellow onion (1 medium)
Dry white wine♁ (just over ¼ cup)

Shopping List:

Indian long-grain pilau or Patna rice or, as a second choice, standard long-grain rice (4 cups)
Almonds (½ lb., in shells, or ¼ lb., shelled and blanched)
Pitted dates (½ lb.)
Indian pistachio nuts, shelled (¼ lb.)
Seedless white raisins (1 cup)

About 35 Minutes Before Serving

We prepare this in a large enameled cast-iron cocotte* with a tightly fitting lid, one big enough to hold the rice as it expands and to allow it to be lifted and turned during the cooking. Begin by steeping 1 tablespoon of the saffron in 1/4 cup of the dry white wine, according to the BASIC RULE (page 27). Next, prepare a *massala* (page 400) by grinding in a mortar: 1/2 teaspoon allspice and 10 whole cardamom pods; add 1/2 teaspoon ground cinnamon and 1/2 teaspoon ground clove, then mix thoroughly and hold, covered. Finely mince the clove of garlic. Peel and finely chop the onion. If necessary shell and blanch the almonds, then coarsely chop them. Coarsely chop the 1/2 pound dates.

We place our cocotte over medium frying heat and melt in it 12 tablespoons (1 1/2 sticks) of the butter, then sauté the onions until just wilted. Add the garlic and the *massala*. Stir around to blend, then add the 4 cups of rice. Keep stirring to coat each grain with spiced butter and continue to color rice for about 5 minutes. In a separate saucepan bring 2 quarts of freshly drawn cold water to a boil. Work saffron-wine mixture into rice, rinsing the saffron pan with a dash of wine plus a fair amount of salt, pepper, and MSG. When water boils pour it over rice, stir again, bring back to boiling, then turn down heat so that water is gently bubbling, put on lid tightly, and do not lift it for the first 15 minutes. Meanwhile, in a sauté pan over fairly low frying heat, melt the remaining 4 tablespoons of the butter, then stir in the cup of white raisins, the chopped almonds, the shelled pistachios, and the chopped dates. These are not to be fried but gently heated and enriched with a coating of butter. After 15 minutes, using a wooden fork, very gently lift and loosen the rice all around and taste a grain to check its progress. Re-cover and continue cooking as required. When rice is just soft through, but still firm and chewy so that there is no danger of its mushing, with a rubber spatula carefully work the entire contents of the sauté pan into it. Replace the lid on the cocotte and continue cooking until rice is perfectly done and all liquid is absorbed.

Finally Building and Decorating the Biriani Pyramid

An Indian family would probably use a golden platter with a pedestal about 10 inches high, like a tall cake stand, so that the pyramid would be high on the table. On such a platter (or any other round dish) gently, without breaking up chicken or mashing rice, combine the *khorrma* with the pilau, including the sauce from the chicken. Build it all up in a sharp, tall pyramid, with pieces of chicken sticking out here and there and some of the raisins and nuts showing on the surface.

Now decorate with the colored wedding-cake tidbits. There is unlimited opportunity for imagination. Finally, the Indian family might place on the peak of the pyramid a small gold or silver elephant with his trunk upraised in salute. As the Moglai *biriani* is placed on the table, with its accompanying array of condiments (page 93), each diner feels like a Mogul emperor.

INDIAN HALVAH SUJI WITH ALPHONSE MANGOES

For a party of 8 to 10

In the Middle East the word "halvah" means a crispy, flaky sweetmeat made from honey, nuts, and sugar, but in India it means a velvety cereal pudding which serves, so to speak, to soothe the mouth after the riotous excitements of the preceding courses. This halvah may be served warm, but we prefer it at room temperature. It is the perfect foil to the bright freshness of the Indian Alphonse mangoes.

Check Staples:

Sweet butter (6 Tbs.)
Milk (about 3/4 cup)
Aromatics: whole cardamom pods (10), whole nutmeg
Granulated white sugar (3/4 cup)

Shopping List:

Imported Indian sliced Alphonse mangoes in syrup✱ (2-lb. can)
Semolina, farina, or milled rice (1 1/2 cups)
Almonds (1/2 lb., in shells, or 1/4 lb., shelled and blanched and/or slivered)
Dark unsulphured molasses (1/4 cup)
White seedless raisins (1/2 cup)

The Day Before or at Least 5 Hours Beforehand—Preparation in About 25 Minutes

If necessary shell the almonds, then blanch, sliver, and toast them, using the BASIC RULES (pages 91 and 253). Cut 10 cardamom pods in half, then scrape out the tiny black seeds into a cup and hold. In a thick-bottomed 1-quart saucepan, mix the 3/4 cup of sugar with the 1/4 cup of molasses and work in just enough of the milk to liquefy, usually 1/3 to 1/2 cup. Bring slowly to a boil, stirring several times, then simmer gently, uncovered, to form a milk syrup. If it starts thickening too soon blend in a little more milk. Meanwhile in a sauté pan over medium frying heat melt the 6 tablespoons of butter, then blend in the 1 1/2 cups of semolina (or alternative) and stir until completely amalgamated. Turn down heat and just simmer, stirring almost continuously, until the cereal is a golden-brown and the butter begins to separate out again, usually in about 7 minutes. Now blend in the milk syrup, plus the 1/2 cup of raisins, then turn up heat and bubble fairly hard to boil off superfluous liquid until the halvah thickens, usually in about 5 minutes. Then spoon into a handsome shallow serving bowl, cool to room temperature, then cover and refrigerate 3 to 4 hours or overnight. Also refrigerate the can of Alphonse mangoes.

Just Before Serving

Decorate the top of the halvah with the toasted almonds, the cardamom seeds, and freshly grated nutmeg. Serve with slices of Alphonse mango and a little of the mango syrup.

Informal Party Menus

Of course we don't plan a foreign menu every time we give a party. Much of our entertaining involves far less time spent on shopping and preparation. Many of our less formal party menus have a French accent, with the stress on balance and simplicity. During the winter months we might entertain with the following:

WINTER PARTY LUNCH I:
Brandade de Morue, page 559
Swiss Cheese Fondue, page 302
Salad with Winter Dressing, page 169
Bananas Flamed with Rum, page 618

WINTER PARTY LUNCH II:
Italian Vitello Tonnato, page 423
Crab Meat with Eggs, page 483

Jerusalem Artichokes in Cream Sauce, page 462
French Poires Bon-Chrétien, page 618

Winter Party Lunch III:
Cream of Inebriated Mushrooms, page 113
Cheese Soufflé, page 147
Green Beans Athenian Style, page 156
Cognac Meringue Pie, page 175

Winter Buffet Supper:
Creamed Consommé Bretonne, page 388
Paella a la Valenciana de Neuva York, page 234
Salad with Winter Dressing, page 170
Cold Pseudo-Soufflé of Raspberries, page 480

Winter Party Dinner I:
Cream of Leek, Potato, and Tomato, page 112
Sea Bass as They Do It on the French Riviera, page 137
Deep-Fried Oyster Plant, page 467
Fruit with Cheese, page 173

Winter Party Dinner II:
Greek and Spanish Olives, page 105
Baked Whole Acorn Squash with Maple Butter, page 155
Cotriade Bretonne, page 143
Our Basic English Applesauce, page 174

Winter Party Dinner III:
Clear Vegetable Bouillon, page 111
French Pot-au-Feu, page 115
Salad with Winter Dressing, page 169
Amaretti with Rum in Chocolate Sauce, page 620

Winter Sunday Lazy Breakfast I:
Vouvray Fruit Cup, page 178
Royal Court English Trifle, page 626
Buttered Toast with Homemade Seville Orange Marmalade, page 183
Coffee or Tea

Winter Sunday Lazy Breakfast II:
Homemade Country Sausage, page 178
Perfectly Poached Eggs, page 151
Various Breads and Jams

THE FAMILY MEALS OF WINTER
Day-to-Day Recipes

IN THE party menus on the preceding pages the concentration was on gastronomic adventure and dramatic presentation, but for day-to-day planning, when one considers also the factors of time and cost and the avoidance of waste, fixed menus are too inflexible and we group the family recipes by courses, foods, and time of day. This makes it easy to find the recipe *after* one has found the food. We resist menu planning by impulse. We avoid saying: "I feel like salmon on Friday." Instead we first ask: "What is at its best on the list of foods in season? What are the bargains in the market?" Then we often save more cost and time by buying a substantial quantity and organizing a sequence of sharply contrasting dishes. (For example, the sequence for a large leg of lamb, page 276.) We often have several meals at various stages of production, the preparatory work conveniently done on leisurely days, to eliminate the shopping and kitchen pressures from busy days. Finally, it takes hardly more than a few minutes to complete one of our regular meals of three courses. The main dish is preceded by what we call a "prologue," (see discussion on next page) and may be followed by a prepared dessert, but much more often by one of the perfect marriages of fruit, cheese, and wine (page 173). Wine is to us not simply an occasional party luxury, but an everyday ingredient of the pleasures of the table (see pages 202–10).

¶ *Prologues (Appetizers)—Canapés · Hors d'Oeuvres · Antipasti · Entremeses · Mezethakia · Zakuski*

Each great gastronomic country seems to have its own style in opening a meal, and we have adopted and adapted some of these national specialities. In France the classic canapé has to be a single bite on a tiny round of toast, served before coming to the table, while the classic hors d'oeuvre (which means, literally, "outside of work," something prepared outside the immediate routine) is always served at the table. In the Italian version of hors d'oeuvres, the *antipasti* are usually dominated by the sliced savory meats, including the surprising *vitello tonnato* (page 423), which is so filling that we serve it as a main dish. In a Spanish restaurant the *entremeses* (both *fríos* —cold—and *caliente*—hot) are often served at the bar before dinner (a succession of delicious small plates, including the universal *escabeche,* page 268). In Greece the *mezethakia* is made exciting by the wonderful tiny fish of the eastern Mediterranean, including the shrimp boiled in wine (page 108). In Russia, before going in to the dining room, the guests assemble in an anteroom around a buffet table set with a dozen or more *zakuski,* which means "little bits." We sometimes serve one such dish (perhaps the mock caviar, page 270) on a small side table from which the diners serve themselves.

A Variety of Olives

The taste of an olive, Lawrence Durrell wrote, is "older than meat, older than wine." After thousands of years it remains the simplest, most natural, and best of all canapé *mezethakia.* But what a mistake to think of the choice among olives being simply either black or green—and almost always from a can! Of all fruits the olive seems to lose most by the process of canning. There are dozens of varieties (both of the unripe green and the ripe black), and the only way to explore them is by picking them out from the huge stone crocks in authentic Greek, Italian, or Spanish groceries.✲ Some are fat and juicy, soaking lazily in oil, vinegar, or brine. Some are lean, shriveled, and dry with a sharp saltiness that shocks the tongue. Some are broken open and pitted, completely permeated by the flavoring marinade. Some have their pits cracked and are strong with the bitterness of the core. We seldom serve less than four contrasting types.

The SPANISH ALFONSO: luxurious, like a large deep-purple grape, with a soft skin and luscious flesh. It should be kept in a mixture of oil, vinegar, and water. The GREEK KALAMATA, named after the port in the Peloponnesus from which the olives are shipped: shaped like a small blackish-purple egg, usually cracked open, with a crispy-tough skin and a slightly bittersweet flavor with an earthy quality, like old wine. It should be kept in the same type of marinade as the Alfonso, above. The GREEK CHIOS, named for the Aegean island where it grows: egg-shaped, dark brown, with flesh so soft that it squeezes out with the first bite. It should be stored dry. The GREEK VOLOS, named for the Thessalian port: grayish-purple, with a salty juice, as if it were the fruit of some seaweed on a Mediterranean beach. Like The Volos, it is also kept dry. The GREEK AMPHISSIS, named for the town on the lower slopes of the Pindus Mountains: large, black, salty, with a flavor of the purest virgin olive oil; it is also stored dry. The GREEN CRACKED NAFPAKTOS from the town near the vineyards of Patras: like a small grape, meaty, oily, rich, yet with a little of the sharpness of a sour apple because it is probably the least ripe of all table olives. It is kept in strongly salted water. The DRIED MOROCCAN: jet-black, small and shriveled, like a large raisin, crisp and nutty; to be stored, of course, dry. The GREEK AGRINION from the town near the Epirus: firm and chewy, almost like biting into a small piece of meat. It should be stored dry. And these are only a beginning . . .

BASIC RULE FOR FRENCH HOME-STYLE HORS D'OEUVRES: No one knows better than the thrifty French housewife how to use up those odd little remnants of food, not enough even for one portion, remaining from previous meals: the half cup of cooked peas, the single boiled potato, the three lonely shrimp. We often wonder why more Americans have not learned this trick. In a French household this is what hors d'oeuvres are all about. The bits and pieces are collected and each is dressed up with one or another of the famous piquant sauces: the *rémoulade* (page 109), the homemade mayonnaise, named for a French General Mahon (page 423), the Italian *maionese tonnata* (page 424), or the simple vinaigrette, or French dressing (page 73). If there is a little more time, the French cook will soak new life into her cooked vegetables with an overnight hot marination known in France as *à la Grecque*—Greek style. This converts mushrooms for example into one of the most delicate and attractive of all prologues (see following recipe).

Then, on a handsome flat platter, the small piles are neatly arranged, decorated with bits of greenery, garnished and expanded perhaps with some green pepper rings, some sticks of white celery, some olives, and possibly a few slices of savory sausage. The result is a good-looking and appetite-whetting first course for lunch or dinner.

FRENCH MARINATED MUSHROOMS

For our family of 4

This is one of the classic appetizers of the French cuisine. Many gourmets consider it a perfect prologue to a delicate meal: with a slight acidity to encourage the appetite, and the interest of the mushroom heightened by the dressing. This recipe can also be used with many other fresh or precooked vegetables. These button mushrooms can be served as canapés on toast rounds, or on small plates with forks.

Check Staples:

Lemon (1)
Aromatics: crystal salt, whole black peppercorns, MSG, whole bay leaves, whole fennel seed, thyme
Fresh parsley (1 bunch)
Watercress (1 bunch)
Olive oil (3/4 to 1 cup)
Tarragon white wine vinegar (1/4 to 1/2 cup)

Shopping List:

Small button mushrooms (1 lb.)

The Day, or Several Days, Before

We like these so much that we often keep a running supply in the refrigerator for several weeks, using the same marinade to prepare fresh batches of mushrooms. Wipe (never wash) the mushrooms, cutting stems off level with the caps, getting rid of any dried ends on stems, the remaining good parts being cooked with the caps. Caps, if small enough, should be left whole. In a 2-quart saucepan, preferably enameled iron or tinned copper, to avoid interaction with the acid, mix: 1 cup freshly drawn cold water, 1/2 cup olive oil, and 1/4 cup vinegar. Bring slowly to simmering, while adding aromatics: about 1 teaspoon salt, 12 whole peppercorns, 1 teaspoon MSG, 2 whole bay leaves, 1 teaspoon fennel seed, 1/2 teaspoon thyme, 3 or 4 whole sprigs of parsley with stems. Simmer, covered, about 10 minutes to bring out flavors, then drop in mushroom caps and stems, making sure there is enough liquid to cover them. If not, add more oil, vinegar, and water in same proportions as above. Bring back to simmering and continue cooking, covered, until mushrooms are just cooked through, usually in 10 to 15 minutes. To check progress the first time, fish out one cap and cut it in half. The flesh should be dark and soft through the center. Let mushrooms cool in marinade, then bottle them, still in marinade, in wide-mouthed screw-top jars and refrigerate until needed.

The flavor of the marinade will continue slowly to impregnate mushrooms and if it becomes too strong they can be drained and stored separately. The marinade can be reused for fresh batches of mushrooms. If the marinade itself gets too strong after a while, strain the liquid and throw away aromatics. Serve mushrooms with lemon quarters on chopped watercress leaves.

GREEK WINE-BOILED SHRIMP

For our family of 4

We know of no better way of boiling shrimp, to be eaten cold or added to a prepared dish. The shrimp absorbs the flavor and remains juicy and tender by being held in the shell until the last minute. When served cold as an hors d'oeuvre we add a mild Creole *sauce rémoulade* (recipe follows).

Check Staples:

Aromatics: crystal salt, freshly ground black pepper, red cayenne pepper, MSG, whole bay leaves, garlic (1 or 2 cloves)
Green Pascal celery, with leaves (2 or 3 stalks)
Tarragon white wine vinegar (1 to 2 cups)
Dry white wine (1 to 2 cups)

Shopping List:

Jumbo shrimp—for number of shrimp per pound, *see* page 62 (1½ lbs.)

Boiled the Day Before and Soaked Overnight

First we prepare the boiling liquor, remembering that it must be very strong to the taste if it is to inject its flavor into the shrimp. In a 2½-quart saucepan put: 1 cup each of vinegar, wine, and cold water. Add the garlic (slivered), 2 whole bay leaves, the celery with its leaves, all finely chopped; at least 1 tablespoon or more of crystal salt, 6 or more grinds of pepper, enough cayenne to make the liquid peppery to the tongue, and 1 teaspoon MSG. Bring to a boil and simmer, covered, for roughly 30 minutes to bring out and mingle the flavors.

Meanwhile wash the shrimp under cold running water, remove legs, but do not shell. When boiling liquor is ready drop in shrimp all at once, adding more vinegar and wine in equal parts, if needed, to cover. Return to a boil as quickly as possible, then time for exactly 5 minutes. Turn off heat and let shrimp cool to room temperature in the liquid. Turn entire contents of saucepan into a storage bowl and refrigerate for *at least* 24 hours. This is when the shrimp absorbs the flavor and the process cannot be speeded up.

Just Before Serving

Drain the shrimp. Shell and devein them. Serve ice cold, with the *sauce rémoulade* (below).

ARNAUD'S SAUCE RÉMOULADE

About 1 cup

The owner of one of the great restaurants of New Orleans, where we have always found the *crevettes à la rémoulade* to be superb, released his secret a few years before he died. This sauce, which has the consistency of a relish, avoids drowning the shrimp in the richness of mayonnaise or dominating them with horseradish. Instead it intensifies the natural flavor of the shrimp.

Check Staples:

Aromatics: crystal salt, freshly ground black pepper, MSG, Hungarian sweet red paprika (1 Tbs.)
Parsley (3 or 4 sprigs)
Watercress (1 bunch)
Olive oil (6 Tbs.)
Spanish Sherry vinegar (2 Tbs.)

Shopping List:

New Orleans Creole mustard, or as second choice, French Dijon (4 Tbs.)
Italian red or Spanish sweet onion (1 small)
White celery (1/2 heart)

The Day Before—Hold, Tightly Covered, in Refrigerator

We work hard to chop very finely: the parsley, the celery heart, and the onion. Mix these in a bowl with the 2 tablespoons of vinegar, the 6 tablespoons of olive oil, the 4 tablespoons of mustard, the tablespoon of paprika, and rather more salt, pepper, and MSG than usual. The flavor should be sharp but not strident. Put mixture into a tightly covered jar and refrigerate for at least several hours to mature.

When Used with Cold Shrimp—About 2 Hours Before Serving

Mix the boiled and shelled shrimp with enough *rémoulade* to coat well and leave in the refrigerator for about 2 hours. Serve on a bed of chopped watercress.

GRILLED OXTAIL DISCS

For our family of 4

This is an "encore" way of making canapés of the pieces of oxtail from the *pot-au-feu* (page 115). They have already gained flavor from having been parboiled in the strong beef broth. Now they are breaded and crisped under the grill.

Check Staples:

Oxtail discs, previously boiled, about ½ inch thick (about 12)
A batch of homemade sauce, either the *rémoulade* from page 109, the *maionese tonnata* from page 424, or one of the winter salad dressings from pages 169–70 (about ¾ cup)
Salt butter (about 2 Tbs.)
Spiced bread crumbs, sometimes called "herb stuffing" (about ½ cup)

About 25 Minutes Before Serving

Preheat oven to 325 degrees. In a small saucepan melt 2 tablespoons of the butter and paint the oxtail pieces with it. Cover each piece thickly and firmly with bread crumbs and put into an au gratin dish or onto a baking sheet. Then bake in the oven until they are warm through, usually in about 15 minutes. About 5 minutes before oxtail comes out of the oven, turn on grill and adjust shelf so that oxtail will be about 2 inches from the heat. Dribble each piece with a few drops more butter and broil until well browned on both sides, usually in 2 to 3 minutes per side. Each diner holds the oxtail disc by its central bone, dips it into a small individual bowl of sauce, then bites off the succulent meat.

¶ *Prologues (Soups)—Bouillons · Consommés · Petites Marmites · Bisques · Crèmes · Potages · Purées*

The great eighteenth-century French gastronome Grimod de la Reynière once said that soup is to a dinner what the entrance is to a house: the first indication of style, the setting of tone and atmosphere. This principle applies equally well to the most exalted and to the simplest dinner. Soup is an alternative to hors d'oeuvres as the prologue to a family meal. The English language provides only the one word "soup," but the French, always particularly precise in the language of gastronomy, have given the world at least a dozen varietal names. There is the rich *bisque,* almost always with shellfish, as in the *Billi-Bi* (page 429). There is the infinity of the *crèmes* and of the expansive farmhouse *potages,* with solid meats and vegetables providing a one-dish meal, as in *la garbure* (page 574), or the smooth, thick *purées,* as in roasted red pimiento (page 565). Then there are the variations of clear broths, the *bouillons,* which means the "boilings" for the extraction of juices from meats and vegetables; the *consommés,* clarified and concentrated versions of bouillons; the *petites marmites,* named for the small earthenware dishes in which they are brought to the table. Each can be served light and clear, with drops of lemon juice, or a dash of dry Sherry, or a floating dab of whipped cream as in *consommé Bretonne* (page 388). Or they can be given body with rice or with such unusual pastas as the melon-seed-shaped *seme di mellone,* or, in the French style, with semolina or tapioca. Or they can be dramatized with the classic meat garnishes, tiny meatballs, German *Leberknödel* (liver dumplings), or the meat-stuffed pastry shapes, either the Jewish *kreplach,* or the Italian *cappelletti* (little hats), or the Siberian *pelmeny.* There is hardly a better midnight snack than a cup of steaming bouillon with a country-ham biscuit (page 484). Finally, these homemade clear broths provide the aromatic stock that is the flavor-foundation of nine out of ten recipes. Our refrigerator is seldom without a supply of the beef bouillon from the *pot-au-feu* (page 115), the chicken bouillon from the *waterzooie* (page 286), the mushroom bouillon (page 273), or the vegetable bouillon (recipe follows). In almost any recipe calling for one of these bouillons another may be substituted, with slight (and often interesting) variations of flavor.

CLEAR VEGETABLE BOUILLON

About ¾ gallon for storage

Check Staples:

Lemon (1)
Aromatics: crystal salt, freshly ground black pepper, MSG, whole caraway seed (1 Tbs.)
Carrots (6 medium)
Parsley (small bunch)
Dry Sherry (a few dashes)

Shopping List:

Cabbage (1 small head)
Leeks (4 medium)
Soft boiling potatoes, *see* list, page 56 (6 medium)
White turnips (4 small)
Dried green split peas (1 cup)

Preparation in About 15 Minutes—Unsupervised Simmering, 2 to 4 Hours

In a large soup pot set 4 quarts of freshly drawn cold water to boil. As it heats up, add: the cabbage, quartered, after removing bruised outer leaves; the 6 carrots, scraped and chunked; the 4 turnips, peeled and quartered; the 6 potatoes, peeled and chunked; the 4 leeks, split and carefully washed under cold running water, then chunked; the cup of split peas, first washed and drained; a handful of parsley, washed but not chopped; 1 tablespoon of caraway, 2 tablespoons of salt, a few grinds of pepper, and 2 teaspoons MSG. When it boils turn down heat to gentle simmering and continue cooking, uncovered, for several hours so that bouillon boils down and concentrates. The time is reasonably flexible: 2 hours is the minimum; 4 hours will extract and concentrate even more of the flavoring juices. When the cooking is finished and the bouillon has cooled enough to handle, we use clean hands to remove, squeeze out, and throw away the vegetables. Finally, strain out the smaller particles through a fine-mesh sieve. The result is a rich and potent broth that will keep perfectly in the refrigerator. Before serving add a dash of Sherry and freshly squeezed lemon juice to each bowl.

CREAM OF LEEK, POTATO, AND TOMATO

For our family of 4

This soup is one of the classic combinations of the French cuisine; it is rich, hearty, economical, easy and quick to prepare, with a regal balance of flavors.

Check Staples:

Salt butter (5 Tbs.)
Milk, for thinning (up to 1 pt.)
Clear vegetable bouillon, *see* previous recipe, or clear chicken bouillon (4 cups)
Aromatics: crystal salt, freshly ground black pepper, MSG
Yellow onions (2 medium)
Fresh parsley (small bunch)
Granulated white sugar (2 tsp.)
Bread croutons

Shopping List:

Leeks (4 medium)
Soft boiling potatoes, *see* list, page 56 (6 medium)
Tomatoes (3 medium)
Light cream (1 pt.)

Advance Preparation in 10 Minutes—Unsupervised Simmering, About 35 Minutes

Use only the white parts of the 4 leeks, cutting off leaves and roots. Carefully wash out every last grain of sand by splitting them open and holding them under fast-running cold water, then cut in ½-inch chunks. Peel and thinly slice the 2 onions. Peel the 6 potatoes and dice into large cubes. Coarsely chunk the 3 tomatoes. In a 3-quart soup pot over medium frying heat melt 3 tablespoons of the butter, then, before it starts bubbling, add the leeks and onion slices. The essential trick now is to adjust the heat so that the leeks and onions do not fry or brown, but just gently simmer. Stir them around occasionally to keep them coated with the butter. When they are just soft, usually in 5 minutes, add the tomatoes, stir again, and continue gently simmering. In a separate saucepan bring the quart of bouillon to the boiling point. When the tomatoes are just beginning to mash add the potatoes and then the boiling bouillon. Stir in the 2 teaspoons of sugar, plus salt, a very little pepper, and MSG to taste. Turn the heat down to gentle simmering, then cover and cook until potatoes are completely soft, usually in 30 to 35 minutes. Cool and pass mixture through a fine-mesh food mill. At this point it can be stored in the refrigerator and will keep perfectly for several days. It will thicken to a paste.

About 2 Hours Before Serving

Remove soup from refrigerator and let it come to room temperature.

About 20 Minutes Before Serving

Prepare croutons by coarsely dicing sliced white bread and frying in a little butter until cubes are crisp. Finely chop enough parsley to fill 1/4 cup. Gently reheat soup, remembering that potato may burn if the bottom of pan is too hot. As it is simmering blend in 1 cup of the cream, using a wooden spoon and carefully scraping the bottom of the pan. Taste and adjust seasonings if necessary. Also judge the richness and texture of the soup. For more velvet on the tongue, continue adding cream, dash by dash. To thin it, simply add milk. When it is exactly right, serve it very hot, in preheated bowls, with croutons, green parsley sprinkled on top, and a pat of butter melting in the center.

CREAM OF INEBRIATED MUSHROOMS

For our family of 4

Generally, mushrooms for soup are first softened in butter. We steam them in wine for a dramatic accent to the basic mushroom flavor.

Check Staples:

Salt butter (4 Tbs.)
Milk (3 cups)
Aromatics: crystal salt,* freshly ground black pepper,* MSG,* garlic (1 clove), ground mace, Hungarian sweet red paprika*
Carrot (1 medium)
Green Pascal celery with leaves (1 inner stalk)
Yellow onion (1 medium)
Parsley (small bunch)
Granulated instantized flour* (several Tbs.)
Dry white wine* (1 cup)

Shopping List:

Mushrooms (1 lb.)
Heavy cream (1 pt.)

About 40 Minutes Before Serving

Wipe clean (never wash) the pound of mushrooms, slice them fairly thick, and put them into a saucepan with a tightly fitting lid. Pour over them the cup of wine and heat to merry bubbling to provide plenty of steam. Cover tightly and keep going until mushrooms are soft, usually in about 15 minutes. Meanwhile in a mixing bowl assemble: the carrot, scraped and sliced; the celery stalk, thinly sliced, the leaves chopped; plus the onion, peeled and thinly sliced. Finely mince the clove of garlic and hold separately. Finely chop enough parsley to fill 1/4 cup. Put the 3 cups of milk in a saucepan and heat it, but do not let it boil.

In the main soup pot, over medium-high frying heat, melt the 4 tablespoons of butter, then lightly brown the vegetables, at the same time adding the garlic and a couple of whole sprigs of parsley. As soon as vegetables are browned, carefully sprinkle on and stir in enough flour to absorb all the butter, usually 3 or 4 tablespoons. Now start blending in the hot milk, slowly at first, stirring vigorously to keep smooth as it thickens. Blend in 1/2 teaspoon mace, plus salt, pepper, and MSG to taste. Keep quite hot but do not let boil, for about 10 minutes, to develop flavor. Then let cool slightly, strain out solids, crushing them with a wooden spoon to release their juices, and put milk back into the rinsed-out soup pot.

About 15 Minutes Before Serving

When mushrooms are soft, drain them, carefully saving the wine, and purée them either by rubbing them through a fine sieve or passing them through a food mill or swirling them for a very few seconds only in an electric blender. Blend mushroom purée back into wine, then mix both into soup, with 1 1/2 cups of the cream. Carefully reheat, at the same time tasting and adjusting seasonings, if necessary, but do not let it boil.

Serving at Table

The soup should be served very hot, in preheated bowls, with more cream floating on the surface. Add color by sprinkling paprika in the center and surrounding it with a ring of chopped green parsley.

¶ *Main Dishes (Meat)*

Our first family meat dish of the year, below, was carefully chosen as one of the most basic of all meat recipes. We were surrounded by the aroma of this dish one Sunday morning while strolling in a middle-class Parisian residential suburb, and realized that in about every second house there was on the fire a *pot-au-feu.* The classic boiled beef is as much a tradition in French bourgeois life as is the weekend roast beef in England or the Saturday night baked beans in Boston. There are sound, practical reasons why the thrifty French housewife conforms. Not only does the *pot-au-feu* provide the hearty and expansive one-dish Sunday dinner for the family, it also sets up a whole week of good eating. There is the magnificent beef bouillon as soup and stock. There is the boiled beef to be sliced and served cold, or reheated and encored *en miroton* (page 120), for a quick week-night dinner. There is the stuffed chicken (although this is optional if one wants to simplify the dish), the sausage, the pork, the veal, the oxtail, plus all the vegetables for "instant" suppers and snacks for the rest of the week.

POT-AU-FEU—CLASSIC FRENCH BOILED DINNER

Several meals for our family of 4, or dinner for a party of 8 to 10

In any version of boiled beef there are always two irreconcilable factors. If the beef is boiled until it has given its best to the broth, one ends up with a rather washed out piece of beef. On the other hand, the more the beef is pampered for the retention of its own flavor, the less richness there is in the broth. We solve this problem luxuriously with two pieces of beef. The first, the "boiling beef," is primarily for the broth but, even as meat, it is by no means wasted. The second, the "poaching beef," is boiled for its own perfection as the centerpiece of the meal. It is extremely important to choose the right cuts for these two purposes. For the boiling beef, the best is the so-called "front section" of fresh brisket, but if this is not available, a compromise choice might be chuck or bottom round. For the poaching beef, one needs a medium-tender cut, say top round or rump. For notes on the later, encore use of the various meats from the pot, see the end of the recipe.

Check Staples:

Salt butter (about 2 Tbs.)
Eggs (2 large)
Lemons (2)
Mayonnaise, our own homemade, page 423, or alternative (about 1 cup)
Southern corn-belly salt pork⊜ (½ lb.)
Aromatics: crystal salt,☧ freshly ground black pepper,☧ MSG,⊜ whole bay leaves, whole dried hot chili pods☧ (optional), garlic (5 cloves), tarragon, thyme, fresh horseradish, which we keep in our freezer, ready to grate☧ (enough,

Shopping List:

Boiling beef, "front section" of fresh brisket or alternative, *see* above (4 to 5 lbs.)
Poaching beef, top round or rump, lean, square block (about 4 lbs.)
Veal knuckle bone, with some meat on it, split in half (about 2 lbs.)
Beef marrow bone, cut in half lengthwise (1)
Beef liver, sliced (¾ lb.)
Oxtail in ½-inch sections (1)
Old boiling hen, optional, *see* shopping notes, page 520 (about 3 lbs.)

Check Staples (*continued*):

grated, to fill 1 Tbs.)
Shallots (small handful)**
Carrots (6 medium)
Green Pascal celery, with leaves (1 head)
Yellow onions (4 medium)
Parsley (1 bunch)
Green scallions (1 bunch)
Spiced bread crumbs, sometimes called "herb stuffing" (about 1½ cups)
Dry Sherry (a few Tbs.)
Dry white wine (1 bottle)

Shopping List (*continued*):

Pork sausage meat, our own homemade, page 178, or alternative (½ lb.)
Garlic sausage, Polish *Kielbasa,* or Hungarian *Kolbasz,* optional (about 1 per person)
Leeks (8 medium)
Parsnip (1)
Small boiling potatoes, *see* list, page 56 (2 lbs.)
Tomatoes (2 medium)
White turnips (4 medium)
French Dijon mustard (1 tsp.)
Sour pickles (small jar)
Any sour fruit in season, *see* list, pages 52–3 (enough, peeled and diced, to fill 1 cup)
Any sweet fruit in season, *see* list, pages 52–3 (enough, peeled and diced, to fill 1 cup)

One or More Days Ahead—Boiling the Beef

Wash the oxtail pieces under cold running water, then soak in warm water for about an hour before putting them into the pot. Also carefully trim off green leaves and roots from 4 of the leeks, split them open and wash them under fast-running cold water to get rid of sand, then soak in cold water until needed. Now begin assembling the ingredients, in order, in a very large soup kettle (about 5 gallons). Put the piece of boiling beef on the bottom, with the two halves of the veal knuckle on top, cut sides down. Wrap each half of the marrow bone in cheesecloth, to save marrow from disintegration, and place at each end of beef. Fill spaces around and on top with the vegetables: 4 whole onions, washed and with skins left on (the skins add color to the broth); 4 stalks of the celery, chunked, with leaves chopped; the 4 washed leeks, chunked; 3 of the carrots, scraped and chunked; 2 of the white turnips, peeled and chunked; the parsnip, scraped and chunked; plus 4 whole cloves garlic, with skins left on. Fill up pot to within 2 inches of top with freshly drawn cold water, turn on heat, and bring to a boil. As it heats up, add seasonings: 4 whole sprigs parsley, 3 whole bay leaves, 2 teaspoons each of tarragon and thyme, 1 dry hot chili pepper if available, 1 tablespoon salt, very little pepper if there is a hot chili, more if not, and 2 teaspoons MSG. Watch pot as it heats up and skim. Meanwhile cut the 2 tomatoes in half, lightly pan-fry in butter, then add them with the pan juices to the pot. When oxtail pieces have soaked for about an hour, drain, and add them to pot. As soon as pot starts bubbling, turn down to simmering. . . .

BASIC RULE FOR TRUE SIMMERING: It is impossible to be a good cook without understanding precisely what is meant by "simmering." This dish, for example, is generally called "boiled beef," but if the beef were actually boiled it would be ruined. The violently rising bubbles would agitate the water under the surface like the paddles of a washing machine and, beating against the meat, would wash away the gelatinous cement that holds the meat together. The result is disastrous. The meat breaks up into its separate fibers, is impossible to slice, and loses all taste and texture. Even gentle bubbling can do considerable damage.

True simmering avoids all bubbling by keeping the water just below the boiling temperature. Even the gentlest bubbling is not true simmering. How, then, is one to know that the water remains very close to boiling? Fortunately, there is a visible sign. When the water is just, just below boiling, the surface slowly moves, to and fro, round and about, as if crisscrossed by tiny currents. The French have a wonderfully descriptive term for it. They say that the water is *riant,* which means "smiling." If the smiling stops, the water has cooled by a degree or two and the heat must be brought up a tiny bit. If bubbles appear, it has become too hot and the heat must be brought down. This fine control of the heat can make the difference between magnificent success and total failure.

Set the heat under the *pot-au-feu* to simmering, "just smiling." This involves watching and adjusting for about the first 10 minutes. Then put on the lid, remembering that this will cause the temperature to rise slightly within about 5 minutes, so that some bubbling will begin and the heat will have to be turned down. Check every 5 minutes, until the simmering is again established under the lid; keep it going for about 4 hours. Then turn off heat and let *pot* cool to room temperature. Now take the *pot* apart. We think this is most efficiently done with clean hands. Remove the 2 halves of veal knuckle, cut off the lean meat, wrap and refrigerate or freeze it, throwing away the bones. Unwrap the 2 pieces of marrow bone, spooning the delectable marrow into a small covered refrigerator jar and throwing away the bones. Gently lift out the beef which, if properly simmered, will still be quite firm, wrap and refrigerate or freeze. Find all the pieces of oxtail, drop into a plastic bag and refrigerate or freeze. Lift out handfuls of the vegetables, squeeze them to release their juices, then throw them away. Finally, strain the broth through a fine sieve to get rid of every last solid particle. This clear liquid (approximately 3 quarts now), magnificent in appearance and taste, is the foundation on which the *pot-au-feu* will be built.

On the Morning of the Day—Stuffing the Chicken

We think that a chicken loses flavor oils by being washed with water. We prefer to clean it by rubbing, outside and in, with the cut side of half a lemon. Next, poach the 3/4 pound of liver slices in a little of the beef broth until they are just stiff enough to handle, then coarsely grind them and put them into a large mixing bowl in which the stuffing is now to be assembled: the 1/2 pound of sausage meat; 4 shallots, finely minced; the scallion bulbs, finely minced; 4 or 5 sprigs of parsley, finely chopped; 1 clove garlic, crushed through a press; 1 cup of the bread crumbs; 1 whole raw egg for binding; plus salt, pepper, and MSG to taste. Blend thoroughly, adding just enough wine, dash by dash, to make a firm yet moist stuffing. If it gets too soft, work in more bread crumbs; if too stiff, more wine. Loosely stuff the chicken, close openings at each end in the usual way and tie down wings and legs so that bird will stay neat in the pot.

About 2 1/4 Hours Before Serving

Put large pot with beef broth on high heat and bring just to a boil. Pinch the chicken and judge its toughness. If it is quite old, it will need 2 hours of simmering; if younger, a bit less. This controls the total cooking time. Let us assume 2 hours. As soon as broth starts bubbling, lower in chicken and reset heat for gentle simmering, "just smiling." Weigh the piece of poaching beef and calculate its cooking time. We like it rare and allow 12 minutes per pound, but for medium-well done allow up to 15 minutes per pound. Let us assume the beef will need 1 hour. Tie up beef with string and provide two string handles with which it can be lifted out of the broth. It must never be pricked with a fork or much of its juice will be lost.

About 1 1/4 Hours Before Serving

Add 1 pint of the white wine to the broth, stir and taste, adjust seasonings if necessary, then lower in poaching beef by its string and bring back to simmering as quickly as possible. In a separate saucepan, start simmering the garlic sausages (if any) and the 1/2 pound of corn belly, starting them in freshly drawn cold water and keeping them gently simmering, covered, for about 1 hour. Start preparing eating vegetables that will eventually go into the main pot. (Since they are hard to find when serving, we like to wrap them all together in a cheesecloth bag for easy withdrawal.) Wash the white parts of the 4 remaining leeks and cut them into 1-inch chunks. Scrape the 3 remaining carrots and quarter lengthwise. Peel the 2 remaining turnips and quarter. Wrap all these together and hold.

About 45 Minutes Before Serving

Lower the bag with vegetables into the broth. Peel the 2 pounds of potatoes and cut into fairly large chunks, then hold.

About 35 Minutes Before Serving

Put in the potatoes. During the final half hour prepare the sauces and garnishes. These are quite flexible and different people have widely different tastes. Some like a plain horseradish sauce. We prefer our homemade mayonnaise (page 423), with the following additions for 1 cup: 1 teaspoon Dijon mustard, 1/4 cup finely chopped scallion tops, 2 tablespoons finely chopped parsley, 1 tablespoon finely grated fresh horseradish, and 1 diced hard-boiled egg. Stir into the mayonnaise and put into a small serving bowl for the table. Another bowl at the table may contain diced sour pickle, yet another, diced tart apple or another seasonal tart fruit; and still another, diced sweet fruit. Finally, uncover big pot and skim off fat. Also, dice the beef marrow as a garnish for broth.

Serving at Table

The beef broth is usually served as a preliminary course, garnished with the marrow, plus a few drops of lemon juice and/or a dash of dry Sherry. As this broth is being ladled out of the big pot, the beef and chicken can be checked for perfect doneness and the final timing adjusted. For the main course we bring two very large shallow platters to the table, the first with the beef and chicken (their strings removed), corn belly and sausages, which are carved at the table, the second with the vegetables. Each diner gets a little bit of everything (not forgetting the chicken stuffing) and makes up his own combination of sauce and condiments.

ENCORE NOTES: The poached beef and chicken are usually so fine in taste and texture that reheating them would be a shame; they are best eaten sliced cold. The beef makes the *miroton,* which follows. It and the veal can also be diced, marinated in oil and lemon juice, then used as the base of various substantial salads. The rounds of oxtail, reheated under the broiler, make fine canapés (page 109). The corn belly can be sliced and fried with breakfast eggs. The *pot-au-feu* makes light work of many succeeding meals.

FRENCH BOEUF EN MIROTON—AN ENCORE WITH THE BOILED BEEF

For our family of 4

This recipe uses the boiled beef from the *pot-au-feu,* but it could also be prepared with other boiled or roasted meats. The flavor can be varied by substituting different wines.

Check Staples:

Slices of the boiled beef from the *pot-au-feu* (enough for 4 people)
Clear beef bouillon, from the same (1¼ cups)
Salt butter (4 Tbs.)
Aromatics: crystal salt,* freshly ground black pepper,* MSG
Yellow onions (3 medium)
Parsley (small bunch)
Watercress (small bunch)
Spiced bread crumbs, sometimes called "herb stuffing" (¾ to 1 cup)
Granulated instantized flour (about 3 Tbs.)
Italian tomato paste (1 or 2 Tbs.)
Spanish Sherry vinegar (¼ cup)
Dry white wine or alternative (½ cup)

About 40 Minutes Before Serving

The boiled beef slices should come to room temperature. Peel and coarsely chop the 3 onions. Chop enough parsley and watercress to fill ¼ cup. Heat up the 1¼ cups of beef bouillon. In a sauté pan over medium frying heat, melt 2 tablespoons of the butter and just gild the chopped onions. Then carefully sprinkle over and work in with a wooden spoon enough flour to absorb the butter, usually between 1 and 2 tablespoons. Carefully blend in the ¼ cup of vinegar and the ½ cup of wine, then begin adding the hot bouillon, dash by dash at first, working the sauce to keep it quite smooth. When all the bouillon is in, add the chopped parsley and watercress, plus more than the usual amount of salt, pepper, and MSG, enough to make a rather strong flavor. Finally, blend in between 1 and 2 tablespoons of the tomato paste, just enough to give a slight body to the sauce. Let it bubble merrily for 4 or 5 minutes, stirring steadily, until it thickens to the consistency of heavy cream. Preheat oven to 375 degrees. For the final baking, choose an open au gratin dish or a shallow ceramic casserole good-looking enough to come to the table, then lightly butter it and cover the bottom with half the sauce. Neatly lay in the beef slices and spoon remainder of sauce over them. Sprinkle fairly thickly with the bread crumbs and dot with remaining butter.

About 20 Minutes Before Serving

Set dish in center of oven and bake uncovered until lightly brown, usually between 15 and 20 minutes. Serve at once on very hot plates, with extra chopped parsley and watercress sprinkled on top.

SAM'S SPICED POT ROAST OF BEEF

2 or 3 meals for our family of 4

In a charming small hotel in the French Quarter of New Orleans we met a Lebanese student at Tulane University and his young wife, a soft-voiced Louisiana girl from the Bayou country. Later, in their first apartment, we shared several delightful meals which were a combination of the breadth of the Lebanese cuisine and the sharp contrasts of the Creole. Sam had been taught to cook lamb by his mother in a farmhouse near Beirut. His wife was showing him American ways with beef. However, we use this recipe interchangeably with beef, lamb, or veal (see Braising Chart, page 59).

Check Staples:

Beef stock (about 1 pt.)
Lemons (2)
Floured butter—*beurre manié*, *see* page 12 (up to 8 Tbs.)
Aromatics: crystal salt, whole black peppercorns, MSG, whole allspice, whole bay leaves, whole cloves, dried whole sage leaf, thyme
Carrots (2 medium)
Yellow onions (2 medium)
Olive oil (3 to 4 Tbs.)
Red wine (about 1 pt.)

Shopping List:

Beef pot roast or alternative, *see* shopping notes, page 59 (4 to 5 lbs.)

The Day Before—Preparing the Marinade in About 15 Minutes

Peel off thinly the yellow outer rind of the 2 lemons and chop. Squeeze juice of both lemons. In a mortar coarsely crush: ½ teaspoon black peppercorns, 2 teaspoons whole allspice. Mix 1½ cups of the beef stock and 1½ cups of the red wine in a saucepan and add: the lemon rind and juice, the spices from the mortar, 3 crumbled bay leaves, 2 teaspoons cloves, 1 teaspoon crumbled sage, ½ teaspoon thyme, 1 teaspoon salt, and 1 teaspoon MSG. Stir and heat carefully almost to boiling. Put the meat in a large bowl and pour on the hot marinade. Cool, then store in the refrigerator overnight, turning the meat several times to keep moist on all sides.

About 6 Hours Before Serving

Take the meat and its marinade from the refrigerator and let come to room temperature.

About 4 Hours Before Serving (or Less, According to Meat Cut)

Scrape and slice the 2 carrots. Peel and chunk the 2 onions. Take meat out of the marinade and dry it. Heat the marinade to just boiling and let simmer, covered, until needed. For cooking the meat we would use either our stainless steel Dutch oven on top of the stove or an enameled cast-iron cocotte* in the oven. First place it over medium frying heat and bring 3 or 4 tablespoons of olive oil almost up to smoking. Quickly brown the onions and carrots and remove them. Sear meat on all sides. Then turn down heat, hiss all of the marinade over meat and surround it with the carrots and onions. Braise the meat in the usual way, with the liquid gently bubbling on top of the stove or in a 350-degree oven, in each case tightly covered. Time and final meat temperature vary according to meat cut used and are shown in the chart on page 59. If liquid boils down during cooking add more stock and wine, in equal proportions, making sure that it continues, gently bubbling.

About 15 Minutes Before Serving

Remove meat from pot and keep warm. Strain gravy and throw away all solids, then pour into a saucepan and thicken . . . with floured butter, according to our BASIC RULE on page 12. Sauce should finally have the consistency of heavy cream. Taste and adjust seasonings if necessary. Bring to table in a very hot sauceboat. Serve with mashed potatoes, rice, or kasha (page 167); and it is particularly good with pan-fried tomatoes (page 97).

SAM'S ONE-DISH MEAL OF BEEF KABOBS—HERO STYLE

For our family of 4

This is another dish adapted from our Lebanese friend in New Orleans (see previous recipe). With the meat marinated in advance, the final preparation, including a variety of vegetables, takes only about 25 minutes.

Check Staples:

Salt butter (¼ lb.)
Lemon (1)
Aromatics: crystal salt,☆ freshly ground black pepper,☆ whole black peppercorns,☆ MSG,▣ garlic (2 or 3 cloves), oregano
Parsley (small handful)
Green peppers (2 medium)
Tomatoes (4 medium)
Watercress (small bunch)
Olive oil▣ (½ cup)

Shopping List:

Sirloin steak, in 1½-inch cubes (about 1½ to 2 lbs.)
French bread (1 long loaf)
Mushrooms (about 1 dozen, medium)
White boiling onions (about 1 dozen)
Red wine, say a medium-priced Beaujolais♁ (½ bottle)

The Day Before—Marinating the Meat

In a covered refrigerator dish large enough to hold the meat, mix: the ½ bottle of red wine, the ½ cup of olive oil, 1 teaspoon oregano, 4 teaspoons salt, 1 teaspoon peppercorns, coarsely cracked in a mortar, plus 1 teaspoon MSG. Put in the meat, making sure that each piece is well moistened. Refrigerate overnight; stir meat around before going to bed and once again next morning.

About 2 Hours Before Serving

Peel and parboil 1 dozen white onions in boiling salted water, about 6 to 7 minutes, until not quite soft. Let the meat, garlic (if kept in the refrigerator, as ours is), and butter come to room temperature. Prepare remaining vegetables. Cut the 4 tomatoes and 2 green peppers into bite-size pieces. Wipe clean (never wash) the mushrooms and pull out stalks, saving them for some other use. In the usual way, stick the pieces of meat, alternating with vegetables, onto shish-kebab skewers—1 skewer per person. Hold at room temperature. Finally, prepare garlic butter . . .

BASIC RULE FOR GARLIC BUTTER: Soften the ¼-pound stick of butter, then cut up and put into a hand mortar. Peel and finely mince garlic, then add to butter, with 1 tablespoon finely chopped parsley, leaf only. Pound and thoroughly work together, adding, to taste, a few squeezes of lemon juice, plus salt, pepper, and MSG. Any quantity of this aromatic butter can be stored almost indefinitely in the refrigerator in a tightly closed screw-top jar.

About 25 Minutes Before Serving

Preheat broiler, setting shelf so that meat will be about 2 inches from heat. Cut the French loaf in half lengthwise, as for a hero sandwich, then lightly spread each half with garlic butter and set to warm. Stir the marinade and liberally spoon some of it over the pieces on the skewers. Place skewers under broiler, and baste every 2 minutes with more marinade for a total of about 8 minutes on the first side. Turn skewers over, baste again, and continue basting every 2 minutes for about 6 minutes on the second side. These times may be varied to control the rareness of the meat. Wash sprigs of watercress for garnish. Take bread out of the oven, cut each length in half, and place one section, cut side up, on each plate. Slide pieces from skewer neatly along top of bread. Spoon on juices from broiling pan so that they soak into the bread. Serve at once, garnished with watercress.

GRENADINE-GLAZED ROAST PORK

A large roast to last for several days

Grenadine is the brilliant red and slightly tart syrup made from the juice of the pomegranate. It is used here both as glaze and sauce for the largest loin roast that will fit into our oven. We make sure that the butcher cuts through the backbone at the bottom and slightly loosens each rib bone for easy slicing.

Check Staples:

Aromatics: crystal salt, freshly ground black pepper, MSG, mace chips, freshly ground nutmeg, dried thyme (if fresh not available)

Shopping List:

Pork loin roast, bones loosened, *see* above (any convenient size—we order 6 to 7 lbs.)

Grenadine syrup (1 pt.—half for glaze, half for sauce, recipe follows)

Fresh thyme, if available (small bunch)

30 Minutes Before Roasting Begins—Preparing the Meat

Wipe pork clean. In a small mortar mix 2 teaspoons mace chips with 2 tablespoons chopped fresh thyme (or 2 teaspoons dried) and pound for a few seconds to amalgamate oils. Then insert mixture into various pockets where butcher has lossened bones, making a few extra cuts if necessary, until contents of mortar are used up. Then refill mortar with second mixture: 3 teaspoons salt, roughly 1 teaspoon black pepper, 1 teaspoon MSG, plus roughly 1 teaspoon ground nutmeg. Pound for a few seconds, then, using the heel of the hand, pound mixture into all sides of pork, especially on back crust. Place pork, fat side upward, on rack in open roasting pan ready to go into oven. At proper time, below, preheat oven to 450 degrees.

Roasting the Pork According to Size and Thickness—20 to 30 Minutes per Pound

We insert a meat thermometer into thickest end of the pork and place it on a rack in the center of the oven to sear until just beginning to brown, usually 15 to 20 minutes. Meanwhile put 1 cup of the grenadine into a small saucepan and heat up, but keep well below boiling at all times. When pork shows first signs of browning, reduce oven temperature to 350 degrees and begin basting with hot grenadine. Repeat every 20 minutes or so using any available pan drippings, plus fresh grenadine being kept hot in saucepan, until pork is done, when thermometer shows internal temperature of 185 degrees. Crust will be scarlet and shiny and usually all grenadine will be used up. Serve with grenadine sauce (recipe follows).

HOT OR COLD GRENADINE SAUCE FOR PORK OR OTHER RICH MEATS

For about 1 pint

This is a modification of a sauce widely used in England with venison, mutton, and certain game birds, when the richness is to be cut by a tart and fruity relish. When served cold it is used as a homemade form of chutney.

Check Staples:

Orange, with thin, unblemished skin (1)
Lemon, the same (1)
Aromatics: red cayenne pepper, Indian ground ginger
Shallots (2)
Ground arrowroot (3 tsp.)

Shopping List:

Grenadine syrup, remaining from pork, preceding recipe (1 cup)
French Dijon mustard (about 3 tsp.)
Sweet vermouth (½ to ¾ cup)

About 20 Minutes to Prepare

We mix and cook this sauce in a small 1½-pint copper saucepan. Using a sharp potato peeler, thinly slice the outer rinds from the orange and lemon, finely chop, and put into saucepan. Separate the cloves of the 2 shallots, peel and slice them, then crush through a garlic or onion press and put into saucepan. Now add: ½ cup of the grenadine, ½ cup of the sweet vermouth, the juice of the orange, the juice of half the lemon, 2 teaspoons of the mustard, a very careful shake or two of the cayenne pepper, ½ teaspoon of the ginger; then blend thoroughly and heat up to gentle simmering for about 5 minutes. In a small bowl or cup put 3 teaspoons of the arrowroot and blend in enough extra grenadine to liquefy. Turn off heat under saucepan and immediately blend in arrowroot mixture, ½ teaspoon at a time, stirring continuously and vigorously to avoid lumping, until sauce is thickened to the consistency of heavy cream. Not all the arrowroot may be needed. Return to simmering, stirring continuously, for a minute or two. Then turn off heat, taste and finally balance flavors toward a sharp, bittersweet taste by adding, as needed, a little more of any or all of the following: grenadine, sweet vermouth, lemon juice, mustard, ginger. (The final balance is a matter of personal taste and judgment, which will come with experience.) Reheat and serve hot, or cool and refrigerate in a tightly covered jar. Cold, the sauce has the consistency of light jelly.

RABBIT IN MUSTARD BUTTER

For our family of 4

Our butcher skins the rabbit and cuts it up into serving pieces. This is the best way we know of preparing it; also one of the simplest and quickest.

Check Staples:

Beef bouillon (a few Tbs.)
Salt butter (about 5 Tbs.)
Aromatics: crystal salt,* freshly ground black pepper,* MSG,▣ whole bay leaf, garlic (2 cloves), rosemary, tarragon, thyme
Yellow onions (2 medium)
Parsley (small bunch)
Shallots* (3)
Olive oil▣ (about 3 Tbs.)

Shopping List:

Young rabbit, skinned and cut up (about 3½ lbs.)
Fresh dill, if available (small bunch)
French Dijon mustard (1 whole pot will be needed, about 6 oz.)

The Day Before—Advance Preparation in About 10 Minutes

Remove the rabbit's liver and hold, covered, in refrigerator. Wash and dry rabbit pieces, then smear thickly with mustard, put into a covered dish and refrigerate overnight.

On the Morning of the Day

Take rabbit out of refrigerator and leave at room temperature for several hours, to hasten absorption of the mustard flavor.

About 1½ Hours Before Serving—Sautéing the Rabbit

Peel and chop the 2 onions. Finely mince the 3 shallots, the 2 cloves of garlic, then hold together in a covered jar. We use an enameled cast-iron cocotte* with a tightly fitting lid, which can be used for the sautéing on top of the stove, for the oven baking, and for serving at the table. In it we melt the 5 tablespoons of butter and the 3 tablespoons of olive oil over low frying heat, being careful not to let the butter brown, then add: 1 bay leaf, crumbled; ½ teaspoon each of rosemary, tarragon, and thyme; about 1 tablespoon each of chopped fresh dill (if available) and parsley; plus salt, pepper, and MSG to taste. Turn down heat and simmer for 3 or 4 minutes to develop flavor. Meanwhile, preferably using a rubber spatula, scrape some of the mustard from the rabbit pieces, leaving on enough mustard to amalgamate with the butter and form a mustard sauce. Preheat oven to 150 degrees (keep-warm temperature) and set in it a pan to hold the rabbit pieces after sautéing. Turn up heat under cocotte to medium frying temperature and quickly sauté rabbit pieces, 2 or 3 at a time, until lightly brown. As each piece is done keep it warm in the oven. When all are done put them back into the cocotte, turning off heat and covering tightly. Turn up oven temperature to 350 degrees.

About 1 Hour Before Serving—Baking with Little Attention

Set cocotte in center of oven. After 30 minutes switch rabbit pieces around, so that the top ones are at the bottom and vice versa. Continue baking, covered, until rabbit is quite tender, usually in 50 to 55 minutes. Meanwhile chop enough dill and parsley to fill 1/3 cup. Take rabbit liver out of the refrigerator and chop finely.

Just Before Serving—Preparing the Sauce

When rabbit is done, take cocotte out of oven and set on top burner, turn off oven and leave door ajar, take out rabbit pieces and keep warm in pan in oven. Turn on heat under cocotte and bring sauce up to gentle bubbling. Stir liver into sauce, with 2 or 3 tablespoons of the beef bouillon. Turn up heat, so that sauce begins to bubble strongly, and reduce, stirring steadily. Taste and adjust seasonings if necessary, also working in a little more mustard if that seems required. When sauce glazes and shows first signs of thickening, turn down heat to simmering, put back pieces of rabbit, spooning sauce over each as it goes in, sprinkle with dill and parsley, cover and bring to the table. Delicious with our 7½-minute cabbage (page 310).

¶ *Main Dishes (Birds)—Chicken · Quail · Duck*

NORMANDY CHICKEN FLAMED WITH CALVADOS

For our family of 4

This is the famous farmhouse dish which combines the riches of that northern region (considered by many gourmets to have the most opulent cuisine of France): the fat chickens, the thick cream, the Calville apples and the Calvados applejack brandy that is distilled from their juice. It can be prepared with the chicken cut up in advance, but we think that keeping it whole seals in the juices. A rich and filling dish, to be teamed with a light first course and dessert.

Check Staples:

Salt butter (10 Tbs.)
Eggs (3 large)
Lemon (1)
Aromatics: crystal salt,☆ freshly ground black pepper,☆ MSG

Shopping List:

Frying-roasting chicken (about 2½ to 3 lbs.)
Heavy cream (½ pt.)
Fresh mushrooms (½ lb.)
French Calvados apple brandy (¼ cup)

About 1¼ Hours Before Serving—Including 40 Minutes Unsupervised Cooking

It is most important that the pot should have a tightly fitting lid, so we choose an oval-shaped enameled cast-iron cocotte,* just large enough for the chicken to fit snugly with not much more than an inch of space all around. This concentrates the aromatic steam. Instead of washing the chicken, clean it by rubbing inside and out with the cut side of half a lemon. We set the cocotte over medium-high frying heat, melt in it 6 tablespoons of the butter, then lightly brown the chicken on all sides, salting and peppering at the same time. In a tiny saucepan, gently heat up the ¼ cup of Calvados until it is just too hot to touch (if it gets anywhere near to boiling, the alcohol evaporates). Turn up the heat full on under the chicken, pour on the Calvados, and flame. Using oven mitts on both hands, lift the cocotte slightly and shake it, to encourage the flames. As soon as they die down, clamp on the lid tightly, turn down heat to simmering, and let the chicken absorb the brandy for 10 minutes. Meanwhile wipe the ½ pound of mushrooms clean (never wash them), cut lengthwise into hammer-shaped slices, and quickly sauté in the remaining 4 tablespoons of butter, continuing until mushrooms are just soft, usually in 3 or 4 minutes, adding a very little salt, pepper, and MSG. Preheat oven to 350 degrees. After chicken has simmered for 10 minutes, shake the mushrooms and their buttery juices into it, turn up the heat for a few seconds to blend the juices at a rolling boil, then re-cover and turn off heat.

About 50 Minutes Before Serving

Set cocotte in center of oven to steam chicken until tender, usually in 30 to 40 minutes. (If there is any doubt as to the tightness of the lid, seal it around the edge with a paste of flour and water.)

Meanwhile prepare the apple rings (see following recipe), which traditionally accompany this dish.

About 10 Minutes Before Serving—the Cream Sauce

Have ready a warm, oval serving platter. Separate the three eggs, reserving the whites for some other use. With a small wire whisk beat ¾ cup of the cream into the yolks. When chicken is done, turn the oven down to keep-warm temperature (150 degrees), then put cocotte on top burner. Lift chicken onto platter, neatly surround with apple rings, then lift out mushrooms with slotted spoon and sprinkle over and around chicken. Set in the oven to keep warm, leaving door slightly ajar. Add a little of the pot juices to the egg-cream mixture and then turn back into the pot, blend, and turn on gentle heat, still beating, until sauce warms up and thickens to the consistency of heavy cream. If it gets too thick, add more cream. Taste, adjust seasonings if necessary, then pour over chicken and serve at once.

BASIC METHOD FOR MAKING FRIED APPLE RINGS

For our family of 4

We go far beyond Normandy chicken in serving fried apple rings. They are among the best of all garnishes, fine with most birds, with many meats, with some of the rich fish (like salmon and swordfish), and even in salads and sandwiches. They come to our table about once a week throughout the year.

Check Staples:

Salt butter (about 4 Tbs.)
Maple syrup🅢 (about 2 Tbs.)

Shopping List:

Tart frying apples, in winter perhaps Cortland or Winesap; at other times perhaps Greening, *see* page 50 (6 medium)

Preparation in About 15 Minutes

Peel and core the apples, then slice into rings about ¼-inch thick. In a sauté or fry pan over medium frying heat melt 2 tablespoons of the butter, then sauté first batch of rings, turning with spatula every minute or so, until soft but not mushy. Repeat with remaining rings, adding more butter as needed. Each batch will usually be done in about 5 minutes. Taste one and if it is too tart, sprinkle a drop or two of maple syrup on each ring. They can be held hot in a keep-warm oven (150 degrees), but never covered, or they become mushy.

BOBWHITE QUAIL UNDER A BLANKET OF GRAPES

For our family of 4

A light main course, to go with a solid first course and perhaps to be followed by cheese. See notes on shopping for quail (page 60). The type of grape is important. The most convenient is the Thompson Seedless, but if it is not available we might use the Belgian White Muscat or the California Emperor. We do not agree with the purists that each grape must be peeled, but seed grapes must be cut in half and seeded.

Check Staples:

Thick-sliced dark smoked bacon (8 slices)
Salt butter (about 3 Tbs.)
Lemon (1)
Aromatics: crystal salt,* freshly ground black pepper,* MSG, whole bay leaves, garlic (2 cloves), thyme
Parsley (small bunch)
Imported Italian tomato paste (½ cup)
Dry white wine (½ cup)

Shopping List:

Young bobwhite quail, eviscerated, *see* above (1 per person)
White or pink grapes, *see* above (1½ to 2 lbs.)

On the Morning of the Day

In our house many hands make light work of halving and seeding the grapes if this is necessary.

About 1¼ Hours Before Serving

It is vital to have a pot with a tightly fitting lid, to hold in the steam from the boiling grape juice, so we use one of our French enameled cast-iron cocottes,* just large enough so that there is very little waste space around the birds. We set the cocotte over low frying heat, then cut 4 slices of the bacon into 1-inch squares, drop them into the cocotte, and slowly melt the fat out of them. Add about 3 tablespoons of the butter and the 2 cloves of garlic, crushed through a press. Do not wash quail; clean them by rubbing inside and out with the cut side of half a lemon. Then, turning up heat to medium frying temperature, gently and lightly brown each quail on all sides. Turn off heat and set them neatly back in the cocotte, breast up. Cut each of the remaining 4 bacon slices in half and lay 2 halves across each quail. Finely chop some parsley and sprinkle over, with 2 bay leaves, crumbled, plus 1 teaspoon dried thyme. Turn on heat to simmering and put on lid so that flavors amalgamate and begin soaking into quail. Preheat oven to 350 degrees. In a small mixing bowl beat together with a wire whisk the ½ cup of tomato paste and the ½ cup of dry white wine. Pour over quail. Add salt, pepper, and MSG to taste. Now fill up pot with grapes, dropping them into the spaces between the birds and adding enough to cover birds completely. Cover tightly and, if there is any doubt about the fit, make a flour-and-water paste and use it to seal lid.

About 1 Hour Before Serving

Set pot in center of oven and let quail steam in grape juice until flesh is quite soft, usually in a few minutes less than 1 hour.

A Few Minutes Before Serving

When quail are soft turn off oven and put cocotte back on top burner. Have a warm kitchen bowl ready to hold quail for a few moments. Also lift out all grapes with a slotted spoon and place in bowl around quail. Set in oven to keep warm, leaving the door slightly ajar. Turn on fairly high heat under cocotte and let juices bubble hard for a few minutes, to reduce and concentrate flavor. Stir continually, and as soon as sauce shows first signs of thickening, turn off heat, taste and adjust seasonings if necessary, then put quail back, spooning sauce over each, and cover again with the grapes. Put back lid and speed to table. It is a dramatic moment, both in appearance and aroma, when the lid is lifted at table.

MALLARD DUCKS WITH CHERRY HEARTS

For our family of 4

Wild mallard duck is another delight of this season (see shopping notes, page 59). Since the mallard is a lean and slim bird, with strongly developed muscles, it lends itself especially well to steaming. This dish may also be prepared with Long Island Duck and there would be more meat on the bone, but also more fat and a less dramatic flavor. On St. Valentine's Day we might follow this rather solid dish with our special Valentine dessert (page 177).

Check Staples:

Thick-sliced dark smoked bacon (2 or 3 slices)
Clear chicken bouillon (1 pt.)
Lemon (1)
Oranges, with unblemished skins (4 large)
Aspic, made from duck or chicken bouillon, *see* page 134 (1 batch)
Aromatics: crystal salt, freshly ground black pepper, MSG, garlic (1 clove), ground mace, thyme
Carrots (2 medium)
Yellow onion (1 medium)
Watercress (1 bunch)
Dry white wine (½ cup)
Plus ingredients for duck giblet bouillon and aspic, pages 133–4

Shopping List:

Large mallard ducks (2—combined weight about 4 lbs.)
Fresh mushrooms (½ lb.)
Maraschino cherries (about 3 dozen)

The Day Before—Preparation in About 30 Minutes, Unsupervised Cooking for About 2 Hours

Start boiling duck giblets to make bouillon (recipe on page 133). Since the ducks are to be pot-roasted in a concentration of steam, the pot must be just large enough so that there is not much more than an inch of spare space all around, and the lid must fit tightly. We find it best to use one of our French enameled cast-iron cocottes.* First, assemble in a bowl: the 2 carrots, scraped and sliced; the ½ pound of mushrooms, wiped clean (never washed) and sliced lengthwise in hammer shapes; plus the onion, peeled and thinly sliced. Finely mince the clove of garlic and hold, covered. Cut the 2 or 3 bacon slices in half, lay them on the bottom of the cocotte, and set over low frying heat to melt. As soon as there is enough liquid fat, put in the vegetables and stir them around, continuing to melt, rather than fry them. Add: the minced garlic, ½ teaspoon mace, 1 teaspoon thyme, plus salt, pepper, and MSG to taste. Continue melting for 5 to 10 minutes. Meanwhile instead of washing the ducks under running water, clean them by rubbing inside and out with the cut side of half a lemon. Firmly rub in, also inside and out, some pepper and MSG; finally, pat and press on plenty of salt crystals. Quarter 2 of the oranges (with skins) and put 1 inside each duck. There is no need to close the opening, but the legs and wings should be tied down with string. As soon as vegetables are soft and have given their aromatic flavors to the fat, carefully remove them with a slotted spoon, letting all fat dribble off. Turn up heat to medium frying temperature and quickly brown ducks on all sides. Then wet with the ½ cup of wine and bubble fiercely, uncovered, for a couple of minutes to reduce and concentrate flavor, turning ducks to absorb wine into skins. In a saucepan bring the pint of stock to the boiling point. The ducks should be turned breast side up now. Put the vegetables on top of and around the ducks, then pour on the hot stock. Preheat oven to 350 degrees. Tightly cover cocotte. (If there is any doubt as to the fit of the lid, make a flour-and-water paste and use it to seal the lid all around the edge.) Set cocotte in center of oven and let ducks steam until quite soft, usually in about 45 minutes, more or less, according to age. Then let cool and set in refrigerator overnight.

At Least 3 Hours Before Serving—the Sauce and the Decoration in About 40 Minutes

Clarify duck bouillon and prepare aspic (pages 133–4). Grate the yellow outer rind of half an orange and hold. Squeeze the juice from both halves of this same orange and hold. Lift ducks out of cocotte, scraping them to remove all adhering fat, and put back in refrigerator for the moment. Skim all fat from bottom of cocotte. Slightly warm cocotte to melt jellied juices, at the same time removing the bacon pieces, then purée remaining vegetables and juices by passing them through a food mill or sieve or by putting them in an electric blender for a few seconds. Then heat up purée to bubbling in a saucepan. Blend in orange rind and juice, plus 2 tablespoons of the syrup from the maraschino cherries. Let it bubble for 1 or 2 minutes, tasting and adjusting seasonings as needed, then let cool.

Set ducks on serving platter and put back in refrigerator to keep cold while preparing aspic (page 134). Then glaze ducks by spooning syrupy aspic over them to make a thin coat. Put back in refrigerator for at least 2 hours to set aspic. When aspic has set, decorate ducks. We cut maraschino cherries in half and use them to make bright red hearts on the ducks' flat breasts.

A Few Minutes Before Serving

Clean up platter, scraping away all superfluous aspic, then decorate with bright green watercress and bright yellow orange slices. Any remaining maraschino cherries are stirred into puréed sauce, which is served separately.

BASIC METHOD FOR MAKING GIBLET BOUILLON

For about 1½ pints

We are working here with duck giblets, but the recipe can also be used with the giblets of chicken, goose, pheasant, turkey, etc.

Check Staples:

The giblets and liver
Good drippings from bacon, ham, etc. (1 Tbs.)
Bacon rind, if available (a few small pieces)
Aromatics: crystal salt, freshly ground black pepper, MSG, rosemary, thyme
Carrots (2 medium)
Yellow onion (1 medium)
Dry white wine (½ cup)

Preparation in About 10 Minutes—Unsupervised Boiling for About 1 Hour

Put about 1 tablespoon of the fat, plus the bacon rind (if any) into a 2-quart saucepan and melt over frying heat. Peel and slice the onion and drop it in; also add the 2 carrots, scraped and sliced. Fry until slightly brown, then add washed giblets and liver and sauté for 1 or 2 minutes, adding 1/2 teaspoon rosemary, 1/2 teaspoon thyme, plus salt, pepper, and MSG to taste. Then stop the frying by hissing in the 1/2 cup of wine and bubble fiercely for a couple of minutes more, to reduce and concentrate flavors. Then add 3 cups freshly drawn cold water and keep gently bubbling, covered, for about 1 hour. Let cool, pour everything into a covered dish, and refrigerate overnight.

The Next Day

Skim off fat from top of bouillon, then reheat slightly, but do not let it get too hot to handle. Remove giblets. They have given most of their heart and soul to the bouillon, but could still be marinated in oil and vinegar and added to a salad. Strain bouillon, squeezing out solids to give up their last drops of juice. If bouillon is to be used for aspic, it should be clarified (below).

BASIC METHOD FOR QUICKLY CLARIFYING BOUILLONS

For 1 to 2 pints

Check Staples:

Bouillon (1 to 2 pts.)
Egg (1 large)
Lemon (1)
Aromatic: tarragon
Ruby Port♁ for dark bouillon, or dry Sherry♁ for light (1/4 cup)

Preparation in About 10 Minutes—Plus About 15 Minutes Unsupervised Boiling

Separate the egg and crush the shell in a 2-quart saucepan. Put away yolk for other use. Slightly beat the egg white and add to saucepan. Also add: a few good squeezes of lemon juice, 1 teaspoon tarragon, plus the 1/4 cup Port (or Sherry). Pour in bouillon and bring rapidly to boil, then turn down heat and bubble gently, covered, for 15 minutes. Meanwhile prepare the strainer. Line a sieve or colander with a piece of thickish flannel that has been soaked in cold water and then lightly wrung out. Let bouillon cool slightly, then pass through flannel, twice if necessary, until crystal clear.

BASIC METHOD FOR MAKING QUICK ASPIC

For about 2 cups

The aspic here is prepared with duck bouillon, but any clarified bouillon of meat, poultry, or fish may be substituted according to the needs of any particular recipe.

Check Staples:

Clarified duck bouillon, or alternative, above (1¼ cups)
Tomato juice (¼ cup)
Aromatics: crystal salt,* freshly ground black pepper,* MSG
Unflavored powdered gelatin (2 envelopes)
Granulated white sugar (½ tsp.)
Dry vermouth (¼ cup)
Dry white wine (¼ cup)

Preparation in About 5 Minutes

Put the 1¼ cups of bouillon into a 1½- to 2-quart saucepan and begin heating up. Empty the 2 envelopes of gelatin into a small mixing bowl and blend in the ¼ cup of tomato juice and the ¼ cup of white wine. Spoon this mixture into the bouillon, stirring steadily until gelatin is dissolved and bouillon has come just to a boil, then turn off heat. Add the ½ teaspoon sugar, then taste for seasoning, and add salt, pepper, and MSG if and as needed. When liquid has cooled to about blood heat, stir in the ¼ cup of dry vermouth.

Working with Aspic

The most important trick is not to let the aspic become too stiff too quickly. There is an easy way to avoid this. Set out 2 large mixing bowls. Fill 1 with ice cubes, the other with hot water. Have ready all the ingredients that are to be either glazed or molded. Stand the saucepan with the hot liquid aspic among the ice cubes. In a surprisingly short time the aspic will begin to set. It is important to learn to recognize the various stages. First it becomes thick and syrupy, like honey. This is the moment to spoon it on for glazing. Next it becomes gelatinous, like raw egg white. This is the moment to pour it into a mold. Then it becomes too stiff to handle. Lift the saucepan out of the ice cubes and half submerge it in the hot water, stirring. Within a few seconds the aspic will be liquid again. Put it back in the ice cubes and wait for it to get syrupy again. Repeat this double play as often as necessary. Of course, all work with aspic must be done several hours in advance of serving, so that it can be fully set in the refrigerator before serving. When glazing do not worry about syrupy aspic dripping and running down on the serving platter. It all scrapes off easily when aspic is fully set.

Making Decorative Aspic Cubes

Pour liquid aspic into a square cake pan until it is about ¼ to ⅜ inch deep. Set in refrigerator until aspic is very firm. Then cut layer in bottom of pan into squares of any desired size and lift out with spatula. These squares catch the light and are extremely decorative.

¶ *Main Dishes (Fish, Shellfish)—Basic Methods · Bay Scallops · Fish Stew · Toheroa*

We have already discussed (page 60) the special problems of buying fish. After we have brought home the "best fish of the day," we choose one of our basic cooking methods, below, adaptable to many fish of similar type (see list of the foods in season, page 50).

BUTTERED TILEFISH IN A POTATO NEST—BASIC METHOD FOR OVEN-BAKING FISH

For our family of 4

It seems almost magical that a recipe so completely simple can produce such a superb result. The secret is in the combination of the qualities of perfectly fresh fish, first-grade creamery butter, and fluffy potatoes, soaked in the rich juices. Tilefish is an excellent seasonal fish; it has handsome pink flesh and the texture of cod. It can be replaced by cod, whiting, haddock, or other fish at other seasons. This is a rich and solid main course and the rest of the menu should be light.

Check Staples:

Sweet butter, the best available (up to 7 oz.)
Aromatics: crystal salt,☆ freshly ground black pepper,☆ MSG
Parsley (small bunch)

Shopping List:

Tilefish, solid center cut or alternative, above (about 2½ lbs.)
Boiling potatoes, soft and fluffy, ***see list, page 56*** **(about 3 lbs.)**

About 1½ Hours Before Serving

We choose a round open casserole about 3 inches deep. (A Mexican earthenware peasant dish does very well and can be brought to table.) Butter the inside liberally. Wash the fish, carefully removing any scales and fins, but leaving center bone in and skin on, then dry and hold. Start peeling potatoes and slicing them thinly. Make two or three layers across the bottom of casserole, staggering slices so that juice may circulate, and sprinkle on salt, pepper, and MSG. Stand fish on layers of potato in exact center of casserole, then continue peeling and slicing the potatoes and building up a nest around fish, adding more seasonings, until casserole is full, with the fish standing well up. Preheat oven to 375 degrees. In a small pan over gentle heat melt ¼ pound of the butter and dribble it liberally over fish and potatoes. Set casserole in center of oven. Every 15 minutes baste fish and potatoes with pan juices, adding more melted butter as it is absorbed. With this dish, the more butter the better. While baking continues, finely chop plenty of parsley and hold for garnishing. Continue baking until potatoes are soft and buttery and fish is opaque and flaky right through. The time varies according to size and shape of fish cut, from about 45 to 75 minutes. Sprinkle liberally with parsley and bring casserole to table. Buttery juice from bottom of casserole is spooned over each serving.

SEA BASS AS THEY DO IT ON THE FRENCH RIVIERA—BASIC METHOD FOR PAN-FRYING FISH

For our family of 4

This classic Mediterranean method teams the fish with the famous products of the French-Italian borderland: the olives and their oil, the anchovies, and the luscious plum tomatoes. The sea bass could be replaced by other lean-fleshed small whole fish: striped bass, young cod, mullet, etc. (see list of foods in season, page 50). This is a solid and exceptionally good-looking main course.

Check Staples:

Salt butter (2 Tbs.)
Lemon (1)
Aromatics: crystal salt, freshly ground black pepper, MSG, garlic (1 clove), shallots (2)
Parsley (small bunch)
Granulated instantized flour (about 1 Tbs.)
Olive oil (a few Tbs.)
Granulated white sugar (½ tsp.)
Italian peeled and seeded plum tomatoes (2 lb. 3 oz. can)

Shopping List:

Whole sea bass, head on, or alternative, above (about 3 lbs.)
Flat anchovy fillets (10)
Black and green pitted olives, for color contrast, *see* page 105 (say, 3 of each)

About 45 Minutes Before Serving

Start boiling the tomato sauce. Empty the can of tomatoes into a 2-quart saucepan, preferably copper for instant response to heat adjustments, and bring up to strong bubbling to reduce liquid and concentrate flavor. Add: the clove of garlic, finely minced; the 2 shallots, chopped; the 1 teaspoon of sugar; 1½ tablespoons of the olive oil; plus salt, pepper, and MSG, making the seasoning fairly strong. Keep bubbling strongly until it just begins to thicken, then turn down heat to keep-warm temperature, cover and hold. Meanwhile prepare anchovy butter . . .

BASIC RULE FOR ANCHOVY BUTTER: Let the 2 tablespoons of butter soften. Cut up 4 of the anchovy fillets, pound in a mortar to a fairly coarse paste, then work in butter with a few drops of lemon juice and 1/4 teaspoon MSG, then hold. (We often prepare several times this quantity and refrigerate in a screw-top jar for general use.)

It is essential to cook the fish in an oval-shaped enameled cast-iron fish pan, first used for the frying, then set in the oven for the final reheating; ours is good-looking enough to come to the table. Wash fish, remove all last scales and bits of fin, but leave head on, then dry, coat with flour, and sprinkle with salt. Set fish pan over medium-high frying heat and add enough olive oil just to cover bottom, usually 3 to 4 tablespoons. When oil is quite hot put in fish and quickly brown on both sides. Turn heat down to gentle frying and keep fish just sizzling, turning every 4 or 5 minutes, until perfectly done, with flesh opaque and flaky, usually in 15 to 20 minutes. About 5 minutes before fish is done, preheat oven to 350 degrees.

About 10 Minutes Before Serving

When fish is done pour tomato sauce over its entire length, completely covering fish and bottom of pan. Set in center of oven to steam for just 5 minutes. Meanwhile slice the 6 olives into rings about 1/4-inch thick and cut 2 or 3 slices of the lemon into fancy shapes for decoration.

About 5 Minutes Before Serving

Decorate fish in any way that suits the fancy. We crisscross it with the remaining anchovy fillets, put contrasting olive rings and lemon slices on top and sprigs of parsley around the dish. Finally, a few seconds before being served, dot with the anchovy butter, so that it is just melting and running down the sides as the pan is set on the table.

BLACKBACK FLOUNDER UNDER A MUSHROOM BLANKET— BASIC METHOD FOR BROILING FLATFISH

For our family of 4

Whenever possible we cook our fish with the head left on and the backbone in. They conduct the heat through to the center of the fish, for faster and more even cooking and a sealing in of the juices. We use this broiling method for any whole small flatfish, including gray sole, Rex sole, fluke, sand dab, yellowtail (rusty dab), etc. It is a solid main course.

Check Staples:

Sweet butter (about 4 Tbs.)
Lemon (1)
Aromatics: crystal salt,* freshly

Shopping List:

Whole blackback flounder or alternative, above (about 2 1/2 to 3 lbs.)

Check Staples (continued):
ground black pepper,* MSG
Parsley (small bunch)
Shallots* (4)
Sliced bread crumbs, sometimes called "herb stuffing" (about 3/4 cup)
Granulated instantized flour (1 Tbs.)
Olive oil (about 2 Tbs.)
Italian tomato paste (1 1/2 to 2 Tbs.)
Dry white wine (about 1 1/4 cups)

Shopping List (continued):
Fresh mushrooms (1/2 lb.)

About 45 Minutes Before Serving

Wash the fish, removing all last scales and bits of fin, but leaving head on, then dry and hold. Peel and chop the 4 shallots. Preheat oven to 400 degrees. Oil the bottom of an oval fish-baking platter of the right size with olive oil, then make a carpet with the chopped shallots and lay the fish on it. Pour in wine until it is about 1/4 inch deep. Sprinkle on a little salt, pepper, and MSG. Tightly cover entire platter with foil and set in center of oven to steam until fish is just barely done, usually in 20 to 25 minutes.

Meanwhile prepare mushroom blanket. Wipe clean (never wash with water) the 1/2 pound of mushrooms, then slice and chop fairly fine. Chop enough parsley to fill about 1/4 cup. In a sauté pan over medium frying temperature melt 1 1/2 tablespoons of the butter and 1 1/2 tablespoons of the olive oil, then lightly and quickly sauté chopped mushrooms, then turn down heat and simmer for a couple of minutes. In a small bowl blend together about 1 1/2 tablespoons of the tomato paste with about 1 tablespoon flour, add a few dashes of wine to make mixture the consistency of thick cream. Blend this into the mushrooms, at the same time sprinkling on the chopped parsley and a little salt, pepper, and MSG. Continue stirring and simmering until it has the consistency of a paste. If it gets too thick, add a little more wine; if too thin, add more tomato paste.

About 10 Minutes Before Serving

When fish comes out of oven, turn on broiler and set shelf so that top surface of fish will be about 2 1/2 inches from heat. Now spread the entire top surface of flounder with mushroom paste. Then lightly press on a not-too-thick layer of bread crumbs and dot with about 2 tablespoons of the remaining butter. Broil until top is a nice solid brown, usually in 3 to 4 minutes. Cut lemon into slices or wedges and place them on top of flounder as it comes to the table.

SEA SMELT WITH LEMON BUTTER—BASIC METHOD FOR DEEP-FRYING FISH

For our family of 4

This method can be used with any small fish and the special, ultra-light batter is of course universal in its application. The lemon butter sauce will dramatize and heighten the flavor of almost any fish. The fishmonger should clean and behead the smelts, and some shoppers also have the fish opened up and the backbone removed. We think that this reduces the juiciness and flavor of the fish and prefer to deal with the backbones on our plates. Often the heat makes them so crisp that they can be eaten, like the bones of sardines.

Check Staples:

Salt butter (1/4 lb.)
Egg (1 large)
Milk (1/2 cup)
Lemon (1)
Aromatics: crystal salt, freshly ground black pepper
Chives, fresh or frozen (enough to fill 1 Tbs., chopped)
Parsley (small bunch)
Granulated instantized flour (1 cup)
Olive oil (3 Tbs.)
Granulated white sugar (about 1 tsp.)
Oil for deep-frying

Shopping List:

Sea smelts, or other small fish, cleaned and beheaded (2 1/2 to 3 lbs.)

About 2 1/2 Hours Before Serving

BASIC RULE FOR ULTRA-LIGHT FRYING BATTER: The object of a frying batter, as Brillat-Savarin once explained to his cook, is to provide a glove to protect the food from the hot oil. The trouble with most batters is that they also intrude their own personalities, often making light foods stodgy and sometimes even dominating a delicate food. The following batter is the lightest and most tactful we know. Put the cup of flour into a mixing bowl. Separate the egg, putting the yolk into a small mixing bowl. Lightly beat into the yolk the 3 tablespoons of olive oil, 1/4 teaspoon of the salt, and the 1 teaspoon of sugar. Smoothly work this into the flour. Just warm the 1/2 cup of milk and add, dash by dash, to flour paste, using only enough milk to make a smooth, very thick cream. The thickness is important, as it controls the thickness of the "glove." Let it stand, uncovered, for 2 hours, stirring occasionally.

At the last moment before using this batter, beat the egg white stiff and lightly fold it in. We are sure that Brillat-Savarin would approve.

While batter is standing, wash and dry the smelts and lightly salt and pepper them, inside and out. Leave them to come to room temperature. Also set out the 1/4 pound of butter to soften.

About 20 Minutes Before Serving

Start heating up the oil in the deep-fryer to 375 degrees. While it is heating up, prepare the lemon butter . . .

BASIC RULE FOR LEMON BUTTER SAUCE: Chop finely enough of the chives to fill 1 tablespoon and enough of the parsley to fill 1/4 cup. Lightly cream 2 teaspoons of the chives and 2 teaspoons of parsley into softened butter, with the juice of half a lemon, plus salt and pepper to taste. The lemon flavor should be fairly strong. If not, work in a squeeze or two more lemon juice. This sauce is excellent on all forms of fish and on many grilled meats.

Turn on oven to keep-warm temperature (150 degrees) and place in it a serving platter for the fish. This is the moment to beat the egg white and lightly fold it into batter. The oil should be hot now. Dip each smelt into batter, turning fish around so that it is fairly thickly coated, then lower at once into hot fat. Fry to deep golden-brown, usually in 3 to 4 minutes. As each batch of fish is done, drain on absorbent paper, place on serving platter, dot with lemon butter, and return to oven to keep warm. When all fish are on platter and all lemon butter is used up, sprinkle on remaining chopped chives and parsley, garnish with a few parsley sprigs, and bring it to the table.

BUTTERED WHOLE YOUNG COD—BASIC METHOD FOR OVEN-POACHING FISH IN FOIL

For our family of 4

The bulky old poaching kettle for fish has been made almost obsolete by the modern uses of aluminum foil. Provided that the foil is tightly sealed all around, the fish simply poaches in its own juices. This is just about the simplest of all methods for cooking fish, since it makes its own sauce inside the package. Naturally, all the flavor is "sealed in."

Check Staples:

Salt butter (1/4 lb.)
Aromatics: crystal salt,⁑ freshly ground black pepper⁑
Parsley (small bunch)

Shopping List:

Whole young cod or alternative whole fish, cleaned by fishmonger, but with head left on (about 3 lbs.)

About 1½ Hours Before Serving—Including 1¼ Hours of Entirely Unsupervised Baking

Cut a piece of foil 8 inches longer than the fish and wide enough to go around the fish, with a double or treble airtight fold along the top. Preheat oven to 300 degrees. Wash and dry fish, then lightly salt and pepper it, inside and out. Butter the inside of the foil copiously, using about 4 tablespoons of the butter. Lay fish on foil and wrap tightly, first bringing long sides together and making an airtight fold, then folding up ends as if they were envelopes. Neither steam nor juices should escape. Place this package on a flat baking sheet and slide into preheated oven. Forget it completely for 1¼ hours. This is one dish where peeking is impossible. If fish is not entirely perfect the first time, because of slight variations in oven temperatures, adapt timing slightly for the second try.

About 10 Minutes Before Serving

Melt remaining butter in a small ½-cup pan. Chop a small handful of the parsley. Set a large oval serving platter in oven to get warm. Finally, very carefully unwrap fish, taking care not to lose a single drop of the juices. At this point, if desired (although we think it unnecessary, except for a party), the top skin and head of the fish may be carefully removed. Then slide onto serving platter and dribble over it all juices from foil. Finally dribble on remaining melted butter from small pan, sprinkle on bright green parsley, and bring to the table.

10-MINUTE BAY SCALLOPS FLAMED WITH COGNAC

For our family of 4

Bay scallops are one of the great gastronomic joys of the season (see shopping notes, page 62). They must however be absolutely fresh, and this is indicated by a creamy-gray color; when they are snow-white they are already stale. This is a light main dish, but it can be the center of an excellent dinner, served on a bed of fairly bland rice pilaf (page 166), with a not-too-assertive vegetable, preceded by a rich cream soup—perhaps the inebriated mushroom (page 113)—and followed by one of the great combinations of fruit and cheese (page 173). When the "baby" bay scallop is not in season, one may substitute the all-year-round deep-sea scallop, but with some coarsening of flavor and texture.

Check Staples:

Aromatics: crystal salt,⁂ freshly ground black pepper,⁂ MSG,▣

Shopping List:

Small bay scallops, very fresh, *see* above (about 1½ lbs.)

Check Staples (continued):

garlic (1 or 2 cloves to taste), plus dried herbs only if fresh not available: dillweed, fennel seed tarragon

Rice flour or light cake flour, to coat scallops (about 3 Tbs.)

Olive oil (about 2 Tbs.)

Shopping List (continued):

A few sprigs each of whichever of the following are available: dill, fennel fronds, parsley, tarragon, watercress

French Cognac, medium-priced, for flaming (1/4 cup)

10 Minutes Before Serving

Once the sautéing begins it must proceed with lightning speed, so all ingredients must be prepared and set out. First, assemble the aromatic bouquet in a small bowl. Finely chop enough of the leaves *only* of each of the fresh herbs to make a combined total of about 1/2 cup: dill, fennel, parsley, tarragon, and watercress. For each of the fresh herbs that is missing, put in 1/2 teaspoon of the dried. Peel and very finely mince the garlic, then hold separately, covered. Quickly wash the scallops (never soak them), then pat dry and lightly coat with flour. We place our tin-lined copper sauté pan over medium frying heat, spread in just enough of the olive oil to cover the bottom, and, as soon as it is fairly hot, sauté the scallops for exactly 3 minutes (set the timer), at the same time adding the minced garlic, plus a little salt, 2 or 3 grinds of pepper, and about 1/2 teaspoon of MSG. Meanwhile warm the 1/4 cup Cognac just to blood heat. When the timer rings after 3 minutes, throw on the aromatic bouquet and toss scallops vigorously for not more than a few seconds, until they are speckled with green and herbs have absorbed and been softened by remaining oil. Then hiss in the 1/4 cup of Cognac and flame. We sometimes do this flaming at the table over a spirit stove or in an electric frypan. For the fullest flavor and tenderest texture, the scallops should be eaten immediately.

COTRIADE BRETONNE—THE FINE FISH STEW OF BRITTANY

For our family of 4

It is wrong to think that the bouillabaisse is the only fish stew of France. There are regional versions wherever fresh fish is caught from sea, lake, or river and is wedded to a local wine. (Compare the *meurette* of Burgundy, in which river fish are cooked in red wine, once and for all disproving the purists' theories, see page 597.) The special quality of the *cotriade* comes from the light and lean Muscadet wine, which is the favorite of the Bretons and is now widely available in the United States. This dish is the perfect example of the basic principles of any fine stew: first, the preparation of an aromatic broth by "boiling out" certain ingredients, which are then thrown away; second, the use of this broth to flavor the main ingredients, which are separately timed for perfect texture. (Compare with the *pot-au-feu*, page 115, where the same principles are applied to meats.) The *cotriade* is simple to prepare, with comparatively low-cost ingredients that combine into a solid and dramatic one-dish meal. It reheats excellently, and is even good cold.

Check Staples:

Salt butter (about 1/4 lb.)
Lemon (1)
Aromatics: crystal salt, freshly ground black pepper, MSG, whole bay leaves, whole cloves, Indian *garam massala* curry blend, garlic (3 cloves), Spanish saffron filaments, thyme
Shallots (3)
Small carrots (1 bunch)
Parsley (small bunch)
Granulated instantized flour (about 2 Tbs.)
Olive oil (about 4 Tbs.)

Shopping List:

A selection of seasonal fish, *see* list, page 50, say, the following:
Mackerel, whole fish, with head (about 1 lb.)
Whiting (the same)
Eel (the same)
All these fish should be boned by the fishman, cut into largish chunks, and the valuable heads and bones wrapped separately.
Boned fillets, preferably a mixture of cod, haddock, flounder, sole, etc. (about 1 1/2 lbs. more)
Extra fish heads and large bones, usually a gift from the fishman (about 2 lbs.)
Leeks, white parts only (5 medium)
Fresh button mushrooms (1 lb.)
Sweet Bermuda or Spanish onions (2 large)
Good, waxy boiling potatoes, *see* list, page 56 (2 lbs.)
Green fronds of fresh fennel, if available, not absolutely essential (small handful)
A good Muscadet (1 bottle for the *cotriade*, more to drink with it)
Long French bread, to serve in the soup bowls (1 or 2 loaves)

On the Morning of the Day—Preparing Aromatic Bouillon in About 40 Minutes

Using chopping block and small chopper, cut fish heads and bones into practical chunks, wash, then hold. Slit open the 5 leeks, wash out any remaining sand under fast-running cold water, then leave soaking in cold water. Assemble in a medium mixing bowl: the 2 large onions, peeled and sliced; the bunch of carrots, scraped and chunked, then hold. Mince finely the 3 cloves garlic and hold, covered. Soak 1 heaped teaspoon of the saffron in 1/4 cup of the wine. Place a large soup pot over medium frying heat and melt in it 4 tablespoons of the butter with 2 tablespoons of the olive oil, making sure that butter does not brown, then add 4 of the leeks, chunked, plus the onions and carrots, then sauté, stirring, until vegetables are lightly colored. Sprinkle in 1 to 2 tablespoons of the flour, just enough to absorb juices, and continue to brown, stirring and scraping the bottom continually, for a couple of minutes or more. Now blend in gradually, still stirring vigorously to avoid lumping, 1 1/2 cups of the wine and 2 cups of freshly drawn cold water. Turn up heat, bringing liquid rapidly to a boil, then add fish heads and bones. If necessary, add a little more water to cover fish. Bring rapidly back to a boil, then turn down heat to gentle bubbling and add: the minced garlic, the saffron in its wine, the juice of half a lemon, 2 or 3 sprigs of parsley, 2 teaspoons of the *garam massala,* 2 whole bay leaves, 6 whole cloves, 1 teaspoon thyme, plus plenty of salt, with pepper and MSG to taste. Continue gentle bubbling, uncovered, for roughly 30 minutes. Meanwhile prepare and hold the following ingredients. Mince together: the 1 remaining leek, the 3 shallots, 2 or 3 more sprigs of parsley, and the fennel fronds (if available). Wipe clean (never wash) the 1 pound of mushrooms and leave whole. In a large sauté pan over medium frying heat melt 4 tablespoons of the butter with 2 more tablespoons of the olive oil, again making sure that butter does not brown, then add the leek-shallot-fennel-parsley mixture and stir around until just beginning to color. Then add the whole mushrooms, plus salt and pepper to taste. Continue stirring for 3 or 4 minutes, allowing mushrooms to absorb flavors, then turn heat down to simmering, cover, and let steam for about 5 minutes, then turn off heat and hold, covered. Finally, turn off heat under soup pot, cover, and let cool.

About 2 Hours Before Serving

Wash all chunks of fish, leaving on skin but removing any last bones. Put them together in large bowl and let come to room temperature.

About 45 Minutes Before Serving

Peel and slice thinly the 2 pounds of potatoes and hold under water. The aromatic bouillon must now be relieved of all its non-edible ingredients. Strain through a large colander, quickly clean out and rinse the big soup pot, then put the bouillon back into it. From the colander pick out and throw away all non-edible items—fish heads and bones, bay leaves, whole cloves, plus all mushy vegetables. We use judgment in deciding what is worth keeping—almost certainly the carrots, plus some of the leeks. Return these to the bouillon, bring rapidly back to a boil, again adjusting seasonings, adding perhaps a little more lemon juice and wine. Add sliced potatoes and simmer, covered, for 15 minutes.

About 20 Minutes Before Serving

Add mushrooms with entire contents of sauté pan and continue simmering 5 minutes longer.

About 15 Minutes Before Serving

Add fish and now boil quite hard, uncovered, so that fish oils remain distributed throughout liquid, until fish is just flaky, usually in about 11 to 14 minutes. Meanwhile cut French bread into large chunks and lightly toast in oven. (Garlic bread is never used with a *cotriade.*) Chop remaining parsley. Warm a large soup tureen or a rough earthenware peasant toupin* in which to bring the *cotriade* to the table.

Serving at Table

Place a chunk of bread in bottom of large soup plate, pile onto it a mixed selection of fish, ladle on the aromatic juice, and sprinkle bright green parsley on top. Drink more Muscadet with the meal.

CREAM STEW OF TIKINUI TOHEROA

For our family of 4

If we want to celebrate New Zealand Day (see International Calendar, page 66), we might serve this great dish. The toheroa is one of the world's rarest foods. The severe problems involved in getting this extraordinary shellfish from the New Zealand coast are discussed in the shopping notes on page 62. Let us now assume that we are the proud possessors of two 1-pound cans of toheroa meat. . . .

Check Staples:

Sweet butter (3 Tbs.)
Milk (2½ cups)
Aromatics: crystal salt,* freshly ground black pepper,* MSG,* rosemary, tarragon
Chives, indoor home-grown, hot-house, or frozen (small bunch)
Parsley (small bunch)
Granulated instantized flour* (3 Tbs.)

Shopping List:

New Zealand toheroas* (two 1-lb. cans)
Heavy cream (2 cups)
Fresh dill, if available (small bunch)

About 40 Minutes Before Serving

Open the two cans of toheroa and carefully separate: (a) the green tomalleys, or livers, which are soft and pasty; (b) the oyster-shaped bodies, and (c) the long, narrow tongues. Pass the bodies through a meat grinder with the coarse cutter, then switch to the fine cutter for the tongues. Bodies and tongues can then be mixed, but tomalleys are held separately. Take the greatest care to preserve the juice in each can as this is the vital flavoring element. However, any last vestiges of sand must be strained out. In a 1½-quart saucepan over medium heat mix 2 cups each of the milk and cream, then heat up, but do not let boil. In a 2-quart saucepan over medium frying heat make a *roux* by first melting the 3 tablespoons of butter, then smoothly blending in the 3 tablespoons of flour. Now work in the milk and cream, slowly at first, stirring vigorously to keep smooth. Gently heat up mixture almost to a boil, still stirring continuously, then blend in toheroa juice. Next smoothly work in the green tomalleys, making sure that no lumps form. Season with 1 teaspoon rosemary, 1 teaspoon tarragon, plus salt, pepper, and MSG to taste. Keep it hot but below boiling, to blend and mature flavors, for 5 to 10 minutes. It should remain a creamy consistency, and if it thickens too much add a few dashes more milk. Add toheroas, which must be cooked neither too hard nor too long or they will toughen. Keep them hot in the stew, but below boiling, for not a second more than 4 minutes. During this time quickly chop and add to stew about 2 tablespoons each of fresh dill (if available) and parsley. Taste to judge seasoning. Serve at once in very hot bowls.

¶ *Main Dishes (Cheese, Eggs)*

We are a family of cheese aficionados (see page 660). Cheese is too good to be relegated to the after-dinner cheese board or the picnic sandwich. We prepare it as a main dish for any meal of the day. It teams perfectly with eggs, and here are two of the most flexible and infinitely useful of these combinations.

BASIC CHEESE SOUFFLÉ WITHOUT BUTTER OR FLOUR

For our family of 4

In order to prepare this recipe to perfection, one should be familiar with the BASIC RULES for soufflés (page 74). The cheese used in this version is sharp Cheddar, but wide variety is possible by substituting other good grating cheeses (page 674).

Check Staples:
Eggs (7 large)
Milk (1 pt.)
Aromatics: fine table salt, freshly ground black pepper,⁑ ground mace
Ground arrowroot⊜ (about 1 Tbs.)

Shopping List:
Sharpest possible Cheddar cheese⊜ (½ lb.)

About 1 Hour Before Serving

Grate the cheese and hold. Separate the eggs, putting 3 of the yolks together in one bowl and each of the 4 remaining yolks in separate cups. Six of the whites go into the copper beating bowl; the seventh is put away for later use. In a 1½- to 2-quart saucepan, preferably copper because it responds so quickly to heat adjustments, heat the pint of milk up to a temperature just too hot to the touch but still well below boiling. Meanwhile into the bowl with the 3 egg yolks put 2 teaspoons of the arrowroot and 1 teaspoon salt and beat with a small wire whisk. When egg yolks are lemon-colored and creamy, gradually beat the warm milk into them. When thoroughly amalgamated, pour back into saucepan and gently reheat, stirring continuously with a wooden spoon and carefully scraping sides and bottom of pan as the mixture thickens to the consistency of pouring custard. Blend in cheese and continue stirring until it melts, adding salt, pepper, and MSG to taste. Then turn off heat and let this *panada* cool. When just warm to the touch, add the 4 remaining yolks, one by one, immediately and thoroughly blending each in before the next is added. Finally blend in ¼ teaspoon mace. Judge the correct final thickness according to the BASIC RULE (page 75). It should have the consistency of an extra-thick custard sauce that drips only slowly from the spoon and offers a solid resistance to stirring when the spoon is held lightly.

Preheat oven to 325 degrees. Now beat egg whites by hand, according to the BASIC RULE (page 75) and, when properly stiff, rapidly incorporate ⅓ of the whites into the *panada* with a rubber spatula, then pour entire contents of saucepan into center of remaining whites. Rapidly fold together, according to the BASIC RULE (page 75). Have ready a 1-quart soufflé dish, unbuttered. Pour soufflé mixture into it. Soufflé dish should be filled to within 1 inch of its top. Set soufflé dish low in oven, about 1½ to 2 inches above floor, with inverted cake pan above it, according to the BASIC RULE (page 76). Bake for at least 25 minutes without opening door. Then check for perfect doneness, according to the BASIC RULE (page 76). In our oven the perfect cheese soufflé usually takes about 30 minutes. Always remember that the diners must be waiting for the soufflé—it cannot wait for them.

BASIC WELSH RABBIT

For 1 person

Out of a dozen people discussing this universal way of "making a meal" out of a piece of cheese and an egg, nine would probably have different recipes, each proclaimed to be "the best." We like to make and serve ours in small individual oval-shaped enameled cast-iron dishes, which keep the rabbit warmer than when it is poured over toast on a plate. This recipe is for one such dish for one person.

Check Staples:

Salt butter (traditionally, a walnut of)
Egg (1 large)
Aromatics: crystal salt,⁑ freshly ground black pepper,⁑ MSG, garlic (½ clove), English dry mustard (1 tsp.), Hungarian sweet red paprika,⁑ Tabasco, Worcestershire sauce (1 tsp.)
Unbuttered triangles of toast

Shopping List:

Natural sharp Cheddar cheese or alternative (¼ lb.)
Heavy cream (2 tsp.)
Beer or ale or dry white wine (up to 2 Tbs.)

Preparation in 15 Minutes—Then Served at Once

Once the cheese starts melting the operation must move forward quickly, without interruption, so all ingredients must be set out in advance. Break the egg into a saucer. Crush the ½ clove of garlic through a press and hold, covered. Make the toast triangles. Cut the cheese into large dice. Then we place our small oval dish over moderate heat and give it continuous attention. Melt the walnut of butter and, as soon as it has liquefied, before it gets too hot, dump in all the cheese at once and begin "worrying" it. A wooden fork is the best tool. (Never, under any circumstances, stir the cheese, or it will suddenly convert to hard inedible strings floating in a pool of butter, and then one has to just start over.) Cheese and butter must be completely amalgamated and this is achieved by gently prodding, pushing to and fro, poking, raking, and scraping the bottom and sides always in different directions. As soon as cheese shows first signs of melting, work in the aromatic condiments. The list is quite flexible and, with practice, one does it by dashes and drips rather than with measuring spoons, but for the first time add in turn: 1 teaspoon dry mustard, 1 teaspoon Worcestershire sauce, 2 or 3 drops of Tabasco, the crushed garlic, the 2 teaspoons of cream, plus a small dollop of salt, a few grinds of pepper, and ½ teaspoon of MSG. When all are fully blended and cheese melted, work in dash by dash enough beer (or alternative liquid) to make it the consistency of a heavy pouring custard. It must get very hot, but *never* bubble. Work fast. Taste for seasoning and adjust by adding more of any or all of the condiments. Turn off heat. Slide egg onto the rabbit and immediately break it and work it in. There is enough heat in the cheese to cook the egg, but it must be continuously blended to keep it smooth and prevent it from scrambling. As egg thickens the rabbit, add more dashes of liquid to keep consistency of pouring custard. The instant the egg is fully cooked, stick toast triangles upright around the dish, sprinkle on a little paprika for color and serve immediately.

Search for Variety with Brunch-Lunch Eggs

The great French gourmet Maurice-Edmond Sailland lived by at least one inflexible rule. He was continually showered with invitations, but felt he could fully appreciate only one rich meal per day and insisted that each of his other meals should be limited to an egg, perfectly prepared in a variety of ways. We follow his example and never feel the boredom of repetition among the dozens of unusual recipes.

Since it is more convenient to take an egg straight out of the refrigerator, all of the following recipes are planned to start with a cold egg.

FRENCH OEUF SUR LE PLAT—EGG BAKED AND SERVED ON A PLATTER

For 1 person

The *plat* is a small French au gratin dish of enameled cast-iron or oven-proof china* that keeps the individual egg warm as it comes to table. The egg looks as if it had been fried sunny-side up, but the texture is quite different and the taste can be varied with dozens of different garnishes.

Check Staples:

Sweet butter, best available (1 to 2 tsp., to taste)
Egg, freshest possible (1 large)
Aromatics: crystal salt,☧ freshly ground black pepper,☧ MSG,▣ savory (use dried only if fresh not available)
Parsley (1 sprig)

Shopping List:

Fresh savory, if available (enough for 1 tsp., finely chopped)

10 Minutes Before Serving

Preheat oven to 325 degrees. Put 1 teaspoon of the butter (or more to taste) into the *plat* and place it in center of oven for exactly 3 minutes (leaving it longer overheats the dish, which results in a tough egg).

While *plat* is heating prepare garnish: 1 teaspoon parsley leaf, finely snipped, and the same amount of fresh savory, if available, or replace with 1/4 teaspoon dried. At the end of 3 minutes swish melted butter around *plat* so that bottom and sides are coated. Sprinkle in parsley and savory, plus salt, pepper, and MSG to taste, then break egg in and set back in oven. Bake until egg is done to individual taste. In our oven yolk and white are still just runny after 5 minutes, white is just set and yolk still soft after 6 minutes, yolk is firmly set after 8 minutes. Place hot *plat* on a plate and serve at once.

VARIATIONS: The parsley and savory can be replaced by any of the aromatic herbs which go with eggs. Or the bed for the egg can be expanded with about 1 tablespoon of chopped or diced cooked meat, or flaked cooked fish, or vegetables, or chopped anchovies, or crisp crumbled bacon, or Bombay duck.🛍 Also, the top of the egg may be sprinkled with grated cheese or masked with an aromatic sauce, but the appearance is better if the yolk is not covered. However, when the top is covered, the heat is enclosed and the egg cooks more quickly.

THE PERFECTLY POACHED EGG

For 1 person

The perfectly poached egg is NOT "steamed" in a metal dish and shaped like a bun. It sets round and light, suspended in the water, unsupported by any gadget. The method involves some slight skill, quickly acquired by practice.

Check Staples:

Sweet butter, best available (enough to spread on 1 slice of toast)
Egg, very fresh (1 large)
Aromatics: crystal salt,⚘ freshly ground black pepper⚘
Tarragon white wine vinegar🛍 (2 tsp.)
Toasted white bread (1 slice)

The Tools Required

In making a perfect poached egg a copper saucepan is virtually essential, since it responds instantly to the rapid changes of temperature. We use a 1-quart size, about 5 inches across and 4 inches deep. To stir the water into a whirlpool a short-handled wooden spoon about the size of a dessert spoon is best. (If the spoon is too large it will slop the water out of the pan.) Also needed are a cup in which to break the egg, a slotted spoon with which to lift it, and a clean white terry towel on which to dry it.

Exactly 5 Minutes Before Serving

Pour hot water into the pan until liquid is about 3 inches deep. Do not overfill. Add the 2 teaspoons of vinegar. (The vinegar or any acid, such as lemon juice or dry white wine, helps to form an immediate skin on the egg so that it holds its shape.) Heat water to gentle simmering. Prepare slice of buttered toast. Break egg into cup and put cup in left hand. Hold wooden spoon in right hand. Turn down heat a small notch so that simmering just stops. Stir water with spoon in a circular motion around the outside of the pan, slowly at first, then faster and faster until there is a deep whirlpool at the center. Still stirring fast, lower cup almost to the surface of the water so that egg will slide in rather than plop down. In an instant remove spoon and place egg at exact center of whirlpool. Put down spoon and cup and turn up heat sharply so that water returns to simmering as quickly as possible. During the 5 seconds it usually takes to gain this heat, set timer to 1½ minutes for a soft egg, or 2 minutes for medium-firm, or 2½ minutes for very firm. Watch closely and the moment first bubbles appear, turn heat down, as bubbles would slap egg out of shape. Turn on hot-water faucet in sink to a gentle stream. When timer rings lift egg out of water with slotted spoon, rinse under hot running water to wash off vinegar, and place on towel to dry. Finally, roll egg back onto spoon and place on toast. Lightly sprinkle with salt and pepper and serve at once.

When Poaching Eggs for Several People

On the burner behind the poaching pan set a sauté pan filled with warm water (about 150 degrees) over keep-warm heat. As each egg is poached, place it in the warm water, which will wash off the vinegar and keep it warm without hardening it until all eggs are done.

FRENCH OEUF EN COCOTTE—EGG STEAMED IN AN INDIVIDUAL POT

For 1 person

The cocotte✱ is a small French earthenware pot, usually brown on the outside and white inside, about an inch deep, in which 1 egg is cooked and served. In a conservative French household this is a classic first course for even a party dinner. We like it for breakfast, lunch, or a midnight snack.

Check Staples:

Egg (1 large)
Aromatics: fine table salt, freshly ground black pepper✱

Shopping List:

Heavy cream (3 tsp.)

Exactly 5 Minutes Before Serving

Choose a sauté pan large enough to hold as many cocottes as will be needed and arrange it as a steamer, with a tightly fitting lid. Put in enough hot water to cover the bottom about 1/4 inch deep. Heat up to merry bubbling and cover to work up a head of steam. Put 1 teaspoon of the cream into cocotte and swish around to coat bottom and sides, then break in egg. Stand cocotte in the boiling water in the sauté pan, replace lid, then set timer to 2 minutes for a very soft egg, or 2 1/2 minutes for medium-firm, or 3 minutes for quite firm. When timer rings and lid is removed, lift it gently, then very quickly swing it away from pan, so that the condensed water does not drip into cocotte. Spoon remaining 2 teaspoons of cream into cocotte, replace lid and steam for 30 seconds longer to heat cream. Place cocotte on small plate, with perhaps white buttered toast, sprinkle egg lightly with salt and pepper, and serve at once.

THE PERFECTLY SERVED BOILED EGG

For 1 person

This method makes use of the handsome French white china egg cups, available in many kitchen-equipment shops.✱

Check Staples:

Sweet butter, best available (1 tsp.)
Egg, very fresh (1 large)
Aromatics: crystal salt,✱ freshly ground black pepper,✱ MSG,✱ basil (use dried only if fresh not available)

Shopping List:

Fresh basil, if available (enough leaves for 1/2 tsp., finely chopped)

About 5 Minutes Before Serving

Heat up the water in a saucepan large enough to hold both the egg and the egg cup. Mash in the egg cup: the teaspoon of butter, the ½ teaspoon of finely chopped basil (or dried, if fresh not available), plus salt, pepper, and MSG to taste. While water is heating stand egg cup upright in pan. When water bubbles put egg in water next to cup and time to taste. Stir melting butter in egg cup to blend in aromatic oils brought out by the heat. When egg is done stand hot egg cup on a plate, break egg into it, and serve at once.

VARIATIONS: Other herbs can replace the basil. Other fats can replace the butter, but use none that is so strong in flavor as to overpower the egg. A pat of *pâté de foie gras* is a luxurious substitute for the butter.

¶ *Vegetables*

Nature provides a marvelous variety in the cycle of the year. If we plan our meals from the list of foods in season (page 55) one vegetable after another comes forward to be greeted with ever-renewed excitement and pleasure, then discreetly fades away until its next entrance. We find a constant delight in the challenge of making the best use of each seasonal crop. How much excitement can be left for the first asparagus of spring if one has been eating frozen asparagus tips all winter? Far better, we think, to make something superb out of the winter parsnips and turnips (page 163). This means flavoring and garnishing each vegetable according to its character and season. When winter weather makes it coarser and tougher, it needs to be marinated and cooked with assertive aromatics and served with dominant sauces. . . .

VEGETABLE SAUCE NUMBER ONE—CARAWAY SOUR CREAM

For our family of 4

This is best made with natural sour cream (what the French call *crème fraîche,* page 326). If only commercial sour cream is available, care must be taken not to overheat it or it will curdle; be sure, too, that it comes to room temperature before you heat it. When it is just hot to the touch, it is hot enough to serve. It is good with broccoli, cabbage, Brussels sprouts, green beans, and baked onions.

Check Staples:

Lemon (1)

Aromatics: freshly ground black pepper,⁑ MSG,⁑ whole caraway seed (1 Tbs.)

Shopping List:

Sour cream, *see* above (1 pt.)

Preparation in About 10 Minutes—Can Be Kept Warm or Stored

Put the pint of sour cream into a saucepan and gently heat up, never letting it get too warm. Carefully blend in, squeeze by squeeze, the juice of half a lemon. Put the tablespoon of caraway seed into a mortar and grind fairly fine, then blend into the sour cream along with a few grinds of pepper and about ½ teaspoon MSG. Finally, taste for seasoning and possibly blend in a few more drops of lemon juice or more ground caraway or pepper. If sauce is not to be served at once, it may be held, covered, over keep-warm heat (but never allowed to come anywhere near boiling), or it may be refrigerated overnight (which actually improves and unifies the flavoring), then carefully and gently reheated.

VEGETABLE SAUCE NUMBER TWO—AROMATIC BUTTER WITH CAPERS

For our family of 4

This sauce is wonderful with green beans or baked eggplant.

Check Staples:

Salt butter (4 Tbs.)
Lemon (1)
Aromatics: crystal salt,☆ freshly ground black pepper,☆ MSG▣
Parsley (enough for 1 Tbs., finely chopped)

Shopping List:

Capers (1½ Tbs.)

Preparation in About 5 Minutes—Can Be Kept Warm or Stored

Finely chop parsley. Melt the 4 tablespoons of butter in a small saucepan, squeezing in the juice of half a lemon, plus a little salt (according to saltiness of butter), a few grinds of pepper, and MSG to taste. Drain the 1½ tablespoons of capers and add to butter with the parsley. Stir and taste for seasoning, gradually adding more lemon juice, squeeze by squeeze, until fairly strongly acidulated.

VEGETABLE SAUCE NUMBER THREE—SAUCE PECANDINE

This sauce is particularly good with broccoli and green beans (recipe on page 306).

BAKED WHOLE ACORN SQUASH WITH MAPLE BUTTER

For our family of 4

This is the best way of cooking any hard-skinned squash, leaving Nature's "perfect packaging" intact to keep flavor and juices sealed in. The trick is to bake it very slowly, but it requires no attention whatsoever during the hour or so that it is in the oven. The first whiff of the bouquet when the squash is cut open is magnificent.

Check Staples:

Sweet butter (4 Tbs.)
Aromatics: crystal salt,✗ freshly
  ground black pepper✗
Pure maple syrup⌷ (about 4 Tbs.)
Olive oil⌷ (about 1 Tbs.)

Shopping List:

Acorn squash (2 fairly large)

About 1½ Hours Before Serving

Preheat oven to 350 degrees. Rub skins of squash with olive oil, so that skins will crisp and hold shape. Place in center of oven, standing on a sheet of foil, and forget for 1¼ hours. (Timing varies slightly with size of squash: very large, up to 1½ hours; smaller, in 1 hour. Experience with one's own oven brings perfection.)

About 10 Minutes Before Serving

Cut squash in half and scoop out seeds and fibers. Using each half skin as a serving cup, mash flesh with a fork, blending in about 1 tablespoon butter per half, about 2 teaspoons maple syrup, plus a touch of salt and pepper. Taste and add a drop or two more maple syrup if needed, but do not allow it to dominate the fine natural flavor of the squash. Finally, fluff it up into a neat pile for appearance and pop back into oven to reheat for a couple of minutes. Serve each half in its own skin.

ATHENIAN GREEN BEANS

For our family of 4

This dish may be served hot or cold. Compare this aromatic method, for the coarser green beans of winter, with the recipe for green beans with rosemary (page 308), where the accent is on the sweet freshness of the spring pods. Other winter vegetables, such as broccoli or Brussels sprouts, may also be cooked in this way.

Check Staples:

Clear beef bouillon (¼ cup)
Aromatics: crystal salt,✗ freshly
  ground black pepper,✗ MSG,⌷
  garlic (1 or 2 cloves, to taste)
Yellow onion (1 medium)
Olive oil⌷ (a few Tbs.)
Italian peeled and seeded plum
  tomatoes (half of 1 lb. 1 oz. can)
Dry white wine⌷ (¼ cup)

Shopping List:

Green beans (1 lb.)

About 30 Minutes Before Serving—Or the Day Before If To Be Served Cold

In our house many hands make light work of topping, tailing, and cross-cutting the fresh beans. Peel and finely chop the onion. Peel and finely mince the garlic. In our large copper tin-lined sauté pan we heat up 2 tablespoons of the oil and very lightly sauté the onion and garlic. Put in the beans and stir around to coat with oil, seasoning to taste with salt, pepper, and MSG. Adjust heat to keep them gently frying, stirring occasionally and, as they expel their water and absorb oil, sprinkle on more oil, just enough to keep the bottom of pan lubricated. The trick is to get some oil absorbed into the beans, but not too much. They should never swim in a pool of oil. Continue for 7 to 10 minutes, when beans should be lightly flecked with brown. Now stop the frying by adding: the ½ pound of tomatoes, the ¼ cup of bouillon, and the ¼ cup of wine. Stir around, breaking up the tomatoes and adjusting heat so that liquid bubbles fairly hard, uncovered, to evaporate water and concentrate flavors. Beans are perfectly done when just tender, but still crisp, usually in 5 to 10 minutes. The trick is to adjust the intensity of the bubbling so that water is all evaporated and sauce has just thickened at precise moment when beans are cooked. Stir once more, adjust seasonings, then serve hot, or refrigerate overnight and serve at room temperature as a ready-dressed salad.

BRUSSELS SPROUTS WITH ITALIAN CHESTNUTS

For our family of 4

This is the season for chestnuts, surely one of the finest of starch foods. Since almost all U.S. chestnut trees were destroyed by the chestnut disease and are only gradually being replanted, most of our chestnuts are imported from Italy. This recipe can be prepared with fresh chestnuts, or the dried, skinned kind (less trouble, but also less flavor), or even with ready-roasted ones bought from the chestnut man's portable griddle on the street corner.

Check Staples:

Clear beef bouillon (1½ tsps.)
Salt butter (to grease dish)
Aromatics: crystal salt,☧ freshly ground black pepper,☧ MSG,▣ whole caraway seed, rosemary, tarragon
Ground arrowroot▣ (2 tsp.)
Olive oil▣ for cooking fresh chestnuts (2 to 3 Tbs.)

Shopping List:

Brussels sprouts (two 1-pt. baskets)
Chestnuts, in one form or another, *see* above (1 lb.)
Heavy cream (1 Tbs.)

Preferably the Day Before—Preparing the Chestnuts

As necessary, according to the type used, shell, skin, and cook chestnuts by our BASIC RULES (immediately following), then refrigerate overnight.

On the Day—About 2 Hours Before Serving

Thoroughly wash the 2 pints of Brussels sprouts, pull off shriveled outer leaves, and soak in cold water to bring out final vestiges of sand. Let chestnuts come to room temperature.

About 45 Minutes Before Serving

Drain and partly cook Brussels sprouts, either by simmering in slightly salted water for about 7 minutes, or, much better, in a steamer,* about 10 minutes, until just soft. Meanwhile preheat oven to 350 degrees and liberally butter an open shallow casserole (we use a Mexican earthenware dish), then put in cooked chestnuts and heat in oven for about 5 minutes. In a small mortar coarsely grind together: 1 teaspoon whole caraway seed, 1/2 teaspoon rosemary, and 1/2 teaspoon dried tarragon, and add to the 1 1/2 cups of bouillon. Add salt, pepper, and MSG if necessary, and heat just to boiling. When Brussels sprouts are ready, distribute them among chestnuts and pour on hot aromatic bouillon. Set in center of oven, uncovered, and bake for about 30 minutes. Meanwhile make a thickening paste with 2 teaspoons of the arrowroot, liquefied with a few dashes of the cream.

Just Before Serving

Without disturbing internal arrangement of casserole, spoon off remaining bouillon into a small saucepan, place over gentle heat, and thicken by stirring in, teaspoon by teaspoon, some of the arrowroot cream. Make sure that no lumps form and use no more arrowroot than is necessary to produce a sauce the consistency of heavy cream. Taste and adjust seasonings if necessary, then pour over Brussels sprouts and serve.

BASIC RULE FOR SHELLING, SKINNING, AND COOKING FRESH CHESTNUTS: Preheat oven to 350 degrees. With a short-bladed oyster knife, make 3 deep cross-gashes on the flat side of each chestnut. Put them in a cake pan on top burner over medium frying heat and sprinkle with 2 or 3 tablespoons of olive oil. Hustle chestnuts around so that each is coated with oil. When they start sizzling, set pan in center of oven, and bake until chestnuts are soft, usually in 20 to 30 minutes. Shells will have puffed out and inner skin will be crisp, so that both can be flaked off as soon as chestnuts are cool enough to handle.

BASIC RULE FOR DRIED PRE-SHELLED CHESTNUTS: In a 3-quart saucepan bring about 2 quarts of freshly drawn cold water up to a rolling boil. Meanwhile wash chestnuts under cold running water. When water in pan is boiling hard, drop in chestnuts, a handful at a time, but do not let boiling stop. Keep boiling hard for 4 minutes, then turn off heat and leave them soaking in hot water for from 1 to 6 hours. The longer period is slightly better, if time allows. Then drain chestnuts and rinse thoroughly under hot running water. Rinse out saucepan and put chestnuts back. Just cover with freshly drawn cold water (or, much better, with bouillon, vegetable stock, or any other available aromatic liquid) and simmer gently to desired degree of softness: either *al dente,* chewy, for serving whole; or very soft, for mashing.

CORSICAN CAULIFLOWER PANCAKES

For our family of 4

This is an unusual and attractive way of serving a large winter cauliflower. When perfectly done the pancake is brown, crackly on the outside, soft and juicy inside, with the cauliflower flavor concentrated and magnified.

Check Staples:

Aromatics: crystal salt, freshly ground black pepper, MSG, garlic (1 clove), whole nutmeg
Olive oil (1 or 2 Tbs.)

Shopping List:

Cauliflower (1 large)

About 25 Minutes Before Serving

Remove outer leaves from cauliflower (putting away leaves and thick stalk for boiling in soups) and divide into flowerets of roughly equal size. We partly cook these in a small steamer* over rapidly boiling water, until flowerets are just soft, usually in 5 to 7 minutes. Meanwhile set a frypan over low frying heat, put in 1 or 2 tablespoons of the olive oil, and let it get quite warm but not really hot. Finely mince the clove of garlic and add to oil. As soon as cauliflower is soft, put it into frypan and season with a few grinds of nutmeg, plus salt, pepper, and MSG to taste. Now, working fast, mash cauliflower with a wooden fork, pressing down and together, until it forms a solid pancake about ½ inch thick. Turn up heat and fry pancake, using a fairly large spatula to turn pancake, until both sides are brown and crisp. Finally, drain pancake on absorbent paper, then serve on a hot platter, cutting into pie-shaped pieces.

BAKED WHOLE EGGPLANT AS THEY DO IT IN BARCELONA

For our family of 4

This is one of the simplest and best ways of cooking an eggplant. It is equally good served hot or cold.

Check Staples:

Corn-belly salt pork (about 1/4 lb.)
Aromatics: crystal salt, freshly ground black pepper, MSG, garlic (2 cloves), oregano
Olive oil (2 or 3 Tbs.)

Shopping List:

Eggplant (2 medium)

About 1 1/4 Hours Before Serving—Advance Preparation in Less than 15 Minutes

Mix thoroughly in a small bowl: 2 teaspoons salt, a few good grinds of pepper, 1 teaspoon MSG, plus 2 teaspoons of crumbled dried oregano. Place eggplants on their sides in a flat-bottomed casserole with a lid, which has first been lightly rubbed with olive oil, one small enough so that eggplant will not roll around. Using a small, pointed knife, cut about 24 small slits in neat rows in the top 1/3 of each eggplant. Each slit should be about 3/8 inch wide and 1/2 inch deep and slits should be about 1/2 inch apart. Now preheat oven to 350 degrees. Peel the first clove of garlic and slice lengthwise into fairly thin slivers. Press a sliver into aromatic salt mixture, turning it around and pressing it down, so that sliver is well coated. Now, using handle of a small spoon to force open the slit, put coated garlic sliver into first slit, pushing sliver right down with small finger and pressing opening of slit back together. Next, cut a sliver of the salt pork about same size as garlic and push down into second slit. Continue alternately with coated garlic and salt pork until all slits of both eggplants are filled. If garlic runs out use extra salt pork. Thoroughly rub eggplant all over with olive oil, and adjust eggplant in casserole so that slits remain at top or the juices will run out during baking.

About 1 Hour Before Serving—Entirely Unsupervised Baking

Place covered casserole in center of oven and leave eggplant undisturbed until done, usually in about 1 hour. It is ready when skin begins to crinkle and flesh is very soft to the touch.

Serving

TO SERVE HOT: Peel back skins and scrape out and mash up flesh, discarding garlic and salt pork, if desired. (We usually prefer to mash them in, since garlic has by now lost its bite.) Taste and adjust seasoning, also possibly working in a few more dashes of olive oil.

TO SERVE COLD: Simply cut eggplant in half lengthwise and serve ½ to each person, spreading ½ teaspoon olive oil onto each half and sprinkling with a little more salt and pepper. Let each diner dig out flesh with a spoon.

MUSHROOMS IN MADEIRA CREAM

For our family of 4

We usually keep a small bottle of a dry Sercial Madeira in our kitchen wine rack (page 43), because it goes so well with mushrooms.

Check Staples:

Aromatics: crystal salt, freshly ground black pepper, MSG, garlic (1 clove)

Dry Sercial Madeira (½ cup)

Shopping List:

Mushrooms, preferably small buttons (1 lb.)

Sour cream (1 cup)

About 15 Minutes Before Serving

Wipe mushrooms clean (never wash); do not peel, but pull off stalks and cut away any woody ends. Put the ½ cup of Madeira into a saucepan with a tightly fitting lid, which is large enough to hold mushroom caps and stalks. Bring up to boiling, then turn down heat to merry bubbling, put in mushroom caps and stalks, sprinkle with salt and MSG to taste, then cover and let steam for 3 or 4 minutes. Meanwhile in a second saucepan, gently heat up the cup of sour cream, stirring in the garlic, peeled and mashed through a press, plus a very little more salt and MSG. Do not let sour cream actually boil. When mushrooms have steamed, without removing them from their pan, pour off Madeira into a holding bowl, then cover mushrooms with aromatic sour cream. Keeping heat under pan moderate so that sour cream does not boil, stir mushrooms around with a wooden spoon for 2 or 3 minutes longer, to impregnate thoroughly with cream. If cream is too thick, work in 1 to 2 teaspoons of the held Madeira. At the last moment stir in a little pepper and serve at once.

OVEN-BAKED ONIONS

For our family of 4

Few people seem to think often enough of serving whole onions as a side-dish vegetable. The English tradition is to serve them on Sundays, boiled with a cream sauce, but a better way, we find, is slowly baking them, like potatoes, in their jackets. There is no crying, no sharpness, and what remains is a delicate, juicy sweetness; a delectable accompaniment to meats and birds. All the principal onion types (page 198) can be prepared in this way and each provides a subtle variation in flavor and texture.

Check Staples:

Salt butter (4 Tbs.)
Aromatics: crystal salt,☆ freshly ground black pepper,☆ caraway seed, marjoram, nutmeg, Hungarian sweet red paprika,☆ ground sage
Parsley (small bunch)
Olive oil (about 1 Tbs.)

Shopping List:

Yellow, Spanish, or Bermuda onions (1 lb.—preferably 1 per person)
Italian hard pecorino cheese, optional (1/4 lb.)

2 Hours Ahead—or Less, According to Oven Temperature

Onions can be baked at almost any oven temperature being used for other foods. The oven time will vary slightly according to size of onion, but will average about 2 hours at 300 degrees, 1 3/4 hours at 350 degrees, or 1 1/2 hours at 400 degrees. To prepare onions do not remove any of the dry skins, but wash lightly under cold running water, rub with a very little olive oil, and preferably place directly on rack in center of oven. Then forget them until they should be done.

About 5 Minutes Before Serving

Prepare an aromatic butter by melting the 4 tablespoons of butter in a small saucepan and stirring in a pinch or two of any or all of the aromatic herbs listed above, with some finely chopped parsley, plus salt and pepper to taste. Now grate cheese, if it is to be used. This, again, is a matter of taste. Finally, slice off root end of each onion and squeeze out the inside, throwing away outer skin. Serve in a hot dish, with the aromatic butter poured over and cheese sprinkled on top. Incidentally, baked onions are excellent cold and may be marinated in a vinaigrette dressing (page 169).

JOHANNA'S SOUTHERN GREENS

For our family of 4

Our friend Johanna remembers, when she was a girl on a farm in South Carolina, how she went out to pick the greens and brought them in to her mother, who taught her to prepare them in this basic Southern way. The trick of course is the balanced mixture of different greens, all soaking up the flavors of the meats. Often the dish was expanded to a main course with extra meats, rice, and crackling corn bread (page 330).

Check Staples:

Corn-belly salt pork⊜ (about 6 oz.)
Aromatics: crystal salt,☧ freshly ground black pepper☧

Shopping List:

A balanced selection of as many as possible of the following greens:
- Collards, basic, must always be included (about 2 lbs.)
- Hanover salad (about 1/4 lb.)
- Kale (about 1/2 lb.)
- Mustard greens (about 1/2 lb.)
- Turnip tops (about 1/2 lb.)

Ham knucklebone, with some meat on it (about 3/4 lb.)

About 1 3/4 Hours Before Serving—Including 1 1/2 Hours of Unsupervised Simmering

Into a 5- or 6-quart lidded soup kettle put 3 pints of freshly drawn cold water and set over high heat to bring to a rapid boil. Wash ham knuckle and put into kettle. When water boils, turn heat down to gentle bubbling, cover, then keep bubbling for 30 minutes to draw flavors from ham. Meanwhile cut the piece of corn belly into 1/2-inch cubes and hold.

About 1 1/4 Hours Before Serving

Put corn-belly cubes into kettle and continue bubbling, covered, for another 30 minutes. Meanwhile prepare greens and assemble them in a large mixing bowl. Wash them all throughly under cold running water. They are usually very gritty. Remove all roots and tough, woody stems. However, a few young and tender stems can remain with the leaves, since they add extra flavor. Now chop everything to about the consistency one would find in a salad of chopped greens.

About 45 Minutes Before Serving

Drop greens into kettle, salt and pepper to taste, then keep merrily bubbling, covered, for about 45 minutes more. By the time they are done, they should have absorbed almost all the liquid. If not, boil hard, uncovered, for 3 or 4 minutes at the end. Finally, remove ham meat from bone and dice into greens. Corn belly will generally have melted away, but if any lumps remain, dice them also. Stir meats into greens, and serve very hot.

WHITE TURNIPS IN MAPLE-MUSTARD SAUCE

For our family of 4

Since the white turnip is generally available the year round and is always low in cost, this is one of our regular standby vegetable dishes. However, there is nothing ordinary about its flavor. Winter parsnips can also be prepared this way.

Check Staples:

Salt butter (4 Tbs.)
Aromatics: crystal salt,* freshly ground black pepper,* MSG,
English dry mustard
Dark-brown sugar (1 Tbs.)
Pure maple syrup (2 Tbs.)

Shopping List:

White turnips, small (2 lbs.)

About 50 Minutes Before Serving

In a 3-quart saucepan bring about 2 quarts of salted water to a boil. While water is heating, peel turnips, slice 1/4 inch thick, and drop, all at once, into rapidly boiling water. Set timer and let bubble for 5 minutes. Meanwhile prepare a heatproof covered casserole or dish, in which turnips will bake. We use an enameled cast-iron cocotte* with a tightly fitting lid, which can also be heated on top of the stove. In it over medium heat melt 4 tablespoons of the butter, being careful not to let it brown or burn. When the 5-minute bell rings, drain turnip slices and leave until cool enough to handle. When butter is melted blend in 1 level tablespoon of the dry mustard, the tablespoon of brown sugar, the 2 tablespoons of maple syrup, plus salt, pepper, and MSG to taste. Preheat oven to 350 degrees. Now, with the fingers, work each turnip slice into maple-mustard sauce and arrange in neat rows or circles in bottom of cocotte.

Exactly 30 Minutes Before Serving

Put cocotte, tightly covered, into oven. Leave 30 minutes, then taste 1 slice. It should be soft, but still slightly crisp. Also check seasoning while tasting and adjust if necessary. We bring our cocotte to the table.

¶ *Foundations—Potatoes · Rice · Whole Grains*

We regard the starch-filler of the meal as the "foundation," the solid base on which the menu comfortably rests. In American and western European kitchens, few cooks seem to think beyond potatoes, rice, or pasta, yet even on this home ground our search for variety has led us to the more unusual ways of preparation. Then there is the much wider world of the grains and legumes of the more exotic cuisines, with starch foods capable of lifting even a simple meal by a touch of the flavor of a foreign feast: the couscous of the Arabs, the kasha of the Cossacks, the *tarhonya* of the

Magyars, the *dalls* of the Bengalis, and the Yorkshire pudding of the English. We include many of these among our foundations.

FRENCH POMMES DE TERRE BOULANGÈRE—BAKER'S POTATOES

For our family of 4

The name of this recipe stems from the custom in many French villages of paying a small fee to the baker for permission to set the dish in his bread oven. Usually the small boy of the family, treading carefully, carries the dish, covered with a white cloth, down the street to the bakeshop.

Check Staples:

Salt butter (about 6 Tbs.)
Clear beef or chicken bouillon (about 2 cups)
Aromatics: crystal salt,⁕ freshly ground black pepper,⁕ MSG⁕
Yellow onions (3 medium)
Parsley (small bunch)
Watercress (1 bunch)

Shopping List:

Fluffy starchy potatoes, *see* list, page 56 (2 lbs.)

About 1¼ Hours Before Serving—Preparation in About 15 Minutes

The choice of dish is important. It should be a shallow, open casserole, perhaps of heat proof earthenware or china, in which the potatoes can be spread out so that they brown; the casserole should also be attractive enough to be brought to the table. Liberally butter this casserole. Finely chop a small handful each of the parsley and watercress, then mix them together in a bowl. Now start peeling the 2 pounds of potatoes, slicing them about ¼ inch thick and laying the slices over the bottom of the casserole. Sprinkle very lightly with salt, pepper, and MSG. Then build a second layer, in overlapping patterns, like bricks in a wall, again lightly seasoning. Peel and thinly slice the first onion, laying slices on top of potatoes. Sprinkle with parsley and watercress. Then add 2 more lightly seasoned layers of potato slices. Now peel and slice the second onion and lay on top of potatoes, along with more parsley and watercress. Continue until everything is used up. The top layer should be unadorned potatoes. Preheat oven to 400 degrees. Dot the top liberally with bits of the butter, then pour in enough of the bouillon just to reach the upper layer of potatoes. The actual top surface should be dry so that it will brown, but the level of the liquid should be just below it.

About 1 Hour Before Serving—Entirely Unsupervised Baking

Set casserole in center of oven and forget it. The potatoes are partly boiled, partly steamed by the liquid, while the top slowly browns and the melting butter seeps down through all the layers. The objective (which may not be perfectly achieved the first time, but will come with practice) is to have the potatoes perfectly done and the top beautifully brown at the precise moment when all the liquid is absorbed. If there is a little liquid left on the bottom, use a little less next time, while keeping temperature and cooking time constant. If liquid is all absorbed before potatoes are quite done, pour on a little more liquid and continue baking a few minutes longer. When the dish is perfectly done it is dramatic in appearance, taste, and texture.

OUR MODIFIED ARABIAN PILAF OF RICE

For our family of 4

This dish may have started out in Mecca, but it ends up in a Boston bean pot when it comes to our table. It is a highly flexible way of preparing rice, in a form either simple and bland or richly aromatic and textured with fruit and nuts. Generally we serve it as a side dish to the main course, but it can also be a supper dish on its own, flecked with meat, poultry, fish, or cheese.

Check Staples:

Salt butter (2 Tbs.)
Beef bouillon (2¼ cups)
Aromatics: crystal salt,☧ freshly ground black pepper☧
Long-grain white rice, say Patna,⊜ if available, or a domestic brand (1½ cups)

Shopping List:

Seedless white raisins (about ⅓ cup)
(As to other garnishes, there is a wide choice: chopped scallion tops, green pepper, watercress, other greens, coarsely diced tomatoes, cooked vegetables, coarsely chopped nuts, lightly sautéed mushroom slices, etc.)

About 50 Minutes Before Serving

The basic trick of this dish is first to half-cook and expand the grains of rice in boiling water, then to complete the cooking in an aromatic bouillon that the rice absorbs. Thus the rice keeps its own character while delicately assuming the flavor of the bouillon. We do the first cooking in a pot of slightly salted boiling water, enclosing the rice in an aluminum rice ball* for easy withdrawal. However rice can also be boiled loose and strained out. Either way, boil the 1½ cups of rice for exactly 7 minutes. Meanwhile preheat oven to 150 degrees and put a 1- to 1½-quart covered bean pot (or alternative) in the oven to warm up. Heat up the 2¼ cups of bouillon just to boiling, and hold hot. Measure the ⅓ cup of raisins and prepare any other garnishes (above).

About 35 Minutes Before Serving

After precisely 7 minutes remove rice from boiling water and drain. Take bean pot out of oven and turn up heat to 350 degrees. Liberally butter inside of pot and put in rice. Lightly blend in raisins (plus other garnishes, if used). Pour in hot bouillon, stir lightly, taste, then add salt and pepper as needed. Dot surface of rice with the 2 tablespoons of butter. Stretch a piece of folded cotton cloth (a handkerchief does very well) across opening of bean pot and press it down with the lid. This helps to seal in the steam and prevent condensation, improving the expansion of the rice. Set bean pot in center of oven and leave for 25 minutes. Then taste rice and check whether all liquid is absorbed. The trick is to have the rice perfectly done just when the pot is dry. If liquid remains put pot back in oven, uncovered, for about 5 minutes. Gently fluff rice in pot with a rubber spatula or wooden fork, then serve in the covered bean pot.

RUSSIAN KASHA—WHOLE-GRAIN WHEAT

For our family of 4

From eastern Europe across northern Asia to the Pacific, this is the staple eaten by millions of people at almost every meal. The wheat grain comes in various forms, under various names, and is easily available by mail-order.✲ We like the whole grain best because it has a nutty flavor and chewy texture. There is also cracked wheat in which the grains are broken in half, like split peas, and there are various other types, known as buckwheat, bulgur, wheat pilaf, etc. They can all be prepared in the following way.

Check Staples:

Salt butter or aromatic beef or pork fat from previous cooking or bits of pork crackling, etc. (about 8 Tbs.—1/2 cup)
Beef bouillon or other aromatic stock (1 qt.)
Eggs (2 large)
Aromatics: crystal salt,✲ MSG◉

Shopping List:

Whole-grain kasha wheat✲ (2 cups —just under 1 lb.)

At Any Time Beforehand—Toasting the Wheat in About 10 Minutes

Spread the 2 cups of wheat across the bottom of a clean and dry cold frypan. Break in 1 of the eggs and start vigorously working it in with a wooden spoon. Every grain must be wetted and coated with egg. If the first egg is not enough, break in the second. The wetted grains will stick together and pile up in lumps; this does not matter. When every grain is egg-coated, turn on medium frying heat under pan and keep stirring and moving grains continuously. Soon the magnificent aroma of toasting wheat rewards your effort. Break up the lumps, separating each grain as it toasts and dries out. Grains will stick to bottom of pan. Scrape them off. Do not worry about a thin layer of browned egg on the bottom of the pan; it will come off during the boiling. Finally every grain is separate and dry, like rice. Turn off heat. At this point grains may be held for later preparation.

Boiling the Kasha in About 1 Hour—Almost Completely Unsupervised

In a separate saucepan heat up the quart of bouillon to boiling, then pour over wheat in frypan and stir well. Turn on heat under frypan and adjust so that liquid simmers gently. Dot top with about 4 tablespoons of the butter (or alternative fat), then cover and keep simmering until grains are tender but still chewy, usually about 25 to 30 minutes. Do not lift lid for the first 15 minutes, but then grains should be gently lifted and loosened with a rubber spatula or wooden fork. More butter or fat may be added for a richer dish, but this is a matter of taste. For the perfect final result, all the liquid should be absorbed at the precise moment when the grains are done. If a little liquid is left on the bottom, boil it away violently at the last moment, with the pot uncovered. If all the liquid is absorbed before grains are quite tender, add a little more hot liquid and continue simmering, covered, for a few minutes longer. Then turn off heat and let kasha stand uncovered for about 30 minutes, to mature the flavor. This is now the basic kasha, which may be stored in the refrigerator, as long as a month if it is very dry, and used in many ways (see below).

About 15 Minutes Before Serving

Reheat required amount of kasha in any convenient way: in a covered buttered casserole in a 350-degree oven; or in a covered saucepan or frypan, with a little butter to prevent sticking. As it heats up it may be further enriched with more butter or fat (the capacity of the grains to absorb fat seems unlimited!). The grains are separate and dry and the kasha is served as if it were rice.

VARIATIONS: An excellent light supper dish can be prepared with kasha by blending into it bits of cooked meat or fish or sliced fried sausage, etc. It may be covered with any cream sauce and is particularly good with our corn-belly gravy (page 628). For a variation in texture it may be combined with an equal quantity of separately cooked elbow macaroni or other small pasta shapes. Kasha also makes a first-class solid winter breakfast dish, served with cream and maple syrup or honey and perhaps combined with sliced bananas or chunks of any other fruit. Many other uses can be imagined. To every dish kasha adds its own character of toasted flavor and firm, *al dente* texture. Oh, yes! Kasha is also excellent for stuffing poultry, and can be added to meat loaf, see *kibbee* (page 185). See also *salade tabbooleh* (page 171).

¶ *Salads*

Just as we flavor our winter vegetables according to the season so we dress our winter salads with more robust and dominant vinegars and herbs to lift and sharpen the winter greens. Compare these winter dressings with those of spring and summer. The best winter salad ingredients are noted in the list of foods in season (page 54).

WINTER SALAD DRESSING NUMBER ONE

For our family of 4

Check Staples:

Aromatics: crystal salt,⚜ freshly ground black pepper,⚜ basil, English dry mustard, garlic (½ clove), savory, tarragon, thyme (dried, only when fresh not available)
Green scallion tops (enough for 2 Tbs., finely chopped)
Parsley (enough for 1 Tbs., finely chopped)
Green virgin olive oil⚱ (4½ Tbs.)
Burgundy red wine vinegar⚱ (1½ Tbs.)

Shopping List:

Any of the following herbs, homegrown or hothouse, if available (enough for 1 tsp. each, finely chopped): savory, tarragon, thyme

Before the Salad Goes into the Wooden Bowl

The precise details of each operation are given in our BASIC RULE on page 73. Rub the inside of the bowl with the cut side of the half clove of garlic. Wash, completely dry, and assemble the salad, then freshen and crisp it.

We Prepare the Dressing at Table

Put ½ teaspoon of the salt into the mortar, grind a few times, then add enough pepper to speckle salt, plus ½ teaspoon of the mustard and ¼ teaspoon each of any of the dried herbs used in place of the fresh ones. Grind again to bring out oils, then add 1½ tablespoons vinegar and the 4½ tablespoons oil. Stir well and hold. In small mixing bowl assemble the fresh aromatic herbs: the 2 tablespoons of chopped scallion tops, the tablespoon of parsley and, as available, the teaspoon each of the savory, tarragon, and thyme.

Just Before Serving

Stir up dressing in mortar. Add chopped fresh herbs and stir again. Spoon dressing over salad. Toss thoroughly and serve instantly.

WINTER SALAD DRESSING NUMBER TWO

For our family of 4

The recipe is exactly the same as for dressing number one above, except that the thyme is replaced by marjoram, fresh or dried, and the green scallion tops by 2 finely minced cloves of shallot.

We think it unnecessary to offer specific combinations for salads. Each salad maker must ultimately stand alone before his salad bowl, experimenting, learning from his mistakes and gaining confident judgment from his successes. However we do have two fixed-ingredient salads which are favorite standbys of our family. . . .

SWISS APPENZELLER SALAD

For our family of 4

This is a hearty cheese salad which makes an excellent lunch or supper dish on its own or can be teamed with a light dish, such as a mushroom omelette, to make an excellent main course at dinner. The Swiss Appenzeller cheese, which originated in the eastern canton of Appenzell, is an extra-nutty first cousin of the Gruyère, but with much smaller holes, or "eyes." The supply is somewhat irregular, but it can be ordered by mail.✠ If it is not available it may be replaced by imported Swiss natural Gruyère (*not* processed) or by imported Swiss Emmenthaler with the very large eyes (generally and inaccurately called simply "Swiss cheese"). The Appenzeller is worth the trouble of ordering, as it gives the salad a most unusual flavor.

Check Staples:

Eggs (4 large)
Aromatics: crystal salt,✠ freshly ground black pepper,✠ whole cumin seed, English dry mustard, fresh horseradish,✠ which we keep in our freezer (enough for 2 tsp., grated)

Shopping List:

Imported Swiss Appenzeller cheese,✠ or alternative, *see* above (½ lb.)
Sour cream (⅓ to ½ cup)
Plus two or three salad greens chosen from the list on page 54, perhaps hand-torn hothouse Bibb lettuce, coarsely torn watercress, chunked and separated Belgian endive, etc.

About 25 Minutes Before Serving

Boil the 4 eggs to make *oeufs mollets* and grate enough frozen horseradish (see BASIC RULE, page 26) to fill 2 teaspoons, then hold, covered.

BASIC RULE FOR OEUF MOLLET: The French define an *oeuf mollet* as an egg that is a good deal harder than soft-boiled, but not nearly as hard as hard-boiled; the white is firm, but the yolk is as soft as a paste. A hard-boiled egg, in almost any recipe, can be replaced by an *oeuf mollet,* which we think has a better flavor and texture. Have water bubbling in a pan and gently lower in the required number of large-size eggs taken straight from the refrigerator. Start timer as first egg goes in. After exactly 5½ minutes, remove first egg and immediately put in cold water to stop the cooking. First egg in is first out, then the rest follow in order. For large eggs starting at room temperature, the boiling time is a few seconds under 5 minutes. Smaller eggs take less time. *Oeufs mollets* require a little extra care in shelling, as they can easily burst open.

About 15 Minutes Before Serving

Put ⅓ cup of the sour cream in a small mixing bowl and blend in the 2 teaspoons of grated horseradish, along with 1 teaspoon of the dry mustard, ½ teaspoon cumin seed, coarsely ground in a mortar, plus salt and pepper to taste. Cut the ½ pound of cheese into ½-inch cubes and hold. Wash, pat dry, and tear up the salad ingredients by hand, then toss them together in a salad bowl. Sprinkle in the cheese cubes. Slice the *oeufs mollets* and drop them in. Stir the cream dressing and taste. If it seems too strong, add a little more sour cream; if not strong enough, grate in a little more horseradish and add a pinch or two more mustard and seasonings. Spoon dressing into salad and lightly blend together. Taste again and work in a little more sour cream if needed. If salad is not to be served immediately, keep cool in refrigerator.

ARAB SALADE TABBOOLEH

For our family of 4

Of all fancy and foreign salads this is the most adaptable and practical. It combines in the one dish the functions of salad and starch-filler foundation. Ideally, it is made with the cooked whole-grain wheat kasha (page 167), but it can also be prepared, as a compromise, with certain packaged grades of milled wheat, sometimes called "wheat pilaf," which are prepared simply by soaking. This salad is dramatic in appearance and wonderful in flavor and texture.

Check Staples:

Cold cooked kasha or alternative, *see* above (1 cup)
Lemons (4)
Parsley (2 large bunches)
Aromatics: crystal salt,⁑ freshly ground black pepper,⁑ dried mint leaves (if fresh mint not available)
Olive oil (½ cup)

Shopping List:

Fresh hothouse or home-grown mint, if available (small bunch)
Italian sweet red onions (3 medium) or Bermuda or Spanish sweet onion (1 large)
Tomatoes (3 medium)

At Any Time Beforehand—Preparing the Grains

Cook a batch of kasha (page 167), or if there is already a supply in the refrigerator, measure 1 cup of it and let it come to room temperature. If packaged milled wheat is used, soak it, according to directions, until it is just tender, but still chewy, usually about 30 minutes.

About 15 Minutes Before Serving

Peel and finely chop the onions, then thoroughly mix them in a bowl with the kasha, seasoning with salt and pepper to taste, and leave

covered for a few minutes, allowing the kasha to absorb the onion juices. If fresh mint is available, finely chop enough leaves to fill ¼ cup, fairly tightly packed, then hold, covered. Chop fairly fine enough parsley leaves to fill 1½ cups, fairly tightly packed, then hold, covered. Hold out a few nice sprigs of parsley for decoration. Chop coarsely 2 of the tomatoes and cut the third tomato into wedges for decoration. Now add to the kasha: the chopped fresh mint (or about 1 tablespoon dried), the chopped parsley, the 2 chopped tomatoes, then thoroughly blend with light strokes of a wooden fork or rubber spatula. Refrigerate for a few minutes, while preparing the dressing in a small mixing bowl. Squeeze juice from the 4 lemons, blend with the ½ cup of olive oil, and lightly season with more salt and pepper. Do not dress salad until . . .

Just Before Serving

Beat dressing with a few strokes of a small wire whisk and pour over salad. Taste for seasoning. There should be a fairly strong accent of lemon. If it is too strong, blend in a little more olive oil. We think the *tabbooleh* looks best when piled up in a small heap in a very shallow bowl or even on a flattish platter. Decorate with sprigs of parsley and the tomato wedges. More parsley may be put around the base. Incidentally, *tabbooleh* should never be runny, but it is unlikely since kasha seems to absorb dressing as fast as it is poured on.

¶ *Desserts*

The modern revolution in refrigerated transportation makes our fruit stands look as if it were June and July the year-round. Every day from New Year's to Christmas fresh strawberries arrive in New York from somewhere in the world. Even on the darkest Winter Dog Days, the market baskets are loaded with cherries, peaches, plums . . . all transported over thousands of miles. Yet the millennium has not quite arrived! At best these out-of-season fruits are expensive party luxuries, and at worst they can be very poor value indeed. For everyday economy we must still rely on the old winter standbys: the apples, bananas, grapefruit, oranges, pineapples . . . but we lift and sharpen them by subtle contact with the fruit brandies and liqueurs (see discussion following). With so many dramatic combinations possible, we sometimes wonder why it is ever necessary to prepare a formal dessert, when the near-perfect ending to almost any meal can so easily be . . .

Fruit with Cheese and "A Glass"

The hospitable French phrase *boire un glas* can include anything from wine to beer, from brandy to liqueur. Accompanied by a sympathetic fruit and a well-matched cheese, the combination takes on the unity of a perfect marriage.

All the fine winter eating APPLES have a special affinity for two of the best winter cheeses, English CHESHIRE and Dutch GOUDA. We join them to a glass of RED BURGUNDY, or, less formally, to a mug of HALF-AND-HALF of, say, India Pale Ale and imported Irish Guinness Stout. With the various California or imported Belgian winter GRAPES, the best combination is an American LIEDERKRANZ and a glass of California GRENACHE ROSÉ or a foaming glass of BLACK VELVET, an equal mixture of New York State champagne and imported Irish Guinness Stout.

With the winter PEARS, our ideal combination is Philadelphia CREAM CHEESE and a powerful white wine, say, a glass of WHITE BURGUNDY.

With an imported Chilean SANTA ROSA PLUM, the cheese is a wedge of BRIE OR CAMEMBERT, with a glass of gentle and delicate red wine, say, a Bordeaux RED CLARET or a CLARETE from the Rioja district of Spain.

Or there might be DATES and FIGS, marinated overnight in brandy, with small pieces of crystallized ginger, some French PETIT SUISSE cream cheese and small liqueur glasses of a dry fruit *eau-de-vie,* say, a MIRABELLE, distilled from the tiny yellow plums of Alsace.

Fruits Marinated in Brandies and Liqueurs

Instead of muddling our fresh-fruit salads together in a bowl, we prefer to chunk the fruits neatly and spread them out on an open platter in circles or wedges or squares of contrasting colors, as if they were hors d'oeuvres. Then, for a dramatic variety of flavors, one can sprinkle different brandies or liqueurs over the different sections of fruits: slices of peeled ORANGE arranged in overlapping rows, sprinkled with superfine-grind sugar, then very lightly spotted with CHERRY KIRSCH or a good American BRANDY; small piles of California GRAPES, cut in half and seeded, then lightly spotted with a half-and-half mixture of MAPLE SYRUP and orange COINTREAU, which have been beaten together first; chunks of fresh PINEAPPLE lightly sprinkled with a pale French Martinique RHUM; thick slices of BANANA, lightly dribbled with a pre-mixed blend of half MAPLE SYRUP and half orange CURAÇAO with a squirt or two of lemon juice.

OUR BASIC ENGLISH APPLESAUCE

A supply for several meals

The trick in this old family recipe is in the use of the apple skins to seal in the flavor and juices and to add some of their nutty oils to the sauce.

Check Staples:

Sweet butter (4 Tbs.)
Lemons (2)
Aromatics: whole stick cinnamon, whole nutmeg
Superfine-grind white sugar (a few Tbs.)

Shopping List:

Baking apples, preferable to tart cooking ones, *see* list, page 50 (12 large, about 4 to 5 lbs.)
Sweet cider (about ½ cup)

Advance Preparation in About 15 Minutes

With a sharp potato parer thinly slice off the yellow outer rind of the 2 lemons, mince finely, and mix in a small bowl with 1/4 cup of the cider. Carefully peel the 12 apples to get fairly large pieces of skin or a fairly wide continuous strip. Then core apples and slice into 1/2-inch rings. It is essential to prepare the apples in a pot with a tightly fitting lid that can be used on top of the stove and in the oven. We use one of our enameled cast-iron cocottes.* Put in two 2-inch sticks of the cinnamon, then the apple rings, pour on the cider and lemon peel. Now completely cover them with the peeled-off apple skins, cut side down, carefully overlapping to make the tightest possible "inner lid." Set cocotte, uncovered, over medium heat on top of the stove until cider in bottom just boils. Be careful not to heat apples too fast or part of flavor may evaporate. While apples are heating, usually it takes 5 minutes, preheat oven to 350 degrees.

Oven-Baking in 15 to 20 Minutes, Entirely Unsupervised

As soon as cider begins to bubble cover cocotte tightly and place in center of oven, leaving until apples are soft and fluffy, usually in 15 to 20 minutes. Overcooking substantially reduces flavor. Remove and throw away all apple peels. Also remove cinnamon sticks, wash them, and save for later reuse. Now coarsely mash apples, preferably with a wooden fork so as to leave small lumps, at the same time beating in the 4 tablespoons of butter, about 3 to 4 tablespoons sugar, or more to taste, plus a few grinds of nutmeg. Adjust thickness of sauce by adding a little more cider if needed. Apple sauce may be served at once, hot; however we prefer to refrigerate it for a while and serve it cold, but not ice-cold. It keeps in the refrigerator almost indefinitely.

COGNAC MERINGUE PIE

For our family of 4, with some left over

This is a sophisticated dessert, to be served after the children have gone to bed. It is so luscious that it comes best after a light main course. The filling can be floated on other kinds of pie shell, but we prefer the contrast between the smooth filling and the crackly meringue shell that has been given extra firmness with ground nuts. The decoration can be any fruit in season or frozen fruit.

Check Staples:

Sweet butter (enough to grease baking sheet)
Eggs (5 large)

Shopping List:

Heavy whipping cream (1/2 pt.)
Shelled Indian cashew nuts, unsalted (1/4 lb.)

Check Staples (continued):

Aromatics: table salt, pure vanilla extract (1 tsp.)
All-purpose flour (enough to flour baking sheet)
Unflavored gelatin (1 envelope)
Superfine-grind white sugar (1¾ cups)
Powdered cream of tartar (½ tsp.)

Shopping List (continued):

Frozen pineapple chunks (12-oz. carton)
Glacé cherries (about 6, for decoration)
Hard maple sugar✲ (enough to fill 3 Tbs., coarsely grated)
French Cognac,♁ medium-priced (3 oz.)
Light French Martinique rhum♁ (3 oz.)

One or More Days Ahead—Preparing the Shell in About 15 Minutes, Unsupervised Baking for 1 Hour

BASIC RULE FOR MERINGUE-NUT PIE SHELL: Preparing the perfect meringue is not as difficult as is often imagined. However it is useless to try it on a very damp day, for then it refuses to dry out and crisp. First, we separate the 5 eggs, putting the whites into our copper beating bowl.* (The yolks are set aside for the filling, covered with milk to prevent skin forming, in a screw-top jar in the refrigerator.) Turn on oven to lowest keep-warm setting (this varies with different ovens, usually somewhere between 150 and 225 degrees). Prepare a flat baking sheet large enough to hold a 9-inch shell with room to spare. Lightly butter and flour it, then hold at room temperature. Finely grind the ¼ pound of cashew nuts and hold. Measure 1 cup of the sugar and hold.

Before starting to beat the egg whites, sprinkle over and stir in ½ teaspoon cream of tartar and ⅛ teaspoon salt. Beat by hand (see BASIC RULE, page 75) until they just hold a stiff peak, but are not yet dry. Now start beating in, 1 tablespoon at a time, ¾ cup of the sugar. The mixture should remain thick and smooth, like marshmallow, and if a little is rubbed between the fingers no grains should be felt. Now shake out beater and switch to rubber saptula. Quickly fold in remaining ¼ cup sugar, ground nuts, and 1 teaspoon vanilla extract, then shape pie shell by spooning meringue onto baking sheet, building up edge about ¾ inch all around. It does not matter if surface is rough. Remember that too much smoothing squeezes out air. Slip at once into oven and bake until just speckled with the lightest brown, usually about 60 minutes at 175 degrees, 45 minutes at 200 degrees, 30 minutes at 225 degrees, but the slower the better. Then turn off heat, but leave meringue in closed oven until quite dry and crisp, usually 15 to 20 minutes longer. Then carefully separate from baking sheet and let come to room temperature on a cake rack. It now should be perfectly dry and can be stored for several days at room temperature, loosely covered with waxed paper, in a well-ventilated place.

The Day Before—Preparing the Filling in About 30 Minutes

Set mixing bowl and beater in freezer. Drain milk from 5 egg yolks and let come to room temperature. Finely chop enough of the frozen pineapple to fill 1/2 cup and hold.

Put 5 egg yolks into mixing bowl and beat until thick and lemon-colored. Gradually beat in the remaining 3/4 cup of sugar, then blend in chopped pineapple. Soften the 1 envelope of gelatin to a paste by adding 1 to 2 tablespoons of the rhum, then gradually work in more rhum to liquefy. Heat gently over boiling water or very low flame, stirring continually, until gelatin is fully melted and all tiny lumps have disappeared, then blend quickly into yolks. Stir in remaining rhum and the 3 ounces of Cognac. Using ice-cold hand beater and bowl, whip cream stiff and, using rubber spatula, fold quickly into yolk mixture. Spoon filling into pie shell and refrigerate overnight, loosely covered with waxed paper.

Shortly Before Serving

Cut about a dozen neatly shaped slices of remaining pineapple. Cut about 6 glacé cherries in half. Coarsely grate or chop the 3 tablespoons of maple sugar. Make a pretty design on top of filling with pineapple and cherries, sprinkling here and there with the maple sugar, but do not cover up too much of the handsome yellow filling. Serve quite cold.

FRUIT-AND-ICE-FILLED MERINGUE HEART

For our family of 4

This recipe should be read in conjunction with the previous one, as the making of the meringue-nut shell is the same in both.

Check Staples:

Eggs (5 large)
Lemon (1)
Aromatics: table salt, pure vanilla extract (1 tsp.)
Superfine-grind sugar (1 1/4 cups)
Powdered cream of tartar (1/2 tsp.)

Shopping List:

Red raspberry sherbet (1 pt.)
Red strawberries, either luxurious fresh from California or Florida or frozen (2 pts. fresh or about 1 1/2 lbs. frozen)
Red glacé cherries, optional, for decoration (about 12)
Shelled Indian cashew nuts, unsalted (1/4 lb.)

One or More Days Ahead—Preparing the Shell in About 15 Minutes, Unsupervised Baking in 1 Hour

Prepare the meringue according to the BASIC RULE in the previous recipe. To make a heart-shaped shell, instead of buttering and flouring the baking sheet wet it with water and cover with unglazed brown paper. Then lightly draw on it in pencil the outline of a heart about 8 inches across and 10 inches long. First spoon the meringue around the edge of the heart, building up the outer wall about 3/4 inch high. Leave it rough; too much smoothing dispels the air from the meringue. Then fill in the floor about 1/4 inch thick, making sure that it is tightly joined to the wall, to avoid leakage of fruit juice. Bake and cool the shell as previously described. It may then be stored for one or more days.

About 1 Hour Before Serving

If fresh strawberries are used, wash and hull them, then let them come to room temperature; if frozen, let them thaw out. Either way, taste and add a little sugar if needed.

About 15 Minutes Before Serving

Cut about 12 glacé cherries in half. Working very quickly, spoon strawberries into a solid mass in center of heart, surround them with a piled-up frame of raspberry sherbet, then decorate the white meringue edge with glacé cherries. Serve at once.

¶ *Family Specialties—Lazy Sunday Breakfast · Bread · Bitter Marmalade*

We have gradually evolved a number of special recipes for our family tradition of Lazy Sunday Breakfast, when we keep an "almost open house." The informality is reflected in the menu, centered around a handsome hot dish with what the French would call *un certain éclat,* and as many homemade accompaniments as possible. Some of these recipes follow here; others are in the spring section (pages 327–32); in the summer section (pages 482–5); and in the fall holidays section (pages 626–32).

MORNING VOUVRAY FRUIT CUP

For 4 people

The sparkling variety of Vouvray from the Loire Valley was the favorite early-morning drink of Balzac. It has been called the "champagne of Touraine," and at its best is a bit sharper on the tongue than true Champagne, so is more perfectly matched to the waking hour.

Check Staples:

Oranges (4)
Superfine-grind sugar (to taste)

Shopping List:

Grapefruit (2 large)
Good sparkling Vouvray (half bottle)
Fresh mint, hothouse, home-grown, or frozen (about 6 sprigs)

The Evening Before—Advance Preparation in About 15 Minutes

Set the bottle of Vouvray to chill overnight in the least-cold part of the refrigerator. We place a pretty cut-glass serving bowl and a tulip champagne glass for each person in the freezer overnight. Cut out grapefruit sections, throwing away skins, then squeeze orange juice, but refrigerate each separately overnight in tightly covered jars; they are not to be mixed until the morning. The trick is to blend them just before serving so that their flavors remain distinct.

In the Morning—About 5 Minutes Before Serving

Quickly mix in serving bowl: the grapefruit sections with their juice, the orange juice, about 1 dozen mint leaves, finely snipped with scissors, plus a minimum of sugar to taste. Stir, then decorate top with sprigs of mint and serve at once.

Serving

Avoiding mint sprigs, ladle fruit mixture into tulip glasses until each is half full. Fill up with Vouvray. Place a crisp mint sprig in each glass.

OUR HOMEMADE COUNTRY SAUSAGE

A supply for the freezer, about 16 servings

We like to boast that we haven't bought a pork sausage in years, such is the revelation in quality of this pure pork version, without "filler" or preservative. Yet it keeps for weeks in the freezer and, when one of our individually foil-wrapped patties goes straight from the freezer into the hot frypan, the bouquet of fresh herbs which bursts into the kitchen raises appetites to the point of desperation. The aromatic seasoning is completely flexible and one can experiment with all kinds of combinations. We use it in all recipes calling for ready-made sausage meat.

Check Staples:

Aromatics: crystal salt, freshly ground black pepper, MSG, whole caraway seed, plus the fol-

Shopping List:

Pork fillet, absolutely lean, ground by butcher or at home (5 lbs.)
White pork fat, no rind, ground by

Check Staples (continued):
lowing dried herbs (only if fresh not available): marjoram, oregano, rosemary
Parsley (2 bunches)
Green scallions (2 bunches)
Watercress (2 bunches)

Shopping List (continued):
butcher or at home (1 lb.)
A small bunch each of as many other fresh herbs as are available: dill, sweet marjoram, rosemary, tarragon, etc.
Dried whole sage leaf (about 4 small packages, enough when crumbled to fill ½ cup)

Preparation in About 20 Minutes if Meat Is Ground at Home—Only 10 Minutes if Meat Pre-Ground by Butcher

We grind the meat and fat in our own electric grinder,* then put them into our largest mixing bowl with: about 1 tablespoon salt, plenty of pepper, about 1 tablespoon MSG, 1 tablespoon whole caraway seed; ½ cup of the crumbled sage leaves; 2 cups of finely chopped parsley; the 2 bunches of scallions, tops finely chopped, bulbs coarsely chopped; the leaves of the 2 bunches watercress, finely chopped; about ¼ cup each of other fresh herbs (or 2 teaspoons each of the dried). All these must now be evenly blended and we know of no more efficient tool than clean fingers. (When we began developing this recipe and were still experimenting with the seasonings, we kept a small frypan hot so that we could fry and taste little bits, to judge the seasoning, as the mixing proceeded.) When everything is evenly blended, we all join in shaping mixture into single-portion hamburger-style patties, wrapping them individually in foil and packing them in the freezer. There is no need to thaw patties before cooking them; they can go straight from the freezer into the hot frypan.

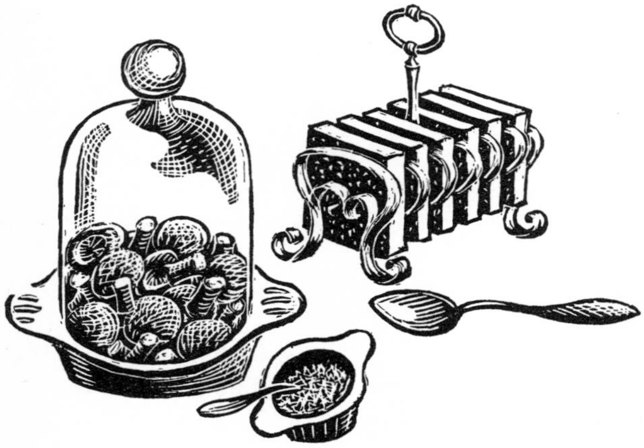

MUSHROOMS UNDER GLASS BAKED AS IN PROVENCE

For 4 people

Several friends have said that after preparing mushrooms in this way they never wanted to return to any other method. Fireproof glass bells of various sizes to fit the various au gratin dishes can be ordered by mail, either a single large one to fit over a central serving dish or several small individual ones. This is a dramatic way of presenting the mushrooms, but of course it makes no gastronomic difference if the dish is prepared in a tightly lidded casserole.

Check Staples:

Sweet butter (1/4 lb.)
Aromatics: crystal salt, freshly ground black pepper, MSG, garlic (1/2 to 3 cloves, to taste)
A few sprigs of one or more of the following, as available: fresh or frozen chives, parsley, watercress

Shopping List:

Fresh mushrooms, medium or small white buttons (1 lb.)

About 30 Minutes Before Serving

Preheat oven to 300 degrees and set to warm in it a single au gratin dish (or 4 individual ones) fitted with a fireproof glass bell. In a suitably sized saucepan (we use enameled cast-iron) over gentle frying heat melt the 1/4 pound of butter and introduce the garlic. The trick is the precise control of the garlic, exactly to one's taste. For minimum garlification, cut 1/2 clove into 2 or 3 slices, stir around in the melting butter, then remove before putting in mushrooms. For maximum effect, chop 2 or 3 cloves so finely that they are almost pulp, then blend in as a permanent addition to the butter. Or do something between the two extremes. Turn down heat, cover pan, let butter and garlic simmer together for 3 or 4 minutes while mushrooms are prepared. Wipe them clean (never wash), then pluck stems from caps and trim off dried ends of stems. Put caps and stems into hot melted butter and stir vigorously with a wooden spoon until thoroughly coated. Sprinkle on a little coarse crystal salt, 1 or 2 grinds of black pepper, and a generous amount of MSG. Continue to stir for hardly more than 2 or 3 minutes. The object is not to cook but to encourage absorption of the aromatic butter.

Take the hot au gratin dish out of the oven and into it pour the mushrooms, sprinkling the remaining butter over them, and cover at once with the glass bell.

About 15 Minutes Before Serving

Set dish in center of oven for about 15 minutes, but the time is not critical and mushrooms may be left in 3 or 4 minutes longer. Meanwhile finely chop enough of the fresh herbs to fill 1/4 cup. Bring herbs to the table in a small bowl. Do not lift bell from mushrooms until everyone is assembled and ready to savor the aroma. Serve on toast or on split and toasted English muffins; sprinkle with fresh herbs. This dish inspires our day.

OUR MODIFIED PERUVIAN CHILI CORN BREAD

For 8 good servings

This is a luxurious and decorative version, but it still holds the simple texture of Southern corn bread. It is so rich that it is best served by itself. We bake it and bring it to table in a shallow open casserole of glazed pottery.

Check Staples:

Salt butter (8 Tbs.—1 stick)
Eggs (2 large)
Milk (3/4 cup)
Aromatic: table salt
Water-ground white cornmeal (1 cup)
Baking soda (1/2 tsp.)

Shopping List:

Cream-style corn (8-oz. can)
Sharp Cheddar cheese (1/2 lb.)
Whole sweet red pimientos, roasted (4-oz. jar or can)
Whole chilis, roasted and peeled, usually packed in California or Mexico—medium strong, or stronger or milder to taste (4-oz. can)

Advance Preparation in About 10 Minutes—Unsupervised Baking in About 50 Minutes, Served Hot or Cold

In a small saucepan over low heat melt 6 tablespoons of the butter and hold, warm. Cut off 2 ounces of the cheese, coarsely grate and hold. Coarsely dice remaining 6 ounces of cheese and hold. Coarsely cut the 4 ounces of chilis and hold. Coarsely chop half of the red pimientos and cut remaining half into strips for decorating top of bread.

Preheat oven to 400 degrees. Put remaining 2 tablespoons of butter into a round, open baking dish, about 8 inches in diameter and 2 inches deep, then set in oven to heat for not more than 4 or 5 minutes, to avoid butter browning. Into a large mixing bowl put the 3/4 cup of milk, then break in the 2 eggs and beat thoroughly. Work in smoothly the 1 cup of cornmeal, the melted butter, the 8 ounces of canned corn, the diced cheese, the chilis, and chopped red pimiento, plus 1/2 teaspoon of the baking soda and about 1 teaspoon salt. Mix carefully and thoroughly.

Swizzle melted butter around inside hot baking dish, then pour in the corn-bread mixture. Sprinkle grated cheese over top and decorate with strips of red pimiento. Bake until a silver knife comes out dry, usually in 40 to 50 minutes. Excellent either hot from the oven or left to cool to room temperature.

OUR SIMPLIFIED BITTER-ORANGE MARMALADE

For about 8 pounds

We usually make this marmalade once a year, during the very short season of the Seville orange (see shopping notes, page 63). Some cooks make a big fuss about first peeling the oranges, blanching the skins, straining and restraining to get out the pulp . . . but we prefer our marmalade slightly rough in texture and a little sharp in flavor, so we eliminate the fuss and divide the work into short periods spread over 3 days, to allow for the full soaking and maturing of the fruit.

Check Staples:

Lemons (2)
Granulated white sugar (16 cups, about 8 lbs., according to taste)

Shopping List:

Bitter Seville oranges,⚜ with reasonably unblemished skins (4 lbs.)
Paraffin wax (for sealing eight 1-lb. jars)

The First Day—Advance Preparation in About 15 Minutes

With a small pointed knife cut away any skin blemishes or coarse ends of oranges and lemons. Do not be afraid to lose some skin. Cut oranges and lemons in ¼-inch slices. Do not remove pits, as they add to flavor. Pack slices down fairly tight in a china bowl or dish and just cover with freshly drawn cold water. Leave to soak at room temperature for 24 hours.

The Second Day—Boiling and Sugaring in About 15 Minutes

Put oranges, lemons, and their soaking water into a suitably sized enamel saucepan and bring rapidly to a boil, stirring occasionally. As soon as water begins bubbling, stir in about 12 cups of the sugar and, as soon as it is all in, turn off heat and keep stirring until sugar is dissolved. Now taste and add more sugar as desired, up to the full 16 cups. Let cool, then pour into storage bowl, preferably of china or enamel since direct contact with metal tends to darken oranges. Leave soaking at room temperature for another 24 hours.

The Third Day—Cooking for About 2½ Hours, Mostly Unsupervised

Put marmalade back into saucepan and again bring to a boil, then turn heat down to gentle simmering, cover, continuing until orange peel is transparent and fairly soft (but we like it still slightly chewy), usually in about 2 hours. Now uncover and turn up heat to rapid boiling, to evaporate water and thicken marmalade. Stir occasionally and, if one is available, insert a candy thermometer. Keep boiling hard until it reaches the "jelly stage," when thermometer shows 220 degrees Fahrenheit, and the liquid falls from the spoon in a "sheet." Turn off heat and, as marmalade cools, sterilize eight 1-pound jars and their caps by immersing in warm water, bringing to the boil, and simmering for 15 minutes. When everything is cool enough to handle, skim foam from top of marmalade, thoroughly drain jars, fill them with marmalade, and seal with two layers of paraffin wax, letting first layer set before second is poured in.

The Budget Pull-Back and Encore Dishes of the Winter Dog Days

As OUR first pull-back recipe—the dishes that we make when we feel we have overextended our family food budget—we have chosen Lebanese *kibbee* because it illustrates some of our rules for eating well at low cost. This is a classic dish of a relatively non-affluent society, where a largely agricultural people has for centuries learned to eat well, not with luxury foods, but by skillful preparation of the raw materials at hand. The *kibbee* has all the simplicity and flexiblity of a dish not hastily "invented" in a test kitchen but gradually evolved and improved from generation to generation. All its ingredients are economical. A relatively small amount of meat is "extended" (and at the same time improved in texture and nutritional value) with nuts and toasted whole-grain wheat. *Kibbee* can be prepared in substantial quantities, is easily stored, and can be served in a dozen different ways. It is typical of a number of low-cost family dishes that we have adopted from various parts of the world.

Perhaps "adapted" would be a better word, for we have had to convert the recipes to the methods of the Western kitchen. In Lebanon the *kibbee* meat is laboriously pounded in a huge mortar; we use an electric grinder. We have added wine (forbidden to a Muslim household). We have slightly changed the balance of the meats, the aromatic herbs, and the texture contrasts. Yet we feel we have kept the true qualities of the original *kibbee* in a dish that delights us again and again with its variety and harmony of natural flavors.

OUR MODIFIED LEBANESE BEEF AND LAMB KIBBEE

3 meals for our family of 4

To call the *kibbee* a "meat loaf" is hardly to do it justice. It is the national dish of Lebanon and is regarded as festive fare over large areas of the Middle East. Anyone who takes a walk through a residential section of Beirut toward the middle of the day can hear the sound of *kibbee*-in-the-making from every second house: the steady pounding of the *jorn* and *modagga,* the huge two-handed wooden pestle and the massive stone mortar on the floor in which the chunks of lamb are hammered to a smooth tenderness.

Check Staples:

Salt butter (½ lb.)
Whole-grain kasha,✲ prepared in advance, or packaged substitute, *see* Shopping List opposite (3 cups)
Aromatics: crystal salt,✲ freshly ground black pepper,✲ MSG,✲ whole allspice, whole coriander seed
Yellow onions (4 medium)
Parsley (small bunch)
Dry white wine✲ (2 cups)

Shopping List:

Lean beef, bottom round or chuck, best when ground at home with onions, but may alternatively be ground by butcher (1 lb.)
Lean lamb, best cut from leg, also preferably ground at home with onions, but butcher may do it, putting it through grinder twice (2 lbs.)
Salted shelled peanuts (½ lb.)
Seedless white raisins (½ lb.)
Plus, if home-cooked kasha not available: processed wheat pilaf or buckwheat groats or bulgur cracked wheat (1-lb. box)

Best Flavor When Made Ahead—Advance Preparation of the Wheat Grain in About 5 Minutes

We usually prepare a batch of whole-grain kasha (page 167) the day before, but it is also possible to use one of the prepared packaged grains, although with some compromise in texture and flavor. If kasha is used, its toasted flavor and chewy texture make a poem of the *kibbee.* Marinate the 3 cups of kasha in the 2 cups of wine for 15 minutes, moving the grains around occasionally, then drain and hold, saving the now-flavored wine for soups. If packaged grains have to be used, follow instructions on box for soaking in hot water, but use wine in place of the water. Since these grains usually expand threefold, start with only 1 cup of the dry grain. During the soaking time, start preparing the meats. . . .

Grinding the Lamb in About 10 Minutes

Peel and chunk 2 of the onions. We first put the lamb, interspersed with the onion chunks, through our electric meat grinder,* starting with the fine cutter in position. Put lamb through grinder twice, so that it is very smooth. Then loosely turn into it—preferably with a wooden fork, and taking care not to mash meat down—about 1 tablespoon salt, a good grinding of pepper, and about 1 teaspoon MSG, then hold. (If lamb was pre-ground by butcher, onions must first be finely minced, then loosely worked into lamb with seasonings.)

Grinding and Sautéing the Beef in About 15 Minutes

Peel and chunk the 2 remaining onions. We now switch from the fine to the coarse cutter on the meat grinder and pass the ½ pound peanuts through, to give them a very coarse texture. About the same result can be achieved by chopping. Or they can be used as they come. Each size gives a different texture to the *kibbee* and is a matter for experimentation and personal taste. Coarsely chop a small handful of parsley and hold. Coarsely grind in a small mortar: 1 teaspoon each of allspice and coriander, 1 teaspoon salt, plus a few grinds of pepper, then hold, covered. Put the beef, interspersed with the onion chunks, through the coarse cutter of the meat grinder, passing through only once, so that it keeps a contrasting texture to the lamb. Then, loosely work into (or if pre-ground, as with lamb, the onions must be minced and added to mixture) the beef: ½ cup of the peanuts (holding the remainder until later), the ½ cup of raisins, the chopped parsley, plus the aromatic mixture from the mortar. We set our tin-lined copper sauté pan over medium frying heat and quickly melt in it ¼ pound of the butter, taking care that it does not brown. Lightly sauté beef mixture, stirring around to absorb butter, until crumbly and lightly browned, usually in about 4 to 5 minutes. Turn off heat and hold. Preheat oven to 350 degrees.

Assembling the Kibbee and Baking for About 1 Hour, Largely Unsupervised

Loosely blend drained wheat grain into lamb mixture. Liberally butter a shallow baking tin, preferably about 2 inches deep, but of any preferred shape so long as it is large enough to hold the *kibbee* below the top edge, to avoid spilling melted butter. Divide lamb mixture into 2 halves and spread first half on bottom of pan as a smooth, even layer, about ½ inch thick. Spread entire beef mixture on top as a middle layer. Spread in remaining lamb as a top layer. Using a fork, prick regular lines of ¼-inch-deep holes over top surface so that melting butter will run in. Neatly sprinkle remaining peanuts on top and liberally dot with remaining butter. Bake in center of oven until top shows first signs of lightly browning, usually in about 1 hour. Finally, just before serving, brown *kibbee* more thoroughly under a grill for about 2 or 3 minutes.

Storing and Serving

Kibbee may be served at once, hot from the grill, or may be foil-wrapped and refrigerated, then reheated a day or two later, or frozen for many weeks. In fact the flavor seems to improve and mellow with keeping. It is excellent sliced, cold (preferably at room temperature). When serving it hot we like *kibbee* with an Italian tomato sauce, or our own corn-belly gravy (page 628), or with almost any of the classic meat sauces.

VARIATIONS: The two meat mixtures, before being cooked, may be shaped and completed in many other ways, but always, as far as possible, with the beef as the stuffing for the lamb. Larger baked meat-loaf shapes may have 5 layers. Hamburger-shaped patties with 3 layers may be quickly pan-fried. Meatballs, called *kofta* in Arab countries, will have a central core of beef with an outer coating of lamb. They may be grilled on skewers or simmered in aromatic bouillon. Individual *kibbee* shapes are excellent at a picnic, grilled over charcoal or an open campfire. For boiling, grilling, or pan-frying, the outer coating of nuts is of course omitted. Incidentally, other nuts can be used to vary the taste and texture. In Lebanon they often use pignolas. There seems to be no end to the flexibility of *kibbee*.

OUR 5-MINUTE CLAM STEW

For our family of 4

Of all the quick dishes in our repertoire this is the one we turn to most often in an emergency. If there were a formula for measuring gastronomic success against culinary effort, this recipe would probably have the highest rating. We serve it several times a month even when we are not pressed for time. We always keep canned clams in the store cupboard and milk may be substituted for the cream.

Check Staples:

Salt butter (6 to 8 Tbs.)
Lemon (½)

Shopping List:

Minced clams (four 10-oz. cans)
Light cream (2 pts.)

Check Staples (continued):

Aromatics: crystal salt, MSG, Hungarian sweet red paprika, Tabasco, thyme, Worcestershire sauce
Watercress leaves for garnish (small handful)

Shopping List (continued):

Heavy cream (4 Tbs.)
Fresh dill for garnish, if available (a few fronds)

With Practice, Just About 5 Minutes Before Serving

Set a 2- to 2½-quart saucepan over gentle heat and melt 6 tablespoons of the butter, making sure that it does not brown. Strain minced clams from their broth and hold. When butter is melted, blend in: 1 teaspoon thyme, no more than 4 single drops of Tabasco, a dash or two of Worcestershire sauce, and a little salt and MSG. Stir around for a few seconds to bring out and blend flavors. Pour in clam juice and turn up heat to bring rapidly to a rolling boil, stirring occasionally. Lower heat slightly and add the 2 pints of light cream, still stirring. Watch carefully as cream heats up almost to boiling, but it must not actually boil. Now add clams, stir again, and let them heat up for not more than 2 minutes or they will become leathery. Have ready hot bowls in which to serve the stew at once.

Serving at Table

Stir into each bowl of stew a squeeze or two of lemon juice and 1 tablespoon of the heavy cream. Float in the center a good pat of the remaining butter. Surround this yellow with a ring of sprinkled red paprika and an outer ring of finely snipped fresh green dill and watercress leaves.

SPANISH MOROS Y CRISTIANOS—BLACK BEANS WITH WHITE RICE

Several meals for our family of 4

This dish has been a phenomenon at our table for many years. The ingredients are so inexpensive, the preparation so simple, and the name so homely that one would hardly expect more than a solid and convenient family meal. Yet guest after guest has fallen in love with it. We have probably given out more copies of this recipe than of any other in our repertoire. However, a word of warning: the balance of flavors and textures is quite a delicate matter and no changes should be made in the ingredients or the method. The large amount of olive oil is completely absorbed into the beans, fattening and enriching them, and this is the secret of the dish.

Check Staples:

Dark smoked bacon,⊜ solid piece (about ¼ lb.)

Corn-belly salt pork,⊜ solid piece (about ¼ lb.)

Aromatics: crystal salt,* freshly ground black pepper,* MSG,⊜ whole bay leaves, garlic (6 cloves, completely lost in the long simmering)

Yellow onions (8 medium)

Baking soda (2 tsp.)

Olive oil⊜ (2 cups)

Boiled white rice, as an accompaniment to each serving (about 2 cups for each meal)

Tarragon white wine vinegar⊜ (2 Tbs.)

English hard cider or dry white wine (1 pt.)

Shopping List:

Black beans, often called turtle beans or, in Spanish stores, *frijoles negros* (2 lbs., about 5 cups)

Italian sweet red onion, chopped as garnish (1 medium for each meal)

Green peppers (3 medium)

The Day Before—Soaking the Beans

In a large 6-quart soup pot set 4 quarts of freshly drawn cold water over high heat and bring to a rolling boil. Meanwhile wash and pick over the beans in a colander under cold running water. When water in the pot is bubbling hard, dribble in beans by handfuls just slowly enough so that water does not stop boiling. When all beans are in, keep water bubbling hard for 4 minutes, then turn off heat and leave beans to soak. At about the end of 1 hour, when water feels hot but not stinging, stir in the 2 teaspoons of baking soda. If pressed for time, beans could be ready for next step in 3 hours, but we usually prefer to soak them at room temperature overnight.

On the Day—Timing Is Entirely Flexible

Drain and thoroughly wash beans under cold running water. We then put them in our 6-quart French earthenware toupin,* pour in the 1 pint of cider or wine, add enough freshly drawn cold water just to cover, put on lid, then place toupin in center of oven and turn on heat to 300 degrees. While it is heating up, assemble in a mixing bowl the aromatic ingredients that will contribute their flavor to the beans: the 8 onions, peeled and chunked; the 3 green peppers, cored and coarsely chunked; plus the bacon and corn belly cut into ½-inch cubes. In a sauté or fry pan heat up the 2 cups of olive oil. When it is fairly hot but still a long way from smoking, add aromatic ingredients from bowl and sauté strongly until lightly browned. Take pot out of oven and add entire contents of sauté pan. Stir around thoroughly but gently with a wooden spoon, then also stir in: 4 whole bay leaves, the 2 tablespoons of vinegar, the 6 cloves of garlic, peeled and thinly sliced, plus about 1 tablespoon salt to begin with, a good few grinds of pepper, and about 2 teaspoons MSG, with more of these added, to taste, as simmering proceeds. Place covered pot back in oven and gradually adjust temperature (according to idiosyncrasies of individual oven) until contents are very gently simmering. As level of liquid falls below top surface of beans, add hot water, 1 cup at a time, so that simmering is not interrupted. Beans will be eminently edible after 2 hours, but much better after 4 or 5 hours, and even still better when reheated the next day. Even if serving them on the same day, we try to arrange to let them cool and then reheat them before serving.

Serving at Table

Have ready about 2 cups of boiled white rice, plus about 3/4 cup of finely chopped sweet red onion. Serve black beans in very hot gumbo bowls or soup plates, with a small pile of white rice in the center and chopped onion sprinkled over. Each diner can mix his rice and onions into beans. The ideal wine to serve with this dish is a Spanish red Rioja.

BASIC METHOD FOR MAKING ITALIAN RISOTTO AS THEY DO IT IN MILAN

For our family of 4

We regard the Italian *risotto* as one of the most useful and flexible of all pull-back and encore dishes. On one day it can expand a small quantity of fresh meat, fowl, fish, or cheese into a solid and dramatically flavored main course. On another day it may be the ideal way of using up the odd bits and pieces remaining from previous meals. It is in the tradition of all the great rice dishes of the world (the Spanish *paella,* the Arab pilaf, the Indian pilau, etc.), yet the Italians have found a unique way of cooking their own soft, short-grain rice into a dish that is, in effect, a light and loosely textured savory pudding. Getting this texture exactly right is the basic trick in making a good *risotto.* Once this trick has been learned, the *risotto* can be varied by mixing in almost anything within reason.

Check Staples:

Salt butter (1/4 lb.)

Any well-flavored bouillon to match the meat, in this case clear chicken bouillon (about 2 1/2 cups)

Shopping List:

Chicken livers (1/2 lb.)

Fresh mushrooms (1/2 lb.)

Hard Parmesan grating cheese (1/4 lb.)

Check Staples (continued):

Aromatics: crystal salt, freshly ground black pepper, MSG, garlic (1 clove)
Yellow onion (1 medium)
Olive oil (¼ cup)
Italian *risotto* rice (1 cup)
Italian Marsala wine (½ cup)

About 45 Minutes Before Serving

Pour the 2½ cups of chicken bouillon into a small saucepan and heat up to just below boiling on the burner nearest to the one on which the *risotto* is to be cooked. Bouillon must be kept hot as long as it is needed for ladling into *risotto*. Next assemble in a mixing bowl: the onion, peeled and finely chopped; the ½ pound of mushrooms, wiped clean (never wash them) and cut lengthwise into hammer-shaped slices; plus the garlic, finely chopped. For the *risotto* itself, we use a 2-quart enameled cast-iron saucepan with enough extra room so that rice can be vigorously stirred around. Pour in the ¼ cup of olive oil and heat up until moderately hot. Put in mixture of garlic, mushrooms, and onions, then sauté fairly strongly, stirring around, until onions just begin to color and mushrooms have thrown off a good part of their moisture. Immediately throw in the 1 cup of *risotto* rice and stir around vigorously until every grain is glazed with oil. At same time melt in 1 tablespoon of the butter. Then, before rice has a chance to brown, stop frying by "hissing in" the ½ cup of Marsala. Adjust heat so that liquid is merrily bubbling, which must continue throughout cooking of *risotto* in order to provide steam to expand the rice. Now ladle in about ½ cup of the hot bouillon, stir again, then put on lid and let steam undisturbed for 5 minutes. (The essential trick in preparing a *risotto*, one which makes it different from all other methods of cooking rice, is that the cooking liquid is added a little bit at a time and is absorbed before the next ladleful is added. There is no need to measure the liquid because one continues to add bouillon until the rice is exactly done. At this point all liquid should have been completely absorbed. Also, contrary to all normal rules for making rice, it is regularly stirred during cooking, so that as the outside of the grains soften they begin to stick together.)

Each time liquid is absorbed, add another ladleful of bouillon, stir the rice fairly vigorously with a wooden spoon, then cover for a few minutes to steam and absorb new liquid. Meanwhile grate the ¼ pound of Parmesan cheese and lightly sauté the ½ pound of chicken livers (cut up into thumbnail-size pieces) in 2 or 3 more tablespoons of the butter, then hold, warm, until *risotto* is almost done. This point should be reached after about 30 minutes, but is best judged by tasting. Now work in about 2 tablespoons of the grated Parmesan, the chicken livers and all their pan juices, plus 1 or 2 tablespoons of the remaining butter. In this way one can precisely control the richness of the *risotto*. During the final few minutes of cooking, set a serving platter in the oven to get warm and season *risotto* with salt and pepper to taste. Finally, when texture is exactly right, with grains sticking lightly together but each still slightly firm at center, spoon and shape *risotto* into a neat pile on serving dish and bring at once to the table.

VARIATIONS: Obviously the chicken livers can be replaced by cubes of fresh or cooked meats, or pieces of chicken or turkey, or chunks of fish, crab, or lobster, or cubes of cheese which will melt, plus chunks of tomato or green pepper, or bits and pieces from the refrigerator. A *risotto* of sorts can also be made with ordinary long-grain rice, but the grains do not soften and stick together in the same way and the texture is somewhat less attractive. If any of the *risotto* remains uneaten, it may be reheated as shown in the following recipe.

ENCORE RISOTTO PANCAKES

For our family of 4

Check Staples:

Remaining *risotto* (about 1 cup—or whatever is left over, adjusting proportions of other ingredients accordingly)
Salt butter (1/4 lb.)
Fine spiced bread crumbs (about 3/4 cup)

Shopping List:

Hard Parmesan grating cheese (about 1/4 lb.)

About 15 Minutes Before Serving

Shape the cooked *risotto* into individual pancakes, each about the size of a fairly large hamburger patty, but not more than about 1/2 inch thick. Cover each fairly thickly with bread crumbs, pressing crumbs in firmly. In a sauté or fry pan heat about 4 tablespoons of the butter and, using a wide pancake spatula with great care so as not to break them, place *risotto* pancakes in hot butter. Brown on one side, then carefully turn over and brown on the other. All this must be done slowly over fairly low frying heat or else the outside will burn before the inside is hot. Meanwhile grate the 1/4 pound or so of Parmesan cheese and melt the remaining butter in a small 1-cup pan. Serve *risotto* pancakes with melted butter dribbled over them and fairly lavishly sprinkled with Parmesan cheese.

Three Encore Ways with Stale Bread

In Greenwich Village in New York City we are lucky to be near several small French bakeries where the bread is sold every morning, warm from the oven. Of course it does dry out quickly, and since we have no intention of wasting it we chunk the hard pieces into a large tin and eventually convert it into one of the three following dishes.

ONE-DISH PORK AND CHEESE STEW

For our family of 4

This recipe comes originally from friends who live in the charming countryside of the Latium, a few miles outside Rome. They learned it from the farmwives of the neighborhood, who call it *zuppa di maiale con formaggio.*

Check Staples:

Salt butter (about 2 Tbs.)
Corn-belly salt pork (about ¼ lb.)
Clear veal or beef bouillon (about 1 qt.)
Aromatics: crystal salt, freshly ground black pepper, MSG, rosemary
Yellow onions (about 6 medium)
Hard, old bread in roughly 1-inch chunks (about 3 qts.)

Shopping List:

Fillet of fresh pork, lean, thinly sliced (about ½ lb.)
Italian Parmesan cheese (about ½ lb.)
Heavy cream (about ¼ pt.)

About 1¼ Hours Before Serving—the Aromatic Bouillon

We prepare the ingredients and hold them separately. Dice the salt pork. Cut the fresh pork slices into roughly 1-inch squares. Peel and thinly slice the 6 onions. In a 2½- to 3-quart saucepan gently fry the diced salt pork. Bits will stick at first and should be loosened with a wooden spoon. As soon as bottom of pan is covered with liquid fat, add fresh pork squares and lightly brown, then remove with slotted spoon and hold. Also remove and hold salt pork pieces as they become crisp. Turn down heat under remaining fat and very gently simmer onion slices until almost melted; they must not brown or burn. Then add the quart of bouillon, 1 teaspoon rosemary, plus salt, pepper, and MSG to taste. Bring to a boil, then gently simmer, covered, for about 30 minutes. Meanwhile grate the ½ pound of cheese, setting aside ¼ cup of it for final sprinkling at the table. Now assemble the dish in a fairly deep 4- to 5-quart oven-proof casserole or cocotte* with a tightly fitting lid, which is good-looking enough to be brought to the table. Liberally butter bottom and sides and put in a layer of about 1/3 of the bread, then in turn sprinkle on 1/3 of the grated cheese, dribble on 1/3 of the cream, lay on 1/3 of the fresh pork squares, and sprinkle on 1/3 of the salt pork dice. Repeat this sequence of layers twice more. At this point, if required, heat may be turned off under bouillon and everything held for a while.

About 25 Minutes Before Serving

Preheat oven to 400 degrees. Bring bouillon up to boiling and pour over bread layers, taking care not to disturb them. Cover, then place casserole in center of oven and leave until hot through, usually in 15 to 20 minutes. The cheese melts and gives an extraordinary flavor and texture. Serve in very hot bowls with the remaining cheese sprinkled over.

MEXICAN CAPIROTADA—A ONE-DISH LUNCH OR SUPPER

For a hungry family of 4

Some of our Mexican friends consider this a dessert, but we never object to an occasional sweet main dish, and the combination of cheese, fruit, and bread gives it both body and a savory quality.

Check Staples:

Salt butter (about 1 Tbs.)
Aromatics: stick cinnamon (2-inch stick), whole cloves
Hard, old bread, in roughly 1-inch chunks (enough to fill a 1-pt. jug, fairly tightly packed)
Pure maple syrup* or dark buckwheat honey* or a mixture of both (1 cup)

Shopping List:

Ripe bananas (2)
Eating apples, according to season, *see* list, page 50 (2)
Seedless raisins (1 cup)
Unsalted peanuts, shelled (1 cup)
Blanched slivered almonds (1/2 cup)
Sharp Cheddar cheese (1/2 lb.)

About 1 Hour Before Serving

Put the cup of syrup or honey into a heavy saucepan (enameled cast-iron is best) and bring very gently to the boiling point. Watch it—it boils over like milk. Drop in the stick of cinnamon and 6 whole cloves. Keep it simmering, uncovered, about 5 to 10 minutes, to thicken. Slice the 2 bananas; peel, core, and slice the 2 apples; coarsely cube the 1/2 pound of cheese. Liberally butter a 2-quart casserole or soufflé dish and cover the bottom with a thin layer of bread; then add a thin layer of banana slices, covered in turn with apple slices; then some of the raisins, both kinds of nuts, and a top layer of cheese cubes. Repeat this sequence until everything is in. Preheat oven to 350 degrees. Pour the hot syrup through a strainer (to get rid of cinnamon and cloves) over the layered mixture in the dish. Set, uncovered, in oven until cheese has melted and all ingredients are soft and hot, usually in 25 to 30 minutes. Bring it to the table in the dish in which it was baked.

SWEET CONCUBINE CAKE—AN ARAB ENCORE DESSERT

For our family of 4

Check Staples:

Sweet butter (1/4 lb., plus 1 tsp. for buttering dish)
Hard, old bread in 1-inch chunks, avoiding the hardest crusts (about 1 1/2 qts.)
Dark-brown sugar (1/4 cup, fairly tightly packed)
Dark buckwheat honey✲ (1 cup)

Shopping List:

For the topping: heavy cream (1/2 pt. or more, to taste)

The Day Before—the Cake Is Served Cold

The preparation requires a heavy saucepan (enameled cast-iron is best) in which we mix: the bread, the 1/4 cup of brown sugar, the 1/4 pound of butter, chunked, and the cup of honey. Heat gently, stirring continuously with a heavy wooden spoon until bread is soft and all is combined into a sticky mass. Lightly butter a pie plate and spread the mass in it with a buttered spatula. Cool slowly at room temperature overnight. It solidifies into a soft and unctuous cake.

Just Before Serving

Top with whipped cream.

MUSSELS ON THE HALF SHELL FLOATING IN A GREEN SAUCE

For our family of 4

A sure way of cutting cost is to make a feast out of ingredients that are in small demand. In most fish markets, on most days, mussels are the cheapest item. The lack of demand is partly understandable, for mussels *can be* scraggy and disconcertingly gritty. There is a secret (see our BASIC RULE, below) known to every fisherman's wife along the northern coasts of Europe. If more American cooks knew it, mussels might soon command the price of oysters.

This main dish of mussels can be served with buttered rice (which absorbs the green sauce) and pan-fried tomatoes (page 97) for color contrast.

Check Staples:
Sweet butter (4 Tbs.)
Eggs (3 large)
Aromatics: crystal salt, freshly ground black pepper, red cayenne pepper, MSG, whole bay leaf, garlic (1 to 2 cloves, to taste), tarragon, thyme
Yellow onions (2 medium)
Parsley (small bunch)
Granulated instantized flour (4 Tbs.)
All-purpose flour (3 or 4 handfuls)
Dry white wine (2 cups)

Shopping List:
Mussels in the shell (3 lbs.)
Heavy cream (½ pt.)
White celery, with leaves (1 heart)

The Day Before

BASIC RULE FOR PREPARING MUSSELS: We pile the mussels in the sink under cold running water and arm ourselves with a stiff wire brush and an old oyster knife. Scrape off all the clinging seaweed and barnacles until the shells "shine." Discard any half-open shells (indicating that their owners are in a poor state of health) or any that are suspiciously heavy from internal sand. Then put them into a large bowl, cover with water, and salt to the taste of the sea. Having made the mussels feel at home, give them a Roman feast with the food that is their caviar. Throw in 3 or 4 handfuls of flour and stir around to distribute evenly. Within a few minutes there will be a gentle stirring and scraping as the mussels open up to gorge on the flour. Set the bowl in the refrigerator, where the feast continues all night, until the mussels have glutted themselves to a fat whiteness, at the same time throwing out all excrement and dirt. In the morning the water is black, and when the mussels have once more been thoroughly rinsed under cold running water they are ready for cooking.

About 40 Minutes Before Serving

BASIC RULE FOR STEAMING MUSSELS AND OTHER SHELLFISH: Into a tall soup pot with a tightly fitting lid pour the 2 cups of white wine and begin heating gently. Add: 1 of the onions, finely chopped; the leaves of the celery, finely chopped; 3 whole sprigs of parsley; the garlic, finely minced; 1 bay leaf, crumbled; 1 teaspoon thyme; plus salt, pepper, and MSG. Turn heat up high and bring liquid to a rolling boil. When pot is filled with steam, put in mussels and cover tightly, leaving the heat on high, for about 4 minutes. When lid is lifted, disclosing mussels enveloped in boiling foam, some are seen to have opened and these are picked out with tongs and put into a bowl to cool. For the more obstinate mussels, replace the lid for 1 or 2 minutes longer, at the same time lifting pot and shaking it. When all mussels are out of pot, turn off heat.

About 25 Minutes Before Serving

Preheat oven to keep-warm temperature (about 150 degrees), then set in it a large flat serving platter. In our kitchen many hands make quick work of dressing the mussels. As soon as each is cool enough to be handled, the top shell is thrown away and the mussels on their half shells are placed on the warm serving platter in the oven. When all mussels are on platter, cover with foil and hold in oven.

About 15 Minutes Before Serving—the Green Sauce

The wine in the big steaming pot is now a wonderfully aromatic mixture with the mussel juices. Strain it through muslin to remove seasoning solids and any last grains of sand. Chop enough parsley leaves to fill ½ cup and hold. Chop enough white celery to fill ¼ cup and hold. Peel and finely mince the remaining onion. Separate the 3 eggs, putting each yolk into a separate cup and reserving whites for some other use. Pour strained wine into the jar of an electric blender and add: the chopped parsley, the chopped celery, 1 teaspoon tarragon, and 2 or 3 shakes of cayenne pepper. Blend at medium speed only until solids are just creamed, usually 20 to 30 seconds, then turn off and hold. Melt the 4 tablespoons of butter in a 1-quart saucepan (preferably copper, for instant response to heat adjustments) and quickly sauté minced onion until just translucent. Smoothly blend in the 4 tablespoons of granulated flour and then begin working in the green liquid from the blender jar. Stir constantly, until sauce is about as thick as heavy cream. Turn off heat and, using a small wire whisk, beat in yolks, one at a time, alternating with good dollops of the heavy cream. Set saucepan back over medium heat, stirring continuously, and as it thickens, continue adding cream, until it has a smooth texture and a bright green color. When sauce is hot but still nowhere near boiling, pour it over the mussels, covering each one, and then bring them to the table. The mussels are served in their shells, preferably on a bed of rice. After the mussels have been eaten, it is permissible to lift the shells and sip the remaining sauce from them.

Chives for Boys, Onions for Men, Garlic for Heroes . . .

. . . As Dr. Samuel Johnson might have said if he had had more experience in the kitchen. Always a demanding perfectionist, he would soon have recognized that a working intimacy with the onion family is one of the first essential skills of the gourmet in the kitchen.

Starting with the frying of the onion, nine out of ten recipes call for sautéing until "just transparent," or "just golden," or "just limp," or "flecked with brown.". . . These directions are meaningless unless the cook understands what happens when the onion meets the hot fat. During the first few seconds the water in the onion is steamed off, concentrating the flavor oils and bringing them to the surface. At the same time the fibers begin to be slightly burned, adding a pleasantly mellow taste. Thus the first minute or so strengthens and improves the onion, but then the flavor oils begin to evaporate and in the next couple of minutes, the onion, as an onion, is lost. It has been converted to nice crisp flakes or rings, but with hardly enough strength to influence the dish. The expert cook will disregard the cliché directions and will sauté the onion by personal judgment as to how strong an onion flavor is required.

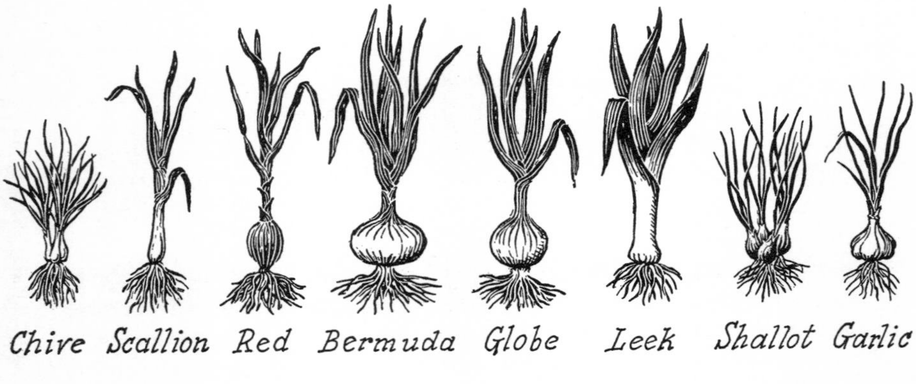

"He knows his onions!" was once a bit of teenage slang for a boy who was smart all around. It is still good advice in the market and in the kitchen. The cook should know the character of each type of onion and how it will change the dish when substituted for another—we mean, of course, fresh onions. We are firm in avoiding all forms of powdered or dried onions or garlic which have no character and in fact distort the original, fresh flavor because of the addition of preservatives.

The CHIVE might be called the most innocent member of the onion family. It is the tiny stalk leaf of an onion picked long before the bulb has had a chance to form. It is so delicate that it can never be cooked, but should always be finely snipped with kitchen scissors and sprinkled over the food just before serving. Marvelous in salads or with eggs, it can be grown in pots indoors and a fresh supply can be kept going all winter.

The GREEN SCALLION, or GREEN ONION, is simply a teenage chive. It is still, we think, best when finely snipped and sprinkled raw over the food, as in the *estouffade* of crawfish (page 299). However it does have enough strength to be lightly cooked, say, in an omelette or in scrambled eggs. Always remember that the white bulb is a good deal stronger in flavor than the green top.

The WHITE BABY PEARL, or COCKTAIL, ONION usually comes pickled in jars and is excellent in salads and in lightly cooked dishes.

The SWEET RED ITALIAN, or CREOLE, ONION, was probably originally developed in Italy and is still imported at certain times of the year, but is now grown in vast quantities in many parts of the United States. It is the eating onion par excellence, sliced paper-thin for sandwiches or on hamburgers, or finely minced in salads. We always use it as a garnish on our black beans with white rice (page 188). Because it is sweet and delicate, the red onion is not strong enough to give much flavor when cooked into stews, soups, etc.

The SWEET BERMUDA, or SPANISH, ONION may have originated in those pleasant places, but nowadays enough are grown in Texas alone to supply the entire United States each spring and summer. It is larger and slightly stronger than the red Italian, but still sweet enough to be sliced paper-thin and eaten raw. Yet, it is just strong enough to be boiled, usually whole, in soups and stews.

A French housewife who comes to live for awhile in the United States is invariably amazed at how little use we make of the LEEK, the *poireau* of France, which when simmered and melted slowly in butter develops an unusual and nutty flavor. It is a basic essential of the *pot-au-feu* (page 115) and adds a rich magnificence to soups. We sometimes prepare our *pissa-*

ladière (page 389) using leeks in place of the onions as a subtle and dramatic variation.

The SMALL WHITE BOILER is too strong to eat raw and too small to chop, but because it is tightly interleaved it holds its shape and texture in soups and stews and is the ideal onion-as-a-vegetable, best, in our opinion, under our corn-belly gravy (page 628).

The workhorse of the family, the YELLOW GLOBE, is actually many different types of yellow onion which come to market at various times of the year and make up 75 per cent of the world's onion supply.

The neglected SHALLOT is the link between the onion and the garlic. Like garlic, it is divided into cloves. Unlike garlic, it does not linger on the breath. A clove or two of shallot, finely minced and sautéed with the other onions, adds its own unusual flavor. We always keep a handful of shallots as a regular staple in our refrigerator vegetable bin.

And last there is the eternally controversial GARLIC, which some of our friends say is "insupportable and abhorrent!" We believe, on the contrary, that while garlic may be a bad master it is, when treated with respect, a fine servant. Some of the greatest dishes in the world owe their excellence to a delicate undertone of garlic. That "delicate undertone" is the key to its use.

The great French chef Francatelli was once asked how he achieved the extraordinary combination of delicacy and excitement in his salads. With a broad, wicked smile he said: "At ze last moment, I chew a leetle clove of garlic between my teeth and zen I breathe gently over ze salad."

No one has defined the dangers and joys of garlic better than the writer Ford Madox Ford, who told the story of the superbly beautiful model who was also a superbly imaginative cook. She had been taught by a Provençal mother and so garlic of course was one of the most important ingredients in her cookery. But how could she possibly hold her job in a high-fashion salon? The answer was that she could not. Even the passengers on the bus on her way to work had complained, and the outcry among the other models and designers was such that she had been dismissed from one salon after another. Finally she decided to live on her savings for a month or two of completely uninhibited garlic cookery. She plunged into the making of a *poulet Provençal à l'ail,* which includes about two dozen cloves of garlic, and then she discovered an extraordinary fact. When garlic cloves, still in their skins, are gently stewed in butter, it is possible to enjoy the flavor without the aftermath on the breath. The beautiful young lady met her aunt in the street and kissed her, with no resultant complaint. She went back to the salon, but there was no outcry. She had learned how to master her garlic.

Any cook can prove this truth in a simple way. . . .

POULET PROVENÇALE À L'AIL—CHICKEN WITH GARLIC AS THEY DO IT IN PROVENCE

For our family of 4

This is a classic recipe in which the garlic is muted and each diner is given the choice of having more, or less, of the garlic flavor.

Check Staples:

Salt butter (4 Tbs.)
Lemon (1)
Aromatics: crystal salt,☆ freshly ground black pepper,☆ MSG▣
Parsley (large bunch)
Olive oil▣ (2 or 3 Tbs.)

Shopping List:

Young broiler-fryer chicken, cut up (2½ to 3 lbs.)
Garlic (24 cloves, usually 3 bulbs)

About 45 Minutes Before Serving

We use a tin-lined copper sauté pan with a fairly tight-fitting lid, just large enough to hold the pieces of chicken without stacking. First rub chicken pieces with cut side of lemon halves, then dab on salt, pepper, and MSG and hold. Place sauté pan over medium-high frying heat and add the 4 tablespoons of butter and 2 tablespoons of the olive oil. Do not let the butter brown. Then put in chicken pieces and brown quickly on all sides. When they are a golden-brown color, turn down heat, season with a little more salt, pepper, and MSG to taste, then cover and simmer for about 15 minutes.

Meanwhile prepare the garlic according to a special technique. Separate the 24 cloves and from each remove only the dry outer skin, leaving the shiny inner skin completely intact. Ruthlessly discard any clove in which this inner skin is cracked or broken. The cloves will go into the dish whole and will be cooked in their skins, but none of the inside flesh must be released. This is absolutely vital to the delicate flavor of this dish.

When chicken has simmered 15 minutes, carefully put in the garlic cloves, distributing them around, making sure that each goes down to the bottom of the pan and is well coated with butter and oil. If necessary for this purpose, sprinkle on 1 more tablespoon of oil. Re-cover and simmer 20 minutes longer. Meanwhile finely chop enough of the parsley to give each person about 2 tablespoons; this is sprinkled over the chicken when it is served. Each diner also gets as many whole cloves of garlic as he wishes. They have now been cooked to a soft mush, which can be squeezed out on the plate by pressing down on the clove with the fork. Garlic lovers spread this soft purée over the chicken or mix it with any accompanying vegetables. Diners who imagine that they hate garlic will have none of it on their plates, but even they will admit that there is a certain mysterious charm about the flavor of the chicken.

AS THE YEAR BEGINS—THOUGHTS ON WINE

AFTER the Christmas and New Year holidays, our small "cellar-in-a-closet," which is discussed more fully on page 498, is usually depleted and as we plan its replenishment we often reassess our family's pleasure in the intelligent use of wine. To us, it is as serious and satisfying a hobby as, for example, collecting stamps or antique china, demanding a certain minimum dedication and the disciplined practice of a few basic rules. Our first is to find and drink the wines we enjoy, regardless of the purists who are forever telling us what we ought to enjoy. A single glass of an honest small wine can frame and enhance the simplest of family meals. Even when our girls were quite young, we let them feel that they were sharing the pleasure by coloring their drinking water with a few drops of red wine. Later, they discovered that the choosing and buying of wine is a fascinating game. It is not a mysterious ritual, involving years of initiation; neither is it as simple as recognizing a trademark on a label. Wine is not the synthesized product of an automated factory, but a delicate growth in nature, subject to the vagaries of sun, rain, and wind. It is this very uncertainty, this eternal search for a perfection that is never fully achieved, which adds the excitement to the wine game.

Rules for Choosing Wines

The range of wines is so enormous that a hundred different people might each choose a different wine for the same meal on the same occasion and each wine would be appropriate. What exactly do we mean by "appropriate"? First, the wine must complement the food, being neither so dominant that it will overpower a delicate dish nor so light that it will itself be overpowered by the dominant aromatics of the food. Second, the wine must be appropriate to the importance of the occasion—Champagne for a birthday, a great wine to honor the return of a long-absent friend. Third, it must be appropriate to the guests, in terms of their knowledge and appreciation of wine. A. J. Liebling, who was as great a gourmet as he was a journalist, once said that he hated to give an unexpected dinner guest a wine that was far too good for him because there happened to be nothing in the cellar between the superlative and the insulting. We keep this dilemma in mind when buying our wines. We try to maintain a balanced supply of "the great," "the fine," and "the everyday."

The truly great and rare wines, naturally, command rare prices and are reserved for rare occasions. It is the simple everyday wine that is the foundation of the family cellar, the wine priced low enough to be bought regularly, to be opened for the simplest family lunch and kept recorked without shame for supper.

Playing the Vintage Game

Although it is true that a wine with a date on the bottle will almost certainly be better than an undated wine, there is much too much stress on vintage years. It has been said that there are no bad years, only bad wines. It is true of course that a vintage year can be good or bad in relation to a single individual vineyard. It cannot be true to say it of a whole area or a whole country. Sudden ice storms can completely destroy the vines over thousands of acres. Yet there are always some vineyards that miraculously escape. One owner has a subconscious premonition of danger and decides to harvest his grapes a few days earlier than usual. His neighbor, half a mile down the road, decides to wait a few days longer and is caught.

The lesson is twofold. First, there are many poor wines produced in good years and it is a serious mistake to buy blindly by vintage year alone. Second and even more important, in bad vintage years there are many good wines to be found at bargain prices. See the directory of table wines at the back of the book for specific suggestions.

Neither Too Cold Nor Too Warm

Many wine drinkers know that white and *rosé* wines should be served cold, and red wines at room temperature, but few seem to realize that the whole character of a wine can be changed by being served either too cold or too warm. Pour two glasses of a light, dry white wine (say from the Moselle Valley of Germany), put one in the refrigerator and the other in the freezer for about half an hour, then taste them side by side. The lovely, fruity flavor and bouquet of the cool wine is entirely absent in the ice-cold wine. To avoid overcooling our bottles, we follow these rules with the almost-too-efficient modern refrigerator:

1. Place bottles of dry white and *rosé* wines on the floor of the refrigerator (NEVER in the freezer), not more than 2 hours before serving.

2. Put in slightly sweet wines about 3 hours before serving.

3. Put in very sweet and luscious dessert wines about 4 hours before serving.

"Room temperature" for a red wine definitely does not mean the 90-degree level of a New York heat wave. We serve our red wines at about 65 degrees and have no hesitation in placing them in the refrigerator for a few minutes, if necessary, to bring them down to that temperature. The common practice of pulling the cork from a bottle of red wine about an hour before serving, and letting the wine "breathe," involves certain dangers as well as advantages. A young and light red wine may mellow in flavor and strengthen in bouquet, while an old wine may lose both character and color. In general, the finer and older a wine the less it should be exposed to the air.

The Right Number of Bottles and the Right Glasses

A general rule is that the host should provide one third of a bottle of each wine for each guest. Thus for a formal dinner party for six there might be two bottles with the opening courses and two bottles with the main course. However, we generally prefer to break this rule and provide only one bottle each of several different wines. The variety heightens the interest and each wine will taste better for the contrast and comparison. As to the order, we serve the gentle wine first, the dominant later.

The proper glass is the last element in the simple routine of enjoying wine. Drink it from a clear and plain glass with rounded sides curving inward. If the glass is colored, the color of the wine is lost. If the glass does not curve, as in a tulip, the bouquet cannot collect at the top. Allow room for the bouquet by filling the glass no more than one third to one half full.

Which Wine with Which Food?

Red wine with red meat, white wine with white chicken, *rosé* wine when in doubt. . . . What a ridiculous system it is to try to match food and wine by color! If the wine is to complement the dish, the flavors must not clash, nor must one be so much stronger as to override the other. If the flavors and characters match, the colors are of no importance. There is a fine regional dish of Burgundy in which rich white river fish are cooked in red wine (see *meurette,* page 597). There are many strong and aggressive white wines that can hold their own with the darkest of red meats.

Some foods are too strong for any wine. We never serve wine with an Indian curry, or an oil-and-vinegar-dressed salad. Some old and very great wines are so dominant in character that any food will be secondary.

Our simplest family rule of thumb is to drink the powerful wines with the strong foods, the gentle wines with the delicate foods, the more expensive wines with the richer party dishes, and the inexpensive everyday wines with the day-to-day meals.

Drinks Before the Meal—Sherries, Madeiras, and Other Aperitifs

One evening at a dinner party in a Chicago "Gold Coast" apartment, we were shocked by the strength of the pre-prandial martinis. We felt our taste buds being anesthetized and knew that neither we nor any other guest would be able to savor the dinner. We mentioned the point to our partner, who said: "Bill gets so tense during a day at the office that he just has to get a slug of alcohol inside him to uncoil his nerves, and he thinks everyone else needs it too." We have never been able to agree that the function of the drink before dinner is medicinal and sedative. It should titillate the taste buds and sharpen the appetite and this means something light and dry.

We think that a dry Sherry is about the best of all before-dinner drinks. The word "Sherry" is a British distortion of the name of a town in southern Spain, Jerez, where the only true Sherry has been blended for hundreds of years. There is no legal copyright on the name, so anyone in any part of the world can make any kind of liquid of any degree of sweetness or strength, or any color, and, provided it is not actually poisonous, may sell it as "sherry." Some of these may be very pleasant drinks, but they have none of the qualities of true Spanish Sherries. Among the Spanish names of these magnificent wines are two in which we find exceptional qualities and values. One is the slightly salty MANZANILLA (the Spanish word for crab apple, perhaps because of a distant tartness in the wine) produced along the seacoast. The other is the extraordinary MONTILLA, a wine so unusual that it does not choose to call itself Sherry, considering itself the original source of all Spanish Sherries. Our own list of the Montillas and Sherries that we have consistently enjoyed is on pages 676–8.

We think it a pity that the aperitif wines of the island of Madeira have fallen out of popular favor. The two dry types, which are excellent before-dinner drinks, are labeled *sercial* (the name of the grape from which the wine was made) and *rainwater* (made from grapes grown on a part of the island where there is no artificial irrigation and the grapes must rely on falling rain). There are also some sweet Madeiras, known by their grapes as *boal* or *malmsey,* but these are best served after dinner. Our list of favorite Madeiras is on page 678.

There is one mixed drink that we serve regularly because we think it meets the requirements of being a good appetizer without being too sweet or too strong: the French "vermouth cassis." This is served over ice. Sherry or Madeira are served slightly chilled.

BASIC METHOD FOR VERMOUTH CASSIS

For 1 person

The unique French fruit syrup Crème de Cassis is made from sweet black currants and is usually fortified with about 16 per cent alcohol. The best quality comes from the city of Dijon.

Check Staples:
Soda water

Shopping List:
French dry vermouth (4 oz.)
Crème de Cassis (1 oz.)

Fill an 8- to 10- ounce tumbler with ice cubes. Pour on the 1 ounce of Cassis, then the 4 ounces of dry vermouth, finally fill up with the soda, and stir vigorously for a few seconds. The amount of the Cassis may be varied to taste, bearing in mind that it is very sweet. For the children too young for alcohol, eliminate the vermouth.

The Great, Dominant Red Wines for the Great Party Dishes

All experts agree that the greatest red wines in the world come from the two most famous French wine areas of Bordeaux and Burgundy. Violent controversy begins at once in any comparison between them. Yet they *can* be compared, for each area produces in its best wines a definite and recognizable unity of character and personality. The great Bordeaux reds, always found in the same, rather prim, straight-sided shape of bottle (see illustration), are gay in color and light on the tongue. Their alcoholic strength, which is often substantial, is always masked by a beautiful balance of flavors. The pleasures they offer are subtle and feminine. They are the most magnificent of party wines. The great red Burgundies, always in a sensuously curving bottle, with not a single straight line about it (see illustration), are dark, powerful, and heavy on the tongue. A good part of the pleasure they offer comes from a marvelous and illusive bouquet, or aroma, which is rich and mellow. They have a solid and masculine flavor, a feel of smooth velvet. A French friend once said that Bordeaux reds reminded him of the qualities of a perfect wife, while Burgundy was the irresistible mistress. A more conservative Englishman said that Bordeaux reminded him of his daughters and Burgundy of his sons. Our own preference inclines toward Bordeaux, but our loyalty is easily swayed!

Bordeaux is the richest wine-producing area of the world. It has more than 4,000 named vineyards, but only a handful produce the great wines. To find them in Bordeaux is simply a matter of knowing their names (pages

678–9). Naturally, they vary from year to year, they improve with age—they are always wines for special occasions and special guests.

Something called "Burgundy wine" now comes from places as far apart as Australia and California, sold by vintners who claim that the name can be applied to any dark-red wine. These may be honest and sound wines, but they have none of the finer qualities of the true Burgundies of France. Finding these great wines is a little more complicated in Burgundy than in Bordeaux, because of some dexterous name-juggling by the always-adroit Burgundians. Each of the wine villages, which includes within its borders one of the world-famous vineyards, has hyphenated its own name with that of the great vineyard. Thus, the village of Gevrey, which includes the great "Chambertin" Vineyard, now calls itself Gevrey-Chambertin. This means that even the least distinguished vineyard of Gevrey can now use the magic Chambertin name on its label. If we want a great Chambertin, we must read the label carefully enough to make sure that the wine was actually produced and bottled in the one Chambertin vineyard and not in just a Gevrey-Chambertin vineyard. The same considerations apply to the other principal villages, where, in each case, if we want a great wine, we make sure that it comes from the famous vineyard that is the second half of each name. For our list of the great Burgundies that we have most consistently enjoyed, see pages 679–80.

The Middle Range of Fine Red Wines for the Simpler Menus

Alongside their great wines, Bordeaux and Burgundy also meet the enormous and worldwide demand for fine wines of lesser quality and price. This huge middle range stretches all the way from a vineyard that is only a shade below the "greats" (for example Château Palmer in Bordeaux) to a fine "community" or "district" wine named, not for a single vineyard but for the village, town, or legally delimited district, where it is blended from the grapes of many small vineyards by a famous wholesale shipper who guards his reputation as jealously as he guards the secrets of his cellars. To the intelligent buyer looking for the finest possible wine at a reasonable price, the name of one of the proud French shippers, or *négociant,* is often the most important information on the label. Between the two extremes of the middle range are hundreds of lesser-known vineyards, and among these it is always true that when one moves from the well-advertised names to the comparatively obscure, the price of the wine falls much more rapidly than the quality. Our list of those names that we have found consistently reliable is on pages 680–1.

Fine red wines are also produced in other parts of France, notably along the valley of the river Rhône north of the historic papal city of Avignon. Many Rhône wines have an attractive spiciness, derived mostly from the Syrah grape from which they are made. They are solid wines to go with the solid winter foods. They should be drunk as old as they can be found. We think that the best wines are not those of the famous "Châteauneuf-du-Pape" (The New Castle of the Pope), although they are usually safe and often splendid, but those wines that come from the mountain slope so consistently bathed by the hot southern sunshine that it is called "Côte-Rôtie" (Roasted Slope). The third group of Rhône wines are named for the spectacular single hill, its rocky terraced slope covered with vines, called "L'Hermitage." Its wines often have a delightful honeyed scent. Finally, at much more economical prices, there are the blended district wines of the area, called not by any single vineyard but by the general name "Côtes-du-Rhône," and these are safest when they also include the name of a trusted wholesale shipper. Our favorite names of Rhône wines are on pages 681–2.

Among the fine red wines of Italy, there are two contenders in the middle range, both dependable because their quality is protected by law. The better of them, we think, is not the world-famous Chianti from Tuscany, but the deeply colored Barolo, made from the *nebbiolo* grapes grown high above the shores of Lake Garda in northern Piedmont. The greatest Chiantis, which can be very fine, come not in the wicker-covered flask, but in straight-sided Bordeaux-type bottles (see illustration on page 207). Our favorite Italian wine names are on page 682.

The Everyday Red Wines and the American Wine Revolution

As wages rise all over Europe and more and more families can afford to drink wine every day, instead of just on Sundays, less and less of the low-priced, good-value wines are available for export to the United States. The great wines and the fine wines continue to arrive at great and fine prices, but the simple and sound European wines are more and more being replaced on the American market by overpriced, inferior wines, done up in fancy bottles with showy labels. Fortunately, the change in Europe has been matched by a revolution in the quality of American wines, so that we can now look to our own country for many excellent everyday types.

The first American growers, almost all Europeans, thought they could best sell their wines by giving them European names. A dry white wine was called a "Chablis," a dark red became a "Burgundy," a sweet wine a "sauterne," and any fortified white wine a "sherry," any fortified red a "port" . . . The growers disregarded the fact that all these names are specific geographic locations in Europe, associated for centuries with a particular character of wine, a character which never has and never will be reproduced thousands of miles away under entirely different conditions of soil and weather. Nevertheless these pioneers built a huge American wine industry, which today produces almost 200 million gallons a year of extremely undistinguished blended wine, mass-produced in automated factories. However, the sons and grandsons of some of the early pioneers, a new generation of young men highly trained as wine-farmer-chemists, have developed the idealism and the determination to try to produce at least a small quantity of fine wines, unblended and estate-bottled in the great European tradition. They have adopted an altogether more accurate and satisfactory way of labeling their wines: by the names of the grapes from which the wine is made. Thus, the light reds are called "Cabernet Sauvignon," the name of the noble grape transplanted from Bordeaux. The dark reds are "Pinot Noir," the magnificent grape of the great French Burgundies. These are the so-called "varietal labels" and their use on an American wine, together with its vintage year, is, in our view, a primary mark of quality.

The best of these vineyards are, without question, in northern California. They may be divided into two groups. First, the very small vineyards, producing the finest of all the wines but in such small quantities that very few bottles ever leave California. The wines are so good and there is such a demand for them that they are entirely consumed, first by the friends and associates of the vineyard owner, then by a few favored wine merchants in the San Francisco area. In general, these small vineyards are run at a loss, financed by wealthy wine connoisseurs, who make it their hobby to try to produce wines as fine as their European equivalents. The second group of vineyards is made up of those large enough to achieve a reasonable distribution throughout the United States, but still not large enough for any sort of mass-production. Each, of course, produces several different types of wine and often several grades within each type. A list of those labels that we have most enjoyed is on page 683.

Although the European imports of good-value, everyday wines have been substantially reduced in recent years, one is bound to add that American wines do still face stiff competition, both as to quality and price, from a few European wines of established reputation and with large enough production to meet both the European and the United States demand. First, among these, we place the light red wines of the high mountain district of Rioja in northern Spain. Some of these wines are aged for more than fifteen years and have an extraordinary elegance of taste and velvety smoothness. Italy produces at least two charming light red wines, often of excellent everyday quality (see pages 683–4). Finally, there is the wine of which one might say that the world has virtually loved it to death—the inevitable warning siren must be sounded about Beaujolais. It has been reckoned that the number of bottles of Beaujolais sold in Paris alone is double the total production of all genuine Beaujolais. You have been warned! Yet, by following certain rules we think it is possible to find truth in a Beaujolais. Our favorite names in all these wines are on page 684.

THE
Spring

March, April, May, and June

EXPLANATION OF SYMBOLS

A symbol appearing after a word refers the reader to a particular section of the book for further details. Example: olive oil, crystal salt, cocotte, dry white wine, Parmesan cheese, Beaujolais, turtle meat.

- stands for Raw Materials and Staples, pages 10–18
- stands for Aromatics, pages 18–29
- stands for Kitchen Equipment, pages 32–41
- stands for Wine in the Kitchen, pages 41–5
- stands for Cheeses, pages 660–75
- stands for Wines for the Table, pages 676–98
- stands for Marketing and Mail-Order Sources, pages 699–714

SPRING FOODS IN SEASON

THE FIRST gastronomic climax of the year brings foods so fresh and young that sauces and spices must be muted. This is the season for cooking lightly and simply, to make the most of the natural flavors. We welcome back beloved delicacies, concentrating on each as it arrives and preparing it in all our favorite versions. Here is a checklist of what we consider to be the best of the spring foods. Obviously it cannot include everything grown in every county of the United States, but we have found it accurate over many years of our own spring shopping on the East, West, and Gulf coasts and in Chicago and other Midwestern cities.

The Special Pleasures of the Season

IT IS the time for SPRING LAMB, but the authentic cuts are often hard to find (page 222). The peak season for baby SPRING PORK also comes in March and April (page 223).

April starts the new season for LONG ISLAND DUCKLING (page 225).

May is often the best time of the whole year for the magnificent new season's Atlantic NOVA SCOTIA and Pacific KING CHINOOK and SILVER COHO SALMON. The biggest and fattest fish are the first to head for the rivers and the run up to the spawning grounds. They are at their finest when caught as they come in from the ocean depths. We relish the Nova Scotia for its subtle flavor, the king for its dramatic size and deep red color, and the silver for its firm and flaky texture. The first fish are luxury foods, but supplies increase rapidly from week to week. In New York spring is always confirmed when the SHAD begins to run up the Hudson River. Our gastronomic joy is not dimmed by knowing that we come late in the shad's six-month-long progress up the East and West coasts (see shopping notes, page 225; recipes begin on page 292).

The spring is also an especially good time for shellfish. In May begins the new season for Atlantic and Gulf LIVE CRAB and the Pacific DUNGENESS CRAB, the peak of Maine and Canadian LIVE LOBSTER, and the new season for Atlantic and Gulf SOFT-SHELL CRAB (page 294). Also, March usually brings the new season for the Louisiana BAYOU CRAWFISH, with peak supplies available through April and continuing through May and into June. They can be ordered direct from Louisiana✻ and we "suffocate" them in an aromatic Creole sauce (page 299). Their main season in the North (where they are called CRAYFISH) comes in summer (page 370).

During March, April, and part of May, we continue to delight in many types of APPLE, which are the only available local fresh fruit until the first new spring arrivals. For a simple dessert we eat chunks of raw apple with the spring cheeses (page 322) and freshly shelled nuts; the best eating apples of the season are Western YELLOW NEWTOWN PIPPIN and the Eastern and Northwestern GOLDEN and RED DELICIOUS. For fried apple rings, such an excellent garnish for the spring meats (page 129), we use the Eastern BEN DAVIS and Northwestern WINESAP. For baking apples with a firm texture to hold their shape in the oven (page 615), our first choice remains the Eastern and Western ROME BEAUTY. For general stewing, applesauce, and pies, our choices are the New York and Michigan GREENING or the Pennsylvania and Virginia YORK IMPERIAL. Toward the end of May, when the soft berries begin to come in, we deliberately drop apples from our menus, skipping the summer varieties until the new crop arrives in October.

In May and June it is the season for the soft berries: BLACKBERRIES; BLUEBERRIES, which we burst in our Sunday pancakes (page 327); CURRANTS, the BLACK mainly for cordials, jams, and jellies, the RED, tart, but good for the spring version of our *rote Grütze* (page 621), the WHITE, sweet for eating raw; GOOSEBERRIES; HUCKLEBERRIES; LOGANBERRIES; RASPBERRIES; and STRAWBERRIES, which we garnish in four favorite ways, according to their ripeness and quality (page 323); also imported French wild baby strawberries, FRAISES DES BOIS, flown across as available. May and June is the season for CHERRIES: the early SOUR MORELLO for cooking (page 326) and the Western and imported Argentine SWEET BING.

The other harbinger of spring is ASPARAGUS, which we garnish and sauce according to its age (page 304). And in June, the time for the sweetest of local GREEN PEAS-IN-THE-POD, to be steamed on lettuce leaves (page 313).

In May, we welcome the MAY WINE and prepare the *Maibowle* (page 331).

In April when the days are warm but the nights still cold, in Vermont, New York, and Canada, the MAPLE SAP is running and we replenish our storage supplies (page 227).

The Freshwater Fish of the Spring Season

These fish have lean flesh and generally respond to similar cooking methods:

River BUFFALO FISH
Great Lakes and river CARP
LAKE HERRING from the Great Lakes, continuing through early part of season as long as cold weather lasts
Great Lakes and river MULLET
Great Lakes and river YELLOW PERCH
Great Lakes PICKEREL
Great Lakes BLUE PIKE, mainly around Chicago
Great Lakes YELLOW PIKE
Great Lakes SAUGER, mainly around Chicago, at end of season
Great Lakes and river SHEEPSHEAD
Lakes Erie and Ontario LAKE SMELTS, in early part of season, in large sizes at this time, often 6 ounces each

These fish have oily flesh and are generally interchangeable in recipes:

Great Lakes CHUB, end of season
River BROOK TROUT, start of season, which we poach in Alsatian Riesling (page 295)
Great Lakes LAKE TROUT
Great Lakes WHITEFISH

The Saltwater Fish of the Spring Season

These are the lean-fleshed fish:

Atlantic SEA BASS
Atlantic STRIPED BASS, early in season only
Pacific WHITE BASS, mainly on the West Coast
Atlantic BLOWFISH, or SEA SQUAB, sometimes sold cut and skinned as CHICKEN-OF-THE-SEA

Atlantic and Gulf BLUEFISH
Atlantic and Pacific COD, both the smaller MARKET type for cooking whole and the larger STEAK COD
Atlantic CROAKER, which some foolish people are trying to rename STRAWBERRY BASS
The members of the FLOUNDER family, always best prepared whole with the bone in (page 138):
- Atlantic BLACKBACK; early in the season it may be from frozen storage
- New England and Pacific SAND DAB
- Atlantic FLUKE
- New England GRAY SOLE
- New England LEMON SOLE
- Pacific REX SOLE
- Atlantic YELLOWTAIL, or RUSTY DAB

Gulf GROUPER, mainly in the South
New England HADDOCK
Atlantic RED HAKE
Atlantic WHITE HAKE, toward the end of season
East and West coast HALIBUT, the giant of the flatfish family, first from Florida, then moving up off New England and Nova Scotia, and in the Pacific
Gulf MULLET, mainly in the South
New England OCEAN PERCH, mainly in the Northeast
New England POLLOCK
Atlantic PORGY, peak season through spring and summer
Imported West Indian SWORDFISH, some from frozen storage
Atlantic TILEFISH, peak spring season
Atlantic WEAKFISH
East and West Coast WHITEBAIT, when available (page 296)
Atlantic KING WHITING

These are the fish with oily flesh:

Atlantic BUTTERFISH
Atlantic EEL, superb when imaginatively prepared (page 242)
Atlantic HERRING
The new season for MACKEREL
- Atlantic BOSTON MACKEREL; early in season it may be from frozen storage
- Giant Florida KING MACKEREL
- Florida SPANISH MACKEREL, late in season

Gulf POMPANO, a magnificent fish, but too often sold frozen (page 297)
Pacific ROCKFISH, West Coast cousin of the Eastern STRIPED BASS
Canadian SEA SMELT
The first BLUEFIN TUNA, late in season (page 268)

The Shellfish of the Spring Season

All have lean flesh:

Pacific ABALONE, a rare delicacy, eaten fresh only in Northern California, shipped elsewhere canned
The varieties of the CLAM family:
- Atlantic CHERRYSTONE, for eating raw on the half shell
- Atlantic HARD CHOWDER, which New Englanders call QUAHOG
- Pacific GEODUCK, mainly around Seattle
- Atlantic LITTLE NECK, also eaten raw on the half shell
- Pacific PISMO CLAM, Pacific RAZOR CLAM } both mainly around Seattle
- Atlantic SOFT STEAMER

Imported South African and West Indian frozen ROCK LOBSTER TAILS
Atlantic MUSSELS (page 339)
Through March and April, the last of the official Atlantic, Pacific, and Gulf OYSTERS (page 371)
Atlantic DEEP-SEA SCALLOPS
The end of the Atlantic and Gulf SHRIMP season; still good fresh supplies during March and April, then increasingly from frozen storage (page 454)
Atlantic and Pacific SQUID, excellent when carefully prepared (page 496)

The Fruits of the Spring Season

We look for best values in:

By mid-season, usually early in May, the first California APRICOTS
Puerto Rican COCONUT

California fresh BLACK MISSION FIG, toward end of season

Spring varieties of GRAPE, excellent at this season with many of the soft cheeses—Brie, Camembert, Liederkranz:

- Imported South African ALPHONSE LAVALLE
- Imported South African BALINKA
- California CARDINAL, with a slight muscat flavor
- California DELIGHT, seedless
- The last of the California EMPEROR
- Puerto Rican and imported Argentine, Chilean, Mexican, and West Indian OLIVET SEEDLESS
- California PERLETTE, also seedless with a slight muscat flavor
- The first of the California THOMPSON SEEDLESS
- Imported South African WALTHAM CROSS

Florida GRAPEFRUIT

California LEMONS

Florida LIMES

Imported Haitian MANGOES

The spring varieties of MELON:

- California, Florida, Texas, and imported Mexican CANTALOUPE
- California CRANSHAW MELON
- Texas HONEYBALL MELON
- Arizona, California, and imported HONEYDEW MELON
- Florida CHARLESTON GRAY WATERMELON, also general watermelon imports from Mexico and the West Indies

California and imported Chilean NECTARINES

Spring varieties of ORANGE

- Imported Israel, JAFFA, large, seedless, short season
- California KING, loose-skinned tangerine type
- California NAVEL, thick-skinned, seedless, end of season
- Florida PINEAPPLE JUICE
- California and Florida TEMPLE, loose-skinned
- Start of the California and continuing of the Florida VALENCIA

Hawaiian PAPAYA, toward the end of the season

The first of the Arizona and New Mexico PRICKLY PEARS

Hawaiian, Puerto Rican, and imported PINEAPPLE

The early spring PLUMS, which we eat with the soft cheeses—Brie, Camembert, Reblochon:

- Imported Argentine and Chilean SANTA ROSA PLUMS
- The first TEXAS BEAUTY PLUMS

Spring RHUBARB, which makes an outstanding sherbet (page 322):

- Early in the season, Michigan and Washington HOT-HOUSE RHUBARB
- Then the mounting supplies, from all over, of FIELD RHUBARB

The last of the Florida TANGERINES

Imported Jamaican UGLIS (page 64)

The Salads of the Spring Season

On these crisp and delicate greens with the shy flavors, we use our lightest salad dressings.

We begin to look for the unusual Italian ARUGULA, the leaf with the extraordinary flavor (page 227)
The end of the Florida and the start of the California AVOCADO
When other greens are expensive, as often at this season, we use the small center leaves of CELERY, or CHINESE, CABBAGE; or we finely shred the RED CABBAGE or the SAVOY CABBAGE
For crispness, diced local WHITE CELERY
California and Florida CHICORY
Local CUCUMBERS, and toward the end of the season BABY PICKLING CUCUMBERS, a rare salad delicacy
The end of the season for the imported Belgian ENDIVE
California and Florida ESCAROLE
Spring varieties of LETTUCE, from greenhouses and often expensive at the start of the season:
- Florida, Indiana, and New Jersey BIBB, or BIBB LIMESTONE
- Connecticut, Delaware, Long Island, and New Jersey BOSTON, or HEAD, type, start of season
- ICEBERG, start of season all over the country
- Connecticut, Long Island, and New Jersey ROMAINE, start of season

Spring salad varieties of the ONION family:
- The delicate new sproutings of CHIVE
- California, Louisiana, Texas, and imported Mexican GARLIC
- Domestic and imported Italian SWEET RED ONION
- Local GREEN SCALLION

Florida GREEN PEPPERS, new crop
Local RADISHES, the young spring bunches; the leaves also go into our salads
We list TOMATOES among the vegetables, as we think they tend to over-soften a mixed salad. We prefer them on their own, either raw (page 321) or cooked (page 605)
And, as always, WATERCRESS, the perfect accompaniment to shad roe

Wild Spring Salads to Gather in the Fields

Early in April, when the spring weather settles in, we sometimes take a country walk to gather a few of the young wild plants for fresh and unusual salads. We carry two light tools in our knapsack: a small aluminum weeder and an asparagus knife, since the roots are often the best parts of the plants. One should also include a moisture-proof shoulder bag in which to bring back the spoils; we use a plastic airline bag.

A few ideas from what could be a long list:

1. WILD CHICORY is about two feet high in the spring. The leaves are dark green, slightly saw-toothed, with a purple midrib. It has large bright blue flowers. Only the very youngest leaves are worth eating, but they are superb. Dig up the whole plant with at least the top part of the root; just above it is a crown of white underground leaves. This is the part to be kept.

2. DANDELIONS are found in fields among the tall grass—a tangle of slightly red leaves. Again we dig up the whole plant, and the edible treasure is the crown of young white leaves. We cut off and throw away the tops. The flavor is brought out by soaking the crowns in cold salted water for about an hour.

3. DAY LILIES are bright orange flowers that grow along the banks of many country lanes. Since each blossom lasts only one day, the withered flower of the day before is usually hanging from the new bloom. The young sprouting stalks are the edible part, cut off just above the root with the large leaves discarded.

4. WILD GARLIC is found in rich, moist meadows. The green leafstalks grow about ten inches high and are tubular like the scallion. Its flavor is more onion than garlic, but wilder, lighter, and gayer.

5. NASTURTIUM flowers make a bright garnish and the young leaves give zip to a salad.

6. PURSLANE grows flat along sandy ground, the stems radiating twelve to eighteen inches from a central root. It has tiny yellow flowers. For our

salads, we pinch off the leafy tips, which have an interesting, slightly sharp flavor.

7. WILD WATERCRESS is abundant along the shallow banks of almost every country stream. We cut the leaves at the surface of the water; the underwater stems are tough. Wild watercress combines wonderfully in the salad bowl with day lilies and wild garlic.

The Vegetables of the Spring Season

We make our sauces and garnishes as light and delicate as these new growths:

California ARTICHOKES, usually during March and April
Local FAVA BEANS (page 602)
From the South spreading northward, the season for GREEN BEANS, excellent prepared with rosemary (page 308)
The first Maryland and North Carolina LIMA BEANS
First from New Jersey hothouses, then the general season for BEETS
The last of the Western and the first Eastern BROCCOLI, superb prepared as an iced cream soup (page 275)
The end of California and Texas BRUSSELS SPROUTS
Spring members of the CABBAGE family:
- California, Florida, North and South Carolina, and Texas GREEN CABBAGE
- New Jersey, South Carolina, and Virginia RED CABBAGE
- Florida, New Jersey, New York, and Virginia SAVOY CABBAGE

New Western CARROTS, delicious teamed with maple syrup (page 311)
Eastern and Western CAULIFLOWER
The peak of Florida and the start of California CORN, outstanding baked in butter (page 311)
Florida and imported West Indian EGGPLANT
California FENNEL, through March and April
New Jersey and Texas KOHLRABI
New York, Pennsylvania, and Western MUSHROOMS
Florida, Georgia, and imported West Indian OKRA, superb served tipped with hollandaise sauce (page 464)
The spring aromatics of the ONION family:
- Idaho large BERMUDA ONION
- Louisiana SHALLOTS

From many states, the WHITE BOILER, excellent with Sicilian sweet-sour sauce (page 312)
And the workhorse of the family, the YELLOW ONION
Virginia OYSTER PLANT, early in the season (page 467)
Spring varieties of POTATO:
Idaho and Ohio large RUSSET BAKER
California LONG WHITE BOILER
Florida NEW RED BOILER
Florida NEW WHITE ROUND BOILER
Maine SEBAGO
The last of the New Jersey SWEET POTATO
The slightly lemon-flavored WILD SORREL, or SOURGRASS, which the French call *oseille* and prepare in several excellent ways (page 468)
The local peak season almost everywhere for new young SPINACH; we cook it by the classic method of Brillat-Savarin (page 533)
Spring varieties of SQUASH:
The first New Jersey ACORN, superb baked whole with maple butter (page 155)
New York BUTTERNUT
The last of the HUBBARD
And the small ZUCCHINI and other summer SOFT SQUASHES
The first New Jersey SWISS CHARD
The best time of year for TOMATOES:
In March, the end of the Florida season, plus imported Mexican and West Indian varieties
In April and May, the start of the Texas and Southern season
In June, at their best locally all over the country
New spring WHITE TURNIP, the tops also, an excellent green vegetable

The Abundant Shopping of Spring

Search for Variety and Value in Lamb

This is the time of year for "genuine spring lamb," but it is not always immediately available. We press our butcher to put in a special order if necessary, and we have learned to differentiate between the three types of lamb:

1. MILK-FED BABY LAMB is a tiny animal not yet weaned, seldom more than 5 to 6 weeks old. It usually appears in time for Easter holiday buying and is often small enough to be roasted whole. We think the meat is too young to have developed flavor and that it is generally overpriced.

2. "GENUINE SPRING LAMB" (so stamped by the U. S. Department of Agriculture) is a larger animal, but not more than 5 to 6 months old. The

butchered leg of such an animal should weigh from 5 to 7 pounds and we consider this to be one of the delicacies of the year (page 276).

3. ALL-YEAR-ROUND LAMB is what the butchers now sell, even in midwinter, as "spring lamb." This animal can be up to 12 months old and is the modern version of what was once simply called "lamb." At this age the butchered leg weighs from 7 to 10 pounds and makes fine eating at any time of the year.

When buying lamb we use the following table to help us compare the relative values of the various cuts. The left-hand column lists the lamb cuts. The middle column shows how to convert the price per pound into the cost of an average serving. (For example: if a leg of spring lamb is 68 cents per pound, we divide by 2 and the cost of an average serving is 34 cents).

When the best-value cut has been decided upon, the right-hand column shows the approximate amount of that cut to buy for each person to be served. For example: in the case of the leg, for a dinner party of 10 people, we need ½ pound per person, or a total of 5 pounds.

LAMB

When buying this cut:	To find approximate cost per serving, divide price per pound by:	And buy this amount per person:
Leg	2	½ lb.
Loin	1⅓	¾ lb.
Shoulder	1⅓	¾ lb.
Ribs	1⅓	¾ lb.
Breast	Cost per pound is price per serving	1 lb.

And the Same for Pork

The above rules for lamb apply also to "spring pork," usually available from April to June. Again, many butchers do not carry the different varieties, so it is essential to know what to put on special order:

1. SUCKLING PIG is the baby, "the young and tender suckling—under a month old" of Charles Lamb, often featured by fancy butchers for Easter dining. It can weigh as little as 15 to 25 pounds.

2. TRUE SPRING PORK is the young porker let out of the barn for the first time since its midwinter birth. It is roughly half the size of the fully grown pig and we consider it a spring delicacy (page 279).

3. ALL-YEAR-ROUND PORK comes from an animal weighing around 350

pounds, and every butcher's cut is about twice the size of the equivalent from the spring carcass.

When buying pork we use the following special table to help us compare the relative values of the cuts. For the background how and why of these

PORK

When buying this cut:	To find approximate cost per serving, divide price per pound by:	And buy this amount per person:
BOSTON SHOULDER BUTT:		
Boned and rolled	4	1/4 lb.
With bone	3	1/3 lb.
HAM, fresh or smoked	2	1/2 lb.
LOIN	2	1/2 lb.
CHOPS	2	1/2 lb.
PICNIC or CALA SHOULDER	1 1/2	2/3 lb.
SPARERIBS	1 1/3	3/4 lb.

tables see page 58; for practical instructions as to how to use this table see the preceding lamb table.

Caviar at Easter

New Year's Eve may be the big night for caviar, but our family tradition is to have it as the supreme luxury prologue to Easter dinner (page 247). What started us was the story of Feodor Chaliapin in Paris (when the city was filled with Russian exiles from the Revolution) leading the men's choir in the Russian Orthodox Church on Easter Sunday and then adjourning to his favorite bistro to lunch on a small mountain of pressed caviar and a jug of vodka. We agree with the great singer that the solidly packed pressed caviar, at about half the price of the whole grain, has the best flavor. When buying caviar it is important to know the meaning of the words used by both the Russian and the Iranian industries: BELUGA is the most expensive type with the largest eggs from sturgeons weighing as much as a ton; OSIETRA has smaller eggs from smaller fish; SEVRUGA has the smallest eggs. After these three grades have been separated, there remains a solid mass of slightly crushed eggs stuck together, and these are called by the Russian name, PAYUSNAYA, pressed caviar. The pressure seems to seal in the flavor. The word MALOSSOL added to any of the above names means "less salt," but has little significance, since U. S. law requires minimum salting of all caviar.

Ducks from Long Island

Almost a hundred years ago a farsighted sea captain brought to Long Island from China a pair of white Pekin ducks, and they have multiplied into millions, making the Long Island name as famous in the duck world as the British Aylesbury or the French Rouen. The season for fresh Long Island duck is from April 1 to November 15 and it is available freshly killed in Eastern cities and areas within a reasonable distance of Long Island. Frozen birds are of course available all over the country all through the year. The average duck is killed when it is 8 to 9 weeks old and when it is oven-ready it weighs 3½ to 5 pounds, enough to serve three to four people. The Long Island duck is prepared as a farm-fattened bird (page 289) and is not to be confused with the wild Mallard (page 131).

Ask for the Right Shad

It seems almost unbelievable that this wonderfully delicate spring fish is a Brobdingnagian member of the strong and lowly herring family. There are various types available: the BONED SHAD FILLETS are usually from the female, since she is generally larger, fatter, and juicier. When the female is left whole (but with the roe cut out), she is known as CUT SHAD. The male, left whole and with the milch intact, is known as BUCK SHAD.

Be Fair to the Flounder Family

If the fishmonger is out of flounder, we don't give up. There are many members of the flatfish flounder family, each with subtle variations of flavor and texture, so it is good to know them all. The correct name of the ordinary flounder is the BLACKBACK. From New England and the Pacific coast, there is the SAND DAB, then the Atlantic FLUKE, GRAY SOLE, and the light-colored

LEMON SOLE. Also from the Pacific is the fine REX SOLE, sometimes confused with the luxurious and extraordinary British DOVER SOLE. Finally, there is the YELLOWTAIL, or RUSTY DAB, always cheap and good. The saddest statistic about all these fine fish is that 90 per cent of them are sold filleted. We firmly advocate buying them whole, with the head left on. The head not only keeps the juices sealed in, but also absorbs the oven or grill heat and transmits it along the backbone so that the center of the fish cooks simultaneously with the outside. The fish cooks faster and the improvement in final flavor is striking.

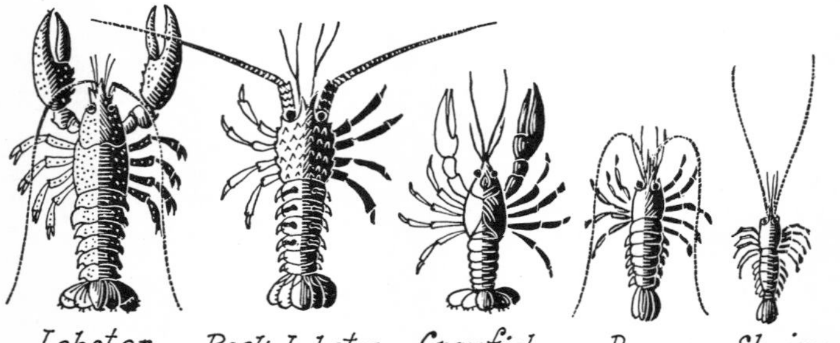

Who Will Kill the Lobster?

The spring lobster season begins when winter storms abate and more small boats can put out to sea to set more traps among the rocks. The largest number of the best lobsters still come from the clear, crisp Atlantic waters off New York, New England, and Canada's Nova Scotia. Attempts to breed them in quantity in the Pacific have so far failed. When buying a lobster is it less cruel to ask the fishmonger to kill it by cutting its spinal cord? A group of rabid be-kind-to-animals British gourmets sponsored a scientific study on the subject supervised by the Royal Society for the Prevention of Cruelty to Animals. The final report was that the most humane way is to put the live lobster (or crab) into a pot of cold fresh salted water, then bring it to the boil as quickly as possible. The rising temperature deadens the lobster's nerves, so that it feels no discomfort (see BASIC RULE, page 86). When lobster is not available or too expensive, it is useful to remember that it can sometimes be replaced in a recipe with at least partial success by one of the other crustaceans: the ROCK LOBSTER TAIL is from a deep-sea type of the spiny rock lobster and has a thin, almost transparent shell; those with a thick and blue-flecked shell are a shallow-water type, with a poor quality of flesh. Any French recipe for LANGOUSTE can be prepared with our Wisconsin CRAYFISH or Louisiana CRAWFISH (page 456). What we call SHRIMP is PRAWN in British recipes, but what the British call "shrimp" is a tiny thing about the size of a quarter and unknown in virtually all our kitchens except those of San Francisco; they are called CREVETTES in France, but the French also give the same name to our jumbo shrimp and the British prawn. Another very small type of rock lobster is fished off the coast of Scotland and is ridiculously called the DUBLIN BAY PRAWN but is generally known in the United States by its Italian name of SCAMPI and in French recipes as the LANGOUSTINE. Finally, in some French recipes there is the ECREVISSE, a type of small, freshwater crayfish caught only in Europe. Perhaps there should be a UN International Conference to straighten things out!

May Wine for the Maibowle

More and more wine merchants across the country are now carrying this light and refreshing wine from Germany. It is the very young wine from the first pressings of the previous year's harvest. It is fresh and thirst-quenching, but has no special character as wine. So the German producers spice it with woodruff, a wild aromatic herb gathered in the German forests and known there as *Waldmeister*. We often begin a party at this season by using the May Wine to make a traditional German *Maibowle* (page 331).

Maple Syrup Must Be Pure

Almost every spring at "sugaring time" we make a pilgrimage to Vermont. We feel Nature's rebirth in watching the sap drip from the tapped trees, in helping to carry the clear liquid to the "sugaring house," and in watching the slow bubbles in the huge tanks until syrup and sugar emerge. We save a substantial part of the cost of our maple syrup by leaving a standing order with one of the Vermont mail-order farms✽ for delivery of the new season's syrup in ½-gallon cans, in which it keeps indefinitely at room temperature. Once a can is opened, we store the syrup in the refrigerator. If in time a little mold forms on top, we skim it off and clear the syrup by bringing it once to the boil; but watch it, it boils over like milk!

Special for Spring Salads

On a visit to Greece we learned to use a musky-green leaf that the Greeks call *roka* and Italo-American greengrocers call variously *arugula* or *rugula*. A few sprigs of it, broken into a salad, add a taste that reminds us of the aroma of Swiss sapsago cheese. *Arugula* is probably a corruption of the scientific name of the plant, *Eruca,* which means rocket. It is known in English as "rocket salad." It is well worth trying.

THE FEASTS OF SPRING
An International Calendar

IN SPRING there are more feast days around the world than we could possibly celebrate at home. Here are a few which we enjoy remembering.

We might plan a Spanish supper party for one of the days between **March 13** and **19**, which is *La Fiesta de San José* in Valencia (St. Joseph being its patron saint). The fiesta brings bullfights, dancing in the streets, magnificent feasting, and on the last night the burning of the *fallas,* the huge set pieces, in gigantic bonfires. We might be there in spirit with an ice-cold *gazpacho* and a huge open platter of *paella a la Valenciana* (page 234).

We are very likely indeed to have an authentic Irish mutton stew on **March 17** for St. Patrick (page 282).

An excuse for a superb Greek dinner comes on **March 25**, when Greece celebrates Independence Day, commemorating her freedom from the Turkish Empire in 1821 (page 239).

Some time in **March** or **April** Easter brings its high celebration of the Christian year, perhaps with the symbolic and traditional roasting of lamb, or we might remember the past glories of the Russian Easter, dramatized in music and opera. Our Russian menu on page 247 might have been served in old St. Petersburg and includes one of the most magnificent of all desserts, the flower-decked pyramid of the Easter Paskha.

We hardly need an excuse for serving some of our favorite Arab, Turkish, or other Middle Eastern dishes, which, with subtle variations, are native to a huge area from North Africa across Arabia and reaching into northern India. We might arrange an Arab supper party on **March 3** or on **April 17**, the independence days, respectively, of Morocco and Syria—Syria having gained her independence from France in 1946, and Morocco in 1956. Our Arab menu is on page 256.

We love Indian food, so we have always been delighted to find that there seems to be at least one Indian feast day every week of the year. We might return to our Indian Moglai dinner of the winter (page 93) on **April 13** or thereabouts (the date varies slightly from year to year, as the Hindu calendar has thirteen months) for the feast of *Baisakhai,* the Hindu New Year. Or we might serve our extraordinary South Indian home dinner (from the summer section, page 398) on **April 22** for the South Indian festival of the Goddess Meenakshi in the great temple of Madurai in the southern province of Madras. These unique South Indian recipes were originally given to us by an expert Madrasi cook.

For a party breakfast, lunch, or light supper on a spring weekend in **April,** we would certainly want to have a Swiss *Bircher müsli,* because it is so wonderfully refreshing as made by our friend Ruedi from Zürich (page ooo). At this time in Ruedi's home town (the date is variable), the feast of *Sechselauten* is celebrated, with streets decorated with flowers for the parades, and on the second day the giant snowman figure of Böögg, Old Man Winter, is exploded with firecrackers on a bonfire in the city's central Bellevue Platz.

The Spring Party and Feast-Day Menus

THE FIRST FOUR menus following are traditional at our table to celebrate the principal spring feasts mentioned in the calendar on the previous pages. They are so good that we also serve them at other times of the year.

A Spanish Fiesta Supper

MENU

	WINES
ERNEST HEMINGWAY'S GAZPACHO	*A Montilla*
PAELLA A LA VALENCIANA DE NUEVA YORK	*A dry white Rioja*
SPANISH MEMBRILLO *with* Greek Feta English Bath Oliver Biscuits	*A sweet Málaga*
Café Latino	*Fundador*

La Fiesta de San José in Valencia

An American tourist once described *gazpacho* as "the national soft drink of Spain." It's a refreshing sight at harvesttime to see the women going out to the fields carrying pails of *gazpacho* to their men working under the hot sun. Each man dips in the ladle and, thrusting his head far back, pours down his parched throat the icy liquid, which tastes of fresh tomato with faint overtones of garlic and olives. At the same time he collects in his mouth the crisp diced vegetables, which he chews after the liquid has gone down.

Although *paella* is always associated with Spain, there is historical evidence that the idea of marrying rice, in a one-dish meal, to meats, fish, vegetables, and seasonings originated in the Arab world, where there are still many versions of "pilaf." The dish traveled eastward to India, where there are infinite variations of "pilau," see page 166. It also traveled westward into Europe, and from Portugal across the Atlantic to Florida, where today, in the Portuguese restaurants of Tampa, one can order a "pilo." In Spain there are dozens of regional variations, but the most famous *paella* is made in the port of Valencia, the fishing center of the garden of Spain, with an abundance of rice and olive oil, wine and vegetables, and boatloads of crustacea—all the ingredients for the perfect *paella.*

After the expansive joys of the main dish, we find that our guests are happy to be invited to leave the table and walk around, while sipping perhaps an extra glass of Spanish Rioja. Then we offer them small plates with an unusual combination as dessert.

Shopping for Spanish Ingredients and Equipment

The growing Spanish population in many of our cities ensures that two vital ingredients of the *paella* are widely available: the pepper-hot, dark-brown Spanish sausage, the *chorizo,*⚜ and the sun-dried, salted shrimp, the *camarones secos.*⚜

But the technique of preparation is more important than the precise imitation of the ingredients. First, it must be cooked on the flat, round hammered-steel pan (which is usually about 1½ to 3 feet or more across) called a *paellera.** This will be bumped about on top of the stove, at times on high heat over two, three, or even four burners, and then will be slammed into a very hot oven, so the handles must be of welded iron and there should be no wood or plastic anywhere. It is part sauté pan, part stewpan, part serving dish. Secondly, the rice must be cooked on this open platter on top of the stove—it is the key to the flavor and texture of a *paella.* This way the rice will absorb the juices resulting from the frying of the meats and fish and it will have a certain firmness and glistening patina which comes only from being glazed in an open pan. As to the dessert, for the *membrillo* paste, the feta cheese, and the English Bath Oliver biscuits, see the "Index of Sources."

Planning and Timing

Once the *paella* has been tried and its special tricks learned, this menu is easy to prepare and presents only a problem in timing. The *gazpacho,* the ice-cold salad-in-a-soup, is prepared the day before and refrigerated overnight. There is then only the final adjustment of seasoning and the frying of a few bread croutons. If all the meats and fish for the *paella* are prepared beforehand, there remains only the boiling of the rice, the building up and decoration of the platter, and the final heating in the oven, a total of about 50 minutes of work. The *paella* should come to the table sizzling. The dessert needs no more preparation than the opening of two cans and the slicing of a piece of cheese. As for side dishes, there might be just one: a small pile of Spanish olives (page 105) to be offered to guests with a first glass of the Montilla aperitif wine. The olives remain on the table throughout the meal.

ERNEST HEMINGWAY'S GAZPACHO

For a party of 8 to 10

There are many versions of *gazpacho* in different parts of Spain. In Seville and Segovia they thicken it slightly with bread crumbs; in Málaga, with mashed rice; in Córdoba, with corn flour. Here we use bread crumbs.

Check Staples:

Aromatics: crystal salt, freshly ground black pepper, garlic (1 or more cloves, to taste)
Scallions (1 bunch)
White bread (3 slices)
Olive oil (several tsp.)
Italian seeded and peeled plum tomatoes (2 lb. 3 oz. can)
Spanish Sherry vinegar (about ½ cup)

White bread (about 2 cups cubed for croutons)
Salt butter (enough to fry the croutons)

Shopping List:

White celery (1 head)
Tomatoes (4 medium)
Green pepper (1 medium)
Cucumber (1 small)

The Day Before

Gazpacho is nothing if it is not refrigerated for at least 24 hours, so that the vegetable juices can mingle with the aromatics. We use a large open punch bowl that holds a little more than ½ gallon. The garlic is thinly sliced into the bottom of the bowl, then bruised with a wooden pestle. The slices of bread are then put in and vinegar is poured over them until the bread is thoroughly soaked and will absorb no more. With the pestle now mash the bread into the garlic, adding a few teaspoons of olive oil, just enough to make a smooth paste. Blend in 1 cup of the canned tomatoes, mashing thoroughly.

Add the vegetables, and extreme accuracy of measurement is not required. They should all be fairly coarsely chopped, since they will be eaten with a spoon in a liquid: the 4 tomatoes, the head of white celery, with a few of its leaves more finely chopped, the green pepper, the scallions, and the cucumber, sliced with the rind. Add salt and freshly ground black pepper to taste, remembering that they will be partly absorbed by the vegetables. Stir well.

The next operation requires judgment, which comes from the experience of making the dish a few times. At this point the *gazpacho* tastes bland; by tomorrow it will have developed a sharp and exciting flavor. Yet today the bowl must be filled up with the right balance of flavoring liquid. First we add 1 quart of cold water, stir, add 2 more cups of the canned tomatoes, stir again, and taste. There should be a definite flavor of tomato, yet diluted by the water so that the anticipated flavor of the vegetables will not be overpowered. Then more canned tomatoes or cold water, or both, are added until the bowl is filled to within 1 inch of the top. Cover and refrigerate overnight. The final balancing will be done tomorrow.

Just Before Serving

We fry bread croutons in butter, and these are served at the table in a side dish. Now comes the final stirring, tasting, and adjustment of flavor. More water or canned tomatoes, or both, are added to fill the bowl. The soup plates are chilled and 1 or 2 cubes of ice are placed in each. The *gazpacho* is ladled so that each diner gets a fair balance of the crisp vegetables and icy liquid. The croutons are sprinkled over the top.

PAELLA A LA VALENCIANA DE NUEVA YORK

For a party of 8 to 10

Can a true *paella a la Valenciana* be reproduced, say, in New York? Certainly not. No more than a true *bouillabaisse à la Provençal.* They depend for subtle flavorings on certain unique types of fish caught only in their local waters. But a very passable imitation can be prepared here. It can either be luxurious for a party or can "extend" cold cooked meats for a family Sunday-night supper. Let us begin with a party version.

Check Staples:

Chicken consommé (about 4 cups for every cup of rice)
Aromatics: crystal salt,✻ freshly ground black pepper,✻ MSG, garlic (4 cloves), Spanish saffron (1 tsp. whole strands), bay leaf, thyme
Yellow onions (2 large)
Fresh parsley (a handful)
Long-grain white rice (½ cup for each man to be served, ¼ cup for each woman, according to the ancient rule)
Olive oil (about 1 cup)
Italian peeled and seeded plum tomatoes (2 lb. 3 oz. can)
Dry white wine (about ½ cup)

Shopping List:

Spanish *chorizo* sausages✻ (5 or 6 of the *picante* type)
***Camarones secos,* sun-dried shrimp✻ (3 oz.)**
Lean fillet of pork (½ lb.)
Frying chicken, cut up (2½ to 3 lbs.)
Large fresh shrimp (½ lb.)
Deep-sea scallops (½ lb.)
Lobsters (2 medium)
Large mussels (about 3 dozen)
Hard-shell clams (1 dozen small)
Red pimientos (1 small can or jar)
Peas (1 package frozen)
Green beans (1 package French-cut frozen or equivalent fresh)

The Day Before (if Desired)—Frying the Meats and Fish

Our medium-sized paellera✻ is 16 inches across and covers two burners on top of the stove. We heat it up to the normal temperature for frying chicken—325 degrees Fahrenheit. We spread over the bottom of it ¾ cup of the olive oil. When this is quite hot (giving off a strong fragrance, but not yet smoking), add the pork, cut into ½-inch cubes, the chicken cut up as for fricassée, and the *chorizo,* cut in ½-inch slices. Each piece, as soon as it is brown and done, is removed to a large covered storage pot. When the paellera is again empty but with the oil now richly flavored, we fry the fish. First, the large shrimp, previously shelled and cleaned, which fry for 4 to 5 minutes and then go into the storage pot. Next, the scallops, previously washed and sliced in half, fried for 2 to 3 minutes and then added to the storage pot, which can now be covered and refrigerated until needed, either later or the next day. The next fried ingredients add the special flavor to the rice: the *camerones secos;* the onions, chopped; and about 4 cloves of garlic, finely chopped. When these are lightly fried they stay in the paellera overnight or until later that same day.

The Morning of the Day—Other Items Prepared Separately

In a large pan of water we boil the lobsters (according to our BASIC RULE, page 86), halve them, and clean them. (A true Valencian *paella* calls for these to rest on top of the dish in their shells and for the guests to pick out the meat, but if the party is formal the meat can be dug out and chunked ahead and blended into the rice—the empty shells then being used for decoration.) Next, in a large covered pot, we steam the mussels and clams (by our BASIC RULE, page 197). As soon as the shells open, we dig out the meats and add them to the shrimps and scallops. We save about a dozen of the handsomest shells for decoration. The wine used for steaming the shellfish is strained through muslin and used as part of the liquor for boiling the rice. The fried meats and fish are brought to room temperature.

In Sequence Before Serving—Boiling the Rice

In a tiny saucepan, soak the saffron in 1/4 cup of the dry white wine (according to our BASIC RULE, page 27). Bring the paellera with its contents up to simmering. Add to the luscious pan juices 1 to 2 cups of the Italian plum tomatoes, holding back the liquid. Mix together equal parts of shellfish wine, chicken consommé, and liquid from the can of tomatoes as the cooking liquor for the rice. In the "open pan" method much more than the usual amount of liquor has to be used, for there is considerable evaporation. Here is a rough guide:

For 1/4 cup of rice—1 cup liquor
For 1/2 cup of rice—1 3/4 cups liquor
For 1 cup of rice—3 1/2 cups liquor

Let us then assume that we will use 3 cups of white rice, boiled in 10 cups of liquor. Gradually, add this liquor to the juices in the paellera, turning up heat so that it quickly begins to simmer. Add the seasonings: chopped parsley, thyme, bay leaves, salt, and MSG (the *chorizo* will supply the pepper). Bring the saffron and wine just to a boil and pour it into the paellera. Now we spread the rice into the bubbling liquid. The rice will rise as it absorbs the liquid and must be spread out again and gently turned over. Also, with the two burners, there will be zones of bubbling and non-bubbling and the rice should be rotated. Our objective is to cook the rice to a point where it is almost done but not yet soft, so that it won't mush when we blend in the meats and fish. This usually takes about 10 minutes, but the exact point can best be judged by tasting a grain or two.

The Blending and the Hot Oven

While the rice is cooking, preheat oven to 350 degrees and put the dish of fried meats in to warm. As soon as the rice is ready and the meats are hot, artistry must join gastronomy. The storage pot comes out of the oven, which is then turned up to 425 degrees. All the meats and fish (except the lobster) go into the rice. Using a wooden spoon and a soufflé technique of gently lifting and folding, the object is to get everything thoroughly imbedded in the rice, yet with many of the pieces showing—part of a shrimp sticking out here, the "handle" of a chicken leg there. . . . From this point on, nothing should be moved. We lay the red lobsters on top, and finally decorate with the mussel and clam shells. It is vital at this point that there still be a good deal of the liquid left at the bottom of the dish, for in the hot oven this is to boil away madly, providing the steam for the final cooking. So one must check the liquid and, if needed, sprinkle on more hot consommé. The whole dish now goes into the oven and is rechecked after 5 minutes; the rice should be tasted and possibly more hot consommé added. Usually 10 minutes in the oven is required to cook the rice, but the final decision must be made by taste.

Final Decoration and Serving

During the time the *paella* is in the oven we quickly cook the shelled peas and the French-cut green beans and heat up the pimientos, which we have cut into strips. (Other vegetables can be substituted, but the

bright green and red colors are a perfect contrast to the yellow rice.) When the *paella* comes out of the oven, we finally decorate it with these vegetables and take it directly to the table, where a large heatproof board must be waiting for it.

MEMBRILLO WITH FETA

For a party of 8 to 10

For many years, we associated the end of a Spanish menu with guava paste or preserve, then we discovered the incomparable delicacy of the Spanish quince paste. Our second discovery was, instead of the bland cream cheese, the slight saltiness of the Greek white goats' milk cheese, feta. With the salt in the cheese, one must be careful to avoid any form of salted cracker. The crumbly dryness of the English Bath Oliver is excellent.

Shopping List:

Imported Spanish *pasta de membrillo,* quince paste✣ (a 2-lb. tin)
Greek feta cheese♔ (2 lbs.)
English Bath Oliver biscuits✣ (1 tin)

Serving

We place the square blocks of *membrillo* and feta on a handsome cutting board and serve slices to each guest with the biscuits.

A Greek Independence Day Dinner

MENU

WINES

TARAMASALATA—A Carp-Roe Dip

Ice-cold Ouzo

GRILLED EEL WITH LEMON SAUCE

STEFADO OF BEEF

with

Rice-Stuffed Moussaka

A Roditis Rosé through the fish and meat courses

MOUNT HYMETTUS HONEY WHIP
WITH NUTS AND FRUIT

Sweet Mavrodaphne

Greek Coffee

Metaxa

A Classic Dinner from Greece

The best *tarama* carp roe is exported from Greece in wooden tubs or boxes and scooped out like an orange-colored ice cream at the Greek grocery (see below). When it is prepared as a *taramasalata* it assumes the texture of a mayonnaise.

The *stefado* is the classic Greek beef stew with nuts and goat's-milk cheese in a tomato sauce.

A Greek *moussaka* is a highly flexible dish. It consists basically of slices of fried eggplant covered by a smooth, light custard. When it is used as a main dish there is a central stuffing of ground beef or lamb, but when we use it here as an accompaniment to a main meat course, we stuff it with a pilaf of rice so that the *moussaka* provides both vegetable and starch foundation.

The dessert is so rich that all thoughts of calories must be put out of mind for a few minutes of luxurious feasting. A quite small portion of the whipped honey is enough, balanced by a larger amount of the fresh fruit. Hymettus is the most famous Greek honey, so heavy in body that it is probably the only honey possible for this dish.

Shopping for Greek Ingredients

The imported Greek *tarama* carp roe is now fairly widely available from Greek groceries✣ or fine food stores. Sometimes it comes packed in individual jars, but it is usually best when bought loose. The imported Greek feta cheese,⌂ made from goats' milk, is also found in Greek groceries or in cheese specialty shops. The imported Mount Hymettus Greek honey is one of the great honeys of the world✣ and is available in most fancy honey shops.

Planning and Timing

The main work of this menu can be completed in advance. We usually serve the *taramasalata* and its "salad scoops" before coming to the table. The eel appears in its sauce at room temperature and is the better for having been marinated for 24 hours. Both the *stefado* and the *moussaka* are reasonably flexible in timing. The whipped honey dessert is best made about 3 hours before the guests arrive and stiffened in the refrigerator. This dinner involves a minimum of last-minute pressure.

TARAMASALATA—A CARP-ROE DIP

For a party of 8 to 10

Check Staples:

Fresh limes (2 or 3)
Milk (about 1 cup)
Aromatics: dill salt, freshly ground black pepper,✲ MSG⊜
White bread (4 or 5 slices)
Olive oil⊜ (about 1 cup)

Shopping List:

Greek *tarama* carp roe✲ (¼ lb.)
Sweet red onion (1 small)
Salad scoops for the dip: green pepper strips, cucumber slices, carrot strips, celery boats, Greek kalamata olives, etc.

On the Morning of the Day

Flexibility is the key to a perfect *taramasalata* dip. We mix, taste, and adjust. We pat 3 slightly heaped tablespoons of the *tarama* into a mortar, reserving the rest. De-crust the bread slices and mash them in a bowl with as much of the milk as they will absorb. Squeeze the juice from the limes. Finely grate the onion, saving the juice. We gently mash the stiff *tarama* with a pestle, gradually working in some of the grated onion and its juice. Adding the olive oil a teaspoon at a time, we soften the *tarama* to a smooth paste and switch from the pestle to a wooden spoon. Squeeze a piece of the bread-mash and work it into the *tarama,* adding more olive oil and onion. Also begin adding spoonfuls of the lime juice. As the fish eggs absorb the oil, the *tarama* expands to the top of our mortar and is spooned into a large round mixing bowl, where it can be beaten with a wire whisk. Continue adding, alternately, squeezed bread, oil, onion, and lime juice, balancing them until the *tarama* begins to fluff like mayonnaise. Then start beating it, with more and more olive oil, until it becomes creamy pink and completely fluffy. Beat in dill salt, freshly ground black pepper, MSG, and adjust for final flavor and texture. More oil thickens. More lime juice thins. When perfect, store in a covered bowl in the refrigerator.

Taramasalata can of course be served on crackers or canapé rounds, but we prefer to make it a dip, with "scoops" of salad greens and vegetables. We cut inch-long chunks of the green peppers, thin lengthwise strips of the carrots and the same of the cucumbers, sticks of the white celery, and we cut the stones out of the olives and stick them on toothpicks. We keep them all crisp in a covered bowl in the refrigerator.

Just Before Serving

We think both the flavor and texture of the *taramasalata* dip are improved by whipping in tiny lumps of fresh *tarama* a few minutes before serving. We put about 1 tablespoon more of the raw *tarama* into the mortar and break it into tiny lumps with a little more lime juice. This is rapidly beaten into the dip with a wire whisk. Pile it like mayonnaise into a pretty glass bowl and set in the center of a large serving platter. Arrange the cut vegetables around the bowl.

ENCORE: Not much *taramasalata* is usually left by the guests, but if any is available the following day it can be blended with mashed potatoes or used in a salad dressing.

GRILLED EEL WITH LEMON SAUCE

For a party of 8 to 10

The fishman will usually skin the eel, but should it be presented freshly caught by a fisherman friend, the job is easy. Cut the skin around the neck and slit it down the belly. Hold the head and, grasping the neck end of the skin, slowly pull it inside out. Cut off the head and tail, clean the fish, and cut it into 2-inch lengths.

Check Staples:

Lemons (2 or 3 for ¼ cup of juice)
Aromatics: crystal salt,⁑ freshly ground black pepper,⁑ MSG,▣ garlic (about 1 clove)
Fresh parsley (a small handful)
Indian chick-pea flour▣ or all-purpose flour (a few Tbs.)
Olive oil▣ (about ½ cup)

Shopping List:

Fresh eel (about 3 lbs.)
French Dijon mustard (about 2 tsp.)
Tomatoes (2 medium)

The Day Before

First we prepare the lemon dressing. Squeeze the lemons to fill ¼ cup with juice. Finely chop the parsley. Mix in a medium bowl: ⅓ cup of the olive oil, the juice of the lemons, about 3 tablespoons of the chopped parsley, the mustard, plus salt, pepper, and MSG to taste. Also add as much crushed garlic as desired. Beat vigorously with a fork and let it stand at room temperature.

Assuming that the eel is prepared in 2-inch lengths (see above), we make a basting sauce with 1 to 2 tablespoons of the olive oil, 1 to 2 tablespoons of the chick-pea flour, plus salt, pepper, and MSG. Set the grill to medium-high. Using a pastry brush, paint each piece of fish with the basting sauce and grill about 3 inches from the heat, turning once and repainting 2 or 3 times with the basting sauce. The eel is done when lightly browned; with our grill this takes about 5 minutes on the first side and 4 minutes on the second, but the time can vary.

Set the browned pieces of fish neatly in a dish, adjust the seasonings of the lemon sauce, and pour it over the eel. Let the flavors blend, covered, in the refrigerator overnight.

2 Hours Before Serving

Remove from refrigerator and let eel come to room temperature; serve on a platter decorated with parsley and tomato wedges.

STEFADO OF BEEF

For a party of 8 to 10

Check Staples:

Aromatics: crystal salt,☆ freshly ground black pepper,☆ MSG,■ bay leaves, garlic (2 or more cloves)
Italian peeled and seeded plum tomatoes (2 lb. 3 oz. can)
Italian tomato paste (6-oz. can)
Olive oil■ (a few tablespoons)
Tarragon white wine vinegar■ (2 or 3 Tbs.)
Red wine ■ (about 1 pt.)

Shopping List:

Top round of beef, cut into 1-inch cubes (about 4 lbs.)
Small white boiling onions (4 lbs.)
Shelled whole pecans (½ lb.)
Greek feta cheese■ (about ½ lb.)

On the Morning of the Day

We first prepare the tomato sauce. In the jug of our electric blender we mix: 2 cups of the plum tomatoes, the 6 ounces of tomato paste, ¾ cup of the red wine, 2 tablespoons of the vinegar, plus salt, pepper, and MSG to taste. Blend for hardly more than 15 seconds, taste and add more of any or all of the above, until the flavor of the sauce is quite strong. Blend for a few seconds more and hold.

We prepare the dish in one of our large enameled cast-iron cocottes,* which can be used for frying or simmering on top of the stove and then with a tight cover can be put in the oven. Let the cubes of beef come to room temperature. Peel the white onions. Heat up enough olive oil in the cocotte just to cover the bottom. When the oil is quite hot but not yet smoking, quickly brown the pieces of meat on all sides and remove them at once to a waiting bowl. Keeping the oil at the same temperature and adding a little more if needed, fry the onions until they have brown patches, and as each batch is ready add it to the waiting meat. Reduce the heat under the cocotte to boiling temperature and put back meat and onions. Switch on the blender for 1 or 2 more seconds to remix the tomato sauce, then pour it into the cocotte. Add 2 or 3 crumbled bay leaves and crushed or slivered garlic to taste. As soon as the liquid in the cocotte reaches the bubbling point, turn the heat down to the lowest possible simmering temperature, cover tightly, and gently simmer for 3 or 4 hours or longer, until the meat and onions are butter-tender. Of course if the heat is too high even 3 hours will demolish the meat into tasteless shreds, so the whole operation must be carefully watched. At various times, as the sauce reduces and thickens, more plum tomatoes and more wine can be added. When the dish is finally done the sauce should be quite thick.

About 1 Hour Before Serving

With an eye on the timing of the meal, the slow stewing in the cocotte can be interrupted at any time (in fact, cooling and reheating improve the flavor) and we usually like to do the final reheating in a 350-degree oven. While this is in progress, cut the feta cheese into large dice and hold. Exactly 30 minutes before serving, gently blend the shelled whole pecans into the stew, using a wooden spoon. Exactly 10 minutes before serving, add the cubes of feta cheese, which will melt around the meat and blend into the sauce. Our cocotte is attractive enough to be brought to the table.

RICE-STUFFED MOUSSAKA—EGGPLANT WITH CREAM CUSTARD

For a party of 8 to 10

Check Staples:

Beef bouillon (about 1 pt.)
Salt butter (a few Tbs.)
Eggs (2 large)
Milk (1 cup)
Aromatics: crystal salt,☆ freshly ground black pepper,☆ MSG,▣ ground cinnamon, nutmeg
Yellow onions (6 medium)
Fresh parsley (a handful)
Olive oil▣ (about 1 cup)
Italian tomato paste (6-oz. can)
Long-grain white rice (2 cups)
Red wine◊ (about 1 cup)

Shopping List:

Ripe eggplants (6 medium)
Heavy cream (½ cup)
Italian Parmesan cheese (about ½ lb.)
Pine nuts (about 2 oz.)
Seedless white raisins (½ cup)

About 2 Hours Before Serving

We begin by making our favorite pilaf of rice according to our basic recipe (page 166), using 1½ cups of rice in a mixture of beef bouillon and red wine, adding white raisins and pine nuts for texture. This version of rice cooks in about 35 minutes and can then be held.

Cut the eggplant, unpeeled, in ¾-inch slices, salt lightly and let stand. Some cooks believe in pressing down on the slices with an inverted plate and a weight, but with the modern heavy eggplant we find this no longer necessary.

Peel and coarsely chop the onions. Bring a sauté pan to medium frying heat, just cover the bottom with olive oil and fry the onions until golden, then remove and hold. Add more olive oil as needed to the pan and bring almost to smoking heat. Fry the eggplant slices, not too many at a time, until well browned. At the same time, the eggs, milk, and cream are brought up to room temperature.

About 1 Hour Before Serving

We use a flat-bottomed open casserole about 6 inches deep. Lightly rub the inside with olive oil. Preheat oven to 350 degrees. Cover the bottom of the casserole with eggplant, then a ½-inch layer of the rice pilaf and a thin layer of fried onions. Repeat until all the eggplant, rice, and onions are in, with a final layer of eggplant on top.

In a mixing bowl beat together with a wire whisk: 1 cup of the beef bouillon, 1 cup of the red wine, the 6 ounces of tomato paste, chopped parsley, salt, pepper, and MSG to taste and about ½ teaspoon of ground cinnamon. Bring this sauce rapidly to a boil in a copper saucepan and pour over the vegetables in the casserole. Set at once in the oven, open for about 30 minutes, until the sauce is absorbed and reduced.

Meanwhile prepare the custard. Grate enough Parmesan to fill 1 cup. In a mixing bowl beat together furiously with a wire whisk: the 3 eggs, the cup of milk, the ½ cup of heavy cream, the grated cheese, and a few grinds of nutmeg. Heat this mixture slowly in a copper saucepan, stirring continuously, until it just begins to thicken. At this point the casserole should be about ready to come out of the oven. If the vegetables were tightly packed in the first place and have bedded down, the custard, when poured on, will fill all the crevices and rest about ½ inch thick over the top. Sprinkle on a thin layer of extra grated Parmesan. Put the casserole back into the oven until the custard sets, usually in 20 minutes, but it should be left until the top is golden-brown. Bring the casserole to the table and serve the *moussaka* by digging the spoon straight down so that each diner receives a balanced share of all the layers.

MOUNT HYMETTUS HONEY WHIP WITH NUTS AND FRUIT

For a party of 8 to 10

Shopping List:

Imported Greek Hymettus honey☆ **(1-lb. jar)**
Heavy whipping cream (½ pt.)
Mixed nuts, say, walnuts, cashews, almonds, brazils, etc. (enough to make about 1 cup of shelled meats)
Fresh fruit of the season, say, 3 kinds to be chunked and eaten by hand

About 3 Hours Before Serving

Keep the cream, copper bowl, and wire whisk cold in the refrigerator. Pour the honey into another bowl and start whipping it with a wooden fork. This will be hard work at first; when it gets frothy and milky we switch to a strong wire whisk. When the honey is stiff enough to hold a small peak, it should be held in the refrigerator.

Shell the nuts. (If we are feeling lazy we buy ready-shelled *unsalted* mixed nuts.) Leave the walnuts in halves. Chunk the larger nuts; leave the smaller ones whole. The objective is to have bite-size pieces. About 1 cup of shelled nuts is needed, but it is good to have a few extra for final blending if needed just before serving.

Whip the cream with the cold wire whisk until it is quite stiff. Using a very soft spatula fold together honey, cream, and nuts. Honey and cream need not be fully blended; there can be broad streaks, provided there is a fair share of each in every part of the mix. The nuts must be evenly distributed throughout. Hold in the refrigerator.

Prepare the fruits for hand eating—perhaps peeled and cored quarters of apples, slices or sections of oranges, and chunks of banana. The choice is dictated by season and weather.

Finally, for each person, set to cool in the freezer a small glass bowl about the size of a custard cup.

Serving at Table

Each diner gets a pretty dessert plate with a small ice-cold bowl holding a rough little pile of the honey mix surrounded by the chunked fruits. The mix is eaten with a small silver spoon; the fruit is picked up by hand.

GREEK COFFEE

Greece and Turkey may be worlds apart politically, but in coffee they are united. Greek coffee is made in the same way as Turkish (page 261).

A Russian Easter Dinner

MENU

	WINES
RUSSIAN OR IRANIAN PRESSED CAVIAR ON A BLOCK OF ICE	*Vodka*
AN AUTHENTIC BORSCH	*A Tavel Rosé*
BEEF STROGANOFF *with* Green Beans with Rosemary Whole-Grain Wheat Kasha	*A red Burgundy from the Clos Vougeot*
A FLOWER-DECKED PASKHA	*A sweet Sauternes from the Château d'Yquem*
Russian Tea with Lemon	*Armagnac Brandy*

Easter Dishes from Old St. Petersburg

Borsch has become so standardized by mass-production in cans, in jars, and in popular restaurants that we seem to have forgotten the freshness, crispness and velvet texture of the loving version, made at home.

Count Paul Stroganoff, a member of the court of Tsar Alexander III, would hardly be remembered were it not for his French chef who one day invented a new way of cooking beef and named the dish in honor of his employer. With the reddish sauce a bright green vegetable looks attractive, and the whole-grain kasha is the ideal starch foundation because it blends with the creamy sauce.

Let's face it, the dessert is a major operation, but in our home Easter wouldn't be a feast without it. When the Paskha comes to the table with its fresh spring flowers, its multicolored religious decorations in glacé fruits, and its base surrounded by colored Easter eggs, it is one of the most magnificent desserts. Taste matches appearance!

Note on the Mold for the Paskha

Some families mold their Paskha in a round flowerpot, letting it drain through the hole in the bottom, but we find the four-sided pyramid offers more opportunities for imaginative decoration, with variations from year to year. First, one needs a four-sided wooden mold, shaped like a large metronome, open at both ends, so that the Paskha can drain. The four sides of the mold should be lightly screwed together, so that it can be taken apart to unmold the Paskha. Ours was made by the girls as a carpentry project in school and has lasted for ten years.

Planning and Timing

This menu involves no special difficulties in cooking or timing, but there is a good deal of work which can be spread over the preceding four days. To make a dramatic show for the caviar we order a block of ice and carve in it (using an old knife repeatedly heated in a gas flame) a bowl-like depression in which the caviar rests. On the day before the party, we complete some of the work on the borsch, slice and sear the beef, do the other advance jobs for the Stroganoff and prepare the kasha, to be reheated.

RUSSIAN OR IRANIAN PRESSED CAVIAR ON A BLOCK OF ICE

For a party of 8 to 10

For a note on buying caviar, see page 224.

Check Staples:

Sweet butter (about ½ lb.)
Lemons (3)

Shopping List:

Unpasteurized, pressed caviar (2 oz. per person)
Westphalian dark pumpernickel, thin-sliced (about 4 small packages)
A neat square block of ice

On the Morning of the Day

Carving the block of ice has always been a fascinating pop-art project for our children. One year the block came to table carved into an egg shell, with the caviar inside. One must work fast, with hot knives, and as soon as the job is done, the carving goes into the freezer until the last moment.

Serving

The ice block containing the caviar within a circle of lemon wedges comes to table on a platter or open bowl deep enough to hold the melting ice water. Each diner receives on his plate a small mound of the caviar, a chunk of sweet butter, lemon wedges, and thin slices of pumpernickel. Each bite of caviar when placed on the buttered bread is refreshed with a drop of lemon juice.

AN AUTHENTIC BORSCH

For a party of 8 to 10

Check Staples:

Strong beef bouillon (3 qts.)
Salt butter (about 4 Tbs.)
Aromatics: crystal salt, whole black peppercorns, MSG
Green Pascal celery (5 or 6 stalks with leaves)
Yellow onions (2 medium)
Indian chick-pea flour (a few Tbs.)
Spanish Sherry vinegar (3 Tbs.)
Red wine (about ½ cup)

Shopping List:

Fresh beets (about 1 dozen medium)
Cabbage (a few young center leaves)
Leeks (4 medium)
Sour cream (1½ pts.)

1 or 2 Days Ahead

The first requirement of a great borsch is a good beef bouillon base, with the added vegetable flavoring. We simmer the bouillon gently for about 1 hour with a few young leaves of the cabbage, cut into large pieces; the onions, chunked; the whites of the four leeks, well washed; the celery stalks with their leaves cut up; and about a dozen whole black peppercorns. Leave the vegetables in as bouillon cools. Strain and hold refrigerated.

On the Morning of the Day

Wash and peel the beets. Finely grate 1 beet and set it to soak in a small bowl with enough red wine to cover. This is to give the rich color. Dice the remaining beets. In a saucepan large enough to hold the beets melt about 4 tablespoons of the butter, put in the beets, and stir them around for 1 or 2 minutes with a wooden spoon until they are heated and well coated with butter. Add about 3 tablespoons of the vinegar, cover, and simmer very gently until just tender, usually in about ½ hour. Let cool and stand until the final preparation.

About 30 Minutes Before Serving

Let the sour cream come to room temperature. Bring the beef bouillon up to the boiling point. Heat the beets in their saucepan and, as soon as bubbling begins, sprinkle on 2 or 3 tablespoons of the flour and carefully blend in with a wooden spoon, avoiding lumps. Continue stirring gently, while adding hot bouillon, tablespoon by tablespoon, at the same time gradually bringing up the heat, until the beets are coated with a creamy, bubbling sauce. Continuing to stir gently, gradually add more of the bouillon, until the beets are just covered. At this point they may need 5 minutes more simmering, depending on their age. Taste and decide, remembering that the beets should still be freshly crisp when the borsch is served. When they are perfect, combine the beets with the rest of the boiling bouillon and add the grated beets with the red wine.

An authentic borsch does not have a dollop of cold sour cream in the middle of the bowl. Put about ½ cup of the sour cream into a small mixing bowl, thin it smoothly with a few tablespoons of the hot soup, then add it to the borsch. Keep adding sour cream in this way, ½ cup at a time, until exactly the right color and softness have been achieved. Then serve the borsch at once. It is equally good ice-cold.

BEEF STROGANOFF

For a party of 8 to 10

Check Staples:

Salt butter (1 lb.)
Lemon (1)
Aromatics: crystal salt,✲ freshly ground black pepper,✲ MSG,Ⓢ chili powder, Hungarian sweet red paprika,✲ Tabasco
Yellow onions (about 6 medium)
Italian tomato paste (6-oz. can)

Shopping List:

Lean wedge-bone sirloin steak—(4 lbs., about 1½ in. thick) the exact way of slicing the beef is very important, so we always do it ourselves
Fresh whole mushrooms (1 lb.)
French Dijon mustard (about 4 Tbs.)
Sour cream (2 pts.)

On the Morning of the Day or Several Hours Before Serving

We begin by cutting the meat. Remove and discard all fat, gristle, and bone. Slice the steak into strips 1½ inches wide and ⅜ inch thick. Pound with a meat hammer on a chopping block to spread and soften them. Cut into 1-inch lengths. Wipe the mushrooms and slice. Peel and finely chop the onions. Take the sour cream out of the refrigerator. Leave all at room temperature.

About 1 Hour Before Serving

Heat a heavy sauté pan to searing temperature. In a fast, continuous operation, drop in butter, a couple of tablespoons at a time, then, before it has time to smoke and burn, drop in pieces of meat, a few at a time, and brown them almost instantly on both sides. Each piece should remain in the pan for only a few seconds. The butter is rapidly absorbed, so more is added every few seconds. Hold the browned meat in a warm cast-iron cocotte.* As soon as the meat is all done, reduce the sauté pan to normal frying temperature. Melt more butter and sauté the chopped onions until they are just golden. Remove them with a slotted spoon and add to the beef. Melt more butter and very lightly sauté the mushrooms, no more than 5 minutes. Also remove with slotted spoon and add to the meat.

Preheat oven to 325 degrees. Let the sour cream come to room temperature. Bring heat under sauté pan down to simmering and smoothly blend into the pan juices: about 3 tablespoons of the tomato paste, any excess juice that has collected in the cocotte where meat is waiting, 1 teaspoon of the paprika, 2 teaspoons of the mustard, about 2 teaspoons of the chili powder, 2 or 3 drops of Tabasco, plus salt, pepper, and MSG to taste. Stirring continuously, let it bubble for a few seconds. Turn the heat down until the bubbling stops completely.

Smoothly blend in 1 pint of the sour cream. Taste and add more of any or all the ingredients, until a highly flavored sauce is achieved. When it tastes good and is smooth and hot, carefully blend it with a wooden spoon into the meat, mushrooms, and onions. There should be enough sauce to coat each slice. If necessary, add up to 1 pint more sour cream, with more flavoring, until the right taste, smoothness, and coverage are achieved. Do not add any salt at this point, as it will toughen the meat.

Cover the cocotte and set it in the oven for about 20 minutes, until the meat is piping hot and the sauce bubbling, but no longer or meat will toughen.

At the Last Minute

Stir in 1 tablespoon or more of salt. Give the pepper grinder a half dozen or so turns, and add MSG to taste. Finally, a few seconds before bringing the cocotte to the table, stir in the juice of half a lemon. Serve at once on very hot plates. Some of the cream sauce goes over the kasha.

GREEN BEANS WITH ROSEMARY

See recipe (page 308), preparing a double quantity for the party.

RUSSIAN KASHA—WHOLE-GRAIN WHEAT

See recipe (page 167), making a sufficient quantity.

PASKHA—A FLOWER-DECKED EASTER PYRAMID

For a party of 8 to 10, and some to take home

Check Staples:

Eggs, large (18 yolks)
Sweet butter (1½ lbs.)
Aromatic: pure vanilla extract (3 Tbs.)
Granulated white sugar (1½ cups)

Shopping List:

Coarse, loose pot cheese (5 lbs.)
Heavy cream (½ pt.)
Mixed candied fruits (1 lb.)
Almonds (1 lb. in shell or ½ lb. shelled)
Optional for the decorations: multicolored jelly beans, maraschino cherries, chunks of candied fruits and angelica, any colored bits for decorating cakes, fresh flowers and green leaves, colored Easter eggs, etc.

4 Days Ahead

We don't feel under pressure yet; there is not much to do today. Line a large colander with a double-thickness of cheesecloth. Break up the pot cheese with a wooden fork and pile it in loosely. Bring the cheesecloth up over the cheese, cover with a plate somewhat smaller than the colander and put a fairly heavy weight on top. Suspend over a basin in the refrigerator overnight to drain some of the whey.

3 Days Ahead

BASIC RULE FOR BLANCHING ALMONDS: If necessary, shell the almonds. Pour boiling water over the shelled nuts and let stand 3 minutes. Drain and immediately cover with cold water. The skins are now loose and slip off easily. If freshly blanched almonds are to be stored, they must be kept tightly covered in the refrigerator. To prevent them from jumping around when chopping them, first warm and wet the nuts slightly. We chop them with a curved steel chopper that exactly fits its own wooden bowl.* One pound of almonds-in-the-shell makes 1 cup of shelled nuts.

We fit the finest cutter to our electric meat grinder* and pass the drained pot cheese through it twice, collecting it in our largest mixing bowl. (It could also be pushed through a sieve or a potato masher.) Separate the 18 eggs, reserving the whites for meringue (page 176) or anything else; beat the yolks with a wire whisk in a round bowl until they are frothy and lemon-colored. Beat in gradually the 3 tablespoons of vanilla, the 1½ cups of sugar, and the ½ pint of heavy cream. Slowly melt the 1½ pounds of butter, cool to lukewarm, and beat into the eggs. Dice the mixed candied fruits and blend into the eggs. Blend in the blanched and chopped almonds. Now combine the egg mixture and the pot cheese, and we have found no better way than to work with the hands, feeling the nuts and fruits to make sure that they are separated and evenly distributed. Another sign that the mixing is complete is the appearance of a uniform golden-white color, without streaks or patches.

Rinse the cheesecloth in cold water, wring out, and carefully line the four-sided Paskha mold with two thicknesses of the cloth, resting the mold upside down on a board. Still using our fingers, we fill the mold bowl, packing in the Paskha mixture firmly but not too tightly. Lift the ends of the cheesecloth and fold them over so as to cover the big open base. The mold still upside down, balance it over a bowl in the refrigerator in such a way that liquid can freely drip from the narrow end for the next 2 days. During this time the Paskha will dry and set.

The Day Before

The Paskha is now as hard as cream cheese, but it must not venture out of the refrigerator for more than 1 hour at a time. Therefore the various decorating operations must be planned in advance and carried out quickly, so that the Paskha can go back to cool off. Choose the large platter on which it is to be brought to table. Unfold the

cheesecloth so that the base of the Paskha can be put exactly in place in the center of the platter, with the wooden mold still around it. Unscrew the four sides of the mold and carefully pull each away from the cheesecloth. Even more carefully peel the cheesecloth off the Paskha, revealing it in its golden-white, but still bare, glory. It is soft enough so that the jelly beans, half cherries, bits of candied fruits, nuts, etc., can be stuck all over it. We outline the edges of the top, down the four corners and the base with colored bits. On two of the four panels, we usually put a Christian cross, on the third, an "XB" of the Russian Orthodox Church (meaning, in the Cyrillic alphabet, "Christ is Risen"), and on the fourth panel perhaps a lamb or an angel. Hold in the refrigerator.

Before Bringing It to Table

Hard-boiled, colored eggs are placed around the base of the Paskha and fruit and nuts are used to prevent the eggs from rolling. Two or three bright fresh flowers, with stems not more than an inch long, are stuck into the top of the Paskha. More flowers and green leaves are arranged on the platter. Then it is carried to table. It is served and eaten with spoons and has the texture of a fruit-and-nut-stuffed cream cheese.

RUSSIAN TEA

After the Paskha is enjoyed, a Russian host in old St. Petersburg would bring in the samovar from which would be dispensed hot, very weak tea with only a little sugar and slices of lemon, served in heatproof glasses, which are held in silver stands with ivory handles. For a general discussion of the various teas, see page 518.

An Arab Feast Day Buffet

MENU

WINES

Hunkar Begendi—An Eggplant Dip

*A dry Mascara Rosé**

Samak Bi Taheeni—Cold Sea Bass
with Sesame Sauce

Shamshiri's Chellow Kebabs of Lamb
with
Green-Garnished Persian Rice
Lavash—Unleavened Bread
'Ayraan—Iced Bubbling Yogurt

Arab Honey-Nut Pastries:
Loukoumi
Halvah
Baklava
Tel Kadayif

A sweet Greek Mavrodaphne

Arab or Turkish Coffee

A Turkish Raki

* True believers in the prophet Mohammed are not, of course, permitted wine, but we infidels might accompany the first three courses with this Algerian native "gulping" wine, now widely available—a simple wine to stress the hearty peasant character of the meal.

Dishes for an Arab Feast Day

We found the mashed eggplant first in Istanbul, but it appears all over the Arab world, sometimes as a hot cream, sometimes as a thick mash accompanying lamb or fish. We like to add Parmesan cheese and serve the mash as a cold, creamy dip, putting it in a small bowl in the middle of a larger platter surrounded by a variety of unusual breads and crackers: thin toasted and buttered rye, Norwegian crisp breads, Swedish limpa, etc.✲

For the fish platter we use a whole sea bass at this time of year, but in winter it would be red snapper and at other seasons it might be any other good baking fish.

Shamshiri's is the famous "bistro" of the Iranian capital, Teheran. It is away from the center of the modern city, in a cellar in the old shoe market, with low prices and always a crowd. Only this one dish is served and what Shamshiri does to the lamb to make it so good is a "secret." Our method is as near as an outsider can come to the truth.

Shopping for Arab Ingredients and Equipment

The *taheeni* sesame paste, which gives a most unusual and dramatic flavor to the fish, is now easily available by mail.✲ The ground sumac seed, an extraordinary Arab spice with a slight flavor of lemon, is not essential but is well worth ordering in advance.✲ So is the *lavash,* the unleavened Arab bread, a flat disc the size of a dinner plate, which is packaged and can be shipped by mail.✲ The special long-grain Persian rice can also be ordered,✲ but as a second choice domestic long-grain rice can be used. Many neighborhood bakeshops or Middle Eastern delicacy shops now sell the Arab honey pastries.✲ The long-handled "imbrik," the Turkish copper coffeepot, and the ultra-finely ground Turkish blends (see page 516) can also be ordered by mail.✲

Planning and Timing

There are no special difficulties in planning or serving this meal, which shares some of the gastronomic character of Turkey, Lebanon, and Iran. The *hunkar begendi,* which means "the king liked it," is best made the day before and refrigerated overnight. The fish is also served cold and is prepared in advance. The lamb for the kebabs is cut and marinated the day before. The final grilling of the meat and cooking of the rice takes hardly more than 30 minutes.

HUNKAR BEGENDI—AN EGGPLANT DIP

For a party of 8 to 10

Check Staples:

Salt butter (2 Tbs.)
Lemon (1)
Milk (2/3 cup)
Aromatics: crystal salt,☨ freshly ground black pepper,☨ whole nutmeg
Granulated instantized flour⊜ (about 2 Tbs.)
Olive oil⊜ (1 or 2 Tbs.)

Shopping List:

Eggplants (2 medium)
Italian sweet red onion (1 medium)
Parmesan cheese (6 oz.)
Plus the assortment of breads and crackers on which to serve it, *see* page 257

The Day Before—Baking the Eggplant in About 1 Hour, Unsupervised

Preheat oven to 400 degrees, prick each eggplant with a fork in about a dozen places, rub with olive oil, and place on an open baking dish in the center of the oven. They are done when skins begin to crisp and split and inside pulp feels soft, usually in under 1 hour. While baking is in progress, finely mince the onion and grate the 6 ounces of Parmesan. Set the 2/3 cup of milk to warm, but do not allow to boil. In a saucepan over medium frying heat melt the 2 tablespoons of butter and very lightly sauté the onion. Blend in just enough of the flour to make a thick *roux*. Keep stirring until flour browns slightly. Now blend in just enough milk to form a smooth, thick sauce. Turn off heat, press waxed paper on surface to prevent skin forming. Cover and hold until eggplant is ready.

Still the Day Before—Final Assembly in About 20 Minutes

When eggplants are done, open them up, dig out inside pulp and put into a second saucepan over medium heat. Mash down and stir continually, to evaporate water. At the same time, gradually squeeze in juice of half a lemon, tasting and squeezing until lemon flavor is strongly asserted. Water should have evaporated and mash be quite thick after about 5 minutes of bubbling and stirring.

Now add white sauce, beating it in with a small wire whisk, using circular strokes to get air and lightness into it. Add: salt, pepper, and nutmeg to taste. Then add grated Parmesan, 1 tablespoon at a time, until there is the right balance of flavor between cheese and lemon. Finally, if necessary a few more drops of warm milk to adjust the thickness of the dip. Hold overnight, covered, in the refrigerator, to blend flavors.

Serving

The dip may be served at room temperature or carefully reheated, surrounded by its assortment of breads and crackers (page 257).

SAMAK BI TAHEENI—COLD SEA BASS IN SESAME SAUCE

For a party of 8 to 10

This recipe appears on page 594, where it is prepared with the red snapper of the fall. However since the snapper is not in season in springtime, we would prepare it now with a whole sea bass. All other details of the recipe are the same.

SHAMSHIRI'S CHELLOW KEBABS OF LAMB

For a party of 8 to 10

Check Staples:

Clear beef bouillon (6 cups)
Salt butter (1 lb.)
Eggs, large (1 yolk per person)
Aromatics: crystal salt,* freshly ground black pepper,* Spanish saffron filaments (1 Tbs.)
Yellow onions (3 medium)
Scallions (2 bunches)
Watercress (2 bunches)

Shopping List:

Lean spring lamb (about 4 lbs., boned leg or shoulder, all fat cut away)
Plain yogurt (4 pts.)
Buttermilk (1 qt.)
Club soda (2 qts.)
Radishes (2 bunches)
Tarragon pickles (1 medium jar)
Arab specialties:
Long-grain Persian rice* (2 lbs.) or, as a compromise, long-grain domestic rice
***Lavash,* unleavened bread* (1 box)**
Ground sumac seed* (1 small package)

The Day Before—Marinating the Lamb

The exact shape of the lamb strips is one of the secrets of the dish. Cut the meat across the grain into strips 5 inches long, 1½ inches wide, and ½ inch thick. Prepare the marinade by blending in a large mixing bowl: 1 pint of the yogurt, the tablespoon of saffron, and the 3 onions, finely chopped. Work in the meat, making sure that each piece is well coated. Pour in just enough buttermilk to cover the meat, usually about 2 cups. Work the meat again to mix everything thoroughly. Refrigerate overnight.

On the Morning of the Day—Preparing the Green Garnish

Cut up fairly fine and put into a large bowl: some of the tarragon pickles, scallions, radishes, watercress, parsley, etc. Add salt and pepper to taste, but no dressing. Mix well. Cover and crisp in the refrigerator.

1 Hour Before Serving—Boiling the Rice

We use a rice ball* large enough to hold 4 cups of the rice, and immerse it in a pot of boiling salted water. As soon as the water returns to a boil, set the timer for 7 minutes and let it bubble steadily. Meanwhile preheat oven to 350 degrees and make ready a 2½- to 3-quart covered bean pot. Lavishly butter the inside. Bring the 6 cups of beef bouillon to a boil. Fish out the rice ball and let hot water from the faucet run over it for 1 or 2 seconds, to loosen the rice inside. Put the rice into the bean pot, dot it with 4 or 5 tablespoons of butter, cover the opening with a clean square of folded cloth, and jam down the lid. The cloth collects the steam and keeps the rice grains separate. Put the bean pot in the oven for 30 to 35 minutes, until the rice is just done. Warm up two platters, one for the rice, the other for the lamb. Separate the eggs, putting away the whites for some other purpose, and resting each yolk in half its shell.

30 Minutes Before Serving—Grilling the Lamb

Preheat the broiler to high temperature. Thread the lamb strips on skewers and rub each with olive oil, salt, and pepper. Grill the lamb close to the heat, turning it several times, and recoating it with oil so that it gets crisp on the outside but remains pink inside. The total time it takes with our grill is usually about 12 minutes, but it can vary slightly.

10 Minutes Before Serving—Preparing the 'Ayraan

For each person fill a tall iced-tea glass half full with the plain yogurt. Now put a couple of ice cubes in each glass and fill them up with soda water. Add a pinch of salt and put a long spoon in each.

The Way Shamshiri Serves It

Both the serving platters and the plates must be quite hot. On the dining table the knives, forks, and spoons are stood up in glasses of hot water, so that nothing sticks to them when the mixing begins. Make a huge mound of the rice in the middle of one of the platters, set the egg yolks in their shells around the top, lavishly dot the mound with lumps of butter, which melt to yellow pools, and surround with the green garnish. Set the hot lamb on the other platter and bring everything to

the table. Set a tall glass of the *'ayraan* beside each wineglass. Each diner is served a small mound of the rice. He makes a depression in the top and pours in an egg yolk. On top of this he puts several spoonfuls of the green garnish and then mixes everything together on his plate. More butter may also be melted in. Arrange pieces of lamb around the *chellow* and sprinkle them with the sumac powder. There may also be a side mound of separate green garnish. The *'ayraan* is stirred to fizz up and is sipped to sharpen the appetite in between mouthfuls of the *chellow kebabs.* Each diner has at his left a large round of the *lavash* bread.

ARAB HONEY PASTRIES

These rich and sweet desserts are the invariable ending to a dinner in Greece, Turkey, Lebanon, Iran, Egypt, and the Muslim states of Arabia and North Africa. From one of the many New York stores that carry them✱ we might choose: *baklava,* made from paper-thin layers of phyllo pastry (never less than 36 layers, sometimes more than 100), interleaved with buttered chopped nuts and honey; *tel kadayif,* like squares of shredded wheat, also with buttered nuts, honey, and clotted cream; halvah, crisp and flaky bars made of butter whipped with cornstarch and sugar syrup; or *loukoumi,* a soft, sticky candy, made from gelatinous rose water, chopped pistachio nuts, and orange sugar. And there are many others. . . .

ARAB OR TURKISH COFFEE

For the authentic version one needs an "imbrik," the long-handled copper or brass Turkish coffeepot,✱ a supply of the special roast of Middle Eastern coffee, ground almost as fine as dust, and granulated white sugar. There are many methods of brewing the coffee and much ceremony surrounding its service. It is offered to the guests in tiny, smaller-than-demitasse cups set out on an inlaid brass tray, and it is considered an essential courtesy that each cup have its share of the foam which develops on top of the coffee during the brewing.

Our Turkish coffeepot makes 4 cups at a time but, since the whole operation takes only 2 or 3 minutes, many people can be served. For each person put into the pot 1 heaping teaspoon of coffee and 1 level teaspoon of granulated sugar. Add 4 ounces of cold water for each person. Bring it rapidly to a boil, without stirring, then take it off the heat, stir, and put it back on the heat. The second time it comes to the boil, it will froth. Take it off, stir it, and put it back on the heat. Let it froth up in this way three times. Then quickly spoon equal quantities of the froth into each cup, stir once more, and fill up each cup. We use an eye dropper to add 2 or 3 drops of cold water to each cup, to settle the grounds. Naturally, coffee spoons are not used.

Informal Party Menus

Of course, we don't plan a foreign menu every time we give a party. Much of our entertaining involves less time spent on shopping and preparation.

SPRING PARTY LUNCH I:
- Wheel of Okra with Hollandaise Sauce, page 464
- Pan-American Escabeche, page 268
- French Clafouti of Bing Cherries, page 326

SPRING PARTY LUNCH II:
- Iced Avocado Cream, page 274
- Grilled Sicilian Shrimp, page 595
- Watercress Salad
- Fresh Strawberries, page 323

SPRING PARTY COLD BUFFET:
- Marinated Mushrooms, page 107
- Circassian Cold Chicken with Walnut Sauce, page 288
- Dutch Tomato Platter with Fresh Basil, page 321
- Concord Grape Kissel, page 479

SPRING PARTY SUPPER:
- Wine-Boiled Shrimp with Sauce Rémoulade, page 108
- Quiche de Georges de Fessenheim, page 301
- Salad of Spring Greens, page 318
- Rhubarb Sherbet, page 322

SPRING PARTY DINNER I:

Hot-Weather Tomato Cream, page 271
Spring Lamb with Dill Sauce, page 277
Pearl Barley with Mushrooms, page 317
Fresh Fruit with Cheese, page 322

SPRING PARTY DINNER II:

Cherrystone Clams on the Half Shell
Sam's Pot Roast of Beef, page 282
French Gratin of New Potatoes, page 314
Modified Spring Caesar Salad with Arugula, page 320
Strawberries with Maple Cheese, page 325

THE FAMILY MEALS OF SPRING
Day-to-Day Recipes

¶ *Prologues (Appetizers)—Canapés · Hors d'Oeuvres · Zakuski*

For a general discussion of what we mean by "prologues," and the various appetizers of different countries, see page 105.

SCOTCH WOODCOCK—A CANAPÉ WITH DUNLOP CHEESE

For our family of 4

This prologue is fairly solid and might be followed by a light main course. Dunlop cheese is named after the small town in the county of Ayr in Scotland. When properly aged it toasts perfectly, the heat bringing out a sharp aftertaste which is a delight.

Check Staples:

Eggs (4)

Shopping List:

Scottish Dunlop cheese (about ½ lb.)
Rolled anchovy fillets (two 2-oz. cans)
Rye bread (1 loaf canapé rounds)

About 2½ Hours Before Serving

Hard-boil the eggs. On each round of rye bread place a thick lengthwise slice of egg and a slice of Dunlop cheese about ¼ inch thick and just large enough to hide the egg. In the center of the cheese, place a rolled anchovy fillet, dribbling a little of the anchovy oil over the cheese. Hold at room temperature for 1 to 2 hours.

Just Before Serving

Set the grill on high heat. Place all the Scotch Woodcocks on a baking sheet under it. They are done as soon as the cheese is flecked with brown and its corners droop. Serve instantly on hot small plates.

PAN BAGNA—A SALAD HERO SANDWICH

For a hungry family of 4

This light hors d'oeuvre (to be followed by a solid main course) comes from the French Mediterranean coast near the Italian border and is obviously influenced by the cuisines of both countries. We usually serve the long stuffed loaf on a bread board. It looks like an ordinary loaf and the guest who cuts a slice is surprised to find the unexpected stuffing, which tastes sharp and refreshing on a hot spring day.

Check Staples:

Aromatics: crystal salt, freshly ground black pepper, MSG, garlic (1 or 2 cloves), Hungarian sweet red paprika
Scallions (1 bunch)
Olive oil (about ½ cup)
Tarragon white wine vinegar (about 1 Tbs.)

Shopping List:

Bread (a long, narrow French loaf)
Ripe tomatoes (4 medium)
Green peppers (2 medium)
Italian red or sweet Spanish onion (1 large or 2 medium)
Olives (about ½ lb., mixed black and green, preferably several of the marinated types available loose at Greek or Italian stores)
Capers (2¼-oz. jar)
Small sour pickles (about 2 oz.)
Red pimientos (4-oz. can or jar)
Flat anchovy fillets (2-oz. can)

Preparation the Day Before—A Must

In this salad mix we are not bound by fixed measurements. We blend and taste and adjust. Into a large bowl coarsely chop the 4 tomatoes, the onion, scallions, the 2 green peppers, red pimientos, pitted olives, pickles, also adding the whole capers, the garlic (crushed), and the anchovies (chopped), at the same time seasoning to taste with the salt, pepper, MSG, and paprika. As the mixing proceeds, with a wooden spoon, add a few drops of the vinegar and a larger amount of the olive oil, but only a little at a time, allowing it to be absorbed. Too much oil makes the bread soggy. Refrigerate for at least 1 hour.

Carefully cut the French loaf in half lengthwise, as if for a hero sandwich, making sure that upper and lower halves are about the same

size. With the fingers, carefully pull out the white center crumb from the full length of each half, leaving the crust-wall of the loaf at least ½ inch thick. If it is too thin, the loaf will break while being served. Treat the crumbs gently, so that they are still fluffy when added to the salad mix. As the bread absorbs the olive oil, add a few drops more if necessary.

Now begins the tricky business of stuffing the loaf. The lower half looks like a long boat and into it the salad mix is firmly pressed. Pile it just high enough so that, when the top half is pressed down over it like a lid the two halves will meet exactly, with neither an air space inside nor a break between the two halves. Tie them firmly together with several loops of string, wrap tightly in aluminum foil and refrigerate for at least 24 hours.

To Serve

When the loaf is untied it will be firmly set and the salad flavors will have soaked into the bread. Serve quite cold. Set the loaf carefully on a large bread board and provide a sharp bread knife. Slice about ½ inch thick and lay flat on small plates. Eat with a fork.

OUR MODIFIED GENOESE PESTO DIP

For our family of 4

Pesto is the famous specialty of the port city of Genoa, made by pounding a type of basil that grows along the Ligurian coast and blending it with sardo cheese, which is made from ewes' milk and comes from the nearby island of Sardinia. Since these ingredients are simply not available in the United States, we use our own combination of greens. The cheese can be either the Argentine version of sardo or a fine Parmesan. Like its Genoese original, it can be used as an appetizer on blinis (see next recipe) or as a dressing for a dish of pasta, or it can be stirred into a hearty soup or spooned into a baked potato.

Check Staples:

Lemon (1)
Mayonnaise, preferably homemade, page 423, or alternative (about 1 cup)
Aromatics: crystal salt, freshly ground black pepper, MSG, garlic (1 to 3 cloves, to taste)
Parsley (small bunch)
Green scallions (1 bunch)
Watercress (1 bunch)
Olive oil (a few tsp. if necessary)

Shopping List:

Arugula, *see* shopping notes, page 227 (small bunch)
Imported Italian or Argentine sardo cheese, or Parmesan, *see* above, or a combination of both (about ½ lb.)

Prepared in About 10 Minutes—Chilled for 4 Hours

The amount of the greens is not critical. We wash and dry them, then pick out enough young leaves and tender stalks to make a small handful of each. We grind them all together in our electric meat grinder,* using the finest blade. (Or they could be finely chopped or pounded, but not too smoothly.) Put the ground greens into a large mixing bowl and begin blending in the mayonnaise, 1 tablespoon at a time, until the greens are worked into a thick but still fairly coarse dip. At the same time work in as much garlic mashed through a garlic press, as wanted; plus lemon juice, squeeze by squeeze; and salt, pepper, and MSG to taste. When pungent flavor and thick consistency have been achieved, set bowl in refrigerator for a few minutes, while grating the ½ pound of sardo or Parmesan cheese. Fold this in, tablespoon by tablespoon, but do not necessarily use all of it. Taste repeatedly and judge whether the flavor seems right. Sauce must be strong and pungent. Then refrigerate, covered, for at least 4 hours, and serve in a bowl as a dip or drop spoonfuls on blinis (recipe follows) or spread on crackers, preferably unsalted, or use more generally as a sauce. If it needs to be thinned, a little olive oil can be worked in.

BASIC METHOD FOR MAKING RUSSIAN ZAKUSKI BLINIS—SMALL CANAPÉ PANCAKES

For our family of 4

The classic Russian pancakes are not very different from ours, except that they are always made quite small (not more than 2 to 2½ inches across) and they are never topped with sweet syrups, but always with savory tidbits, etc. They are excellent with dabs of the *pesto* (preceding recipe).

Check Staples:

Salt butter, for frying blinis (several Tbs.)
Eggs (2 large)
Milk (1½ cups)
Double-acting baking powder (1 tsp.)
Granulated instantized flour▣ (1 cup)
Granulated white sugar (1 tsp.)

Shopping List:

Sour cream (½ pt.)

About 30 Minutes Before Serving

Assemble the batter in a mixing bowl. Spread the cup of flour across the bottom. Sprinkle over, in turn, the teaspoon of baking powder and the teaspoon of sugar, then make a crater in the center and pour in 1 cup of the milk. Blend with fingers until all dry ingredients are incorporated into a fairly stiff dough. Break the 2 eggs into a separate bowl, beat hard with a wire whisk, then blend into dough, at the same time incorporating 3 tablespoons of the sour cream. Blend lightly but thoroughly, then gradually thin down to the consistency of thick whipping cream by adding, alternately, dash by dash, more milk and sour cream. Cover and let stand at room temperature for 20 minutes.

About 5 Minutes Before Serving

Heat up a frying pan or griddle to medium-high frying temperature; grease bottom with butter as needed; then beat up batter and readjust consistency with more milk, as necessary, and quickly fry small pancakes until brown on both sides. These blinis can be used in place of toast under almost any savory prologue canapé.

PAN-AMERICAN ESCABECHE—A FISH SALAD

For our family of 4

This hors d'oeuvre appears on the menus of many Latin-American countries, with regional variations and sometimes different names. It is a fairly solid dish and should be followed by a light main course, or it could itself be a main course for a luncheon or supper. It is always served cold and improves by being kept overnight in the refrigerator.

Check Staples:

Salt butter (¼ lb.)
Eggs (4 large)
Clear bouillon (a few Tbs.)
Lemons (3)
Aromatics: crystal salt, freshly ground black pepper, MSG, chervil, garlic (1 or 2 cloves), oregano, tarragon, thyme
Yellow onion (1 medium)
Fresh parsley (1 bunch)
Shallots (3 or 4)
Watercress (1 bunch)
Indian chick-pea flour or all-purpose flour (a few Tbs.)
Olive oil (about 1 cup)
Tarragon white wine vinegar (a few Tbs.)
Dry white wine (1 cup)

Shopping List:

Fresh tuna or other oily fish, *see list, page 216* (1 lb.)
Heavy cream (1 Tbs.)
Tomatoes (2 medium)
Green hot peppers (fresh or canned, a few slices)
Italian red onion (2 medium)
Pine nuts (about 2 oz.)
Black olives (about ¼ lb.)

Can Be Made the Day Before—Improves with Keeping

We cut the fish in pieces roughly 2 inches by 2 inches and about ½ inch thick. In a bowl large enough to hold the fish mix a marinade: ⅓ cup of the olive oil, the juice of 2 of the lemons, about 2 tablespoons of chopped parsley, 1 or 2 cloves of garlic, crushed, about ¼ teaspoon each of the dried chervil, tarragon, and thyme, plus salt, pepper, and MSG to taste. Marinate the fish for several hours, covered, in the refrigerator.

Bring fish back to room temperature and prepare to fry. Break 2 of the eggs onto a plate and beat lightly with the tablespoon of cream. On a second plate spread 2 or 3 tablespoons of the chick-pea flour. Finely chop the yellow onion and shallots. Bring a sauté pan up to medium frying heat (325 degrees), covering the bottom with a half-and-half mixture of olive oil and butter. Sauté the onion and shallots until just golden. Take the pieces of fish from the marinade, roll each first in the egg, then in the flour, and fry to a golden-brown. Then sprinkle over 2 tablespoons each of the white wine and the bouillon, bring heat down to simmering, cover, and let fish steam for about 7 minutes, basting 2 or 3 times with the pan juices. Remove fish to a covered storage dish and hold in the refrigerator.

When the sauté pan is cool we prepare the sauce, tasting and adjusting as we blend. Add to the pan: about 2 tablespoons of the pine nuts, about 3 tablespoons of the original fish marinade, plus extra olive oil and tarragon vinegar, if necessary, to taste. We try to achieve the basic flavor of French dressing. Hold in a covered jar in the refrigerator.

1½ Hours Before Serving

Hard-boil the remaining 2 eggs. Peel the red onions and slice into wafer-thin rings and put in a bowl. Pour in the sauce and let stand while it comes to room temperature. Cut the tomatoes in wedges. Wash and chop enough watercress to make a bed on the serving platter. Sliver the hot peppers. Hold these decorative vegetables crisp in the refrigerator.

Arranging the Serving Platter

On a large oval platter we make a bed of the watercress, neatly arrange the fish, pour over the sauce with the onion slices, and decorate with tomato wedges, black olives, slivered hot peppers, and half-moon wedges of the hard-boiled eggs. Pan-American gourmets consider this as a salad first course and expect it to be served quite cold.

A RUSSIAN ZAKUSKA—FALSHIVANNAYA IKRA (MOCK CAVIAR)

For our family of 4

It is not caviar, but it is so cheap and easy to prepare and has such variety that it is one of the most useful kickshaws to have available in the refrigerator. It can be a light start to almost any meal, or provide an excellent cocktail or midnight snack.

Check Staples:

Lemon (1)
Aromatics: crystal salt, freshly ground black pepper, MSG, garlic (1 to 3 cloves, to taste), Worcestershire sauce
Italian tomato paste (6-oz. can)
Olive oil (about 4 Tbs.)
Spanish Sherry vinegar (about 3 Tbs.)

Shopping List:

Ripe eggplant (3 medium)
Italian sweet red onion (2 small)
Green pepper (1)
Fresh herbs (2 or 3 from the following to make ⅓ cup: basil, chive, dill, tarragon)

At Least 2 Days Before

The secret is in the slow-baking of the eggplant. Neither fast-baking, boiling, or frying seems to bring out the flavor to the same extent or make the pulp as black and grainy. Rub the eggplant with olive oil, place in an open baking dish and, just before going to bed, set it in the slowest possible oven (200 to 225 degrees) and leave it there all night.

The Next Morning

The eggplant will have collapsed, the skins will be black and partly crisp, and the bottom of the baking dish will be covered by an ink-black liquid. Carefully scrape out the good pulp and put it in a large mixing bowl, pouring over it the black ink, and throwing away the skin. Crush through a press as many cloves of garlic as taste permits and add to the eggplant. Now add: the onions, green pepper, and fresh herbs, all finely chopped. Using a two-pronged steel carving fork, which helps to break up the pulp, start mixing vigorously, adding little by little: about 4 tablespoons of the tomato paste and about the same amount of olive oil, about 3 tablespoons of the vinegar, about 1 teaspoon of Worcestershire sauce, the juice of a lemon, plus salt, pepper, and MSG to taste. We try to recapture the flavor we know and like, by tasting and adjusting. Refrigerate for at least 24 hours, tightly covered.

Serving

To serve as a canapé, put small piles of it on buttered squares of thin-sliced back Westphalian pumpernickel; or chill in a serving bowl and set on a small buffet table, along with sardines, bits of pickled herring, slices of salami, smoked salmon rolls, etc., and let the guests help themselves. It is also excellent eaten with cold meats, fish, chicken, turkey, game birds, etc.

¶ *Prologues (Soups)—Light Hot Creams · Bouillons · Iced Creams*

Even on warm days we find a cup of hot soup a soothing appetite-whetter. We insist, though, that our spring and summer soups be light and delicate. The same rule applies to a few cold soups, which have become family "regulars." Since they require chicken broth, we often team them with a Belgian *waterzooie* (page 286), which provides an excellent main course and a fine, clear broth.

HOT-WEATHER TOMATO CREAM

For our family of 4

This is a light soup, to go with a substantial main dish.

Check Staples:

Clear chicken broth (about 2 cups)
Milk (about 2 cups)
Aromatics: crystal salt,⁑ freshly ground black pepper,⁑ MSG,▣
Yellow onion (1 medium)
Watercress (1 bunch)
Ground arrowroot▣ (about 2 tsp.)

Shopping List:

Tomatoes (2½ lbs., preferably vine-ripened as soon as their season starts)

Preparation in About 30 Minutes

Chunk the tomatoes into a saucepan. Add the onion, chopped, about 2 teaspoons of salt, plus black pepper and MSG to taste. Bring mixture to a boil, stirring and crushing the tomatoes with a wooden spoon, then simmer, covered, until the tomatoes are quite mushy, usually about 15 minutes. Let cool slightly, then pass through a food mill. In a small bowl blend 2 teaspoons of the arrowroot with just enough cold milk to liquefy it and blend into the tomatoes. Return to the saucepan and reheat, stirring continuously to keep it smooth as it thickens slightly. In another saucepan combine the chicken broth and remaining milk and heat to just below boiling. Slowly pour this hot liquid into the tomato purée, stirring steadily. Do not let boil, but keep quite hot for about 5 minutes. We like it fairly thin. If it gets too thick, add a bit more milk. If too thin, add another teaspoon of arrowroot liquefied in milk. If lumps form, pass once more through the food mill.

To Serve

We garnish each bowl with finely chopped watercress.

HOT-WEATHER CREAM OF SORREL

For our family of 4

Sorrel (*oseille* in French cookbooks) is a wild grass that grows in sandy soil, often not far from beaches, and is now gathered commercially in many parts of the country, so that it is available in the spring in the stores. It has a slight flavor of lemon, a refreshing sharpness in a soup, and a strong affinity with eggs (page 348) and with mussels (page 429).

Check Staples:

Salt butter (2 Tbs.)
Clear chicken broth (2½ cups)
Eggs (3 large)
Aromatics: crystal salt, freshly ground black pepper, MSG
Yellow onion (1 medium)

Shopping List:

Fresh sorrel (1 bunch, enough when shredded to make 2 cups)
Light cream (1 cup)

About 30 Minutes to Prepare

Thoroughly wash the sorrel, discard the tough stalks, and finely chop the leaves. Peel and finely chop the onion. Melt the butter in a saucepan and gently sauté the onion until just transparent. Add the sorrel and stir it around until it begins to melt into a purée. Gradually blend in the chicken broth, stirring continuously to keep everything smooth. Let simmer 5 minutes. Meanwhile separate the 3 eggs, putting the yolks in a small bowl and reserving the whites for some other purpose. Add the cup of cream to the yolks and beat until smooth.

Just Before Serving

Blend a little of the hot broth into the egg-cream mixture, then a little more, up to a cup. Reduce the heat under the saucepan so that it is not quite boiling and then add egg-cream mixture; under no circumstances allow it to bubble. Adjust the seasonings with salt, pepper, and MSG.

CLEAR MUSHROOM BOUILLON

For our family of 4

This has remained one of our favorite clear soups, hot or cold, for twenty years. It is also an excellent base stock for many recipes, so we usually prepare it in double or triple quantity.

Check Staples:

Aromatics: crystal salt, freshly ground black pepper, MSG, whole caraway seed, sweet marjoram
Green scallions (1 bunch)

Shopping List:

Fresh mushrooms (1½ lbs.)
French, Italian, or Chinese dried field mushrooms (2-oz. package)
Sweet Bermuda onion (1 large)

The Day Before—Preparing the Basic Bouillon in About 1½ Hours

Put into the deep soup pot 2 quarts of freshly drawn cold water and the dried mushrooms, the larger pieces broken up. Simmer, uncovered, for about 30 minutes (set timer). We do all the boiling of this bouillon uncovered, so that the flavor is strengthened as some of the water boils away. Wipe 1 pound of the fresh mushrooms clean with a damp cloth (never wash or peel) and slice fairly thinly. Peel and chunk the onion. When the timer rings, add the fresh mushrooms, the onion, and a full tablespoon of the caraway seed, but no salt yet. Gently simmer, "just smiling," uncovered, for 1 hour or so. Cool and store overnight in the refrigerator, with the solids left in the bouillon, to intensify the flavors.

The Next Day—2 Hours or More Before Serving

Reheat to a gentle simmer and add: about 1 teaspoon of dried marjoram (or better still, some leaves of fresh marjoram), 2 or 3 teaspoons of salt, plus black pepper and MSG to taste. Continue gently simmering, uncovered, about 1 hour more. During these repeated simmerings the liquid should be reduced by approximately one third.

Now strain out the remaining solids, carefully squeezing them to make sure that not one drop of their highly flavored essence is lost. This is the finished bouillon, which should now be tasted and adjusted for seasoning. Its delicate flavor can be strengthened, if desired, by being rapidly boiled down to less volume. It can be stored almost indefinitely in the refrigerator.

Serving Suggestions

TO SERVE HOT: Choose about 8 of the remaining mushroom caps. Clean them carefully and peel off any stains. Coarsely grate them into a serving bowl and blend into them about 1 tablespoon of lemon juice and 2 or 3 tablespoons of the finely chopped green scallion tops. Spoon some of this mixture into each serving of the hot bouillon.

TO SERVE AS ICED CONSOMMÉ: On top of each serving float 1 to 2 teaspoons of heavy cream, then lightly sprinkle on grated mushroom so that it floats on top.

TO SERVE JELLIED: Jell according to our basic method (page 134). Sprinkle grated mushroom over each serving.

ICED AVOCADO CREAM

For our family of 4

The avocado seems to magnify the flavor of garlic, so be careful.

Check Staples:

Clear chicken broth (2 cups)
Lemons (2)
Aromatics: crystal salt, freshly ground black pepper, MSG, garlic (1 clove)
Green scallions (1 bunch)
Dry Sherry (a few Tbs.)

Shopping List:

Ripe avocados (2 large)
Light cream (1 cup)

Prepared in About 10 Minutes, But Chilled for Several Hours

We use an electric blender, but the avocado can be sieved or mashed, though preparation time is a little longer. We cut the avocados in half, remove the stones and, with a small melon scoop, dig out and hold a few neat balls for later garnish. The rest of the avocado flesh is spooned into the jar of the blender. Add the clove of garlic, crushed through a press, plus about ½ cup of the cream. Squeeze juice from the lemons and add about 1 tablespoon to the avocado mix. Add chicken broth to the blender jar until it is three quarters full. Blend at high speed for the minimum number of seconds to achieve a smooth cream—5 seconds should be enough. Over-blending seems to destroy the flavor of the avocado. Transfer the purée into a mixing bowl. Then add, a little at a time, tasting and adjusting to achieve the right flavor and thickness: more cream, chicken broth, or lemon juice, plus salt, pepper, and MSG to taste. The final consistency should be of thin cream. Chill for several hours, or overnight.

To Serve

Chill the soup bowls. Stir 2 tablespoons of dry Sherry, or more to taste, into each serving. Garnish with the avocado balls and finely chopped green scallion tops.

ICED BROCCOLI CREAM

For our family of 4

Check Staples:

Clear chicken broth (4 cups)
Aromatics: crystal salt, red cayenne pepper, MSG, rosemary
Carrots (2 or 3 small)
Yellow onions (2 medium)
Fresh parsley (1 bunch)
Green scallions (1 bunch)
Ground arrowroot (about 1½ Tbs.)

Shopping List:

Broccoli (1 bunch, about 1 lb.)
White celery (1 heart)
Light cream (1 cup)

About ½ Hour to Prepare, But Several Hours to Chill

Heat the chicken broth in a large saucepan. Cut off the tender flowerets of the broccoli and hold. Coarsely chunk the stalks and drop into the simmering broth. Add: the onions, coarsely chunked; the carrots, scraped and sliced; a small handful of the parsley, chopped; plus salt, pepper, and MSG to taste. Simmer, covered, for 15 minutes. Put the broccoli flowerets into a small saucepan and ladle enough of the hot liquid out of the larger saucepan to cover. Simmer flowerets for 5 minutes, strain their liquid back into the main pan and chill the flowerets in the refrigerator for later garninsh. Put 3 teaspoons of the arrowroot into a cup and liquefy with 1 to 2 tablespoons of the cream. Turn off the heat under the main saucepan and blend in the arrowroot, stirring vigorously, until the liquid is thickened to the consistency of light cream. If the first blending of arrowroot is not enough, stir in more in the same way. Cool for a few minutes, then purée in the electric blender at high speed for not more than 20 seconds. Pour into a covered storage dish, stir in about ½ teaspoon dried rosemary, and chill for several hours, or overnight.

Just Before Serving

Blend in the remaining cream. Check and adjust the seasonings. Chill the serving bowls. Garnish each serving with broccoli flowerets and finely chopped green scallion tops.

¶ *Main Dishes (Meats)—Lamb · Pork · Beef · Veal*

Economy Cuts with a Leg of Lamb

At all times of the year, but especially in spring, we find very good value by buying the largest available leg of lamb and cutting it up in our own special way, as shown in the accompanying illustration. Arming ourselves with a

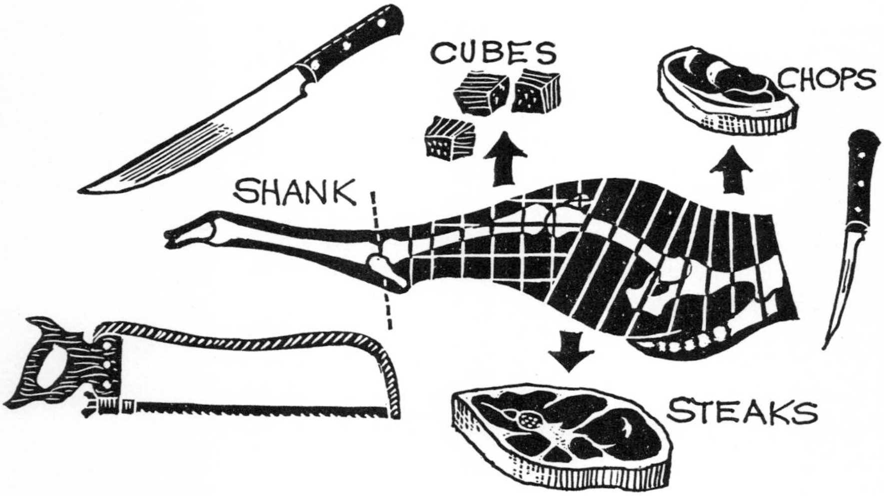

long carving knife, a short pointed knife, and a hacksaw,* we place the leg on its back on a cutting board, with the shank end at the left, as shown. First, we cut off the four or five chops at the right, cutting straight through the bone with the hacksaw and slightly at an angle, so as to square-off the widest part of the leg. Then, cutting straight across the widest part, we remove two or three 1-inch-thick steaks. (These are best marinated for a day or two in a mixture of olive oil, soy sauce, and garlic, then grilled or pan-fried until just pink in the center.) Next, cut off the shank bone at the left, surrounded by a solid chunk of a couple of pounds or so of the less-tender tip of the meat. (We convert this into a low-cost main dish by simmering it with lentils, page 334.) Finally, there is the large center cut of solid lean and tender meat. We feel for the spot where the bone is nearest to the surface, make a long cut exposing the bone; then, using the small knife, we cut closely around the bone and remove it. (It can be boiled with aromatic vegetables to make an excellent lamb broth.) Then, the solid meat is cut into 1½-inch cubes, some of which can be prepared with a dill sauce (recipe follows), while the others are marinated as described in the *arni souvlakia* (page 278) then refrigerated in a covered dish. These marinated chunks of lamb will keep perfectly for a week or more and are among the most useful of all quick, standby meats. As many chunks as needed can be removed from the marinade about 15 minutes before a mealtime, threaded onto skewers with appropriate vegetables and grilled in 8 or 9 minutes. Of course our butcher would, if pressed, do all this cutting for us, but, first, he would not have the time to be as careful and accurate as we are and, second, we find a great pleasure in the skillful use of tools.

SPRING LAMB WITH DILL SAUCE

For our family of 4

This is a light dish and could be teamed with a fairly substantial first course and a solid dessert. Too often the charming flavor of young lamb is lost in complicated preparation or dominated by too-powerful aromatics. Here, the lamb is cosseted in the cooking and set off by fresh spring dill. An excellent lamb stock remains for general use.

Check Staples:

Floured butter—*beurre manié, see* page 12 (2 or 3 Tbs.)
Eggs (1 or 2 yolks)
Aromatics: crystal salt, freshly ground black pepper, MSG, basil, sweet marjoram, thyme
Young carrots (3 or 4)
Yellow onions (2 or 3 medium)
Fresh parsley (1 bunch)
Granulated white sugar (a few Tbs.)
Tarragon white wine vinegar (a few Tbs.)

Shopping List:

Spring lamb, lean (about 1½ lbs.)
Lamb bones (about 2½ lbs.)
Heavy cream (1 or 2 Tbs.)
Fennel (2 or 3 stalks, plus some of the green fronds)
Fresh dill (1 bunch)

The Day Before—Preparing the Stock

Put into a medium stockpot the lamb bones; the onions, carrots, and fennel stalks, all chunked; several sprigs of parsley; plus salt, pepper, and MSG to taste. Cover with freshly drawn cold water and simmer gently for about 2 hours. Cool and refrigerate overnight.

About 1 Hour Before Serving—Gentle Cooking of the Lamb

Skim the fat from the stock. Bring to a simmer. Cut the lamb into 1½-inch cubes and put into a saucepan, surrounded by stalks of the dill and the coarser green fronds of the fennel, chopped. (Hold the finer fronds of both for the sauce.) Add about ½ teaspoon each of basil, marjoram, and thyme, plus salt, pepper, and MSG to taste. Ladle in enough of the hot lamb stock to cover and simmer very gently until the lamb cubes are barely cooked through and very tender, usually in 30 to 40 minutes.

10 Minutes Before Serving—the Sauce

Take out the lamb cubes and keep warm, covered. Strain the liquid in which they were cooked, and if needed add more stock from the main pot to make 1 pint. Put stock back into the saucepan and place it over gentle heat (making sure that it stays below boiling) ; thicken stock to the consistency of heavy cream by carefully stirring in lumps of floured butter. As soon as it is smooth blend in: 1 tablespoon of the sugar, about 1½ tablespoons of the vinegar, the remaining green fronds of dill and fennel, finely chopped, plus salt, pepper, and MSG. Taste and add more sugar or vinegar if needed.

Just Before Serving

Separate the egg and beat the yolk and 1 tablespoon of the cream lightly together. Take the sauce off the heat and quickly and smoothly blend in the egg yolk. If the sauce is now too thick, add a little more stock. If too thin, add a second egg yolk in more cream. Bring the lamb to the table in a hot, covered dish, with some of the sauce poured over. The rest is served in a sauceboat. We like to accompany this with boiled or mashed potatoes and more chopped parsley can be sprinkled onto each serving.

ARNI SOUVLAKIA—GREEK SPRING LAMB ON SKEWERS

For our family of 4

This is a simple and light main dish, to be surrounded by solid courses. As in the preceding recipe, we use cubes of lamb cut from the center of the leg, but the different preparation gives it an entirely different flavor and texture.

Check Staples:

Lemons (3)
Aromatics: crystal salt,⚘ freshly ground black pepper,⚘ sweet marjoram, oregano
Fresh parsley (1 bunch)
Olive oil⛁ (a few Tbs.)

Shopping List:

Spring lamb, boneless lean, from center cut of leg (about 1½ lbs.)

At Least 3 Hours Before Serving, or the Day Before

Cut the lamb into 1½-inch cubes and put in a bowl. Squeeze juice from 2 of the lemons. Rub the lamb cubes with olive oil and lemon juice, then press into the flesh salt, pepper, marjoram, and oregano. Sprinkle over a little more oil and lemon juice. Cover and marinate refrigerated for several hours, or overnight.

20 Minutes Before Serving

Set the grill to high temperature and let it heat up for 5 or 6 minutes. Divide the lamb cubes into 4 portions and thread onto 4 skewers. Grill close to the heat, turning once and basting with the marinade until the outside of each cube is brown while the inside remains pink. With our grill this takes about 5 minutes on the first side and 4 minutes on the second.

Serving at Table

Serve the meat still on the skewers, heavily sprinkled with coarsely chopped parsley. A pilaf of rice (page 166) is an excellent accompaniment.

NOTE: For more spring lamb recipes, see "budget pull-back dishes," page 333.

SPRING PORK CHOPS BURIED IN FARFALLE

For our family of 4

This is a substantial main course, to go with a light prologue and perhaps fruit for dessert. We get variety in our Italian pasta dishes by using the more unusual shapes. Farfalle is a bowtie noodle.

Check Staples:

Salt butter (about 2 Tbs.)
Chicken broth (2 cups)
Floured butter—*beurre manié,* *see* page 12 (4 or 5 Tbs.)
Aromatics: crystal salt, freshly ground black pepper, MSG, Mexican chili powder, sage leaf (crumbled)
Fresh parsley (1 bunch)
Watercress (1 bunch)
Dry bread crumbs (about 1/4 cup)
Granulated instantized flour (a few Tbs.)
Olive oil (about 2 Tbs.)
Italian tomato paste (6-oz. can)

Shopping List:

Spring pork (3/4-inch loin chops, 1 or 2 per person)
Large farfalle (1/2-lb. box)
Fresh mushrooms (1/2 lb.)

About 1 1/4 Hours Before—Frying the Pork Chops

Rub the chops with salt, pepper, MSG, and the crumbled sage leaf, pressing the aromatics into the meat. Spread flour on a plate and lightly coat the chops. Heat a sauté pan to medium frying temperature, covering the bottom with a half-and-half mixture of the olive oil and butter. Slowly fry the chops until well browned, usually in about 20 minutes. Remove from pan and, as soon as cool enough to hold, make a handle at the end of each bone by cutting off about 1 inch of the meat and fat. Keep chops warm, covered.

About 1 Hour Before—the Farfalle and the Sauce

Bring a large pot of salted water to a rolling boil. Drop in the farfalle and let bubble until chewy, *al dente*. Meanwhile heat the chicken broth to just simmering and thicken it by working in lumps of floured butter until the sauce has the consistency of heavy cream. Gently simmer, covered, for 5 minutes. Meanwhile wipe the mushrooms (never wash) and slice them lengthwise; then sauté slices in the pan in which the pork chops were fried, adding more floured butter if needed; finally, add mushrooms to sauce. Also add, tasting and adjusting: a small handful of the parsley, finely chopped, 1 tablespoon each of the tomato paste and chili powder, plus the bits of pork that were cut off the chops. Stir well.

Remove farfalle from pot, rinse under hot running water, and drain. Butter an open casserole (we use one about 6 inches deep, with a flat bottom) and slide in farfalle. Using a wooden spoon as a digging tool, stick the meaty part of the pork chops vertically into the bed of farfalle, so that the rib bones stick up, curving outward, all around the casserole, like a crown roast. Decorate the bare tip of each bone with shiny aluminum foil. Preheat oven to 400 degrees. Quickly sauté the bread crumbs in 1 to 2 tablespoons of butter. Now pour sauce carefully into casserole so that it covers and soaks into farfalle but does not touch the exposed part of the chops. Spread the buttered bread crumbs over farfalle. Place casserole in hot oven and leave until bread crumbs are browned and pork chops are done, usually in about 30 minutes.

Serving at Table

The great attraction of this casserole when it comes to the table is its picnic quality. The foil handles cool almost immediately, so that each diner can pull out his own chop while the head of the house spoons the sauce-filled farfalle. We garnish each plate with crisp watercress.

SPRING PORK CHOPS WITH ROME BEAUTIES IN VALPOLICELLA

For our family of 4

This is a substantial dish and it requires only light surrounding courses.

Check Staples:

Salt butter (about 1/4 lb.)
Aromatics: crystal salt,☆ freshly ground black pepper,☆ MSG,☐ oregano, summer savory
Yellow onion (1 medium)
Pure maple syrup☐ (a few Tbs.)
Dark-brown sugar (2 or 3 Tbs.)

Shopping List:

Spring pork (3/4-inch loin chops, 1 or 2 per person)
Rome Beauty baking apples (4 to 6)
Italian peeled and seeded plum tomatoes (1 lb. 1 oz can)
Indian sweet chutney☆ (small bottle)
Italian Valpolicella red wine☐ (1 bottle, enough for cooking and drinking)

Early in the Day

We butter a French earthenware casserole (wide and shallow, with a straight handle like a frypan and a close-fitting lid). Quickly fry the pork chops in a sauté pan (usually their own fat is enough) until they are just brown, then layer them neatly in the casserole. Sprinkle them with salt, a few grinds of pepper, and MSG. Finely chop the onion and sprinkle it over the pork. Cover the casserole and let chops marinate while making the sauce.

Put into a small saucepan, preferably copper, about 1/3 cup of the Italian tomatoes and gently heat. Now we add, tasting and adjusting: about 2 tablespoons of the Indian chutney and about 1/2 cup of the Valpolicella. The flavors should be balanced, none should dominate. The sauce will be thin, but will reduce and thicken in the casserole. Finally, in a small mixing bowl, blend together about 2 tablespoons of the sugar with about 1 tablespoon of the maple syrup.

About 1 1/2 Hours Before Serving

Preheat oven to 400 degrees. Spoon about half of the tomato-wine sauce onto the pork chops, making sure that each is coated. Cover casserole and set in oven for 30 minutes. Meanwhile cut the Rome Beauty apples in half and core but do not peel (at other times of the year, other baking apples may be used). At the end of the first 30 minutes make a circle of apple halves, cut sides up, around the pork chops, then spoon the rest of the tomato-wine sauce over the apples. Any remaining sauce goes over the pork chops, or they can be basted with the liquids from the bottom of the casserole. Also spoon the sugar mixture over the apples. Put the lid back on the casserole and set it in the oven for another 15 minutes. Baste again and return to the oven, now uncovered, for the last 15 minutes, basting every 5 minutes. We bring the casserole to the table and serve it with the rest of the wine.

AUTHENTIC IRISH STEW

For our family of 4

Of all the great national dishes, Ireland's is the simplest: three ingredients, blended in a big pot, to make a substantial main dish. Many cooks can't believe it and try to improve the stew—with disastrous results. It is an insult to Irish patriots to add the orange of carrots. Enriching it with more meat spoils the flavor balance. Economizing with extra potatoes spoils the texture. The meat must be mutton, and, if we plan to serve the stew on St. Patrick's Day, we order a leg about March 10. The cut pieces must never be browned in advance or the stew will be coated with a heavy grease which the potatoes, wisely, refuse to absorb. An authentic Irish stew has no visible fat.

Check Staples:

Aromatics: crystal salt, freshly ground black pepper, MSG

Shopping List:

Mutton, preferably from the leg, with a small amount of fat (about 2 lbs.)
White boiler onions (2 lbs.)
White boiling potatoes, *see* list, page 222 (2 lbs.)

Well in Advance—the Flavor Improves with Keeping

Cut the mutton into fair-sized chunks. Peel the onions and leave whole. Peel and cut the potatoes to the size of the onions. In the large soup pot put a layer of potatoes on the bottom (this is important, as they melt first and give body to the liquid), then salt, pepper, and MSG, next a layer of the mutton, salt, pepper, and MSG, then a layer of the onions, and repeat until all the ingredients are in. Barely cover the mixture with freshly drawn cold water. Bring to a boil and gently simmer, "just smiling," for several hours. The mutton should be butter-tender, the potatoes mashing into the unctuous gravy, the onions dissolved completely. The soup bowls in which the dish is served should be as hot as the stew.

BOEUF À LA MODE FRANÇAISE

For our family of 4

This is a solid main course, which should be teamed with a light prologue and dessert. Here the meat does not rule the dish. The dominant role is given to the young spring vegetables, and they must be cooked to perfection.

Check Staples:

Floured butter—*beurre manié,* *see* page 12 (a few Tbs.)
Sweet butter (4 to 6 Tbs.)
Mushroom bouillon, page 273, or as second best, clear meat bouillon (2 cups)
Aromatics: crystal salt, freshly ground black pepper, whole bay leaves, garlic (1 clove), thyme
Young carrots (about 6)
Fresh parsley (1 bunch)
Watercress (1 bunch)
***Glace de viande* (1 Tbs.)**
Granulated instantized flour (a few Tbs.)
Italian tomato paste (about 1 Tbs.)
Dry Sherry (2 Tbs.)
Dry white wine (1 cup)

Shopping List:

Top round of beef, lean (1½ lbs.)
White celery (1 heart)
Fresh mushrooms (½ lb.)
White boiler onions (about 12)
New potatoes, small white (1½ lbs.)
White turnips (about 6 small)
French Marc brandy (about ½ cup)

The Day Before

We prepare this dish in one of our enameled cast-iron cocottes,* which can be used for the frying and simmering on top of the stove and which has a tightly fitting lid and can go into the oven. Remove all fat and cut the meat into 1-inch cubes. In bottom of cocotte over medium-high frying heat melt 2 tablespoons of the butter and, as soon as it is hot, quickly sear and brown the pieces of meat lightly on all sides. Then at once pour in ¼ cup of the brandy and flame. When the fire dies down, take out meat with a slotted spoon and make the sauce. Turn down heat to gentle simmering and carefully blend into pan juices: about 1 tablespoon of the tomato paste, about 1 tablespoon of the *glace de viande,* and about 3 tablespoons or a bit more of the flour, to make a firm and smooth *roux.* Turn up heat slightly and blend in the cup of white wine. Turn up heat a little further and keep stirring until sauce bubbles gently and is very smooth. Begin working in the 2 cups of mushroom bouillon or stock, but only enough to give sauce the consistency of heavy cream. Add the aromatics: salt and pepper to taste, 2 whole bay leaves, ¾ teaspoon dried thyme, the clove of garlic, peeled and finely chopped, and a few sprigs of parsley. Put pieces of meat back into cocotte and distribute them evenly in the sauce. Gradually add more mushroom bouillon or stock until meat is barely covered, stirring with a wooden spoon to make sure that the thickened sauce and the new stock are fully blended. Stir in 2 more tablespoons of the brandy, bring it all up to the boiling point, and let it simmer very gently, "just smiling," covered, for 30 minutes. Cool and refrigerate overnight, to blend and mature the flavors.

About 2 Hours Before Serving

Skim the fat from the stew and let it come to room temperature. Peel the onions; scrape the carrots with a wire brush and cut into 1-inch lengths; peel the turnips and quarter; cut the celery heart into quarters lengthwise; and wipe the mushrooms clean and quarter or halve them according to size. The objective is to cut each vegetable into a uniform size for accurate control of cooking time. Preheat the oven to 325 degrees and . . .

Exactly 1½ Hours Before Serving

Put cocotte in oven, covered. Set a sauté pan, preferably copper, over medium-high frying heat and melt in it 2 tablespoons of the butter. When it is hot, lightly sauté each of the vegetables separately till they are specked with brown and then add them to the cocotte according to a staggered schedule. The onions must have 60 minutes of simmering in the cocotte. The carrots and turnips can be sautéed together and simmered 40 minutes; the celery for 30 minutes. The mushrooms are sautéed last, with additional butter if necessary, and require about 10 minutes in the cocotte. Reserve the juices in the sauté pan.

40 Minutes Before Serving

Scrape or peel 1½ pounds of new potatoes, cut the larger ones so that all pieces are roughly the same size, put them in a steamer, salt and pepper them to taste, and steam them separately. They will take roughly 30 minutes.

Just Before Serving

Turn oven down to 200 degrees. Pour the liquid from the cocotte through a strainer into the sauté pan in which the vegetables were browned. Put the cocotte, covered, back into the oven to keep warm. Bring the sauce in sauté pan up to simmering; taste and adjust the seasoning. Stir in 2 tablespoons of the dry Sherry, or a bit more according to taste. Now consider the thickness of the sauce, which should be that of heavy cream. To thicken, turn down the heat and blend in as many small lumps of floured butter as may be needed. Add the steamed potatoes to cocotte, gently distributing them among the meat and vegetables. Pour back the sauce. Over a medium-high heat on top of the stove bring the cocotte back to bubbling; then serve at once. Our cocotte is handsome enough to come to the table. Each serving is sprinkled with finely chopped parsley and watercress.

FILLET OF VEAL STUFFED WITH BING CHERRIES

For our family of 4, with some remaining to be served later

This is lighter than the average main course of roast meat, so it can be preceded by a fairly substantial first course and followed by fruit and cheese. Although it can be prepared with canned cherries, it is outstanding with the fresh Bing cherries of spring. It is excellent cold and can be a handsome centerpiece for a buffet supper, enclosed in a slightly sweet aspic, decorated with whole cherries.

Check Staples:

Salt butter (¼ lb.)
Corn-belly salt pork (about ½ lb.)
Clear veal stock (about 1 cup)
Aromatics: crystal salt, freshly ground black pepper, MSG, whole cardamom pods, ground cinnamon
Arrowroot liquefied with cream, *see* page 14 (1 or 2 tsp.)
Indian chick-pea flour or all-purpose flour (a few Tbs.)
Granulated white sugar (about 1 Tbs.)

Shopping List:

Veal (whole fillet, about 4½ lbs.)
Sweet Bing cherries, ripe (2 lbs.)
Sweet vermouth (about 1 cup)

The Day Before—Advance Preparation of the Meat

We do the most tiresome job first: pitting the cherries (we try to make it a family project) . The veal fillet is like a long sausage about 4 inches in diameter. With a small sharp knife, we cut a deep slit, starting and finishing about 2 inches from each end and cutting down to within 1 inch of the bottom of the meat. We then have a pocket, about 3 inches deep and perhaps 12 to 15 inches long. Into this pocket we pack: first, a lining of 1-inch-square slices of the salt pork, then as many pitted cherries as the pocket will hold (usually about half the total) , among them about a dozen or so whole cardamom pods, then we sprinkle it liberally with ground cinnamon, salt, pepper and MSG, and finally put a few more bits of salt pork at the top. Cut more slices of salt pork like slices of bacon and, pressing the pocket closed, lay the slices over the top of the veal. Tie everything firmly in place with tight rounds of strong string along the full length of the fillet. Rub the outside with salt and refrigerate overnight.

About 3 Hours Before Serving—the Sauce and the Roasting

Let the stuffed meat come to room temperature. Cut about 6 more cardamom pods in half, dig out the little black seeds, and pound them to powder in a mortar. Mix them with about 3 teaspoons of ground cinnamon and hold. Preheat oven to 400 degrees in time for the meat to go into the hot oven 2¼ hours before serving time. We cook the veal in an oval enameled cast-iron cocotte* with a tightly fitting lid; butter the inside of it and press the veal in, making sure that the opening of the pocket is at the top, so that the basting juices will seep in. Rub the exposed parts of the veal with butter, with the cardamom-cinnamon mixture, and with flour. Set cocotte, open, in oven and brown the meat, usually in 20 minutes. Then turn oven down to 350 degrees, baste veal with freshly melted butter, cover and put back in oven for 45 minutes longer (set timer).

Meanwhile into a 2-quart saucepan put the remaining pitted cherries and barely cover with veal stock. Make it just sweet to the taste by stirring in a little granulated sugar. Make it sweeter still by adding 2 tablespoons or so of the sweet vermouth. Bring gently to the boil and simmer, covered, for 10 minutes. Let cool. When the timer bell rings for the meat, pour the consommé-vermouth liquid from the saucepan over it, through a strainer, holding the cherries. Sprinkle a few more tablespoons of the sweet vermouth over veal and baste again with freshly melted butter. Replace cover and return to oven for about 1 hour more, but from now on baste every 20 minutes with pan juices. Just 10 minutes before serving, add the cherries and put a serving platter in the oven to warm.

Just Before Serving

Test veal for doneness and put it on hot serving platter. Skim excess fat from cocotte, then put cocotte over simmering heat on top of stove, add 2 more tablespoons of the sweet vermouth, check the seasoning and adjust; then if necessary thicken sauce to consistency of heavy cream with 1 or 2 teaspoons of ground arrowroot liquefied with cream (see BASIC RULE, page 14). This sauce, with its whole cherries, comes to the table in a sauceboat.

¶ *Main Dishes (Birds)—Chicken · Duck*

BELGIAN WATERZOOIE OF CHICKEN

2 or 3 meals for our family of 4

This is a light main course, to go with solid accompaniments. The *waterzooie* is a practical and economical dish, which converts a cheap old stewing hen into a richly smooth dinner, with the bonus of a basic supply of first-class chicken broth. Failing the hen, we use a large capon. It can be prepared in advance and reheated several times, or the cold meat can be the basis of the magnificent Circassian chicken (page 288).

Check Staples:

Eggs (3 or 4 yolks)
Salt butter (1/4 lb.)
Lemon (1)
Aromatics: crystal salt, freshly ground black pepper, MSG, whole bay leaf, whole cloves, freshly ground nutmeg, thyme
Carrots (2 medium)
Green Pascal celery (1 head)
Fresh parsley (1 bunch)
Granulated instantized flour (about 4 Tbs.)
Dry bread crumbs (about 1/2 cup)
Dry white wine (2 cups)

Shopping List:

Boiling chicken—best: stewing hen; second best: capon (6 to 8 lbs.)
Heavy cream (about 1/2 cup)
Leeks (4 medium)
Sweet Bermuda onion (1 large)

At Any Time Beforehand

BASIC RULE FOR OUR BEST CHICKEN BROTH: We put the cleaned chicken or capon into our large deep soup pot, which holds about 6 quarts, and surround it with coarse chunks of: the head of celery (its leaves chopped); the white stems of the 4 leeks, carefully washed; the 2 carrots, scraped; the onion; plus salt, pepper, and MSG to taste. Into a tiny muslin herb bag we put: 2 or 3 whole bay leaves, the parsley, about 1 teaspoon of dried thyme, and 4 whole cloves. Tie tightly and deposit alongside chicken. Finally, we give a few turns to the nutmeg grater, pour over 1 cup of the wine, add freshly drawn cold water to cover, and bring up to simmering. Let it "just smile," covered, until a sliver cut off chicken tastes perfectly tender. The time depends entirely on the age of the chicken—anywhere from 1 to 3 hours. With chicken kept moist in broth, this entire production can be cooled, refrigerated (the fat skimmed off), and reheated.

About 30 Minutes Before Serving—the Sauce

Reheat chicken in its broth until hot, then put the 1/2 cup of bread crumbs into a small bowl and ladle in hot broth to cover and soak them. In a small saucepan melt 4 tablespoons of the butter and blend into it, over low heat, 4 tablespoons of the flour to make a smooth white *roux*. Gradually work in enough hot broth to make about 2 cups of sauce with a consistency of heavy cream. Let simmer very gently for a few minutes. Take the chicken out of the pot and keep it warm. Strain the vegetables out of the broth and purée them (not the herb bag) either for a few seconds in an electric blender or by passing them through a food mill or sieve. Squeeze the juice from the lemon. Now blend into the sauce, tasting and adjusting, a little bit of each of the following in turn: the vegetable purée, the soaked bread crumbs, the rest of the wine, and small dribbles of the lemon juice. The flavors should blend and none should dominate; the final result should be smooth and intense. It will now be a good deal thinner than when it started. Keep it very gently simmering, covered.

Cut all the meat off the chicken in strips about 3 inches long and 1 inch wide. Place in a hot serving dish with a cover. Separate the 4 eggs and beat together the yolks and 1/4 cup of the cream. (Save the whites for some other purpose.) Turn off the heat under the sauce and finally thicken and enrich it by carefully blending in the yolk-cream mixture. Reheat very gently, stirring continuously, but under no circumstances allow it to boil. It should now return to the thickness of heavy cream. If it becomes too thick, blend in a little more plain cream. Pour about half of this sauce over the chicken and serve the rest in a sauceboat. A pilaf of rice (page 166) is the ideal accompaniment, as it absorbs and projects the velvety sauce.

TURKISH SHERKASIYA TAVUGU—CIRCASSIAN COLD CHICKEN

2 or 3 meals for our family of 4

This is one of the richest of dishes and deserves only the lightest accompaniments. The extraordinary juxtaposition of the pounded nuts with the solid chicken meat makes it one of the great experiences of gastronomy. Decorated with an imaginative design in red paprika, it is a magnificent centerpiece for a cold buffet. We first boil and carve the chicken exactly as in the preceding recipe.

Check Staples:

Cold boiled chicken (prepared and carved as in previous recipe)
Salt butter (about 3 Tbs.)
Clear chicken broth (3 cups)
Milk (about 1/2 cup)
Aromatics: crystal salt,⁑ MSG,❂ red cayenne pepper, Hungarian sweet red paprika⁑ (about 2 Tbs.)
Yellow onions (2 medium)
White bread (4 or 5 slices)

Shopping List:

Almonds (about 1/2 lb. in shells or 1/4 lb. shelled)
Filberts (same amount)
Walnuts (same amount)
Pure walnut oil⁂ (about 1/2 pt.)

With the Chicken Already Boiled—About 1 Hour Before Serving

A Turkish housewife might spend half a day pounding the walnuts in a mortar and squeezing them by hand, to extract the oil. We save several hours by buying the oil already prepared. Blanch the almonds by our BASIC RULE (page 253), then finely grind all the nuts by passing them 2 or 3 times through the finest cutter. Put into a large mixing bowl. Peel and finely chop the 2 onions and quickly sauté them in 2 or 3 tablespoons of the butter, until just transparent. Blend into nuts. Soak the bread slices in the milk, mashing them around with a wooden spoon, then squeeze dry and begin working into nuts. Season to taste with salt, cayenne pepper, and MSG. We find that the longer and more vigorously we work the mixture the smoother and more luscious it becomes. Begin blending in spoonful after spoonful of the hot chicken broth, until the paste becomes a sauce but still is so thick that it will hardly pour from the bowl.

Cut the meat from the chicken in strips about 3 inches long and 1 inch wide and pile on a large oval platter, to form a slight dome in the center. Now cover this completely with nut sauce. The surface should be rounded and smoothed with the back of the wooden spoon. Mix about 1 tablespoon of the paprika with about ¼ cup of the walnut oil and dribble or lightly pour or spoon this reddish liquid over the mound of nutted chicken, so as to make an attractive design. Picasso once decorated a dish of Circassian chicken for Gertrude Stein.

LONG ISLAND DUCK WITH FIGS

For our family of 4

This is a solid and rich main dish and it requires that the rest of the menu be light. See shopping notes on Long Island duck (page 225). This dish can be prepared either with dried figs or with the fresh California Mission figs during their short season.

Check Staples:

Salt butter (about ½ lb.)
Orange (1 whole)
Aromatics: crystal salt, freshly ground black pepper, MSG, whole bay leaf, garlic (2 to 4 cloves, to taste), sweet marjoram, thyme
Carrots (2 medium)
Yellow onions (2 medium)

Shopping List:

Long Island duck (3½ to 5 lbs.)
Veal bones (about 1 lb.)
Fresh or dried figs (about 2 dozen)
Sweet Sauternes (½ bottle)

The Day Before—a Quick Veal Stock

We put the veal bones in our medium stockpot along with the giblets of the duck, the onions and carrots (both chunked), 1 or 2 crushed cloves of garlic, and about ½ teaspoon each of dried sweet marjoram and thyme. Just cover with freshly drawn cold water and simmer about 3 hours. While the stock is simmering, pour the ½ bottle of sweet wine over the figs and let them marinate in the refrigerator overnight. Cool and refrigerate the stock until needed (skimming off fat when it solidifies).

About 2 Hours Before Serving

We do the entire preparation of the duck in an oval enameled cast-iron cocotte* with a tightly fitting lid, which can be used for frying and simmering on top of the stove, and in the oven. Set cocotte over high frying heat and quickly brown the cleaned duck on all sides. A good deal of fat will be released and it is to be removed from cocotte, but it should be cooled and stored, as it is excellent for general cooking purposes. Firmly rub the browned duck, inside and out, with salt and pepper, then put inside: 1 teaspoon or so of MSG, 4 tablespoons of the butter in four separate lumps, 1 or 2 slivered cloves of garlic, a couple of whole bay leaves, and the orange in its skin, quartered. Preheat oven to 400 degrees. Melt 4 more tablespoons of the butter in cocotte and put in duck, breast down. Rub the exposed parts of the duck with more butter, then set cocotte, uncovered, in the oven, for the duck to develop a deeper-brown crust. This will usually take from 10 to 20 minutes. Meanwhile strain the wine from the figs and put in a saucepan with about 1 cup of the clear veal stock; bring to a boil. Pour this over duck as soon as it is sufficiently brown. Now turn the duck breast up. Lower heat to 250 degrees, cover cocotte, and return duck to oven for very slow cooking. The duck should be butter-tender in about 1 hour. Meanwhile bring figs to room temperature. Turn on oven to keep-warm temperature (150 degrees) and set a platter to warm.

About 15 Minutes Before Serving

As soon as duck is done, remove from cocotte and keep warm on serving platter in oven. Skim as much fat as possible from cocotte juices, then set over high heat so that it bubbles fiercely; this reduces and thickens sauce while concentrating the flavors. It usually takes about 10 minutes. In the last 5 minutes or so add the figs to heat them up, but carefully avoid mashing them. Finally, arrange figs around duck, and when sauce has the consistency of thick honey pour it over bird and fruit.

BASIC RULE FOR CARVING DUCK—I. FORMAL: Some of our friends tell us that they don't serve duck because they are afraid of carving it. Armed with a sharp knife that has a fairly narrow blade and a strong

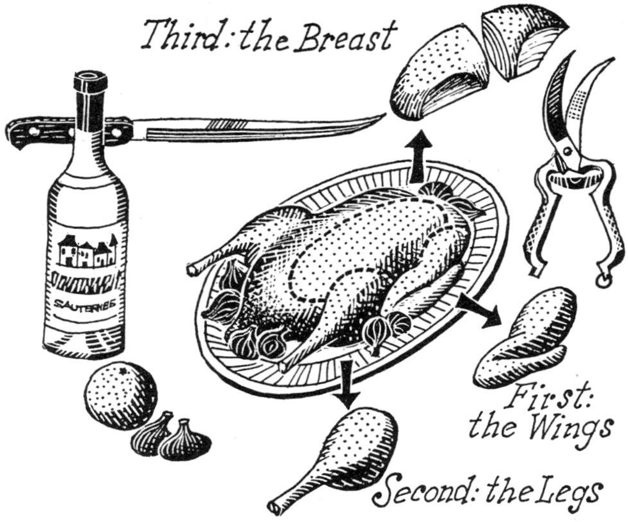

pair of poultry shears, nothing could be simpler. We start by placing the duck breast upward with the legs pointed toward the carver. Cut off the wings. Cut off the legs at the body end of the thigh bone, then separate the drumsticks and thigh sections. Cut straight down on either side of the breastbone, keeping the knife so close to the bone that it scrapes it, then turn the knife outward and remove the entire breast on each side by cutting underneath it. The fork can be used to lift the breast as it comes away and more or less scrape it off the bone. Cut each breast in half crosswise. Each diner gets half a breast, plus either a drumstick or a thigh section. If the party is so formal that no one is permitted to lift a bone with the fingers, the wings and the rest of the carcass are sent back to the kitchen. We strongly object to this and much prefer . . .

BASIC RULE FOR CARVING DUCK—II. INFORMAL: We again start by placing the duck breast upward, but with the legs now pointed to the right of the carver. With the poultry shears cut through the bird from end to end right at the top, as close as possible to one side or the other of the breastbone. Turn the duck over and do the same along the center of the back. We now have two halves. Again with the shears cut each of these crosswise, just ahead of each thigh. At first thought this may not seem quite fair, but in fact it is. Two of the diners get drumsticks and thighs but only a small amount of the breast; the others get not only the wings but also the major part of the breast meat. With this method of carving, we permit reasonable use of the fingers to lift the various pieces of bone as they are separated.

¶ *Main Dishes (Fish, Shellfish)—Shad · Crab · Trout · Whitebait · Pompano · Estouffade*

SPRING SHAD GRILLED IN MILK

For our family of 4

The prime fish of the season makes a light main dish, to be preceded by a solid first course and followed perhaps by cheese and fruit. Many cooks seem to feel that shad cannot quite stand on its own merits. They stuff it with lobster, crab, or shrimp, or fill it with a highly spiced mousse, or even smother it in an overpowering curry sauce. We do sometimes stuff it, but best of all we like it as prepared with complete simplicity (below). The original for this recipe comes from our Italian "fish-mama," who knows her fish.

Check Staples:

Salt butter (1/4 lb.)
Lemon (1)
Milk (about 1 pt.)
Aromatics: crystal salt, freshly ground black pepper, MSG, Hungarian sweet red paprika, tarragon
Dry bread crumbs (about 1/2 cup)
Tarragon white wine vinegar (a few Tbs.)

Shopping List:

Shad, boned fillet (about 2 lbs.)

About 30 Minutes Before Serving

We choose an oval enameled cast-iron platter, which holds the heat and is good-looking enough to come to the table. Butter it. Wash and dry the fish and lay it, skin down, on the platter. Set broiler to high heat and arrange shelf so that fish will be about 3 inches from heat. Pour enough milk over and around fish to be about 1/4 inch deep in the platter. Stir in about 1 teaspoon of dried tarragon and enough vinegar to give a slightly sharp taste to the milk, usually about 2 or 3 tablespoons. Sprinkle the fish in turn with: salt, pepper, and MSG to taste, a few good squirts of lemon juice, then cover the whole surface lightly with bread crumbs, dot very liberally with the butter, and finally just color it with a few shakes of the paprika.

20 Minutes Before Serving

Slide shad platter under broiler, keep heat at high for 5 minutes, then turn down to medium-low and watch fish until it is nicely browned. When opened with a fork, the flesh should be flaky. If it browns too quickly before the inside flesh is done, baste with the milk. The total time under the broiler is usually from 15 to 20 minutes.

SHAD ROE UNDER GLASS

For our family of 4

This light main course would be the superb center of a solid menu. We have prepared the exquisite shad roe of spring in many ways, but this is so much better than any other way that we have stopped experimenting. The essential accompaniment is the crisp salted watercress, which seems to lift and support the soft-textured roe. For the preparation we use the same fireproof glass bell, tightly fitted into an open enameled-iron au gratin dish, as described for the mushrooms under glass (page 181).

Check Staples:

Dark smoked bacon (about 12 thick slices)
Salt butter (1/4 lb.)
Lemon (1)
Aromatics: crystal salt, dill salt, freshly ground black pepper, MSG, turmeric
Watercress (2 bunches)
Dry Sherry (about 2 Tbs.)
Dry white wine (about 1 Tbs.)

Shopping List:

Shad roe (1 large single roe or 1 medium pair per person)
Fresh herbs, as available; dried simply will not do: fresh dill (small bunch), fresh parsley (small bunch), fresh tarragon (small bunch)
Tomatoes (about 4 medium)

About 45 Minutes Before Serving

We are usually so excited about having shad roe that the preparatory chores are a pleasure. Finely chop about 3 tablespoons each of the dill, parsley, and tarragon. Finely dice 4 slices of the bacon and lightly sauté to remove most of the fat, but do not let them crisp because a little of the fat is needed to flavor the roe. Preheat oven to 400 degrees. Carefully rinse and dry the roes. Liberally butter the au gratin dish and cover its bottom with some of the chopped dill, parsley, and tarragon. On top of this carefully lay the roes. Dot with small chips of the butter, then sprinkle on: more chopped dill, parsley, and tarragon, then salt, pepper, and MSG to taste, and finally the diced bacon. Tightly cover the au gratin dish with the fireproof bell and set in the oven until the roes are just firm, usually in 20 to 25 minutes.

Meanwhile quickly wash and dry the watercress, arrange it loosely in a salad bowl, liberally sprinkle it with dill salt, and keep fresh in the refrigerator. Fry the remaining 8 slices of bacon until they are quite crisp, then drain and keep warm. Pour the bacon fat from the sauté pan and fry the tomatoes in some of the remaining butter, according to the method on page 91, using some of the fresh dill, a pinch or two of turmeric, and the Sherry.

Serving at Table

We bring the dish with its glass bell to the table, so that the diners can enjoy the concentrated aroma as the bell is lifted. Serve the roes with all the accumulated juices, bits, and greenery from the dish. Each diner is also served a quarter of a lemon, a grilled tomato, and a pile of watercress, the latter to be eaten by hand.

CHESAPEAKE BAY SOFT-SHELL CRABS FLAMED IN PERNOD

For our family of 4

This is a light main course and the rest of the menu should be fairly solid. A sound reason for living on the East Coast in the springtime is to be near Chesapeake Bay, which calls itself "the soft-shell crab center of the world."

Check Staples:

Salt butter (1/4 lb.)
Lemons (2)
Milk (about 1/2 cup)
Aromatics: crystal salt,☧ freshly ground black pepper,☧ MSG⊜
Fresh parsley (1 bunch)
Indian chick-pea flour⊜ or all-purpose flour (a few Tbs.)

Shopping List:

Soft-shell crabs (8 to 12, according to size; the smaller have better flavor)
Pernod (1/4 cup for flaming)

About 30 Minutes Before Serving

Assuming that the crabs have been cleaned by the fishman, wash and dry them. Set out two open dipping plates, one with milk, the other with chick-pea flour. Finely chop a good handful of the parsley. In a sauté pan, preferably copper, over medium-high frying heat melt enough of the butter to cover the bottom about 1/8 inch deep. Get the butter fairly hot, but do not let it brown. Dip each crab first in milk, then roll in flour, then dribble with the juice of 1 of the lemons and sprinkle with salt, pepper, and MSG. Quickly sauté them in the hot butter, turning them over, until each is a delicate brown and has a crisp edge, usually in 5 to 10 minutes. Meanwhile turn on oven to keep-warm temperature (150 degrees) and set an open serving platter to warm. When crabs are perfect pour the 1/4 cup of Pernod over them and flame. As soon as the fire dies down, lift crabs with a slotted spoon and keep warm on the serving platter in oven. Throw a handful of chopped parsley into the sauté pan, stirring it around and turning up the heat so that the juices bubble fiercely for a few seconds, to sharpen the flavor, then pour sauce over crabs. Quarter the remaining lemon and give each diner a lemon wedge. Serve with a pilaf of rice.

APRIL BROOK TROUT POACHED IN ALSATIAN RIESLING

For our family of 4

This light main dish usually comes to us in April, when the brook trout season opens and a fishing friend brings us a gift of the long slender fish with bright blue skin. It generally comes cleaned, but we are prepared to do the scaling, filleting, and skinning ourselves. We can also buy brook trout at some of the local fish stores. It has a remarkable affinity with the slightly acid flavor of the dry white wine pressed from Riesling grapes in Alsace.

Check Staples:

Salt butter (3 or 4 Tbs.)
Lemon (1)
Aromatics: crystal salt, freshly ground black pepper, MSG, tarragon
Shallots (a handful)
Carrot (1)
Fresh celery leaves (small handful)
Fresh parsley (small bunch)

Shopping List:

Brook trout (1 large or 2 medium, total about 3 lbs.)
Alsatian dry white Riesling (1 bottle, enough for cooking and drinking)

On the Morning of the Day—the Fish Bouillon

Assuming that the trout has first been cleaned, scaled, and washed, we lay it on a wooden cutting board and have ready the saucepan in which the bouillon is to be boiled. Using a small, very sharp knife, cut off the head, the tail, and any remaining fins and put them in the saucepan. Slit the trout open from belly to tail and, working along the backbone, separate the top and bottom halves until the fish lies open and flat. Carefully cutting under the backbone, remove it and put it into the saucepan. Turn the trout over, carefully pull off the skin and add it to the saucepan. Keep the filleted trout refrigerated. Add to the saucepan: 1 cup of the wine, the juice of the lemon, the carrot (scraped and sliced), the celery leaves (coarsely chopped), about ½ teaspoon of the tarragon, 2 or 3 sprigs of parsley, plus salt, pepper, and MSG to taste. If the wine does not quite cover all this, add a little more. Gently simmer this aromatic bouillon, uncovered, for at least 1 hour. Meanwhile skin and finely chop the shallots. Also finely chop enough of the remaining parsley to make about 4 tablespoons. Finally, strain and hold the liquid, throwing away the solids.

1 Hour Before Serving

Let the trout fillets come to room temperature. Bring the bouillon gently back to simmering; keep it hot.

About 30 Minutes Before Serving

The trout is best cooked in a shallow casserole with a tightly fitting lid, one which is good-looking enough to be brought to the table. Preheat oven to 400 degrees. Liberally butter the inside of the casserole and make a bed for the fish with about half the chopped shallots and 2 tablespoons of the chopped parsley. Put in the fillets, slightly overlapping if necessary. Sprinkle over them the rest of the shallots, about 2 more tablespoons of the parsley, and possibly a very little salt, pepper, and MSG, remembering that the bouillon is already seasoned. Liberally dot the fish with the butter and carefully pour the bouillon around so as not to disturb the arrangement. Cover tightly and bake until the trout is flaky when slightly opened with a fork, usually in 15 to 20 minutes. Bring it to the table at once—the perfection of flavor fades if it is allowed to overcook even for a few minutes. Drink the rest of the Alsatian Riesling with it, quite cold, to lift it to a "gastronomic delight."

WHITEBAIT WHENEVER POSSIBLE

For our family of 4

This dish makes a light main course. Occasionally when the fishing boats are far out to sea, they come across shoals of millions of tiny fish, each hardly more than an inch long. Out go the finest-mesh nets and in comes a catch that is a prize for gourmets from Paris to Singapore to New York. There is some mystery about them. Are they baby herring? or a fully-grown pigmy species? One can seldom count on finding them, but our Italian "fish-mama" has strict instructions to call us whenever they are available. They are so tiny that they need no cleaning and are eaten head, tail, and all.

Check Staples:

Lemons (2 or 3)
Aromatics: dill salt, red cayenne pepper, English dry mustard
Coarse white stone-ground cornmeal🅢 (about 1 cup)
Green virgin olive oil🅢 (about 1 cup)

Shopping List:

Whitebait (1½ lbs.)

About 3 Hours Before Serving

Wash the whitebait in a colander under cold running water, then put them in a large bowl and cover them with ice water, adding plenty of ice cubes. Refrigerate for at least 2 hours. This expels and removes the last particles of grit.

About 20 Minutes Before Serving

Drain the whitebait, dry them on absorbent towels, and roll them in the cornmeal and coat them thickly. Set a large sauté pan, preferably copper, over high frying heat, and cover the bottom about 1/4 inch deep with olive oil. Bring up almost to smoking heat, then slide in the first load of whitebait, shaking the pan to prevent the bottom ones from sticking, and lifting and turning them all carefully with a wooden spoon. Each layer is done when the fish are brown, usually in about 30 seconds. We preheat our oven to keep-warm temperature (about 150 degrees) and heat a large platter on which to pile the loads of whitebait. Each fish should be crisp and slightly curled, with a luscious and juicy center. There are varying degrees of crispness, and it is wise at first to experiment with a few seconds more or less frying, until the family's taste is established. When all the crisp fish are on the platter, sprinkle to taste with dill salt, a little cayenne pepper, a very little dry mustard, and plenty of freshly squeezed lemon juice. We think they need no sauce or other accompaniment, but occasionally, for friends who like to paint the lily, we may serve a *sauce rémoulade* (page 109).

POMPANO BAKED IN FOIL

For our family of 4

This beautifully firm fish from the tropic waters of the Gulf of Mexico makes a solid main course, the perfect center of a light menu. It used to be *pompano en papillotte* (pompano baked in paper) before we had aluminum foil, which is easier to handle and more efficient as a conductor of heat and protector of flavor. The foil packages come to the table in individual au gratin dishes and each diner has the intimate pleasure of his own first scent of the bouquet. This dish is also excellent made with the lean-fleshed bluefish, flounder, or sole.

Check Staples:

Salt butter (1/2 lb.)
Eggs (2 large)
Lemon (1)
Aromatics: crystal salt, freshly ground black pepper, red cayenne pepper, MSG
Yellow onion (1 medium)
Fresh parsley (1 bunch)
Glace de viande **(about 2 tsp.)**
Dry bread crumbs (about 1/2 cup)
Dry vermouth (about 3/4 cup)

Shopping List:

Pompano (1/2- to 3/4-lb. fillet per person)
Ham, boneless, lean (about 1/2 lb.)
Fresh mushrooms (1/2 lb.)
Fresh shrimp (1/2 lb., plus the ingredients for wine-boiling, page 108)

The Day Before—Advance Preparation of the Stuffing

Wine-boil the shrimp according to the recipe on page 108, but remember to use only one third the amount of each ingredient since you are making only one third the amount of shrimp. Refrigerate the shrimp in its marinade overnight. Now prepare the stuffing as follows.

BASIC RULE FOR MODIFIED DUXELLE STUFFING: We prepare this in a fairly large copper saucepan, which is instantly responsive to changes in heat. Wipe the mushrooms clean and hold. Finely chop the onion and sauté it in about 3 tablespoons of the butter until golden, usually in 5 minutes. Finely dice enough of the ham to make ½ cup and stir cubes into onion sauté. Turn down heat and let it just simmer for as long as it takes to finely chop enough of the mushrooms to make 1 cup. Add to mixture and let mushrooms absorb the butter for about 3 minutes, then add about ¼ cup of the dry vermouth, turn up the heat, and let bubble strongly until almost all the liquid has evaporated. Stir in 2 teaspoons of the *glace de viande* and the remaining ¼ cup of vermouth. Again, let bubble strongly until there is only about 1 tablespoon of liquid left. Absorb this by stirring in ½ cup of the dry bread crumbs. Turn off heat and cool slightly. Separate the 2 eggs and in a small mixing bowl beat the yolks hard until they are lemon-colored. (Reserve the whites for some other purpose.) Finely chop enough parsley to make about 2 tablespoons. As soon as mixture is cool enough, bind it with the egg yolks and season to taste with salt, pepper, MSG, a touch of cayenne, and the chopped parsley. The mixture should now have the consistency of a *risotto.* It can be thinned with a few drops more vermouth or thickened with more bread crumbs. Refrigerate, covered, overnight.

On the Morning of the Day

Drain, shell, coarsely chop the shrimp, and blend the bits into the *duxelle.* Let it come to room temperature and make sure that it has not become too thick; if it has, add a bit more vermouth. We set out one small enameled cast-iron dish per person and line it with a good-sized square of foil, leaving the corners sticking up, to be folded down later. Cut a ¼-inch-thick slice of ham to fit the bottom of each foil-lined dish. These slices are then lightly browned in butter and set in place. Liberally butter each portion of the pompano fillets and lay them on the ham. Remove the stems from 3 or 4 small mushroom caps and sauté the caps lightly in butter in which ham was fried, adding a little more butter as needed. Divide the *duxelle* stuffing into 4 parts and spread 1 part in a thick layer on top of each portion of fish. Top with the sautéed mushroom caps, a few dots of butter, more chopped parsley, and a little more seasoning if needed. Now fold the foil down, twisting and crimping it all around to form a tight package. The flavors will be nicely blended if these packages are left at room temperature for a few hours.

About 30 Minutes Before Serving

Preheat oven to hot 425 degrees. Put in the dishes with their foil packages and bake until the pompano is just flaky. In our oven this takes about 20 minutes, but the first time this dish is prepared it is best to open one of these packages and check. Put a lemon wedge on the side of each portion. Now bring the packages unopened to the table and let each diner open his own package in its dish.

ESTOUFFADE OF LOUISIANA CRAWFISH

For our family of 4

One of the joys of the American gastronomic year is that we have two seasons for the "lobster-in-miniature," the crayfish (or crawfish, as they call it in Louisiana), while most other countries of the world have only one. The main supply comes in high summer (page 370), but from March to May they are also dredged up from the Louisiana bayous and are available there, or can be shipped by air freight to many parts of the country.✱ The French *estouffade* literally means "suffocated," a method of cooking in aromatic steam with a minimum of liquid; this enhances the pungent flavor of the Louisiana crawfish. A rich and luxurious main course, the *estouffade* is best accompanied by a light and delicate prologue and dessert.

Check Staples:

Salt butter (2 Tbs.)
Aromatics: crystal salt,✱ freshly ground black pepper,✱ red cayenne pepper, MSG,✱ basil, garlic (2 or 3 cloves, to taste), marjoram, oregano, rosemary, thyme
Yellow onion (1 medium)
Green scallions (1 bunch)
Olive oil✱ (3 Tbs.)
Italian peeled and seeded plum tomatoes (1 lb. 1 oz. can)

Shopping List:

Whole live Louisiana crawfish✱ (100)
White goose fat,✱ which has a remarkable affinity with crawfish; it can be replaced by chicken fat or sweet butter, but with a compromise in flavor (⅔ cup)
Clam juice (8-oz. bottle)
Plus ingredients for the preliminary boiling of the crawfish, page 456

The Day Before—Preparing the Crawfish in About 15 Minutes

Boil the crawfish according to the basic method (page 456).

On the Morning of the Day—Shell the Crawfish: All Hands Can Do It in About 30 Minutes

Follow the directions given on page 456.

About 1 Hour Before Serving—Preparing the Estouffade

Peel and chop the onion and finely mince the 2 or 3 cloves of garlic. We use a tin-lined copper sauté pan and heat about 2 tablespoons of the olive oil in it over medium frying temperature, then quickly sauté onion and garlic for hardly more than 1 minute. Pour in the canned tomatoes, add about 1 teaspoon MSG, plus salt and pepper to taste. Then bubble fairly hard, stirring occasionally, to boil away tomato liquid, until it is all quite thick. Then turn off heat and hold.

About 40 Minutes Before Serving—the "Suffocation" of the Crawfish

For this we use an enameled cast-iron cocotte* with an especially tightly fitting lid that holds in the steam and is the key to a successful *estouffade*. With a not-too-tight lid it is advisable to use foil as an extra cover or to seal the edge with a flour-and-water paste. Finely chop tops and bulbs of the scallions. In bottom of cocotte over medium frying heat melt the 2 tablespoons of butter with 1 tablespoon more of the olive oil, then quickly sauté half the chopped scallions for hardly more than 30 seconds. Blend in sauce from sauté pan and stir in just enough of the clam juice to ensure adequate steam, usually not more than 1/4 cup. Next blend in shelled crawfish tails and the 2/3 cup of goose fat (or alternative) and keep everything gently bubbling while blending in aromatics: 1/2 teaspoon each of basil, marjoram, rosemary, and thyme, 1/4 teaspoon oregano, 1 teaspoon MSG, plus salt, black pepper, and a very little red cayenne to taste. Blend very carefully with wooden spoon so as not to crush crawfish. Each will be coated with red sauce, but will be resting above boiling liquid. Cover tightly, sealing lid if necessary (above), and keep bubbling moderately so as to provide plenty of steam; do not remove lid for 30 minutes.

Then taste. Crawfish should be just cooked, still crisp and juicy.

Serving at Table

We use gumbo bowls and rest crawfish on a bed of white rice. The remaining small quantity of thick sauce is then spooned over and chopped green scallions are sprinkled on top. No other sauce is ever served, for it might mask the delicate flavor of the crawfish. However, the hot rice may be dotted with bits of butter.

¶ *Main Dishes (Cheese, Eggs)*

QUICHE DE GEORGES DE FESSENHEIM

For our family of 4

The *quiche* is still the great specialty of Alsace-Lorraine, with dozens of local variations of the meat-and-cheese-filled savory custard pie. When our young friend Georges came to the United States for a year of study as an exchange student, he brought with him, among the dollar bills in his wallet, a hand-written copy of the recipe for this *quiche* as his mother makes it at home in the village of Fessenheim near Strasbourg.

Check Staples:

Sweet butter (½ lb.)
Eggs (5 large)
Milk (1 cup)
Ice water (about 4 Tbs.)
Aromatics: crystal salt, red cayenne pepper, MSG, freshly ground nutmeg
Granulated instantized flour (1½ cups)
Granulated white sugar (about 1 tsp.)

Shopping List:

Imported Swiss Gruyère cheese (½ lb.)
Dark smoked boiled ham, lean (about ½ lb.)
Heavy cream (1 cup)
Leeks (6 medium)

If to Be Served Hot, 2 Hours Beforehand—the Pie Crust

Stir the salt into the instantized flour (no sifting necessary; with ordinary flour, they would be sifted together). Let a ¼-pound stick of the butter come to room temperature, then work into flour, moistening gradually with the 4 tablespoons of ice water. Roll dough into ball and refrigerate for 1 hour.

Coarsely dice the ham. Thinly slice the cheese, making each slice about 1-inch square. Wash and slice the white parts of the leeks and sauté them slowly in 2 or 3 tablespoons of the remaining butter. When they are almost a purée, add the ham, salt to taste, and keep warm. Let eggs, cream, and milk come to room temperature.

1 Hour Before Serving

On a floured board, roll out the dough fairly thinly—about ⅛ inch thick. Lightly butter a 10-inch pie pan and line it with dough. Cut and crimp the edges. Preheat oven to 450 degrees. Spread the ham-leek mixture as the bottom layer, the sliced cheese as the second. Hold while making the custard.

Put into a round-bottomed bowl: 4 whole eggs plus 1 extra yolk, the 1 cup each of milk and heavy cream, the teaspoon of sugar, plus salt, cayenne pepper, and freshly ground nutmeg to taste. Beat hard with a wire whisk and pour into the pie. Set at once in the oven and leave on high heat, to harden the crust, for exactly 12 minutes. Then turn oven down to 350 degrees and leave *quiche* until the custard sets, usually in 30 to 40 minutes. Test by inserting a silver blade into the custard to see if it comes out clean. In our oven the top of the *quiche* is usually golden-brown at this point, with a crack across the custard. However if the custard sets before browning it can be toasted under the grill for a minute or two. The *quiche* is equally good hot or cold.

SWISS CHEESE FONDUE

For our family of 4

The fun of a fondue is its *gemütlichkeit.* It's hard to be formal at dinner while eating from a communal dish. The fondue is prepared in a casserole (ceramic or iron), which comes to table boiling hot and is kept gently bubbling on a spirit stove, a chafing dish, or an adjustable electric hot plate. Each diner is armed with a long-handled fork on which he impales pieces of bread to soak in the fondue. The trick is to fish up a thick crust of cheese without losing the bread.

Check Staples:

Aromatics: crystal salt, freshly ground black pepper, MSG, garlic (2 or 3 cloves, to taste), freshly ground nutmeg
Granulated instantized flour (about 3 Tbs.)
Swiss kirsch liqueur (2 oz.)

Shopping List:

Swiss Emmenthaler cheese (½ lb.)
Swiss Gruyère cheese (½ lb.)
Swiss Neufchâtel dry white wine (1 bottle)
French Cognac (1½ oz.)
French Martinique rhum (1½ oz.)
French bread (2 long loaves)

About 40 Minutes Before Serving

Arrange the spirit stove, chafing dish, or electric hot plate on a heatproof board in the middle of the dining table, within reach of each diner. Coarsely grate the two cheeses and lightly mix them in a bowl with the 3 tablespoons of flour. Peel and very finely chop the garlic and spread it inside the casserole. Put in 1 pint of the white wine and heat it almost to boiling. When small air bubbles start to rise intermittently, begin adding large spoonfuls of cheese mix, carefully stirring with a wooden fork until each lot is melted before dropping in the next. Scrape bottom to avoid sticking. Break up lumps and, above all, stir gently to avoid having cheese become stringy. When mixture becomes quite thick, adjust heat to maintain gentle bubbling. Season to taste with salt, pepper, MSG, and a couple grinds of nutmeg. Do not stop stirring with the wooden fork for even a moment. Add the 2 ounces of kirsch, the 1½ ounces of Cognac, and the 1½ ounces of

rhum. Keep stirring. Meanwhile a second person starts the heater on the dining table and begins to cut the bread into ¾-inch-thick slices; these are then quartered. Place before each diner a plate with about a dozen or so of these bread triangles and a long-handled fork. Bring casserole from kitchen and set it on dining-table heater, adjusting temperature so that fondue continues to bubble gently. The eating begins at once.

How to Avoid Losing the Bread and Messing up the Table

Impale a piece of bread on the fork, passing the points through the white crumb first, then firmly embedding them in the crust. Each diner in turn sticks his bread into the fondue, where his first duty is to continue the stirring, first at the top and then, more importantly, scraping the thicker cheese that is settling on the bottom.

As the bread is lifted from the fondue it is twisted until it stops dripping, then quickly brought over the diner's plate, which is held out to meet it, and allowed to cool for a second or two. Still bubbling, the fondue gradually thickens and, if needed, a little more heated white wine can be stirred in. Finally all that is left is a firm crust of cheese on the bottom of the casserole. The heat is turned off, the crust scraped off with a knife, and the pieces are divided among the diners, as a special last delicacy. It is crisp and crackly. One essential of a fondue is that no ice-cold drinks be served with it; they would harden the cheese in the stomach and cause indigestion. Hot tea or coffee are excellent.

¶ *Vegetables*

Spring Asparagus in Six Ways

We vary the preparation of asparagus according to its age and texture. When the first thin, delicate spears from local beds come to market, we simmer and sauce them with loving gentleness. The stronger, peak-season spears can support bolder sauces. With the big, fat end-of-season thumbs, the sauce dominates. We apply this principle to many seasonal vegetables, often with the same sauces. We like to serve asparagus as a separate course, before the main dish.

BASIC METHOD FOR COOKING ASPARAGUS

For our family of 4

The problem of cooking asparagus is simple. The tips are tender and should never be in contact with boiling water. The stems, on the other hand, must be boiled. We use an asparagus boiler.*

Check Staples:

Aromatic: table salt for the boiling water (about 2 Tbs.)

Shopping List:

Asparagus (2-lb. bunch, with spears all the same thickness and length)

25 Minutes Before Serving

We do not follow the rule about breaking each spear at its weakest point. This only results in spears of unequal length and with no handle by which the diner can hold them. We measure the bunch against our tall stockpot and if necessary, with a single cut, trim an inch or so from the bottom of the bunch. Fill the pot two thirds full of hot water. Salt the water until it tastes of brine and bring to a rolling boil. Meanwhile undo the bunch, wash the spears under cold running water, scrape off the scales, which often hold sand, then retie the bunch and stand it in the middle of the pot as soon as the water boils. Adjust heat so that water continues to bubble fairly hard, filling top of pot with steam. Clap on lid and set timer. Very young and narrow spears are usually done in 12 minutes, the bigger ones in 15 minutes. The very large ones sometimes take as much as 18 minutes. The tips control the timing. Taste one. It should be warm through and soft, but still with a slightly crisp texture. While the asparagus cooks, place a white towel or napkin on a serving platter and set both in a keep-warm oven (150 degrees).

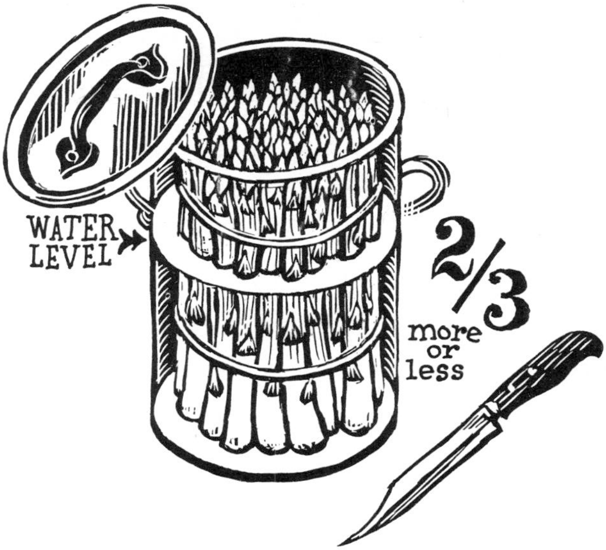

Serving the Asparagus Dry and Warm

With a pair of tongs lift the bunch and lay it on a wooden board to drain for about 1 minute. Cut the strings and lay the spears on the towel, folding it over so as to wrap the asparagus. Bring to the table with one of the following sauces.

ASPARAGUS SAUCE NUMBER ONE—PLAIN BUTTER FOR THE TINY, YOUNGEST SPEARS

Check Staples:

Salt butter (½ lb.)
Aromatic: MSG

5 Minutes Before the Asparagus Is Served

Melt the butter in a small saucepan (we use a pretty copper one, which can be brought to the table). Stir in MSG, to taste—about 1 teaspoon. Arrange the asparagus on plates and serve.

ASPARAGUS SAUCE NUMBER TWO—LEMON BUTTER FOR THE LARGER SPEARS

Check Staples:

Salt butter (½ lb.)
Lemon (1)
Aromatic: MSG

5 Minutes Before the Asparagus Is Served

This is exactly the same as the plain butter sauce above, except that after the MSG has been added lemon juice is squeezed in until the lemon flavor is as dominant as family taste demands. Serve exactly as in previous recipe.

ASPARAGUS SAUCE NUMBER THREE—FRENCH CRÈME CHANTILLY

Check Staples:

Aromatics: fine table salt, MSG

Shopping List:

Heavy cream (½ pt.)

10 Minutes Before the Asparagus Is Served

Whip the cream and work into it equal parts (about 1 teaspoon altogether) of salt and MSG to taste. Arrange the asparagus on plates and pile the whipped cream on the tips.

ASPARAGUS SAUCE NUMBER FOUR—OUR SAUCE PECANDINE

Check Staples:

Salt butter (½ lb.)
Tarragon white wine vinegar (2 tsp.)

Shopping List:

Pecans (enough for ½ cup shelled meats)

10 Minutes Before the Asparagus Is Served

We run the pecans through the coarsest cutter of our grinder; however they could be finely chopped by hand. Melt the butter in a small saucepan (preferably copper) and when it is quite hot but not yet browning, add the ground nuts. Stir around for a few seconds until they just turn color, then throw in, all at once, the 2 teaspoons of vinegar. There will be a violent hissing and frothing. Stir once more and spoon immediately over the asparagus, being careful to divide the nuts equally. This is perhaps the best of our asparagus sauces. The highest compliment paid to it was by a young graduate gourmet from Yale who said: "Why bother with the asparagus? Just serve this sauce over bits of string!"

ASPARAGUS SAUCE NUMBER FIVE—SAUCE POLONAISE

Check Staples:

Salt butter (¼ lb.)
Egg (1 large)
Lemon (1)
Aromatics: crystal salt, freshly ground black pepper, MSG
Fresh parsley (small bunch)
Dry bread crumbs (½ cup)

About 15 Minutes Before the Asparagus Is Served

Hard-boil the egg, separate it, and put the yolk through a sieve. Squeeze the juice from the lemon and blend it into yolk. Finely chop the parsley. In a small saucepan (preferably copper) heat the ¼ pound of butter until it just begins to brown. Add the ½ cup of bread crumbs and let them color for about 30 seconds. Season to taste with salt, pepper, and MSG. We spread the lemon-yolk mix on the asparagus tips, then pour over the hot buttered bread crumbs. When the hot butter meets the cold lemon juice, the sauce foams and makes a Lilliputian show for the diners.

ASPARAGUS SAUCE NUMBER SIX—CHEESE FOR THE FADING, FAT SPEARS

Check Staples:

Salt butter (1 to 2 Tbs.)
Floured butter—*beurre manié*, *see* **page 12 (about 5 Tbs.)**
Eggs (4)
Milk (1 pt.)
Lemon (1)
Aromatic: crystal salt
Yellow onion (1 medium)

Shopping List:

Imported Italian Parmesan cheese (about ¼ lb.)

About 20 Minutes Before the Asparagus Is Ready to Serve

We use a 1-quart copper saucepan to heat the pint of milk to just below boiling. Thicken to the consistency of heavy cream by carefully blending in pieces of floured butter, making sure that it dissolves quickly, without lumping. The milk will usually absorb about 4 tablespoons. At this point it is best stirred with a small wire whisk. When sauce is smooth and creamy, let it gently simmer, "just smiling," with lid on, for as long as it takes to peel and chop the onion finely. Add it to sauce, with salt to taste. Replace cover and let it continue "smiling" while separating the 4 eggs and beating the yolks until lemon-colored. Grate enough of the cheese to fill ½ cup. Squeeze juice from the lemon. Add 1 tablespoon of the butter to sauce, plus about half the grated cheese, and stir steadily until both are melted. Turn off heat and carefully blend in beaten egg yolks. Finally, tasting and adjusting flavor of sauce, add more grated cheese, 1 teaspoon at a time, alternately with dribbles of lemon juice. The flavor of the Parmesan should dominate, backed up by the sharp punch of the lemon. Serve in the same way as the preceding sauces, poured over the tips of the asparagus.

GREEN BEANS WITH ROSEMARY

For our family of 4

This is the time for the most delicate of the new green beans. So we prepare them with gentle concern, pampering them with sweet herbs and sweet butter. Prepared in this way, they can stand on their own as a separate course.

Check Staples:

Sweet butter (1/4 lb.)
Lemon (1)
Aromatics: crystal salt,✻ MSG,✻ dried herbs (if fresh not available)

Shopping List:

Green beans (1 1/2 lbs.)
Fresh herbs, a few sprigs each, as available: basil, parsley, rosemary, summer savory

About 40 Minutes Before Serving

In our 2-quart copper saucepan we bring 1 pint of freshly drawn cold water to a boil. While it is heating, put 2 or 3 sprigs of fresh (or 1 teaspoon of dried) summer savory into a tiny muslin herb bag and dunk in the boiling water. Simmer, covered, for as long as it takes to wash and cut the beans. If they are small (as they should be at this time of year), we merely top and tail them. If larger, they can be snapped, chunked, or "frenched" through a cutter. Remove herb bag from simmering water and drop in beans. They should be just covered by liquid, and if needed a little more hot water can be added. Mix into beans 2 or 3 sprigs of fresh (or a teaspoon of dried) rosemary. Keep the water bubbling quite strongly, uncovered, so that beans are partly steamed as liquid boils down, for about 15 minutes. Soften 4 tablespoons of the butter in a mortar and prepare basil butter by our basic method (page 23). Hold until beans are served. Finely chop a small handful of parsley and hold. After the first 15 minutes, stir 2 tablespoons of the plain butter into beans and begin tasting to judge exact moment when they are perfectly done. They should remain almost crisp. Immediately pour off remaining liquid (saving for basic stock) and put beans back on low heat for about 3 minutes to dry out. Pile on a hot serving platter, dot with the basil butter, and sprinkle with the chopped parsley.

SPRING BEETS IN A SAUTÉ PAN

For our family of 4

The trick here is to use very little water and to concentrate the steam by covering the beets with the large cabbage leaves.

Check Staples:
Salt butter (3 Tbs.)
Lemon (1)
**Aromatics: crystal salt,✗ freshly
ground black pepper,✗ MSG☷**
Fresh chives (very small bunch)
Parsley (small bunch)
Pure maple syrup☷ (2 tsp.)

Shopping List:
Small beets (about 2 lbs.)
**Large outer leaves of Chinese cab-
bage or lettuce, not to be eaten (5
or 6, according to size, enough to
cover sauté pan)**
Heavy cream (1 Tbs.)

About 35 Minutes Before Serving

Peel and thinly slice the 2 pounds of beets. Wash the cabbage leaves
under cold running water and let soak in a bowl of cold water until
needed. Put the 3 tablespoons of butter and the 2 teaspoons of maple
syrup into a sauté pan and melt over fairly low heat, tilting pan this
way and that until bottom and sides are well coated. Put in beet slices
and carefully stir around with a wooden spoon to coat with butter and
syrup. Then spread out evenly, sprinkle with the tablespoon of cream,
plus salt, pepper, and MSG to taste. Then, bringing the bowl with the
cabbage leaves over to the sauté pan, lift each leaf out of the water and
place it, dripping wet, over beets until they are fully covered. Water
adhering to leaves is all that is needed to provide steam. When hissing
subsides, turn down heat to merry bubbling, cover, then leave until
beet slices are crisply soft, usually in 20 to 25 minutes. Meanwhile set a
serving dish in oven to get warm and chop 1 tablespoon each of chives
and parsley. When beets are perfect, remove and throw away cabbage
leaves, salt and pepper beet slices to taste, turn out onto serving dish,
pour over all juices from sauté pan, and sprinkle with chopped chives
and parsley.

PURÉE OF BRUSSELS SPROUTS

For our family of 4

Check Staples:
**Aromatics: crystal salt,✗ freshly
ground black pepper,✗ MSG☷**
Granulated white sugar (¼ tsp.)

Shopping List:
Brussels sprouts (about 1 qt.)
Sour cream (about 2 Tbs.)

About 50 Minutes Before Serving

Wash Brussels sprouts and soak in cold water for 15 minutes.

About 35 Minutes Before Serving

Trim Brussels sprouts, cutting off stalks and removing any soiled outer
leaves. We would then steam them until very soft, usually in 15 to 20

minutes, but they could also be simmered in salted water, with a slight loss of flavor. During steaming, we sprinkle them with the 1/4 teaspoon of sugar, and salt, pepper, and MSG to taste. When quite soft, pass them through a Foley hand food mill.* Some of the firmer fibers will remain inside the mill, but will have been thoroughly mashed by the pusher and should be scraped out and worked into the purée to give it more body. Put purée into a saucepan and gently reheat, at the same time working in just enough of the sour cream to give smoothness and richness, usually 1 or 2 tablespoons. Finally, adjust seasoning and serve very hot.

7½-MINUTE CABBAGE

For our family of 4

We have prepared green cabbage in more ways (and in more places) than we can remember. This is the way we now choose most often, for simplicity, for speed, and for crisp aromatic excellence.

Check Staples:

Salt butter (2 or 3 Tbs.)
Aromatics: crystal salt,* freshly ground black pepper,* MSG,* and 1/2 tsp. each of not more than 2 of the following (we vary them each time we prepare the dish): whole caraway seed, sweet marjoram, oregano, thyme

Shopping List:

Young green cabbage (1 small)
Not more than 2 of the following added flavorings (we vary each time): green scallion tops (enough for 1/4 cup, chopped), fresh tarragon (a few sprigs), Italian Parmesan cheese (enough for 1/4 cup, grated)

15 Minutes Before Serving

Discard the tough outer leaves of the cabbage, cut head in half, wash under cold running water, and finely shred enough to fill a 1-pint jug, tightly packed. We cook this cabbage in an enameled cast-iron 1½-quart saucepan with a tightly fitting lid and add: 1/3 cup of freshly drawn cold water, 2 tablespoons of the butter, a selection of the aromatic herbs as listed above (but if using cheese, do not add it at this point), plus salt, pepper, and MSG to taste. Set saucepan on high heat and bring liquid rapidly to a rolling boil, uncovered. Then immediately cover tightly and turn down heat to simmering. Simmer exactly 7½ minutes so that cabbage retains its crispness and character. Drain off any remaining liquid. Melt in more butter to taste and grated cheese, if it is being used. Bring at once to the table, in a hot covered dish, before it has a chance to get soggy.

MAPLE-GLAZED SPRING CARROTS

For our family of 4

Our family is in complete agreement as to how to prepare the small new carrots of this season.

Check Staples:

Salt butter (3 Tbs.)
Lemon (1)
Aromatics: crystal salt,☧ freshly ground black pepper☧
Pure Vermont maple syrup (3 Tbs.)

Shopping List:

Small spring carrots (2 bunches)

30 Minutes Before Serving

We do not peel very young carrots; we simply scrub them with a wire brush. Then we preserve their flavor by steaming them in the four-way multiple steamer,* dribbling them with a few drops of lemon juice, until they are just soft, usually in about 15 minutes. Then cut them into ¾-inch lengths. In a sauté pan (preferably copper) melt the 3 tablespoons of butter and blend in the 3 tablespoons of maple syrup. Slide in carrots and move around to coat them on all sides. Take care that butter does not brown and syrup does not burn. After 2 or 3 minutes carrots will develop a glossy brown glaze. Serve at once.

NICK'S FRESH CORN PUDDING

For our family of 4

This used to involve hard work until we discovered our corn scraper.* The dish is nothing if not made with absolutely freshly scraped corn. The flavor is so delicate and rare that we serve it as a separate course.

Check Staples:

Salt butter (about 6 oz.)
Aromatic: crystal salt☧

Shopping List:

Fresh corn (8 large ears or 12 medium ones)

Allow Enough Time for Scraping the Corn

Our corn scraper scrapes an ear of corn in about 1 minute. More old-fashioned methods will take longer. Make sure that all the corn milk is collected in the bowl with the kernels. If they are to be held even for a few minutes, they should be refrigerated, covered.

1 Hour Before Serving

We use a soufflé dish, choosing a size to ensure that it is not more than ¾ full, to allow for expansion of the corn in baking. Butter the dish and put in corn and corn milk. Stir in 1 tablespoon of the butter for each ear of corn and plenty of crystal salt. Set the oven to 325 degrees and, without waiting for it to heat up, put in the dish, uncovered. Let it bake slowly for 50 minutes, thoroughly stirring it once, at the halfway point.

Just Before Serving

Turn on the broiler to medium-high and set the shelf so that the top of the corn pudding is about 3 inches from the heat. Leave until well browned—in our broiler this takes about 2 minutes. Serve at once.

SICILIAN WHITE ONIONS IN MARSALA

For our family of 4

This is one of the best of all ways of preparing onions as a side vegetable; it is so dramatic in flavor and texture that we often serve it as a separate course, just before the main dish. We usually keep a small bottle of the slightly sweet Sicilian Marsala in our kitchen wine rack.

Check Staples:

Aromatics: crystal salt, Tabasco
Parsley (small bunch)
Pure maple syrup (3 Tbs.)
Olive oil (3 Tbs.)
Red wine vinegar (¼ cup)
Italian Marsala wine (¼ cup)

Shopping List:

Small white boiler onions (2 lbs.)
Dried apricots (enough to fill ¾ cup, coarsely chopped)

About 50 Minutes Before Serving

Peel the onions, leaving them whole. Coarsely chop the ¾ cup of apricots and hold.

About 35 Minutes Before Serving

Put the 3 tablespoons of olive oil into a sauté pan, heat up until fairly hot but definitely not smoking, then put in onions and sauté vigorously, stirring around, until all have a few light-brown patches. Then "hiss in" the ¼ cup of Marsala and the ¼ cup of vinegar. Turn heat down to merry bubbling and stir in: the 3 tablespoons of maple syrup, the chopped apricots, plus 2 or 3 drops of Tabasco, and salt to taste. Now turn up heat, so that liquid bubbles hard for 1 minute or so and stir onions around until all are well coated with sauce. Then turn heat down again to merry bubbling (enough to provide steam), cover, and let onions steam until quite soft, usually in 25 to 30 minutes. Set serving dish to warm. By the time onions are done, sauce should have boiled down to a thickish syrup. If not, uncover and boil hard for 1 or

2 minutes, until sauce begins to glaze and thicken. Then turn onions out onto serving dish, scraping out all contents of sauté pan and spooning over onions. They will have an attractive sweet-sour flavor.

SPRING PEAS STEAMED IN A SAUTÉ PAN

For our family of 4

This is our best recipe for preparing young peas; they are just bathed in steam and their natural green is retained and made glossy by a gently aromatic butter. We learned this method many years ago from a French farmer's wife.

Check Staples:

Sweet butter (a few Tbs.)
Aromatic: crystal salt☧
Green scallions (enough for ¼ cup, chopped)

Shopping List:

Spring peas in the pod (2 lbs.)
Lettuce (4 large outside leaves)

30 Minutes Before Serving

Shell and wash the peas, holding 2 empty pods for extra flavoring (save rest of pods for cream of pea-pod soup, page 333). Finely chop enough scallion tops to fill ¼ cup. We use a fairly large copper sauté pan with a tightly fitting lid, and prepare it for the peas before turning on the heat. Cut 2 tablespoons of the butter into small pieces and dot the bottom of the pan. Choose 2 large outside lettuce leaves, wash under cold running water and, without shaking them out, lay them in the pan as saucer-shaped cradles for the peas. The clinging water provides the steam. Divide peas equally between the 2 leaves, lay reserve pea pods on top, sprinkle on chopped scallions, and lightly dot with more butter. Wash 2 more lettuce leaves and, with plenty of dripping water, invert them over the cradles. Cover sauté pan tightly and place immediately on high heat. Listen carefully, first for the sound of the boiling water, then for the sizzling of the butter. At once turn heat down to simmering, and steam for exactly 15 minutes. With a pair of tongs, fish out and throw away the lettuce leaves and the pea pods. With a wooden spoon, lightly stir the peas around in the butter sauce, salting to taste. If any water is left, evaporate it away by bubbling over highest heat for about 1 minute. Serve at once, preferably as a separate course.

BABY WHITE TURNIPS IN SWEET SEMILLON

For our family of 4

Semillon is the name of a grape from which an excellent, slightly aromatic, sweet wine is made, in, among many places, California.

Check Staples:
Salt butter (4 Tbs.)
Aromatic: crystal salt☧
Pure maple syrup⛁ (2 tsp.)

Shopping List:
Small white turnips (about 2 lbs.)
Heavy cream (2 Tbs.)
California sweet Semillon wine (1/2 cup)

About 25 Minutes Before Serving

Peel turnips and dice into 1/4-inch cubes, sufficient to fill 4 cups. This measurement must be accurate in relation to the amount of liquid used. We prepare this dish in a 2-quart enameled cast-iron saucepan with a tightly fitting lid, which will hold in the steam. Put into saucepan the 4 tablespoons of butter and the 1/2 cup of wine, then heat up rapidly to a rolling boil. As soon as liquid boils, working fast to avoid wasting steam, put in turnips, sprinkle on the 2 teaspoons of maple syrup, the 2 tablespoons of cream, plus salt to taste, and stir around thoroughly. Turn down heat to merry bubbling (enough to continue providing steam), cover tightly, then let turnips steam until crisply soft, usually in 10 to 15 minutes. Finally, add a little more salt if necessary, then serve very hot.

¶ *Foundations—Potatoes · Pasta · Beans · Grains*

We have already discussed our theory that the starch-filler is the foundation of the meal and can make or spoil the final effect. Our search is always for variety, not only in the preparation of the eternal potato but also in its occasional replacement by other interesting and unusual starch foods.

FRENCH GRATIN OF NEW POTATOES

For our family of 4

This is one of the many French regional ways of baking potatoes.

Check Staples:
Salt butter (1/4 lb.)
Egg (1 large)
Milk (about 1 qt.)
Aromatics: crystal salt,☧ freshly ground black pepper,☧ MSG,⛁ garlic (1 clove), freshly ground nutmeg

Shopping List:
New potatoes (2 lbs.)
French Gruyère cheese (1/2 lb.)

About 1 1/2 Hours Before Serving

Peel and cut the potatoes evenly into 1/4-inch slices, putting them into a large mixing bowl. Coarsely grate the cheese. Beat the egg. Scald 3 cups of the milk and hold, warm. Add to potatoes in bowl, but do not mix for the moment: a few grinds of nutmeg, the beaten egg, half the grated cheese, plus plenty of salt and pepper. Now wet everything down with the hot milk and move the potatoes around with a wooden spoon, the object being to coat them without breaking them. Preheat oven to 400 degrees. For the baking we use a shallow, open earthenware dish, which we butter thickly, then smear with crushed garlic. Now carefully spoon in the entire contents of the mixing bowl, making sure that potato slices are horizontal and reasonably separated. The milk should come almost to top of potatoes. Sprinkle on rest of grated cheese and liberally dot with butter. Bake, uncovered, until potatoes are soft and brown on top, usually 1 hour. The earthenware dish is brought to the table.

MACARONI MARUZZE WITH BLUEBERRIES

For our family of 4

This is one of the more attractive and practical types of macaroni pasta, each piece shaped like a small sea shell, holds its share of sauce, and when the blueberries are stirred in one black pearl usually enters each maruzze oyster. The idea of serving fruit with the main meat course is not unusual: orange with duck, apple sauce with goose, sweet mint jelly with lamb. . . . We find this an excellent replacement for potatoes with various meats and birds.

Check Staples:

Salt butter (¼ lb.)
Aromatic: crystal salt
Italian tomato paste (6-oz. can)
Dry red wine (about ½ cup)

Shopping List:

Maruzze macaroni shells (½-lb. box)
Fresh blueberries (1 cup)
Swiss Gruyère cheese (¼ lb.)

About 45 Minutes Before Serving

We cook the maruzze as if they were macaroni, in a large pot filled with salted, boiling water, until they are *al dente,* still chewy. Drain, rinse under hot running water, then carefully drain again, shaking vigorously to get all water out of the shells. While they are cooking we make the sauce in a small copper pan. Melt the butter, thicken it by blending in 1 to 2 tablespoons of the tomato paste, thin it with 1 to 2 tablespoons of the red wine, season to taste with the salt, and finally adjust by thickening or thinning to the consistency of heavy cream. Let it gently simmer, covered, until needed. Wash and dry the blueberries. Coarsely grate the cheese. Liberally butter an shallow, open baking dish. Put in the drained maruzze with the blueberries on top. Alternately shake the dish and gently stir the contents with a wooden spoon. After 2 or 3 minutes of this, almost all the blueberries

will have disappeared into the shells. Pour on the sauce and stir so that the sauce too runs into the shells. Finally, sprinkle the top with the grated cheese.

25 Minutes Before Serving

Preheat oven to 350 degrees. Put in the dish and leave it until the sauce begins bubbling, usually in 20 minutes.

BLACK-EYED PEAS WITH SOUR CREAM

For our family of 4

The staple ingredient of so many charming Southern dishes makes an excellent alternative to the potato.

Check Staples:

Thick-sliced dark smoked bacon (6 slices)
Beef or chicken bouillon (about 4 cups)
Aromatics: crystal salt, freshly ground black pepper, MSG, whole caraway seed, oregano
Yellow onion (1 medium)

Shopping List:

Black-eyed peas (½ lb.)
Sour cream (½ pt.)
Cucumber (1 medium)
Fresh dill (small bunch)

On the Morning of the Day

BASIC RULE FOR BLACK-EYED PEAS: Bring 1½ quarts of water to a rolling boil in a large saucepan. Keeping the heat high, dribble the black-eyed peas in slowly enough through the fingers so that the water does not stop boiling. When they are all in let them boil violently for exactly 2 minutes, then turn off the heat and leave them to soak for not more than 1 hour. Then they are drained and will need about 45 minutes more of gentle simmering in whatever aromatic liquid is called for by the dish.

About 1 Hour Before Serving

Peel and chunk the onion. Cut the 6 slices of bacon into 1-inch squares and fry gently, starting in a cold pan, until crisp and crumbly, then drain on absorbent paper and hold. Peel and coarsely dice the cucumber. Chop enough fronds and stems of the dill to fill ⅓ cup. Drain black-eyed peas and put them in a saucepan with enough of the bouillon to cover, adding 1 teaspoon of caraway, ½ teaspoon oregano, plus salt, pepper, and MSG to taste. Simmer very gently, "just smiling," covered, until soft (do not overcook), usually in about 45 minutes.

15 Minutes Before Serving

We usually present this dish in a wide-mouthed bean pot. Preheat oven to 300 degrees. Put into the bean pot the cup of sour cream, the diced cucumber, the crumbled bacon, and the chopped dill; cover, and set in the oven to warm up—but for not more than 10 minutes or the cucumber will wilt. Drain the black-eyed peas (saving any remaining liquid for basic stock) and carefully spoon them into the bean pot. Very gently stir everything around with a wooden spoon so as to avoid mashing the peas. These peas are especially good with slices of meat from a roast.

PEARL BARLEY WITH MUSHROOMS

For our family of 4

We regard each grain of barley as a tiny sponge, eager to absorb any aromatic liquid. We shape it in a ring mold and often fill the center with sauced chunks of meat (for example, the spring lamb with dill sauce, page 277).

Check Staples:

Beef or chicken bouillon (about 3 cups)
Salt butter (about 6 oz.—12 Tbs.)
Aromatics: crystal salt,☆ freshly ground black pepper,☆ MSG,▣ garlic (2 or 3 cloves)
Yellow onions (2 medium)
Dry white wine▯ (1 cup)

Shopping List:

Whole-grain pearl barley (1 cup)
Small button mushrooms (½ lb.)

About 1¼ Hours Before Serving

We use an enameled cast-iron cocotte* with a tightly fitting lid. Peel and coarsely chop the onions. Set the cocotte over medium frying heat, melt 4 tablespoons of the butter, and fry the chopped onion until it is just transparent. Add the barley and stir around, so that each grain is coated and slightly browned. Slowly add ½ cup of the wine, stirring constantly, and turning the heat up full so that the liquid comes to a rolling boil as quickly as possible. At once start adding 2½ cups of the bouillon, a little at a time, continuing to stir, waiting for each new batch to come to a boil before the next is added. When all liquid is in, turn heat down to a gentle simmer, season to taste with salt, pepper, and MSG, cover tightly and keep simmering until all liquid has been absorbed and barley is soft but still slightly chewy. If liquid is absorbed before barley is perfect, add about ¼ cup more hot bouillon and/or wine and continue simmering. If barley is perfect before all liquid is absorbed, evaporate final liquid over high heat, uncovered, for a couple of minutes. The entire operation usually takes 1 hour.

While barley is cooking, cut the stems off the mushrooms, leaving small buttons whole and quartering large ones. Prepare buttons and stems in the Provençal manner, with garlic and butter, according to our recipe (page 181), and hold warm until barley is ready. Butter a ring mold. Gently blend cooked mushrooms into cooked barley. Lightly press the mixture into mold. Unmold onto a hot platter and, if possible, fill the center of the ring with a main dish or a vegetable of contrasting color.

¶ *Salads*

This is the time to combine the youngest of greens into one of the most delicate salads of the year, with the lightest of dressings. Some combinations need no dressing, only a sprinkling of crystal salt or a few added drops of virgin olive oil over the top, not tossed in. We replace vinegar with lemon juice, onion with chive. We think that no salad is ever complete without a touch of garlic, but now it should be as if a whiff of its aroma had merely been blown through the salad, just a few rubs of a cut clove round the inside of the bowl. Now is the time to practice tasting the leaves as they are torn by hand into the bowl to learn to judge the balance of flavors and textures. Our BASIC RULE for assembling a salad is on page 73. The best salad greens of the season are noted in the list of foods in season (page 220).

SPRING SALAD DRESSING NUMBER ONE

For a salad for 4

Check Staples:

Lemons (1 or 2, according to juiciness)
Aromatics: crystal salt,⁑ freshly ground black pepper,⁑ garlic (½ clove to rub around bowl), dried tarragon (if fresh not available)
Fresh chives (enough for 2 tsp., finely chopped)
Fresh parsley (enough for 1 Tbs., finely chopped)
Green virgin olive oil (4½ Tbs.)

Shopping List:

Fresh tarragon (enough for 2 tsp., finely chopped)

Before the Salad Goes into the Wooden Bowl

Rub the inside of the bowl with the cut side of the clove of garlic. How many rubs is a matter of trial and error within the taste of each family; we go around five times.

We Prepare It at Table

Put ½ teaspoon of salt into a small mortar and pound for 1 or 2 seconds with the pestle. Grind on black pepper until the salt is speckled gray. Squeeze lemons; we use a 1-ounce graduated medicine glass* to measure exactly 1½ tablespoons of the lemon juice. Add to the mortar and stir around to dissolve the salt. In the same way, measure exactly the 4½ tablespoons of olive oil and add to the mortar. Stir around and let it rest, so the flavors will blend, until the salad is ready to be dressed. Finely chop and put into a small separate bowl: 2 teaspoons of chives, 1 tablespoon of parsley, and 2 teaspoons of fresh tarragon leaf (or add ½ teaspoon of the dried).

When the Salad Is About To Be Served

Stir up the oil mixture in the mortar. Add the chopped fresh herbs and stir again. Spoon the dressing over the salad. Toss thoroughly and serve instantly.

SPRING SALAD DRESSING NUMBER TWO

For a salad for 4

Use the same ingredients as for the preceding dressing, except replace the fresh tarragon with finely chopped fresh dill (dried dillweed is not possible as an alternative); prepare and serve in the same way.

MODIFIED SPRING CAESAR SALAD WITH ARUGULA

For our family of 4

Presumably the "Caesar" is the usual reference to the ubiquitous "Caesar Ritz," although it is doubtful whether he ever operated widely in California, the original home of the dozens of versions of this salad. It is usually made piquant with mashed anchovies and Parmesan cheese but we omit these in the spring and rely on the delicate flavor-texture balance of the young greens and vegetables.

Check Staples:

Salt butter (2 or 3 Tbs.)
Egg (1 large)
White bread (6 slices)
Salad dressing number one, *see* page 319 (1 batch)

Shopping List:

Fresh arugula (a few leaves)
White cauliflower (1 very small, young)
Boston lettuce (2 small heads)
Fresh button mushrooms, the whitest available, for appearance (¼ lb.)
Green pepper (1 medium)
Radishes (small bunch)
Spinach (a few young leaves)

A Few Hours Beforehand

Cube the 6 slices of bread, later to be fried in the butter as croutons. Wash, dry, and crisp in the refrigerator: the lettuce leaves, spinach, arugula, green pepper, and radishes. Wash and dry the cauliflower and break off about a dozen flowerets, each about the size of a small cherry. Wipe the mushrooms clean (never wash) and slice them lengthwise into hammer shapes. Hold everything cold and dry.

About 30 Minutes Before Serving

Coddle the egg to half-set the white, but do not yet break it. Fry the bread cubes in 2 tablespoons of the butter (adding a bit more if needed) to brown and crisp, then drain and cool on absorbent paper. Start preparing salad dressing number one (page 319). Thinly slice about a dozen of the radishes and hold in the refrigerator. Coarsely dice the green pepper.

5 Minutes Before Serving

Assemble the salad in the bowl. The exact amount of each ingredient can only be decided by judgment borne of trial and error. Rub salad bowl with cut garlic. Break egg into bowl. Toss in a balance of: lettuce leaves (hand-torn into bite-size pieces), radish slices, diced green pepper, cauliflowerets, about 3 or 4 leaves each of the spinach and arugula (hand-torn), a good handful or more of the sliced mushrooms, and the fried croutons. Dress the salad and toss it vigorously, bringing the egg up from below to meet the salad dressing, working down from above. Each crouton absorbs some of the dressing and seems to magnify its aroma.

DUTCH TOMATO PLATTER WITH FRESH BASIL

For our family of 4

We start making this good-looking and good-tasting salad as soon as the local vine-ripened tomatoes and bunches of fresh basil come into the market. Through spring and summer the family asks for it again and again. No dish in our repertoire better demonstrates the affinity of basil with tomato, but for the perfect wedding of the flavors a few hours in the refrigerator is essential.

Check Staples:

Aromatics: crystal salt, freshly ground black pepper, MSG, dried celery seed
Fresh chives (small bunch)
Granulated white sugar (a few pinches)

Shopping List:

Vine-ripened tomatoes, in perfect condition (4 medium)
Sweet red onion (1 medium)
Sweet white Bermuda or Spanish onion (enough for about 1 Tbs., finely chopped)
Fresh basil (small bunch)
Fresh dill (small bunch)

About 2½ Hours Before Serving

We prepare this on a flat oval platter. Peel the red onion and cut into ¼-inch slices. Break up into rings and completely cover the platter with them, but not too many and none overlapping. The object is to lift tomato slices off platter to allow them to drain. Cut the tomatoes crosswise into ⅜-inch slices and lay on top of onion rings, none overlapping. Sprinkle with a few pinches of: sugar, celery seed, salt, pepper, and MSG. With kitchen scissors, coarsely snip onto the tomatoes the basil leaf, dill fronds, and chives. Make sure that each tomato slice is well covered with about equal parts of chive and dill and double the quantity of the basil. It is a good trick to crush a few basil leaves in the fingers to bring out the oil. Finely chop enough of the sweet white onion to fill about 1 tablespoon and sprinkle over the top of tomatoes. Finally, tightly cover entire platter with aluminum foil and refrigerate for about 2 hours.

Just Before Serving

Without taking off foil, open up one end, hold an inverted plate on top of the platter to prevent the tomatoes from slipping, and very carefully pour off the tomato water that will have accumulated around onion rings. Unwrap, see that everything is neat, and serve.

¶ *Desserts*

Again Fruit with Cheese and "A Glass"

We have already discussed (page 173) some of the extraordinary dessert combinations of fruits, with cheese and a glass of an appropriate wine, beer, brandy, or liqueur. Some of the spring fruits and cheeses are especially well matched.

With the APPLES which remain crisp and juicy, the YELLOW NEWTOWN PIPPIN, plus the GOLDEN and RED DELICIOUS, we serve chunks of the new season's cheeses, the Swiss APPENZELLER, Canadian SHARP CHEDDAR and Dutch EDAMMER and a glass of a good Italian red BAROLO, or less formally, a foaming glass of imported Irish GUINNESS STOUT.

With the impressive California EMPEROR GRAPE, a cube of soft American LIEDERKRANZ and a refreshingly cold glass of French white MUSCADET or a tall glass of BLACK VELVET, an equal mixture of New York State champagne and imported Irish Guinness Stout.

With the various types of spring PLUM, a wedge of BRIE or CAMEMBERT and a glass of a good tawny PORT or a mug of HALF-AND-HALF, a 50–50 mixture of India Pale Ale and imported Irish Guinness Stout.

With STRAWBERRIES or some of the other soft berries, we serve PHILADELPHIA CREAM CHEESE and a first-class Alsatian PINOT NOIR ROSÉ or a small liqueur glass of a Swiss KIRSCHWASSER, the colorless brandy distilled from cherries.

OUR BEST HOMEMADE SHERBET—WITH SPRING RHUBARB

1 load for a 4-quart freezer

We have prepared this magnificent sherbet in each of the three types of electric home-freezer: the small model, which fits into the refrigerator freezer and has two plastic propellors to stir the mixture* (for this we use about half the quantities listed below); the larger rotary machine, which also fits into the refrigerator freezer,* and the electrically driven equivalent of the old-fashioned chipped-ice-and-rock-salt model.* The result is first-class in each case, although the textures differ. Some friends have even made it in ice trays, stirring every few minutes as it hardens and then, just before it finally solidifies, blending in whipped, sugared heavy cream.

Check Staples:

Eggs (4 large)
Lemons (2 or 3, according to juiciness)
Oranges (3 or 4, enough for 1 cup of juice)
Aromatic: crystal salt☆
Pure maple syrup☐ (1 cup)
Granulated white sugar (2¼ cups)

Shopping List:

Young spring rhubarb (3 lbs.)

Preparation in About ½ Hour—Freezing in 2½ Hours Longer

Wash the rhubarb, discard leaves and tough parts and finely cut up enough to fill 8 cups. Put rhubarb into a 4-quart saucepan with 1 cup of freshly drawn cold water and boil briskly, covered, stirring occasionally, until rhubarb mashes down, usually in 10 minutes. Meanwhile break the 4 eggs into a mixing bowl and beat with a wire whisk until blended and frothy. Gradually add the 2¼ cups of sugar, beating until very stiff. Finely chop enough outer yellow rind of the lemon to fill 2 teaspoons. Squeeze enough lemon juice to fill ¼ cup and enough orange juice to fill 1 cup. When rhubarb is soft, add: the cup of maple syrup, the lemon and orange juices, and the lemon rind. Stirring continuously, bring all rapidly to a boil. Pour at once into a heatproof mixing bowl, cover and set in the freezer to cool rapidly. It should be cold and syrupy in about 10 minutes. Sprinkle on about ½ teaspoon of salt and beat in the egg-sugar mixture. Pour at once into the container of the freezer and follow instructions for the particular machine being used.

Four Ways With Strawberries

Each of the ways given is best suited to a particular quality and ripeness of the fruit.

STRAWBERRIES (WHEN PERFECT, FRESHLY PICKED, RIPE AND SWEET)—OUR VERSION OF THE FRENCH WAY

For our family of 4

Check Staples:

Pure maple syrup☐ (about 4 Tbs.)
Ice water (about ½ cup per person)
Ice cubes (1 or 2 per person)

Shopping List:

Strawberries (about 1 qt.)

About 5 Minutes to Prepare

This wonderful way of serving strawberries is also the simplest. Do not wash or hull them. Make a balanced circle of strawberries around a

dessert plate for each person. In the center of each plate we place 2 roly-poly glass bowls: the tiny one on the left contains about 1 tablespoon of the maple syrup, the larger, on the right, about ½ cup of ice water with an ice cube floating in it.

How to Eat in the French Way

Hold the strawberry by its stem and wash-it-yourself by dipping it several times in and out of the ice water, then hold it up to let the water drip off. Then dip the strawberry into the maple syrup and, leaning forward over the plate, bite the strawberry off the stem. Sweet-tooths may bite only half and give the second half another dip in the syrup. The affinity of the natural syrup with the natural fruit is extraordinary.

STRAWBERRIES (WHEN SLIGHTLY UNDERRIPE AND JUST TART)—WITH SUGARED CREAM OR FRENCH-STYLE CRÈME FRAÎCHE

Check Staples:

Confectioners' sugar (a few Tbs.)

Shopping List:

Strawberries (about 1 qt.)
Heavy cream or homemade *crème fraîche,* recipe follows (about ½ cup)

About 10 Minutes to Prepare

Chill bowl and whisk in freezer, then whip the cream until stiff and beat in sugar to taste. This time wash the strawberries in advance and dry them, but leave the stems on. Make a balanced circle of berries around the edge of each individual chilled dessert plate. In the center make a small rough pile of whipped cream. Hold each strawberry by its stem and dip into the cream.

STRAWBERRIES (WHEN JUST PAST THEIR PRIME AND SLIGHTLY MUSHY)—WITH SOUR CREAM

Check Staples:

Granulated white sugar (a few Tbs.)

Shopping List:

Strawberries (about 1 qt.)
Sour cream (about 3/4 pt.)

About 15 Minutes to Prepare

These strawberries are eaten with a fork, so they are washed, dried, and hulled beforehand. Again they are placed in a circle around chilled dessert plates. Blend the sour cream with the sugar to taste, divide into 4 parts and pile 1 part in the center of each plate; sprinkle over a little more sugar. Spear a strawberry on the fork, twist it around in the sour cream to coat on all sides, and crunch the gritty sugar in the mouth.

STRAWBERRIES (WHEN THEY HAVE TO BE MASHED)—WITH MAPLE CHEESE

Check Staples:

Granulated white sugar (a few Tbs.)
Pure maple syrup (about 6 Tbs.)

Shopping List:

Strawberries (about 1 qt.)
Philadelphia cream cheese (two 3-oz. packages)
Sour cream (1/2 pt.)
French Calvados brandy (a few tsp.)

The Day Before

Soften the cream cheese at room temperature, then mash with the cup of sour cream and 1/4 cup of the maple syrup. Blend vigorously with a wooden spoon until smooth. Spoon into individual custard cups, filling each not more than two thirds full. Refrigerate, covered, overnight.

About 15 Minutes Before Serving

Take custard cups out of refrigerator and check texture of maple cheese. It should be a little stiffer than a baked caramel custard. If too stiff, blend about 1 more teaspoon of maple syrup into each cup. A little untidiness does not matter. Lightly mash the strawberries with sugar to taste and fill each cup, piling it up. Dribble on a few drops more maple syrup and about 1 teaspoon of the Calvados per cup. Serve at once, still slightly chilled.

BASIC METHOD FOR MAKING FRENCH CRÈME FRAÎCHE—MATURED, THICKENED CREAM FOR FRESH FRUIT

Makes 1 pint, will keep for 2 weeks

Although France is the homeland of Pasteur, the French do not seem to rely on pasteurization as much as Americans do. When one buys *crème fraîche* from a French dairy, it is not fresh at all, but has been allowed to stand in a warm place to mature. (At this stage it is not yet sour, like American sour cream.) *Crème fraîche* is thick, has a faint flavor of crushed almonds, and is the perfect foil for fresh fruit. We have found a way of preparing a close imitation at home, and since it keeps better than fresh cream we maintain a supply in our refrigerator.

Shopping List:
Heavy whipping cream (1 pt.)
Commercial buttermilk (1 Tbs.)

Preparation in 5 Minutes—Then 8 to 24 Hours of Patient Waiting

This is the same process as is used in making yogurt, but with a different bacillus. We stir cream and buttermilk together in a small copper saucepan and very gently heat to a temperature no higher than 75 to 85 degrees. Above that temperature the vital bacilli are "burned to death," and nothing happens. The easiest way to control the temperature is to remember that one's index finger normally registers about 98 degrees; therefore if one just touches the cream, it should still feel very slightly cool. Turn off heat at once, pour cream into a 1-pint bowl, cover with a single thickness of paper toweling (so that air may circulate in without dust), and stand bowl on the pilot light of the stove, on the lukewarm stand of an electric yogurt-maker or in an oven that is kept just warm by its pilot light. Depending on the temperature, cream will thicken in 8 to 24 hours. Every 8 hours or so, it should be checked and stirred. As soon as it thickens, refrigerate, covered.

FRENCH CLAFOUTI OF BING CHERRIES

For our family of 4

A *clafouti* is a baked batter pie, a specialty of the Limousin region of southern France, where cherries are abundant.

Check Staples:
Sweet butter (1 tsp., to grease dish)
Milk (1¼ cups)
Eggs (3 large)
Aromatics: crystal salt,☧ pure

Shopping List:
Sweet, ripe Bing cherries (1½ lbs.)
Crystallized ginger (2 oz.)

Check Staples (continued):

vanilla extract (1 Tbs.)
Granulated instantized flour (about 1 cup)
Granulated white sugar (about ½ cup)
Confectioners' sugar (a few Tbs.)

Well Ahead—the Usual Family Chore

We all pit enough cherries to fill about 3 cups, fairly tightly packed; the exact amount is not critical. Also chop the ginger.

About 1¼ Hours Before Serving

Preheat oven to 350 degrees. We make the batter in our electric blender, but it can also be beaten by hand. We put into the blender container: the 1¼ cups of milk, ⅓ cup of the granulated sugar, the 3 whole eggs, the tablespoon of vanilla, ⅔ cup of the flour and about ½ teaspoon of salt. Stir ingredients together before switching on the machine, cover, and run at high speed for about 30 seconds. We prepare this size *clafouti* in a 9″x9″x2″ enameled cast-iron open baking dish, which is brought to the table. The size is important. The batter must be deep enough to cover the cherries. Butter the dish and pour in enough batter from the blender container to cover the bottom with a layer ¼ inch deep. Place the dish on a top burner over medium frying heat, until the batter is lightly set, usually in about 2 minutes. Turn off heat at once and drop cherries on this batter foundation, making a solid, single layer. Sprinkle with the chopped ginger and more granulated sugar to taste. Pour over the rest of the batter, submerging the cherries. Put the dish in the center of the oven and bake until the top is brown and puffy. A shiny silver knife plunged into the center at this point should come out dry. The total baking time is usually 1 hour. Immediately sprinkle the top with the confectioners' sugar and bring to the table piping hot.

¶ *Family Specialties—Party Breakfasts · Lunch · Breads · Cakes · Drinks*

LAZY SUNDAY BREAKFAST—DO-IT-YOURSELF BLUEBERRY PANCAKES

For 4 people

When the spring blueberries arrive in the market, we bring our electric frypan into the living room on Sunday morning and take turns at "making a load."

Check Staples:

Sweet butter (about ½ lb.)
Eggs (4 large)
Milk (2 cups)
Aromatic: crystal salt☧
Double-acting baking powder (4 tsp.)
Granulated instantized flour⛁ (2½ to 3 cups)
Pure maple syrup⛁ (for pouring over)
Dark-brown sugar (for sprinkling over)

Shopping List:

Blueberries (about 1 pt.)

1 or 2 Hours in Advance

BASIC RULE FOR BATTER FOR PANCAKES, CRÊPES, ETC.: We just throw the staples together in a mixing bowl and whip them up thoroughly with a wire whisk. With the instantized flour, even sifting is eliminated. Spread 2½ cups of the flour over the bottom of the bowl. Sprinkle on the 4 teaspoons of baking powder and about 1 teaspoon of salt and stir around with a wooden spoon. Break in the 4 eggs, whole, and start blending them in with the wire whisk, at the same time adding, bit by bit, 1 cup of the milk. It will all still be quite thick. Melt ½ cup of the butter over gentle heat, so that it liquefies without becoming very hot, and blend it into the batter. Now adjust the thickness by adding, bit by bit, more milk as needed. For thin pancakes, the final consistency should be just a shade thicker than heavy cream. If it gets too thin, a little more flour can be blended in. It will always get thicker as it stands and should then be thinned with more milk. It can be held, covered and refrigerated, for several days and can be used for many purposes.

Preparing and Serving Blueberry Pancakes in the Living Room

The electric frypan must be quite hot so that the lubricating lumps of butter sizzle. As soon as butter is melted, ladle on batter and immediately dot it with as many blueberries as it will comfortably hold. The batter should still be soft enough for them to sink in. When bubbles begin to form and edge becomes crinkly, turn pancake over and let blueberries burst. This looks messy and requires a continuing supply of lubricating butter, but it tastes luscious. Serve with maple syrup and/or brown sugar.

FRUIT LUNCH FOR SPRING—RUEDI'S BIRCHER MÜSLI

For 4 people

This is the recipe that our friend Ruedi brought from his home in Zürich, where April is the month of celebration. When he first prepared it for us, he explained that the *Bircher* refers to a Dr. Bircher of Geneva, who invented the dish as a health food, while the *Müsli* is Swiss-German dialect for a "mousse." With a hearty soup ahead of it, this "fruit mousse" makes a refreshing lunch or brunch. The whipped cream adds glamour but can be omitted.

Check Staples:

Lemons (4)
Milk (about 1 pt.)
Oranges (2 or 3)
Granulated white sugar (½ to 1 cup)

Shopping List:

Quick-cooking oatmeal (about 4 cups, uncooked)
Heavy cream (½ pt.)
Apples (4 firm)
Apricots, nectarines, or peaches (2 or 3)
Bananas (2 ripe)
Seedless grapes (½ lb.)
Ripe strawberries (1 qt.)
Maraschino cherries (4-oz. jar, for decoration)
Unsalted mixed nutmeats (about 2 cups)

About 1½ Hours Before Serving

Ruedi always stresses that the balance of ingredients is flexible. The oatmeal gives body and solidity and more or less of it can be used to taste, but it is wise the first time to put in the full 4 cups. The character of the whole dish can be changed by varying the balance of the fruits. Follow Ruedi's recipe the first time, then start experimenting.

We use our large punch bowl and spread over the bottom of it the 4 cups of oatmeal. Add as much milk as needed to cover and soak oatmeal. Let stand at room temperature for 30 minutes, adding more milk as needed, until the result is a fairly thin oatmeal gruel. Meanwhile prepare fruits and nuts and put together in a large mixing bowl. Peel, core, and coarsely grate the apples. Cut the bananas into ¼-inch slices. Separate the oranges into sections and remove pips. Chunk the apricots, nectarines, or peaches. Hull and wash the strawberries. Wash the grapes. Coarsely grate the 2 cups of nutmeats. Do not mix ingredients now; hold in the refrigerator.

1 Hour Before Serving

Squeeze the juice from the lemons. When oatmeal is soaked and soft, pile over it all fruits and nuts and start folding and mixing with a large wooden spoon, making sure that the fruits are not crushed. At the same time add lemon juice and sugar alternately, tablespoon by tablespoon, and keep tasting until a good balance between tartness and sweetness is achieved. Then refrigerate for not more than 30 to 40 minutes. A slight chill gives tang, but if it is too cold some of the flavor is lost.

10 Minutes Before Serving

Whip the cream stiff and then spread it thickly and roughly over the top of the fruit. Decorate with the maraschino cherries. Bring at once to the table.

AUNT ANNA'S BANANA-DATE-NUT BREAD

For 6 to 8 people

This bread, more than the cake, was what we looked forward to when our Aunt Anna invited us to tea. We often asked for the recipe, but she always refused, saying she wanted to make sure that we would keep on coming to see her. She sent us the recipe shortly before she died. We prepare it often and remember Aunt Anna.

Check Staples:

Sweet butter (1/4 cup)
Egg (1 large)
Aromatic: fine table salt
Double-acting baking powder (1 tsp.)
Granulated instantized flour (2 cups)
Granulated white sugar (3/4 cup)

Shopping List:

Bananas (2 or 3, according to size)
Pitted dates (enough to fill 1/2 cup, chopped)
Walnuts (in the shell or ready-shelled, enough to fill 1/2 cup, chopped)

About 1/2 Hour to Prepare—1 Hour in the Oven

The instantized flour needs no sifting (with ordinary flour, sift with the baking powder and salt). Prepare all ingredients, holding them separate: let butter come to room temperature, break egg into small bowl; in another bowl carefully stir the 2 cups of flour with the teaspoon of baking powder and 1 teaspoon salt; mash bananas, coarsely chop nuts and dates. In a good-sized mixing bowl, cream butter with sugar, then add quickly beaten egg and continue beating mixture vigorously. Then blend in one by one: the flour mixture, mashed bananas, chopped dates and walnuts. Preheat oven to 350 degrees. Lightly butter a loaf pan, smooth in dough and bake until it has risen and a silver knife comes out clean, usually in 1 hour. Cool on a rack. Cut bread in very thin slices and just butter lightly; to spread jam on it would be a crime.

JOHANNA'S CRACKLING CORN BREAD

For our family of 4

Whenever we have pork, there are usually lumps of fat which can be fried out to make crackling and then stored in a screw-top refrigerator jar. When we have about 1 cup, we are ready to bake corn bread. It can also be made (and is almost as good) without the crackling.

Check Staples:

Pork crackling, ***see*** **above (about 1 cup)**
Butter (1/4 lb.)
Eggs (2 large)
Milk (about 1 cup)
Aromatic: crystal salt☧
Double-acting baking powder (about 2 tsp.)
Coarse white water-ground cornmeal⛁ (2 cups)
Granulated instantized flour⛁ (1/4 cup)

About 45 Minutes Before Serving

Set 1/4-pound stick of butter out to soften.

About 35 Minutes Before Serving

Preheat oven to 350 degrees and put in a 9- or 10-inch cake pan to heat up. Assemble in a large mixing bowl: the cup of crackling, the 2 cups of cornmeal, then sprinkle on in turn, the 1/4 cup of flour, the 2 teaspoons of baking powder, about 1 teaspoon salt. Mix thoroughly, then begin lightly to work in the 2 eggs, which first have been slightly beaten, and the 1/4 pound of butter, cut into bits—but hold back about 2 teaspoons to use for greasing pan. Continue working together, lightly but thoroughly, adding enough of the milk to make a batter that will just pour. Remove hot pan from oven, quickly butter it, using a pastry brush, then pour in batter and bake in center of oven until top is lightly browned, usually in 20 to 30 minutes.

MAIBOWLE NUMBER ONE—FOR A SMALL, INFORMAL PARTY

For 12 people

When the new May Wine arrives from Germany we serve one of these traditional German punch bowls, either as a prologue to a light supper on a hot evening or as the centerpiece of what would otherwise be a cocktail-and-canapé party. We sharpen the already spiced May Wine by adding more of our own aromatic woodruff.

Check Staples:

Aromatic: dried woodruff☧ (1 or 2 Tbs.)

Shopping List:

Sweet, ripe strawberries (1 qt.)
Imported German May Wine (5 bottles)

The Day Before

We spread over the bottom of our punch bowl about 1½ tablespoons of the woodruff. Pour over it 1 bottle of the May Wine, making sure with the back of a spoon that all woodruff is submerged. Cover and refrigerate overnight. Also chill the other 4 bottles.

About 15 Minutes Before Serving

Hull, wash, and slice the strawberries. Strain woodruff out of wine and put strained wine back in punch bowl. Add the other 4 bottles. Float sliced strawberries as garnish. Stand bowl on bed of ice. Serve sliced strawberry in each cup.

MAIBOWLE NUMBER TWO—FOR A BIG, FORMAL PARTY

For 25 people

Check Staples:

Aromatic: dried woodruff (about 4 Tbs.)

Shopping List:

Tiny wild wood strawberries—*fraises des bois*—if available, *see* list, page 214, if not, use domestic strawberries as in previous recipe (about 1 qt.)

French Cognac, medium-priced (1 bottle)

Imported German May Wine (8 bottles)

Champagne, medium-priced (1 bottle)

The Day Before

This is the same basic method as used in the previous recipe. Spread the 4 tablespoons of woodruff in the punch bowl, pour in all the Cognac, and refrigerate, covered, overnight. Chill all other bottles.

About 15 Minutes Before Serving

The tiny wild strawberries can be left whole, but they may need washing and hulling (if domestic strawberries are used, prepare as in previous recipe). Strain woodruff out of Cognac and put strained Cognac back in bowl. Add the 8 bottles of May Wine and, at the last moment, the champagne. Float strawberries on top. Stand punch bowl on ice.

The Budget Pull-Back and Encore Dishes of Spring

For a general discussion of our cost-control budget system, see page 6.

CREAM OF PEA-POD SOUP

A basic supply for several days

This is the dish for the cook who likes to get something for virtually nothing. Our note on this recipe after we had tried it for the first time: "Lots of work, but worth it!" The young pods of spring peas give the best flavor.

Check Staples:

Pea pods (we save them until we have about 6 qts., 5 to 6 lbs.)
Salt butter (1/4 lb.)
Floured butter—*beurre manié,* *see* page 12 (about 1/3 cup)
Aromatic: crystal salt
Yellow onions (2 medium)
Fresh parsley (small bunch)

Shopping List:

Romaine lettuce (2 small heads)
Light cream (1 1/2 cups)

Preparation in About 30 Minutes—Before Cooking Begins

We prepare this in our large, deep soup pot with 2 1/2 quarts of freshly drawn cold water. Prepare and add: the washed and de-stemmed pea pods, the 2 lettuce heads, the 2 onions (coarsely chopped), the parsley in whole sprigs, 4 tablespoons of the butter, and a good dose of salt.

Cooking in About 45 Minutes

Bring the ingredients in the pot to a brisk boil and keep bubbling merrily, covered, until the inside green flesh of the pods is pulpy and comes away easily from the thin outer skin, usually in 30 to 40 minutes.

Pounding and Sieving in 30 Minutes

Strain the solids from the liquid and return latter to the pot. Put the solids, batch by batch, into a large mortar and pound hard. The idea is to loosen all the green pulp from the pods and squeeze all the juices from the aromatic vegetables. Then push the pounded solids through a strong sieve held over the pot, rubbing through with the pestle, so that pulp and juices fall back into the soup. This is the "basic mix," which can be stored in the refrigerator for several days.

Final Preparation in About 15 Minutes

Assuming that we are preparing 1 quart of the basic mix, to serve 4 people, bring it up almost to boiling, then thicken to the consistency of cream soup by adding small bits of the floured butter, stirring around so that it melts immediately without lumping, usually 3 to 4 tablespoons are absorbed. When mixture is smooth, bring to a boil, then reduce heat to just below boiling and stir in 1 cup of the cream; it must not boil again. Taste and adjust seasoning and if it needs thinning add a little more cream. Serve very hot.

ONE-DISH MEAL OF SPRING LAMB WITH LENTILS

For our family of 4

A solid dish for a hungry family on a busy day.

Check Staples:

Salt butter (a few Tbs.)
Aromatics: crystal salt,* freshly ground black pepper,* MSG,* basil, sweet marjoram, thyme
Yellow onions (4 medium)
White rice (1 cup, raw)
Dry white wine* (1 cup)

Shopping List:

Lean spring lamb, perhaps cut from the shank end of a leg, page 276 or cubed by butcher (1 lb.)
Jumbo Argentinian lentils (1/2 lb.)

About 1 3/4 Hours Before Serving

The dish requires about 15 minutes of work and almost no attention for the rest of the time. We do all preparation in a single 4-quart enameled cast-iron cocotte* with a tightly fitting lid. The lamb should be cut up and a few pieces of bone add to the flavor. Set cocotte over high frying heat and quickly brown lamb pieces, adding 1 to 2 tablespoons of the butter as needed. When brown, lift out pieces with a slotted spoon and hold. Meanwhile peel and slice the 4 onions and separate into rings. As soon as cocotte is cleared of meat, turn heat down to low frying temperature and slowly brown onion rings, adding more butter as needed. When done, take out half the onion rings with a slotted spoon and hold. Put lamb cubes on top of the remaining onions. Turn heat up high and gradually add, bringing rapidly to a boil: the cup of wine and 2 cups of freshly drawn cold water. Now put in: 1/2 teaspoon each of basil, marjoram, and thyme, plus salt, pepper, and MSG to taste. Lower heat to gentle simmering and continue cooking, covered, for about 45 minutes. Meanwhile wash the cup of lentils and after the first 45 minutes add them to lamb. Turn up heat to bring back quickly to simmering, then adjust to continue simmering, covered, for 15 minutes more. Add 2 cups of hot water and as soon as stew is again boiling gently blend in the cup of raw rice. Continue simmering, covered, until rice is soft and almost all liquid is absorbed, usually in 20 to 25 minutes. The final mixture should be rich, solid, moist, and aromatic. At the table garnish each serving with fried onion rings.

Three Foreign and Fancy Ways with Kidneys

Our friend Steve was a kidney-phobe of long standing. He said that every mouthful of a kidney reminded him of its past, unsavory activity. One Sunday evening, he and his wife, Barbara, arrived at suppertime from a country hike absolutely starving. All we had to offer was a dish of Dutch veal kidneys (recipe below). For a few seconds Steve's face was contorted by the struggle between hunger and distaste. Barbara seized the opportunity. For years she had been pointing out that kidneys were among the cheapest and most nutritious meats in the market and that in millions of homes in Europe and all over the world they are an honored delicacy. . . .

Steve is a true gourmet. After he had slowly savored the first kidney, he allowed neither pride nor obstinacy to dilute the sincerity of his praise. We have proved again and again that we can convert any reasonable kidney-phobe with any one of our kidney recipes, for each includes the same basic technique of pre-preparation. We never use a kidney until it has passed through the ceremony of purification from its questionable past. We name this recipe in honor of the brilliant cook who first taught us "the kidney trick."

DUTCH VEAL KIDNEYS SLIJPER FLAMED WITH GIN

For our family of 4

Check Staples:

Salt butter (½ lb.)
Aromatics: crystal salt, freshly ground black pepper, MSG, whole dried juniper berries (1 Tbs.)

Shopping List:

Veal kidneys (6, whole)
Heavy cream (½ cup)
Buttermilk (1 qt.)
Mushrooms (½ lb.)
Dutch Bols gin (⅓ cup)

The Day Before

BASIC RULE FOR PRE-PREPARATION OF KIDNEYS: All types and sizes of kidneys should be marinated. The smallest lambs' kidneys and the medium-sized pork and veal kidneys should be soaked whole. The large beef kidneys, having the most tenacious aroma, are best quartered or sliced before soaking. Marinate the kidneys in the buttermilk overnight, covered and refrigerated, stirring and turning occasionally. The acid of the buttermilk is drawn into the tiny tubes of the kidneys, cleaning and sweetening them. In the morning half fill a large saucepan with water and bring to a rolling boil. Wash kidneys under cold running water, drop them into boiling water and leave there for the exact time for that size and type of kidney: lambs' kidneys, 15 seconds; pork or veal, 30 seconds; quartered or sliced beef, 2 minutes. The heat expels the acid from the inside of the kidneys, leaving them virgin-pure. They are then ready for further preparation, or they can be refrigerated for later use.

About 30 Minutes Before Serving

The basic requirement of all kidney dishes is that they shall not be overcooked to a leathery texture. Timing must be exact, so that they remain just pink in the center. To achieve this, the following operation must be quick and continuous, and all ingredients must be prepared and measured in advance. Clean (never wash) and quarter the mushrooms. Coarsely crack the tablespoon of juniper berries in a mortar. Place a large sauté pan (preferably copper) over high heat; in it melt 6 tablespoons of the butter almost to browning. Trim all fat and membrane from kidneys, then put into hot butter and quickly sear on all sides for not more than 2 minutes. Then add the quartered mushrooms and the cracked juniper berries, and stir around, still turning kidneys for another 2 or 3 minutes. Lower heat and blend in enough of the cream to make sauce rich and smooth. Stir for another 30 seconds, tasting and adding salt, pepper, and MSG and slightly warm the 1/3 cup of gin according to the BASIC RULE for flaming (page 44). Turn up heat, pour over the 1/3 cup of gin and flame. Before the flame dies down, we rush the whole pan to the table. This dish is excellent served with a pilaf of rice (page 166) to absorb the sauce.

FRENCH LAMBS' KIDNEYS IN CHAMPAGNE

For our family of 4

This is among the quickest of all quick dishes. From the moment the heat is turned on under the pan to the serving of the kidneys at the table we take not more than 15 minutes. This is an excellent main dish for dinner on a busy day, with a hearty soup and solid dessert; a superb lazy Sunday breakfast; or a fine hot centerpiece for a buffet supper. The character of the dish can be sharply varied by substituting for the champagne: dry white wine, light red wine, dry Sherry, dry vermouth, medium-dry Madeira, or brandy.

Check Staples:

Salt butter (1/4 lb.)
Lemon (1)
Aromatics: crystal salt, freshly ground black pepper, MSG
Fresh parsley (small bunch)
Granulated instantized flour (a few Tbs.)

Shopping List:

Lambs' kidneys (8 whole)
Buttermilk (1 qt.—for the pre-preparation, *see* preceding recipe)
Fresh button mushrooms (1/2 lb.)
Champagne, medium-priced (1/2 bottle)

The Day Before

Soak the kidneys in the buttermilk and scald them briefly, according to the BASIC RULE in the preceding recipe.

About 20 Minutes Before Serving

Cut each kidney in half lengthwise, then cross-cut to halve again, and cut away any tough membranes. Wipe mushrooms clean (never wash) and thickly slice lengthwise into hammer shapes. Put sauté pan on medium frying heat; quickly melt in it 4 tablespoons of the butter and, as soon as it begins to froth, slide in the kidneys. Stir and turn steadily with a wooden spoon for 1 minute, slightly increasing heat, so that they sizzle. Add mushrooms and keep stirring steadily for 1 minute more. Turn heat down to low frying temperature and stop stirring; let kidneys bleed and mushrooms give up their water. After 2 or 3 minutes of brisk bubbling, season to taste with salt, pepper, and MSG. Then begin sprinkling on flour, stirring and testing consistency of sauce, until all liquid is absorbed, usually with about 3 tablespoons of flour. Immediately start thinning the *roux* with the champagne, 1 tablespoon at a time, stirring continuously until the sauce has the thickness of heavy cream, usually after adding about 1/2 cup of the champagne. As mixture boils up, turn heat down to simmering. Cut the lemon in half and add juice, squeeze by squeeze, stirring and tasting to achieve best balance of flavor. Serve instantly on very hot plates. It is fine served on a bed of fluffy mashed potatoes with chopped green parsley sprinkled on top.

ITALIAN BEEF KIDNEYS IN SWEET VERMOUTH

For our family of 4

Check Staples:

Thick-sliced dark smoked bacon (1/2 lb.)

Shopping List:

Beef kidneys (2 large or 3 medium, total about 2 lbs.)

Check Staples (continued):
Salt butter (1/4 lb.)
Aromatics: crystal salt,* freshly ground black pepper,* MSG,* basil, sweet marjoram
Shallots* (1/4 lb.)
Granulated white sugar (a few Tbs.)

Shopping List (continued):
Buttermilk (1 qt., for soaking kidneys, *see* page 335)
Sour cream (1/2 pt.)
Fresh mushrooms (1/2 lb.)
Ripe tomatoes (1 lb.)
Italian sweet vermouth* (about 1 cup)

The Day Before

Cut kidneys into slices about 1/2 inch thick, cut away any tough membranes, soak overnight in buttermilk and scald, according to the BASIC RULE (page 335).

About 1 Hour Before Serving

We prepare this dish in an enameled cast-iron cocotte* with a tightly fitting lid. Skin and chop the 1/4 pound of shallots. Wipe mushrooms clean and cut off stems, leaving small heads whole and quartering larger ones. Set cocotte over gentle frying heat, melt in it about 3 tablespoons of the butter, add shallots and mushrooms (heads and stems), and stew until latter have expelled their water and absorbed the butter, adding a bit more if needed. Meanwhile wash and coarsely chunk the tomatoes, with skins and seeds, adding them to the cocotte and stewing them until they mash down. Stir in 1 teaspoon dried basil leaf, 1 teaspoon sweet marjoram, 1 tablespoon of the sugar, 1/2 cup of the sweet vermouth, plus salt, pepper, and MSG to taste. Let it all bubble briskly until it shows the first signs of thickening, usually in 5 to 10 minutes. Taste and adjust seasoning with more aromatics, sugar, or vermouth as needed.

While contents of cocotte are bubbling, cut bacon into 1-inch squares (no need to separate the slices) and begin melting their fat in a sauté pan over medium frying heat. As each square becomes crisp, lift out with slotted spoon and drop into cocotte. When all bacon is out of sauté pan (and making sure that remaining fat is quite hot), put in all the kidney slices at once and sear quickly on both sides, turning up heat as needed so that they brown in 2 or 3 minutes. If kidneys are cooked for even 1 minute too long they will become leathery. Turn off heat and transfer kidney slices to cocotte with a slotted spoon (letting fat drip off). Simmer them in the tomato-vermouth sauce for not more than 2 minutes, then finally smooth and blend the sauce with a few tablespoons of the sour cream, judging the exact amount by tasting and balancing the seasonings. Heat up once more (but do not boil) and serve immediately. This dish is extremely good accompanied by the black-eyed peas baked in buckwheat honey (page 610).

FRENCH MOULES MARINIÈRE—MUSSELS IN AROMATIC SAUCE

For our family of 4

Of all foods that are cheap because few people know or care about them, mussels seem to offer the greatest opportunity for unusual and attractive preparation. This dish, perfectly prepared, is one of the glories of the French cuisine. How many Americans serve it regularly? For a general discussion of mussels and rules for their pre-preparation see page 195.

Check Staples:

Salt butter (4 Tbs.)
Aromatics: crystal salt, freshly ground black pepper, MSG, garlic (2 cloves), whole bay leaf, thyme
Yellow onion (1 medium)
Fresh parsley (small bunch)
Granulated instantized flour (a few Tbs.)
Dry white wine (about 1 cup)

Shopping List:

Very fresh mussels in the shell (5 lbs. or 3 qts., whichever way the fishman sells them)
White celery (1 center stalk, if possible with some leaves)

The Day Before

Wash and clean the mussels and "feed" them overnight according to our BASIC RULE (page 196).

About 30 Minutes Before Serving

First prepare the base for the sauce. Peel and finely chop the onion, finely chop the celery stalk and leaves, and crush the garlic through a press. In a 2-quart saucepan melt 4 tablespoons of butter and add the onion, celery, and garlic. Stir until slightly colored. Spoon in flour, 1 tablespoon at a time, stirring after each addition, until there is a thick *roux*. Season to taste with salt, pepper, and MSG. Keep warm, covered. Put a large covered tureen to warm in the oven.

Finely chop the parsley. Cook the mussels according to the BASIC RULE (page 197), and as each shell opens lift it out with tongs and drop it in the hot tureen. When all mussels are removed, strain the aromatic juice through muslin and start blending the clear liquid into the *roux*, bit by bit, stirring continuously and turning up heat as needed, until there are about 3 cups of a lightly creamy sauce. Add a good handful of the chopped parsley and pour at once over the mussels in the tureen. Sprinkle more chopped parsley over the top.

Serving at Table

Each diner gets a large, hot, open soup plate, a fork with which to pick the mussels out of their shells, a soup spoon for the sauce, and plenty of lightly toasted thick chunks of French bread. Within easy reach of the diners there must be a large bowl for the empty shells. Each portion consists of about a dozen mussels in their wide-open shells, with some sauce ladled over them and more parsley sprinkled on top. The final remnants of sauce in the plate are mopped up with the last of the bread.

SQUID WITH GINGER ROOT AS THE CHINESE DO IT

For our family of 4

This is a light main course, to be surrounded by solid accompaniments. Squid is one of those excellent foods that are cheap in the market because not enough people know how good they can be. We think that well-prepared squid is equal in taste and texture to lobster. The squid is a shellfish, but the shell is inside the outer skin. It is a tube shaped like a large fountain pen and can easily be slid out by following the instruction in our BASIC RULE on page 496. The fishman is usually willing to prepare the squid, but, we find, not as neatly as we do it ourselves.

Check Staples:

Aromatics: crystal salt,* freshly ground black pepper,* MSG,* fresh ginger root (which we keep frozen, page 25; 2 tsp. grated) or, if absolutely unavailable, Jamaican dry ginger (1 tsp.)
Green scallions (1 bunch)
Ground arrowroot (about 1 Tbs.)
Olive oil (2 to 3 Tbs.)
Chinese soy sauce (2 to 3 Tbs.)
Dry Sherry (2 to 3 Tbs.)

Shopping List:

Fresh squid (about 2 lbs., the smaller are sweeter)

At Any Time Beforehand

All ingredients must be prepared and measured before the heat is turned on. The actual cooking takes exactly 6 minutes and requires split-second timing. The worst mistake is to overcook the squid, for then it loses its flavor and becomes leathery. Cut, wash, and dry squid. Measure 2 teaspoons of the arrowroot in a cup and liquefy it with about 1 tablespoon of the Sherry. Into another cup measure 2 tablespoons of the soy sauce. Into still another, measure 2 more tablespoons of the Sherry. Finely chop enough of the green scallion tops to fill 1/2 cup. Skin the ginger root with a potato scraper, cutting away any dry sections, then grate enough to fill 2 teaspoons. (Alternatively, but second-best, we measure about 3/4 teaspoon of the ground ginger.)

Exactly 10 Minutes Before Serving

We set our copper sauté pan over medium-high frying heat and cover the bottom with about 2 tablespoons of the olive oil. When the oil is quite hot but before it smokes, slide in all the squid at once and stir around 2 or 3 times with a wooden spoon to coat each piece with the hot oil. Add the ginger. Keep stirring for exactly 30 seconds longer, then add the scallion tops. Stir 30 seconds, then add the soy sauce. Stir 30 seconds longer, then add the Sherry. Stir for 1 minute. Turn off heat. Stir up the arrowroot-Sherry mixture in the cup to make sure that it is well mixed, and add to the sauté pan, stirring vigorously. Turn on the heat again and keep stirring firmly to make sure that no lumps form, until the sauce thickens to the consistency of heavy cream. If not thick enough, add another teaspoon of the arrowroot, liquefied with more Sherry. If too thick, add a little more Sherry and soy sauce in equal parts. Work very quickly and bring it at once to the table. It is excellent served on a bed of rice pilaf (page 166).

Easter Exposé on Omelettes

THE EGG is hardly a true symbol of Easter any more. Once, after each winter of off-tasting "preserved" eggs, Easter brought the exciting first flood of "new-fresh-laid" eggs. Now, scientific progress provides an even flow of eggs almost every month of the year. Nevertheless, to us the egg is still the embodiment of the spring feeling of rebirth. So we find it a good time to eat eggs and to discuss the making of an omelette, the finest and most flexible way of cooking the egg, and also one of the simplest, regardless of the fantastic and nonsensical old wives' tales that have grown up around it. It is time for these monstrous myths to be debunked once and for all.

OLD WIVES' TALE NUMBER ONE: That the omelette is the most difficult of all dishes to prepare.

THE TRUTH: In fact there is hardly a dish that is easier. It is about half as difficult as poaching an egg, where one is trying to work under scalding water. It takes eggs, sweet butter, a flexible spatula, a frypan, some heat, and a little courage. Wherever these are available, so is a first-class omelette.

OLD WIVES' TALE NUMBER TWO: That you must have a frypan which (a) is never used for anything but omelettes, (b) is never scrubbed or washed with water, but is cleaned only with a dry cloth or paper towel.

THE UNVARNISHED TRUTH: Forty or fifty years ago, when the only available type of frypan was of black cast-iron, it was perfectly true that the surface was like very coarse sandpaper with thousands of tiny nicks and depressions. A fat steak seared over highest heat in such a pan would leave tiny specks of meat, burned to black charcoal, in the irregularities of the surface. This would make an omelette stick and give it a bitter-burnt flavor. So it was true at that time that a separate pan should be kept for the more delicate, lower-heat omelette operation. As to washing the pan with water, it *was* true that water might cause a cast-iron pan to rust—and rust would be unfriendly to omelettes.

But now consider the modern frypan of aluminum, tinned copper, or stainless steel, with a rustless shiny surface . . . True, there is such a thing as a special omelette pan.* It is made shallow and with a curving side so that a flexible spatula can more easily be slipped under the omelette during the brief cooking. To that extent only might it be called a "special pan" for omelettes, but provided it is kept scrupulously clean (with soap and water, of course) it can also be used to fry fish, onions, or Mexican Magüey worms.

OLD WIVES' TALE NUMBER THREE: That an omelette should be brought to table shaped like a bolster—thick in the middle, thin at the ends.

THE TRUTH: Any omelette that is stiff enough to be molded into a bolster, or any other shape, is vastly overcooked.

How to Make a Perfect Omelette

Having disposed of these fearful bogies, let us prepare an omelette.

ESSENTIAL TRICK NUMBER ONE: The size of the pan is important. Too few eggs in too large a pan make an omelette that is too thin. Conversely, if an omelette is too thick, the bottom will be overcooked before the top is properly set. We keep two omelette pans: one 8½ inches in diameter, for 3 to 5 eggs; the other, 10½ inches in diameter, for 6 to 8 eggs. But this is not essential. One could make do with only the smaller pan and repeat with as many 5-egg omelettes as may be needed for a larger party. Even with two sizes of pan one often has to do this, because it is physically impossible to make a satisfactory omelette larger than an 8-egg one. Once one has the proper pan, one must get to know and love it—get the feel of its handle and balance, and how it reacts over various kinds and degrees of heat.

ESSENTIAL TRICK NUMBER TWO: At least an hour ahead, we take the eggs out of the refrigerator and break them into a deepish mixing bowl, adding the "garnish." (In the recipes that follow, "garnish" always means those herbs, spices, salts, peppers, chopped leaves, etc., which are stirred into the raw eggs—as opposed to the "filling," which is mixed and heated separately and put inside the omelette only when it is almost done. Some omelettes have no "filling"—the *omelette aux fines herbes,* for example (page 346). We beat the eggs lightly with a fork or small whisk, just enough to mix yolks and whites. Tens of thousands of omelettes are ruined every day by being overbeaten. Contrary to the instructions of most cookbooks, we do *not* add even a single drop of milk, cream, or water.

ESSENTIAL TRICK NUMBER THREE: We turn on the heat to "low frying," or 325 degrees. This is only a rough guide for the first try, since all stoves vary in their heat efficiency. For the first three or four times one must experiment. If the omelette at the table turns out to be overdone in the center, it was cooked too slowly and the next one should be cooked for less time over slightly higher heat. If there is too much soft egg in the center, the reverse is true. The essential trick is to make a careful note of the heat setting each time and then, when the exact setting for that stove has been found, stick to it forever. All omelettes are cooked over a single heat setting, although one achieves slight variations by lifting the pan up over the heat during the operation.

Having set the heat to the correct temperature we put on the empty pan to heat up. We put a single drop of water in the center and, when it boils and evaporates, we drop in a *small* piece of butter, just enough to make a film across the bottom. Nothing is worse than an over-fat omelette. We take the pan by the handle, not hesitating to lift it an inch or so above the heat, and slosh the butter around, so as to grease the sides as well as the bottom. The butter should be hot before the eggs go in. The exact point is after the butter has stopped spitting, but before it has started to turn brown.

ESSENTIAL TRICK NUMBER FOUR: The other indispensable tool is a flexible spatula, about 1 to 1½ inches wide, which, when pushed down from the edge under the eggs, will bend to the curve of the pan and not break the setting egg mass (this is why we need a low pan with a curved side).

The hot butter in the pan is now exactly right. The eggs, once more lightly beaten in their bowl, are at room temperature. We virtually "throw" (not "slowly pour") them into the pan with courageous abandon. They will immediately make frills around the edges and often huge bubbles in the center. Keep calm. It's all part of the game. Grasp the spatula in the right hand, firmly grip the pan handle in the left, and . . .

ESSENTIAL TRICK NUMBER FIVE: As soon as the edge has begun to set, lift it with the spatula and, raising and tipping the pan, run the top liquid underneath. Do this all the way around. Don't be afraid to run the spatula

right in under the center of the omelette. Try to visualize the operation as "building the omelette," layer after layer, from the bottom upward. (In fact, the word "omelette" is said to derive from the Old French *amelette* or *alemette,* which meant a thin, flat, round, *laminated* object.) As fast as each layer is set on the bottom, one must instantly rush a fresh layer of liquid egg under it.

The whole operation goes forward at split-second speed. None of the layers must be left in contact with the bottom for more than 2 or 3 seconds. It must be lifted and the next layer run in underneath. From the moment the eggs go into the hot pan to the point when the omelette is turned onto the serving dish usually takes 50 to 60 seconds.

When there is no more liquid to run underneath (although there are still some glistening golden pools on top and these will go on cooking during the trip from kitchen to table) it is the precise moment to turn off the heat and . . .

ESSENTIAL TRICK NUMBER SIX: In the mind's eye we divide the orb of the omelette into two halves, with the dividing equator at right angles to the axis of the pan handle. The "filling," separately prepared according to the following recipes, now goes onto the half that is farthest from the handle. Now slide the spatula way under the non-filled half (nearest the handle)

and with a quick, firm flip, fold it over the filled half. There's the finished, half-moon omelette.

ESSENTIAL TRICK NUMBER SEVEN: Have a *hot* platter ready. Toss the spatula into the sink and change grip on the handle. Switch it from the left to the right hand, but grasp it like a golf driver, with the wrist under the handle. Flip the pan over onto the dish, with the handle describing an

upward arc (see illustration). The first time, the omelette will probably land half off the platter. From the third time on, it will be a perfect tour de force.

Decorate the omelette on the platter according to the recipe. Sometimes multicolored bits go around the edge or over the top. At other times bright sauces are dribbled over it in free-form designs.

Rush the finished production to the table. At this point its internal heat and the heat of the platter are still cooking it, so the diners must be waiting for the omelette—it cannot wait for the diners. It will be slightly sunburned on the outside, with a few trickles of golden juice oozing out from the center.

This is the perfect omelette!

Here are four basic omelettes which for many years have given us repeated delight.

BASIC OMELETTE WITH GARDEN HERBS

For our family of 4

Let's face it, the perfect *omelette aux fines herbes* is only possible when the cook can step out of the back door into the kitchen garden and pick the fresh herbs, then finely snip the leaves with kitchen scissors. A passable imitation is possible, however, for the exile in the city, by using reasonably fresh, first-quality dried herbs, as in this recipe. If fresh herbs are used, the quantities should be about trebled. Note that there is no filling in this omelette.

Check Staples:

Salt butter (about 1 Tbs.)
Eggs (6 large)
Aromatics: crystal salt,* freshly ground black pepper,* MSG,* marjoram, rosemary, savory, thyme
Chives (enough when chopped to fill 2 tsp.)
Parsley (enough when chopped to fill 1 Tbs.)

About 1 Hour Before Serving

Break the 6 eggs into a bowl and beat with a small wire whisk only enough to break yolks and mix with whites. Sprinkle on top, but do not yet stir in, the aromatic garnish: ¼ teaspoon each of the marjoram, rosemary, savory, thyme, the 2 teaspoons of finely chopped chives, the tablespoon of finely chopped parsley, plus ½ teaspoon salt, ½ teaspoon MSG, and a few grinds of the pepper. Gently stir in and hold, covered, so that eggs come to room temperature and aromatics are thoroughly soaked to bring out flavor oils.

About 3 Minutes Before Serving

Heat the butter in the omelette pan, as described above, then lightly stir the eggs once more, pour into the pan, and make omelette; fold and serve at once.

OMELETTE WITH CRAB MEAT

For our family of 4

This is the basic technique for any omelette filled with diced (or flaked) cooked fish or meat. The possibilities are limitless.

Check Staples:

Salt butter (about 2 Tbs.)
Eggs (6 large)
Aromatics: crystal salt, red cayenne pepper, MSG
Chives (enough when chopped to fill 1 Tbs.)

Shopping List:

Shelled crab meat, in small chunks or flakes (1 lb.)
Heavy cream (½ cup)
French Cognac, medium-priced (1 oz.)

About 1 Hour Before Serving

In a small saucepan, preferably copper because it responds so quickly to heat adjustments, over very gentle heat, very slowly warm up the pound of crab meat with the ½ cup of cream, 1 tablespoon of the butter, plus a couple of pinches of salt and a shake of the cayenne. Lightly stir occasionally. Meanwhile finely chop the tablespoon of chives, soak in the ounce of Cognac, and hold, covered. Break the 6 eggs into a bowl, add about ½ teaspoon of salt and about ¼ teaspoon MSG, then beat with a small wire whisk only enough to break yolks and mix with whites. Let stand, covered, to warm up.

About 4 Minutes Before Serving

Lightly stir chives and Cognac into warm crab meat. Heat butter in the omelette pan, as described above, then pour in eggs and make omelette. Using a slotted spoon, fill omelette with solid crab meat, fold and flip out onto hot platter, then pour the hot Cognac cream over it and serve at once.

OMELETTE WITH MUSSELS

For our family of 4

This involves a slightly more complicated advance preparation, but the final technique of the omelette is the same.

Check Staples:

Salt butter (about 1 Tbs.)
Eggs (6 large)
Aromatics: crystal salt, freshly ground black pepper, MSG, whole bay leaf, garlic (2 cloves), thyme
Yellow onions (2 medium)

Shopping List:

Mussels, in shell (2 lbs.)

Check Staples (continued):
Parsley (small bunch)
All-purpose flour (a couple of handfuls)
Olive oil (1 Tbs.)
Dry white wine (about 1 cup)

The Day Before—Cleaning and Soaking the Mussels

Let the clean mussels soak and feast overnight, according to our BASIC RULE (page 196).

About 1 Hour Before Serving

Break the 6 eggs into a bowl, add about ½ teaspoon salt and about ¼ teaspoon MSG, then beat with a small wire whisk only until yolks are broken and mixed with whites. Let stand, covered, to warm up.

About 25 Minutes Before Serving—Cooking the Mussels

Wash and steam open the mussels, according to our BASIC RULE (page 197), with the cup of wine; 1 clove garlic, finely minced; 1 of the onions, chopped; a few sprigs of parsley; crumbled bay leaf; and thyme; plus salt, pepper, and MSG to taste. Remove cooked mussels from shells and hold. Carefully strain mussel-wine juice through muslin and hold.

Finely mince remaining onion, then add it to the remaining clove of garlic, finely minced, plus 2 or 3 more sprigs of parsley, finely minced, then hold. In a fairly small sauté or fry pan, over medium temperature, heat up the tablespoon of olive oil, then fry aromatic onion mixture until just transparent. Add just enough of mussel-wine juice, usually about 1 tablespoon or so, to make a thickish sauce. Stir in cooked mussels and let them heat up very gently. Just before starting omelette, check mussels for seasoning and adjust if necessary.

About 3 Minutes Before Serving

Heat up the butter in the omelette pan, as previously described, then pour in eggs and make the omelette. Fill it with mussels and onion sauce, then fold over and serve at once.

OMELETTE WITH SORREL

For our family of 4

When the lemon-flavored wild grass, sorrel (the *oseille* of so many French recipes), is in season (see page 222), it can be used in the preparation of this unusual and dramatically flavored omelette. This is also the basic technique for other omelettes filled with chopped vegetables.

Check Staples:

Salt butter (about 1 Tbs.)
Eggs (6 large)
Aromatics: crystal salt,☓ freshly ground black pepper,☓ MSG

Shopping List:

Sorrel (small bunch)
Heavy cream (4 Tbs.)
French Cognac, medium-priced (1 Tbs.)

About 1 Hour Before Serving

Break the 6 eggs into a bowl, add about ½ teaspoon salt, about ¼ teaspoon MSG, plus a few grinds of pepper, then beat with a small wire whisk only enough to break yolk and mix with whites. Wash and fairly coarsely chop enough of the sorrel to fill ½ cup, then lightly stir into the eggs and let soak.

About 10 Minutes Before Serving

Very gently heat the 4 tablespoons of cream, without letting it come anywhere near the boiling point. At the last moment before starting the omelette add the tablespoon of Cognac to the warm cream.

About 3 Minutes Before Serving

Heat up the butter in the omelette pan, as previously described, then lightly stir the eggs once more, pour into pan, and make the omelette. No filling goes inside before folding it and flipping out onto hot platter. With a small sharp knife make a fairly deep incision down almost the full length of the center of the omelette, dribble the warm Cognac-cream into the incision, and pour the remainder over top of omelette, then serve at once.

SPRING THOUGHTS ON WINE

Wine Tasting

April usually brings an invitation from our nearby wine merchant, to one of the reception rooms of a local hotel, inviting us to a "private tasting" of the newly arrived shipments of the young white and *rosé* wines—the wines that are served chilled to prevent or quench a spring thirst. In England it is the common practice for a wine merchant to offer his patron a glass of wine before buying, but U.S. liquor laws prevent this. Yet we feel strongly that many more responsible wine merchants should take the trouble to rent a hall and invite their regular customers to taste the new wines. Then perhaps there would be less mumbo-jumbo surrounding the simple and enjoyable game of judging wine.

Wine tasting is a minor art that is easy to learn. It is a pleasure even for the very beginner, and the more one practices it the deeper the pleasure becomes. We can appreciate a Mozart concerto without playing the piano; we can marvel at a Rembrandt without learning to draw. So we can enjoy wines as an amateur.

Yet it seems to be the fashion to tell stories that cast the wine taster as a sort of magician-hero. In a hushed silence, he holds the glass up to the light. He breathes slowly as his nose goes down into the glass. He sips and rolls the wine around his tongue. Then, step by step, he unfolds to his awed audience all the details of the label (kept carefully hidden from him) and of the history of the wine: the precise acre of land on which the grapes were grown, the precise month and year of the vintage, and so on. Such stories prove absolutely nothing beyond the luck of an accident. Wine tasting is not a guessing game. Does a literary critic expect immediately to identify the author by hearing five words at random from the text? The best way to learn about wine is to drink it often and there are few fixed standards of judgment. The ultimate decision for each taster is his own personal preference.

A Chart to Help the Wine Taster

Many professional tasters in the wine business use charts as tools of their trade. With some of these as models, we have worked out our own wine-rating chart. There is no magic about it. It does not make our decisions. It merely helps us separate in our minds (and thus independently judge) the different qualities of sight, smell, and taste, which combine to make the total effect of a wine. Here is our chart, followed by instructions for its use.

WINE-RATING CHART

A COLOR IN RELATION TO TYPE:	B CLARITY AGAINST LIGHT:	C AROMA—BOUQUET:	D FIRST TASTE—GENERAL QUALITY:	E SUGAR:	F ACIDITY:	G BODY—TEXTURE:	H ALCOHOL:	I AGE:
Light—Thin 1	Clear 1	Just volatile 1	Just agreeable 1	Dry—No sweetness 1	Steely 1	Thin—Watery 1	Dully weak 1	Too young 1
Full—Warm 2	Bright 2	Fresh but undistinctive 2	Pleasantly fresh 2	Delicately sweet 2	Pungent 2	Thin but delicate 2	Good average strength 2	Mature 2
Deep—Rich 3	Brilliant 3	Fresh with character 3	Light but interesting 3	Nobly sweet 3	Vinous 3	Smooth body 3	Smoothly heavy 3	At peak 3
		Delicate bouquet 4	Robust but rough 4			Elegant body 4		
		Strong bouquet 5	Robust with harmony 5			Broad, bity body 5		
		Fine, fruity bouquet 6	Mellow—Satisfying 6			Juicy body 6		
		Spicy 7	Fine 7			Full, oily body 7		
		Exquisitely great 8	Nobly great 8			Powerful, velvety body 8		
			Superbly great 9			Supremely great 9		

Under 10 Undrinkable   10–20 Normal consumption   21–28 Good to Superior   29–38 Fine to Noble   39–44 Superb to Great

Each vertical column represents a separate judgment of a separate quality of the wine. We half fill the glass and first judge, in a good light, the quality of the color against the definitions in the boxes of column A. We don't dwell on it. We try to avoid indecision. This is like one of those psychological test papers in which one is asked to tick off one's instant reaction to a word or phrase. We immediately pick one of the definitions and write down the number associated with it on a slip of paper. Column B defines the clarity of the wine when held up against the light. We quickly choose the appropriate definition and write this number under the first on the slip of paper. Next, we swirl the wine in the glass, sniff its bouquet, define it from column C and write down the third number. Take the first sip, roll it around the tongue, swallow it, and carefully note the aftertaste, then define it from column D, and set down the fourth number. Take one more sip for each succeeding column, concentrating each time on the particular qualities to which that column applies: sweetness, acidity, body—texture (which means the "feel" or "weight" of the liquid on the tongue), alcoholic strength, and degree of maturity (the development of the wine in relation to its vintage year). We now have nine figures on the slip of paper, and when they are added together the total is a personal rating of this particular wine. Check it against the categories at the bottom of the chart. This places the wine in perspective against others of its type.

Any number of people can play this game, but each person should make his own decisions, in silence, without reference to anyone else. Then, when each person has a final rating, the inevitable discrepancies can be discussed. (It is often surprising how close all the figures are.) During the discussion we sometimes persuade each other to adjust the individual figures slightly, so as to arrive at a final agreed rating to be noted on the file card for that wine. Perhaps the most interesting use of the chart is in comparing two or three different wines of approximately the same type, tasted one against the other.

Finally, we sometimes use the chart to estimate the value of a wine in relation to its price. First, we rate the wine by the chart, then we divide the bottle price by the rating and the resulting figure gives us the "cost-per-rating-point." If this calculation is made for each of several comparable wines, they can be compared for value. We often find, for example, that a more expensive wine of a much higher rating is really a far better buy than a much cheaper, low-rated wine.

The Great, Dominant White Wines for the Great Party Dishes

Through the spring and summer months, the stress in our small cellar is more on the white and *rosé* wines to be served chilled. Again, as with the red wines, we divide our buying into three categories. The foundation of the cellar is always the everyday wine, inexpensive enough to be served regularly at family meals or to quench a thirst at any time of the day. Second, we choose from the wide middle range of fine wines for the simpler party menus, where the wine should support but not dominate the food. Finally, we look for a few of the always-expensive great white wines for the festive occasions when the food is superb and the guests are connoisseurs.

Our order of preference with the white wines is slightly different from that of the reds. We place Bordeaux first among the reds, but turn to Burgundy for the greatest white wines. These magnificent vineyards are south of the city of Beaune, along the old Roman road that passes through the twin villages of Chassagne and Puligny. They share the glory of the vineyard called "Le Montrachet" (The Bald Mountain), which can produce, in a good year, a wine that is perhaps the greatest of all whites.

There is a story, which may or may not be true, that all the lands of this district once belonged to a single Montrachet vineyard. Then when the great seigneur died he willed that the land should be divided among his children. He left part to his eldest son, and this vineyard is known today as "Le Chevalier-Montrachet" (The Knight). The seigneur also had another son, whose birth was somewhat less legitimate, and his inheritance is known today as "Le Bâtard-Montrachet" (The Bastard). To his elder daughters he left the vineyard which became known as "Les Demoiselles-Montrachet"; then to his younger daughters, the vineyard he optimistically named "Les Pucelles" (The Virgins). Over the years the fact that Le Chevalier was alongside Les Demoiselles led to so many rude jokes that, it was said, the wine began to curdle. So the name of the Demoiselles vineyard was changed to "Cailleret" (The Curd). These and a few others (page 685) can, when rain and sunshine are propitious, all produce great white wines.

Second to those of Burgundy, we place the white wines of Germany from grapes grown on the towering hillsides above the valley of the Rhine. Since there is often a shortage of sunshine in these northern latitudes, the harvesters do not pick the grapes in large bunches, but handcut only those that are sufficiently ripe, returning the next day or the next week, as the later grapes ripen. These different pickings are separately pressed and the various wines are identified by different colors of cork seal and by the use of certain words on the labels: *auslese* means from selected, riper grapes; *spätlese* means from late-picked, sweeter grapes; *trockenbeeren* refers to grapes so ripe that they are beginning to dry and shrivel like raisins, producing (as with the French Sauternes) a sweeter, richer wine. Some vineyards use special identifying names, including the word *Kabinett,* to indicate that the wine was made from a special picking and reserved in separate storage. We list our favorite Burgundian and German names on pages 685–7.

The Middle Range of Fine White Wines for the Simpler Menus

Again, as with the red wines, the middle range is extremely wide, stretching from wines that are only a shade below the "greats" in both quality and price to the honorably blended wines bearing simply the names of village *communes* or regional districts. There are many splendid white-wine vineyards in Burgundy, but one must remember that over the centuries almost all of them have been broken up into many small holdings, with different owners, each with a varying degree of wine-making skill. Thus, for example, when one buys a bottle of "Les Charmes," one may actually be getting any one of 31 different wines made by 31 different owners, with substantial variations in quality. Therefore one must again get to know the names of the reliable owners and wholesale shippers, who guard their reputations with an extreme discipline. This is especially important among the *commune* labels of the principal white-wine villages: Chassagne-Montrachet, Puligny-Montrachet, or Meursault. (The latter was named by the Roman soldiers under Julius Caesar. When they came to this spot, they found a tiny river which was so narrow that they could leap across it. So they named the place "Muris Saltus"—the Leap of the Mouse.) Finally, there is the wine from the two adjoining villages of Pouilly and Fuissé which have combined their cellars to produce "Pouilly-Fuissé." Although its popularity is rising and one must be increasingly alert in watching the labels for the names of the reliable shippers, the relatively moderate price of a sound "Pouilly-Fuissé" set against its above-moderate quality usually puts it among the best values of the white wines of Burgundy. Our favorite names among all these Burgundian wines are on pages 687–8.

There are fine, luscious, and fruity German white wines at almost every level of quality and price, but to find the best of them the serious amateur buyer must take the trouble to learn a few of the basic German rules. Almost always on a German wine label the name of the vineyard is immediately preceded by the name of the town. For example, "Bernkasteler Doktor" means the famous Doktor Vineyard of the town of Bernkastel (the suffix *er* means "of," as in New York*er*). All German wines are sold in tall, tapered bottles, quite different in shape from those of Bordeaux or Burgundy. Rhine wines are sold in bottles of brick-red glass; those from the valley of the Moselle, in blue-green glass. Also of great importance on a label are the names of the old families which have owned many of the vineyards for centuries. We list on pages 688–9 the names of the vineyards, towns, and owners that we have found consistently reliable.

There are several fine white wines from the valley of the river Loire and from Alsace, on the French side of the Rhine, which we regularly enjoy. An offbeat wine with which to surprise one's guests is the "Pouilly Fumé" (not to be confused with Burgundy's "Pouilly-Fuissé") from the village of Pouilly-sûr-Loire, which does in fact have a gunflint smoky personality. Across the river from Pouilly is the lovely old hill town of Sancerre, which gives its name to some of the best white wines of the Loire, wines with a light, clean taste and a refreshing charm, young and limpid, perfect with the foods of spring. As to the wines of Alsace, many people make the mistake of thinking that they should all be cheap. Anyone foolish enough to buy a nondescript, vaguely labeled "Vin d'Alsace" at less than a dollar should not be surprised at being disappointed. The better Alsatian wines have "varietal" labels, with the names of the grape from which they were made. Although there are few individual vineyard names in Alsace, there are several famous and honorable wholesale shippers and we list on page 690 those whom we have found to be most consistently skillful.

From southern France there is the pale-gold wine with the bouquet of honeysuckle from the mountain slope of "L'Hermitage" in the valley of the Rhône. Finally, there is the most elegant wine of Switzerland, the habit-forming "Dézaley" from the canton of Vaud, a wine par excellence to cure a spring fever. See page 690.

The Everyday White Wines from Home and Abroad

Wine lovers in the United States are fortunate in having excellent white wines produced here at home, and the extraordinary progress of the American wine industry is a matter for astonished admiration. Some of the noblest of the European wine grapes have been successfully transplanted to

California (especially the Pinot Chardonnay of Burgundy, the Riesling of Germany, and the Traminer of Alsace). Of course the character of the wine is different due to differences in soil and climate, so it is quite inaccurate to speak of, say, a "California Chablis," but many of these wines have a superb quality in their own right. Incidentally, all the best producers follow the honorable practice of labeling the wine by the name of its grape. The pattern of these vineyards is much the same as for the red wines (pages 690–1). The best white wines, without question, come from the small vineyards, which are for the most part owned by wealthy amateurs who can afford to make quality rather than profit the cardinal objective. Unfortunately for the rest of the United States there is so little of this wine and it is so much in demand that few bottles ever travel beyond the area of San Francisco. Then there are the larger vineyards with sufficient production for a reasonable national distribution, but not enough, thankfully, for any form of mass-production.

Quite fair American "varietal" wines are also produced in the Finger Lakes region of New York State, along the Lake Erie shore of northern Ohio, and in single vineyards in favored locations in other parts of the country. However, these wines are made, not from the so-called "noble wine grapes" but from native American grapes with such charming and homely names as Catawba, Delaware, Elvira, Isabella, Moore's Diamond, etc., which produce wines of a somewhat earthy, peasant character. Wine snobs call the flavor "foxy," and look down their noses. We do not agree. Without claiming any special sophistication or breeding for all of these native American wines, we enjoy their straightforward simplicity.

Although imports of many of the simple, good-value, everyday European white wines have been reduced by the increasing European demand, it must be conceded that wonderfully good and inexpensive small wines are still arriving to compete powerfully with their American counterparts. First among these imports we place the famous French "Muscadet" from the area around the city of Nantes in southern Brittany. It is a lean and hungry young wine with a taste as if it had a faint squeeze of lemon in it, and an ice-cold glass is an ideal refresher on a hot day. Almost equally clean is the dry mountain wine of the French Alps, the "Seyssel Blancs de Blanc" from the Savoyard village of Seyssel—a wine that often feels as if it is about to burst into bubbles on the tongue. There is the honest and unpretentious "varietal" wine of Burgundy (made from the hardy Aligoté grape, which grows on the more exposed hilltops), charming in both taste and price, simply called "Bourgogne Aligoté." Italy sends at least one dry white wine that is light on the pocket and good for every thirsty occasion, the "Soave," from the village of that name near the city of Verona. Sometimes when we are tasting several important wines at a dinner party we serve a glass of Soave in between the others, to cleanse and sharpen the palate for the next taste. Such cleanness and sharpness are fine qualities in any wine at any price.

Finally, some of the dry white table wines of Yugoslavia are now being nationally distributed. At least two of them—one made from the "Traminer" grape in the Slovenian wine district of Radgona, and the other made from the native Yugoslavian "Chipon" grape in the Slovenian wine district of Ljutomer—are of sufficiently high quality and low price as to be among the best bargains in all light wines for the everyday occasions of spring and summer. In all these low-priced wines the name of an honorable shipper is all-important, and we list on page 692 those that we have found most consistently reliable.

T H E

Summer Harvest

July, August, and September

EXPLANATION OF SYMBOLS

A symbol appearing after a word refers the reader to a particular section of the book for further details. Example: olive oil, crystal salt, cocotte, dry white wine, Parmesan cheese, Beaujolais, turtle meat.

- stands for Raw Materials and Staples, pages 10–18
- stands for Aromatics, pages 18–29
- stands for Kitchen Equipment, pages 32–41
- stands for Wine in the Kitchen, pages 41–5
- stands for Cheeses, pages 660–75
- stands for Wines for the Table, pages 676–98
- stands for Marketing and Mail-Order Sources, pages 699–714

SUMMER FOODS IN SEASON

WHAT wealth there is in the swelling flood of summer fruits! This is the lush season of peaches and pears, melons and grapes, and we believe in eating them simply, sweetened only with the honeys of the season. The hot days bring fewer formal dinners, more simple suppers and cold buffets, less use of the hot oven and more of the sauté pan, and dishes prepared ahead in the cool of the early morning. Here is a checklist of what we consider to be the best of the summer foods. Not everything is available everywhere, of course, but this list is based on our own experience of summer shopping in many parts of the country.

The Special Pleasures of the Season

OUR FAVORITE summer meat is VEAL, which, when properly spiced and larded, is execellent cold in aspic (page 433), or it can be prepared in the sauté pan (page 432). Notes on shopping for veal are on page 368. For cost-saving main meat dishes we turn to BEEF TONGUE, which can be flavored and garnished in various interesting ways (page 487). No staple meat is more flexible and useful than a cold boiled DARK SMOKED COUNTRY HAM, which is in no way related to the bland pale pink stuff of the average cold-cuts counter. We order it by mail from one of the Southern farms (see shopping notes, page 369) and serve it in a variety of ways (page 437).

This is still the peak season for the Pacific KING CHINOOK and SILVER COHO SALMON, shipped out mainly from Seattle. We serve salmon steaks dramatically in a *selianka* (page 449). It is also the high season for North Atlantic Canadian and Pacific SWORDFISH, which we serve with shrimp and gray sole in fettuccelli (page 451).

Summer is a high-quality and good-value time for shellfish. Maine and Canadian live LOBSTER continues in good and slightly lower-priced supply (page 226) and we flame it in Pernod (page 454). In September fresh South Atlantic and Gulf SHRIMP return to market (page 61) and we celebrate by grilling them in garlic butter as the Sicilians do (page 595). This is also the new season for the tiny San Francisco BAY SHRIMP, an increasingly rare delicacy. Also available are Atlantic and Gulf HARD-SHELL BLUE CRAB, the Pacific ROCK CRAB and, at its peak in August, the Chesapeake Bay SOFT-SHELL CRAB (page 294). August and September is CRAYFISH time and we send to Green Bay, Wisconsin (page 370), for our annual feast. September opens the new season for the Atlantic, Gulf, and Pacific OYSTER, including the BABY OLYMPIA OYSTER from the Pacific Northwest, but we prefer to wait (page 371). Also in September is the start of the new season for the Atlantic and Gulf BAY SCALLOP, so small, sweet, and tender that it needs only a minute or two of cooking (page 142).

For dessert, this season for us is one long fresh fruit fiesta and we are in revolt against cooking or fancy preparation. As a variation from the fruit bowl, in which half the fruit is hidden, we like to set them out on a huge flat platter in contrasting colors and designs (a fruit version of a French *salade composée*), the larger fruit chunked, the less sweet dribbled with a few drops of one of the summer honeys (see page 521). Through July the SOFT BERRIES continue (page 480), also the ebb and flow of the STRAWBERRIES (page 323), the CHERRIES still red on the trees (page 477), and our Sundays still start with BLUEBERRY pancakes (page 327). Then, after midsummer, comes the celestial thirst-quenching of the Western BARTLETT PEAR, which, in one of the supreme combinations of gastronomy, is served stuffed with Roquefort cheese (page 476); the multitudinous PEACHES, MELONS, and PLUMS (page 372), and the California and Eastern GRAPES (page 371), around which we sometimes plan an ancient Greek cheese-and-fruit supper (page 459). Usually from July to September, we expect the peak season for the lush HAYDEN MANGO from Florida, Puerto Rico, and the West Indies and we eat it in the Indian way (page 479).

September is the brief time for the California fresh BLACK and GREEN MISSION FIG, a supreme delicacy, which makes a fine accompaniment for baked duck (page 289). This month also, when we visit New York's Chinatown, we watch for the small shipments flown in from Florida of "the grape with the hard shell," the fresh CHINESE LITCHI.

For a summer salad platter we slice the local vine-ripened TOMATOES with the now abundant fresh basil (page 321). We marinate the CHERRY TOMATOES, or LOVE APPLES, and stick them on toothpicks. We convert the local fresh CORN into a corn pudding (page 311).

The Freshwater Fish of the Summer Season

These fish have lean flesh and generally respond to similar cooking methods:

River BUFFALO
Great Lakes and river CARP
Great Lakes HERRING, mainly in Chicago
Great Lakes and river MULLET
Great Lakes and river YELLOW PERCH
Great Lakes PICKEREL
Great Lakes YELLOW PIKE
At the end of the season, Great Lakes SAUGER, mainly around Chicago
Great Lakes and river SHEEPSHEAD

These fish have oily flesh and are generally interchangeable in recipes:

Great Lakes CHUB, mainly around Chicago
Great Lakes TROUT, also in Chicago
During the first half of the season, Great Lakes WHITEFISH

The Saltwater Fish of the Summer Season

These are the lean-fleshed fish:

Pacific BLACK BASS
The last of the Atlantic SEA BASS
Also, later in the summer, Pacific WHITE BASS
Pacific COD, both the smaller MARKET COD for cooking whole and the larger STEAK COD
Atlantic CROAKER, which some foolish people are trying to rename STRAWBERRY BASS, peak of season
The members of the FLOUNDER family, always best prepared whole with the bone in (page 138):
Atlantic BLACKBACK
Atlantic FLUKE, peak of season
New England GRAY SOLE, which we pound for the sauce of our fettuccelli (page 451)
New England LEMON SOLE
Pacific REX SOLE, mainly on the West Coast

Pacific and New England SAND DAB
Atlantic YELLOWTAIL, OR RUSTY DAB
Gulf GROUPER, mainly in the South
New England HADDOCK
Atlantic RED HAKE
Atlantic WHITE HAKE, peak of season
East and West Coast HALIBUT, the giant of the flatfish, peak of season
South Atlantic and Gulf MULLET
New England OCEAN PERCH, mainly in the Northeast
New England POLLOCK
Atlantic PORGY, in high season through the summer
Pacific ROCKFISH, the West Coast variety of the Eastern STRIPED BASS
Atlantic WEAKFISH, sometimes called SEA TROUT
Atlantic WHITING and KING WHITING

These are the fish with oily flesh:

Atlantic BUTTERFISH
Atlantic EEL, superb when imaginatively prepared (page 242)
The summer members of the MACKEREL family:
Atlantic and St. Lawrence BOSTON MACKEREL
Giant Florida KING MACKEREL
Florida SPANISH MACKEREL
Gulf POMPANO, a magnificent fish, but too often sold frozen (page 297)
Pacific and Canadian SEA SMELT
Atlantic BLUEFIN TUNA (page 268), peak of season

The Shellfish of the Summer Season

All these have lean flesh:

Pacific ABALONE, a rare delicacy, eaten fresh only in northern California, shipped elsewhere canned (page 85)
The summer varieties of the CLAM family:
Atlantic CHERRYSTONE, for eating raw on the half shell
Atlantic HARD CHOWDER, which New Englanders call QUAHOG
Pacific GEODUCK, mainly around Seattle
Atlantic LITTLE NECK, also raw on the half shell
Pacific PISMO CLAM }
Pacific RAZOR CLAM } both mainly around Seattle
Atlantic SOFT STEAMER

Pacific and imported South African and West Indian frozen ROCK LOBSTER TAIL

Atlantic MUSSEL, mainly around New York (page 195)

Atlantic SQUID, excellent when carefully prepared (page 340), peak of season

The Fruits of the Summer Season

We usually disregard the rather bland summer APPLES, preferring to wait for the first of the new harvest which begins in October (see page 508)

July and August bring the high season for the Western APRICOTS; the tree-ripened fruit sold near the orchards has superb flavor

Imported BANANAS from the West Indies, Central and South America, Taiwan, and the Canary Islands; the fruit that flames dramatically with rum (page 618)

Western and imported Argentine BING CHERRIES

New York State wild baby CRAB APPLES

Arizona, California, and imported Iraqi fresh DATES

First the California, then the Arizona, Florida, and Texas GRAPEFRUIT

Western, Southern, and imported Greek and Turkish LEMONS, peak of season

California, Florida, and imported Mexican LIMES, peak of season

The summer family of the MELON:

- Local CANTALOUPE, peak of season
- California CASABA MELON, new season
- Local CRANSHAW MELON
- Local HONEYBALL MELON
- Western HONEYDEW MELON, peak of season
- California PERSIAN MELON, high season
- Imported SPANISH MELON and the Southern WATERMELON, both the CANNONBALL and the CHARLESTON GRAY types

California NECTARINES, high season

The summer varieties of the ORANGE:

- The Florida and Louisiana JUICE ORANGE
- Early in the summer, the Florida VALENCIA ORANGE

First from the Rio Grande Valley, then in turn from Florida, the West Indies, and Hawaii, the glamorous PAPAYA

Small New York SECKLE PEARS

Hawaiian, Puerto Rican, and imported Mexican and West Indian PINEAPPLES

Late in the summer, from California and the Gulf states, the historic POMEGRANATE, its juice excellent for marinating meats

California PRICKLY PEARS

The Salads of the Summer Season

We now switch to our summer salad dressings (page 474), to frame and accentuate the more mature greens of this season:

We continue to watch for the green ARUGULA, the leaf with the highly unusual flavor (page 277)

California, Florida, and imported West Indian AVOCADOS, also variously called CUSTARD APPLES, BUTTER PEARS, or ALLIGATOR PEARS

California and Florida CELERY, both the GREEN PASCAL and the WHITE HEARTS

Local CHICORY

Mainly California and Florida CUCUMBERS

Eastern and Western DANDELION GREENS

California and Florida ESCAROLE

The summer varieties of the LETTUCE:

- Indiana BIBB or BIBB LIMESTONE
- New York ICEBERG
- California and Florida ROMAINE

The summer salad varieties of the ONION family:

- The delicate CHIVE, peak of season
- From California, Louisiana, Texas, and Mexico, the eternally controversial GARLIC (see page 200)
- Domestic and imported ITALIAN SWEET RED ONIONS
- Local GREEN SCALLIONS, peak of season

Local GREEN PEPPERS and, at this season, handsome, fully ripe RED PEPPERS

Local RED RADISHES

Local WATERCRESS

The Vegetables of the Summer Season

Toward the end of the summer, the extraordinary JERUSALEM ARTICHOKE, a rare delicacy when properly prepared (page 462)
Eastern and Western GREEN, or SNAP BEANS
Local fresh LIMA BEANS, including the BABY and the LARGE GREEN LIMA, peak of season
Eastern and Western RED BEETS, high season
At midsummer, the new season for Eastern and Western BRUSSELS SPROUTS
The summer members of the CABBAGE family:
- Midwestern CELERY CABBAGE, or CHINESE CABBAGE
- Local GREEN CABBAGE
- Eastern SAVOY CABBAGE

California and Texas CARROTS
Eastern and Western CAULIFLOWER
Southern COLLARD GREENS
California, Florida, and New Jersey EGGPLANT, or AUBERGINE, high season
Local KOHLRABI
Local MUSHROOMS, usually in slightly shorter supply at this season
Local MUSTARD GREENS, peak of season
California, Jersey and Southern OKRA, which does not *have* to be sticky (page 464), high season
The summer aromatic members of the ONION family:
- Idaho large SWEET BERMUDA ONIONS
- The always-in-season local LEEK, for which we give round-the-year thanks
- In several states, the summer harvest of the BABY WHITE PICKLERS
- Local SHALLOTS
- Local SWEET SPANISH ONIONS
- Local WHITE BOILERS
- Local all-purpose YELLOW ONIONS

Local OYSTER PLANT, excellent deep-fried (page 467)
Peak summer harvests of Colorado, Idaho, and New York GREEN PEAS
The summer members of the POTATO family:
- Idaho and Western LARGE RUSSET BAKER
- California LONG WHITE BOILER
- Toward the end of the summer, the Western RED BLISS BOILER
- Long Island, New Jersey, and Pennsylvania WHITE BOILER

Wherever it is gathered locally, the wild SORREL, or SOURGRASS, the *oseille* of so many fine French recipes (page 468)
Local summer harvest of SPINACH, excellent prepared according to our master recipe (page 533)
The summer varieties of SQUASH:
- Southern CROOKNECK
- Eastern and Western HUBBARD
- California PATTYPAN

Local ZUCCHINI, which we grill with butter, garlic, and sardo cheese (page 469)
Local SWISS CHARD
Local WHITE TURNIPS, excellent baked in a maple-mustard sauce (page 163)
Southern YAMS

The Lavish Shopping of Summer

Search for Variety and Value in Veal

We buy most of our veal for the light suppers and cold aspics of summer, but French gourmets buy it the year-round and rank milk-fed veal above all other meats. By comparison the U.S. produces precious little of the true "milk-fed" veal, so the efficient shopper must know exactly what it is and where to find it. There are two main types:

1. *True Milk-Fed, Dairy-Bred Veal* is the meat of a baby calf, slaughtered when it is 4 to 8 weeks old and weighing between 75 and 125 pounds. During its short life it has been fed on nothing but skimmed milk. The lean meat of such an animal is a beautiful whitish-pink and the fat is the color of milk. These animals are mostly bred on dairy farms that specialize in this, one of the finest of all meats; it usually can be bought only in fancy-butcher shops.

2. *Older, "Beef-Bred" Veal* is from a calf raised mainly on Western ranges, where the animal runs free and lives first on its mother's milk and then on range grass. By the time it is slaughtered its flesh has already taken on some of the qualities of the beef which it would become if it were allowed to grow up. The meat from the older animals should probably be sold as "calf," but some butchers still call it "veal." About 95 per cent of all butchers just sell this type of veal and there are great variations in the age of the meat sold.

When buying veal, we use the following table to help us compare the relative values of the various cuts. For an explanation of how and why we developed these special tables see page 58. In the table below the left-hand column gives the names of the various veal cuts. Opposite each name, the middle column shows how to convert the price per pound into the cost of an average serving. For example, if the best-quality veal rib chops cost $1.40 per pound, we divide by 2 and the cost of an average serving is thus 70 cents. When the best-value cut has been decided upon, the right-hand column shows the approximate amount of that cut to buy for each person to be served. For example, for veal *scaloppini,* which are all edible meat, we would order 1/4 pound per person, or a total of 2 1/2 pounds for a dinner party of 10 people.

VEAL

When buying this cut:	To find the approximate cost per serving, take price per pound and divide by:	And buy this amount per person:
Escalopes—Scaloppini	4	1/4 lb.
Loin chops	3	6 oz.
Rib chops	2	1/2 lb.
Round roast	4	1/4 lb.
Rump roast	3	6 oz.
Leg	3	6 oz.
Boned shoulder	3	6 oz.
Loin, ribs	2	1/2 lb.
Ground lean	4	1/4 lb.
Liver	4	1/4 lb.
Brains, Sweetbreads	4	1/4 lb.
Tongue	4	1/4 lb.
Heart, Kidneys	4	1/4 lb.

The Real Taste of Ham

A whole new generation of young eaters is growing up without having ever really tasted ham. The processing of a fine ham is too leisurely an operation for the modern world: the months of special feeding of the live porker, the weeks of curing in salt and sugar, the hand-pounding with black pepper, the days of smoking over hickory and apple woods for flavor (with oak for color), and finally the aging, often taking up to two years. So the modern factory-mass-produced, pressure-cooked ham has been developed and has all but replaced the real stuff. However, fine hams are still being produced in various parts of the world, usually named after the places where they are cured—and these names are internationally famous: the YORK, or CUMBERLAND, of Britain; the BAYONNE of France; the WESTPHALIAN of Germany; the PARMA of Italy; and, among the greatest of them, the SMITHFIELD of the United States. In fact, the small town of Smithfield, in Virginia, is so jealous of its international reputation that it will only allow its name to be attached to hams actually cured within a circle of three miles around the town. However, magnificent dark smoked hams are also produced by skilled farmers elsewhere in Virginia as well as in other states, especially Kentucky, Tennessee, Georgia, and Florida.

We have found that the only way to taste ham at its finest is to order a whole uncooked ham from one of these Southern farms,* then to boil it ourselves in a spiced wine bouillon (page 437). We order either one of the two main types:

1. A TRUE SMITHFIELD is a dark, nutty-dry, slightly crumbly, almost wine-flavored ham, with such strong character that it is best not to serve it in large quantities as a main dish. It is magnificent as an hors d'oeuvre, in sandwiches, crumbled into omelettes and salads, baked in hot biscuits (page 484), or in other ways where its powerful flavor (the result of the all-peanut diet of the porker) is projected with restraint. A famous Southern hostess once told the story of a buffet supper where a superb Smithfield ham was the centerpiece. The guests, realizing the rare perfection of this ham, modestly cut themselves paper-thin slices—all the guests except one, that is, a Yankee attorney recently moved to the South, who began hacking off ½-inch chunks, wolfing them, and hacking off more. As the hostess approached him with a face of thunder, he fatuously murmured between bites: "I never, in all my life, tasted such good ham!" He was *never* asked to that house again.

2. A COUNTRY HAM is smoked for days and aged for a year or more, but is softer, less dominant in flavor (and less expensive) than the Smithfield and is more suitable for thick-slicing or cutting into steaks as a main course. The difference in flavor comes from the mixed peanut-and-grain diet of the porker, providing more fat and moisture than in the Smithfield.

Adventure with Live Crayfish

The crayfish (the *langouste* of French recipes, see page 256) looks like a small lobster and is a rare and wonderful delicacy, having a short Northern season from about mid-August to mid-September. Each year we are alerted by the arrival of a postcard from one of the Great Lakes fisheries at Green Bay, Wisconsin, on Lake Michigan,⌘ saying: "Crayfish beginning to come in fine. Very large this year. Shall we send you the usual 200?" This is the cue for one of the adventures of our gastronomic year. We mail back our order with check and some days later the Railway Express man brings to our front door a large slotted rough-wood crate, which is usually leaking water (from the melting blocks of ice inside) and is buzzing with energetically crawling crayfish. Today they can be sent more rapidly by air express, but the shipper should make certain that the order receives special rapid handling. Be careful opening the crate; once, after prying open the lid, I made the mistake of being drawn away by a ringing telephone. Twenty minutes later, a circular area of about twenty feet around the crate was nicely filled with highly active crayfish, briskly crawling each toward his own notion of the direction of the nearest water! We start by washing, humanely killing, and boiling them in dill bouillon, just as the Swedes have done it over the years for their national feast (page 456). In fact, Scandinavian stores⁂ in most large cities almost always stock crayfish, alive or already cooked, during the season. (In Louisiana, the crayfish feast is celebrated on the shores of the bayous, where the crayfish are caught, but there they call them crawfish and their season is in the spring.) Our recipes are given on pages 456–8.

Wait For an "O" in the Month for Oysters

On September 1, when there is again an "r" in the month and oysters are legally in season, the inhabitants of the great oyster-fishing centers of England, Colchester and Whitstable, go wild and eat oysters for three meals a day for several days in a row. We think that this excitement is premature, that September oysters are not good in flavor, and that it is much better to wait until October. This is because most oysters spawn in June and July (the exact date depends upon the temperature of the sea) and they have not yet recovered from this exhausting activity by September. We would prefer that the legal oyster season begin on October 1. We always open our oysters at home, a few minutes before serving. It is hard work, but not too difficult once the knack is learned, and the gain in flavor is worth the effort. As the shell opens, the oyster is left on the deep side, which serves as a cup from which the juice can be sipped. It is harder and harder, these days, to indulge one's preference for a specific type of oyster. All small oysters are sold as "Bluepoint," even if they come from beds a hundred miles away from Bluepoint Bay on Long Island. Large oysters, regardless of their source, are generally sold as "Cotuit," or "Cape Cod." So these names no longer have any usefulness. Very occasionally, friends on the shore at Greenport, Long Island, send us a small quantity of the local Greenport oyster, and we consider it the best of all in the Northeast—strong, salty, and firm.

Contrasts in Summer Grapes

We are blasé about the fat and juicy Western grape, which brings us steady pleasure, in one variety or another, almost every month of the year. On the other hand, the Eastern grape comes for only a few summer weeks and we make a fuss of it because of its sharp contrast, its slightly acid bite, its wild and winey flavor, and its strong texture. The principal varieties, most of them grown in New York State, are the CATAWBA, the CONCORD, the DELAWARE, and the NIAGARA. We convert the Concord into an excellent *kissel* (page 479). As for the California grape, at this season our special favorites are the RED MALAGA, colored pink to reddish-purple, big and crisp in the mouth, its season usually runs from July to October; and the superb BLACK RIBIER, with its thick showy skin and meaty texture, available through the summer and winter. Other varieties of the California grape for which we watch and which we often eat with the summer soft cheeses—Brie, Camembert, Triple-Crème—are the ALMERIA, starting in October; the CARDINAL; the EMPEROR; the WHITE MALAGA; the THOMPSON SEEDLESS; and the TOKAY.

Concentrate on the Ripe Mango

To get the greatest pleasure from a mango the fruit must be at its peak of ripeness. If there is any green at all on the skin, it is still unripe. When every last speck of green has faded and the skin is pink and gold, it is the perfect moment. It is best to buy the mango a few days early and watch it daily at home. Never let the brown flecks of over-ripeness develop, for then the skin will weaken and burst when the fruit is squeezed.

Search for Variety in Plums

There are more than 200 kinds of plum, so it is worthwhile to learn a few of the names and decide which plums one likes best. Usually our first choice is the Western ELDORADO, handsomely heart-shaped, with reddish-purple skin. For a large showy plum, we choose the Western EMPRESS, also reddish-purple in color. For a color contrast, we choose the green Western KELSEY. Our other specials are the Western LARODA, reddish-purple, with a grape-like flavor; the Western NUBIANA, or CHERRYSTONE, heart-shaped, reddish-purple; the Western SUGARPLUM, blushing-red in color, oval in shape, always very juicy, but slightly bland in flavor. For easy cutting-up in fruit salads, we use the California ITALIAN PRUNE (which, illogically, is neither from Italy, nor is the type used for the dried prune), a small, bluish-purple freestone with a strong flavor. Other fine plums of the summer season are the Texas BEAUTY, the California BURBANK, the Western DUARTE, the Western SANTA ROSA, and the California TRAGEDY.

THE SUMMER FEAST DAYS
An International Calendar

MANY of the dishes of other nations have become such favorites of our family that we hardly need an anniversary on which to hang them. However here are a few of the summer dates that we sometimes remember in our own home.

On **July 4** we often try to represent various gastronomic areas of our country with a regional party buffet supper (page 375).

On one of the most important days of the year for every lover of freedom, the day when the French stormed and destroyed the prison of the Bastille, **July 14**, perhaps an open-air French party buffet on a lawn or terrace (page 387).

On **July 28**, the National day of Peru, the day in 1821 when she declared her independence from Spain, we might start dinner with the extraordinary raw-fish appetizer *seviche* (page 268).

On the Independence Day of Switzerland, **August 1**, when the first three cantons united to break away from the Hapsburg Empire in 1291, we might serve the wonderful one-dish fresh-fruit lunch *Bircher müsli* (page 328), or a Swiss cheese fondue (page 302).

In Sweden on **August 7** is the start of *Kräfttiden* ("Crayfish Time"), the opening of the new crayfish season, when gardens and balconies are festooned with garlands and paper lanterns and effigies of crayfish. We have our own source for live crayfish, which we prepare in various ways (pages 456–8).

A national religious holiday in Spain on **August 15**, Assumption Day, will probably take us back to our *paella* buffet supper (page 231). Assumption Day is also the national holiday of Belgium, which we might celebrate with a *waterzooie* of chicken (page 286) or a *carbonnade flamande* (page 567).

On our honeymoon in Hungary many years ago, we participated on **August 20** in the national holiday for *Szent Istvan Kiraly Nap* (the Day of Saint Stephen), when the relics of the nation's patron saint (who was murdered by previous oppressors) were carried high above the Danube, through the steep and narrow streets of the historic city of Buda, which forms half of the capital city of Budapest. We might remember with a Hungarian party dinner (page 408).

There are many South Indian festivals to give us an excuse for serving the extraordinary and delicate South Indian home dinner. In August there are the Krishna Festival of Janamashtami, and the water festival on the river Kaveri, and usually in September the South Indian Feast of *Asuj Dasehra.* We might join in any of these with our South Indian recipes beginning on page 398.

The Summer Party and Feast-Day Menus

THE FIRST two menus below have been served at our table again and again in celebration of the two great feasts of our gastronomic year. When our children were younger, it was our tradition on the Fourth to read the Declaration of Independence, and on the Fourteenth, from Dickens's *A Tale of Two Cities,* the magnificent description of the fall of the Bastille. The South Indian and Hungarian feasts are quite unusual and extraordinarily good; they would make a party at any time of the year.

☆

An American Dinner for the Fourth

MENU

WINES

PHILADELPHIA CLAM PIE

A Great Western dry white Moore's Diamond

≈

PACIFIC KING SALMON
STUFFED WITH OLYMPIA OYSTERS
with
Green Mayonnaise

A Wente Pinot Blanc

≈

CALIFORNIA AVOCADO AND ORANGE SALAD

≈

NEW ORLEANS CHICKEN AND SHRIMP GUMBO
with
Chinese-American White Rice
and
Southern Hush Puppies

A light red wine, perhaps a Louis Martini Cabernet Sauvignon

≈

VERMONT BLUEBERRY GRUNT
with Wisconsin Blue Cheese

A dry California champagne, perhaps a Korbel Naturel

≈

Antoine's French Quarter Café
Diabolique with Orange Brûlot

A California brandy in the coffee, perhaps an Almaden Centennial 4-year-old

☆

Regional Dishes of the United States

To friends who ask: "How can you have a traditional American dinner without beef?" we have always replied that this menu stresses the unusual in our gastronomy. A few places remain obstinately and magnificently regional and they are honored here.

We continue to think, through year after year of repetition, that the New Orleans gumbo is among the greatest of native American gastronomic inventions. It has something of France about it, a touch of Spain, and the trick for the final flavor and texture was contributed by the Choctaw Indians of Louisiana. They taught the early Spanish and French settlers how to thicken and darken the gumbo with ground sassafras leaf.

Each of our Southern friends has a different story as to the origin of the name "hush puppies." The one we find most believable is that these small corn biscuits were fried over campfires on hunting expeditions and when the dogs smelled the delectable scent of frying corn they howled. So the cook would fry a few extra biscuits and throw them to the dogs, yelling: "Hush, puppies!" and the dogs devoured them, were satisfied, and hushed.

Shopping for the Ingredients

The baby Olympia oysters are available absolutely fresh only on the Northwest coast, but they are now being shipped air express to other parts of the country.✽ However they can be replaced by scallops. The ground sassafras leaf comes from the leading spice companies in jars labeled *gumbo filé*.✽

Planning and Timing

In spite of the generous proportions of this menu, it presents no special problems in preparation or timing. The clam pie is made a day or two in advance and served at room temperature. The salmon is cooked the day before, decorated on its platter on the morning of the day and served cold. The gumbo is prepared the day before, then reheated and thickened at the last minute with the sassafras. The rice is timed for the usual 20 to 30 minutes and can be kept warm longer. The dessert is prepared the day before and served cold. The coffee is flamed at the table. Our children used to be so expert at reversing the orange skins for the orange *brûlot* that they did the job at the table and kept the guests fascinated by their dexterity. A meal to sleep after!

PHILADELPHIA CLAM PIE

For a party of 8 to 10

Although one 10-inch pie provides only a small portion for each guest, this menu offers so many riches to follow that we find it best to cut the pie into finger-thin wedges and serve them simply as an appetizer.

Check Staples:

Salt butter (4 Tbs.)
Sweet butter (½ lb.)
Eggs (2 large)
Lemon (1)
Ice water for crust (½ cup)
Aromatics: table salt, freshly ground black pepper, MSG whole bay leaf, garlic (2 cloves), Worcestershire sauce
Carrots (2 medium)
Yellow onion (1 medium)
Parsley (small handful)
Ground arrowroot (4 Tbs.)
Granulated instantized flour (3 cups)
Dry white wine (1 pt.)

Shopping List:

Cherrystone clams, unopened (3 dozen)
Heavy cream (¼ cup)
Fresh mushrooms (¾ lb.)
French Dijon mustard (2 tsp.)
French Armagnac or brandy (2 Tbs., a 1-oz. jigger)

Everything Is Done the Day Before—the Crust

Let the ½ pound of sweet butter come to room temperature. There is no need to sift the new instantized flour; just put the 3 cups into a fairly large mixing bowl and stir in 1 teaspoon of salt (with ordinary flour, these would have to be sifted together). Using a pastry cutter, work in butter, moistening with a minimum of the ice water, added a dash at a time, until dough has consistency of niblet corn. Lightly gather into a ball and refrigerate for 1 hour or more.

Steaming the Clams in About 15 Minutes

Wash and scrub clams under cold running water. In a tall soup pot large enough to hold all the clams, bring the pint of wine to a boil. Scrape the 2 carrots and thinly slice them into the wine as it heats up; also add the onion, peeled and chopped. Add the aromatics: 1 whole bay leaf, the handful of parsley, the 2 cloves of garlic, chopped, plus 2 or 3 grinds of pepper, and MSG to taste. Cover and simmer for about 5 minutes, to develop flavor. Then bring wine up to a rolling boil so that pot is filled with aromatic steam; now slide in clams and cover immediately. Leave heat on high for 6 minutes, giving pot a vigorous shake about every minute, to encourage clams to open. Remove lid, standing back from steam, and use tongs to fish out all open clams. Put back lid and leave more obstinate clams to steam for a couple of minutes longer. When last clam is out of pot, turn off heat and strain aromatic wine (now wonderfully fortified with clam juice) through a fine strainer or through cheesecloth. This liquid is the heart of the sauce. As soon as open shells are cool enough to handle, remove clams and throw away shells. Chop clam meats and set aside. Wipe (never wash) the 3/4 pound of mushrooms and slice them lengthwise into hammer shapes, then sauté slices lightly in about 4 tablespoons of the salt butter and hold.

The Sauce—a Modified Velouté

Put the 4 tablespoons of arrowroot in a small mixing bowl and wet it down with 4 tablespoons of the cream. Measure 2 cups of the strained aromatic liquid from the clam pot, put it into a 2-quart saucepan, and heat it to gentle simmering. Lower heat and stir in, 1 tablespoon at a time, the creamed arrowroot, firmly blending it in and making sure that it melts without lumping. Continue working in creamed arrowroot until sauce has consistency of very thick cream (not all the creamed arrowroot will be used), cover and gently simmer for about 5 minutes, stirring 2 or 3 times. Separate 1 of the eggs and put the yolk and the white into separate mixing bowls; beat the yolk lightly. Now add to the sauce: the juice of 1/2 of the lemon, 2 teaspoons of the mustard, 1 tablespoon of Worcestershire sauce, the cut-up clams, the egg yolk, the sautéed mushrooms, and the 2 tablespoons of Armagnac. Separate the remaining egg and add the second white to the first, but do not beat yet. (Reserve the yolk for painting pie crust later.) Keep the filling warm, well below boiling, while the crust is rolled out.

Building and Baking the Pie in About 1 Hour

Very lightly butter a 10-inch pie plate. Preheat oven to 450 degrees. Take ball of dough from refrigerator and divide into two halves, one slightly larger than the other. Roll out this larger lump on a lightly floured board until it is about 1/4 inch thick; line the bottom of the pie plate with dough, leaving a 1/2-inch skirt hanging over edge all around. Roll out second half of dough also to 1/4-inch thickness and roughly 1 inch larger than pie plate all around. Hold ready on waxed paper. Stir the filling in the saucepan, taste, and finally adjust seasoning. Also adjust thickness. If too thick, add 1 or 2 more dashes of the clam wine. If too thin, stir in a little more creamed arrowroot and reheat. The final result should be quite thick. Then beat egg whites stiff and lightly blend into the filling. We usually lift the filling into the pie plate with a slotted spoon, making sure that all the solids go in, but holding back a little of the sauce if the pie plate becomes too full. Place top crust in position, wet the edges, and roll together, pressing them down to the edge of the plate. Cut 3 or 4 small gashes in the top and paint with the remaining egg yolk, slightly beaten with a little water. Bake in the hot oven for 15 minutes, then lower heat to 350 degrees and continue baking until top is brown, usually in 25 to 30 minutes. Let pie cool to room temperature, then loosely wrap in waxed paper and refrigerate until about 2 hours before needed. Serve at room temperature.

PACIFIC KING SALMON STUFFED WITH OLYMPIA OYSTERS

For a party of 8 to 10

This is the great regional dish of the Northwest, particularly in Seattle, and although it may not be possible to reproduce it exactly in all other parts of the country, it still makes a magnificent party dish, visually and gastronomically, even with less luxurious types of salmon.

Check Staples:

Thick-sliced dark smoked bacon (about ½ lb.)
Salt butter (about ½ lb.)
Aromatics: crystal salt, freshly ground black pepper, MSG, tarragon leaf, thyme
Yellow onion (1 medium)
Fresh parsley (small bunch)
Olive oil (a few Tbs.)
Day-old bread (enough for 4 cups, diced)
Dry white wine (about 1 pt.)

Shopping List:

Whole King salmon, cleaned, but head left on, scaled, with fins and tail trimmed (about 5 to 7 lbs.)
Shucked Olympia oysters (1½ to 2 lbs.) or, as second best, deep-sea scallops (1½ to 2 lbs.)
White celery (1 or 2 hearts, according to size)

The Day Before—Preparing the Stuffing in About ½ Hour

Peel and dice the onion. Dice enough celery to fill about ¾ cup. Dice enough day-old bread to fill a 1-quart jar. Chop a small handful of parsley. If using Olympia oysters, leave whole; if scallops, slice about ⅜ inch thick. We use a large copper sauté pan and melt in it 1½ sticks (6 ounces) of the butter. When it sizzles add chopped onion and celery and lightly color. Then add bread and stir around until thoroughly impregnated with butter; add more butter if necessary. Add: 1 teaspoon tarragon, 1 teaspoon thyme, ¼ cup chopped parsley, and flavor to taste with salt, pepper, and MSG. Finally, add oysters (or scallops) and gently blend. If stuffing is now too dry, add a few splashes of the oyster (or scallop) liquor. Stuffing must be moist yet stiff enough to stay inside fish.

Lightly rub inside of fish with crystal salt. We use clean fingers to pile in stuffing, making sure that packing is neither too loose nor too tight. Close cavity with small skewers laced with string.

Baking in 1 to 1½ Hours

Rub fish and large platter on which it is to be baked with olive oil. Preheat oven to 400 degrees. Lay fish on platter and cover with strips of bacon laid crosswise. Pour over enough wine to cover platter ¼ inch deep, cover entire platter with foil, and slide carefully into oven. For this size fish, which is usually about 2½ inches thick, we allow 10 to 12 minutes per pound. Do not disturb for the first ½ hour, then discard foil and baste fish with hot wine from platter. Repeat basting roughly every 15 minutes. Fish is perfect when it flakes easily from the bone. Cool to room temperature, refrigerate, covered, overnight, then lay out and decorate with remaining parsley on handsomest platter. Bacon can be crumbled and laid around fish or blended into mayonnaise (recipe follows).

GREEN MAYONNAISE

For a party of 8 to 10

Check Staples:

Homemade mayonnaise, *see* page 423 (1 pt.)

Shopping List:

Spinach (¼ lb., fresh, or ½ standard frozen package of chopped spinach)

Two or three sprigs each of available fresh aromatic herbs: basil, chives, dill, parsley, tarragon

The Day Before—As Soon as the Mayonnaise Is Ready

Set about a pint of water to boil in a 1-quart saucepan. Pick best leaves from aromatic herbs, discarding stalks. Drop them, with the washed spinach, into boiling water and scald for about a minute. Drain and, as soon as greens are cool enough to touch, squeeze out remaining water with clean hands. Chop, then press through fine sieve or food mill. This aromatic paste is now blended with the mayonnaise. Refrigerate, covered, until needed.

CALIFORNIA AVOCADO AND ORANGE SALAD

For a party of 8 to 10

Check Staples:

Lemon (1)

Aromatics: crystal salt,⁑ freshly ground black pepper⁑

Shopping List:

Ripe avocados (2 or 3, according to size)

Large eating oranges *see* list, page 365 (4)

Raspberry honey, *see* page 521 (about 1 Tbs.)

1 or 2 Hours Before Serving

Cut oranges in half and, using serrated grapefruit knife, carefully cut out segments so as to eliminate all skin and pits. Build a pyramid of these segments in the center of a medium-sized salad bowl. Peel avocados and cut flesh lengthwise in narrow strips. Use these to make a nest into which to put the orange pile; place the avocado strips around the bowl in a crisscross pattern. Cover and refrigerate until needed.

About 15 Minutes Before Serving

Very lightly salt and pepper, then sprinkle a few drops of honey over oranges and a few good squeezes of lemon juice over avocados. Serve quite cold.

NEW ORLEANS CHICKEN AND SHRIMP GUMBO

For a party of 8 to 10

The dish can be prepared with chicken parts, but we find it better and cheaper to buy a large stewing hen, and, after cutting off the meat for the gumbo, we boil the remaining carcass to give us the best possible chicken broth for the gumbo and to provide a good deal of extra chicken for later meals. For a really fine gumbo, it must be made at least 24 hours ahead, as it needs time for the flavors to blend and mature before final reheating and thickening with the sassafras.

Check Staples:

Bacon or salt-pork fat (3 or 4 Tbs.)
Chicken broth, *see* above (3 qts.)
Aromatics: crystal salt, freshly ground black pepper, MSG, whole bay leaves, whole cloves, garlic (2 cloves), *gumbo filé,* freshly ground nutmeg, thyme
Carrots (2 medium)
Green Pascal celery (1 bunch)
Yellow onions (2 medium)
Fresh parsley (1 bunch)
Granulated instantized flour (a few Tbs.)
Dry white wine (3 cups)

Shopping List:

Stewing hen, *see* page 520 (4 or 5 lbs.)
Lean ham, solid chunk, at least ½ inch thick—this could be from our boiled country ham, page 369 (1 lb.)
Crabs, whole in shell, cleaned (6 fairly small)
Jumbo shrimp—for number per pound, *see* page 62 (1 lb.)
Leeks (4 medium)
Sweet Bermuda onion (1 large)

2 Days Before—the Chicken and Its Broth

Cut raw chicken meat off breasts and legs of stewing hen and chunk enough to fill 3 cups. Hold, refrigerated and covered, for use the next day. Gently boil the rest of the chicken to make a fine broth, according to our BASIC RULE (page 117), adding the celery, leeks, carrots, Bermuda onion, wine, and aromatics as indicated. Skim and reserve 3 quarts of the final broth for the gumbo. The rest of the chicken and its broth can be used for other purposes.

1 Day Before—Preparing the Gumbo

We do the whole job in a 6-quart enameled cast-iron cocotte* with a tightly fitting lid, which is good-looking enough to be brought to table. Cut ham into ½-inch cubes, leaving on small quantities of fat. Peel and devein shrimp. Peel and slice the 2 yellow onions. Thoroughly wash crabs under cold water. Set cocotte over fairly high frying heat, dry. Add ham and stir around as it starts sizzling, to prevent sticking. Ham should release enough fat to fry, but if not, add about 1 tablespoon of the bacon fat. After 1 or 2 minutes, as soon as bottom of cocotte is lubricated, add shrimp and continue stirring around until just gilded. Turn off heat, remove ham and shrimp with slotted spoon and reserve. Pour off fat into small bowl and measure it back into cocotte, adding more bacon fat, to make exactly 6 tablespoons. Turn heat back on and, in this fat, sauté the sliced onions until lightly colored. Now blend in, 1 tablespoon at a time, enough flour to absorb fat and make a *roux,* usually about 5 tablespoons. Keep stirring and smoothing until flour is well browned, then begin working in, dash by dash, the remaining cup of wine. Keep it bubbling fairly hard and put back ham and shrimp, stirring around to absorb flavor of wine. After a couple of minutes, begin adding, gradually at first and continuing to stir, the 3 quarts of chicken broth. Turn up heat and bring it to boil as quickly as possible. Drop in crabs, whole, in shell. Also add: the 3 cups of chicken meat, 2 whole bay leaves, the 2 cloves of garlic, finely minced, plus salt, pepper, and MSG to taste, remembering that the chicken broth is already seasoned. When it comes to a boil, turn down to simmering and keep bubbling for about 1½ hours. Do not cover. Enough bubbles and steam should be released so that liquid boils down, over the full time, by about one third, to magnify and concentrate flavor. Then cool, cover, and refrigerate for 24 hours. No gumbo can be really great without this essential rest.

On the Day—About 3 Hours Before Serving

Let gumbo come to room temperature. Stir it gently around and, if meal is to be quite formal, remove crabs, open up shells, dig out meat, and drop into gumbo, discarding shells. However, there is comparatively little meat in these small crabs and we generally prefer to leave them whole in the gumbo as a dramatic garnish. All parts of the shell, claws and body contribute flavor. This contribution is increased by now leaving gumbo standing, covered, at room temperature for a couple of hours.

About 1 Hour Before Serving

Very slowly heat gumbo just to boiling point. Heat should be adjusted so that this takes about 1 hour. It can be done over medium-high heat on top of stove, or in a 300-degree oven. Stir gently about once every 15 minutes.

Just Before Serving

Gumbo should now be gently bubbling. Roughly estimate amount of liquid in pot, to determine amount of *gumbo filé* to be added—proportion is roughly 1 teaspoon *filé* to 1 pint liquid, but *filés* vary in strength according to age and quality, so final decision is based on tasting. Turn off heat and as soon as bubbling dies away, begin very carefully stirring in *filé,* teaspoon by teaspoon, until gumbo becomes dark and slightly gummy to the taste. It can now be kept warm for not more than a few minutes over low heat, but it must not boil again, or *filé* will "rope" into long rubbery strands. Do not overdo the amount of *filé;* it is better to have too little, until one has gained experience. Serve gumbo in very hot gumbo bowls with a white island of rice in the center of each. Each spoonful should include a little of this rice.

CHINESE-AMERICAN WHITE RICE

For a party of 8 to 10

Check Staples:

Salt butter (about ¼ lb.)
Long-grain white rice (½ cup for each man, ¼ cup for each lady)

About 35 Minutes Before Serving

We use the Chinese rule-of-thumb for calculating the amount of raw rice for the number of people to be served: ¼ cup for each lady, ½ cup for each man.

Put this amount of first-quality long-grain white rice into a heavy saucepan with a tightly fitting lid. Cover the rice with double its quantity of freshly drawn cold water (that is, 2 cups of water for each cup of rice). Stir and set over high heat. While it is heating up, float on top of the water 1 tablespoon of butter for each cup of rice. This prevents the water from frothing up and boiling over. As soon as it boils, quickly stir, pop on lid tightly, turn down heat to simmer and do not even peek for 30 minutes. Then, preferably with a wooden fork, gently loosen and lift rice, at the same time making a hole in the center to see whether all water has been absorbed. If not, put back lid and continue simmering for a few minutes longer. Rice should be perfectly done at the exact moment when all water is absorbed. Finally, rice may be dried out, so that all grains are separated, by leaving saucepan over low heat, uncovered, for last 2 or 3 minutes.

SOUTHERN HUSH PUPPIES

For a party of 8 to 10

Check Staples:

Eggs (2 large)
Milk (about ½ cup)
Aromatic: crystal salt*
Yellow onions (2 medium)
Double-acting baking powder (4 tsp.)
Coarse-ground cornmeal (2 cups)
Oil for frying

About 15 Minutes Before Serving

Peel and finely chop the 2 onions. In a mixing bowl firmly stir together: the 2 cups of cornmeal, 1 teaspoon salt, and the 4 teaspoons of baking powder, then blend in chopped onion. Break in the 2 eggs and beat hard with a wooden fork until mixture is a smooth, stiff paste. Now gradually blend in milk, dash by dash, using only enough to achieve soft dough, yet still firm enough to hold together. We sometimes shape the hush puppies into 2-inch-long, fairly thin ladyfingers; sometimes into smallish doughnut rings. Keep them thin. The chief attraction is the crisp fried crust. Thick parts tend to be soggy in the center.

Into a heavy frypan pour frying oil to about 1 inch deep. Heat up almost to smoking. Put in hush puppies and fry to deep brown. Serve piping hot.

VERMONT BLUEBERRY GRUNT WITH WISCONSIN BLUE CHEESE

For a party of 8 to 10

Check Staples:

Sweet butter (about ½ lb.)
Lemon (1)
Aromatics: crystal salt,* ground cinnamon
Dry bread crumbs (1 qt.)
Granulated white sugar (1½ cups)
Red food coloring

Shopping List:

Blueberries (2 qts.)
Wisconsin blue cheese (about 6 oz.)
Heavy whipping cream (1 pt.)

The Day Before—About 30 Minutes to Prepare and Bake

In a mixing bowl combine the blueberries with the 1½ cups of sugar, ½ teaspoon salt, 1 teaspoon cinnamon, and the juice of the lemon. These amounts can be varied with later experience, but better be conservative the first time. In a small saucepan just melt 6 tablespoons of the butter. Put the quart of bread crumbs into a second mixing bowl and add the cheese, finely crumbled. Add the melted butter, dribbling it around, and lightly mix everything with a wooden fork. Preheat oven to 400 degrees.

Butter well a 4-quart covered casserole and fill with alternate layers of blueberries and the bread-cheese mix, ending with the latter on top. Cover casserole, place in oven, and leave undisturbed for exactly 20 minutes. Then uncover, lightly dot top layer with more butter, and continue baking for a few minutes longer, until top is browned. Let cool to room temperature, then refrigerate, covered, until next day.

About 2 Hours Before Serving

Let the grunt come to room temperature. Divide the pint of cream equally between two beating bowls. A few minutes before serving, beat both stiff, coloring one red and leaving the other white. Decorate the grunt with the red and white cream, leaving the blue to the blueberries. Always serve this dish at room temperature.

ANTOINE'S FRENCH QUARTER CAFÉ DIABOLIQUE AND ORANGE BRÛLOT

For a party of 8 to 10

Some of our New Orleans friends own all the equipment to reproduce exactly Antoine's service of his flaming coffee. The large round silver-plated bowl fitted onto the spirit stove at the table, the long-handled ladle, the tall cups with the picture of Satan painted in red. It tastes exactly the same in normal coffee cups, prepared as we do it, in a small bright electric copper saucepan, and stirred with an ordinary soup ladle. A reasonably deep chafing dish also works well. Roy Alciatore, the grandson of the original Antoine, taught us the flaming-orange trick. It can be omitted from the coffee ceremony, but we like to end our party with a blaze in all directions.

Check Staples:

Aromatics: stick cinnamon, whole clove, lemon peel (piece about the size of a half dollar per person), orange peel (same amount)

Shopping List:

Thin-skinned orange (1 per person)
French Cognac🍶 (1 oz. per person)
Swiss kirsch🍶 (1 oz. per person)

Check Staples (continued):
Strong black coffee ($1\frac{1}{2}$ oz. per person)
Lump sugar (4 large cubes per person)

The Café Diabolique

Into our small copper electric saucepan, which is to be heated at the table, we put *for each person:* 2 cubes of the sugar, a $\frac{1}{2}$-inch length of the stick cinnamon, 2 whole cloves, 1 piece each of the lemon and orange rind, then pour on $1\frac{1}{2}$ ounces of steaming black coffee. Bring to a light boil at the table, stirring almost all the time with the ladle, to melt the sugar and cook out the aromatic oils. Meanwhile put 1 ounce of the Cognac per person into a small butter-melting pan, warmed slightly over a candle lamp. Do not let it get too hot or the alcohol will evaporate too soon. After 1 or 2 minutes pour Cognac into coffee and set on fire, at the same moment turning out the room lights. Ladle vigorously to make the most of the blue fire. After another minute or so, when the flames die down, ladle coffee through small strainer into cups and serve.

The Orange Brûlot

While the guests are sipping their coffee, our two daughters would prepare the *brûlot* at the table. However the job can be done in advance. With the point of a sharp knife, make a single straight cut right around the equator of the orange, but only just through the skin. Now, with the handle end of a silver teaspoon, begin to loosen the skin (being careful not to tear it) around the cut, until about $\frac{1}{2}$ inch of skin is loose on either side of the cut and all the way around. Next, with the fingers, very slowly and carefully, reverse the skin, until there is a cup at each end, one attached to the orange at the North Pole, the other at the South Pole. If the job has been properly done, the orange will now stand firmly on one end and the other will be a goblet from which to drink. Place one lump of sugar in the goblet and pour over 1 ounce of the slightly warmed kirsch. On a signal, each guest lights his goblet and the room is again darkened. Using a silver teaspoon, each guest stirs and plays with the individual fire. It's more fun than fireworks! It also has a serious purpose, for fire both melts the sugar, and burns out the oils from the orange skin. When the flames have died down and the room lights are back on, each guest lifts his orange to his lips and drinks the warm liqueur.

A French Supper for Bastille Day

MENU

WINES

CREAMED CONSOMMÉ BRETONNE

A very dry Sherry (say a Tio Pepe)
served before the start of the meal
and continued through the first two courses

PISSALADIÈRE PROVENÇALE—An Anchovy-Onion Pie

MELON DE FILETS DE SOLE—A Spiced Fish Mousse
with Puréed Tomato Sauce

A fine dry white Pouilly-Fuissé

BOEUF FARCI EN GELÉE

A great red Bordeaux,
say a Château Haut-Brion

MELON FARCI DE FRUITS DE SAISON—
A Watermelon Basket of Fruit

A fine French Champagne

Café

A first-class French Cognac

Summer Dishes for a French Feast

Like all good French menus, this one is basically simple. The *pissaladière* is the other great savory pie of France. What the *quiche* is to Lorraine, the *pissaladière* is to Provence, especially around Nice, where the French and Italian cuisines so successfully intermingle. Later, the *pissaladière* was carried to Naples, where it was violently transformed and given to the world as *pizza*. Now no one remembers the charming, subtle, and gentle *pissaladière!* The name comes from the *pisala* of Nice, an aromatic anchovy conserve, homemade by the wives of the fishermen from freshly caught anchovies.

The fish mousse is an exciting contrast in textures. Brightly glazed and sauced, it makes a fine show on the buffet. We serve small portions; it is smooth and rich.

For all its simplicity, the watermelon basket is a handsome dessert and never fails to stop the conversation when it is brought in. Preparation offers almost unlimited opportunity for variety in color and design, with different combinations of fruits and colors of ice cream or sherbet.

Planning and Timing

In spite of its simplicity, this menu still requires a certain skill in achieving the perfection of detail. The trick with the *pissaladière* is to gild and soften the onions without frying or mushing them. The delicate texture of the mousse comes from lightness in handling it, always in contact with the ice. The slices of beef must be put together so neatly that the whole rump looks like a solid chunk, with the stuffing as a surprise. However, there need be no pressure about these details, for everything is prepared at least the day before. All that needs to be done while the guests are in the house is to heat up the consommé and, just before serving, to trim the fruit-stuffed melon with the yellow sherbet. Small portions are in order, for there are many riches.

CREAMED CONSOMMÉ BRETONNE

For a party of 8 to 10

This is probably the simplest recipe in the book. If preparation takes more than 5 minutes, there is something wrong. It will be just good or wonderfully good, according to the quality of the chicken broth. It is also good ice-cold, but we prefer to stress the warmth of our welcome by offering each arriving guest a cupful, no more, piping hot.

Check Staples:

Chicken broth, the best available (3 pts.)

Shopping List:

Clam juice (3 pts.—six 8-oz. bottles)
Heavy whipping cream (1/2 pt.)

Check Staples (continued):

Aromatics: crystal salt,☧ freshly ground black pepper,☧ Hungarian sweet red paprika☧

On the Morning of the Day

Combine chicken broth and clam juice, then adjust seasoning with salt and pepper. Hold refrigerated until needed.

A Few Minutes Before Serving

Heat up the broth and the clam juice to just below simmering. Whip cream with a balloon beater. As each cup of consommé is served, float in the center a dollop of whipped cream the size of a cherry. Then color the cream with a pinch of the bright red paprika. The guest stirs in the cream with a teaspoon before drinking.

PISSALADIÈRE PROVENÇALE—AN ANCHOVY-ONION PIE

For a party of 8 to 10

There are dozens of versions of the *pissaladière*. After trying many of them, this, with a crumbly, buttery crust, is our favorite.

Check Staples:

Sweet butter (7 oz.)
Ice water (about 2 Tbs.)
Aromatics: crystal salt,☧ freshly ground black pepper,☧ MSG⊜
Granulated instantized flour⊜ (1½ cups)
Olive oil⊜ (3 to 4 Tbs.)

Shopping List:

Yellow onions (2 lbs.)
Anchovies, flat fillets (about 2 dozen—usually two 2-oz. cans)
Ripe black olives, perferably bought loose in an Italian store (about 2 dozen, say ½ lb.)

The Day Before—the Crust

Let butter come to room temperature. Put the 1½ cups of flour into a large mixing bowl, stir in 1 teaspoon salt, then work in the butter with a pastry cutter, adding the minimum of ice water a few drops at a time, until there is no dry flour left and it all has the consistency of niblet corn. Then gather with light fingers into a ball, wrap loosely in waxed paper, and refrigerate for at least 1 hour, or longer, until needed.

Making the Onion Filling in About 40 Minutes

Peel and thinly slice the 2 pounds of onions. We cook them in a copper sauté pan with a cover. Put in about 3 tablespoons of the olive oil, heat to gentle frying temperature, then add onions and stir around to coat with oil. Now comes the most sensitive part of the making of the *pissaladière*. In the next 15 minutes, the onions must be gently cooked so that they turn golden, yet remain firm. Cook them too fast and they will fry and brown, too slow and they will mush. As soon as they are golden, check whether pan is dry and, if necessary, add a bit more oil. Then put on the lid and let them just simmer for about 15 minutes more. They are perfectly done when still slightly chewy, but smooth and gentle in flavor. Adjust seasoning with salt, pepper, and MSG.

Building and Baking the Pie in About 1 Hour

Lightly butter a 10-inch pie plate. Roll out dough ¼ inch thick on a flour-covered board and line pie plate; you will have some dough left over. Lay about 18 anchovy fillets on bottom of pie. (With experience, this number can be increased or decreased to taste, but it is best to use 18 the first time. There is a certain magic about the proper blend of anchovy and onion flavors.) Now fill pie with cooked onions. Preheat oven to 400 degrees. Gather together the remaining uncooked dough and roll and cut into thin, ⅜-inch-wide strips, using these to make a neat lattice on top of the pie. With remaining anchovy fillets, make a star in the center. Now quickly pit the black olives and press 1 into each open space between lattice. Also make a ring of black olives around edge. (Obviously this design can be varied at will.) Bake pie until lattice crust is brown, usually in 25 to 30 minutes. This *pissaladière* cannot be served hot from the oven as crust is too crumbly to cut. Let cool to room temperature, then refrigerate, lightly covered, until needed. Serve at room temperature, or very slightly warmed.

MELON DE FILETS DE SOLE—A FISH MOUSSE

For a party of 8 to 10

We own a 2-quart melon mold* with a watertight lid and we use it at the end of the year to boil the Christmas plum pudding. Now it serves equally well to shape this classic French fish cream flecked with fresh green herbs and enclosed by solid fillets.

Check Staples:

Lemon (1)
Aromatics: crystal salt,* freshly ground black pepper,* MSG,* freshly ground nutmeg
Powdered gelatin (2 or 3 envelopes)
Olive oil* (a few Tbs.)
Italian peeled and seeded plum tomatoes (1 lb. 1 oz. can)
Spanish Sherry vinegar* (2 tsp.)

Shopping List:

Fillets of sole, skinned, well-shaped, very white (6 to 8, according to size, about 2 lbs.)
Solid center cut of pike, or if not available, whiting (about 2 lbs., to produce 1 lb. of flesh, after all skin and bone removed)
Heavy whipping cream (½ pt.)
Small bunch each, as available: chive, dill, parsley, tarragon, watercress
Dry white Alsatian Riesling* (1 bottle)

The Day Before—Lining and Stuffing the Mold in About 45 Minutes

The cream must be very cold for beating, so the first step is to place in the freezer the balloon wire whisk and the round copper bowl (or if bowl is too large, set over a basin of ice). Lightly oil the melon mold and put it also into freezer. Wash and dry sole fillets and lay out on a platter. Now line the ice-cold mold with fillets, setting the best-looking side toward the mold. Each fillet is laid at a slight angle and just overlapping; the final result looks better if the fillets are on the bias (see illustration). For the moment the ends hang over the edge of the mold, until it is lined like a nest. Place at once in coldest part of refrigerator.

For the filling, take chunk of pike (or whiting) apart, removing all skin and bone and cutting up flesh. Put into freezer for a few moments, while preparing an ice-cooled mixing bowl in which to work by half filling larger bowl with ice cubes and setting smaller bowl in it. Now pound pike (or whiting) flesh in a mortar, until quite pasty, then pass through food mill into ice-cooled bowl. Finally force through fine sieve, again returning it to iced bowl. With kitchen scissors coarsely cut leaf only of the various aromatic herbs (chive, dill, parsley, tarragon), leaving pieces large enough so that the fish stuffing will be clearly flecked with green. Add to sieved fish but do not mix for the moment. Quickly beat the cream until stiff enough to hold tall peaks, then, using wooden or rubber spatula, lightly blend into the fish and herbs. Bowl must remain in contact with ice all the time. Taste and add salt, pepper, MSG, and a few grinds of nutmeg.

Bring out fillet-lined mold and fill with stuffing, pressing down lightly into every corner. Fold the hanging ends of the fillets over the stuffing, enclosing it. Cover with a piece of foil, tucking it down well, then put on watertight lid.

Cooking the Fish in About 30 Minutes

The mold is now heated in boiling water. Into a large enough pot to permit handling the mold, pour hot water to come up to within 1 inch of the lid of the mold, then bring up to simmering, covering pot so that steam will also heat top of mold, and simmer for 20 minutes. At once remove mold from water, take off lid but not foil, and let cool to room temperature. Then remove foil and carefully turn mold over onto rack, allowing condensed moisture to drip out for a few minutes. Then put back lid of mold and refrigerate until needed.

On the Morning of the Day—Final Preparation and Decoration

Cool oval platter on which fish is to be served. Unmold fish in usual way, by dipping mold for a few seconds into hot water, then shaking firmly onto platter. The final decoration is a matter of taste and there are endless possibilities with green leaves, golden rounds of carrots, shapes of hard-boiled egg or tomato, etc. We think it a pity to hide the snowy whiteness of the fish itself, so we proceed as follows:

BASIC RULE FOR INSTANT FISH GLAZE: We use a slightly sharp, dry white wine, say a good Alsatian Riesling. Empty 1 envelope of the dry powdered gelatin into a small mixing bowl and blend in 3 ounces of the wine. Now, in a small copper saucepan, we heat up (but keep well below boiling) 1½ cups of the wine, flavoring it with 2 teaspoons of our best sherry vinegar. When the gelatin mix is pasty, spoon into the hot wine, continuing to heat and stir only as long as it takes for gelatin to dissolve. Turn off heat at once and put ice cubes into a bowl just large enough and deep enough so that small copper saucepan will stand in it. Watch aspic and stir every 30 seconds or so. In a remarkably short time it will show signs of thickening, then it will become syrupy and now is ready to be spooned over fish. If saucepan is left on ice too long, aspic glaze will be too thick to handle. If this happens, put saucepan back on heat for a few seconds, stirring, until aspic becomes liquid again, then put back on ice.

We carefully spoon this syrupy aspic-glaze over fish mold until entirely covered. We control thickness of covering by refrigerating for about 15 minutes after first coating, then spooning on a second coating, and so on. Now we prepare a bright-red base for the fish by pouring the remaining aspic glaze into the container of an electric blender, adding 2 cups of the canned tomatoes, the juice of a lemon, and the contents of the remaining envelope of dry powdered gelatin. Cover and blend at high speed for not more than 15 seconds. Pour back into the saucepan and heat almost to boiling, stirring a few times. Put the pan back on the ice and cool until the contents become thick enough to hold a small peak. Then spoon irregularly around the base of the fish. Finally, decorate the top with a few sprigs of watercress. When the fish is cut and served, the tomato base is served with it as a sauce.

BOEUF FARCI EN GELÉE—STUFFED BEEF IN ASPIC

For a party of 8 to 10

The success of this dish is largely in the hands of the butcher. He must be persuaded to provide a rectangular and well-shaped piece of solid, lean rump of beef, which is then to be brought home, cut apart, stuffed, and put together again so skillfully that the meat looks as if it had never been touched. This is only possible with the "exactly right" size and shape.

Check Staples:

Thick-sliced dark smoked bacon (¼ lb.)
Salt butter (½ lb.)
Corn-belly salt pork (¼ lb.)
Aromatics: crystal salt, freshly ground black pepper, MSG, whole bay leaves, garlic (5 to 6 cloves), nutmeg, orange peel (piece the size of a half dollar), thyme
Green celery leaves (small handful)
Yellow onions (6 medium)
Parsley (1 bunch)
Green scallions (1 bunch)
Shallots (4)
Granulated instantized flour (a few Tbs.)
Granulated white sugar (a few tsp.)

Shopping List:

Prime or choice beef rump, a straight-sided, rectangular chunk (about 5 lbs.)
Calf's foot, split lengthwise (1)
Pig's foot, split lengthwise (1)
Veal knuckle, split (1)
Carrots (10 medium)
White boiler onions (¾ lb.)
Green peas (1 pt., shelled, or a little over 2 lbs. in the shell)
Ripe tomatoes (2 medium)
White truffles (2 medium, if pocketbook allows), if not, mushrooms (1 lb.)
White turnips (2 small)
French Cognac (2 or 3 Tbs.)

2 Days Before—Marinating the Beef

Put the chunk of beef in a deep bowl or pot in which there is hardly more than 1 inch of space all around the meat, thus not using up too much of the wine. Drop in around the meat: 2 or 3 of the yellow onions, coarsely chopped; 3 or 4 of the carrots, scraped and sliced; 2 whole bay leaves, 3 or 4 sprigs of parsley with stalks; 1 teaspoon thyme; 2 cloves of garlic, sliced; and the piece of orange peel. Pour in enough of the wine to come just to the top of the meat. Cover and refrigerate overnight.

The Day Before—Stuffing and Cooking the Beef

For the stuffing, put into a fair-sized mixing bowl: 3 finely minced cloves of the garlic; the 4 shallots, finely chopped; 3 of the yellow onions, finely chopped; a small handful of coarsely cut parsley; the bunch of scallions, coarsely cut; a few grinds of nutmeg, plus salt, pepper, and MSG to taste. Mix thoroughly and then store, tightly covered, in the refrigerator until needed.

We simmer the beef in a large enameled cast-iron cocotte* and in this we now prepare the spiced bouillon. Remove beef from marinade and set aside. Pour marinade with its vegetables and aromatics into the cocotte and add: the washed pieces of veal knuckle, calf's and pig's feet; 2 tablespoons of the Cognac; 2 teaspoons of the sugar; a small handful of the celery leaves; the 2 tomatoes, coarsely chopped; the 2 turnips, peeled and sliced; then taste and add more salt and pepper if needed. Add freshly drawn cold water just to cover, bring to a boil and simmer, covered, for about 1 hour. Meanwhile stuff the beef.

We just cover the bottom of our large sauté pan with a thin film of the olive oil and bring up to fairly high frying heat. Quickly pat the beef dry, then lightly brown it on all sides in the sauté pan. Pour 2 tablespoons of the Cognac around meat and flame. When fire has died down, turn off heat, put meat onto cutting board, and, using a long and very sharp carving knife, carefully cut beef lengthwise into ½-inch slices. Lay slices on top of each other in correct order, to maintain shape of meat. Starting with the bottom slice, begin constructing a giant club sandwich. Cover this first slice with: a layer of thin slices of the truffles (or mushrooms), then a layer of thin slices of the corn-belly salt pork, plus a third layer of part of the prepared stuffing. On top of this, carefully position the second slice of beef and cover it with the same three layers. Repeat this operation with remaining slices of beef, neatly dividing truffle slices and stuffing so that they are all used by the time the final slice of beef is on top. The meat should now have returned almost to its original shape. Tie tightly with string. When bouillon has completed its first hour of simmering, lower the stuffed beef into the cocotte (making sure that it rests on the bottom and is covered by the bouillon), let it all gently simmer, "just smiling," covered, for about another 2½ hours.

Meanwhile peel and dice remaining carrots, fry lightly in butter until just tender (hardly more than 1 or 2 minutes), and hold. Peel and cook small white onions until just tender, and hold. Shell and steam peas until just done and hold.

Still the Day Before—Molding the Beef

For the final shaping of the beef aspic as it will come to the table, choose a deep mold or an oval cocotte* deep enough and large enough to hold the beef with about 1 inch of space all around. There should not be more than about 1 inch of aspic all around the meat when it is unmolded. On the bottom of this mold make an even layer of the diced carrots and peas, mixing them together so that the two colors will show evenly. When meat is done, lift it out of the hot bouillon and lower it gently onto carrots and peas, making sure that it is in the exact center of mold and standing straight. Cut strings and very carefully pull them out. Set cooked white onions neatly around bottom of meat. Strain hot bouillon through a fine sieve, discarding all solids, which by now will be boiled out. Clarify bouillon according to our basic method (page 134) and pour over meat in mold, making sure that vegetables are not disturbed, until level of liquid is just up to top of meat. Remember that this is the base on which meat will stand. Let cool to room temperature, then, moving it very carefully so as not to disturb anything, set mold in refrigerator, making sure it is level, cover and let it set overnight.

On the Morning of the Day—Unmolding and Decorating

About 30 minutes before the unmolding ceremony, set the large oval platter on which meat is to be served in the freezer. Unmold in the usual way, setting mold in a basin of hot water for a few seconds, then inverting onto the ice-cold platter and giving it a good shake. The top, handsome with its green and orange peas and carrots, needs no decoration beyond perhaps a sprig of green watercress stuck in the center. The sides and the surrounding space of the platter offer plenty of opportunity for imaginative arrangement. Keep refrigerated until a few minutes before serving, then finally scrape away any aspic that may have run during the unmolding. It is a fine sight on the buffet and a magnificent combination of flavors and textures.

MELON FARCI DE FRUITS DE SAISON—A WATERMELON BASKET OF FRUIT

For a party of 8 to 10

The final touch of the snowy frosting is optional.

Check Staples:

Egg (1 large)
Granulated white sugar (1½ cups)
Confectioners' sugar (½ cup)

Shopping List:

Whole watermelon, in perfect condition (1 medium)
4 or 5 kinds of fruit for stuffing the

Shopping List (continued):

melon, according to season, a variety of shapes and colors to contrast with the watermelon's pink, enough to provide about 1 pt. of each when prepared, including perhaps: apricots, Bartlett pears, Bing cherries, nectarines, peaches, pineapple, etc.

Lemon sherbet for contrast, or alternative color (1½ pts.)

Freshly squeezed orange juice (¾ cup)

Fresh mint (small bunch)

Early on the Morning of the Day

Cut the watermelon lengthwise, but not exactly in the center, so that the better-looking half will be bigger than the other. The bigger half is the one to be used. Cut a small slice off its bottom to make sure it stands straight and true. Get rid of seeds, then, with a melon-ball scooper of appropriate size, cut out flesh in balls, leaving a reasonably thick wall. Smooth inside and cover with waxed paper. Put back melon balls, cover with more waxed paper, and refrigerate until needed.

Into a heavy pan, put the 1½ cups of granulated sugar with the ¾ cup of orange juice and boil fairly hard for about 5 minutes, until syrup just coats spoon. Let cool. Prepare the fruits, peeling, stoning, and cutting them as needed, both for appearance and convenience in serving. Lightly coat each piece of fruit with sugar syrup and set all in refrigerator until needed.

A Couple of Hours Before the Guests Arrive

Now comes the opportunity for artistic imagination. Remove balls from watermelon and discard now soggy waxed paper. Neatly line watermelon with aluminum foil, shiny side up. Now set all the fruits, including the balls, into the watermelon, playing the colors for maximum effect. Sometimes we make pie-shaped designs, sometimes circles, sometimes bars, or surrealistic designs. As needed, dribble on more sugar syrup here and there to make everything glisten. Refrigerate again until needed.

About 10 Minutes Before Serving

Separate the egg and use the white to make a modified meringue by beating until it holds a stiff peak, then lightly blending in the ½ cup of confectioners' sugar. Now make a frame for the fruit by putting a line of the lemon sherbet right around the edge of the watermelon. Dab haphazard lumps of the white meringue here and there over the pyramid of fruits, to make it all look as if there had been a sudden snowfall. Stick up a few sprigs of mint at the top center, put on a handsome serving platter, and bring to the table.

A Madrasi Harvest Dinner

MENU

WINES

RASSAM—Spiced Tamarind Juice

MADRASI LAMB OR MUTTON CURRY
WITH FRIED POTATOES

*A good dark beer**

with

MADURAI MIXED VEGETABLES

and

MASSOOR DALL—Indian Orange Lentils
PURIS—Hot Pan-fried Bread
SWEET LEMON-LIME PICKLE
GREEN-TOMATO CHUTNEY

INDIAN ALPHONSE MANGOES

The usual brandies or liqueurs

Darjeeling Tea

* Curry kills the taste of wine, so we serve the beer through the meal.

Dining at Home in South India

In several ways, this is an extraordinary Indian meal, different from anything we have read or tried before. Most authentic Indian recipes (apart from those invented in England by retired Anglo-Indians) come from professional chefs and involve much fancier dishes than would normally be served by an Indian housewife in her home. These recipes have come to us privately from just such a housewife, an expert home cook who lives in Madras and who might serve exactly this meal to a group of friends on a hot summer evening. These dishes differ sharply from the normal North Indian menu. South Indian curries are much gentler; potatoes are served in place of rice; and instead of the usual array of small dishes with various fruits and nuts, two homemade chutneys are served. These should be prepared about a week in advance. Everything else can, and in fact should, be prepared the day before, for the flavors mellow and blend overnight. The *rassam* is a remarkable South Indian specialty, a savory drink with a tart and exciting flavor, which in Madras is often served after the meat course, either hot or cold, sometimes even as a sauce over the vegetables. We prefer it as an ice-cold first-course appetizer and we like it so much that we often prepare it quite apart from the rest of the menu and store it bottled in the refrigerator for continuing use. The Alphonse mangoes are quite different in flavor from our own Hayden mangoes and now are imported from India.✻

Shopping for Indian Ingredients

See the general discussion of Indian foods on page 94. The semi-dry flesh of the tamarind fruit is now available in plastic bags in many fancy-food stores and by mail.✻ Bottled tamarind juice is also beginning to be widely distributed, but it is better to start with the semi-dry tamarind. Rice is by no means the only, or even the principal, starch food in India. There are hundreds of different kinds of dried beans, lentils, and split peas, and each is prepared in dozens of different ways. A few are now available in the United States—including *massoor dall,* which has an excellent flavor and a bright color—by mail order from Indian importers.✻ Indian pappadum wafers are available in fancy-food stores or by mail from Indian importers.✻ Alphonse mangoes are available canned.✻

Planning and Timing

There are simply no problems whatever, since everything is far better if made the day before and carefully reheated.

RASSAM—SPICED TAMARIND JUICE

For a party of 8 to 10

Check Staples:

Very light and clear chicken bouillon (1 pt.)

Aromatics: crystal salt,☆ whole black peppercorns,☆ MSG,☐ whole coriander seed, whole cumin seed, garlic (3 cloves), English dry mustard

Shopping List:

Semi-dry tamarind fruit☆ (4- to 6-oz. bag)

Green pepper (1 medium)

At Least 2 Days Before Serving—Soaking the Tamarind

Measure exactly 1 pint of freshly drawn cold water into a 1-quart mason jar. Pull the tightly packed pieces of tamarind pulp apart (this is very much like undoing a package of dates) and drop into the water, including pits. Screw on lid and refrigerate overnight.

The Following Morning—Preparing the Massala

For the *massala* (the aromatic blend of herbs and spices, freshly pounded in a mortar a few minutes before using) put into the mortar: 4 teaspoons whole coriander, 2 teaspoons whole cumin, 1 teaspoon whole black peppercorns, and 1 teaspoon dry mustard. Pound and rub with the pestle until whole seeds are coarsely cracked, but not powdered, then hold. Pour entire contents of mason jar into a 2-quart saucepan and, with clean fingers, lift out and squeeze tamarind pulp to give up all juice and throw away, with any pits. No need to strain liquid at this point, but it is worth tasting the sharp citrus flavor. Now add: the pint of chicken bouillon, the *massala* from the mortar, the 3 cloves of garlic, finely minced, plus crystal salt and MSG to taste. Bring slowly to simmering heat. Meanwhile quickly dice the green pepper and put into a dry sauté pan with 1 more teaspoon whole cumin seed. Turn on heat to low frying temperature and quickly toast pepper and cumin, stirring continuously, for about 2 minutes, then add to *rassam*. Continue simmering, covered, for about 5 minutes. (With experience, one can weaken or strengthen the flavor of the *rassam* to taste, by simmering for shorter or longer periods.) Let the *rassam* cool slightly, strain through a fine sieve, bottle in screw-top mason jar, and refrigerate until needed. We use this as an essence, diluting it with ice water to taste, before serving it in small glasses, exactly as if it were a tomato juice cocktail.

MADRASI LAMB OR MUTTON CURRY WITH FRIED POTATOES

For a party of 8 to 10

This is a comparatively "cool" curry, containing no pepper at all, with the accent on delicacy and subtlety of flavors and the only "heat" provided by a small amount of ginger. As with all authentic Indian recipes, there is no curry powder or paste, for the Indian cook never relies on a standardized "ready-mix" but blends the separate spices into *massalas* (see preceding recipe), varying them with each dish to control flavor and color. In South India oil is used in place of the clarified butter of the North.

Check Staples:

Clear beef bouillon (3 to 4 cups)
Aromatics—for the first *massala:* whole caraway seed, whole coriander seed, Indian ground ginger; for the second *massala:* whole bay leaves, whole cardamom pods, ground cinnamon, ground clove
Other aromatics added separately: crystal salt, MSG, Mexican chili powder, garlic (about 4 cloves), crystallized ginger (about 2 oz.), ground turmeric
Yellow onions (4 medium)
Watercress (1 bunch)
Olive oil (¼ to ½ cup)
Imported Italian peeled and seeded plum tomatoes (2 lb. 3 oz. can)

Shopping List:

Lean lamb or mutton, preferably cut from the leg (4 lbs.)
Small potatoes (3 lbs.)
Green peppers (2 medium)
Plain yogurt (1 pt.)
Coconut (1 whole, fresh, or prepared coconut chips—1 pkg., about 7 oz.)

The Day Before

Cut meat into bite-size chunks, discarding all fat, and marinate overnight in the pint of yogurt in the refrigerator. Meat need not be fully covered with yogurt, but each piece should be well wetted and all should be stirred around last thing at night and again in the morning.

About 2 Hours Before Serving

Turn meat, with yogurt and juices, into a saucepan, stir in about 2 teaspoons salt, and simmer, covered, until all liquid is absorbed. If not, uncover, and boil strongly for last few minutes. Total time depends on tenderness of meat, usually in 30 to 50 minutes.

Meanwhile prepare the first *massala*. Put into mortar: 2 teaspoons whole caraway seed, 2 teaspoons whole coriander seed, and 2 teaspoons Indian ground ginger. Pound and blend until whole seeds are coarsely cracked. Then hold mixture until needed in a screw-top jar, to avoid evaporation of flavor oils. In the same mortar, put together the second *massala:* 4 whole bay leaves, crumbled, 10 whole cardamom pods, 1 teaspoon ground cinnamon, and 1 teaspoon ground clove. Again pound, then hold in a second screw-top jar. Make ready the other ingredients and hold separately. Peel and thinly slice 2 of the onions. Finely mince the 4 cloves of garlic. Chop the crystallized ginger. Peel potatoes and cut into bite-size cubes. Coarsely dice the 2 green peppers. Wash and coarsely chop the watercress. Put coconut in preheated oven for 15 to 20 minutes, then shell and skin the meat and coarsely grate enough to fill 1/3 cup (or just measure prepared flakes).

About 1 Hour Before Serving

We cover the bottom of our large copper sauté pan with 3 or 4 tablespoons of olive oil, heat to low frying temperature and gently color sliced onions. (All frying in Indian recipes is gentle, to avoid evaporating spice oils.) After a couple of minutes, add potatoes and stir around to coat with oil, adding a little more if needed. Now sprinkle first *massala* over potatoes, carefully blending in. Then sprinkle on separately: the minced garlic, 2 teaspoons chili powder, and 1 teaspoon turmeric. Taste, look and adjust. More chili powder for more bite to the flavor. More turmeric for a richer brown color. When balance seems right, pour on canned tomatoes, plus enough of the beef bouillon to cover potatoes. Simmer, covered, for 10 minutes. Then carefully mix in cooked meat, at the same time tasting and adjusting seasoning by adding crystal salt and MSG. Turn up the heat so that the liquid bubbles merrily and continue cooking, uncovered, until potatoes are just tender, usually in 10 more minutes. By this time, contents of pan should be almost dry. The entire operation can now be held, by turning heat down to keep-warm temperature and replacing lid. Delay actually improves flavor.

About 15 Minutes Before Serving

We usually do the final operation in a large enameled cast-iron cocotte* in which we bring the curry to table. Peel and chop the last two onions. Cover the bottom of the cocotte with 3 or 4 more tablespoons of the olive oil and heat to gentle frying temperature. Put in the chopped onions and, after stirring around for a couple of minutes, blend in the second *massala,* stirring everything around for a couple more minutes to develop flavor, then add in turn: the chopped crystallized ginger, the diced green peppers, the chopped watercress, the grated or flaked coconut. Continue gently frying, blending and coating everything with the *massala* flavors, which now rise out of the pan in a swelling bouquet. Turn the entire contents of the sauté pan into the cocotte and carefully blend everything with a wooden spatula, at the same time turning up the heat, so that any remaining liquid is quickly evaporated and the potatoes fried briskly until they are slightly browned. Then the cocotte is brought piping hot to table.

MADURAI MIXED VEGETABLES

For a party of 8 to 10

Check Staples:

Aromatics: crystal salt,⁑ whole cumin seed, fresh ginger root⁑ (3 tsp. grated) or, if not available, crystallized ginger (about 2 oz.), English dry mustard, ground turmeric
Yellow onion (1 medium)
Watercress (1 bunch)

Shopping List:

Good white cauliflower (2 medium large)
Eggplant (about 2 lbs.)
Green pepper (1 medium)
Plain yogurt (1 pt.)

The Day Before

Break up cauliflower into bite-size flowerets and put into steamer, sprinkling over them about 1 teaspoon of turmeric, which will color them a bright yellow. Steam for about 12 minutes. Meanwhile peel and cut eggplant into bite-size cubes and add to cauliflower at 12-minute mark, continuing to steam until cauliflower is just soft but still chewy. Put the pint of yogurt into a mixing bowl and stir in: 1 teaspoon turmeric, about 2 teaspoons crystal salt to taste, the fresh ginger (grated) or the crystallized ginger (thinly sliced), the water cress leaves, coarsely chopped, then stir vigorously to break up yogurt, and hold. Coarsely dice the 2 green peppers and begin frying lightly in 1 or 2 tablespoons of olive oil in a sauté pan, adding at the same time: 1 teaspoon dry mustard and the yellow onion, fairly finely chopped. Continue to fry, stirring, until the onion is just golden. Now carefully blend in the yogurt mixture, keeping heat hot until it just begins to simmer. By this time vegetables in steamer should be ready, and these too are carefully blended in. Finally, check taste, adding salt and pepper if needed; also check color, adding more turmeric for brighter effect, if desired. Put in covered casserole and refrigerate overnight, for flavors to mellow and blend. Next day, reheat casserole in 350-degree oven for 30 to 40 minutes before serving.

MASSOOR DALL—INDIAN ORANGE LENTILS

For a party of 8 to 10

Check Staples:

Aromatics: whole cumin seed, garlic (2 cloves), English dry mustard, ground turmeric
Yellow onion (1 medium)
Watercress (1 bunch)
Olive oil⊜ (a few Tbs.)

Shopping List:

Indian *massoor dall*☫ (2 lbs.)
Green pepper (1 medium)
Tomatoes (about 6 medium)

The Day Before

In a 4-quart soup pot bring 2 quarts of freshly drawn cold water to a rolling boil. Measure 1 quart of the *massoor dall* and dribble it through the fingers into the boiling water. As soon as it returns to the boil, bring down heat to gentle simmer. Now stir in: 2 teaspoons turmeric, 2 tablespoons of olive oil, the 2 cloves of garlic, finely minced, then cover and simmer until *dall* is just soft but still slightly crunchy, usually in about 15 minutes. The *dall* must not be allowed to mash. Meanwhile prepare aromatic vegetables: peel and chop onion, slice green pepper, coarsely chop watercress leaves, and peel and slice tomatoes. Then, in our large copper sauté pan, we heat up to medium frying temperature a couple of tablespoons of the olive oil and, when it is hot, add: the chopped watercress, 2 teaspoons dry mustard, 1 teaspoon whole cumin seed, the chopped onion, the diced green pepper, stirring and frying until onion is just golden. Now add the sliced tomatoes and when their juice begins to boil, turn down heat so that everything simmers, still stirring, and letting tomatoes mash into sauce, usually in about 5 minutes. By this time *dall* should be done. Drain and blend carefully into sauté pan. When *dall* is thoroughly impregnated with sauce, turn off heat, let cool, put into covered casserole, and refrigerate, covered, overnight. Before serving, reheat casserole in 350-degree oven until *dall* is just hot, usually in about 30 minutes. Do not let cook any longer or *dall* will mash.

INDIAN PURIS—HOT PAN-FRIED BREAD

For 24 to 30 rounds

This is not an essential part of the menu and can be replaced either by normal Western bread or by the ready-made packaged Indian pappadums (thin rounds which only need to be heated to make them crisp and puffy), available in fancy-food stores or by mail from Indian importers.☫ However, these *puris* take only a few minutes to prepare and are a most attractive and authentic part of an Indian meal.

Check Staples:

Ice water (1 cup)
Aromatic: table salt
Indian Besan chick-pea flour (1½ cups)
Granulated instantized flour (1½ cups)
Olive oil (a few Tbs.)
Very clean frying oil (enough to fill frying pan ½ inch deep)

1 or 2 Hours Before Serving—Preparing the Dough

Into a large mixing bowl put the 1½ cups of instantized flour and sift over it the 1½ cups of Indian flour with 2 teaspoons salt. Lightly fold flours together. Sprinkle on 2 tablespoons of the olive oil and start to rub in with clean fingertips, at the same time adding, dash by dash, up to 1 cup of ice water, but less if possible. Dough should be smooth and pliable. Divide into balls each about the size of a plum. Roll out on a lightly floured board to ⅛-inch thickness and cut into roughly 4-inch-diameter rounds with a biscuit cutter or tin lid. Stack with waxed paper between and refrigerate until needed. They can be fried ahead and held in 150-degree (keep-warm) oven, but we prefer to fry them at dinner in view of our guests, and serve hot from the pan, below.

Frying the Puris in 40 Seconds

We set up a picnic table with a burn-proof top across the room from the dining table and use an electric frypan. Fill with absolutely new frying oil to a depth of ½ inch and heat to 375 degrees. Fry each *puri* until puffy and just brown, usually about 20 seconds on each side, putting, of course, as many as frypan will hold. Drain on absorbent paper and serve at once. Do not butter them.

SWEET LEMON-LIME PICKLE

Makes about 1½ pints

These pickles must be made a few days in advance. We often prepare them quite apart from an Indian meal, since they are an excellent accompaniment to many cold meats, birds, and fish.

Check Staples:

Aromatics: crystal salt, whole black peppercorns, whole caraway seed, whole cardamom pods, Mexican chili powder, whole cinnamon stick, whole cloves, whole

Shopping List:

Lemons (about 4)
Limes (about 4)

Check Staples (*continued*):

coriander seed, ground turmeric

Dark-brown sugar (3/4 cup, tightly packed)

About 10 Minutes to Prepare

Wipe the skins of the lemons and limes and cut lengthwise into eighths, removing all pits but leaving skin intact. Prepare the aromatic *massala* that must always be made for an Indian meal by mixing in a mortar: 1½ teaspoons salt, ½ teaspoon whole black peppercorns, 1 teaspoon whole caraway, 8 whole cardamom pods, 1 teaspoon whole coriander, ½ teaspoon whole cloves, then pound and grind with the pestle until whole seeds are coarsely cracked, but not powdered. Then add to mortar and mix in: ½ teaspoon turmeric and 1 teaspoon chili powder, and hold. Now mix everything in a large bowl: the cut fruit, the ¾ cup of brown sugar and the *massala*. After it has all been thoroughly blended, put into pint mason jars, with a 1-inch stick of cinnamon in each, screw on lid tightly and keep in a warm place near the stove for a week. Whenever possible, move them to a spot where they will be warmed by the sun. Shake each jar vigorously once every day. Do not open until the week has elapsed, then shake again and taste. The pickle is done when the fruit skins are quite soft. If not, reseal jars and leave for 2 or 3 days longer. If cinnamon flavor becomes too dominant, remove cinnamon stick. Once "cooking" of pickle is completed, it will keep for several months in the refrigerator but jar should be shaken every 2 days.

GREEN-TOMATO CHUTNEY

Makes about 2 pints

This also should be made a few days in advance, but we often keep a supply of it on hand for general use, quite apart from Indian menus.

Check Staples:

Aromatics: crystal salt,* whole black peppercorns,* MSG, whole caraway seed, whole cardamom pods, Mexican chili powder,* whole stick cinnamon, whole cloves, whole coriander seed, garlic (15 cloves, do not become alarmed, *see* below), fresh ginger root* (4 tsps., grated) or, if not available, crystallized ginger (1/4 lb.)

Dark-brown sugar (1 lb.)

Tarragon white wine vinegar (1½ cups)

Shopping List:

Firm green tomatoes (2 lbs.)

Preparation in About 1½ Hours, Including About 1 Hour of Unsupervised Cooking

This preserve seems to consume garlic without any of it showing at the end. We strongly advise that the full amount of garlic be used. It is hardly evident at all in the finished chutney. The other essential is that the cooking be done in an enamel pan, since the acid is not compatible with metal. Wash, shake dry, and coarsely chunk tomatoes into the pan. Peel the 15 cloves of garlic and finely mince or press over the tomatoes. Finely grate enough fresh ginger to make 4 teaspoons (or finely chop the crystallized ginger) and add, together with the pound of brown sugar, the 1½ cups of vinegar, then stir thoroughly with a wooden spoon and leave to blend while preparing the aromatic *massala*.

Mix in a mortar: 1 tablespoon crystal salt, 1 teaspoon whole black peppercorns, 2 teaspoons whole caraway, 10 whole cardamom pods, 1 teaspoon whole cloves, 2 teaspoons whole coriander, then pound and grind with pestle until whole seeds are coarsely powdered. Then mix in 2 teaspoons chili powder and blend complete *massala* into tomatoes. Now bring pan up to simmering heat, stirring intermittently, and continue cooking, covered, until tomatoes are thoroughly soft, usually in 50 minutes to 1 hour. Stir every few minutes and, once tomatoes begin to get soft, do not be afraid to crush them lightly. When done, turn off heat and let pan cool to room temperature, then put chutney into pint mason jars, with a 1-inch stick of cinnamon in each. Refrigerated, this chutney keeps for several months. If cinnamon flavor tends to become too dominant, remove cinnamon stick.

INDIAN ALPHONSE MANGOES

For a party of 8 to 10

Shopping List:

Indian sliced Alphonse Mangoes✲ (two 30-oz. cans)

Serving at Table

Mango is a fruit which lends itself excellently to canning. The Indian canned mangoes are peeled, sliced, and packed in a very light syrup. We serve them cold in small glass dessert bowls. The aroma and flavor are delicate and subtle. The perfect ending to an unusual menu is provided by this dessert and cups of . . .

DARJEELING TEA

For a general discussion of tea, see page 518.

Hungarian Szent Istvan Dinner

MENU

WINES

CSERESZNYELEVS—Cold Cherry Soup

HALKOCSONYA—Jellied Paprika Carp

A dry white wine from the Somlo district of Hungary, say a Furmint

---

SZEGEDI GULYAS—Pork Goulash of Szeged

A light red from the Egri district, say a Bikaver

VARACK FUJT—Apricot Soufflé

A fine, sweet Tokay

KAVE—Coffee

Barack Pálinka, the apricot liqueur of Hungary

We might offer our guests, before coming to table, a small glass of the powerful Hungarian Slivovitz, but let the soup be a break.

Dinner for an Ancient Magyar Feast

We consider the cuisine of Hungary as among the finest in Europe. It is the land where the strong spices from the East met and were wedded to the subtle finesse of meat and fish cookery from Western Europe. Hungarian food is always dramatic and the gastronomic riches include freshwater fish from the famous Lake Balaton, river fish from the Danube, with beef and pork from the wide plain of the Hortobagy.

Various Hungarian cities are famous for their specialities. Debrecen has its beef goulash and its *kolbas* sausage. There are veal goulashes in the south, and lamb goulashes in the west, but the most unusual is the pork goulash of the old city of Szeged, a remarkable blending of the meat with sauerkraut and potatoes.

Shopping for Hungarian Ingredients

It is essential to use a good medium sweet Hungarian paprika and this can be found in the small Hungarian neighborhood of New York City, where there are several stores that accept mail orders.

Planning and Timing

An elaborate Hungarian menu might contain twenty courses and take a week to prepare. This one is comparatively simple. Soup and fish are made the day before and served cold. The goulash is a one-dish course which is very flexible in timing. The dessert soufflé does require close timing, but the base can be prepared before the guests arrive, then the egg whites beaten and folded in while the fish course is being cleared, and the soufflé goes into the oven as the goulash is served.

CSERESZNYELEVS—COLD CHERRY SOUP

For 8 to 10 people

This is best with fresh sour cherries, but sweet Bing cherries are also good. If canned fruit has to be used out of season, the first choice is the canned "dietetic" unsweetened sour cherries, the second choice the sweet Bing, without the sugary syrup.

Check Staples:

Aromatics: whole cassia buds, whole stick cinnamon, whole cloves
Granulated instantized flour (about 2 Tbs.)
Granulated white sugar (up to 2 cups, depending on sweetness of cherries)

Shopping List:

Sour cherries (3 lbs., pitted)
Heavy cream (about 1½ cups)
A dry red Hungarian wine, say an Egri Kadarka or, if unavailable, a light young Beaujolais (1 bottle)

The Day Before—About 45 Minutes to Prepare

Put the 3 pounds of cherries, with 5 cups of freshly drawn cold water, into a 3-quart saucepan (preferably enameled or tinned copper to avoid interaction with the acid of the fruit) and bring slowly to simmering heat. Add: 2 teaspoons whole cassia buds, 2 teaspoons whole cloves, a 2-inch stick of cinnamon, and enough sugar to make liquid just sweet, but not too sweet, usually about 1½ cups. Cover and simmer until cherries are soft, usually in 20 to 30 minutes. Then pass through a colander, returning liquid to saucepan and leaving cherries and aromatics to cool slightly. In a small mixing bowl put 2 tablespoons of the flour and gradually liquefy it smoothly with a little of the red wine, added dash by dash, usually 4 or 5 tablespoons. Turn on low heat under saucepan and gradually thicken the cherry liquid by carefully stirring in the liquefied flour, until the liquid assumes the consistency of heavy cream. Then bring up heat until it is just below boiling, stirring continuously. If it is now too thick, add a few dashes of wine. If too thin, more liquefied flour. Turn off heat. Pick cherries in colander out from among the aromatics and drop them back into the saucepan. Aromatics are thrown away. Let saucepan come to room temperature, then pour cherry soup into a covered pot and refrigerate overnight. Also, chill remaining red wine and, of course, the cream.

A Few Minutes Before Serving

Thin the soup with the red wine to about the consistency of light cream; this usually requires 1½ to 2 cups of wine. Then stir in about 1 cup of the cream. Now, by adding more wine and cream, a little at a time, carefully balance the flavor, the thickness, and the color. Put back in refrigerator until ready to serve.

HALKOCSONYA—JELLIED PAPRIKA CARP

For a party of 8 to 10

If carp is not available, we prepare this with one of the other whole freshwater fish with lean flesh (see list on page 363). The bright red jelly surrounding the fish makes a handsome show.

Check Staples:

Salt butter (a few Tbs.)
Eggs (4 large)
Aromatics: crystal salt, MSG, Hungarian sweet red paprika
Yellow onions (3 medium)
Dry white wine (1 cup)

Shopping List:

A fine whole carp or other whole fish, *see* above (about 6 lbs.)—fishman should cut fish lengthwise, removing head and backbone, but these should be kept, with 2 or 3 other heads and bones, for the *court-bouillon*
Green peppers (3 medium)
Tomatoes (5 medium)

The Day Before—About 1 Hour to Prepare

To make the *court-bouillon* and simmer the carp, we use a long fish boiler with a removable tray,* which avoids the danger of breaking the fish in lifting it out. However a wide Dutch oven could also be used, or the fish could be cut in half and fitted into a smaller cooking pot. In the bottom gently fry the 3 onions, peeled and chunked, in 2 or 3 tablespoons of the butter. When onions are just turning golden, stir in 1 teaspoon salt, 1 teaspoon MSG, plus 1 tablespoon of the paprika. On this aromatic foundation, lay the well-washed fish heads and bones, add the 1 cup wine, freshly drawn cold water just to cover and bring to simmering. Add 1 of the green peppers and 3 of the tomatoes, both chunked. After a few minutes of simmering, taste and add more salt and MSG as needed. Keep simmering, covered, for about 30 minutes. Meanwhile wash the carp and put the two halves together on the fish boiler tray, ready to be lowered into the *court-bouillon.* After the 30 minutes strain fish heads and bones and all solid aromatics from the *court-bouillon,* returning the now-clear and reddish liquid to the fish boiler. Gently lower the fish into the liquid, which should just cover it, and simmer, "just smiling," until fish is barely cooked, usually in 20 to 30 minutes, according to size.

We serve this dish in a longish oval bowl about 2½ inches deep in which the whole fish can come to table. However a round bowl will also do, but it should be shallow so that the fish can be seen resting in its red jelly. As soon as fish is cooked, lift it out carefully and place it on the serving dish. Now bring the liquid to a boil to reduce and strengthen it, and keep it bubbling hard for about 10 minutes. At the same time balance its flavor and color by adding salt, as needed, plus paprika until liquid is bright red and just slightly peppery. Then clarify it according to our basic method (page 134), strain through 2 or 3 thicknesses of cheesecloth (this removes any last vestige of fat), pour over fish until it is just covered, and let cool to room temperature, then cover bowl with foil and refrigerate overnight.

1 or 2 Hours Before Serving

Prepare the decorations. Hard-boil and slice the 4 eggs. Cut the 2 remaining green peppers into rings. Slice the 2 remaining tomatoes. Decorate the bright red jelly with green pepper rings, slices of hard-boiled egg, and slices of tomato. Keep chilled until the moment it is served.

SZEGEDI GULYAS—PORK GOULASH OF SZEGED

For a party of 8 to 10

Check Staples:

Salt butter (about ¼ lb.)
Aromatics: crystal salt,* freshly ground black pepper,* MSG,* whole caraway seed, Hungarian sweet red paprika*
Italian tomato paste (6-oz. can)
Dry white wine* (about 1 cup)

Shopping List:

Lean fresh pork, cut into 1-inch cubes, perhaps from the shoulder (about 3½ lbs.)
Fluffy boiling potatoes, *see* list, page 367 (about 6 medium)
Wine-cooked sauerkraut* (2 lbs.)
Sour cream, at room temperature (1 qt.)

On the Morning of the Day—Preparation in 30 Minutes, 1½ Hours of Unsupervised Cooking

We prepare this dish in a 5-quart enameled cast-iron cocotte* with a tightly fitting lid. Peel and chop the 6 onions, and gently fry in the bottom of the cocotte in 4 or 5 tablespoons of the butter, until onions are just transparent. Remove onions with slotted spoon and hold in a fair-sized bowl. Melt a few more tablespoons of the butter in the cocotte and lightly brown the pieces of pork, as many at a time as cocotte will hold, transferring them when done to the bowl with the onions. Finally, turn off heat and put all meat and onions back into cocotte. Put into a small mixing bowl: ¾ cup of the dry white wine, the 6-ounce can of tomato paste, 3 teaspoons salt, 2 teaspoons caraway seed, 1 slightly heaped tablespoon of the paprika, then beat together with a small wire whisk and pour over pork. The secret of the flavor is the steaming of the meat in this small amount of liquid. Turn on heat, bring wine in bottom of cocotte to a merry bubbling, and keep it that way, tightly covered, for 30 minutes (set timer). Steam hissing out during this period is a danger signal, indicating that heat is too high and cocotte may be boiling dry. Only if necessary, add ¼ cup more wine.

Meanwhile prepare sauerkraut according to type: sharp, vinegar-boiled sauerkraut needs repeated washings under cold water; the imported German wine-boiled kind, which we use, needs no advance preparation. Peel potatoes and coarsely grate into sauerkraut, loosely blending together. When the timer bell rings, add sauerkraut and potatoes to pork in cocotte, thoroughly blending everything together with a wooden fork and spoon. Bring back to gentle bubbling, replace lid, then simmer for 1 hour longer. At this point, dish can be left standing at room temperature until shortly before needed—or it could be refrigerated and held overnight.

About 45 Minutes Before Serving

The dish must now be at room temperature and so must the sour cream. Preheat oven to 300 degrees and put the cocotte in, covered, to warm goulash through without further cooking, usually in about 25 to 30 minutes.

15 Minutes Before Serving

Take cocotte out of oven and turn up heat to 350 degrees. Carefully blend in with a wooden spoon 1½ cups of the sour cream. Taste and finally adjust seasonings, adding salt, pepper, MSG, or paprika as needed. Put back in oven for exactly 10 minutes, so that cream heats without boiling. This rich and unctuous goulash tastes best when served very hot, so we usually bring it to the table in the cocotte. For a buffet, where service is slower, we often put it in an electric casserole, plugged in on the buffet. At service, an extra dollop of sour cream is placed in the center of each portion. Unlike almost all other goulashes, there is almost no juice with this one and it can be eaten with just a fork.

VARACK FUJT—APRICOT SOUFFLÉ

For a party of 8 to 10

This recipe should be read in conjunction with the one on page 74, where we give our BASIC RULES for soufflés. General instructions for judging the thickness of the *panada*, for beating the egg whites, and for the oven technique are not repeated here.

Check Staples:

Sweet butter (¼ lb.)
Eggs (12 large)
Ground arrowroot (4 Tbs.)
Confectioners' sugar (½ to 1 cup)

Shopping List:

Dried apricot halves (1 lb.)
Walnuts, to be coarsely chopped (enough to fill ¼ cup)
Heavy cream (about ½ cup)
A good sweet Hungarian Tokay (½ bottle)

1 or 2 Hours Beforehand—Advance Preparation

Wash apricots and put into a smallish saucepan in which they just fit; it is best to use a minimum of wine. Add exactly 1 cup of the Tokay and boil gently, covered, until apricots mush, usually in 15 to 20 minutes. Be careful that they do not boil dry and burn. If necessary add a dash or two more wine, but apricots should be almost dry when done. Pass through a food mill, then through a fine sieve, and hold.

Separate the 12 eggs, putting the whites into lemon-rubbed

round copper bowl (page 74) and the yolks into a large mixing bowl. It is best to use separate balloon wire whisks for beating yolks and whites, but if this is not possible, the whisk that has been used for the yolks first must be thoroughly washed with soap and water, completely dried, and rubbed all over with a cut lemon before it is used for the whites. Even a single speck of yolk getting into the whites would ruin the entire soufflé. Start beating yolks, gradually blending in about ½ cup of the sugar (or more for an extra-sweet soufflé) and keep beating until smooth and lemon-colored. Now gradually beat in the sieved apricots and 2 tablespoons of the arrowroot. Lightly butter two 2-quart soufflé dishes. Put into the freezer a small beating bowl and small wire whisk to be ready for beating the cream. Coarsely chop the walnuts. Now everything can be left until the exactly timed point at dinner.

Exactly 45 Minutes Before Serving

Beat the egg whites to the proper stiffness (page 75) and fold quickly into the egg-apricot *panada.* Preheat oven to 325 degrees. Fill both soufflé dishes to within about 1½ inches of the top.

Exactly 35 Minutes Before Serving

Put both soufflé dishes onto lower shelf in oven, with reflectors above them (page 176). Do not open oven door for 25 minutes, then check for perfect doneness (page 177).

2 or 3 Minutes Before Soufflés Come Out of Oven

Whip cream, then, working very fast, decorate soufflé with cream and chopped walnuts and rush to table.

Buffet for a Summer Birthday

July 16 is a doubly important day in our home, for both our girls were born on that date (although three years apart). To avoid disagreement, the rule was that they would take turns, year by year, in choosing the arrangements for the party. The New York City night is usually hot and sticky, creating a lethargy unfavorable to gaiety, but on this occasion Christina had chosen to give a party for a group of foreign summer students newly arrived in the city. It was a difficult party to get going. There were severe language barriers. However much we circulated the cold drinks and canapés, and played soft music, there remained an awkward hush in the room. So we decided to begin serving the buffet supper half an hour earlier than planned.

We switched on the light over the table and brought in our huge blue punch bowl on its matching platter, filled almost to the brim with one of the most dramatic and colorful dishes in our repertoire, an *Okrochka,* the famous main-dish cold vegetable and meat soup of Eastern Europe, the Middle East, and southwestern Russia. The colors, in symmetrical rings, appeared brilliant under the light: on the outside, tiny brown Polish *Kielbasa* sausages, then pink shrimp, the yellow of sliced hard-boiled eggs, the red of tomatoes, white cubes of chicken meat, all resting in the creamy white liquid and linked with the green of parsley, chives, and dill. Immediately, our guests began to gather around it. Lois, the English girl said: "Oh, it's so lovely, it's a shame to spoil it by serving it. How is it made? What does the name Okrochka mean?" Lolita, a blond Latvian doing advanced Russian studies, said it meant "little minced soup." All were amused by the way we served it, in hand bowls with ice cubes. Then they tasted it, and the memories and the anecdotes began. A Polish student, Janak, said: "My mother used to make this in Warsaw, but we call it *chlodnik.*" Ahmed, from Turkey, said, with great firmness: "This is neither an *Okrochka* nor a *chlodnik;* it is a Turkish *cacik.*" "Not at all, it's a Greek *tarata,*" said Dimitrios from Athens. Soon there were strong arguments about the ingredients of the various versions and Claudine, a French girl, was taking down reference books from the shelves and proving that the Turkish *cacik* would have had no meat in it, that the Greek *tarata* would have been heavy with eggplant, and that the Polish *chlodnik* would have been bright red with beets. Then we were going back into history. Did a knight returning from the Crusades bring the Turkish recipe to Greece? Did a Turkish traitor sell the recipe as a state secret to the Polish enemy at the Siege of Vienna? One fact was certain—our party was a success.

OKROCHKA

For a party of 8 to 10

Check Staples:

Eggs (2 large)
Milk (1 pt.)
Aromatics: crystal salt,☆ freshly ground black pepper,☆ MSG,◘ dried fennel seed (if fresh fennel is not available, but the latter is infinitely preferable)
Scallions (1 bunch)

Shopping List:

***Okrochka* is a highly flexible dish and can include all kinds of cooked flaked fish, chunked shellfish or chopped meats. One of our favorites would have:**
Cooked chicken, white meat (2 cups, diced)
Wine-boiled shrimp, page 108 (1 lb.)
Sausages, Polish *Kielbasa* or tiny cocktail frankfurters (1 lb.)
Cucumber (enough for 1 cup, chopped)

Shopping List (continued):

Dill pickles (enough for ½ cup, chopped)
Cherry tomatoes (1-pt. basket)
Fresh fennel, with plenty of green fronds (1 head)
Small bunch each of fresh dill, chives, parsley, tarragon
Plain yogurt (½ pt.)
A fairly dry white wine, say a French Graves (½ bottle)

The Day Before

Okrochka must be refrigerated for at least 12 hours for the vegetables to marinate in the liquids. We choose an open punch bowl so that there is a good surface in view on which to make handsome designs with the meats and garnishes. The appearance of an *Okrochka* is an important part of its enjoyment.

Into the punch bowl we put: ½ cup finely snipped fennel fronds (or 1 tablespoon dried fennel seed), ½ cup finely chopped fennel stalks (if available), ¼ cup chopped fresh dill, 1 tablespoon chopped fresh tarragon leaves, ¼ cup chopped scallion tops, 1 cup diced peeled fresh cucumber, and ½ cup diced dill pickles. In a separate mixing bowl, we beat together with a wire whisk the 1 cup of yogurt, with 1 cup of the milk and ½ cup of the wine. Now begins the important tasting. The liquid should definitely have the tang of the yogurt added to the slight astringency of the wine, all softened by the milk. We don't hesitate to add more wine, but we don't let it override the flavors. At the same time, the crystal salt and the MSG are added and the black pepper is ground over, making everything at this point just a bit too strong, because a good part of the flavors will be absorbed by the vegetables. Then the liquid is poured over the chopped ingredients in the punch bowl, which is covered and refrigerated overnight. A few more jobs are completed: the eggs are hard-boiled, shelled, and refrigerated, covered; the shrimp is boiled (page 108), shelled, and refrigerated, covered; the sausages are boiled briefly and refrigerated, covered.

About 3 Hours Before Serving

We begin by stirring the contents of the punch bowl, and tasting the liquid. We adjust the seasoning and may add, if necessary, an extra dash of milk or wine.

The vegetables will have expanded overnight to form a semi-solid platform on which to make designs with the remaining ingredients. Sometimes we make rings, sometimes pie-shaped segments. The diced white chicken meat is piled in the center. The hard-boiled eggs are sliced and gently laid on to form areas of yellow. The shrimp adds pink, the sausages perhaps an outer ring of brown. The chopped parsley and chives add their green, the tomatoes, halved or quartered, add the red.

Serving at Table

The guests eat it from chilled bowls, with tiny ice cubes in the bottom. *Okrochka* is filling and is much more of a main dish than a soup.

OKROCHKA—A RUSSIAN VARIATION MADE WITH KVAS

There are, of course, many versions in different parts of the Soviet Union, all made roughly in the manner described in the preceding recipe, except for the fact that the Russians use their homemade beer, *Kvas* (recipe follows), in place of the wine. It changes the flavor of the *Okrochka* and is worth the extra time spent on making the *Kvas* about a week ahead. It is also a good drink.

Check Staples:

Indian chick-pea flour or all-purpose flour (1 Tbs.)
Dark-brown sugar (¼ lb.)

Shopping List:

Rye bread, darkest available (1 loaf). In the White Russian neighborhood of New York City, one can get Black Rye, which is best
Dark unsulfured molasses (small bottle)
Yeast (2 envelopes)
White seedless raisins (a handful)
Fresh mint (small bunch)

About 1 Week Ahead—Preparing the Kvas

The bread is sliced and placed on the grid of a 200-degree oven and dried to crisp. The slices are then transferred to a large saucepan, covered with boiling water, and left to soak, with a lid on, for 3 to 4 hours. Then we strain off the liquid through a cheesecloth. In a mortar we pound until smooth: the ¼ cup of dark-brown sugar, the tablespoon of chick-pea flour, the 2 envelopes of yeast, a good handful of mint leaves, and enough dark molasses to make a smooth paste. This is then carefully stirred into the liquid; make sure that it does not settle on the bottom. All is then left severely alone for 12 hours in a warm room, until the start of fermentation is signaled by the bubbles rising to the top.

We used to use corked bottles for our *Kvas*, but the tremendous explosions when the cork accidentally blew out were more than our nerves could stand. So now we collect quart gin bottles with screw tops. Into these is strained and decanted the fermenting liquid, and 4 or 5 raisins are dropped into each bottle before the tops are screwed on very tightly. The bottles stand in the coolest, darkest corner of the house for about a week. Then the *Kvas* is ready for the *Okrochka*.

Informal Party Menus

During the summer months when we are not making a foreign menu for a special occasion, we might entertain with the following:

SUMMER PARTY LUNCH I:
- Iced Avocado Cream, page 274
- Calves' Liver Sautéed in Aromatic Wine, page 570
- Salade La Belle Vaughan, page 613
- Bing Cherries in Armagnac, page 477

SUMMER PARTY LUNCH II:
- Peruvian Seviche—Raw Fish in Lime Juice, page 425
- Poached Eggs on Celeriac Mashed Potatoes, page 543
- Bartlett Pears Stuffed with Roquefort, page 476

SUMMER PARTY LUNCH III:
- Scotch Woodcock, page 264
- Boiled Beef Tongue in Port Wine, page 488
- Okra with Hollandaise, page 474
- Concord Grape Kissel, page 479

SUMMER PARTY LUNCH IV:
- Grilled Zucchini with Sardo Cheese, page 469
- Celia's Shellfish Marinara, page 555
- Jerusalem Artichokes in Cream Sauce, page 462
- Strawberries with Maple Cheese, page 325

SUMMER BUFFET SUPPER:
- Light Watercress Cream, page 426
- Cold Stuffed Veal in Aspic, page 433
- Baked Acorn Squash with Maple Butter, page 155
- Homemade Peach Ice Cream, page 478

SUMMER PARTY DINNER I:
- Wine-Boiled Shrimp in Sauce Rémoulade, page 108
- Sautéed Pork Chops in Ginger Cream, page 436
- Pilaf of Rice, page 166

Green Peas Steamed in a Sauté Pan, page 313
Homemade Rhubarb Sherbet, page 322

SUMMER PARTY DINNER II:
Cream of Carrot Soup, page 564
French Riviera Sea Bass, page 137
White Onions with Burnt Glaze, page 466
Potatoes Mashed with Wine Bouillon, page 471
Lona's Rote Grütze, page 621

SUMMER PARTY DINNER III:
Pissaladière Provençale, page 389
Sauté Pan Chicken with Cognac, page 441
Creamed Sorrel, page 468
El Dorado Plums with Reblochon

SUMMER PARTY DINNER IV:
Iced Broccoli Cream, page 275
Red Carpet Lobster Flamed with Pernod, page 454
Fresh Corn Pudding, page 311
Summer Greens Salad, page 474
Cold Pseudo-Soufflé of Raspberries, page 480

THE FAMILY MEALS OF SUMMER
Day-to-Day Recipes

¶ *Prologues (Appetizers)—Canapés · Hors d'Oeuvres · Zakuski*

OUR SIMPLE TERRINE OF HAM WITH CHICKEN LIVERS

About 30 servings—it keeps for 2 weeks or more

When we boil a Southern country ham (page 369), this is one of the excellent ways to use it cold. We work with a long, narrow, heavy cast-iron *terrine,*✱ handsomely enameled red on the outside and gray inside, which first goes into the oven, then is good-looking enough to come to table and, finally, with its heavy lid is sufficiently airtight for refrigerator storage. The *terrine* is about 11 inches long and produces single portion slices about 3-inches square. The following recipe provides exactly the right amount to fill this *terrine* or a 1¼-quart loaf pan.

Check Staples:

Dark smoked ham, preferably our own boiling (1½ lbs.)
Salt butter (about ¼ lb.)
Eggs (6 large)
Aromatics: crystal salt, freshly ground black pepper, MSG, whole allspice
Dry Sherry (about 1½ cups)
Flour-and-water paste for sealing the lid

Shopping List:

Fresh chicken livers (2½ lbs.)
Fat bacon, to be ground (1 lb.)
Fat bacon slices, to cover top of *terrine* (4 or 5 slices)
White truffles, if pocketbook allows (2), or fresh mushrooms (½ lb.)
Small bunch of: dill, parsley, scallions, watercress
French Cognac (about 1 Tbs.)

The Day Before—Marinating the Chicken Livers

Into a covered pot which will be refrigerated overnight put: the 2½ pounds of chicken livers, lightly rinsed under cold running water; the 2 truffles, sliced (or the ½ pound of mushrooms, wiped clean and sliced) ; 2 teaspoons allspice, coarsely cracked in a mortar; and enough sherry poured over to wet everything. Cover and refrigerate overnight; stir once at bedtime and again in the morning.

The Next Day—Preparation in About ½ Hour, Unsupervised Baking for 2 Hours

Let marinated livers come to room temperature, then dry by dabbing with paper towels. Melt 5 tablespoons of the butter in a sauté pan and lightly fry livers until just stiff, no more. Remove with slotted spoon and, as soon as they are cool enough to handle, trim off all dangling bits from large well-shaped pieces. Large pieces are held whole; small bits will be ground with ham. We attach the fine cutter to our electric meat grinder* and put through the liver bits with the 1½ pounds of ham and the pound of fat bacon, putting ground meats into a large mixing bowl. Separate the 6 eggs and add yolks to meats, reserving whites for some other use. Also add to meats: 2 more teaspoons coarsely cracked allspice, ¼ cup each of coarsely cut dill, parsley,

scallion tops, and watercress leaves, plus salt, pepper, and MSG to taste. Thoroughly mix. This is best done by kneading with clean hands. Preheat oven to 300 degrees.

Butter well inside of *terrine* or loaf pan. Divide ground meats into two equal halves and put first half as even layer on bottom of *terrine,* pressing well down into corners and smoothing top surface with fingers. On this surface now make a second layer of whole chicken livers, fitting them in neatly and keeping them away from sides and ends of *terrine,* so that they will eventually be entirely enclosed by the ground meats. Now fill in spaces between livers with truffle or mushroom slices taken from the marinade and sprinkle over this layer 1 tablespoon of sherry from the marinade and 1 tablespoon of the Cognac. Cover with the second half of the ground meats, pressing firmly down all around the liver layer and into corners, finally smoothing top, which should be level with top of *terrine*. Cover completely wth bacon slices, cutting to fit exactly. Put on *terrine* lid and quickly mix enough flour-and-water paste to seal lid all around. Seal air vent with small blob of dough. Stand *terrine* in tray with 1 inch of water, then slide tray into oven and bake 2 hours.

Let *terrine* cool enough to be handled. We find it easier to get dough off while *terrine* is still reasonably hot and we are careful not to scratch its handsome surface. Place it on sink top, next to cold running water and, with continually rewetted fingers, break and push off chunks of dough. Recalcitrant bits are carefully eased off with back of a stubby knife. Let *terrine* cool to room temperature, remove lid, and discard bacon strips, then replace lid and refrigerate.

Serving at Table

The cold *terrine* can be unmolded and served, decorated, on an open platter, and this is fine if it is all to be used up immediately for a large party. However, keeping it in its lidded mold prevents it drying out. The *terrine* can also be cut up into small squares and put on bits of toast as canapés.

SAVORY HAM CORNUCOPIA

For our family of 4

Another way (see previous recipe) of using cold boiled Southern country ham. Or one can compromise with "ordinary" ham, sliced thickly enough to hold its shape.

Check Staples:

Dark smoked ham (8 slices, well-shaped)
Eggs (2 large)
Aromatics: crystal salt,☧ freshly ground black pepper,☧ English dry mustard, Indian *garam massala*☧
Fresh chives (small bunch)
Watercress (small bunch)

Shopping List:

Large-curd cottage or pot cheese (½ pt.)
Sour cream (½ pt.)
Red salmon-roe caviar (2-oz. jar)
For the decoration: pitted green olives (about ½ dozen), sweet red pimiento (2-oz. jar)

About 10 Minutes to Prepare

Hard-boil the 2 eggs. Slice olives into about 24 rings. Mixing stuffing gives scope for individual taste and judgment. Start with equal parts of cottage cheese and sour cream and the chives and watercress leaf, coarsely chopped; then add, about ½ teaspoon at a time, the English mustard and Indian curry mix, and finally adjust with salt and pepper. Spread mixture on each slice of ham, then carefully roll into cornucopia, put a teaspoon of the red caviar into each open end, and plug with rounds of hard-boiled egg. Decorate top of each cornucopia with olive rings, with bit of red pimiento in the center of each ring.

ITALIAN VITELLO TONNATO—AN ANTIPASTO OF VEAL WITH TUNA MAYONNAISE

Several meals for our family of 4

This extraordinary combination of flavors and textures is served in many parts of Italy as an appetizer or as a luncheon entrée. We often serve this also on a hot evening as a light supper main dish, followed by fruit and cheese. Methods of preparation vary, but we think that roasting the veal separately and then preparing our own tuna mayonnaise makes the most smooth and delicious *vitello tonnato.*

Check Staples:

Eggs (4 large)
Lemons (2)
Aromatics: crystal salt,⁑ freshly ground black pepper,⁑ MSG,⊜ English dry mustard
Green virgin olive oil⊜ (¾ to 1 cup)
Tarragon white wine vinegar⊜ (1 to 2 tsp.)

Shopping List:

Lean milk-fed veal, *see* page 369, best from leg, boned, rolled and tied into a fat sausage (about 2 lbs.)
Tuna fish in pure olive oil; if domestic not available, some good imported Italian brand (7-oz. can)
Flat anchovy fillets (2-oz. can)
Capers (2¼-oz. bottle)

At Any Time Beforehand—Roasting the Veal in About 1 Hour, Unsupervised

Preheat oven to 325 degrees. Set veal on rack standing in roasting pan. Stick meat thermometer into thickest part. Roast to internal temperature of 155 degrees, usually in 30 to 35 minutes per pound. We do not season meat, since it will be dominated by the sauce. Let veal cool to room temperature, then wrap and refrigerate.

At Any Time, in About 10 Minutes

BASIC RULE FOR QUICK AND FOOLPROOF MAYONNAISE: Most failures come from trying to make too little, too quickly. With 1 egg yolk, the proportion of oil rises much too sharply; 2 egg yolks make it easier, but our secret is to start with 3. We separate them into a heavy mortar standing on a damp cloth on a wooden surface, so that the mortar will not slide around even when there is no spare hand to hold it. Have all ingredients ready, as there must be no pause once blending begins. To hold the oil, we use a small Spanish drinking bottle, with a tiny spout in its side which precisely controls the pouring; a 1-cup jug will also do. Measure out 1 cup of the oil, so that one can judge how fast one is using it. Pour a little of the vinegar into a cup, so that it can be spooned in, a 1/4 teaspoon at a time. Also have ready salt, the pepper grinder, the dry mustard, and half a lemon. For stirring, we use a very light boxwood spoon,* about halfway in size between a teaspoon and a tablespoon. Mayonnaise-in-the-making must never be beaten with a whisk, or even stirred violently. It requires a smooth, steady, continuous rotary motion.

Now the fun begins. Sitting in a comfortable chair, this is one of the most soothing and relaxing of kitchen tasks. It also has its moments of excitement when the mixture suddenly begins to thicken and shine. Add to the yolks in the mortar: about 1/2 teaspoon salt, MSG, a few grinds of pepper, and 1 teaspoon of the mustard. Break the yolks and steadily stir for at least 10 to 15 seconds. Holding the oil jug in the left hand and continuously stirring with the right, add oil, drop by drop. Each drop must be fully incorporated before next goes in. After about 1 dozen drops, add 1/4 teaspoon vinegar, and about now the miracle should suddenly happen. It will start thickening and begin to glaze. Now oil can be poured in a steady thin trickle. Do not get excited and stir too quickly. Soon mayonnaise will stand up in the spoon. Not all the oil need be used. Depending on the weather and the quality of the eggs, sometimes 3/4 cup is enough. Taste and cut the richness of the oil with squeeze after squeeze of lemon juice and, if needed, more vinegar, salt, pepper, or mustard. When exactly right in taste and texture, let it rest for as long as it takes to boil a little freshly drawn cold water. Blend exactly 1 tablespoon of the boiling water into the mayonnaise. This ensures that it will not separate even if refrigerated for as long as 2 weeks.

With this method there is so little chance of anything going wrong that it seems tactless to mention the possibility of curdling or separation. Yet, if it should happen, do not scream. Immediately separate the extra egg yolk and drop it into a mixing bowl. Break this new yolk and begin spooning and blending the separated mayonnaise into it, stirring fairly quickly and strongly, until there is a second miracle and the rebellious mayonnaise returns to peaceful normalcy.

When the Mayonnaise Is Ready—Adding the Tuna in About 7 Minutes

BASIC RULE FOR ITALIAN MAIONESE TONNATA: Pound the 7 ounces of tuna in a mortar, then grind through a food mill or rub through a sieve. Put this purée into a mixing bowl and blend mayonnaise into it, tablespoon by tablespoon, until it becomes a spreadable paste. Then blend in lemon juice, squeeze by squeeze, plus salt and pepper if needed, until there is a nice blend of competing flavors. It should be fairly sharp, for this highly flexible sauce will be used to lift other, often bland, foods.

Final Assembly of the Vitello Tonnato—in Hardly More Than a Couple of Minutes

For each person, cut 1 slice of veal about 3 inches across and 1/4 inch thick. Spread on it a fair thickness of the tuna mayonnaise. Neatly place 2 anchovy fillets on top, sprinkle on some capers, plus a few more drops of lemon juice, and serve.

PERUVIAN SEVICHE—RAW FISH IN LIME JUICE

For our family of 4

No one should be put off by the word "raw." The fish is as firmly cooked by the acid of the lime juice as if it had been put under a grill. The strips of fish are white and solid; in fact, the whole dish is solid and should be followed by a fairly light main course, or it could be the main course of a light luncheon or buffet supper. We might serve it on July 28, the National Day of Peru.

Check Staples:

Aromatics: crystal salt,☆ freshly ground black pepper,☆ red cayenne pepper, Hungarian sweet red paprika☆
Olive oil▣ (2 Tbs.)
Crisp buttered toast (to serve with the dish)

Shopping List:

Any firm, white, lean-fleshed fish, *see* list, page 363, filleted and skinned (about 1 lb.)
Small bay scallops, if in season, otherwise omit, (1/2 lb.)
Fresh limes (8 to 12, according to size); lemons may be used as a compromise alternative
Fresh corn (3 ears)
Ripe black olives, pitted (about 1 dozen)
Italian sweet red onions or mild white Spanish or Bermuda onions (3 medium)
Green peppers (2 medium)
Chinese parsley, Italian *cilantro,* or Spanish *culantro*☆ (small bunch); alternatively, but less interesting, fresh dill or watercress
Yams or sweet potatoes (2 medium)

A Day or Two Ahead

We prepare and serve this in a wide china or glass bowl. Wash fish and cut into narrow strips, about 3/8 inch wide and about 1 1/2 inches long, then put into bowl. If small scallops are used, cut in half or slice slightly larger ones, but do not use large sea scallops, which may become tough. Clean peppers, cut into narrow, bite-size strips and add to fish. Peel 2 of the sweet onions, slice absolutely paper-thin, and also add. Blend everything thoroughly with wooden spoon and then begin adding juice from limes, enough barely to cover contents of bowl. Season with a very little black pepper, just a touch of cayenne, and salt to taste. Cover with lid or foil, then refrigerate overnight, or for 2 or 3 days. Stir occasionally. Fish will be magically cooked, firm and opaque.

A Few Hours Before Serving

Cook corn in usual way and, on a chopping block with a sharp and heavy knife, cut each ear crosswise right through the cob in ½-inch-thick slices, so that each is a circle of yellow corn surrounding the cob. Peel and cook the yams or sweet potatoes, then slice them about ⅜ inch thick and trim into decorative triangles. Delicately stir 2 tablespoons of the olive oil into the fish, then add at least part of the third sweet onion, this time mincing it very finely. Taste and add more salt if needed. Decorate with corn circles, yam triangles, olives, a general sprinkling of chopped green herbs, plus a few dashes here and there of red paprika. Hold bowl in refrigerator and serve ice-cold with buttered toast triangles. We usually use a slotted spoon so as not to include too much juice. Peruvian experts usually stick a fork into the cob of each corn round, lift it to the mouth and nibble off the corn around the edge.

¶ *Prologues (Soups)—Creams · Hot · Cold*

These are interchangeable with our spring list (page 271) and again we demand of our hot-weather soups that they be fresh and light. On a sun-broiled day it is always a temptation to serve an ice-cold soup, but we still think that a few spoonfuls of hot soup whet the appetite and give a sense of well-nourished satisfaction.

LIGHT WATERCRESS CREAM

For our family of 4

Check Staples:

Salt butter (about 1 tsp.)
Clear chicken bouillon, entirely without fat (1 pt.)
Eggs (2 large)
Aromatics: crystal salt,☆ freshly ground black pepper,☆ MSG
Fresh chives (small bunch)
Parsley (small bunch)
Green scallions (1 bunch)

Shopping List:

Watercress (4 bunches)
Boiling potatoes (enough for 2 cups, peeled and diced)
Light cream (½ cup)
Clam juice (about 1 pint—two 8-oz. bottles)

About 30 Minutes Before Serving—or Prepare at Any Time Beforehand and Reheat

In a 2½-quart saucepan mix the pint of chicken bouillon and the pint of clam juice and bring to a boil. Meanwhile peel and dice enough of the potatoes to fill 2 cups, coarsely chop 2 bunches of the cress, including most of the stalks, finely chop the white bulbs of the scallions, then add all three to boiling liquid, with salt to taste, usually 1 to 1½ teaspoons. Cover and boil until potatoes are quite mushy, usually in about 15 minutes, then pass entire contents of saucepan through food mill. At this point soup can be held for several hours, or several days.

About 10 Minutes Before Serving

Bring potato-watercress purée up to gentle simmering, keeping heat reasonably low and stirring occasionally to avoid sticking. Hold 4 sprigs of watercress, then finely chop remaining leaves and stir into simmering soup. (It is important that watercress should not be heated too long or it will lose its bright color.) Separate the 2 eggs and beat the yolks with ¼ cup of the cream, then, first turning off heat, blend carefully into soup. Now gently reheat, stirring continuously, but do not let boil. At same time, taste for seasoning, adding pepper, MSG, and, if needed, more salt. If soup becomes slightly too thick, add a little more cream. Serve in piping-hot bowls, with a neat sprig of watercress floating on top of soup and surface sprinkled with finely chopped parsley and chives.

COLD CUCUMBER CREAM

For our family of 4

Check Staples:

Salt butter (3 or 4 Tbs.)
Clear chicken bouillon, entirely without fat (1 qt.)
Aromatics: crystal salt,⚘ freshly ground black pepper,⚘ MSG▣
Fresh chives (small bunch)
Yellow onion (1 medium)
Granulated instantized flour▣ (3 or 4 Tbs.)

Shopping List:

Cucumbers (6 medium)
Light cream (½ cup)
Fresh dill (small bunch)

Prepare at Any Time in About 30 Minutes

We cook this in our large copper sauté pan, which has a lid. In it we melt just enough of the butter to cover the bottom, say 3 to 4 tablespoons, according to the size of the pan, heating it slowly to medium frying temperature. Quickly peel the 6 cucumbers, thinly slicing them into the hot butter, then adding the onion, finely minced. Stir around with a wooden spoon to coat all slices with butter, then let sauté gently, uncovered, until cucumber is soft, usually in about 10 minutes. Now thinly sprinkle flour over everything, 1 tablespoon at a time, carefully blending in each spoonful before adding more and continuing until all remaining butter is absorbed into the *roux*. This usually requires 3 to 4 tablespoons of flour. Now turn up heat and start adding chicken bouillon, in single dashes at first, carefully blending in each dash and letting it come to a boil before adding the next, to make sure that the *roux* is smoothly liquefied. No matter now if the cucumber begins to break up, since it will shortly be puréed. After about the first cup of the chicken bouillon has been added slowly, the rest can be added all at once and heated to gentle simmering. Taste and add salt, pepper, and MSG, as needed. Let simmer and thicken, covered, but stirring every 5 minutes or so, for about 10 minutes. Then purée through food mill (or in electric blender), store in covered pot and refrigerate until needed.

Just Before Serving

Finely chop chives and dill. Thin down and smooth the soup with the cream, using more or less to achieve the right thickness. Taste and finally adjust seasonings. Serve ice-cold, with chives and dill sprinkled on top.

CREAM OF SUMMER CORN

For our family of 4

In summer, of course, we prepare this with fresh corn, scraping the whole niblets from the corncob with our special corn scraper.* However, it can also be made with canned whole niblet corn. The essential trick is to put it through the food mill as many times as may be needed to get it absolutely smooth and to eliminate every trace of the husks.

Check Staples:

Salt butter (2 or 3 Tbs.)
Clear chicken bouillon, entirely without fat (about 1 pt.)
Milk (1 pt.)
Aromatics: crystal salt,* freshly ground black pepper,* MSG,* Hungarian sweet red paprika*

Shopping List:

Fresh corn (enough for about 2 cups scraped niblets, usually 4 or 5 medium ears), or whole niblets (1-lb. can)
Light cream (½ cup)

Preparing in About 10 Minutes—Plus 30 Minutes of Unsupervised Cooking

Scrape fresh corn by one method or another, as described on page 311. Put corn in a 3-quart saucepan, season fairly heavily with salt, lightly with pepper and MSG, add enough of the milk to cover and gently simmer, covered, for about 30 minutes. Check once or twice, stir and add more milk, if needed, to keep corn covered. When corn is very soft, pass everything through a food mill at least twice (and possibly even three times) until soup is a thick, smooth purée. Now we put this back into the saucepan over gentle heat and use our judgment in blending in the remaining ingredients, with more seasonings, as needed, until we achieve the right consistency and flavor: melting in the butter, adding, dash by dash in turn, the chicken bouillon, more milk and part of the cream. Serve hot, with a dusting of paprika on top, for color contrast.

ROGER CHAUVERON'S BILLI-BI—HOT OR COLD MUSSEL SOUP

For our family of 4

Roger Chauveron, who has organized some of the best restaurants in New York City, is also a good cook and a loyal son of the French district of Périgord. He claims that this dish with the extraordinary name is native to his home. However, Normandy also claims it and it is a specialty of restaurants in the city of Rouen. It is a rich and solid first course and is best followed by a light main dish. Or it could itself be the main course for a light lunch or supper.

Check Staples:

Salt butter (2 or 3 Tbs.)
Eggs (4 large)
Aromatics: crystal salt, freshly ground black pepper, red cayenne pepper, MSG, whole bay leaf, garlic (2 cloves), thyme
Yellow onion (1 medium)
Parsley (small bunch)
Shallots (4 or 5 cloves)
All-purpose flour (a couple of handfuls)
Dry white wine (about 2 cups)

Shopping List:

Fresh mussels in their shells (3 lbs.)
Heavy cream (1 pt.)
White celery (1 heart)
Sorrel, sometimes called sourgrass, *see* list, page 367 (enough to fill ½ cup, chopped)
A dry Muscadet wine from the Loire Valley (1 bottle)

Prepare at Any Time in About 30 Minutes

Prepare and steam the mussels according to our BASIC RULE (page 196). Remove from shells and hold, throwing away shells. Strain wine in which they were steamed (now rich with their juices) through a double thickness of cheesecloth and hold. These are the foundation ingredients of the dish. Finely shred the sorrel and let it simmer, covered, in a small saucepan with about 1 tablespoon of the butter, until it is quite soft, usually in 5 to 10 minutes. Stir it once or twice and add more butter if it gets dry. Separate the 4 eggs, storing the whites for some other use, then beat yolks into the pint of cream. Combine this with the mussel liquor in a 2-quart saucepan and heat slowly, stirring continuously and scraping sides and bottom with a wooden spoon, until it all thickens. Do not under any circumstance let it boil. Now blend in the cooked sorrel, together with any butter surrounding it, then taste and season, as needed, with salt and black pepper and a very little cayenne. While soup is kept hot, but well below boiling, quickly pick through mussels and, with kitchen scissors, trim off any dark edges, and drop mussels into soup. Allow them to heat for 1 or 2 minutes, but no longer or they will toughen. At the same time, check the thickness of the soup and, if needed, thin with a dash or two more wine. The *Billi-Bi* may now be served at once, piping hot, or allowed to cool, then refrigerated and served cold later.

¶ *Main Dishes (Meat)—Veal · Pork Chops · Boiled Ham*

Some lucky summer cooks have air-conditioned kitchens. Others cook in a breeze-cooled kitchen overlooking a beach. We are not so fortunate. We battle 90-degree New York heat waves in our postage-stamp-size city kitchen and one of our most useful weapons is the sauté pan. The tin-lined copper pan with straight sides, a long handle, and a well-fitting lid can cook a main dish on top of the stove with far less radiation of heat than either the oven or the grill. A sauté of meat (recipes follow) or chicken (page 441) or fish (page 449) is almost always quick and simple. Whether it is also very good depends on perfect attention to the details. One of the basic rules in using a sauté pan is that the bottom of the pan must always be fully covered by the food being cooked. One cannot sauté 2 chops in a pan designed for 4 or 6. If part of the bottom of the pan is left uncovered by the food, that part will overheat and the sauce will burn. The answer is to have 2 or 3 sauté pans* of different sizes. We begin with our favorite summer meat, veal (see shopping notes, page 368).

SAUTÉ PAN VEAL SCALOPPINI WITH TALEGGIO CHEESE

For our family of 4

There must be hundreds of ways of preparing a thinly pounded slice of veal (usually cut from the leg): the *escalopes* of Paris, the veal birds of London, the *Schnitzel* of Vienna, the *zrazniki* of Warsaw, and the inevitable *scaloppini* of any Italian menu. Since the veal is slightly bland, it is almost always served either smothered by a savory sauce or fried in an aromatic batter or rolled around a dominant stuffing. We have tried many of the recipes; this is the one to which we return most often. The taleggio is a wonderfully rich and aromatic softish cheese made from the milk of cows which graze on mountain slopes of the northern Italian district of Lombardy, especially around the resort town of Bergamo.

Check Staples:

Salt butter (about 1/4 lb.)
Dark smoked country ham, preferably our home-boiled kind, page 369 (four 1/4-inch-thick slices, each 3 x 3 inches)
Lemons, for garnish (2)
Aromatics: crystal salt, freshly ground black pepper, garlic
Parsley (small bunch)
Indian chick-pea flour or all-purpose flour (about 1/2 cup)
Dry white wine (about 1 cup)

Shopping List:

Dairy-bred veal, *see* shopping notes, page 368 (8 thin slices for *scaloppini,* each of about 4 x 4 inches, either pounded thin by the butcher or with a toothed meat hammer at home)
Italian taleggio cheese (four 1/4-inch-thick slices, each 3 x 3 inches, total usually between 6 oz. and 1/2 lb.)
Italian white truffle, if pocketbook allows (1 medium); as an alternative, fresh mushrooms (3 or 4 medium)

About 30 Minutes Before Serving

With a little practice, the preparation of this dish is a fast breeze. Slice 2 lemons for garnish. Spread the 1/2 cup flour on a soup plate and mix well with it 1 teaspoon salt, plus pepper to taste. Flatten out 4 slices of veal on heavy chopping board. Slice ham and lay 1 slice on top of each slice of veal. Trim ham to exact size so that about 1 inch of veal shows all around. Thinly slice truffle and distribute on top of ham (if mushrooms are used, slice and sauté for 1 or 2 minutes in butter with minced garlic, before distributing on ham). Slice taleggio and lay on top, trimming exactly to fit ham. Now cover completely with spare slice of veal, fitting edges exactly, then pound all around the edge with small hammer or the blunt back edge of a heavy knife, so that each pair of veal slices is sealed all around. The final result should be 4 fat, stuffed cushions. Put 4 tablespoons of the butter into the sauté pan and make it very hot, without allowing it to burn. Meanwhile lift each veal cushion carefully, holding at both edges, then thoroughly dredge with seasoned flour. When butter is hot, quickly brown veal cushions on both sides, usually in about 2 minutes per side. Turn heat down to simmering temperature and add a dash of the wine. When violent hissing subsides, add the full cup of wine and keep it bubbling merrily so that it reduces and concentrates the flavor of the sauce while steaming the veal cushions. Turn each cushion every 5 minutes and continue bubbling, uncovered, until cheese is thoroughly melted inside. This can be tested by poking top with finger, to feel whether cushion is softly resilient, usually in 10 to 15 minutes. Meanwhile chop the parsley, turn on oven to keep-warm temperature (150 degrees) and heat up a flat serving platter. When veal cushions are done, lift carefully with slotted spatula, place on platter, and keep in oven for 1 or 2 minutes while sauce in sauté pan is bubbled hard, stirring continuously, until it shows the first sign of thickening. Then at once melt 2 or 3 tablespoons of the remaining butter, to taste, into the sauce, and pour over veal cushions. Garnish with lemon and parsley and serve at once.

SAUTÉ PAN VEAL CHOPS

For our family of 4

We usually buy what our butcher calls a "rack" of rib chops, a solid joint about 8 to 12 chops long. He just chops through each connecting bone, so that it takes us only a second or two to cut off each chop as we need it. Veal chops are cheaper to buy in this way and the meat keeps fresher in the solid chunk. The essential trick in this method of preparation is in the French way of "buttering" the sauce at the last moment.

Check Staples:

Salt butter, for frying (3 or 4 Tbs.)
Sweet butter, for sauce (4 Tbs.)
Lemon (1)
Aromatics: crystal salt, freshly ground black pepper
Parsley (small bunch)
Indian chick-pea flour or all-purpose flour (about 1/4 cup)
Dry vermouth (about 1/2 cup)

Shopping List:

Dairy-bred veal rib chops, ***see*** **shopping notes, page 368 (4, each about 1 inch thick)**

About 50 Minutes Before Serving

Keep the solid chunk of sweet butter in coldest part of refrigerator, as it must be quite cold when used at the last minute. Spread the 1/4 cup of flour on a soup plate and mix with it about 1/2 teaspoon salt and pepper to taste. Cut and trim chops, wipe dry and clean with paper towels, then dredge thoroughly with seasoned flour. Put 3 tablespoons of the salt butter into the sauté pan and fry until very hot but not burning or smoking. Quickly brown chops—usually it takes about 3 minutes on each side—adding more butter if needed. Reduce heat to simmering, cover pan, then let chops steam in their own juices until done, turning about every 10 minutes. They are done when fork-soft, usually in 30 to 35 minutes. Meanwhile turn on oven to keep-warm temperature (150 degrees) and heat up flat serving platter. Chop parsley for garnish. When chops are done, lift with slotted spatula, place on platter and keep warm in oven while sauce is prepared. Add about 3 ounces of the dry vermouth to the pan, turning up heat so that sauce bubbles briskly to reduce and concentrate flavors. Stir with wooden spoon, scraping bottom of pan to loosen and blend in aromatic bits of crust. When sauce shows first signs of thickening, usually in 3 to 4 minutes, add the juice of half a lemon, stir again, turn down heat to gentle simmering, and leave uncovered while preparing the sweet butter.

Just Before Serving

BASIC RULE FOR BUTTERING A SAUCE AS THEY DO IT IN FRANCE: Half fill a small mixing bowl with ice cubes or coarsely crushed ice. Place the ice-cold solid chunk of sweet butter on cutting board and cut thinly into slices, dropping each immediately onto the ice. Taste sauce in pan, adding more seasonings and a little more dry vermouth if needed. Now place iced butter on stove immediately to right of pan and hold small fork in right hand. Hold handle of sauté pan in left hand. Working fast, lift butter slices, one by one, with fork and float them all over surface of sauce. At the same time, lift pan with left hand about 1/4 inch above flame and swirl pan gently so that butter moves around in circles. In this way butter melts more slowly than if it were stirred in and forms thin layer on surface of sauce. As soon as all butter slices are in pan and even before it has all melted, while there are still tiny solid lumps floating around, and without again stirring the sauce, pour over the meat, garnish with chopped parsley and serve at once. This method of finishing a sauce adds the natural flavor of fresh butter, so only best quality sweet butter should be used.

COLD STUFFED VEAL IN ASPIC

Several meals for our family of 4

This is one of the most practical ways of spicing and serving a piece of veal cold. The aspic protects it, keeping it fresh and moist for several days in the refrigerator, ready to be sliced for summer cold plates or for picnic sandwiches. The key to success lies in persuading the butcher to provide exactly the right-sized piece of meat, evenly cut to a neat rectangle. He then cuts it in half horizontally and the layer of stuffing goes in the center, in the manner of a huge sandwich. It is cooked wrapped in a large piece of cheesecloth.

Check Staples:

Aromatics: crystal salt,☆ whole black peppercorns,☆ MSG,◘ whole allspice, whole bay leaves, whole cloves, garlic (2 or 3 cloves, according to taste), mace chips, sweet marjoram, thyme
Carrots (2 medium)
Yellow onions (2 or 3 medium)
Parsley (1 bunch)
Shallots☆ (4)
Watercress (1 bunch)
Brandy◊ (about ½ cup)
Dry Sherry◊ (about ½ cup)

Shopping List:

Veal rump, entirely lean and boneless (a square-cut box-shaped piece, about 12 inches long, 7 inches wide, and 5 inches thick; then cut in half horizontally by the butcher to give 2 pieces, each about 2½ inches thick)
Ground lean veal (1 lb.)
Ground bacon (½ lb.)
Italian salami sausage (½ lb., in 1 piece)
Veal knuckle, with some meat on it (1)
White truffles, if pocketbook allows —optional (2 small)
Leeks (2 medium)

2 Days Before—Preparing the Meats in About 30 Minutes

Using our heaviest chopping block and the meat hammer with the metal teeth,* we pound the slabs of veal until they are soft and pliable. Both pieces will get wider and thinner, but should be pounded in a way to keep them equal in size and shape. Put them in a fairly shallow dish, with a cover, in which they will marinate for the night in the refrigerator. Dice the salami sausage into large cubes and distribute these around veal in dish. Add: about 1 tablespoon whole allspice seeds, 2 bay leaves, crumbled, ½ teaspoon whole black peppercorns, salt to taste, then, if the truffles are being used, tuck them, still whole, in among the meats, to work their special flavor-magic. Pour over all the ½ cup each of brandy and Sherry, then cover and refrigerate overnight.

There is one other advance job. Slowly work together in a large bowl the pound of ground veal and ½ pound of ground bacon. At the same time work into it: a small handful of the parsley, finely chopped; the 3 or 4 shallots, peeled and finely minced; salt, freshly ground black pepper, and MSG to taste. Work it thoroughly, then cover and let it mature in the refrigerator overnight.

The Following Day—Preparation Before the Cooking in About 30 Minutes

Spread on the worktable a large piece of cheesecloth, folded double or more so that the final size is a square about 24 inches each way. Take the first slab of veal out of the marinade, carefully removing all adhering aromatics, then lay it in the exact center of the cheesecloth. The diced salami is also picked out of the marinade and added to the ground veal and bacon, together with the truffles, finely chopped. The remaining unabsorbed brandy and Sherry are drained off the marinade and are added, dash by dash, to the ground meat as the salami is worked in, until it is all quite smooth and reasonably soft. Not all the liquid may be needed to achieve this result. Do not let stuffing become mushy. Now spread stuffing, in an even, tight layer, on top of the slab of veal on the cheesecloth. Then place on top the second slab of veal, also disengaging it from its adhering aromatics. See that everything is neat, even, and firm, then bring the cheesecloth up around it, like the wrapping paper of a parcel. Tie it tightly in several places with strong string, both crosswise and lengthwise.

The Cooking, in About 2½ Hours, Relatively Unsupervised

This operation requires our largest pot, which holds about 10 quarts; the veal package can rest flat in it, with room to maneuver around it. But do not put the veal in yet. First prepare the spiced bouillon. Bring about 3 quarts of freshly drawn cold water to a boil in the pot and, as it is warming up, add: the pieces of veal knuckle; the 2 leeks, well washed; the 3 or 4 onions, peeled and each stuck with a pair of cloves; the 2 carrots, scraped and chunked; the 2 or 3 cloves of garlic, chopped; 1 teaspoon each of thyme and marjoram; a small handful of chopped parsley; 2 or 3 whole bay leaves, ½ teaspoon whole black peppercorns, ½ teaspoon mace chips, plus salt and MSG to taste. Let all this bubble merrily for about 10 minutes, to bring out the aromatic oils, then carefully lower the veal package into it, using a wooden spoon to clear a space, so that the package rests level on the bottom, covered by liquid. If necessary, add more boiling water. When pot returns to boil, lower heat to gentlest simmering, "just smiling" (this is absolutely essential or the veal will break up), cover and see that it remains "just smiling" for 2 hours.

Carefully lift out veal package and place on a board, drain, and cool. We lay on top our heaviest chopping block (a 6-inch section of a tree trunk) to press the veal sandwich down solid and tight. Meanwhile boil up bouillon in pot and let bubble hard for a few minutes to reduce and concentrate it. Then strain, clarify according to our basic method (page 134), and let cool.

Final Assembly in the Aspic

We choose a square mold or a loaf pan just large enough for the veal sandwich to fit in with about ½ inch to spare all around. Cut 8 rounds of carrot, each exactly ⅛ inch thick, and place evenly on bottom of pan as a pedestal on which veal will stand. Carefully unwrap the veal and place on carrots in pan. If bouillon has already jelled by this time, reheat to liquefy, then pour enough around the veal just to cover. Cover with foil and set in refrigerator for a few hours, or preferably overnight. Carefully scrape off the layer of fat that will have formed on top and unmold in the usual way (page 394) onto a flat serving platter. Decorate with sprigs of watercress on top and around base. We usually store it by reversing it back into its mold, where it will keep in perfect condition, refrigerated, for many days. It can then be treated as a *terrine* and later slices can be cut without again unmolding it. It is a most excellent standby to have available in summer or at any time of the year.

SAUTÉ PAN PORK CHOPS IN GINGER CREAM

For our family of 4

Check Staples:

Clear beef bouillon (1 pt.)
Salt butter (2 Tbs.)
Aromatics: crystal salt, freshly ground black pepper, MSG, whole caraway seed, garlic (2 cloves), fresh ginger root (1 tsp., grated) or, if unavailable, Indian ground ginger, sweet marjoram, English dry mustard, oregano, rosemary, Worcestershire sauce
Green scallions (1 bunch)
Indian chick-pea flour or all-purpose flour (about 2 Tbs.)
Olive oil (1 or 2 Tbs.)
Italian tomato paste (1 or 2 Tbs.)

Shopping List:

Lean pork chops (4, each about ¾ inch thick)
Sour cream (1 pt.)
Dill pickles (3 medium)

About 1 Hour Before Serving—Preparing the Sauce

Coarsely chop green scallions, both stalks and bulbs, then hold. Chop the 3 dill pickles fairly fine and hold. Peel and grate the fresh ginger root, then hold in a small covered jar (if not available, we use more of the powdered ginger). Put the pint sour cream into a medium-sized mixing bowl and add: 1 tablespoon of the tomato paste, the 2 cloves garlic, mashed, 2 teaspoons dry mustard, the chopped dill pickles, 2 teaspoons Worcestershire sauce, the grated fresh ginger and ½ teaspoon powdered ginger (or 1½ teaspoons powdered ginger alone), ¼ teaspoon rosemary, ¼ teaspoon sweet marjoram, ¼ teaspoon oregano, ½ teaspoon caraway seed, plus salt, pepper, and MSG to taste. When all has been blended and tasted again, a little more tomato paste may be added if needed.

About 45 Minutes Before Serving—Sautéing the Chops

We use a tin-lined copper sauté pan with a fairly tight-fitting lid. (The 4 chops just fill it—see note on page 430.) Put into the pan just enough of the olive oil to moisten its bottom, usually 1 or 2 tablespoons. Lay the chops out on a board and pound into each side of them with the heel of the hand some salt, pepper, oregano, and whole caraway seed. Then quickly sauté chops in the oil until nicely browned —it usually takes about 6 minutes on each side. Preheat oven to keep-warm temperature (about 150 degrees) and heat up the open platter on which chops will be served. As soon as chops are brown, place on platter and keep warm in the oven while sauce is assembled.

About 30 Minutes Before Serving—Saucing and Steaming the Chops

Quickly melt into the hot sauté-pan juices the 2 tablespoons of butter and add the minced scallions, sautéing until just beginning to turn brown. Sprinkle on and smoothly blend in, a single tablespoon at a time, enough chick-pea (or all-purpose) flour just to absorb the liquid fat, usually about 2 tablespoons, a little more or less. Now liquefy this *roux* with about ¼ cup of the beef bouillon. Next, begin working in, 1 tablespoon at a time, the spiced sour-cream mixture, until it is all incorporated. If sauce now seems too thick, it can be thinned to consistency of very heavy cream with a little more of the beef bouillon. As sauce begins to bubble turn down heat, so that cream remains always at a gentle simmer. Now put chops back in pan, embedding them deeply into sauce and covering them completely with it. Keep everything gently simmering, covered, until chops are very soft, usually in about 30 minutes. Sauce generally thickens and clots and is spread over the chops on the serving platter. We sometimes place a slice of orange on top of each chop for decoration.

BASIC METHOD FOR BOILING A HAM

For a 16-pound ham

At least once or twice each summer we order a Southern ham (see shopping notes, page 369). It must first be treated according to the instructions of its producers. Some need washing and scrubbing to remove the surface crusts from the smokehouse and aging. Others need soaking overnight in cold water. Do not be disturbed by the look of the black pepper, which is usually pounded into the surface. Such hams range in size from 12 to 20 pounds, but we never have any difficulty in using them up. Here is the first sequence for boiling, glazing, and serving as the principal course. Then we list the recipes in which the cold ham is used in other ways. The flavor of a ham home-boiled in this way is unique. It simply cannot be bought in a store.

Check Staples:

Aromatics: whole allspice, whole bay leaves, whole cloves

Pure maple syrup (½ cup); or, as a second choice, the same amount of honey or brown sugar

Shopping List:

Whole Smithfield or country ham, uncooked (from 12 to 20 lbs., according to need)

Spanish dry Sherry (1 bottle)

At Least 24 Hours Before Ham Is Needed

This operation requires one piece of special kitchen equipment, a very large and deep oval pan known as a "ham-boiler,"* in which the ham lies flat on its back. We think every family should own one. Apart from its ham-boiling function, ours is used occasionally for preparing enormous quantities of stew for very large parties, but for the rest of the time (since it is too large to "put away") it doubles as a wastebasket next to the typewriter at the desk. After ham has been prepared according to maker's instructions, it is laid, skin side down, on bottom of ham-boiler, which, in our case, spreads over two burners of the stove. Thoroughly moisten ham by dribbling all over it about ⅓ of the bottle of Sherry; allow it to soak for 5 minutes. Then dribble on next ⅓ of the Sherry and let it soak 5 minutes more. Then add the remaining Sherry and again leave it alone for 5 minutes. Now moisten ham with the ½ cup maple syrup (or alternative) and let it soak for 15 minutes. During this wait, throw in the aromatics: 2 teaspoons whole allspice, 5 whole bay leaves, 2 teaspoons whole clove. After the 15 minutes are up, turn burners on high and run in freshly drawn cold water—at side of ham so as not to disturb the syrup on top—until the level of liquid is about ¾ of the way up the ham. Heat up to gentle simmering, then at once run in more cold water, again at the side, until the liquid gently laps over ham and rises to about ½ inch above it. Continue with heat full on until it returns to gentle simmering. It is absolutely vital that the liquid should not bubble at any time but should gently simmer, "just smiling." With such a large quantity of water, the heat will have to be turned down slightly several times. Cover and keep simmering gently for a total time calculated at 20 minutes per pound: for example, 5 hours 20 minutes for a 16-pound ham. Then turn off the heat and let it cool in the liquid for at least 12 hours, preferably 24. It is during the cooling process that the ham absorbs the aromatic flavors.

Finally, carefully remove ham from pan, set on a large board to drain and, with small sharp knife, remove skin, exposing the dome of white fat, which will be decorated and glazed (see method following).

Some cooks suggest that the water in which the ham was boiled can be used for soups, stews, etc. We do not agree. If the flavor of the water is strong enough to impregnate the ham, it is invariably too strong for separate consumption. This is one of the basic principles of cookery. Our ham-water is cloyingly sweet and powerfully spiced; very good for the ham but then it must be thrown away.

BASIC METHOD FOR DECORATING AND GLAZING A BOILED HAM

For a 16-pound ham

It is always difficult to decide whether the ham should be served hot or cold the first day. We think the flavor of a Southern country ham is better cold, so we put it in the oven only long enough to brown and crisp the coating of fat and to give it the shiny glaze, which makes it look attractive and helps to sharpen and frame the flavor.

Check Staples:

Aromatics: large number of whole cloves, all with good round heads; Tabasco

Shopping List:

German Düsseldorf mustard, (½ cup)
Dark unsulfured molasses (½ cup)
Orange curaçao liqueur (¼ to ½ cup)

About 1 Hour Before the Ham Is Needed

Preheat oven to 425 degrees. Using a small, sharp-pointed knife, score the dome of fat around the ham with diagonal straight lines, about 1 inch apart, both ways, so that crisscross cuts make a diamond pattern. In center of each diamond, insert 1 whole clove with a good round head on it. Set ham in hot oven and leave until fat is slightly brown and cuts made with knife have opened up. This usually takes 20 to 30 minutes. During this period, baste thoroughly several times with plenty of curaçao. Meanwhile mix in bowl: the ½ cup of mustard, the ½ cup of molasses, and ½ teaspoon Tabasco. As soon as surface effect is achieved on ham, turn oven setting down to 350 degrees, take out ham and ladle glaze mixture thickly over top surface. Some glaze will run off into pan, but a thick coating should remain. Put back into oven and leave until glazed surface is set and very shiny, usually in about 20 minutes. We then let ham cool again and, if necessary, refrigerate until needed.

BASIC RULES FOR CARVING A COLD HAM: There are two schools as to the carving of ham. The first method suggests that a single deep cut be made, right down to the bone, across the ham at its central thickest point. V-shaped slices are then removed from either side of the first cut and, gradually, this opening is enlarged in both directions. We prefer the second method, the French way, which is much more thrifty and makes better use of all sections of the ham. Using napkin in the left hand, hold the shank bone as if it were a handle and start slicing the small pieces at the tip of the shank end. The first cuts will be a little dry and small, but after an inch or two the lean meat opens out and then one continues cutting in the same direction right through the ham, the best center cuts being used simultaneously with the less desirable outside cuts.

OTHER USES FOR THE COLD HAM: We grind the ham into a *terrine* of chicken livers (page 420); roll slices of it around aromatic cheese for hors d'oeuvres cornucopia (page 422); combine it with eggs in a *Basque pipérade* (page 461); cut it into a pineapple salad (page 475); bake it in hot biscuits (page 484); and use up the last of it, with the bone and even the skin, in Johanna's gumbo (page 489).

MUSTARD SAUCE FOR HAM

For our family of 4

Check Staples:
Clear beef bouillon (1 cup)
Aromatics: crystal salt,✱ MSG▣
Granulated instantized flour▣ (4 to 5 Tbs.)
Granulated white sugar (3/4 cup)
Tarragon white wine vinegar▣ (1/2 cup)

Shopping List:
German Düsseldorf mustard (1/3 cup)

Preparation in About 30 Minutes, Then 1 Hour to Cool

In 1-quart saucepan mix and bring to a boil: the 1/3 cup of mustard, the cup of bouillon, the 1/2 cup of vinegar, the 3/4 cup of sugar, plus salt and MSG to taste, then carefully stir in 4 tablespoons of the flour. Keep stirring until it almost reaches a boil and thickens. It should have the consistency of very thick cream. If too thick, add a little more bouillon. If too thin, sprinkle a bit more flour over the top, then stir it in at once. This simplified method of preparation can only be used with the special instantized flour. We let this sauce cool until it is just warm, then serve it with cold boiled ham.

¶ *Main Dishes (Birds)—Chicken · Guinea Hen · Squab*

Again with chicken, we often use our sauté pan to avoid overheating the kitchen on summer days. In September, we add luxury to our chicken with the new season's oysters (page 376). Although the game birds have to wait until the cold weather of November (page 507), we can usually find farm-bred squab through the summer months.

SAUTÉ PAN CHICKEN WITH COGNAC

For our family of 4

It is particularly important in this recipe that the sauté pan be of such a size that its bottom will be entirely covered by the pieces of chicken. If the pan is too large, so that parts of its bottom are left uncovered, they will overheat and the sauce will burn.

Check Staples:

Clear chicken bouillon (about ½ cup)
Salt butter (about 3 Tbs.)
Floured butter—*beurre manié,* see page 12 (a few pieces)
Lemon (1)
Aromatics: crystal salt, freshly ground black pepper, MSG, outer rind of orange (enough for 1 tsp., grated)
Fresh parsley (small bunch)
Shallots (4 or 5)
Olive oil (about 2 Tbs.)
Indian chick-pea flour or all-purpose flour (a few Tbs.)
Italian peeled and seeded plum tomatoes (1 lb. 1 oz. can)
Dry white wine (about ½ cup)

Shopping List:

Young broiler-fryer chicken, cut up (2½ to 3 lbs.)
Fresh mushrooms (1 lb.)
French Cognac (3 oz., about ⅓ cup)

About 45 Minutes Before Serving

We never wash chicken with water, as drops remain in crevices and cause severe splattering. Instead, we cut a lemon in half and rub the cut side all around the chicken pieces. This cleans and adds flavor at the same time. Spread a few tablespoons of the flour on a flat plate. Rub salt, pepper, and MSG into chicken pieces, then press into flour, coating on all sides. We use a tin-lined copper sauté pan. Into it put the 3 tablespoons of butter and the 2 tablespoons of oil and heat up to medium-high frying temperature, taking care not to let butter brown or burn. Quickly brown chicken pieces on all sides, then turn down heat, cover, and let simmer (turning pieces about every 10 minutes) until chicken is fork-tender, usually in 20 to 25 minutes. Meanwhile preheat oven to keep-warm temperature (150 degrees) and heat up flat serving platter. Also, while chicken is simmering, peel and mince 4 or 5 of the shallots, grate about 1 teaspoon of the outer rind of the orange, chop plenty of parsley for sprinkling on at serving, wipe mushrooms clean (never wash), leaving small ones whole, cutting larger ones, so that all pieces are roughly the same size.

When chicken is soft, turn up heat fairly high, pour on 1/4 cup of the Cognac and flame. When flames die down, turn off heat, remove chicken pieces with tongs or slotted spatula and keep warm on platter in oven. Turn heat back on to frying temperature, put in shallots and orange rind and bubble hard for 2 to 3 minutes. Add mushrooms and continue bubbling, stirring to evaporate liquid while lightly steaming mushrooms. After 3 or 4 minutes, add: 1 cup of the tomatoes, drained of juice, the 1/2 cup of wine, the 1/2 cup of chicken stock, the remaining ounce of Cognac; mix and bubble hard for 2 or 3 minutes more. Taste for seasoning and adjust as necessary. Return pieces of chicken to pan, spreadng well down into sauce. Keep bubbling hard, spooning sauce over chicken, for 3 or 4 minutes more. Put chicken pieces back onto serving platter and finally check texture of sauce. It should have thickened slightly by this time, but if not, melt in a few pieces of floured butter and bring to boil for a few minutes. Then pour sauce over chicken, sprinkle liberally with parsley, and bring to the table. We like to serve this with a pilaf of rice (page 166) into which coarsely chopped watercress has been incorporated.

CHICKEN IN CREAM WITH OYSTERS

For our family of 4

Check Staples:

Clear chicken bouillon (1/2 to 1 cup, according to amount of oyster liquor)
Salt butter (6 oz.—1 1/2 sticks)
Lemon (1)
Aromatics: crystal salt,* freshly ground black pepper,* MSG,* garlic (2 cloves), thyme
Shallots* (4 or 5)
Indian chick-pea flour* or all-purpose flour (a few Tbs.)
Granulated instantized flour* (about 1/2 cup)
Olive oil* (a few Tbs.)
Granulated white sugar (2 tsp.)
Dry, crisp bread crumbs, to be buttered (1/2 cup)
Dry white wine* (1/2 cup)

Shopping List:

Young broiler-fryer chicken, cut up (2 1/2 to 3 lbs.)
Shucked oysters with liquor (1 pt.)
Heavy cream (1/2 cup)
Italian pecorino hard grating cheese* (1/4 lb.)

About 1¼ Hours Before Serving—Preparing Ingredients and Frying Chicken

Preheat oven to keep-warm temperature (150 degrees). Butter the ½ cup of bread crumbs in small frypan with 4 tablespoons of the butter and hold. Finely mince the 2 cloves of garlic and hold in a small covered jar. Grate the ¼ pound of cheese and hold. Peel and finely mince 4 or 5 of the shallots, then divide into 2 equal parts and hold. Spread a few tablespoons of the chick-pea flour (or alternative) on a flat plate. Clean chicken pieces (see previous recipe) by rubbing each well with cut side of half a lemon, then rub in salt, pepper, and MSG and press into flour to coat all around. We fry the chicken in a tin-lined copper sauté pan of the right size (just large enough to accommodate the pieces) with a fairly tight-fitting lid. First put into pan 3 tablespoons of the butter and 2 tablespoons of the olive oil and bring up to medium-high frying temperature, without letting butter brown or burn. Add half the shallots and sauté for not more than 1 minute, then add chicken and quickly brown on all sides. Now sprinkle on 1½ teaspoons thyme, pour on the ½ cup of wine, turn heat down to gentle simmering, cover, and cook until chicken is just tender, usually in 15 minutes. (It will be brought to perfect doneness later in oven.) Meanwhile in the oven heat up an open baking dish, about 2 to 3 inches deep, which will be brought to the table. We use a low, open 1½-quart Mexican clay casserole. As soon as chicken is done, lift pieces out with tongs or slotted spatula and keep warm in baking dish in the oven.

About 40 Minutes Before Serving—Preparing the Oyster Sauce

Pour all juices from sauté pan into a 1-pint measuring cup and add enough of the oyster liquor to make measured liquid up to 1½ cups. Melt in sauté pan 4 more tablespoons of the butter, heat up to medium frying temperature, then quickly sauté remaining minced shallots and garlic. After 1 or 2 minutes smoothly blend in 6 tablespoons of the instantized flour. This will make a thick paste. Turn heat down to a gentle simmer and gradually blend in, stirring continuously, the ½ cup of heavy cream. The sauce will still be very thick. Now gradually blend in, still stirring continuously, the liquid from the measuring cup. Use only enough of this liquid to bring sauce to thickness of heavy cream. However, if sauce is still too thick when all liquid is in, add a little more oyster liquor. Stir in the 2 teaspoons of sugar, taste for seasoning and adjust if necessary, then simmer very gently for 5 minutes, stirring a couple of times.

At this point, sauté pan can be turned off and dish can be held.

About 30 Minutes Before Serving—Final Assembly and Baking

Drain oysters. Take casserole out of oven. Turn oven up to 375 degrees. Slowly heat cream sauce up to gentle bubbling, add oysters, stirring them around and coating them with cream, then time their cooking from the moment sauce returns to bubbling—they must not cook a second more than 2 minutes. Turn off heat. Quickly mix grated cheese with buttered bread crumbs. Pour sauce on chicken, neatly tucking oysters into spaces between pieces of chicken. Cover all with bread-cheese mixture, then bake casserole in oven until sauce is bubbling and crust is lightly browned, usually in 20 minutes.

PALOMBACCI ALLA PERUGINA—SQUABS AS THEY DO THEM IN PERUGIA

For our family of 4

On the wooded hills of the Italian province of Umbria the hunters often catch wild pigeons, which are then prepared in this way over open wood fires. We use domesticated squab (young pigeon, available in summer from fancy butchers). One essential is a supply of the fresh green and black olives sold in Greek and Italian stores out of huge stone crocks. Canned or bottled olives are just too bland, although they can be used as a compromise.

Check Staples:

Thick-sliced dark smoked bacon (4 to 6 slices)
Salt butter (¼ lb.)
Lemon (1)
Aromatics: crystal salt, freshly ground black pepper, MSG, whole juniper berries (2 Tbs.), whole sage leaves
Shallots (4 or 5)
Ground arrowroot (a few tsp.)
Red wine (½ to 1 cup)

Shopping List:

Squabs (4, each about 1 to 1¼ lbs.)
Italian or Greek ripe black olives (about 6 oz.)
Italian or Greek green olives (about 6 oz.)
Fresh tarragon leaves (small bunch)
Italian Barolo red wine (1 bottle, about ½ cup for cooking, the rest to be drunk with the dish)
Sweet sauterne (1 or 2 Tbs.)

Earlier in the Day—Advance Preparation in About 15 Minutes

We begin by preparing a "juniper butter" (*beurre de genièvre,* page 71). Place finished butter in refrigerator to stiffen, while squabs are made ready. Cut the lemon in half and rub the cut sides thoroughly over the outsides and insides of the squabs. Rub them again, inside and out, with juniper butter (we do it with the fingers). Cover breasts of squabs with bacon slices, cutting to size and securing with tiny skewers. Divide remaining juniper butter into 4 parts and loosely pile 1 part into inside of each squab. Refrigerate, covered, until needed.

About 1½ Hours Before Serving

Let squabs come to room temperature.

About 1 Hour Before Serving—Lightly Browning Squabs

Preheat oven to 400 degrees. Place squabs, breast side up, on a rack in an open baking pan, and as soon as the oven is hot slide the pan in, making sure that squabs are in center of oven. Some juniper butter will run out into pan. Use it to baste squabs every 10 minutes. After 20 minutes, remove bacon from breasts, dropping slices into pan to crisp, then let breasts roast to light brown, usually in about 10 more minutes. Meanwhile we make ready one of our enameled cast-iron cocottes,* which has a tightly fitting lid and which is large enough to hold 4 squabs. We warm up this cocotte, still empty, over gentle heat on top of stove.

About 30 Minutes Before Serving—Steaming Squabs in Wine

As soon as the squab breasts are brown, turn oven down to 350 degrees, then arrange birds in the cocotte, at the same time inserting about 6 black and 6 green olives in each squab. Distribute the remaining olives around between birds. Pour over ¾ cup of the red wine, plus all juices and juniper butter remaining in oven pan, and crumble on the now-crisp bacon. Cover tightly and set in oven to steam; open up cocotte and baste squabs with wine every 10 minutes. They are best served when slightly underdone, so that when pricked with fork, meat juice oozes out pale rose in color; this point is usually reached in 20 to 30 minutes. Finally, we remove squabs from cocotte and keep warm for 1 or 2 minutes, while we thicken red-wine sauce with 1 or 2 teaspoons arrowroot liquefied with about 1 tablespoon of the sauterne. Then return squabs to the cocotte, spoon sauce over them, and bring to the table.

¶ *Main Dishes (Fish, Shellfish)—Sauté Pan Fish · Chilled Fish Steak · Poached Fish · Flamed Crab Meat, Lobster · Crayfish Stew*

WHOLE GRAY SOLE IN MUSCADET—BASIC METHOD FOR SAUTE PAN FISH IN WINE

For our family of 4

Almost any flat or small round fish can be prepared by this method, also any fish fillets, of course, but we think that fish always has a better flavor and texture when cooked with the bone in. Although any dry white wine can be used, the French Muscadet of the lower Loire Valley—a wine that is lean, extra-dry and lightly astringent—marries particularly well with fish in cooking.

Check Staples:

Salt butter (1/4 lb.)
Lemons (2)
Milk (1 cup)
Aromatics: crystal salt,⁑ freshly ground black pepper,⁑ MSG▣ dried tarragon leaf (if fresh not available)
Fresh chives (small bunch)
Fresh parsley (small bunch)
Indian chick-pea flour▣ or all-purpose flour (about 1/2 cup)
Olive oil▣ (about 2 Tbs.)

Shopping List:

Whole gray sole or alternative—*see* list on page 363—cleaned, but head left on (about 2 lbs.)
Fresh tarragon (small bunch)
French Muscadet▯ (1 bottle, enough for cooking and drinking)

About 30 Minutes Before Serving

Pour enough milk into an open, flat dish so that cleaned fish can soak in it for a couple of minutes on each side. Spread enough flour on open platter so that the milk-wet fish can be dredged in it, at the same time patting in salt, pepper, and MSG. Put 4 tablespoons of the butter into a small mixing bowl and let soften to room temperature. Then cream into it about 1 tablespoon of chives, coarsely chopped, about 2 tablespoons each of coarsely chopped parsley and tarragon (or 1 teaspoon of dried tarragon), plus 1/2 teaspoon MSG. We choose one of our tightly lidded copper sauté pans, just large enough to hold fish (see discussion of sauté pan sizes in Introduction, page 430). Before putting in fish, melt in sauté pan 3 tablespoons of the remaining plain butter, and 2 tablespoons of the olive oil, taking care so that the butter does not brown. Then put in fish and lightly brown, about 3 minutes on each side. Put the best-looking side of fish upward, turn the heat down to simmering, pour in enough Muscadet to cover the pan about 1/4 inch deep (usually about 3/4 cup), sprinkle the juice of half a lemon over fish, and dot with about half of the herb butter. Turn up heat so that wine bubbles merrily, then cover and cook for about 15 minutes. Meanwhile turn on oven to keep-warm temperature (about 150 degrees) and heat up a flat, oval serving platter. Test fish with fork to see that it is opaque and firm right through to the bone, and cook a few more minutes if necessary. Then lift carefully onto hot platter and keep warm in oven. Quickly bring juices in pan to a rolling boil, to reduce liquid and concentrate flavors, for about 2 to 3 minutes, then, when just beginning to thicken, pour over fish. Dot with the remaining herb butter, squeeze on the juice of the second half of the first lemon, decorate with slices of the second lemon, and bring at once to the table. Drink remaining Muscadet with meal.

SWORDFISH WITH RUSSIAN DRESSING—BASIC METHOD FOR CHILLED DECORATED FISH STEAK

For our family of 4

A French cook, much more often than an American, will prepare a piece of fresh fish especially to be served cold. Any wide center-cut steak from a large fish may be treated in this way. Preferably using homemade mayonnaise (page 423), the decoration may be a simple matter of 5 minutes or it may be a "big production." We give the latter method here, leaving it to the reader to simplify, as desired. This is a rich dish and is best served between a simple prologue and a light desert.

Check Staples:

Homemade mayonnaise, page 423 (1½ to 2 cups)
Lemon (1)
Aromatics: crystal salt,☆ freshly ground black pepper,☆ whole black peppercorns☆ (15), MSG, whole bay leaves, whole cloves, tarragon, thyme (dried, if fresh not available)
Carrots, small (1 bunch)
Parsley (small bunch)
Shallots☆ (4)
Dry vermouth (1 cup)

Shopping List:

Swordfish steak, large center cut about 1½ inches thick, or alternative fish (about 3 lbs.)
Anchovies, flat fillets (2-oz. can)
Green beans (½ lb.)
French-style *petits pois* (8- to 12-oz. frozen package)
Boiling potatoes (4 medium)
Fresh thyme, if available (a few sprigs)
Tomatoes (2 medium)
Red pimiento, roasted (3-oz. jar)

On the Morning of the Day Before—Preparation in 10 Minutes, Plus 1 Hour of Unsupervised Simmering

BASIC RULE FOR FISH COURT-BOUILLON: A French "short bouillon" is a comparatively quickly made (as compared to a meat bouillon, which may be simmered for 5 hours), highly aromatic broth in which some special food (a piece of fish, for example) is first simmered, then allowed to rest to absorb the aromatic flavors. This classic recipe is excellent for any fish or shellfish. It is best made well in advance and allowed to cool, so that the fish can be put into it cold and brought slowly up to the simmering point, thus absorbing more flavor. The shape of the pot in which this takes place is most important since the fish must be lifted out of the *bouillon* without being broken. If a fish boiler with a removable tray* is not available, a fairly shallow pan is best, one which is just deep enough for the fish to be well covered by the broth. As an alternative, the fish may be lightly wrapped in a large piece of cheesecloth, with two long ends left hanging over edge of pan, ready to be used as handles for lifting fish out.

Partly fill the chosen pan with enough freshly drawn cold water so that when the fish is eventually lowered in, it will be well covered, but the liquids will not rise and flood over edge of pan. Bring water up to boiling over high heat. While it is heating up add: 3 fairly thick slices of the lemon, enough crystal salt so that water tastes slightly salty, 15 whole black peppercorns, 2 teaspoons MSG, 2 whole bay leaves, 3 whole cloves, 1 teaspoon tarragon, 3 or 4 sprigs of fresh thyme (or ½ teaspoon of the dried), the cup of dry vermouth, the 4 onions (peeled and coarsely sliced), 3 of the carrots (scrubbed and chunked), the 4 whole shallots (divided into cloves, peeled and coarsely sliced), plus 4 or 5 whole sprigs of parsley. Let all this gently bubble, covered, for 1 hour or so, then turn off heat and let cool to room temperature. The *court-bouillon* is then ready for use.

Meanwhile wash and dry the swordfish steaks and neatly trim off any outside bones, but do not remove skin or large central bone. Let fish rest for 1 or 2 hours at room temperature before going into the *court-bouillon.*

At Any Time Later on the Day Before—Simmering the Fish in About 20 Minutes

Carefully lower fish into *court-bouillon,* letting it rest evenly on the bed of vegetables. Turn on moderate heat under pan and bring slowly up to simmering. It is absolutely vital that the liquid does not boil or fish will break up and disintegrate. What is needed is true simmering, "just smiling" (page 117), until flesh of fish is just firm and flaky; usually, for this amount of fish, about 15 to 20 minutes from the time simmering begins. Then turn off heat and let fish cool in *court-bouillon.* When it has cooled to room temperature, lift fish out with ultra-care and put it into a large, flat refrigerator dish, pour in enough *court-bouillon* to cover, then put on lid and refrigerate overnight. (Even better, if refrigerator is large enough, refrigerate whole pan without disturbing fish.)

On the Morning of the Day—Preparing Decorative Vegetables in About 30 Minutes

The vegetables for decoration are chosen largely for color and the list is fairly flexible. However they must all be cooked separately and only until just tender. We would steam them in our 4-tier vegetable steamer,* but rapid boiling in slightly salted water is a satisfactory second choice. In one of these ways cook: the ½ pound of green beans, 3 of the remaining carrots, the package of frozen *petit pois,* and the 4 potatoes, preferably in their jackets. As soon as vegetables are cool enough to handle, and still keeping them separate, cut green beans into small lozenges, peel and slice carrots into rounds, and peel and dice potatoes. Then store all vegetables in refrigerator, each covered, until needed for the decoration. If mayonnaise has not already been made, now is the time (see BASIC RULE, page 423).

About 3 Hours Before Serving—Decorating the Fish

Lift the fish with ultra-care onto a handsome serving platter and now, with fingers and a sharp-pointed knife, trim it beautifully, removing all skin and the central bone. Gently fold into 1 cup of the mayonnaise as many of the *petit pois* and the potato dice as it will comfortably hold, making a fairly stiff paste. Spread this evenly on top of the fish. Now use all the other vegetables, including the green beans, carrot rounds, parsley sprigs, remaining *petit pois,* pieces of red pimiento, remaining potato dice, plus the 2 tomatoes, cut into small wedges, to make stunning designs on and around the fish—perhaps colored circles on top, with wedges and small piles around the sides, all punctuated with dollops of the remaining mayonnaise. Finally, make a star in the center with about 6 of the anchovy fillets. When decoration is complete, cover very lightly with waxed paper and place in refrigerator to cool and set.

Serving at Table

This is really a one-dish course, since potatoes and vegetables are included within the dish. For final perfection, it needs the accompaniment of a light and dry white wine, perhaps a Seyssel Blanc de Blancs🍷 from the mountains of the Savoy.

CASPIAN SELIANKA—SALMON STEAKS POACHED IN A SAUTÉ PAN

For our family of 4

This is an extremely handsome dish, with the bright sauce framing the reddish-pink salmon and the decorations of black and green olives and yellow lemon. If the fish *fumet,* the aromatic bouillon, is made the day before, the final preparation takes only about 30 minutes. It is a fairly light main dish, excellent served on a bed of boiled rice. It should be preceded by a solid first course and followed perhaps by cheese and fruit. A good wine to drink with the *selianka* is a dry white Muscadet.🍷

Check Staples:
Salt butter (4 Tbs.)
Lemon (1)
Aromatics: crystal salt,✱ freshly ground black pepper,✱ MSG,✱ whole bay leaves, tarragon
Carrots (3 medium)
Green Pascal celery, with some leaves (about 4 stalks)
Yellow onions (3 medium)
Parsley (small bunch)
Granulated instantized flour✱ (2 Tbs.)
Italian tomato paste (2 Tbs.)
Dry white wine✱ (1 cup)

Shopping List:
Fresh salmon, preferably King Chinook or Silver Coho, *see* page 361 (1 steak per person—about 1½ to 2 lbs.)
Fish heads and bones, for the *fumet* (about 2½ lbs.)
Nova Scotia smoked salmon (4 thin slices)
Heavy cream (½ cup)
Capers (1 Tbs.)
Pitted black olives (6)
Pitted green olives (6)
Dill pickles (3 medium)

The Day Before—Preparing the Fish Fumet in 10 Minutes, Plus 30 Minutes of Unsupervised Simmering

Prepare a fish *fumet,* according to the BASIC RULE (page 70), using the fish heads and bones, carrots, celery, onions, wine, bay leaves, and tarragon. After simmering, cool, strain, and refrigerate it overnight.

About 1 Hour Before Serving

Let fish *fumet* come to room temperature.

About 30 Minutes Before Serving

Clean and neatly trim the 4 salmon steaks. Cut the 4 slices of smoked salmon into small squares and hold. Finely chop the 3 dill pickles and hold. Now prepare sauce in a 1½- or 2-quart saucepan. Melt in it 2 tablespoons of the butter, then work in the 2 tablespoons of tomato paste and keep stirring while heating up for 2 or 3 minutes. When thoroughly hot, work in the 2 tablespoons of flour. As it becomes very thick, begin adding, dash by dash, enough of the fish *fumet,* blending each addition in before the next is added, until sauce is the consistency of very thick cream. Stir in the chopped dill pickles and the tablespoon of capers, plus salt, pepper, and MSG to taste. Now blend in a good deal more of the *fumet,* until sauce is the consistency of light cream. Adjust heat so that sauce simmers very gently and leave, covered, to develop flavor. Place salmon steaks in a cold sauté pan just large enough to hold them side by side. If sauté pan is too large, sauce will spread out too much.

About 20 Minutes Before Serving

Pour hot sauce over and around salmon steaks. Liquid should come about three quarters of the way up sides of steaks and, if necessary, add a little more *fumet*. Turn on heat under sauté pan and adjust to gentle bubbling, cover and leave undisturbed to steam for exactly 7 minutes. Then carefully turn steaks over, cover again, and continue steaming until fish is just opaque and flaky, usually in 6 or 7 minutes more. Meanwhile warm an open, shallow serving bowl about 1½ to 2 inches deep. Also, prepare the decorative garnish: slice the black and green olives into rings; slice the lemon into pretty shapes. Finally, put the ½ cup of cream into a very small saucepan, stir in the squares of smoked salmon, and place over gentle heat to warm up, but do not allow it to boil. Chop a small handful of parsley, leaves only. When fish is done, with a slotted spatula carefully lift steaks into serving bowl. Blend cream and smoked salmon into sauce in sauté pan, adjusting heat to avoid any danger of boiling. Then pour contents of sauté pan around fish. Quickly scrape off any sauce which has splashed onto top of salmon steaks and decorate them with olive rings and lemon slices. Sprinkle parsley over salmon and bring very hot to the table. Serve in hot gumbo bowls or wide soup plates, topped with a pat of remaining butter.

ITALIAN FETTUCELLI WITH SHRIMP AND SWORDFISH AS THEY DO IT IN VENICE

For our family of 4

Fettucelli is one of the almost endless varieties of pasta, a thick oval spaghetti. It is used here in a one-dish casserole, which, with light soup and dessert, makes a rich and attractive meal. The sauce is raw fish puréed with spiced cream, either in an electric blender or in a hand mortar.

Check Staples:

Salt butter (about ¼ lb.)
Lemon (1)
Aromatics: crystal salt,⁂ freshly ground black pepper,⁂ MSG,▣ Indonesian Sambal Petis⁂ (hot pepper paste)
Yellow onions (2 medium)
Dry white wine▲ (about ¾ cup)

Shopping List:

Thick swordfish steak (about 1 lb.)
Jumbo shrimp—for number per pound, *see* page 62 (½ lb.)
Gray sole, center-cut fillet entirely without bone or skin (½ lb.)
Fettucelli (1-lb. box)
Light cream (1 pt.—2 cups)
Italian pecorino hard grating cheese▣ (about 6 oz.)

At Any Time Beforehand—Advance Preparation in About 25 Minutes

Peel, chop, and hold onions, covered. Wash swordfish and shrimp (in their shells) and gently simmer together in the ¾ cup of wine in a sauté pan just large enough to hold them, adding: onions, juice of half the lemon, plus salt, pepper, and MSG to taste. Cover for 4 minutes, turn swordfish over and continue simmering, covered, only until just firm and flaky, usually in 7 to 10 minutes. After 7 minutes remove shrimp, cool, shell, devein, and hold. Let swordfish cool in wine, uncovered. We cut up raw sole into ½-inch cubes and place in the container of the electric blender. Add about ½ cup of the cream, plus about ¼ teaspoon of the sambal pepper paste, then blend at high speed for only as long as required to form a thick smooth paste, usually from 10 to 15 seconds. Add more cream, ¼ cup at a time, running blender for 2 or 3 seconds more, until a sauce is obtained with the consistency of very thick cream. Fish usually absorbs more than ¾ pint of cream. During this operation add more sambal if desired, plus salt and MSG, until flavor is noticeably, but not too strongly, peppery. Finally, grate cheese and cut swordfish into bite-size cubes. Now everything may be held until needed.

About 45 Minutes Before Serving—Final Assembly and Baking

Cook fettucelli *al dente* in a large quantity of salted water, according to package directions, for about 10 minutes, then drain, rinse, and hold. Preheat oven to 350 degrees. Now butter a deep 4-quart oven-proof casserole and cover bottom with a 1½-inch layer of fettucelli, then a layer of swordfish and shrimp, sprinkled with a little of the cheese, then more layers in same order, topping with fettucelli. Liberally dot with butter. Check fish-cream sauce and, if it has thickened, thin with a few spoonfuls of the wine in which the fish was simmered, then pour sauce over casserole. Top with remainder of grated cheese and bake, uncovered, only until ingredients are thoroughly hot, usually in 20 to 25 minutes. A final, optional touch of perfection is to brown the top for a last minute or two under the grill. Bring casserole to table at once.

VARIATIONS: Incidentally, this dish is excellent cold. We break it up into salads, dressed with a little oil and our best Sherry vinegar. Also, we drain and save the wine in which fish was simmered. Thickened, it makes an excellent sauce for later reheating of fettucelli or for any other fish dish.

QUICK CRAB MEAT FLAMED IN A SAUTÉ PAN

For our family of 4

We generally prepare this in a bright copper sauté pan and often bring it to the table for the flaming. The final preparation takes only about 15 minutes. This is a light main dish, excellent served on a bed of boiled rice.

Check Staples:

Salt butter (4 Tbs.)
Eggs (2 large)
Aromatics: crystal salt,* freshly ground black pepper,* MSG
Chives (very small bunch)
Parsley (small bunch)
Green scallion tops (enough for 1/4 cup, chopped)
Shallots* (4 cloves)
Italian tomato paste (1 1/2 Tbs.)

Shopping List:

Crab meat, large lumps, preferably not frozen (1 lb.)
Heavy cream (1 1/4 cups)
Button mushrooms (1/2 lb.)
Fresh tarragon (enough for 2 tsp., chopped)
French Calvados apple brandy (2 oz.)

About 25 Minutes Before Serving

Finely chop and assemble together the 1/4 cup of scallion tops and the 4 cloves of shallot, then hold, covered. Wipe clean (never wash) the 1/2 pound of mushrooms, then slice lengthwise into hammer shapes and hold. Finely chop 2 teaspoons each of chives, parsley, and tarragon (as available), then mix them together in a small bowl and hold, covered. Separate the 2 eggs (reserving the whites for some other use), then beat 1/4 cup of the cream into the yolks and hold.

About 15 Minutes Before Serving

Place a sauté pan over medium heat and melt in it the 4 tablespoons of butter. When moderately hot, throw in scallion-shallot mixture and sauté vigorously for not more than 1 minute. Add mushroom slices, stir around to absorb aromatic butter, and sauté for about 2 minutes more. Then work in the 1 1/2 tablespoons of tomato paste to absorb butter and form a thickish paste. Now turn down heat to very low, to avoid any danger of boiling, and work in, dash by dash, enough of the remaining cream (usually about 3/4 cup) to make a smooth, fairly thick, sauce. Gently stir in the pound of crab meat, working very carefully to coat each lump but avoid breaking them up. Season with salt, pepper, and MSG to taste. Heat may be turned up slightly, but there must be no bubbling. When crab meat is thoroughly warm, give creamed egg yolks a few more strokes, then carefully blend into sauce. As it begins to thicken, adjust final consistency by adding a few more dashes of the cream if needed. At the last moment, stir in the chopped fresh herbs. Now place the 2 ounces of Calvados in a 1/2-cup saucepan and warm gently to just above blood heat, according to our BASIC RULE for flaming (page 44), then pour over sauté pan and flame. If preferred, the sauté pan may be brought to the table and flamed there. Serve as soon as flames subside.

RED CARPET LOBSTER FLAMED WITH PERNOD IN A SAUTÉ PAN

For our family of 4

This recipe came to us originally from the chef of the famous Chicago restaurant The Red Carpet, but we have somewhat adapted and simplified it. The French licorice-flavored spirit Pernod has an extraordinary affinity with lobster. This is a rich, but still fairly light, main dish and it should be surrounded by a reasonably solid menu. It is excellent served on a bed of boiled rice.

Check Staples:

Salt butter (4 Tbs.)
Aromatics: crystal salt,✱ freshly ground black pepper,✱ MSG
Olive oil (2 Tbs.)
Dry white wine (¼ cup)

Shopping List:

Live female lobsters, 2 or more, according to size (total weight about 3 lbs.)
Heavy cream (½ cup)
French Pernod (2 ozs.)

About 30 Minutes Before Serving—Preparing the Lobsters

Kill the lobsters in the humane way (page 86); then boil, clean, and cut them up, according to our BASIC RULE (page 86). After removing the corals and tomalleys, put them in a small mixing bowl and cream them together with 2 tablespoons of the butter. Then transfer mixture to a small saucepan and gently heat it up, at the same time blending in the ½ cup of cream, plus salt, pepper, and MSG to taste. Cover and keep warm over a very low flame.

About 15 Minutes Before Serving

In a sauté pan melt the remaining 2 tablespoons of butter and the 2 tablespoons of olive oil, but do not let butter brown. When thoroughly hot, put in lobster pieces, still in shells, and sauté for 2 or 3 minutes, turning the pieces over to color and heat them through. Then pour on the 2 ounces of Pernod and flame, according to the BASIC RULE (page 44). When flames subside, turn down heat to gentle simmering and, using two forks, quickly remove all lobster meat from shells, throwing shells away. Pour in warm coral-tomalley sauce, adjusting heat to avoid boiling and stirring around to coat lobster. Finally, check seasoning and serve very hot.

GREEK SHRIMP WITH FETA CHEESE

For our family of 4

Feta is the Greek goat's-milk cheese with a slight taste of lemon and a strong affinity with shrimp. There are dozens of versions of this dish in various parts of Greece. We have tried several and combined what we liked best of each into our own family recipe.

Check Staples:

Salt butter (a few Tbs.)
Lemon (1)
Aromatics: crystal salt,☨ freshly ground black pepper,☨ MSG,◘ basil, garlic (4 cloves), sweet marjoram, Tabasco
Fresh parsley (small bunch)
Greek olive oil◘ (1/3 cup)
Italian tomato paste (6-oz. can)
Italian peeled and seeded plum tomatoes (1 lb. 1 oz. can)
Red wine◘ (about 1/2 cup)

Shopping List:

Jumbo shrimp, preferably not frozen —for number per pound, *see* page 62 (2 lbs.)
Greek feta cheese, the sharp type◘ (1/2 lb.)
Sweet Bermuda onion (1 large)
Sweet red pimiento (4-oz. jar or can)

About 1 Hour Before Serving—Preparing the Sauce and the Shrimp

Put the 1/3 cup of olive oil into a medium-sized saucepan and heat slowly to medium frying temperature while peeling and chopping the onion, then sauté until just golden. Now add: the 4 cloves of garlic, finely minced; the pimiento, chopped and with its juice; the can of tomatoes; 1 teaspoon basil and 1 teaspoon marjoram; 3 ounces of the tomato paste; 1/4 cup of the wine; and finally, salt, pepper, 1 or 2 drops of Tabasco, and MSG to taste. Mix thoroughly and simmer gently, uncovered, for about 30 minutes. Most of the water should evaporate and sauce should begin to thicken but not dry. If it gets too thick, add more wine. If it remains too thin, turn up heat and bubble briskly for the final 2 or 3 minutes. If the sauce shows any signs of sticking, it is becoming too thick.

Meanwhile wash, shell, and devein the 2 pounds of shrimp. In a sauté pan heat 3 or 4 tablespoons of the butter to low frying temperature and quickly sauté the shrimp until they turn just pink, hardly more than 2 minutes on each side. For the final baking, we use an enameled cast-iron au gratin dish large enough to hold shrimp in a tight single layer, with sauce and cheese on top. When done, lift shrimp out of butter with slotted spoon and lay neatly in baking dish, which has been buttered. Preheat oven to 400 degrees. Squeeze the juice of half the lemon into sauce, stir once more, and pour over shrimp, covering completely. Cover sauce in turn with 1/4-inch-thick slices of feta cheese, using up the full 1/2 pound. Bake until cheese is very soft, usually in 15 to 20 minutes. Meanwhile chop the parsley and hold.

Just Before Serving

Squeeze the juice of the last half of the lemon over top of dish, plus 2 or 3 more grinds of pepper, then sprinkle liberally with chopped parsley. Serve at once, before cheese has time to set. We think the ideal wine with this is an ice-cold Greek Robola, a white wine that is not too dry.

BASIC METHOD FOR BOILING CRAYFISH

For 100 crayfish

When we receive a shipment of live crayfish, as we usually do once or twice a year (page 370), we immediately start the preparation in the following way.

Check Staples:

Lemons (4)
Aromatic: crystal salt✻
Yellow onions (2 medium)
Granulated white sugar (3 tsp.)
Dry white wine✻ (1 cup)

Shopping List:

Live crayfish✻ (100)
Fresh dill (3 or 4 large bunches)
Refined rock salt (½ lb.)

At Least 24 Hours Before Serving

Put the live crayfish in the sink (making sure that none of them crawl out!), then spray or douse them with fresh cold water. Use tongs to lift them and pull away bits of seaweed, but keep fingers away from snapping claws. Then load them into a large pail, cover with fresh cold water, and stir in 1 cup of the rock salt. This helps them clean themselves. Leave them soaking and rustling around for at least 1 hour. Meanwhile prepare the bouillon in which they will be cooked. Into a large 5-quart soup pot put: 3 quarts of freshly drawn cold water, 4 teaspoons of crystal salt (not the rock salt), the 2 onions (peeled and chunked), the 3 teaspoons of sugar, the cup of wine, plus at least 3 or 4 handfuls of the dill (coarsely cut). After they have had their hour of soaking, pour the crayfish back into the sink, wash the salt off them, then drop them into the still-cold bouillon in the soup pot. Now bring it to a boil as quickly as possible. This is the humane way to kill the crayfish (page 86). Let them gently simmer for 12 minutes, then turn off heat and let them cool in the bouillon for about 4 or 5 hours. Then refrigerate, in several dishes if necessary, pouring in enough strained bouillon just to cover.

The Next Day Onwards—Serving Crayfish Cold

As the main dish of a cold supper, the normal portion for one person is 25 crayfish; some people can eat 50 at a sitting! With a strong sharp knife, cut off the head just behind the eyes. Turn crayfish over onto its back and make a straight cut just through the belly shell, from head to tip of tail. Now peel off entire shell. With a lobster pick dig out the edible lumps of meat from the back of the head, also the coral, which is a delicacy, but keep away from the stomach, which is bitter. We like to set aside the tail, as the final top prize, when all the hard work is done. Crack the claws and suck out the meat. Suck the aromatic juices from the larger legs. Last, and best, slowly savor the superb flavor of the soft tail meat. We think that even the best homemade mayonnaise is too strong. All that is needed is a drop or two of lemon juice (serve each person a quartered lemon with the crayfish). The best accompaniment is a bland cucumber salad, dressed with dry white wine in place of vinegar. The traditional drink served with crayfish in Sweden is aquavit, and in Russia, vodka; each is served ice-cold.

When we are tired of cold crayfish, we serve them hot in . . .

CREAMED CRAYFISH STEW

For our family of 4

This recipe begins with the assumption that 100 crayfish have been boiled and shelled as described in the preceding recipe, so it is a three-day operation: boiling the crayfish on the first day, shelling them on the second, and, on the third, proceeding as follows.

Check Staples:

Salt butter (¼ lb.)
Milk (1 cup)
Aromatics: crystal salt,* freshly ground black pepper,* MSG,* garlic (3 cloves, to taste), thyme
Yellow onions (2 medium)
Fresh parsley (1 bunch)
Granulated instantized flour* (about 1 Tbs.)
Granulated white sugar (about 1 Tbs.)
Dry white wine* (1 cup)

Shopping List:

Crayfish (the meat of 100, including the coral of the females, boiled and shelled, *see* preceding recipe)
The 100 empty shells
Deep-sea scallops (1 lb.)
Fresh mushrooms (½ lb.)
Italian tomato purée (8-oz. can)

About 1¼ Hours Before Serving

Put the empty crayfish shells into a suitable-size saucepan and add: 1 of the onions, peeled and chunked; 1 of the cloves of garlic, sliced; 1 teaspoon thyme; ½ cup of the wine; plus 1 teaspoon salt, a few grinds of pepper, and about ½ teaspoon MSG. Pour in freshly drawn cold water just to cover, then heat and simmer, covered, for about 30 minutes. Peel the second onion and chop it fairly fine. In a 2-quart saucepan bring 2 tablespoons of the butter to low frying temperature, then sauté chopped onion until golden. Add: the 8 ounces of tomato purée, the second clove of garlic, finely minced, 2 teaspoons of the sugar, plus salt, pepper, and MSG to taste. Mix and simmer very gently, covered, for about 25 minutes, or until other ingredients are ready. Meanwhile wash scallops and cut into bite-size pieces. Wipe clean (never wash) mushrooms and thickly slice lengthwise into hammer shapes. Chop enough parsley to fill about 1/2 cup. In a sauté pan bring 4 more tablespoons of the butter to low frying temperature, then quickly sauté scallops, stirring around and coating with the butter. After about 2 minutes add the mushrooms and keep stirring. Sprinkle over about 2 tablespoons of the chopped parsley. After about 5 minutes, when scallops should be just done and mushrooms have just softened and darkened, stir in the crayfish, remembering that they need no more cooking, but are to be warmed and impregnated with butter. Add more butter if needed. Cover and turn heat down very low, just high enough to keep crayfish warm.

About 20 Minutes Before Serving—Finishing and Assembling

We finally put the dish together in one of our large enameled cast-iron cocottes,* which is handsome enough to be brought to the table. Set it over low heat on top of stove. Pour in entire contents of saucepan number two (with the spice tomato purée) and turn up heat to keep gently bubbling. Drain spiced bouillon from crayfish shells and add to cocotte, with the remaining 1/2 cup of wine. Mix and bring up to a sharp boil for 3 or 4 minutes, to reduce the liquid and concentrate flavors. Meanwhile in a small bowl mix 1/2 cup of the milk with the 4 tablespoons of flour, then turn down heat under cocotte until it stops boiling, and carefully blend in milk-flour mixture, 1 tablespoon at a time, until hot liquid thickens to the consistency of light cream. Do not necessarily use all the milk-flour. Bring back to gentle simmering and, after stirring continuously for 1 or 2 minutes, check the consistency again. If it is too thin, turn down heat and add more milk-flour. If it is too thick, add a dash or two of plain milk. Now add fish, mushrooms, and all juices from sauté pan. Stir again, taste, and finally adjust seasonings. Recheck consistency and readjust if needed. Reheat to just below boiling, liberally sprinkle top with chopped parsley, and bring steaming to the table. The stew should be served in piping-hot soup bowls and any remaining parsley can be sprinkled onto the individual servings.

¶ *Main Dishes (Cheese, Eggs)*

SUMMER VEGETABLES IN CHEESE SAUCE

For our family of 4

We often make a light meal of the fresh and luscious vegetables of this season. The recipe is entirely flexible. Almost any combination of vegetables can be included.

Check Staples:

Sweet butter, for bread (¼ lb.)
Salt butter (6 Tbs.)
Milk (½ cup)
Aromatics: crystal salt,* freshly ground black pepper,* MSG

Shopping List:

A combination of 3 or 4 vegetables, say: green beans (½ lb.), fresh lima beans (1 lb.), small carrots (1 bunch), cauliflower (1 small head), or alternatives
English Cheshire cheese (½ lb.)
French bread (1 loaf)

About 40 Minutes Before Serving

Prepare and just cook the vegetables in any way preferred, making sure that each is brought to the same degree of doneness. Break cauliflower into flowerets and scrape and cut carrots into sticks. We prefer to steam vegetables, and we can do three or four at a time in our multiple steamer.* It usually takes 10 to 15 minutes. Meanwhile grate the cheese. We bake and serve the meal in an enameled cast-iron au gratin dish of a suitable size; first it is well buttered and then the cooked vegetables are arranged in it in a good-looking pattern. They can be in circles, pie wedges, or squares of contrasting colors. Sprinkle cheese over and around them, also salt, more black pepper than usual, and MSG to taste. Preheat oven to 350 degrees. Pour over the ½ cup of milk and dot liberally with the salt butter. Bake in oven until cheese is melted, sauce has formed, and everything is bubbling hot, usually in about 20 minutes. Bring at once to the table, accompanied by a long French loaf and plenty of sweet butter. This is a much more substantial dish than may appear from the description.

AN ANCIENT GREEK CHEESE-AND-FRUIT SUPPER

For our family of 4

On a summer Sunday evening we sometimes like to imagine ourselves in ancient Athens, preparing a meal that might have been offered to Socrates and Plato. It is a cold menu of bread and cheese, of fruits and various honeys, of milk and wine, a simple but immensely satisfying repast with rare combinations of flavors. The total effect depends largely on the perfection of each separate ingredient, so it is worth taking some trouble with the shopping and advance preparation.

Shopping List:

Bread, preferably home-baked, but if not possible, Greek sesame loaves from a local Greek baker, or long thin French loaves, locally baked on the morning of the day

Sweet butter, the best available locally, worth paying the higher price for butter churned and brought in by a local dairy

Cheese, say a ½ lb. chunk of each of several simple, unsophisticated varieties: Greek sharp feta, Spanish Queso Manchego, Italian Cacio a Cavallo, English white Wensleydale, California Monterey Jack, Dutch Gouda (not all these at one sitting, of course!)

Whole milk, preferably non-homogenized, so that there is a layer of cream on top

Fruit, a rough ceramic bowl lined, if possible, with grape leaves and piled with seasonal varieties of grapes, chosen from the list on page 371, say Concord, White Malaga, Red Emperor, plus Valencia oranges, Bartlett pears, and a few bananas, for color contrast

Honey, a selection of 4 or 5 of the new season's crop, chosen from the list on page 521, some still in the comb

Wine, to end the meal, Greek sweet Mavrodaphne

The Table Setting Is Important

The leaf-lined bowl, filled with a handsome arrangement of fruits, is chilled for several hours. The milk and wine also come to the table ice-cold. The whole loaves are served on a wooden cutting board, so that each person can cut his own chunks. The cheeses, at room temperature, are put on another cutting board, with serving knives and spatulas. The honeys in their original pots and boxes are placed on a serving platter, with a long jam spoon for each one. Obviously there are dozens of different combinations of these foods, but we find it good to follow a certain sequence. We start with bread and cheese, with milk, alone. Then, one by one, we add the fruits to the cheeses. Then, gradually, we increase the sweetness by taking the honeys and leaving the cheeses. Finally, more or less as dessert, we eat only the fruits with the honeys, at the same time bringing in the Mavrodaphne wine. The very last bite can be a small piece of one's favorite cheese, as a savory climax to a charming meal.

BASQUE PIPÉRADE—SCRAMBLED EGGS WITH PEPPERS AND HAM

For our family of 4

One more way of using the cold boiled country ham from page 369. This is the famous egg dish of the Basque country of southwestern France on the Spanish border where the two cultures meet. On its home ground, in the country behind Biarritz and Saint-Jean-de-Luz, it almost always includes the ham cured in Bayonne, which might be called the Smithfield of France.

Check Staples:

Cold dark smoked ham (4 fairly thick slices)
Flavorful fat in which to cook the vegetables lightly, either white goose fat, white pork or bacon drippings, or olive oil (1 to 2 Tbs.)
Eggs (6 large)
Aromatics: crystal salt, freshly ground black pepper, MSG, basil, garlic (1 clove), sweet marjoram
Yellow onion (1 medium)
Fresh parsley (small handful)
Granulated white sugar (about 1 tsp.)

Shopping List:

Green peppers (4 medium)
Vine-ripened tomatoes (2 lbs.), or Italian peeled and seeded plum tomatoes (2 lb. 3 oz. can)

About 20 Minutes Before Serving

Peel and finely chop the onion. Remove the seed pod from inside each of the peppers and then cut them lengthwise into narrow, bite-size strips. Finely mince the garlic clove. Peel the tomatoes (if using the fresh), cut in half, remove seeds and water, then coarsely chunk. Chop parsley and hold. Break the eggs into a mixing bowl, add ½ teaspoon basil, ½ teaspoon marjoram, plus salt, pepper, and MSG to taste, and beat them with a fork for 1 minute. We use a tin-lined copper sauté pan, in which 1 tablespoon of the fat is brought up to fairly high frying heat. Quickly sauté onions to just golden. Add pepper strips and stir around to coat with fat. Add the minced garlic, then the chunked tomatoes (or alternative) and the teaspoon of sugar. Turn heat down, but keep it simmering fairly vigorously, uncovered, so that water is evaporated and vegetables begin to thicken. Meanwhile in a separate frypan lightly brown the ham slices in a little more of the fat. Preheat oven to keep-warm temperature (150 degrees) and heat up a flat serving platter. When ham slices are brown, keep warm on platter in oven. Pour fat from frying pan into vegetables in sauté pan. Stir and, as soon as tomatoes show signs of thickening, turn off heat, give eggs in mixing bowl a final beat, then incorporate them rapidly into vegetables in sauté pan, preferably using a flexible spatula. Turn on heat to gentle simmering and continue to stir and fold eggs until they are lightly and finely scrambled, with no large curds. At the same time taste and adjust seasonings. Even before eggs are fully set, pile them onto the serving platter and arrange the ham slices neatly around them. Sprinkle liberally with chopped parsley and serve immediately.

¶ *Vegetables*

TOPINAMBOURS AS THEY DO THEM IN FRANCE— JERUSALEM ARTICHOKES IN CREAM SAUCE

For our family of 4

When this potato-like root is in its short season at the end of the summer, it is well worth chasing for its delicate nuttiness and crisp juiciness. It is the root of a sunflower, and was first eaten by American Indians. When the colonists arrived and established trade with Europe, seeds of this sunflower were carried to Italy, where, because the flower gyrated toward the sun, it was called *girasole.* When the plant reached England, the British again demonstrated their flair for "gobbledygooking" foreign names (they had previously converted the Spanish *Jerez* into "Sherry") and changed *girasole* to "Jerusalem." The French call them *topinambours,* but when they make a soup from them, they bow with a smile to their British cousins and call the soup *potage Palestine.*

Check Staples:

Floured butter—*beurre manié, see* page 12 (a few Tbs.)
Aromatics: crystal salt, freshly ground black pepper, MSG, garlic (1 clove), freshly grated nutmeg
Yellow onion (1 medium)
Fresh parsley (small bunch)
Olive oil (a few Tbs.)
Granulated instantized flour (about 1 Tbs.)
Dry white wine (about 1/2 cup)

Shopping List:

Jerusalem artichokes, preferably small (1 lb.)

About 30 Minutes Before Serving

We prepare this in a 1 1/2- or 2-quart enameled cast-iron casserole with a tightly fitting lid, which is good-looking enough to be brought to the table. Scrape the tubers exactly as you would potatoes. Peel and chop the onion. Finely mince the clove of garlic. Heat about 1 tablespoon of the olive oil in the bottom of the casserole and quickly sauté the onion to just golden. Blend in enough flour to absorb the oil, usually about 1 tablespoon. Blend in, dash by dash, enough of the wine to make a thick cream sauce, turning up heat to keep mixture bubbling. Add: the minced garlic, a few grinds of nutmeg, plus salt, pepper, and MSG to taste. Make sure the artichokes are all about the same size, if necessary halving or quartering large ones. Put them into casserole, stir around with a wooden spoon to coat with sauce, add freshly drawn cold water just to cover, at the same time turning up heat to bring to a boil just as quickly as possible. When bubbling begins, turn down heat at once to gently simmering, "just smiling," cover and cook until artichokes are fork-tender, usually in about 15 minutes—but watch them fairly closely. If they are overcooked, they fall apart and mash. Meanwhile turn on oven to keep-warm temperature (150 degrees) and place in it a bowl large enough to hold artichokes. Chop enough parsley to fill about 1/4 cup. When artichokes are done, carefully lift them out with a slotted spoon and keep them warm in the bowl in oven while finishing sauce. Thicken it to the consistency of heavy cream by carefully blending in, lump by lump, some of the floured butter. At the same time, taste for seasoning and adjust as needed. When sauce is right, blend in parsley, put artichokes back into casserole, gently poking them around until they are well covered with sauce, then reheat to just bubbling. Serve at once or keep covered in warming oven until needed.

OKRA TO EAT BY HAND

For our family of 4

Some of our friends say they don't like okra because it is gooey and slimy. Here is how we prove that this is not a fair criticism. We think okra so good this way that we usually serve it as a separate course.

Check Staples:

Hollandaise sauce, homemade, ***see*** **following recipe (about 1 cup)**
Aromatic: crystal salt☆

Shopping List:

Fresh okra, young, small, evenly sized pods (1 lb.)

About 20 Minutes for the Hollandaise, Plus 10 Minutes for the Okra

When the hollandaise is almost ready, bring about 1½ quarts of freshly drawn cold water, slightly salted, to a rolling boil. Wash okra. Do not trim them or cut skin anywhere. Drop all at once into boiling water and timing from moment water returns to a boil, cook exactly 7 minutes. Be ready to drain and serve immediately. Meanwhile turn on oven to keep-warm temperature (150 degrees) and put in 4 shallow soup bowls. We serve okra as we do asparagus (page 304), placed like the spokes of a wheel, the points toward the center. Spoon onto the points a pile of hollandaise. We lift the pods by hand, after dipping them into the hollandaise. The okra remain crisp, with full flavor preserved and no trace of stickiness or slime.

BASIC METHOD FOR WHOLE-EGG HOLLANDAISE SAUCE

Makes about 1 cup

We neither agree with the alarmists who say that the making of a good hollandaise is too difficult for the average cook, nor with the purists who claim that it should be composed only of butter, egg yolks, and lemon juice. Preparing a hollandaise is easy (although it does require patience) *provided* that one has the proper tools. The ideal double boiler is the one with the lower half of copper, to respond instantly to heat adjustments, and the top half of thick, heavy china, to transmit heat slowly. This type of double boiler can be ordered,☆ or a pyrex is a fair second choice. One can improvise with a china or glass bowl set into a suitably sized pan of hot water. The only other essential tool is a small wire whisk for stirring and beating. As to the ingredients, we find that a so-called "classic" hollandaise is too bland and smooth. We add extra aromatics, in different combinations for the sake of variety, and also (and this is most shocking to the purists) we use the whole egg instead of just the yolk. This gives a slightly coarser, stiffer texture, with a more individual character to the sauce. Also, since fewer eggs and less butter are used, our hollandaise is more economical and less rich and fattening.

Check Staples:
Sweet butter (1/4 lb.)
Eggs (2 large)
Lemon (1)
Aromatics: crystal salt,☧ red cayenne pepper, tarragon
Tarragon white wine vinegar (2 Tbs.)

Shopping List:
Heavy cream (1 Tbs.)

It Requires About 20 Minutes of Continuous Concentration

The fundamental principle to remember is that one is in fact cooking the eggs, but in such tiny grains, so continuously broken up by the stirring, as to produce a smooth fluff. This cooking must be done slowly. If it is done too fast, the eggs "scramble"—the basic cause of all hollandaise failures. However much time can be saved by having the ingredients warm, but not hot. And it is essential to have exactly the right temperature in the double boiler.

Pour hot water into the lower half of the double boiler until the surface *just touches* the bottom of the top half. Set heat so that water is *just below* simmering. Place china or ceramic top half in position over the water to heat up thoroughly while ingredients are prepared.

Cut the stick of butter into thin slices, spread on a soup plate, and put in a warm place (we stand it over the pilot light of our cooker) to soften almost to the point of melting. Break the 2 eggs into a small bowl (do not separate), beat hard until very frothy, and also put in a warm place. Cut lemon in half and hold. Put the 2 tablespoons of vinegar into a small 1/2-cup saucepan, add 1 teaspoon tarragon, then boil hard for about 2 minutes to reduce liquid to roughly 1 tablespoon. Strain this into double boiler. Give the eggs a final hard beat and add them to double boiler. Now begins the continuous stirring and beating with the wire whisk, which must not be interrupted or slowed down until sauce is ready. Stir eggs and vinegar until just beginning to thicken. At the same time incorporate a shake or two of cayenne pepper plus, dash by dash, the 1 tablespoon of cream. As soon as egg shows first sign of thickening, begin adding butter, bit by bit, stirring continuously and vigorously to incorporate each bit fully before next is added. Soon the magic transformation begins. One feels the resistance in the wire whisk. The sauce begins to expand and fluff up. Our test for the finished sauce is that it should stand up in a spoon. Finally, carefully blend in salt to taste, a tiny bit more cayenne if needed, plus a few squeezes of lemon juice.

There is always a great deal of loose talk about the difficulty of holding a hollandaise warm. We find no problem, up to even an hour. The trick is to keep it lukewarm. If one tries to keep it hot, it will probably separate. We turn down heat under the double boiler very low or put an asbestos mat between, then leave sauce in top half, covered. Incidentally, if you have a bright copper double boiler, you can bring it to the table and serve the hollandaise directly from it.

VARIATIONS: By making a few simple changes in the basic hollandaise, one can produce three other classic sauces. (1) By adding to the vinegar 2 or 3 teaspoons of chopped shallot, a crumbled bay leaf, and 1 teaspoon of thyme, boiling them down, then straining them out, one finishes up with a slightly modified, but excellent, *sauce béarnaise.* (2) By blending into the finished hollandaise ¼ cup of whipped heavy cream, one has a *sauce mousseline.* (3) By blending into the *béarnaise* 2 tablespoons of meat glaze, one has a *sauce foyot.*

WHITE ONIONS WITH A BURNT GLAZE

For our family of 4

Check Staples:
Clear chicken bouillon (½ cup)
Salt butter (4 Tbs.)
Aromatics: crystal salt, freshly ground black pepper, MSG
Parsley (small bunch)
Dry white wine (½ cup)

Shopping List:
White boiler onions (1½ lbs.)

About 35 Minutes Before Serving—Including About 25 Minutes of Unsupervised Simmering

Peel the onions, keeping them whole but pricking each one to its center with a fork. Put them into a saucepan large enough that they form not more than two layers. Pour in the ½ cup of bouillon and the ½ cup of wine. This should provide a depth of about ½ to ¾ inch of liquid in bottom of pan. If not deep enough, add a little water. Sprinkle on salt, pepper, and MSG to taste. Heat up rapidly to a rolling boil, turn down heat to merry bubbling, to provide plenty of steam, then cover and steam for 12 minutes. Then stir them around so that top and bottom layers are transposed. Cover again and continue steaming until onions are just crisply tender, usually in 12 to 15 minutes more. Meanwhile set a serving dish in the oven to warm and chop the parsley. Drain onions and dry them on a towel.

About 5 Minutes Before Serving

Melt the 4 tablespoons of butter in a sauté pan over moderately high frying heat. When hot, put in onions and sauté vigorously, stirring around until each onion has at least one or two burnt brown patches. Sprinkle on more salt and pepper if needed. Finally, turn out onto warm dish, sprinkle on chopped parsley, and serve very hot.

DEEP-FRIED OYSTER PLANT

For our family of 4

This unusual root vegetable, which does in fact have a faint flavor of shellfish, looks somewhat like an earthy-gray, gnarled carrot. The oyster plant, also called salsify by some greengrocers, usually comes to market toward the end of summer and is sometimes hard to find. It is so good that we always serve it as a separate course.

Check Staples:

Egg (1 large)
Lemons (3)
Milk (about ½ cup)
Aromatics: crystal salt, freshly ground black pepper, MSG
Fresh parsley (small bunch)
Granulated instantized flour (about 1½ cups)
Olive oil (about ½ cup)
Granulated white sugar (about 1 tsp.)
Tarragon white wine vinegar (about 5 Tbs.)
Oil for deep-frying

Shopping List:

Oyster plants, small young (2 lbs.)

The Day Before—Preparation and Boiling in About 45 Minutes

As soon as oyster plant is peeled it discolors in the air in a few seconds, so we have ready a bowl of cold water, about 1½ quarts, mixed with the juice of 1 lemon. Quickly scrape oyster plants, trim all ends, and drop instantly into acidulated water. Into a 5-quart soup pot put 3 quarts of freshly drawn cold water and bring to a boil. In a small bowl mix: 4 tablespoons of the flour with 2½ teaspoons salt and work into a smooth cream by adding, dash by dash, 4 tablespoons of the vinegar. The result should be a thick liquid, but not a pasty one. If necessary add a bit more flour or vinegar. Then thin it down with a few tablespoons of hot water from the soup pot, and now add it to the main cooking water, stirring to avoid lumping. This basic trick keeps the oyster plant milky-white. When the water is bubbling merrily, drain oyster plant, drop into cooking water, and simmer until fork-tender, usually in 25 to 35 minutes. Meanwhile in a covered refrigerator dish large enough to hold the oyster plant, prepare a marinade by mixing: the juice of the remaining 2 lemons, 4 tablespoons of the olive oil, a small handful chopped parsley, plus a good sprinkling of salt and a little black pepper. When oyster plant is done, drain it and let it stand. As soon as it is cool enough to handle, work each piece thoroughly into marinade and refrigerate, covered, overnight. It is good to stir them around a bit in the marinade last thing at night and again first thing in the morning.

About 2 Hours Before Serving—Preparing the Batter and Frying

Prepare the ultra-light frying batter according to the BASIC RULE (page 140). Then take the oyster plant out of the refrigerator and let come to room temperature.

About 15 Minutes Before Serving

Heat deep-frying oil to 375 degrees. Drain each oyster plant from marinade, cover thoroughly with batter, and lower gently into hot frying oil. Fry to a golden-brown.

CREAMED SORREL, OR SOURGRASS

For our family of 4

We have already discussed this unusual lemon-flavored leaf, which grows wild and is generally available in our neighborhood groceries through the summer. It is used here as a vegetable, in the manner of spinach, and although the texture is roughly the same the flavor is entirely different.

Check Staples:

Salt butter (about 3 Tbs.)
Egg (1 large)
Aromatics: crystal salt,☧ freshly ground black pepper,☧ MSG⊜

Shopping List:

Sorrel, or sourgrass, young, fresh (enough for 2 qts. of chopped leaves, usually about 2 lbs.)
Heavy cream (about 4 Tbs.)

About 25 Minutes Before Serving

As with spinach (page 533), we usually work this with two people. Number 1 throws all the sorrel into the sink, thoroughly washes the leaves under the cold spray, tears off and throws away the stalks, then cuts the leaves into large but manageable pieces. Meanwhile Number 2 sets a large pot on the stove over high heat and quickly melts in the bottom of it about 2 tablespoons of the butter. Number 1 then brings over handfuls of leaves without shaking out water, and dumps them with much hissing into the pot, where they steam in the water adhering to the leaves. As each load is dumped in, Number 2 stirs it around and presses it down with a long wooden spoon, keeping the heat high. For the first few seconds the sorrel takes up a lot of room, but it wilts and mashes down almost immediately. When it is all in and mashed down, turn heat down to simmering, stir thoroughly to absorb butter, put on lid, and let simmer for about 10 minutes, stirring once or twice. Then turn off heat and let cool until it can be handled.

Have ready a large chopping board and heavy chef's knife. Grasp a not-too-large handful of sorrel and squeeze out water, then place this now-tight lump on chopping board. Repeat until all sorrel is on chopping board in a tightly packed pile, then chop vigorously. Then put chopped sorrel into a 2-quart saucepan (preferably enameled cast-iron because it will prevent burning). Separate the egg and lightly beat the yolk with about 3 tablespoons of the cream and blend into sorrel. (Reserve the white for some other purpose.) Set pan over medium heat, adding salt, pepper, and MSG to taste, plus a little more butter and cream to achieve smoothness.

GRILLED ZUCCHINI WITH SARDO CHEESE

For our family of 4

This is an unusual way of preparing zucchini. Sardo is a hard goat's-milk cheese shaped like a cannonball, made originally on the Mediterranean island of Sardinia. Nowadays, however, it comes also from other parts of Italy and from Argentina. If it is hard to find, it can be replaced here by Parmesan or pecorino Romano.

Check Staples:

Thick-sliced dark smoked bacon (4 slices)
Salt butter (about ¼ lb.)
Aromatics: crystal salt, freshly ground black pepper, MSG, garlic (1 clove)
Fresh parsley (small bunch)

Shopping List:

Zucchini, small ones, about 4 inches long (8)
Sardo cheese (about ¼ lb.)

About 15 Minutes Before Serving

Since the grilling operation goes very fast, first prepare all ingredients. Finely dice bacon and hold. Finely mince garlic and put into a small mixing bowl. Chop enough parsley to fill ¼ cup and mix with garlic. Grate the sardo cheese. Wash zucchini, cut exactly in half lengthwise, and arrange, cut side upward, in a suitably sized au gratin dish that has been well buttered. Turn on broiler to high and let heat up for about 5 minutes. Adjust grill shelf so that zucchini will be about 3 inches below heat. Now lightly dot each zucchini face with butter, spread with garlic-parsley mix, sprinkle with a little salt, pepper, and MSG, then a layer of grated cheese, and finally top with diced bacon. All ingredients except cheese will be completely used up—remember that too thick a layer of sardo would dominate the fresh zucchini flavor.

About 6 Minutes Before Serving

Slip au gratin dish under broiler and watch carefully. Bacon must fry slightly and cheese melt, but zucchini must not become mushy; when perfectly done, they remain crisp and juicy. Since broilers vary in efficiency, it is unwise at first to rely only on timing. However, under our grill, it usually takes 6 minutes. Serve at once, piping hot. Bring the remaining grated cheese to the table; each diner can sprinkle some over his zucchini.

¶ *Foundations—Potatoes · Flageolets · Red Lentils*

In summer we choose starch foods that are light, simple, and quick to prepare, with minimum added heat in an already sun-baked city kitchen. We enjoy the gay colors of the delicate green of the French beans and the orange-red of the Egyptian lentils.

OUR SIMPLIFIED CREAMED POTATOES

For our family of 4

The new type of granulated instantized flour, which requires no sifting and disperses immediately in cold liquids, allows us to simplify many kitchen techniques. Here is our quick way of cooking potatoes and blending them into a cream sauce in a single step. The Asiago cheese is from the Asiago Plateau in the Alps of northern Italy, where the cows eat a slightly sweet clover, which brings to the cheese a faintly honey-sweet flavor.

Check Staples:

Salt butter (2 Tbs.)
Milk (1 cup)
Aromatics: crystal salt, freshly ground black pepper, MSG, freshly-ground nutmeg, Hungarian sweet red paprika
Yellow onion (1 small)
Parsley (enough for 2 Tbs., chopped)
Granulated instantized flour (2 Tbs.)

Shopping List:

Boiling potatoes, *see* list, page 367 (enough to fill 3 cups with bite-size cubes)
Italian Asiago cheese, or second best but less interesting, sharp Cheddar (¼ lb.)

Preparation in 10 Minutes—40 Minutes of Unsupervised Baking

We prepare this dish in a 1½-quart enameled cast-iron casserole with a tightly fitting lid, which goes into the oven and then comes to the table. Peel the onion, finely mince, and hold. Peel and dice potatoes into bite-size cubes, then put into casserole. Preheat oven to 350 degrees. Dot potatoes with the 2 tablespoons of butter and sprinkle on onion, along with about 1½ teaspoons salt, about ½ teaspoon MSG, plus 2 or 3 grinds each of pepper and nutmeg. Sprinkle on the 2 tablespoons of flour and wet everything thoroughly with the cup of milk. Stir with a wooden spoon, cover, then set in oven until potatoes are done, usually in about 40 minutes. Meanwhile grate the cheese and chop the parsley.

Just Before Serving

Sprinkle cheese into casserole and, working carefully with wooden spoon to avoid crushing potatoes, blend in cheese and bring cream sauce up from bottom. Decorate top with green parsley and a few shakes of red paprika.

POTATOES MASHED WITH WINE BOUILLON

For our family of 4

This method for mashed potatoes is almost infinitely variable. Different combinations of aromatics and crisp greens can be used and we sometimes fold in about a tablespoon of grated Swiss sapsago cheese (page 675).

Check Staples:

Beef bouillon (¾ to 1 cup)
Salt butter (3 Tbs.)
Aromatics: crystal salt, freshly ground black pepper, MSG, dried celery seed (only if fresh leaves not available), summer savory
Celery leaves, fresh (enough to fill ¼ cup, chopped)
Green scallion tops (enough to fill 1 Tbs., finely chopped)
Watercress (enough to fill 1 Tbs., finely chopped)
Dry white wine (¼ cup)

Shopping List:

Fluffy boiling potatoes, *see* list, page 367 (about 10 medium)

About 30 to 40 Minutes Before Serving—According to Size and Type of Potato

Since the potatoes are to be steamed, they must be cooked in a saucepan or cocotte* with a reasonably tight-fitting lid. Put in enough of the celery leaves, coarsely chopped, to fill ¼ cup, then pour in enough of the bouillon to cover bottom of pan about ½ inch deep. Set over high heat, meanwhile stirring in ½ teaspoon summer savory and ½ teaspoon MSG. (If celery leaves are not available, also stir in ½ teaspoon celery seed.) When liquid boils, turn heat down to simmering, cover and allow flavors to develop. Peel potatoes thinly and immediately immerse each in salted water, then, as necessary, cut larger ones so that all pieces are roughly the same size. Put them into the boiling bouillon, turn up heat slightly for merry bubbling, clamp on lid for a minimum of 25 minutes. Then prod potatoes with fork and, if necessary, continue steaming until quite soft. Meanwhile let the 4 tablespoons of butter soften, also finely chop enough of the green scallions and watercress to fill about 1 tablespoon each.

About 5 Minutes Before Serving

Turn on oven to "keep-warm" temperature (about 150 degrees) and put in a covered serving dish. When potatoes are soft, lift out with a slotted spoon and mash. Strain bouillon to get rid of celery leaves, etc. Stir the ½ cup of wine into bouillon. Lightly fold into potatoes the scallion and watercress, the butter, enough wine bouillon to achieve the proper texture, plus a good deal of pepper and a little salt to taste. Then lightly fluff into warm serving dish.

FRENCH FLAGEOLET BEANS

For our family of 4

These tiny, elongated pale-green beans are one of the special joys of French cooking, the lightest and subtlest members of the bean family and now widely available in dried form. In France they are often teamed with various types of sausage as a complete one-dish meal. Here we prepare them simply as a starch-foundation side dish. They are particulary delicious with almost all meats and birds, and are especially good with lamb dishes.

Check Staples:

Clear chicken bouillon (2 cups)
Salt butter (¼ lb.)
Aromatics: crystal salt, freshly ground black pepper, MSG, dried dillweed (if fresh not available), garlic (1 clove), sweet marjoram, summer savory
Yellow onions (2 medium)
Fresh parsley (small bunch)
Italian peeled and seeded plum tomatoes (1 lb. 1 oz. can)
Tomato juice (½ cup)
Dry white wine (½ cup)

Shopping List:

Dried French flageolets (1 cup, about ½ lb.)
Fresh dill (small bunch)

The Night Before and in the Morning

Scald, soak overnight, and gently simmer the cup of flageolets in a bouillon made of: the 2 cups of chicken broth, the ½ cup of tomato juice, the ½ cup of wine, a small handful of fresh dill (or 1 teaspoon of the dried), 1 teaspoon marjoram, 1 teaspoon savory, plus salt, pepper, and MSG to taste. Simmer, "just smiling," covered, until flageolets are perfectly tender but not mushy, usually in 1 to 1½ hours. Much of the liquid will be absorbed and flageolets will double in volume. Hold in liquid until needed.

About 35 Minutes Before Serving

Preheat oven to 300 degrees and warm up a heatproof covered dish in which the flageolets will be brought to the table. Drain flageolets, saving excellent bouillon for other soups or sauces. Put drained flageolets into hot covered dish and set in oven to heat up; it usually takes about 25 to 30 minutes. Meanwhile prepare a modified *sauce Bretonne*. Peel and finely chop the 2 onions. In a heavy 1½-quart saucepan melt the ¼-pound stick of butter, then sauté onions until just golden. Add the canned tomatoes and the clove of garlic, finely minced, mashing tomatoes down to a rough pulp. Add a small handful of the parsley, finely chopped, plus salt, pepper, and MSG to taste. Simmer, uncovered, stirring occasionally, until sauce shows first sign of thickening, then gently blend into flageolets. If necessary, put back in oven for another 5 minutes, but do not leave too long or flageolets may begin to dry out. Serve them very hot.

EGYPTIAN RED LENTILS WITH SEEDLESS GRAPES

For our family of 4

These bright red-orange lentils, shaped like tiny split-peas, are cooked quite differently from ordinary brown lentils. They must not be soaked or they will mash to a purée. The Indians grow a similar red lentil, which they call *massoor dall* and serve with their curries (page 399). We serve them with pork, veal, and the more solid types of fish.

Check Staples:

Salt butter (2 Tbs.)
Clear chicken bouillon (about 2 cups)
Lemon (1)
Aromatic: crystal salt☧
Yellow onions (2 medium)

Shopping List:

Egyptian red lentils (1 cup, about ½ lb.)
Thompson white seedless grapes, or alternative, *see* list, page 371 (enough to fill 1½ cups when pulled from stems, say, ½ to ¾ lb.)

About 30 Minutes Before Serving

We prepare this dish in a 1½-quart enameled cast-iron cocotte* with a tightly fitting lid, which is good-looking enough to come to the table.

Put in the lentils, just cover with the chicken bouillon, and bring slowly to a boil, gently stirring occasionally with wooden spoon. Meanwhile peel and finely chop the 2 onions, then quickly sauté to just golden in the 2 tablespoons of butter. Gently blend onions and butter into lentils. The instant they boil, turn down heat to gentle simmering, cover, and cook until lentils are just tender but still chewy, usually in 10 to 15 minutes, according to type of lentil. Timing is quite critical, so check after 10 minutes and, if boiling liquid has fallen well below surface of expanding lentils, add a little more chicken bouillon. Turn up heat for 1 or 2 minutes to bring back to a boil, then turn down to gentle simmering and cover until done. Meanwhile squeeze 1 tablespoon of lemon juice, wash the grapes and pull enough from stems to fill 1½ cups. Preheat oven to 200 degrees. When lentils are perfect, carefully blend in lemon juice and salt to taste, then also check texture. Lentils should be stiff, but not too dry. If necessary, blend in 1 or 2 more tablespoons of chicken bouillon. Now dig a hole in the center of the lentils, piling them up around the side of the dish, then fill this hole with the grapes. Cover and put into oven for 4 or 5 minutes to reheat lentils and warm grapes. Incidentally, this dish is also excellent served cold.

¶ *Salads*

Our general rules for spring salads (page 318) apply through the summer, but now, as the salad ingredients become more mature and robust, we slightly sharpen our salad dressings. A basic discussion of salad-making in general is on page 73. The best salad greens of spring are noted in the list of foods in season (page 366).

SUMMER SALAD DRESSING NUMBER ONE

For our family of 4

Check Staples:

Lemons (1 or 2, according to juiciness)
Aromatics: crystal salt,⚕ freshly ground black pepper,⚕ dried basil (if fresh not available), garlic (½ clove to rub around bowl), dried thyme (if fresh not available)
Fresh parsley (enough for 1 Tbs., finely chopped)
Green scallion tops (enough for 1 Tbs., chopped)
Green virgin olive oil⛁ (4½ Tbs.)

Shopping List:

Fresh basil (enough for 1 Tbs., finely chopped)
Fresh thyme (enough for 2 tsp., finely chopped)

Before the Salad Goes into the Bowl

Rub the inside of the bowl with the cut side of the clove of garlic. How many rubs is a matter of trial and error within the taste of each family; we go around 5 times.

We Prepare It at Table

We put ½ teaspoon salt into a small mortar. Pound for 1 or 2 seconds with the pestle. Grind on black pepper until the salt is speckled gray. We use a 1-ounce graduated medicine glass to measure exactly 1½ tablespoons of the squeezed lemon juice. Add to mortar and stir around to dissolve salt. Measure 4½ tablespoons of the olive oil and add to mortar. Stir around and let it rest, for the flavors to blend, until salad is ready to be dressed. Into a small separate bowl finely snip with scissors: 1 tablespoon of the basil and 2 teaspoons of the fresh thyme (or ½ teaspoon of either of these dried) ; then add 1 tablespoon of the parsley and 1 tablespoon of the scallion tops, both finely chopped.

When the Salad Is About to Be Served

Stir up oil mixture in mortar. Add the chopped fresh herbs and stir again. Spoon the dressing over the salad. Toss thoroughly and serve instantly.

SUMMER SALAD DRESSING NUMBER TWO

For our family of 4

Follow the same procedure as above, but replace the lemon juice with tarragon white wine vinegar,⊜ the basil with fresh dill (dried dillweed is not possible) , and the scallion tops with minced sweet red onion.

COUNTRY HAM AND PINEAPPLE SALAD

For our family of 4

We find this salad particularly refreshing on a hot summer day. Again we make use of our dark smoked country ham (page 369) .

Check Staples:

Lean dark smoked ham (enough to fill about 1½ cups when cut up, about 10 to 12 oz.)

Homemade mayonnaise, *see* page 423 (1 cup)

Shopping List:

Pineapple chunks, preferably fresh, or canned frozen (2 cups, about 1 lb.)

Fresh mint, optional (a few sprigs)

Preparation in About 10 Minutes—Chill for at Least 1 Hour

Cut ham into thick matchsticks. Drain pineapple from juice (if canned type is used) and dice into large cubes. Blend with ham in serving dish. Thin the mayonnaise to consistency of very thick cream with some of the pineapple juice. Blend with ham and pineapple. Serve quite cold. At the last moment it may be sprinkled with a very little finely chopped fresh mint, if available.

THE DUTTONS' FROZEN FRUIT SALAD

For our family of 4

Check Staples:

Lemon (1)
Homemade mayonnaise, *see* page 423 (1/3 cup)
Aromatic: crystal salt
Watercress (1 bunch)
Granulated vanilla sugar (1 Tbs.)

Shopping List:

Heavy whipping cream (about 1/2 cup)
Cream cheese (3-oz. package)
Pineapple, frozen, crushed (1 cup, 8-oz. can)
Cherries, pitted, fresh or canned (1/3 cup)
Pecans, shelled meats (1/3 cup)

Preparation in About 15 Minutes—Freeze for at Least 2 Hours

We begin by putting our round copper beating bowl and balloon whisk into the freezer, to ensure very stiff whipped cream. As the ingredients are prepared, they are combined in a large mixing bowl. Squeeze 1 1/2 tablespoons of lemon juice, put into bowl, and beat it with the 1/4 cup of mayonnaise. Add 1/2 teaspoon salt, the tablespoon of sugar, and work in, breaking it up with a wooden fork, the package of cream cheese. Then blend in the cup of crushed pineapple and the 1/3 cup of cherries, drained, if canned. Cut enough pecan meats into quarters to fill 1/3 cup and add to bowl. Finally, whip cream very stiff and fold into mixture lightly and quickly with flexible spatula. At once, smooth mixture into an ice-cold 9 × 9 × 2-inch pan and freeze for at least 2 hours. Cut each portion as a neat rectangle and serve on a bed of coarsely cut watercress.

¶ *Desserts*

BARTLETT PEARS STUFFED WITH ROQUEFORT CHEESE

We think this is one of the great combinations of all gastronomy. Each part brings out and magnifies the other's flavor. It is also one of the most useful and flexible standbys. Half a pear makes a fine dessert for one person; two halves, with a little extra cheese and a glass of wine, a thoroughly satisfactory quick lunch. As soon as the Bartlett pears start coming in, usually in July, we order a whole wheel of Roquefort, weighing around 5 1/4 lbs., store it in the refrigerator in a covered dish, and dig down into it from the top with a spoon. This gives the rounded blobs of cheese to fit the pears.

Shopping List:

Ripe Bartlett pears (½ or whole per person)
Roquefort cheese (walnut-sized piece per person)

The Tool to Use Is a Melon-Ball Scooper

Remove stem from pear and cut exactly in half lengthwise. With the right size of melon-ball scooper, neatly cut out core. With a small sharp knife, cut out hard stem that runs from core to tip. Place a rounded piece of Roquefort cheese, about the size of a walnut, in the depression where the core was cut out. This combination is at its best when the pear is exactly ripe and the Roquefort is well veined with blue.

BING CHERRIES IN ARMAGNAC AS THEY DO IT IN FRANCE

For our family of 4

We like Bing cherries best as they are picked from the tree. Yet there comes a moment when even this delight palls. Then we cook the cherries in one of two favorite French ways (the other is on page 326).

Check Staples:

Aromatic: whole cloves
Granulated vanilla sugar (1 cup)
Dry red wine (1 pt.)

Shopping List:

Bing cherries (2 lbs.)
French Armagnac brandy (about 2 Tbs.)
Swiss Kirsch (about 2 Tbs.)

The Day Before—a Family Chore

Many hands make light work of pitting the cherries. We count about 30 of the pits, crack them with a hammer, and put them into a tiny muslin herb bag along with 4 whole cloves. Submerge this little bag in the pint of red wine in a saucepan and add the cup of sugar. Stir and boil fairly rapidly for about 10 minutes, then add pitted cherries, turn heat down to simmering, and cook until cherries are quite soft, usually in 10 to 15 minutes. Lift out cherries with a slotted spoon and put them into a serving bowl, which is to be refrigerated, covered, overnight. Fish out and throw away the little bag from the wine sauce, then boil rapidly, stirring now and then, until it becomes thick and syrupy. Let cool, strain into a covered storage dish, and refrigerate overnight.

Just Before Serving

Stir 2 tablespoons each of the Armagnac and Kirsch into the wine sauce (or more to taste), then pour over the cherries. Serve chilled.

OUR QUICK AND SIMPLE PEACH ICE CREAM

Enough for several days for our family of 4

We make quantities of this ice cream every summer when the peaches are at their peak. It can be frozen directly in freezer ice trays and, even without further stirring, the texture is not at all bad, but of course it is smoother when finished in an electric ice-cream freezer.

Check Staples:

Lemons (4)
Granulated vanilla sugar (4 cups)

Shopping List:

Peaches (about 24 medium, roughly 6 to 8 lbs.)
Sour cream (2 qts.)
Crystallized ginger (½ lb.)
French Martinique rhum (½ cup)

Preparation in About ½ Hour—Freezing for About 4 Hours

The first job is to stone the peaches and mash flesh to a purée. People who like an extremely smooth ice cream may prefer to skin them and pass the flesh through a food mill. We think there is more flavor and a more interesting texture when the fruit is slightly coarser, so we simply chunk the peaches, with the skin, then churn them in the electric blender for only a few seconds. In a large mixing bowl combine: the 2 quarts of sour cream, the 4 cups of sugar, the ½ pound of ginger, chopped, the ½ cup of rhum, plus 6 or more tablespoons of lemon juice to taste. When this is thoroughly blended, add peach purée and blend again. Freeze by any preferred method (see above).

THE SAFE INDIAN WAY TO EAT A MANGO

There are some foods which it seems impossible to enjoy to the fullest extent in a formal atmosphere. We remember eating a barrel of freshly dredged oysters on a rocky beach, when we wore bathing suits and soaked ourselves with seawater and oyster juice as we opened and ate them from the shells.

The problem is the same with the mango, the fruit with the thick rubbery skin and the pulp with such an excess of juice that it runs through one's fingers and stains clothes and table linen a bright yellow. Some people say that the only practical place to eat it is in the bath. One of our New York neighbors, an Indian gourmet importer of delicacies from his native land, has taught us the safe Indian way to eat a mango.

Choose a ripe mango, but not overripe for the skin must be firm and intact with no weak brown patches. Wipe it with a damp cloth until the skin shines. Now start turning the fruit in the fingers, pressing it gently but firmly all over, so that the pulp is squeezed and mashed inside without the skin breaking. By continuing this process for three or four minutes, without ever squeezing the mango so hard that it bursts (that would be a disaster!), the fruit will at last feel like a small rubber bag full of water. Now carefully inspect the two ends of the mango and find the spot where the stalk was once attached. Here there is a small round seal, which can be edged off with the thumbnail, leaving a small round hole. Before the juice has time to ooze out, put the hole to the lips and start sucking, at the same time gently squeezing the bag. For a glorious few minutes one sucks and squeezes, until there is nothing left of the mango but the large stone surrounded by the crumpled skin. The bag is empty. The essential trick of course is developing skill at the pressing and pummeling, so that all the pulp is completely mashed and fully detached from the central stone. Then the pleasure can be sucked from the mango with one's hands remaining completely dry. The Florida Hayden mangoes of this season are excellent for this charming game.

CONCORD GRAPE KISSEL

For our family of 4

Kissel is the simple, everyday dessert most often served in an average Russian home: a slightly thickened and sweetened purée of tart fresh fruits. It is most refreshing when properly made with exactly the right sweet-sour balance and served ice-cold with whipped cream. This recipe can be used with almost any of the summer soft berries, but we like it especially with the slightly "foxy" flavor of the semi-wild Eastern Concord grapes when they come into the market (see the list of foods in season, page 366).

Check Staples:

Lemon (1)
Granulated vanilla sugar (3 or 4 cups)
Ground arrowroot (about 4 Tbs.)
Dry white wine (a few Tbs.)

Shopping List:

Concord grapes (2 or 3 lbs.)
Heavy whipping cream (½ cup)

Preparation in About 25 Minutes—Several Hours to Chill

Wash grapes, pull off stalks, put into saucepan, almost cover with freshly drawn cold water, and boil, with steady bubbling, uncovered, for 10 minutes. With experience, this timing can be varied slightly, for fine adjustment of taste and texture. (It will also vary for other fruits, but 10 minutes is always a good starting point.) Next, press grapes through a wire sieve with mesh fine enough to hold back pits as well as skins. Measure the resulting purée, which should be very smooth. Sweeten to taste with the sugar. A good starting rule is 1 cup of sugar to 3 cups of purée, and this is roughly what we use for the Concord grapes. The trick is to balance the acidity of the fruit, without drowning the fresh flavor in sickly sweetness. (For variation, we sometimes replace part of the white sugar with brown, or with pure maple syrup or honey.) We also add at this point a squirt or two of lemon juice, but this is optional.

Prepare the thickening mix. A good starting rule is 2 teaspoons of arrowroot for each pint of sweetened purée. For this amount of Concord grapes, we would put 3 tablespoons of arrowroot into a small bowl and use just enough of the white wine to liquefy it smoothly. Put fruit purée back into saucepan and bring back to a boil, stirring continuously, to dissolve sugar and blend flavors. Let bubble gently for a couple of minutes, then turn off heat. Give a final stir to the arrowroot, then spoon into the purée, vigorously stirring in each spoonful before adding the next, until purée shows first signs of thickening. Turn heat up again and bring back just to boiling, stirring continuously with a wooden spoon and scraping bottom and sides of pan as purée increases in thickness. Let simmer gently, still stirring, for 2 or 3 minutes. Then finally adjust thickness, either by adding a little more of the arrowroot mix, or thinning with a dash or two of the wine. Let it cool, then pour into a covered storage or serving dish and refrigerate until chilled and set. Serve cold, with the cream, whipped with a balloon whisk. At the moment of eating, we discuss our preferences as to thickness, sweetness, and flavor, so that we can adjust the preparation the next time.

COLD PSEUDO-SOUFFLÉ OF RASPBERRIES

Enough for 2 days for our family of 4

This is a dramatic showpiece. The trick is to make the raspberry mousse rise about 2 inches above the edge of the soufflé dish, then accentuate this lift with about another inch of whipped cream on top. At first sight, it seems magical. To make the fluff smoother and higher, we churn the gelatin in an electric ice-cream machine,✲ but it can be beaten by hand.

Check Staples:

Eggs (5 large)
Granulated vanilla sugar§ (3/4 cup)
Unflavored powdered gelatin (2 envelopes of 1 Tbs. each)
Dry white wine§ (1/3 cup)

Shopping List:

Fresh raspberries (1 qt.—could also be done with frozen raspberries, but taste is not nearly so good)
Heavy whipping cream (2 1/2 cups)

The Day Before—Preparation in About 1 Hour

We start with the "paper trick," using a lightly buttered soufflé dish of exactly 1-quart capacity. Cut a piece of waxed paper 10 inches wide and long enough to go around the soufflé dish with about a 2-inch overlap. Fold in half lengthwise, so that it is now a double-thick strip 5 inches wide. Lightly butter one side of it. Wrap it around soufflé dish, with the buttered side in and the folded edge at top, with 2 inches of the paper in contact with the sides of the dish and 3 inches sticking up in the air—in effect, making the dish 3 inches deeper. Hold in place with a couple of tight rubber bands and refrigerate until needed.

Put the 3/4 cup of sugar into a heavy saucepan with 1 1/2 cups of water and boil fairly hard until it just turns syrupy, usually in about 5 minutes. Meanwhile measure 3 1/2 cups of the raspberries, wash and drain, then add to sugar syrup, bring back to a boil and let bubble 5 minutes longer. Then purée through a food mill and put back into saucepan. Put 1 1/2 tablespoons of the powdered gelatin into a small mixing bowl and blend to smooth paste with the 1/3 cup of wine. Stir, by spoonfuls, into the raspberry purée and bring back to boiling, still stirring, to dissolve gelatin. Now we let mixture cool slightly, then load into an electric ice-cream machine and churn, over ice or in freezer, to fluff gelatin as it begins to set, usually in 15 to 20 minutes. (This could also be done by hand, in a bowl set in ice cubes, first letting it rest on the ice for about 20 minutes, then beating with a wire whisk, still on the ice, for about 10 minutes longer.)

While gelatin is being churned, or beaten, prepare final ingredients. We put 2 round copper beating bowls and a wire whisk in freezer to get cold—or if the freezer is too small, place bowls over cracked ice—in preparation for beating cream and egg whites. Separate the 5 eggs, storing the yolks for some other use. Now work fast. When raspberry purée is fluffy but still runny, put into a large mixing bowl, beat egg whites until just stiff (see our BASIC RULE, page 74), then fold lightly into raspberries. Now measure 1½ cups of the cream into the other bowl, then beat stiff and also lightly fold in. Bring paper-collared soufflé dish out of refrigerator and pour in raspberry fluff, which will rise about 2 inches above edge of dish, but be thick enough to be held in by paper. Make sure that paper has no folds and is nicely rounded. Put back in refrigerator to chill and set overnight.

About 1 Hour Before Serving

Again set a beating bowl and wire whisk in the freezer, for the whipping of the decorating cream. Bring soufflé out of refrigerator and carefully run a sharp knife around the sides of the paper, to separate it from the soufflé. Remove the paper, and, if necessary, slightly smooth and shape the soufflé with a small spatula where it stands out of the dish. Beat the remaining cup of cream and roughly pile it to cover the top and accentuate the height. Decorate cream with remaining ½ cup of whole raspberries. Then hold in the refrigerator until it is to be served.

¶ *Family Specialties—Party Breakfasts · Breads · Preserves*

SUNDAY BREAKFAST BAKED EGGS WITH CHICKEN LIVERS

For our family of 4

We were once given a set of individual ceramic onion soup dishes with lids. We also use them for baked dishes, including this one.

Check Staples:

Salt butter (4 Tbs.)
Eggs (8 large)
Aromatics: crystal salt,☆ freshly ground black pepper,☆ MSG,▣ sweet marjoram

Shopping List:

Chicken livers (1 lb.)
Light cream (½ cup)

About 45 Minutes Before Serving

Cut chicken livers into bite-size pieces and quickly sauté in 3 tablespoons of the butter until just brown outside but still quite soft inside, usually in about 6 minutes. Preheat oven to 350 degrees. Lightly butter 4 individual ceramic casseroles (above) and place equal portions of chicken livers in bottom of each. Break the 8 eggs into a mixing bowl, add the ½ cup of cream, 1 teaspoon marjoram, season to taste with salt, pepper, and MSG, then beat vigorously with a wire whisk until quite frothy. Pour at once, in equal parts, into the 4 casseroles, put in oven, uncovered, then bake until eggs are just set, usually in 25 to 30 minutes. Put on lids to keep hot and serve instantly. They are best eaten directly out of the casseroles.

SUNDAY BREAKFAST BAKED EGGS WITH MUSHROOMS

For our family of 4

Check Staples:

Dark smoked bacon (4 slices)
Salt butter (1 Tbs.)
Eggs (8 large)
Aromatics: crystal salt, freshly ground black pepper, MSG, thyme

Shopping List:

Mushrooms (½ lb.)
Light cream (1 cup)

About 45 Minutes Before Serving

Follow the same procedure as in the preceding recipe, except replace the chicken livers with the ½ pound of fresh mushrooms and the 4 slices of bacon, replace the marjoram with thyme, and increase the quantity of light cream to 1 cup, to allow for extra absorption by the mushrooms. We prefer not to sauté the mushrooms in advance, so only enough butter is needed to lubricate the insides of the individual casseroles. Fry bacon until crisp, then crumble into casseroles. Wipe mushrooms clean and cut lengthwise into hammer shapes, then divide between casseroles. The baking time is the same.

SUNDAY BREAKFAST BAKED EGGS WITH CRAB MEAT

For our family of 4

Check Staples:

Salt butter (1 Tbs.)
Eggs (8 large)
Aromatics: crystal salt, freshly ground black pepper, MSG, tarragon

Shopping List:

Fresh lump crab meat (½ lb.)
Light cream (½ cup)

About 45 Minutes Before Serving

Again follow the same procedure as for the baked eggs with chicken livers (page 482), except now replace the livers with the ½ pound of fresh lump crab meat, replace the marjoram with tarragon, and the light cream remains at ½ cup. Since the crab meat requires no advance sautéing, only enough butter is needed to lubricate the insides of the casseroles. Equal parts of the crab meat are placed in the bottom of each casserole and the frothy egg is poured in on top. The baking time is the same.

SUNDAY BREAKFAST HOT COUNTRY-HAM BISCUITS

About 18 biscuits

Here is one more excellent use for our boiled country ham from page 369.

Check Staples:

Boiled dark smoked country ham, coarsely ground (¾ cup)
Bacon or ham drippings (2 Tbs.)
Milk (¾ cup)
Aromatic: crystal salt
Granulated instantized flour (2 cups)
Double-acting baking powder (2 tsp.)

About 25 Minutes Before Serving

Put the 2 cups of flour into a mixing bowl, carefully sprinkle on the 2 teaspoons of baking powder, then stir thoroughly together (with ordinary flour they must be sifted together). Blend the ¾ cup of ground ham into the flour, with a very little salt to taste. Using a pastry cutter, now mix in the 2 tablespoons of drippings, until dough has the consistency of coarse cornmeal. Add the milk, dash by dash, using as little as possible to achieve a soft dough. Preheat oven to 450 degrees. Using a light touch, gather dough into a ball and place on a lightly floured pastry board. Knead gently for about 30 seconds. With a lightly floured rolling pin, roll out dough to about ⅜ inch thick and cut into 1½-inch rounds.

About 5 Minutes Before Serving

Set biscuits on baking sheet and put into oven. Bake until lightly brown, usually in 12 to 15 minutes.

SUMMER PEACHES SPICED AND BOTTLED FOR WINTER

About 6 1-pound jars

When peaches are at their peak, we often preserve a batch and give jars of them as Christmas presents. By December they are perfect. They are a fine accompaniment to various cold meats and particularly good with slices of boiled country ham.

Check Staples:

Aromatics: ground cinnamon, whole cloves, Indian ground ginger*☆*
Granulated vanilla sugar⊜ (2 lbs.)
Tarragon white wine vinegar⊜ (1½ cups)

Shopping List:

Ripe peaches (6 lbs.)

Skinning and First Boiling in About ½ Hour

We use a wide Dutch oven for this operation, so that the peaches can be spread out and not too great a depth of water is needed. First, put them all into this pan and measure the exact amount of water needed just to cover. Remove peaches and add more water to fill pan about half full. Bring water quickly to a rolling boil. Drop in peaches and let them scald for 3 or 4 minutes. Drain, throwing away water, then peel —the scalding makes this easy. Stick 2 whole cloves in each, on opposite sides, pushing heads well in. Measure into pan the exact amount of freshly drawn cold water needed to cover peaches. Bring quickly to a boil and, while heating up, stir in the 2 pounds of sugar, 1 teaspoon ground cinnamon, and 1 teaspoon ground ginger. When this spiced syrup boils, slide in the peaches, bring back to simmering and continue cooking, uncovered, for 15 minutes. Let peaches cool in syrup and leave them soaking for at least 4 hours.

The Second Boiling in About 1 Unsupervised Hour

Drain peaches, taking care not to lose any of the syrup. Add the 1½ cups of vinegar to the syrup and bring to a boil. Let it simmer gently, uncovered, for 30 minutes. Do not let it bubble hard or the liquid will be reduced too much. Put in peaches, bring back to simmering, and let bubble until peach flesh is very soft, usually in 15 to 25 minutes, according to ripeness of fruit. Let cool and leave peaches soaking overnight.

The Next Day—Bottling in About ½ Hour

Sterilize the required number of mason jars. Lift peaches out with slotted spoon, letting syrup drain back into pan, then pack peaches into jars. Bubble syrup hard on high heat, until it begins to thicken, then pour into jars, filling each to the brim. Seal and store. No need to refrigerate until a jar is opened.

The Budget Pull-Back and Encore Dishes of Summer

A PÂTÉ OF CHICKEN GIBLETS

For our family of 4

In the list of ingredients below, we show the chicken parts as they might be bought specially. However once one has the measure of this recipe, one can improvise with all kinds of bits and pieces that might be marooned in the refrigerator. The livers are always basic. We usually prepare two or three times the quantity below and refrigerate the *pâté* in a number of smallish jars, each kept airtight until it is opened for use.

Check Staples:

Salt butter (4 Tbs.)
Eggs (2 large)
Clear chicken bouillon (2½ cups)
Aromatics: crystal salt, freshly ground black pepper, MSG, whole bay leaves, freshly ground mace, freshly ground nutmeg
Yellow onions (2 medium)
Parsley (small bunch)
Green scallions (1 bunch)
Watercress (1 bunch)
Brandy (3 or 4 Tbs.)

Shopping List:

Chicken parts:
gizzards (3)
hearts (3)
necks (3)
backs (3)
wings (6)
Chicken livers (½ lb.)

Preparation in About 45 Minutes—Chilled for Several Hours Before Serving

Bring the 2½ cups of chicken bouillon to a boil in a 2-quart saucepan and, while heating up, add: all chicken parts except livers, the 2 onions, peeled and sliced, 2 whole bay leaves, plus salt, pepper, and MSG to taste. Simmer, covered, until gizzards are tender, usually in 30 to 40 minutes. Meanwhile prepare the other ingredients. Hard-boil the 2 eggs. In a sauté pan bring the 4 tablespoons of butter to medium frying temperature, then quickly sauté chicken livers until slightly brown outside but still soft and rare in the center, usually in about 6 minutes. Finely chop enough parsley, green scallion tops (hold white bulbs for later), and watercress leaves to fill ¼ cup of each, fairly tightly packed. When chicken parts are done, drain, let cool enough to handle, then pick off all meat from bone. We use the fine cutter of our electric meat grinder,* passing through all boned and boneless chicken parts, plus the drained livers, the eggs, and the scallion bulbs. Then grind a second time and put into a fairly large mixing bowl. Add: the chopped parsley, green scallion tops, and watercress, all the liver juices from the sauté pan, 5 or 6 good grinds each of the mace and nutmeg, plus 2 or 3 tablespoons of the brandy. Work everything thoroughly together (most efficiently with clean fingers), then taste and adjust seasonings if necessary, and finally check texture, bearing in mind that it will stiffen as it chills. If an extra tablespoon of liquid is required, this may either be the brandy or the chicken bouillon, according to taste. Chill in an airtight jar until needed. Serve on toast triangles, with remaining parsley and watercress sprinkled over.

TWO WAYS TO SPICE A BEEF TONGUE

Method 1—Cold Aspic of Beef Tongue

At least 2 meals for our family of 4

Check Staples:

Clear beef bouillon (2 cups)
Eggs (4 large)
Aromatics: crystal salt,⚗ freshly ground black pepper,⚗ MSG,🥫 whole allspice, whole bay leaves, whole cloves, Worcestershire sauce (about 1 Tbs.)
Yellow onion (1 medium)
Watercress (1 bunch)
Unflavored powdered gelatin (1 envelope containing 1 Tbs.)
Red wine vinegar🥫 (1/4 cup)
Plus mayonnaise, preferably homemade, page 423, to serve with it (1 cup)

Shopping List:

Fresh beef tongue (1 medium, about 3 lbs.)
White celery (1 heart)

The Day Before

BASIC RULE FOR BOILING A BEEF TONGUE: Wash tongue, place in a suitably sized pot, cover with freshly drawn cold water, and bring quickly to boil. While heating up, add: the onion, peeled and sliced, 1 tablespoon salt, 1 teaspoon MSG, a few grinds of pepper, about a dozen whole allspice, 2 whole bay leaves, about 8 whole cloves, plus the 1/4 cup of vinegar. Gently simmer, "just smiling," covered, until tongue is fork-tender, usually in about 2 hours. Then let cool in the liquid for at least 5 or 6 hours, to absorb aromatics. Next skin tongue and cut away any small bones and rough bits from the root end. If whole tongue is now to be stored, it should be kept refrigerated in enough of the drained boiling-liquor to cover.

Assembling the Aspic in About ½ Hour

Hard-boil the 4 eggs. We use the fine cutter of our electric meat grinder✱ and now pass through it: the hard-boiled eggs; the tongue, cut into manageable pieces; the celery heart, with its leaves; about ½ bunch of the watercress. Then put these ground-up ingredients into a fairly large mixing bowl. Liquefy the tablespoon of gelatin with about 3 tablespoons of the beef bouillon. Bring the remaining beef bouillon quickly to a boil in a small saucepan, stir in gelatin paste, and keep stirring until it is completely dissolved. Then pour into ground tongue, adding 1 tablespoon Worcestershire sauce and working everything thoroughly together. Taste and adjust seasonings. Turn into a mold and refrigerate overnight.

A Few Minutes Before Serving

Unmold in the usual way onto a bed of the remaining watercress. Serve with homemade mayonnaise.

Method 2—Boiled Beef Tongue in Port Wine

For our family of 4

This recipe starts with the assumption that a beef tongue has been boiled according to the preceding recipe and is then kept whole so that slices may be prepared as follows.

Check Staples:

Salt butter (2 Tbs.)
Clear beef bouillon (about ¾ cup)
Glace de viande **(1 tsp.)**
Aromatics: crystal salt, whole black peppercorns, MSG, whole bay leaf, ground cinnamon, whole cloves, orange rind (enough to fill 1 tsp., grated)
Yellow onion (1 medium)
Ground arrowroot (2 to 3 tsp.)
Italian tomato paste (about 2 tsp.)

Shopping List:

Beef tongue, cold boiled (about 16 cross-cut slices)
Red-currant jelly (about ¼ cup)
A fairly good ruby port (about ¾ cup)

About 40 Minutes Before Serving

Preheat oven to keep-warm temperature (150 degrees). We put enough sliced tongue for 4 people into a suitably sized enameled cast-iron cocotte✱ with a tightly fitting lid, which is good-looking enough to come to the table. Cover and put in oven for tongue to get warm. We prepare the sauce in a tin-lined copper sauté pan. First, melt the 2 tablespoons of butter and quickly sauté the onion, peeled and minced, to just golden. Turn heat down to simmering and blend in: 1 teaspoon of *glace de viande* and the 2 teaspoons of tomato paste. In a small bowl liquefy 2 teaspoons of the arrowroot with 1 or 2 tablespoons of the bouillon, then blend carefully into sauté pan. Turning up heat slightly to maintain simmering, work in ½ cup of the bouillon and ½ cup of the port. Turn up heat, so that sauce bubbles and thickens to consistency of heavy cream. If it remains too thin, turn down heat and add a little more liquefied arrowroot. If it becomes too thick, add a little more port. Grate enough of the orange rind to fill 1 teaspoon and add to sauce. Also stir in: ¼ teaspoon cinnamon, 1 bay leaf, crumbled, ¼ teaspoon clove, plus salt, pepper, and MSG to taste. Simmer, covered, for about 15 minutes, stirring occasionally to blend and mature flavors. If texture of sauce becomes a little "rough," it can be strained at this point, but generally this is not necessary. Now blend in 4 tablespoons of the red-currant jelly, then finally recheck seasoning and texture, and if required either thicken with more arrowroot or thin with more port. Pour sauce over hot tongue in cocotte, place over heat on top of stove, and bring just to the boiling point, then carry cocotte to the table.

JOHANNA'S CHARLESTON HAM GUMBO

Several meals for our family of 4

Johanna is a remarkable natural cook. She never uses a formal recipe, but her feeling for putting in "a little bit of this and a little bit of that," coupled with a fine sense of timing for each of the ingredients, produces some superb dishes. This is the way we use up the last of our dark smoked country ham. When ¾ of the bone is bare and there is only about 2 pounds of meat left at the butt end, we prepare this gumbo which Johanna learned from her mother on a South Carolina farm and which we learned by watching Johanna.

Check Staples:

Largest possible ham bone, with about 2 lbs. lean meat on it
Corn-belly salt pork (about ¼ lb.)
Aromatics: salt, whole dried red chili pod, basil, whole juniper berries, oregano, rosemary, summer savory, thyme
Parsley (small bunch)
Italian peeled and seeded plum tomatoes (2 lb. 3 oz. can)
Italian tomato paste (6-oz. can)

Shopping List:

Fresh okra, small young pods (1½ lbs.)
Large fresh lima beans (1 lb., shelled)

About 1½ Hours Before Serving

Johanna would first cut all the ham off the bone, put the bone into the big soup pot, cover it with about 2½ quarts of freshly drawn cold water and bring it to a boil. Meanwhile she would cut the meat into bite-size chunks, but in her own special way, saying: "I pick at the meat and feel it with my fingers and cut off all the dry bits and rough skin and fat. I decide which is the meat worth eating and hold that back in a bowl; and which are the bits to give flavor to the broth and I drop those into the boiling water." Johanna also collected any odd flavorful bits she could find in the refrigerator: a piece of dark smoked bacon rind, odd pieces of cooked meats, any and all bones, etc. Lean bits would be dropped straight into the boiling broth. Anything fatty went into her frypan with the ham fat. Next she added to this pan 4 or 5 good slices of the corn belly, then fried everything gently until most of the fat ran out and the various bits were slightly brown; then they would all go into the boiling broth. During this first phase, the water is kept bubbling fairly strongly to draw out the flavors from the bone and various bits, and continue bubbling for about 1 hour. Meanwhile the principal ingredients are prepared.

Johanna would say: "I look at the okra and pinch it, then I decide whether it's young and tender or old and tough. That makes the difference whether I cook it in the pot for 40 minutes, half an hour, or 20 minutes. If the pods are old, I may top and tail them. Then I cut them all in pieces about ½ inch long. When they get into the pot, the heat drives out the juice and that's what thickens the broth and makes the gumbo." If the lima beans are fresh, they are shucked. If fresh aromatic herbs are available, use a few good sprigs of each, cutting off any woody stalks.

Either 40, 30, or 20 Minutes Before Serving, According to the Age of the Okra

Remove from the pot and throw away all the bits and pieces, which have by now given up their flavor and are of no further use, including, of course, all bones. Next all the main ingredients of the gumbo go into the pot: the okra, the lima beans, the canned tomatoes, the tomato paste (first diluted in a small bowl with some of the hot broth), plus the cubed ham; also add the aromatics, 2 or 3 sprigs each of the fresh, or the following amounts of the dried: 1 teaspoon basil, ½ teaspoon oregano, 1 teaspoon rosemary, 1 teaspoon summer savory, 1 teaspoon thyme, plus 2 teaspoons of juniper berries, 1 small dried hot chili pepper, and salt, pepper, and MSG to taste.

For the next few minutes watch the heat very carefully, to make sure that the liquid keeps at the gentlest simmering. This continues, for 40, 30, or 20 minutes, according to the needs of the okra. For the last 5 minutes Johanna would have the lid off and would hover continually over the pot, stir and taste and adjust the seasonings, take out and throw away odd inedible sprigs of herbs, until everything was exactly right.

It is served of course in piping-hot open gumbo bowls. When the cold fall days begin to bite into the end of summer, Johanna says: "A gumbo is as good as an extra blanket. It talks to you as it goes down."

FRENCH RATATOUILLE AUX OEUFS—A RAGOUT OF VEGETABLES AS THEY DO IT IN PROVENCE

For our family of 4

This is another Franco-Italian dish from the border area around Nice, where the two cultures so successfully intermingle under the Mediterranean sun. There is an obvious similarity between this hot *ratatouille* and the Italian cold *caponata,* the appetizer in which the vegetables are combined and cooked in much the same way. This is a deceptively substantial dish and we often serve it, with two eggs per person, as a one-course meal. It is important to maintain the exact balance of the vegetables listed below. If one of them is omitted or another is allowed to dominate, the unusual quality of the dish can be lost.

Check Staples:

Thick-sliced dark smoked bacon (4 slices)
Salt butter (2 Tbs.)
Eggs (4 large—or 8 for hungry people)
Aromatics: crystal salt, freshly ground black pepper, MSG, basil (only if fresh not available), whole coriander seed, garlic (2 cloves)
Yellow onions (3 medium)
Parsley (1 bunch)
Olive oil (½ cup)
Italian peeled and seeded plum tomatoes (1 lb. 1 oz. can)

Shopping List:

Parmesan cheese (¼ lb.)
Eggplants (2 medium)
Green peppers (3 medium)
Potatoes (3 medium, or 1 lb.)
Zucchini (3 medium)
Fresh basil (1 bunch)
French bread, to dip in juices (1 loaf)

Preparation in 15 Minutes—Cooking, with Minimum Attention, for 1¼ Hours

We prepare this in one of our enameled cast-iron cocottes* with a tightly fitting lid, which is good-looking enough to be brought to the table. Put into it the ½ cup of olive oil, but do not heat it up until the vegetables have been prepared. Peel the 3 onions, coarsely chop and hold separately. Finely mince the 2 cloves of garlic and hold in small covered jar. Other vegetables, as prepared, can be assembled in a single bowl. Cut off stem ends of the 2 eggplants and cut into bite-size chunks, without peeling. Remove the central seed pods from the green peppers and also chunk. Peel and chunk the 3 potatoes. Chunk the 3 zucchini without peeling. Now heat up the oil in the cocotte and quickly sauté the chopped onion until just transparent. Add all the chunked vegetables, plus the garlic, stir around to coat with oil, turn heat down to simmering, cover, and gently bubble in their own juices for 40 minutes. Almost no attention is required, except occasional stirring and checking to make sure that juices keep bubbling to maintain steam inside cocotte. Meanwhile prepare the remaining ingredients. Dice the 4 slices of bacon and hold. Measure 1½ teaspoons of the whole coriander into a mortar, coarsely grind, and hold. Grate the ¼ pound of Parmesan and hold. Chop a good supply of parsley and the fresh basil, if available.

About 30 Minutes Before Serving

Vegetables in cocotte will now be swimming in a good deal of juice. Gently stir them around once more, then add: canned tomatoes, with juice, the ground coriander, plus salt, pepper, and MSG to taste. Blend everything well together, but do it carefully—remember, we are not making a mash. The next objective is gently to boil away all excess water so that flavors are concentrated and focused. Leave lid off from this point onward. Turn up heat slightly so that merry bubbling continues, and every 10 minutes or so, without really stirring, gently move vegetables around to give moisture a chance to escape. The dish is ready to be served when there are no more runny liquids on the bottom but while vegetables are still very moist, though not mushy. At this point, gently blend in chopped parsley and basil, fresh or dried.

About 15 Minutes Before Serving—Baking the Eggs

We prepare the eggs in our small individual cast-iron au gratin dishes.* Preheat oven to 350 degrees. Put ½ tablespoon of the butter into each dish and set in oven for 3 minutes to melt. Then swish butter around in each dish, to lubricate bottom and sides, make beds of the diced bacon, dividing equally between 4 dishes, and add salt, pepper, and MSG to taste. Break 1 or 2 eggs into each dish, cover with a layer of grated Parmesan and bake until eggs are as soft or firm as preferred, usually between 5 and 7 minutes.

Serving at Table

The contents of each egg dish, including crumbled bacon, are slid onto the top of each portion of the *ratatouille* and sprinkled with the remaining Parmesan. We also serve chunks of unbuttered French bread, which can be dipped in the juices.

A Fish Stew Better Than Bouillabaisse

NECESSITY is the mother of most of the world's great fish stews. From the jagged Pacific coast of Chile to the Russian sands on the Black Sea, the fishermen send their best fish to market for profit and bring the rough, bony, spiny fish home to their wives. These endlessly resourceful cooks have learned over centuries of trial and error that these fish, often too rough to stand alone, can be combined with each other in a complementary balance of flavors, textures, and aromatic herbs and spices. The character of the great fish stews is of course different for every sea and every climate: from the *chupe de pescado* of Chile to the *zuppa di pesce* of Sicily, from the Psaro of Athens to the *Ghentsche waterzooie* of the North Sea coast of Belgium.

But it is the *bouillabaisse* of Provence that has been glamorized beyond all the others. Poems have been written and songs sung about it. Gourmets who try to describe it seem to lose their critical judgment: "This incomparable soup of gold, which glides down one's throat like a glorious ecstasy. . . ." The poet Monselet even added aphrodisiac qualities. He described how, if one consumed bouillabaisse anywhere near the sea, beautiful women (preferably not mermaids) would come up out of the water:

And chilly beauties, not a few,
Will do whate'er you wish,
Partaking, tête-a-tête with you,
Of this perfidious dish.

Yet we dare to disagree. We think there is one fish stew that is even better than bouillabaisse—better on its home ground; certainly better when prepared, with strange and foreign fish, in New York or San Francisco. This is the *cacciucco* of the glowing Mediterranean coast of Tuscany.

One summer, many years ago, a very young university student was spending a few months in Pisa doing a research paper on the life of Galileo.

On Sundays he would go with his friends to the beach and there would meet Papa Pasquale, the retired fisherman who made a living out of Sunday beach picnics for visitors from Pisa, taking the men of the party out in his boat. He would steer to the floating markers above his fish traps, which he had loaded at dawn, drop anchor, and begin hauling up the seaweed-coated underwater baskets. As the lids came off, the feet and legs of the crew were sloshed and slapped by the live *cacciucco*—the furiously wriggling *calamaretti,* the snapping *arigusta* and *scampi,* the *branzino, scorfano, gallinella, pesce cappone,* and the large *anguille,* and when one of these large eels slithered out, Papa yelled to jump away, as they could be dangerous until he had knocked them on the head with a wooden club. He always avoided killing any of the fish, because they were all supposed to be alive until they were in sight of the pot. When Papa Pasquale had sorted the fish and organized a properly balanced load of all the various kinds required in two wooden boxes, he pushed the extra fish back into the traps to keep healthy for the next party of picnic customers. Then up came the anchor and Papa headed his hungry crew toward the beach cove where Mama Pasquale was already at work.

A wood fire was roaring beneath a huge black cauldron with the first aromatic ingredients of the *cacciucco* already heating up: olive oil, tomatoes, garlic, onion, lemon rind, hot pepper, the *basilico, timo, salvia, alloro,* and the bottles of *rosé* Ravello waiting to be poured in at the right moment. As the bow of the boat touched the beach, Mama leaped aboard, followed by as many of the children as were old enough to handle knives and scrapers. The fish were scaled, cleaned (the entrails going straight back into the sea), washed in seawater, chunked, divided up into baskets—soft fish in one, hard fish in another, lobsters, *scampi,* and squid in a third—carried up the beach and, in a planned sequence and with exact timing, were tumbled into the pot.

CACCIUCCO TOSCANA—THE GREAT FISH STEW OF ITALY

For a party of 8 to 10

Of course it will not be quite the same when prepared in our city kitchen, but its basic attractions remain: the careful balance of several kinds of fish combined in an aromatic broth with unsophisticated simplicity. Much of its glamour as a party dish lies in the expansive atmosphere of its service: the huge pot in the center of the table, the quarts of red liquid tumbling out, the shapes and colors of the piled-up fish.

We usually visit our local fish-mama the day before and warn her that we are planning a *cacciucco.* She is a Tuscan and knows exactly what we mean. She sets aside several large fish heads, some substantial backbones, plus fins and trimmings—all essential ingredients of the spiced bouillon in which the edible fish will be boiled. She also reserves some live squid, without which a *cacciucco* is not authentic. When properly cooked, squid is delicious.

Check Staples:

Salt butter (1½ sticks)
Lemon (1)
Aromatics: crystal salt, freshly ground black pepper, whole dried hot red chili pepper, MSG, whole bay leaves, garlic (6 to 10 cloves, to taste), whole sage leaves, thyme
Green Pascal celery (3 or 4 stalks, with leaves)
Yellow onions (3 medium)
Fresh parsley (large bunch)
Olive oil (about 1½ cups)
Italian tomato paste (6-oz. can)
Italian peeled and seeded plum tomatoes (1 lb. 1 oz. can)
Red wine (about 1 cup)
Dry white wine (about 1½ cups)

Shopping List:

Solid chunks of at least 3 or 4 kinds of fish from the following list (total about 3 lbs.): sea bass, fillet of cod, eel, fillet of flounder, fillet of haddock, fillet of halibut, whole whiting, bone in, or alternatives from list, page 363
Whole squid, with ink sacs intact (1 lb.)
Deep-sea scallops (1 lb.)
Whole live lobster (1 small, about 1 lb.)
Jumbo shrimp—for number per pound, *see* page 62 (1 lb.)
Fish heads, bones and trimmings, for the bouillon (usually free from our Tuscan fish-mama)
Clam juice (two 8-oz. bottles)
Long Italian loaves for garlic bread (2)

Early in the Day—Simmering the Bouillon for 1 Hour, Unsupervised

We use our largest tall soup pot, which holds about 10 quarts, put in ½ cup of the olive oil, and bring up to medium frying heat. Even before it heats up add: 3 cloves of garlic, finely minced; 1 teaspoon thyme; 3 or 4 sprigs of parsley with stalks; a small handful of celery leaves, pulled apart; and 2 teaspoons salt, several grinds of black pepper, 1 teaspoon MSG, and 1 whole hot chili pepper. Stir around to coat with oil and let fry gently for about 5 minutes. Meanwhile wash and chop the fish heads, bones, and trimmings into large but manageable pieces, then add to pot, slosh around to coat with now-spiced oil, and wet down with ¾ cup of the red wine and ¾ cup of the white wine. Put 4 tablespoons of the tomato paste into a mixing bowl and, with wooden spoon and small beater, gradually work in enough of the clam juice to liquefy it, then add along with remaining clam juice to pot. Finally, add freshly drawn cold water just to cover, bring rapidly to a boil, then turn down heat and keep just bubbling merrily, covered, for about 1 hour. Let cool, strain bouillon into a large bowl, and throw away the solids. This is the liquid foundation of the *cacciucco*.

About 1½ Hours Before Serving

BASIC RULE FOR PREPARING WHOLE FRESH SQUID: Some people find it unpleasant to handle squid, a distant cousin of the octopus, but our girls have always enjoyed dissecting this extraordinary sea animal. The average fishman will do the job, of course, but he seldom has enough time to be as careful as we are, and the ink sac is usually lost. The ink is an essential part of the final flavoring and coloring. The body of the squid is like a large fountain pen, generally 6 to 12 inches long and 1 to 1½ inches in diameter. It is technically a shellfish, but the shell is under the skin inside the body and looks like a long clear plastic tube, which must be removed.

Wash squid thoroughly under cold running water, then lay on its back on a cutting board. With a small, sharply pointed knife, carefully cut through the skin and outer flesh all around the base of the head. The point of the knife should not penetrate more than ¼ of an inch, or the ink sac will be destroyed. When the head has been severed, carefully pull it off the body. The ink sac should come out with it. Cut off arms where they join head and hold head and ink sac in a small bowl. Now cut open the other end of the body. Grasp the body in the left hand, pull out the shell tube, then the internal organs and throw away. The body now is a hollow flexible tube, which is again washed under running water, then cut into ½-inch-wide rings. Finally, cut arms into inch lengths and add to the rings. The first squid is now ready for cooking. Repeat with as many more squid as may be needed, according to size. Carefully hold all the heads and ink sacs.

About 1 Hour Before Serving—Assembling and Cooking the Cacciucco

We start again with our large soup pot, empty. Put into it ¾ cup of the olive oil and heat to gentle frying temperature. Without waiting for it to be fully heated, add: the 3 onions, peeled and chopped; 3 whole bay leaves; 3 cloves of garlic, finely minced; 1 teaspoon thyme; another small handful celery leaves, coarsely cut; about 1 tablespoon whole dried sage leaf, crumbled; then stir around for 1 or 2 minutes to amalgamate the flavors. When oil is hot add previously prepared squid, turn down heat slightly, and let simmer, covered, until squid is quite soft, usually 15 to 25 minutes.

Meanwhile prepare the other fish. Wash, shell, and devein the shrimp. Wash and cut the scallops into bite-size rounds. Wash and cut all fish fillets into 1½-inch squares. Chunk all whole fish, throwing away heads, tails, and fins, but leaving in backbones. As soon as squid is soft, add shrimp and scallops, stirring around to coat them with the spiced oil, and let them simmer for no longer than 5 minutes. Now add: the canned tomatoes in their juice, a small handful of parsley, coarsely cut, and grate in the outer yellow rind of the lemon. Turn up heat and as soon as tomato boils, put in lobster, washed and whole, then pile around and above it the rest of the fish. Now pour in the previously prepared bouillon, enough just to cover the fish. If not enough, add ½ cup more of white wine and freshly drawn cold water just to cover. Turn heat up full and bring to a boil as quickly as possible. Then reduce heat to simmering and continue cooking until fish is just opaque, usually in about 20 minutes.

About 20 Minutes Before Serving

BASIC RULE FOR GARLIC BREAD: Preheat oven to 350 degrees. Very finely mince 4 cloves of garlic and put them into a mortar. Finely chop enough parsley (leaf only) to fill 1 tablespoon and add to garlic. Pound in 1 stick (¼ pound) of the butter, adding at the same time salt, pepper, MSG, and a few dashes of lemon juice to taste. Pound and blend completely. Make diagonal cuts about 1 inch apart in loaf of bread, cutting only a little more than halfway down. Insert cherry-size lumps of garlic butter into each cut, spreading it around with small spatula. Completely wrap loaf in foil and place in oven until bread is toasted and thoroughly impregnated with the butter, usually in 10 to 15 minutes. Bring bread to table, still wrapped, and only unwrap each piece as it is broken off.

Serving the Cacciucco

At the last moment the squid ink sacs are held over the pot and punctured, so that the ink runs out and is stirred into the *cacciucco.* We serve the dish in a preheated deep earthenware casserole. A chunk of garlic bread is placed in the center of each hot soup bowl. Then a variety of fish, scallops, shrimp, and squid is piled in and the soup ladled over. A plate or dish for depositing bones should be within easy reach of each person. When the lobster is uncovered, it can be lifted, allowed to drain for a few seconds, then placed on a cutting board, opened up, and its edible flesh equally divided. This is almost as good, but not quite, as when served on a Tuscan beach.

SUMMER THOUGHTS ON WINE

How do you begin to buy wine? What is involved in starting one's own small cellar? These are the questions most often asked by beginners who would like to start playing the wine game, but are appalled by the multiplicity of labels on the shelves of a well-stocked wine merchant. The first answer is to expose the out-of-date snobbery surrounding the use of the word "cellar." A hundred years ago the producers of fine wines catered mainly to a comparatively small group of wealthy clients, almost all of whom lived in large houses with expansive stone cellars. Here, often as many as 3,000 or 4,000 bottles of wine could be slowly and comfortably aged, sometimes for as long as 20 years. Today, the wine industry caters to a mass market and the chemical composition of even the greatest wines has been deliberately changed, so that they mature much more quickly. Most "average" wines are ready to be drunk within 12 to 18 months. The fine wines are matured by their producers for perhaps two or three years, the great wines for perhaps five or six. These bottles are normally not released to the retail merchant until the wine is ready to be drunk. Our own records show that the longest time that we are likely to store an average bottle is 90 days. What nonsense, in these circumstances, to continue to talk about the need for "a cool, dark cellar"! A wine is hardly likely to change, for better or worse, in 3 months, provided simply that the bottle be laid on its side (to keep the cork moist) and away from either the high heat of a radiator or direct sunlight. We cover these basic requirements in the simplest possible way, in a fourth-floor New York City apartment, with a . . .

24-Bottle-Cellar-in-a-Closet

A standard metal rack, with 4 rows of 6 bottles each, stands against one wall of a clothes closet. The fact that coats and pants are dangling around the bottles is, we think, an advantage, since it helps to keep away the light. The rack is well designed, so that the bottles rest with their necks pointing slightly downward. Naturally, the exact contents of the rack varies from week to week, but in general, we keep white wines on the bottom row, red wines on the row above, then fortified and aperitif wines, and, on the top row, spirits, whiskeys, and liqueurs. A fairly typical arrangement might appear as follows:

How do we stock and maintain this reasonably small storage reserve, which keeps us prepared for any unexpected guests? We think that the

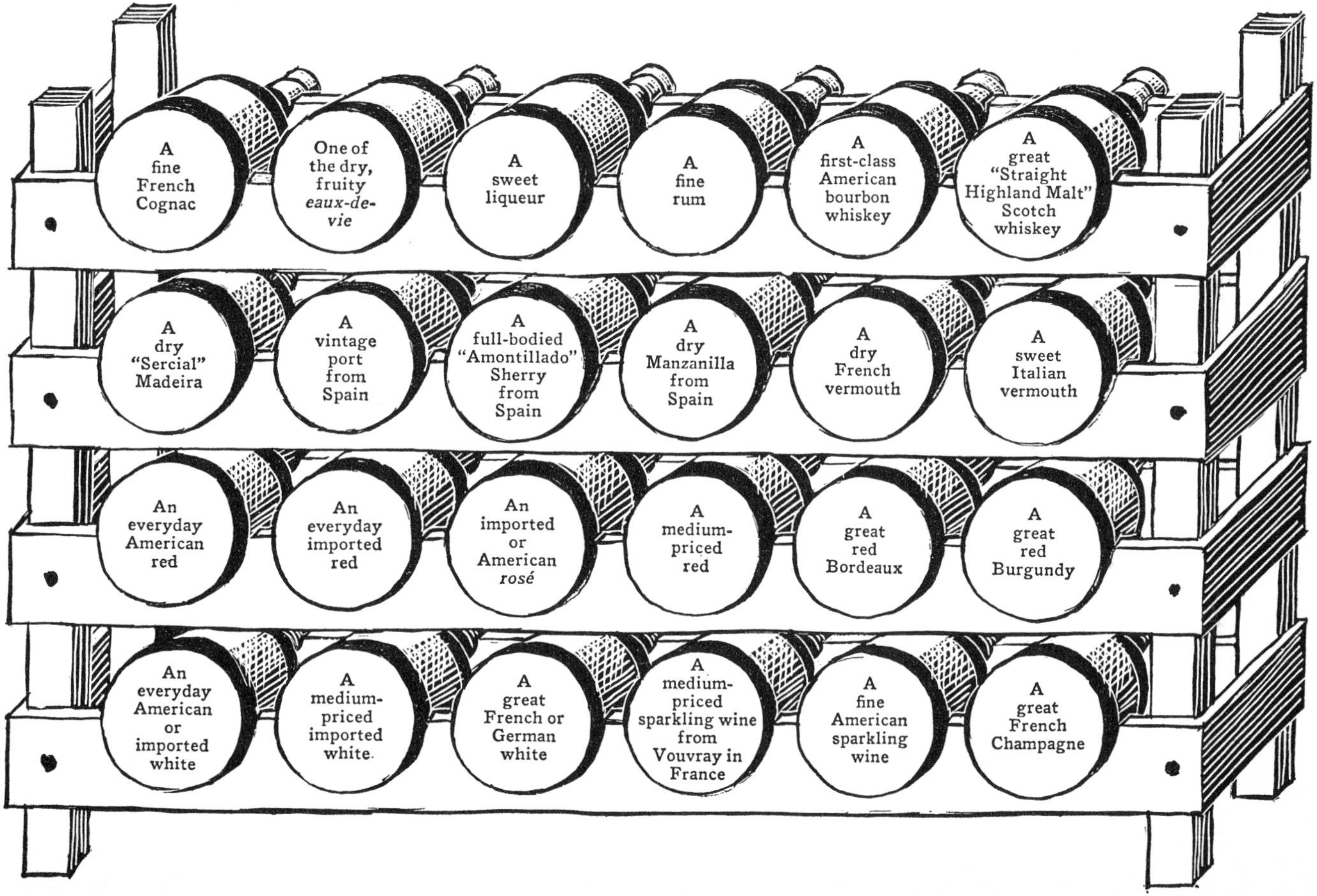
A fine French Cognac
One of the dry, fruity *eaux-de-vie*
A sweet liqueur
A fine rum
A first-class American bourbon whiskey
A great "Straight Highland Malt" Scotch whiskey
A dry "Sercial" Madeira
A vintage port from Spain
A full-bodied "Amontillado" Sherry from Spain
A dry Manzanilla from Spain
A dry French vermouth
A sweet Italian vermouth
An everyday American red
An everyday imported red
An imported or American *rosé*
A medium-priced red
A great red Bordeaux
A great red Burgundy
An everyday American or imported white
A medium-priced imported white.
A great French or German white
A medium-priced sparkling wine from Vouvray in France
A fine American sparkling wine
A great French Champagne

problem of buying wine is neither more nor less difficult than buying any of the items that are the normal tools of family living. It is a good deal less difficult and less risky than, say, buying a new automobile. We must first have a clear idea of what type of car we want. With wine, we must decide first whether we need red or white, dry or sweet, light and fruity or rich and powerful, expensive for a party or low-priced for every day. With the car, we must at least know the names of the leading manufacturers and the general features that they offer. With wine, we must at least take the trouble to learn the names of a few of the important vineyards, associating them in our minds with the types of wine that each produces steadily year after year. In time, one can build a relationship of mutual trust with a responsible automobile dealer and a responsible wine merchant, letting each know that if he gives honest advice and good service one will remain a regular customer.

A young friend asked: "Isn't it really true that every bottle of wine you buy is something of a gamble?" Entirely untrue. The only gamble, however slight, is in the first ½-bottle we buy of a new wine of a new vintage year. Even then, if the name on the label is that of one of the proud vineyards the risk is really a matter of personal taste. Then, if we like that wine of that year, the pleasure can be repeated as often as we please for at least a year, and possibly, if the wine is important, for three or four years. The first and most vital step is to keep a small notebook with a record of one's likes and dislikes. We divide our "Wine-Buying Notebook" into three parts: first, the wines that we have tasted and liked and that are currently in plentiful supply; second, the new wines that are always coming in and that we are anxious to taste as soon as we can afford to do so; third, a short nostalgic list of some of the great wines that we have enjoyed in the past few years and that are now no longer available, except perhaps for an odd single bottle discovered in a dark corner while browsing in a wine merchant's shelves.

Even these slight complications, however, do not apply to the vast majority of the everyday wines and spirits. Whether it be a young white Muscadet from the valley of the river Loire, or a red Beaujolais from the town of Fleurie, or a Scotch whiskey from the valley of Glenlivet, or a Spanish Sherry, or a brandy, or a vermouth, the producer with a proud name blends his product from year to year, trying to maintain an unchanging quality and character so that his particular label and shape of bottle is always associated with a particular drink. All we have to do is to experiment until we find the product that suits our fancy for any particular occasion and then repeat it as often as we wish. Our own list of the wines and spirits that we have most consistently enjoyed is on pages 676–900.

Champagnes and Other Sparkling Wines

The name "Champagne" has always been surrounded by controversy. Shall the word be classified strictly as the geographic name of a particular area of France, or shall it be regarded as a general term to be applied, as it now usually is, to any sparkling wine made by any producer in any part of the world? A few years ago, a British court of law ruled that a sparkling wine made in Spain could not legally be sold in Britain as "Spanish champagne." True Champagne is made from grapes grown in the French Champagne district around the town of Epernay in the valley of the river Marne, near the ancient city of Reims. The trick that originally created the sparkle in the wine was to bottle it before the fermentation was fully completed, so that the process continued inside the bottle. Fermentation is the natural chemical reaction which converts the sugar in the original grape juice into alcohol and carbonic acid gas. When this takes place in a huge open vat, the liquid heaves and bubbles and the gas disappears into the air. When fermentation is encouraged inside the bottle after it is corked, the gas is imprisoned in the liquid until the cork comes out, when the gas races to escape.

French Champagne is not normally sold under the name of any particular vineyard, but under the trademark of a wholesale shipper, who carefully combines the wines from various surrounding vineyards, trying to produce, year after year, his own blend, or *"cuvée,"* of a consistent quality and character. In an especially good year, he may use mainly the wines of that particular year, and the blend is then known as a "vintage *cuvée*" and the year is printed on the label. When there is no year on the label, the Champagne is "non-vintage" and is usually less expensive. We often find that these non-vintage Champagnes, being young and lively, are exceptionally good value. Incidentally, the term "Nature" or "Naturel" on a Champagne label should mean that the wine is drier than one marked "Brut," which in turn should be drier than one marked "Extra Dry," which finally should be drier than one marked "Dry" or "Sec." If this appears to be nonsense, it is, for most producers have their own ideas of what constitutes dryness or sweetness.

There are many other sparkling wines, both white, *rosé,* and red, from various parts of the world. There are a few outstanding ones from California, and some very fair and reasonably priced examples from the Finger Lakes region of New York State. There is also one other brilliant sparkling wine from France (with its own unique flavor and personality) produced in the valley of the river Loire and called "Sparkling Vouvray." It was beloved by the great French writer Balzac in the early 1800's, and it remains a lovely wine to quench a summer thirst or to enliven a breakfast fruit cup on a lazy summer Sunday morning (page 178). With all Champagnes and sparkling wines there is one golden rule: always drink them in tulip-shaped glasses, never in those flat, impractical miniature soup plates on stems. We list the important and reliable names in Champagnes and sparkling wines on pages 692–3.

True and False Rosés

There has been an explosion in the demand for *rosé* wines and now there seems to be a reaction against the flood of mediocre types that has swamped the market. Many of these false *rosés* are hurriedly made simply by mixing red and white wines; others, by adding a tasteless red dye to white wine. This does not give it any of the character of a true *rosé.* It is simply a colored white wine. The fine *rosés,* produced in their own special way, were there before the fad began, are there today, and will always be superb wines of strong individuality.

The *rosé* explosion was set off by millions of indecisive hosts, unable to make up their minds as to whether red or white wine was correct for the particular menu at hand. *Rosé,* touted as "right with everything," seemed to be the easy answer. It is a bad answer. A true *rosé* is not a compromise. At the correct time and place, it can be the perfect choice. It is a simple and informal wine which goes, in an informal setting and always well chilled, with almost any simple and solid dish.

To understand a true *rosé,* one must know how wines are naturally colored. The red of a red wine comes from the skins of black grapes. If the black skins are removed immediately after the pressing, the result is a pure white wine. If the black skins are left soaking for several days, the result is a red wine. If they are left for only a few hours, the result is a true *rosé.*

The truest of them all, unique and unforgettable, not to be missed, comes from a small town on a tiny river, which joins the river Rhône a few miles from Avignon. The town, the valley, and the wine—slightly brown-tinged and dry almost to the point of stinging—are called "Tavel." There are many producers in the dry and dusty valley, and their wines, always blended, vary widely in quality and price. The names of the reliable shippers are all-important. Rivers of *rosé*, most of it to be avoided, flow from other wine areas of France, especially from Anjou in the valley of the Loire. Here there is a simple rule which helps to find the best quality. We choose a *rosé* with a "varietal" label, showing that the wine was made from the noble Cabernet Sauvignon grape, as, for example, "Rosé Cabernet d'Anjou." There is an exceptional *rosé* from Alsace, made from the great Pinot Noir grape, also with a "varietal" label, as, for example, "Pinot Rosé d'Alsace." A very fair *rosé* comes from California, with the "varietal" label of the Grenache grape, usually named "Grenache Rosé" and, from the New York Finger Lakes, a good *rosé* with the "varietal" label of its grape, "Isabella." Finally, there is a charming and refreshing *rosé* from Greece, now stocked by many reputable wine merchants, called "Roditis." With all of these, the important name on the label is that of a reliable shipper and we list those of our experience on page 694.

Natural Sweet Wines

It is easy, anywhere in the world, to produce a sweet wine by adding syrup to a dry wine. The result (except in the cases of the famous fortified wines, the Ports, Madeiras, Sherries, etc.) is not generally a happy one. However, there are some sweet wines produced by a combination of natural factors and the most luscious and creamiest of these come from the two French districts of Sauternes and Barsac along the Garonne River a few miles south of the city of Bordeaux. Here, the extraordinary aromatic sweetness of the wine comes partly from the sugary Semillon grape that thrives in the soil and partly from a bacterial germ that floats in the air of this small, sunny, and protected area. When the grapes are ripe, the germs attack them, forming on the skin a mold which is known in France as *la pourriture noble* ("the noble decay"), which punctures the skin with millions of tiny holes. From these, tiny droplets of the water from the grape escape and are evaporated by the heat of the sun. The grapes begin to shrivel, as if turning to raisins, thus concentrating and distilling the sweet flavors. In this complicated process of harvesting and pressing grapes, the name of one vineyard stands entirely alone, that of the "Château d'Yquem." In the sunniest years, it produces wines that are so rich in flavor, so luscious on the tongue, and so strong in alcohol that they provide an entirely unique experience. In less sunny years, the wines have a delicate and lovely fruitiness. There are other, nearby vineyards that also produce some of the finest of sweet wines by the same natural methods (page 694).

Wonderfully sweet and fruity wines, of the *trockenbeeren* type (page 686), also come from many of the finer German vineyards. There is at least one excellent natural sweet wine from California, laboriously produced from the Semillon grape as nearly as possible by the traditional European method. Since the bacteria of the "noble mold" do not grow in the California air, the grapes are first picked, then spread out on huge trays in an enormous shed, where the temperature and humidity are controlled so that the bacteria may flourish, the mold form, and the grapes shrivel. The wine is then given a "varietal" label, "Premier Semillon." Our favored names among all these sweet wines are listed on page 694.

THE

Fall Holiday Season

October, November, and December

EXPLANATION OF SYMBOLS

A symbol appearing after a word refers the reader to a particular section of the book for further details. Example: olive oil, crystal salt, cocotte, dry white wine, Parmesan cheese, Beaujolais, turtle meat.

- stands for Raw Materials and Staples, pages 10–18
- stands for Aromatics, pages 18–29
- stands for Kitchen Equipment, pages 32–41
- stands for Wine in the Kitchen, pages 41–5
- stands for Cheeses, pages 660–75
- stands for Wines for the Table, pages 676–98
- stands for Marketing and Mail-Order Sources, pages 699–714

FALL FOODS IN SEASON

WHEN Halloween has passed and Thanksgiving is approaching, the stores assume their festive colors, with the fragrant delicacies of the world: the dried muscat raisins, still on the bough, from Australia; red-wrapped plum puddings from England; cinnamon-scented *Christstollen* from Germany; hazelnut *baci* from Italy; crisp almond *turrón* from Spain; lush dates and figs from Araby. . . . Nature outdoes man with the brilliance of her own "packaging": from the rich persimmon to the gay kumquat. . . . During the busy shopping days of the holiday season, there is a dualism about our cuisine—we seem to alternate between the unstinted preparations for the Thanksgiving or Christmas menus (page 523) and quick meals-on-the-run. Here is our checklist of favorite holiday foods.

The Special Pleasures of the Season

IF OCTOBER brings the first solid spell of wintry weather, VENISON makes its festive return to our table, as do the other game animals, wild birds, and the farm-bred small birds. The fancy butcher calls to say that he has his first DEER and offers a choice of cuts, one of which may make the main dish for our Christmas feast (page 538). The local game farm lets us know that they have fattened up their flocks of QUAIL, SQUAB, OT GUINEA HEN. Usually there will be a letter from the mail-order game specialist in Chicago, announcing that he is ready to ship MALLARD DUCK, CANADA GOOSE, RINGNECK PHEASANT, and also cuts of BROWN BEAR.

October is the peak season for LARGE STEWING HENS at moderate cost. (See shopping note, page 520.)

One of the best-looking and best-tasting fish of the season is the RED SNAPPER, now coming in from the Gulf of Mexico. We serve the fish whole, under a blanket of sesame (page 594).

We welcome back the BAY SCALLOP, so small, sweet, and tender that it needs only 3 minutes of cooking (page 142). Its short season is at its peak in November and December. (See shopping note, page 62).

At this season we delight in the enlarging variety of the new APPLE crop. For biting into, the crisp, slightly sharp, local MCINTOSH is followed by the almost-winy Illinois, Virginia, and Washington GOLDEN DELICIOUS, the slightly acid local RED DELICIOUS, the New Jersey CORTLAND, and the Northwestern JONATHAN. The medium sizes taste better than the so-called "Giant Fancy." These apples have a remarkable affinity with two other foods now in season: the new shipments of aged Dutch EDAMER and GOUDA and English CHESHIRE cheeses and the new crop of WALNUTS in the shell. Eaten together, they make the perfect simple dessert. For the ideal baking apple, firm enough to hold its shape in the oven (page 615), we watch for the first of the local ROME BEAUTY, the first Michigan, New England, and New York NORTHERN SPY, and the first New Jersey WINESAP. For fried apple rings (which we serve with various meats, poultry, and game, page 129), for pies, and for general cooking, we use the Michigan and New York GREENING; the early Midwestern, New England, and New York BALDWIN; the New Jersey STAYMAN and JERSEY RED; the Pennsylvania and Southern YORK IMPERIAL; and the Virginia and Western NEWTOWN PIPPIN.

Three other fruits which must be enjoyed quickly during their short season are: the imported fresh LINGONBERRY from Newfoundland, Norway, and Sweden (available in cans all year, but the taste of the fresh is a revelation, page 627); the lovely orange-red California and Florida PERSIMMON, which when softly ripe can be cut in half, sprinkled with a few drops of lime juice, and eaten with a spoon; and the Florida KUMQUAT, also imported from Hong Kong, Japan, and Taiwan. This is the miniature orange beloved of Chinese gourmets (page 521).

It is the peak season for the fresh CRANBERRY, the eastern half of the country supplied from the bogs of Massachusetts and New Jersey, the western half from Oregon and Washington.

We watch for the magnificent California EMPEROR GRAPE, a fine heart for the fruit bowl with its unusual elongated shape and red to reddish-purple color.

In October we celebrate the return of the regal RED CABBAGE, which we prepare with smoked pork, in the German style (page 646).

A few years ago the entire United States' crop of CHESTNUTS was wiped out by disease. Gradually the trees are being replanted, but meanwhile holiday supplies are imported from Italy. It is not difficult to shell and skin chestnuts (page 158); however, the Italians also send ready-to-cook DRIED

CHESTNUTS (page 159). We use chestnuts to stuff our Thanksgiving turkey (page 531), for a nourishing cold-weather soup (page 560), as the solid base of a great stew (page 574), to replace potatoes (page 607), and as a dessert (page 614).

It is sometimes forgotten that HONEY is a seasonal food and that its flavor is strongest when it is freshly gathered from the harvest, which is at its peak in October (see shopping note, page 521).

The Freshwater Fish of the Fall

These fish have lean flesh and respond generally to similar cooking methods:

- Late in the season, river BUFFALO FISH, often called WINTER CARP; the small sizes especially good
- Great Lakes MULLET
- Great Lakes YELLOW PIKE
- Great Lakes SAUGER, mainly around Chicago
- Great Lakes SHEEPSHEAD, at this season in small sizes of about 2 pounds, fine for poaching in foil (page 141)

These fish have oily flesh and are generally interchangeable in recipes:

- Great Lakes HERRING, small and sweet, mainly fished through ice holes
- Great Lakes WHITEFISH

The Saltwater Fish of the Fall

These are the lean-fleshed fish:

- Atlantic STRIPED BASS
- Last of the Atlantic and Gulf BLUEFISH
- Atlantic COD, both the large STEAK size and the smaller MARKET COD, fine baked whole in a casserole (page 141)
- The members of the FLOUNDER family, always juiciest when baked,

poached, or fried whole, with the bone in (pages 136, 141, 137)
Atlantic BLACKBACK
New England GRAY SOLE
Atlantic YELLOWTAIL, or RUSTY DAB
New England POLLOCK
South Atlantic WEAKFISH, sometimes called SEA TROUT
Atlantic KING WHITING, peak of season

These are the fish with oily flesh:

The members of the MACKEREL family:
Atlantic BOSTON MACKEREL
Gulf and South Atlantic SPANISH MACKEREL
South Atlantic ROCK SALMON
Atlantic fresh SARDINE, which, of course, is baby HERRING, one to a mouthful
Imported Canadian SEA SMELT, a small and juicy fish caught by Quebec fishermen in the mouth of the St. Lawrence, peak of season

These fish, at this season, are almost invariably from frozen storage and should be carefully checked for quality:

Atlantic and Pacific HALIBUT, lean flesh
Pacific KING SALMON, oily flesh

The Shellfish of the Fall

All have lean flesh:

Pacific ABALONE, a rare delicacy, eaten fresh only in California, shipped elsewhere canned✠
The members of the CLAM family:
Atlantic CHERRYSTONE, for eating from the half shell
Atlantic HARD CHOWDER, which New Englanders call QUAHOG
Atlantic and Pacific LITTLENECK, for eating from the half shell
Atlantic SOFT-SHELL STEAMER
Pacific DUNGENESS CRAB
Also frozen CRAB MEAT in cans, usually at three prices, for the large chunks, the small chunks and flaked
Maine and Massachusetts LOBSTER, fresh from the icy traps
Pacific SPINY LOBSTER, at its peak in November

Atlantic MUSSELS, mainly from the bays around New York
Atlantic and Gulf OYSTERS in the shell, also ready-shucked, mainly from Chesapeake Bay
Pacific baby OLYMPIA OYSTERS, a magnificent delicacy, now also shipped, across the country, shucked and frozen ☆
Atlantic and Gulf SHRIMP, one of the best times of the year, see shopping notes (page 61)

The Fruits of the Fall

Apart from the apples and other native and exotic fruits mentioned in the preceding "Special Pleasures," the following will add color and sweet delight to our holiday menus:

Imported BANANAS, as always, from the West Indies, Central and South America, Taiwan, and the Canary Islands, delicious flamed in rum (page 618)
New York State wild baby CRAB APPLES
Arizona, California, Florida, and Texas GRAPEFRUIT
The other varieties of GRAPE, besides the EMPEROR, mentioned above, all excellent when teamed with Liederkranz cheese:
- California ALMERIA
- Imported Belgian BLACK COLMAR, very luxurious, hothouse-grown and shipped by air
- California BLACK RIBIER
- Last of the New York CATAWBA
- Last of the California THOMPSON SEEDLESS
- California TOKAY
- Last of the California WHITE MALAGA
- Imported Belgian WHITE MUSCAT, very luxurious, hothouse-grown and shipped by air

Southern, Western, and imported Greek and Turkish LEMONS
Arizona, California, and Florida KEY OF PERSIAN LIMES
The fall varieties of MELON:
- Last of the local CANTALOUPE
- Southern CASABA MELON
- Arizona and California HONEYDEW
- Last of the California PERSIAN MELON
- Imported SPANISH MELON

The strangely named fall members of the ORANGE family:
- Last of the Florida, first of the California HAMLIN

Florida PARSON BROWN
California and Florida TEMPLE, with the loose skin
California VALENCIA
First of the California WASHINGTON NAVEL
Florida, Hawaiian, and imported West Indian PAPAYA
The varieties of WINTER PEARS; all make a fine dessert poached in wine (page 618):
Northwestern ANJOU
Northwestern BOSC
Northwestern COMICE
Imported British Columbian FLEMISH
California WINTER NELIS, peak of season
California, Oregon, and Washington small, brown SECKLE, with an especially aromatic flavor
Hawaiian, Puerto Rican, and imported Mexican PINEAPPLE
California and Gulf States POMEGRANATE, the historic fruit, its juice excellent for marinating meats, peak of season
California fresh winter RASPBERRY, to provide the "scarlet overcoat" for our Thanksgiving menu (page 536)
California fresh winter STRAWBERRIES, these and the raspberries always a luxury at this season
Florida TANGELO
Arizona, California, and Florida TANGERINE

The Dried Fruits for the Fall Holidays

A few steps from the Place Saint-Michel in the Latin Quarter of Paris, down the narrow alley of Git-le-Coeur, there is a tiny Corsican bistro, which serves only one dessert. The owner's wife, Dolores, who is also the waitress, places before each diner a plate, a nutcracker, and a fruit knife, and sets on the table a wooden bowl piled high with the fruits of the season, a second with nuts in their shells, and a third with a fragrant assortment of dried fruits. The possible taste combinations are almost infinite and often magical. We like to reproduce this dessert at our own table. Here are our checklists of the dried fruits and nuts:

California APRICOT halves
Imported Australian whole pitted APRICOTS
Arizona, California, and imported Iraqi DATES
The domestic and imported dried varieties of FIGS:
California BLACK MISSION
California CALIMYRNA, a cross between California and Smyrna types
Middle Eastern SMYRNA
California PEACH halves } both outstanding, but always expensive
California PEAR halves }

California semi-dried pitted PRUNES, moist and ready-to-eat
Imported Australian giant MALAGA and MUSCAT RAISINS, still in bunches on their stems
And at the holiday season, always a choice of many assortments of CRYSTALLIZED and GLACÉ FRUITS

The Nuts for the Fall Holidays

There is of course no truth in the rhyme, "Here we come gathering nuts in May." Nuts are harvested in August, September, and early October and come to market in time for the holidays. We deplore the lazy habit of buying nuts already shelled and usually fried and salted so heavily that they all taste alike. Often peanuts are included in these assortments, although the peanut is not a nut but a bean-type legume with such a powerful flavor and aroma that it dominates the entire package. Even untreated nutmeats dry out quickly, losing their flavor oils. Far better to rely on Nature's perfect packaging and crack open the nuts at the table:

California and imported Italian and Spanish ALMONDS
Northwestern FILBERTS, the large, cultivated version of the small, wild HAZELNUT
Southern, Southwestern, and Texas PECANS
California and imported French, Italian, and Turkish WALNUTS or, more correctly, ENGLISH WALNUTS
California BLACK WALNUTS, with quite a different flavor and can also be bought pickled to serve with cold meats and cheeses

The above are the four main types, which seem to be available everywhere, but in the fancy-food stores we find a wider variety:

Imported Amazon River BRAZIL NUTS, actually gathered in May by Indian tribesmen who climb the towering trees
Imported African and Indian CASHEWS
Hawaiian MACADAMIA NUTS
Imported Mexican PEPITAS
Southwestern and imported Italian and Spanish PIGNOLAS can often be bought still nestling in the folds of the handsome pine cone
California and imported GREEN PISTACHIOS from Afghanistan, Iran, Italy, and Turkey

Finally, there is the ubiquitous Southern PEANUT, the legume which first grew wild on the slopes of the Andes Mountains in Peru. It was carried by explorers and missionaries to Africa and the Orient. When the slave-ships began plying their vicious trade from the African west coast, sacks of peanuts were the cheapest and most easily portable food for the chained slaves during the voyage. So the peanut came to the United States.

The Salads of the Fall

Almost all salad greens are a little hard and sharp at this season and we counter this by making our vinaigrette dressing slightly stronger, using a more forceful balance of aromatic herbs and spices (page 612).

California and Florida AVOCADOS, or ALLIGATOR PEARS
The tender center leaves of local CELERY CABBAGE, or CHINESE CABBAGE
California, Florida, New Jersey, and Ohio CHICORY
Local DANDELION LEAVES
Continued imports of Belgian ENDIVE
California and Florida ESCAROLE
California and Florida BIBB LETTUCE
Arizona and California ICEBERG LETTUCE
Florida fresh MINT, for an occasional touch in the salad bowl
Southern MUSTARD GREENS, only the smallest and tenderest leaves
The salad members of the ONION family:
  Frozen green CHIVES
  California, Louisiana, Texas, and imported Mexican GARLIC
  Domestic and imported ITALIAN SWEET RED ONIONS
  California and Texas GREEN SCALLIONS
California, New York, and Texas GREEN PEPPERS, with the slightly hot, tropical type from Florida
Local RADISHES
California, Texas and the first Florida TOMATOES
Imported Bahamian CHERRY TOMATOES
And always the indispensable local WATERCRESS

The Vegetables of the Fall

With the hardier and harder cold-weather vegetables, as with our salads, we use more dominant flavorings and sauces (see page 602).

California ARTICHOKES from Castroville, which modestly calls itself "the artichoke capital of the world"

Local JERUSALEM ARTICHOKE, a rare root vegetable, but worth a search, for its remarkable flavor and texture when properly prepared (page 462)

California FAVA BEANS, which we team with Spinach (page 156)

Last of the local GREEN BEANS, which we prepare with tomatoes, Athenian style (page 602)

California LIMA BEANS and local BABY LIMAS

California, Texas, and Virginia BEETS, bringing thoughts of borsch (page 246)

Local BROCCOLI

California and last of the Long Island BRUSSELS SPROUTS, which team magnificently with Italian chestnuts, (page 157)

The winter members of the CABBAGE family:

- Local and imported Dutch GREEN
- Local SAVOY

California and New York CAULIFLOWER, the fine Eastern crop continuing until the first frost

Local and Puerto Rican CELERIAC, or CELERY ROOT, which combines superbly with mashed potatoes (page 543)

California, Florida, and New Jersey EGGPLANT, or AUBERGINE

The return of California, Florida, Long Island, and New Jersey FENNEL, also called SWEET ANISE and by Italians, FINOCCHIO, which is delicious prepared in Sherry (page 603)

New Jersey, New York, and Virginia KALE

New Jersey and New York KOHLRABI

New York and Pennsylvania MUSHROOMS, peak of season

Southern OKRA

The cooking members of the ONION family:

- Local large SWEET BERMUDA ONIONS
- Local SHALLOTS
- Local small WHITE BOILERS
- And the workhorse of the family, the local YELLOW ONIONS

Local PARSNIPS, which, like turnips, we serve baked in a maple-mustard sauce (page 163)

California GREEN PEAS

The fall members of the POTATO family, with wide variety of taste and texture:

- Florida RED BLISS, a small, new potato for boiling
- Nebraska RED PONTIAC, a medium-sized boiler
- Idaho LARGE RUSSET, mealy, for baking
- California LONG WHITE, large, with waxy texture and good color, for boiling, frying, and steaming
- Long Island and Maine WINTER WHITE, the Eastern brother to the Californian
- Delaware, Maryland, New Jersey, and Virginia SWEET POTATO

Louisiana, South Carolina, and Virginia SOFT YAM, which we bake in a casserole with apricots and sunflower seeds (page 532)

Local everywhere, PUMPKIN, the fruit we use as a vegetable (page 633), as a soup (page 527), and as a dessert (page 634)

Imported Canadian RUTABAGA, the SWEDE of British recipes

Florida SPINACH, the peak of the late season

Three kinds of WINTER SQUASH, which we bake whole (page 155):

- Local ACORN
- Local BUTTERNUT
- Local HUBBARD

New season for fresh Italian WHITE TRUFFLES, for those who can afford them!

Local and imported Canadian WINTER WHITE TURNIP

Shopping in the Fall

Search for Variety and Value in Coffee and Tea

When the return of wintry days increases our demand for hot drinks, we tend to reappraise our coffee and tea. Even the most exciting taste begins to pall with repetition and we find stimulation in experiment and change.

There are many reliable firms in the coffee business which put out excellent blends under famous brand names, but we prefer to do our own blending. In every large city where we have shopped, we have found small neighborhood coffee-roasting stores, which import their own sacks of green coffee beans and will roast and blend to order. This is a fascinating game, which can easily be played by mail.✣ One begins by asking the coffee merchant to send samples of his own standard blends. Next one lets him know which qualities one likes or dislikes about these blends. The merchant then sends out variations of his blends, keeping a careful record of each variation, until he has found the perfect blends for one's personal taste. (There might be a sharp, wake-up blend for breakfast, a rich and winy blend for after dinner, etc.) These blends can then be re-ordered. However, a personal talk with a knowledgeable coffee merchant can bring out fascinating information about the qualities of different types of beans from various coffee-producing parts of the world, about the degrees of roasting (from "American light," to "French dark," to "Italian black caffè espresso") and about the fineness of the grind which should be adjusted to the method of brewing. After tasting one batch, more of this bean or that can be added until one achieves a flavor, body, and aroma that seem perfectly in balance. Here, as a starter, are some of the blends and a few of the coffees which we have enjoyed:

1. One of the "safest" blends is a 50–50 Mocha-Java. MOCHA is the oldest coffee in the world, first discovered by the Arabs, then cultivated by them, on the mountain slopes of the Arabian peninsula. In the early days it was shipped through the port of Mocha on the Red Sea. The Arabs would not allow Christian "infidels" into their country to visit the coffee plantations, but they permitted foreign traders to set up offices and warehouses in Mocha. The name is an anachronism today since no more coffee is shipped through Mocha, but it is known to so many millions of people that it continues to be used for Middle Eastern coffees now grown mainly in Yemen. These coffees are oily, heavy, and have an aggressive aroma—qualities which make them a good base for many blends.

JAVA is the name given to coffees grown in the Far East and developed originally by the Dutch on the island of Java. It is usually the most expensive because only very small quantities are available. During World War II the plantations were destroyed by the Japanese armies and very few have been replanted. Java coffee is light and delicate, with an almost impalpable fragrance like an essence of spices—a perfect foil for the Mocha.

2. After the Mocha-Java, a sharp contrast would be a blend of 40 per cent Brazilian Bourbon Santos, 40 per cent Colombian Medellín Excelso, and 20 per cent Venezuelan Maracaibo. BRAZIL grows more than half of the world's supply of coffee, from some of the cheapest grades to a few of the best, so one must be specific about the type. "BOURBON" is the name of a certain botanical variety of the coffee bush, which finds its ideal conditions of climate and soil on the mountain slopes behind the port of SANTOS, from which the beans are shipped. Thus the three words "Brazilian, Bourbon, Santos," form the essential definition of the coffee. Tasted on its own, it is sharp, with a slightly angular bitterness and an almost astringent aftertaste.

COLOMBIA is the second largest coffee producer of Latin America, with many grades from poor to first class, so again one must be specific. Some of the best climatic and soil conditions are near the city of MEDELLÍN, and the finest local bean is called "EXCELSO." It is light in body, with a bitterness that is slightly nutty. It is not a good soloist, but makes an excellent partner.

VENEZUELA ships its best coffees through the port of MARACAIBO. They are light and delicate, with a subtle and magnetic aroma. Too tender to stand by themselves, they supply the feminine grace to the masculine power of the other two.

3. Another blend to try might be a 50–50 Colombian Medellín Excelso and Ethiopian Jimma: some of the best African coffees come from the ETHIOPIAN town of JIMMA, in the interior, about 200 miles from Addis Ababa, where the government is developing a high-grade coffee industry. Previously unskilled tribesmen are being trained in the special techniques of harvesting the ripe coffee fruit and of extracting the two beans from the center of each olive-sized berry.

These blends are only a beginning. For many years we have added variety to our coffee tasting by including in our blends small quantities of some of the other good coffees: from Mexico and Central America: MEXICAN OAXACA, GUATEMALAN ANTIGUA, NICARAGUAN MATAGUALPA, COSTA RICAN CARTAGO; from the West Indies: PUERTO RICAN SANTO DOMINGO.

When we are on the West Coast we buy HAWAIIAN KONA, for which there is so much demand that very little of it gets beyond California.

When we travel abroad, there are other coffees unique to foreign capitals. In London, we find INDIAN MYSORE and JAMAICAN BLUE MOUNTAIN. In Paris, we try to duplicate the blend made famous by Balzac, who kept himself awake through night sessions of writing with ". . . infusions of coffee prepared from a blend of Brazilian Bourbon, Martinique and Mocha beans, bought by his servant from three different shops."

With coffee, nothing has changed since Balzac's time. It is still best to buy the whole bean, roasted and blended to individual taste. Finally, it is essential to have a home grinder and only enough should be ground for each separate brewing, for once the skin of the bean has been cracked, most of the flavor-oils evaporate in a few hours.

Even Greater Variety in Tea

There are several hundred different coffees, but more than 3,000 varieties of tea. Again, as with coffee, the world-famous companies sell their blends under brand names such as "Queen X's Choice," or "Prince Y's Breakfast," which do not define the quality of the tea. The factor which makes teas similar or different is the varietal type, and we have found it worthwhile to learn a few so that we can experiment and find the teas that please us best. It is also essential to learn what *not* to do. . . .

It is a serious mistake to think that the phrase "Orange Pekoe" on a label is the name of some rare and exquisite tea. It merely defines the size and shape of the leaf. Any tea, from the worst grade to the best, can be an "Orange Pekoe"! The same rule applies to such words as "Young Hyson,"

"Souchong," or "Fannings," which are traditional definitions of leaf size, after they have been dried, broken up, and sifted. Fannings are the almost granulated residue which passes through the last, fine-mesh sieve. They are not necessarily to be despised. The fannings of a great tea are many times superior to even the largest leaf of a poor grade. The point is that these words have nothing to do with quality.

As to "Earl Grey," perhaps the best known name in the world of tea, it has, after more than a hundred years of use, lost virtually all of its original meaning. Earl Grey was a British nobleman, a pioneer investor in the sailing ships which brought teas from the Orient, who had a special blend made up for his private use and, later, authorized its sale to the public under his name. After the earl's death the copyright on his name expired. Today, any company can throw together any blend of teas and call the result "Earl Grey." This is not to say that some of the "Earl Greys," put up for sale by reliable companies, are anything but first-class blends. The point is that the name "Earl Grey" by itself is not a guarantee of quality.

We buy our teas by varietal type and usually keep three kinds on hand. First, one or other of the sharp, robust teas, as a waker-upper first thing in the morning before breakfast and perhaps for a mid-morning break. Second, one of the soft, delicately smoky or flowery teas for the late afternoon. Third, one of the subtle and almost mystical teas for after dinner, or the last sip before bed.

Morning Teas

KEEMUN is, to us, one of the sharpest of the black fermented teas. When the taste buds are receptive after the night's rest, the slight shock of Keemun is the best possible awakener. The flavor has been described as winey. Keemun is named after the Chinese province where it was first grown, but supplies now come from Taiwan.

FORMOSA OOLONG is half-green, half-fermented, more delicate than Keemun, but still with a slight shock of aftertaste.

CEYLON, from the great island at the southern tip of India, is grown on the high mountain slopes, where the leaf matures slowly, holding in the oils. The flavor is delicate, the aroma rich and almost startling.

Afternoon Teas

LAPSANG SOUCHONG was grown originally in a valley of China where the July sun was so hot that the leaves were toasted while still on the bush. In other places, where it is cultivated, the leaves are baked over smoking fires to develop the special flavor of this extraordinary tea. It is another tea originally grown in China but is now cultivated in Taiwan.

JASMINE is a blend of black fermented leaf with dried Jasmine petals. The leaves are picked in the spring before the heavy rains dilute the oils, then dried and stored until the summer jasmine flowers.

Evening Teas

DARJEELING is named for the town in the high Himalayas of north-eastern India. Here the tea gardens are mostly above 7,000 feet and in this comparatively temperate climate the leaf matures very slowly, bringing a soft roundness of flavor with a lingering aroma.

GUNPOWDER PEARL is a small leaf, rolled by hand into tiny gray nuggets. A very light tea, best drunk without cream or sugar.

Even the greatest tea can be ruined in the brewing. The vital fact is that the first dash of absolutely boiling water during the first fraction of a second uncurls the leaf, opens its pores and brings out the flavor oils. This is the justification for the ritual. This is why the English-made brown earthenware teapot is best, because it holds in the heat. It is thoroughly warmed and dried before the tea is put in, then taken to within an inch or two of the spout of the boiling kettle. (We put in about 2 teaspoons of tea for the pint teapot, 4 teaspoons for the quart.) Stir at once and then brew for not less than 5 minutes. Stir again and pour. To swamp good tea with milk and sugar or completely dominate it with lemon is a crime. We use a minimum of sugar with a drop or two of heavy cream to add a slight body without affecting flavor.

Less Cost, More Flavor with Old Hen

October is the time when many egg farms (or should one call them factories these days?) begin reducing their laying flocks before the winter. The hen that is almost a year old and is now losing some of her energy and efficiency is killed off and comes to market as a "stewing fowl." It is a good value, not only in low per-pound cost, but also because its "aged" flesh (like aged beef) is rich in the flavor essences that simply do not exist in the younger broiler-fryers. So we look for a stewing hen with a broad breast, with plenty of yellow fat showing through the skin and weighing from 4 to 8 pounds. Then we bring out the flavor by gently stewing it in a *waterzooie* (page 286) or in a pot with a dozen vegetables and herbs (page 643). The cold meat can be sliced and served Circassian style with pounded walnuts (page 288).

The Smallest Orange of All?

The holiday season brings back the Florida KUMQUAT, which might be described as an orange the size of a large grape. This tiny citrus fruit was once imported only from Japan and China, but now it is widely grown in Florida and arrives in the stores usually in November. It adds a brilliant color to the fall fruit bowl and has a bright and delightful taste, eaten whole, skin and all. It is also available canned in syrup.✽

A World of Honeys

Just as milk achieves hundreds of variations in cheeses, and grape juice in wines, so natural sugar is converted into hundreds of varieties of honey. What a mistake to go to the store and ask for "some honey." The word should never stand alone, but always be associated with the flower from which the bees drew the nectar and the place where they wrought their magic. We find that a honey tasting is often as much fun as a wine tasting, but the honeys must be tasted against each other in pairs, for human taste buds have almost no memory. Honey flavors are at their sharpest when freshly packed from the harvest and the newest season's crop usually begins arriving in October. Some specialty shops offer lists of hundreds of honeys from all over the world.✽ Each year we balance old favorites against new tryouts. Here are a few suggestions.

Among domestic honeys in our New York area, we give first place in summer to a New Jersey RASPBERRY honey, which is light, delicate, but with so much character that it dominates with its charm; in winter we replace it with a New Jersey BUCKWHEAT, sold in the Polish and Ukrainian district of the city, where it is known as "Ukrainian style," one of the most powerful of honeys, excellent for cooking; also Wisconsin ALFALFA with a candied flavor like spiced sugar; then Colorado DANDELION, with a chewy texture like liquid toffee; also California MANZANITA, Arizona SAGE BLOSSOM, Washington State FIREWEED, Florida ORANGE BLOSSOM, Georgia GALLBERRY, Illinois HEARTSEASE, Indiana SPEARMINT, Iowa ANISE-HYSSOP, Maryland TULIP-TREE, and New York State LINDEN.

Among the imported honeys, one of the greatest is the Tasmanian LEATHERWOOD, with a chewy texture and an extraordinary perfumed after-taste; the oldest of all honeys, the French WHITE NARBONNE ROSEMARY, discovered and "mentioned in dispatches" by Julius Caesar when he invaded Gaul; the Greek MOUNT HYMETTUS WILD THYME, from the slopes of the famous mountain; the English BUCKFAST ABBEY MOORLAND HEATHER, a most unusual, granular and half-bitter honey, collected and packed by the Benedictine monks; Spanish ROSEMARY, powerful and dominant; Chilean DOGWOOD ULMO, used by Caruso to soothe his throat, and Bavarian PINE BLOSSOM, are among dozens of possibilities for gastronomic study of the honeys of the world.

THE FALL FEAST DAYS
An International Calendar

Christmas Before Thanksgiving

During the first few days of October we usually mix the Christmas pudding (page 648), give it its first steaming and let it mature for two months at room temperature, sealed in its mold. We plan the Christmas and Thanksgiving menus side by side to avoid gastronomic overlapping. If we choose turkey (page 528) for the November feast, we shall probably sit down in December to a roast of venison (page 540), brown bear, or suckling pig (page 546).

Other fall feast days that may tempt us to celebrate at our table include:

On **October 10,** the Chinese "Double Ten," the tenth day of the tenth month, when China celebrates its freedom from the Manchu Dynasty, overthrown in 1910, might lead us back to our Chinese feast (page 80).

Turkey's national holiday on **October 29,** the "Foundation of the Republic Day," when she consolidated her independence from the Ottoman Empire in 1923, could bring Circassian chicken (page 288).

We prepare our traditional specialties on **October 31,** for Halloween (page 630).

On **November 1,** the Independence Day of Algeria, commemorating the beginning in 1954 of the rebellion against France, we might salute the day with an Arab buffet supper (page 256) or a decorated platter of Moorish Couscous (page 578).

We demand our pumpkin on **Thanksgiving Day,** but for variety we often serve it as a rich and creamy soup (page 527).

On **November 30,** Scotland's "Saint Andrew's Day," the *haggis* is piped in at celebration dinners around the world. If we are not attending one of these, we will certainly celebrate at home with our non-intestinal *haggis* (page 642), followed by tipsy laird (page 624).

On **December 13,** Saint Lucia Day in Sweden, when the eldest daughter of each family is installed as "Queen of the home," with a crown of seven lighted candles, we might celebrate at breakfast with a Swedish omelette served with imported fresh lingonberries (page 627).

On **Christmas Eve,** our traditional family schedule in New York City is, first, to sing carols with our neighbors in the central courtyard of our apartments; then to join the celebration around the community tree in

Washington Square; then back home to light the candles on our own tree and serve a buffet of dishes to remind us of the unity of many families in many countries on this special night: perhaps from a French *Reveillon,* a *boeuf en gelèe* (page 393) ; or from a Chilean or Peruvian *Noche Buena,* an *escabeche* (page 268) or a *seviche,* (page 425) ; from a Danish *Yuleaften,* an aspic of tongue (page 487) ; or from an Austrian *Weinachtsabend,* a *Schmarren* of apples (page 616) .

On **New Year's Eve,** we adopt a German ceremony, serving hot *Berliner Pfannkuchen* (page 551) on the first stroke of midnight.

A Thanksgiving Dinner

MENU

WINES

CREAM OF PUMPKIN SOUP

With the hors d'oeuvres, before dinner and carrying into the soup, a dry Spanish Montilla

---

ROAST TURKEY WITH FRUIT AND CHESTNUT STUFFING
with
Yams with Apricots and Sunflower Seeds
Brillat-Savarin's Spinach
Marian's Cranberry-Orange Relish

One of the finest of the white Burgundies, perhaps a Bâtard Montrachet, or a first-class California white Pinot Chardonnay

---

APPLES MOLDED IN A SCARLET OVERCOAT

A sweet Sauternes from France, say a Château La Tour—Blanche

DEMITASSE

A Cognac, Marc, or Calvados; or a fine American 4-year-old brandy

The Fall Party and Feast-Day Menus

Day for Giving Thanks

This menu, while being exceptionally easy to prepare, has sufficient drama, elegance, and surprise to make it equally suitable for a small family celebration or a large gathering. The usual tidbits for nibbling before, during, and after the meal are not listed since they are a matter of personal taste, but an imaginative choice can make them a memorable part of the feast. Because this is a fairly solid menu, we would begin with nothing more than a selection of Spanish, Greek, and African olives (page 105). As part of the central decoration of the table, we would have three handsome wooden bowls filled with bright delicacies chosen from the list of foods in season (page 512): fresh fruits, fancy nuts in their shells, and dried fruits, including perhaps the wonderful giant muscat raisins in bunches on the bough and whole dried, pitted apricots, both imported holiday specialties from Australia. Spread around on the table, we would have small serving bowls with salad, savory and sweet bits, including perhaps tiny raw button mushrooms cut into fancy shapes; crackling slivers of Bombay duck✲; the holiday specialty candy from Italy, hazelnut-stuffed *baci Perugina,*✲ or the holiday specialty from the Spanish province of Alicante, crushed-almond *turrón.*✲ If pumpkin reigns supreme from Halloween to Christmas, there is no better way of consuming it than in this rich and luxurious soup. We think that the historic recipe for the spinach is still, after more than 150 years, the best of all ways of preparing it. The high-heat method of cooking the turkey is the one used by almost all professional chefs to achieve a crispness of the skin with juiciness of the flesh.

Planning and Timing

The first thing to do is to prepare the cranberry-orange relish about 3 days ahead. The pumpkin soup is better if it is prepared the day before, refrigerated and carefully reheated. The same rule applies to the turkey stuffing and to the casserole of yams. As to the spinach, its final richness depends on the slow absorption of the butter during gentle cooking in advance. The apples are cooked and molded the day before and the red sauce prepared, then both are refrigerated overnight, the apples unmolded and the sauce poured over just before serving. On the day, the full concentration is on the roasting of the turkey, which does require fairly steady attention.

CREAM OF PUMPKIN SOUP

For a party of 8 to 10

The trick to this soup is to avoid mashing the pumpkin to a cream. Tiny bits should burst in the mouth, releasing the freshness of the pumpkin juices. Warning: it does have a slight tendency to stick, so it should be heated slowly in a thick-bottomed pan and be gently stirred.

Check Staples:

Clear beef bouillon (1 qt.)
Salt butter (about ½ lb.)
Meat extract, or meat glaze, French *glace de viande*⊜ (about 1 Tbs.)
Milk (1 qt.)
Aromatics: crystal salt,☧ freshly ground black pepper,☧ MSG,⊜ Hungarian sweet red paprika☧
Yellow onions (3 medium)
Fresh parsley (small bunch)
Watercress (small bunch)
Plus fried bread croutons for garnish

Shopping List:

Fresh whole pumpkin (about 2½ lbs.)
Heavy cream (½ pt.)

The Day Before—Advance Preparation in About 30 Minutes, Unsupervised Simmering for About 30 Minutes More

We use an enameled cast-iron cocotte✱ that holds about 6 quarts. Cut open the pumpkin, scrape out seeds and central pulp, dig out the meat, chop coarsely, and hold. Finely chop the 3 onions. We set the big cocotte over medium frying heat, melt 3 tablespoons of the butter in it, and sauté the onions to just golden. Meanwhile in a separate pan heat the quart of beef bouillon to boiling, then pour over the sizzling onions. Return to a boil, add the chopped pumpkin and simmer, covered, until soft, usually in 20 to 30 minutes. Overcooking will harm the flavor. Then drain (reserving the beef liquid), press pumpkin through a coarse sieve or a hand food mill. (An electric blender can be used, but only for a few seconds or it will reduce the pumpkin to an over-smooth cream.) The pumpkin purée will now be very thick and some of the beef liquid should be stirred in, but only enough to make it smooth. In this form it rests overnight, covered, in the refrigerator. The remaining beef liquid is also refrigerated.

About 30 Minutes Before Serving

Prepare the garnish and set in serving bowls to be brought to table: fried croutons, finely chopped parsley, and watercress. As the pumpkin mixture is carefully reheated in a thick-bottomed pan, it is steadily stirred with a wooden spoon, the tablespoon of meat extract blended in, while the soup is gradually thinned with alternating cupfuls of the milk and the beef liquid, until the best flavor balance is achieved. The final consistency should be that of a cream soup. At the same time, season to taste with salt, pepper, and MSG.

Serving at Table

The soup and the bowls in which it is to be served must be piping hot. It is best for two people to do the serving: one ladling, the other performing the final ceremony with each bowl. Quickly stir in a tablespoon of heavy cream. Float a nut of yellow butter in the center, surround this with a circle of red paprika from a shaker, then a larger ring of green parsley and watercress, and finally sprinkle with fried croutons.

ROAST TURKEY WITH FRUIT AND CHESTNUT STUFFING

For a party of 8 to 10

Check Staples:

Salt butter (about 4 Tbs.)
Lemon (1)
Corn-belly salt pork (1 lb.)
Aromatics: crystal salt, freshly ground black pepper, MSG, rosemary, thyme
Carrots (5 medium)
Green Pascal celery (3 stalks)
Yellow onions (4 medium)
Ground arrowroot (a few tsps.)
Olive oil, if necessary (enough to moisten cheesecloth)
Dry white wine (1 cup)

Shopping List:

Fresh turkey, oven-ready (about 16 lbs.)
Heavy cream (about 2 Tbs.)
Plus ingredients for the stuffing, *see* next recipe

The Day Before—the Giblets and the Stuffing

Wash and pat dry the giblets, including the liver. Peel and chop 1 of the onions. Scrape and slice 2 of the carrots. Cut one good-sized slice of the salt pork and dice it. Into a 2-quart saucepan over medium frying heat, put 1 tablespoon of the butter and the diced salt pork. As soon as there is enough hot liquid fat, put in onion and carrots, sauté until lightly brown, then put in giblets and continue sautéing, stirring around, until liver is just firm. Stop the frying by hissing in the cup of wine, letting it bubble vigorously for 1 or 2 minutes, at the same time adding ½ teaspoon rosemary, ½ teaspoon thyme, plus salt, pepper, and MSG to taste. Add 1 quart of chicken bouillon, then let gently bubble, with lid on, until gizzard is just soft, usually in about 45 minutes. Then turn off heat and let cool. Meanwhile begin preparing stuffing . . .

BASIC RULE FOR AMOUNT OF STUFFING: We apply this rule to any bird of any size. Weigh the oven-ready but still unstuffed turkey and allow about 3/4 cup, or 5 ounces, of loosely packed stuffing for each pound of unstuffed weight. This turkey weighing 16 pounds will need about 12 cups, or about 5 pounds.

Clean turkey by rubbing all over, inside and out, with cut side of half a lemon, then wrap tightly in foil and refrigerate, unstuffed of course. Prepare stuffing according to recipe following and refrigerate. When giblets are cool enough to handle, dice meats, strain bouillon, then put diced meats back into it and refrigerate, covered.

On the Day—About 8 Hours Before Serving

Take turkey, stuffing, and giblets out of refrigerator and let come to room temperature.

About 5 Hours Before Serving

Assemble stuffing and loosely pack into turkey, closing openings and pinning down legs and wings with small skewers. Liberally rub skin with butter. Cover entire breast area and tops of both legs with 1/4-inch-thick slices of salt pork, holding them in place with 3 tightly fitting bonnets of aluminum foil: a large one over the breast and two smaller ones over the legs. Preheat oven to 350 degrees. Place turkey, breast side up, on a rack which will hold it about 2 inches above roasting pan. Now we work out on a piece of paper the exact oven-timing schedule, which must be precisely followed.

About 4 1/4 Hours Before Serving

BASIC RULE FOR HIGH-HEAT METHOD OF OVEN-ROASTING: One must start by knowing the unstuffed weight of the bird. If this first step has been forgotten, one can also calculate, with slightly less accuracy, from the stuffed weight. The total oven time will be 15 minutes per pound of unstuffed weight, or roughly 12 minutes per pound, stuffed weight. This 16-pound bird will thus be 4 hours in the oven. Divide the total time by 2 and write down this halfway point—with our bird, 2 hours. Place turkey in center of oven and do not open oven door for first 30 minutes. While setting timer, note also clock time for judging 2-hour halfway mark. Meanwhile in a mixing bowl assemble remaining vegetables: the 3 onions, peeled and left whole; the 3 carrots, scraped and left whole; plus the 3 celery stalks, washed and halved, then hold. Have at hand the tools for basting: a large spoon and a bulb baster. At the 30-minute bell, working quickly, take turkey out of oven, close oven door as quickly as possible and turn oven temperature up to 375 degrees, baste turkey thoroughly with pan juices, then set back in oven at once, without waiting for higher temperature to be reached, and set timer to 20 minutes. At the 20-minute bell, repeat the routine, turning oven temperature up to 400 degrees and setting basted turkey back immediately, without waiting for new temperature to be reached. Oven now stays at 400 degrees for remainder of cooking time, but basting must be repeated every 20 minutes. Any laxity on this score may result in a disastrous drying-out of the bird. At precisely the halfway mark (for this bird, 2 hours), spread the vegetables in the roasting pan under the turkey. They provide an essential small amount of steam to keep meat moist and also add flavors to the pan gravies. During the second half of the oven time, the basting routine continues every 20 minutes. Everything inside the oven is now crackling and spitting, but we do not allow the nasty noises to unnerve us and dull the necessary judgments during the final hour.

About 1¼ Hours Before Serving

Judge the crispness of the exposed skin, by pressing lightly with a finger wrapped in a paper towel, then decide when the breast and leg bonnets should be removed for the final browning. This point is usually about 45 minutes before the end. If the browning is too fast, it can be held back by draping any part of the turkey with a blanket of several thicknesses of cheesecloth moistened with olive oil. When the aluminum bonnets come off, the now-crisp slices of salt pork are crumbled into the pan gravies. During final 20 minutes, begin testing for perfect doneness. First, unpin one of the legs and, holding bone with paper towel, move leg gently up and down. At the point of doneness, joint is soft and flexible. Second, again using a paper towel, pinch fleshiest part of leg. At the point of doneness, it gives slightly. Third, prick the fattest part of the leg with a fork. At the point of doneness, juice is pink. The ultimate trick is to achieve perfectly done flesh at the precise moment when the skin is perfectly browned and crisped. Then turn off the oven. Have ready a hot serving platter, place bird on it, and let it rest for a few minutes for flavors to mature. Meanwhile, deal with the pan gravies in the roasting pan on the top burner.

About 15 Minutes Before Serving

Of course, one can prepare a normally strained and thickened gravy from the pan juices, but we prefer to make what we call a "rough garnish." We skim off the fat, mash the vegetables down to a coarse purée with a steel fork, then blend in the diced giblet meat and a few spoonfuls of the giblet bouillon. While it all simmers over a low flame, we use a strong steel spoon to scrape off all crusty bits from the bottom of the pan. Usually the puréed vegetables add sufficient body, but, if necessary, extra thickening can be provided by first turning off the heat, then blending in a few teaspoons of arrowroot, liquefied with a few dashes of the heavy cream. If it gets too thick, blend in a few more dashes of giblet bouillon. Finally, taste and if necessary adjust seasonings. Remove all skewers from turkey before serving.

FRUIT AND CHESTNUT STUFFING

For a 16-pound bird

Check Staples:

Salt butter (about 3/4 lb.)
Aromatics: crystal salt,✲ freshly ground black pepper,✲ MSG,◘ marjoram, rosemary, thyme
Yellow onions (3 medium)
Parsley (small bunch)
Stale white bread (small loaf) or packaged "Herb Stuffing"
Olive oil,◘ for cooking chestnuts (2 to 3 Tbs.)

Shopping List:

The choice of fruit is flexible—it should be tart and juicy—we like a combination of the following, which are in season:
Tangerines (6)
Cranberries (up to 1/2 lb.)
Fresh Swedish lingonberries✲ (up to 1/2 lb.)
White celery (1 heart)
Fresh chestnuts (2 lbs.)
Fresh mushrooms (1/2 lb.)
Corn bread (small loaf); we bake our own (page 330)
Pork sausage meat (1 lb.); we use our homemade (page 178)

The Day Before—Advance Preparation of Chestnuts, Corn Bread and Fruit in About 1 Hour

We bake, shell, and skin the 2 pounds of chestnuts according to our BASIC RULE (page 158). We quickly mix and bake a batch of Johanna's crackling corn bread (page 330) or we use a commercially baked corn loaf or crumbled corn muffins. We grind the stale white loaf to crumbs or use a bag of pre-crumbed "herb stuffing." While chestnuts and corn bread are baking, assemble the vegetables: the 3 onions, peeled and finely chopped; the white celery heart, washed and finely chopped; the 1/2 pound of mushrooms, wiped clean (never washed) and sliced lengthwise into hammer shapes, plus a handful of parsley, finely chopped. Separately assemble the fruit: the 6 tangerines, peeled, sectioned, and pitted; the 1/2 pound each of fresh cranberries and lingonberries, washed; or any other fruits, prepared and cut to a uniform size. We put the pound of our own homemade sausage meat (page 178) or commercial sausage meat into a sauté pan and fry it, crumbling it with a fork, until lightly brown. Our own sausage meat has very little fat, but with commercial meat, the excess fat must be drained off. Now add to sauté pan ½ pound of the butter plus the chopped vegetables and sauté lightly for 4 or 5 minutes, then turn off heat. Now mix all ingredients, except fruits. Coarsely mash chestnuts with a steel fork or pass them through the grinder with the coarse cutter in position, then put into largest mixing bowl. Blend in about 2 cups of crumbled corn bread and about 1 cup of white bread crumbs, using judgment as to exact amount, remembering that corn bread gives body, the chestnuts, weight, and the bread crumbs, lightness. Now blend aromatics into warm contents of sauté pan: 1 teaspoon each of marjoram, rosemary, and thyme, plus about 3 tablespoons salt, a dozen or so grinds of black pepper, and MSG to taste. Now lightly work entire contents of sauté pan into chestnut-bread mixture. Finally, taste and adjust both seasonings and texture. For more body, add more corn bread. For more lightness, use more white bread crumbs. For more moisture, add more melted butter. Above all, use a light touch in mixing, preferably with a wooden fork. When mixture seems right, cover and refrigerate overnight. Separately cover and refrigerate prepared fruits.

About 3 Hours Before Turkey Is Ready to Be Stuffed

Take both parts of stuffing out of refrigerator and let come to room temperature.

When Turkey Is Ready—the Final Assembly

Sometimes the most efficient tool in the kitchen is a set of clean fingers. The mixing must be thorough, yet so light that none of the fruit is crushed. Then loosely fill the turkey and proceed as in previous recipe.

YAMS WITH APRICOTS AND SUNFLOWER SEEDS

For a party of 8 to 10

Check Staples:

Salt butter (about ½ lb.)
Eggs (2 large)
Fresh limes (2)
Aromatics: crystal salt,☧ freshly ground black pepper,☧ MSG,◘ ground cinnamon, whole nutmeg
Pure maple syrup◘ (about 2 Tbs.)
Dark-brown sugar (about 2 Tbs.)

Shopping List:

Yams (about 8 medium)
Dried apricot halves (½-lb. box)
Skinned sunflower seeds, available in health-food or specialty shops (½ lb.)
Large marshmallows (about 1 dozen)
Glacé cherries, optional, for decoration (about 6)
Sweet vermouth (½ cup)

The Day Before—Advance Preparation in About 45 Minutes

Boil or steam the 8 yams, then peel and mash them smoothly and lightly. Meanwhile just melt 1/4 pound of the butter, then turn off heat and blend in: the juice from the 2 limes, the 2 tablespoons of brown sugar, and the 2 tablespoons of maple syrup. Blend this mixture into yams as mashing is completed, at the same time working in the aromatics: about half a nutmeg, freshly ground, 2 teaspoons ground cinnamon, a few pinches of salt, a very few grinds of pepper, and about 1 teaspoon MSG. Work very lightly, preferably with a wooden fork. Then taste and adjust seasonings and ingredients if necessary. Each flavor should be clear, none dominant; the sour lime should balance the two sugars. When all seems right, cover and refrigerate overnight. Complete two more small separate operations. Quarter enough of the dried apricots to fill 1 cup, then marinate overnight in the 1/2 cup of sweet vermouth, in tightly covered jar, at room temperature. Sauté about 3/4 cup of the sunflower seeds in 1 or 2 tablespoons of butter, until lightly brown and crisp, then hold overnight, covered, at room temperature.

On the Day—About 2 1/2 Hours Before Serving

Let yams come to room temperature.

About 45 Minutes Before Serving

Break the 2 eggs and just lightly beat with a few strokes of a fork. Drain apricot quarters, holding vermouth aside. Lightly work the eggs, the apricots and the sunflower seeds into yam fluff. Final fluff should be stiff enough to stand up in peaks, but not too stiff. If it needs slight moistening, blend in a dash or two of the sweet vermouth marinade. Preheat oven to 350 degrees. Butter a fairly shallow, open casserole, one which is good-looking enough to come to the table, then lightly spoon yam fluff into it. Smooth top, but do not press down. Decorate top with marshmallows and glacé cherries, then dot with butter.

About 30 Minutes Before Serving

Set casserole in center of oven and bake until marshmallows are brown and puffy, usually in about 25 minutes. Apricots will now be soft and chewy with sunflower seeds providing a crunchy texture contrast.

BRILLAT-SAVARIN'S SPINACH

For a party of 8 to 10

On Sundays in the village of Bresse the great French gourmet would lunch with his priest after church. When spinach was in season, it was always on the menu, so superbly prepared that, again and again, Brillat-Savarin begged the good priest for the recipe. He kept his secret until, in his will, he bequeathed it to his friend. Many years later it was published in a Paris newspaper. . . .

"You must begin to prepare the spinach for the following Sunday on the previous Wednesday. In the morning, pick the spinach yourself in the garden, choosing young leaves of a good green and with ribs not too thick. In the afternoon, wash it, cut off the stalks, and cook it only until it is just tender. Drain the leaves by pressing them with your hands and chop them finely. Now put them into a glazed earthenware pan with some fine fresh butter and put it onto a very low fire. Cook them for about half an hour, then let them cool in the same pan. Resist tasting them. They are not to be touched today.

"On Thursday add another piece of butter about the size of a large walnut and melt this into the spinach, again over a very low fire. After about 15 minutes let them cool again. Do not taste them. They are not to be touched yet.

"On Friday repeat the same operation: the same added quantity of butter, the same length of cooking . . . there will now be an exceedingly tempting aroma. Do not be tempted.

"On Saturday, again the same as on the previous days. Beware of a fierce temptation. The spinach will be giving out an almost irresistible aroma. Resist.

"At last, on Sunday, about half an hour before your guest is due to arrive, put a final and extra-large piece of butter into the spinach and put the dish again over a low fire. After about 15 minutes, when the final butter has been fully absorbed and the spinach is piping hot, turn it out onto a very hot serving dish and bring it at once to table. The secret, my dear Brillat-Savarin, is that in the course of the 5 days of preparation, each pound of spinach will have absorbed almost three quarters of a pound of butter!"

We began by following this recipe exactly, but found it no longer entirely valid in terms of modern cooking utensils and controlled heating. We achieve his results in 2 days. However, that much time is essential, for what happens is that the water is slowly expelled from the spinach and replaced by the butter. However, we think the flavor is better with less butter.

Check Staples:

Sweet butter, best available (1 lb.)
Aromatic: crystal salt☧

Shopping List:

Young spinach leaves (5 lbs.)

2 Days Before

The first cooking of the spinach works best with two people: one in charge of the washing at the sink, the other, armed with a long wooden spoon, at the big pot on the stove. The pot should be the largest available soup boiler (preferably stainless steel or enameled cast-iron to avoid a reaction with the spinach). The spinach is washed under fast-running cold water. There is fairly high heat under the pot. The wet spinach is thrown in by handfuls. The only liquid used is the water caught in drops in the crinkles of the leaves. Each layer is immediately pressed down into the hissing water with the wooden spoon and fairly heavily salted. The operation is continuous. Each layer follows at once, until the pot is almost completely filled. But the spinach wilts in 1 or 2 minutes and as soon as it has mushed down, the cooking is complete. It takes only 4 or 5 minutes. Let the spinach cool in the pot until it can be handled. We pick up the spinach by handfuls and squeeze out the juice through our fingers. Each squeezed handful goes onto a chopping block and is finely cut with a large chef's knife. Then it all goes into a cast-iron saucepan of suitable size with a tightly fitting lid, placed over simmering heat. Put in 3 to 4 tablespoons of the butter and leave it covered for about 10 minutes. Stir it gently with a wooden fork; dig a hole in the center and see whether there is any loose melted butter on the bottom of the pan. If not, add 1 to 2 tablespoons more butter. The whole operation is extremely flexible. Leave it covered for another 10 minutes. Stir, check again and, if necessary, add a bit more butter. After 30 minutes, let the whole pan cool, until it is possible to put it in the refrigerator overnight.

The Day Before

This is simply the reheating and rebuttering repeated: leave the spinach covered, on simmering heat, for 30 minutes, checking every 10 minutes, and the test is always how much loose butter is left on the bottom of the pan. There is a limit to the amount of butter which the spinach will absorb on any one day.

On the Day—About 2 Hours Before Serving

Let the spinach come back to room temperature. Simmer for 30 more minutes, covered. More butter is added gradually, up to maximum absorption, but this time one must be careful that there is no excess butter in which the spinach might swim to the table. At the last moment, a final check as to salt is made.

MARIAN'S CRANBERRY-ORANGE RELISH

For a party of 8 to 10

Ideally, this should be made about 3 days ahead and kept refrigerated in a screw-top jar, so that the flavors can blend and mature. However it is not entirely inedible, even if made only a few hours beforehand!

Check Staples:

Granulated white sugar (1½ to 2 cups)

Shopping List:

Fresh cranberries (3 pts.)
Oranges, preferably thin-skinned, large (3)
Orange curaçao liqueur (1 Tbs.)

Preparation in 5 to 10 Minutes

Peel the 3 oranges, saving the outer yellow skin, but removing and discarding all white skin, which makes relish bitter. Separate orange flesh into 4 quarters, removing and discarding central white strings and any pits. Wash, drain, and dry the 3 pints of cranberries. Use the coarsest cutter of the grinder and pass through it the yellow orange skin, orange flesh, and cranberries. Blend into the coarse mash the tablespoon of curaçao and only enough of the sugar to achieve a slight sweetness. Stir well, spoon into tightly covered jars and refrigerate, preferably for about 3 days. Finally, a few hours before serving, taste and add more sugar if needed, but do not under any circumstances make it too sweet.

APPLES MOLDED IN A SCARLET OVERCOAT

For a party of 8 to 10

Check Staples:

Sweet butter (about 1 Tbs.)
Lemon, for its skin (1)
Dark-brown sugar (1 lb.)
Dry white wine♁ (2 cups)
Confectioners' sugar, if desired by the children, *see* body of recipe (about 1 Tbs.)

Shopping List:

Greenings, or other stewing apples, *see* list, page 508 (4 lbs.)
Fresh winter California raspberries, or frozen (1½ lbs.)

The Day Before

Peel, core, and chunk the apples into a large saucepan (preferably copper because it responds instantly to heat adjustments and it is essential that the apples be brought up to high heat very quickly). Add 2 tightly packed cups of the dark-brown sugar, 1 cup of the wine, and the thin outer rind of the lemon, finely chopped. Set over high heat, and as soon as the wine comes to a rolling boil stir continuously with a wooden spoon for 1 or 2 minutes, to prevent the apples from burning. When the apples begin to bog down, stop stirring, turn down the heat and keep bubbling gently, uncovered, until apples show signs of thickening, usually in about 30 minutes. The objective is to boil away a good part of the water.

Meanwhile butter the inside of a deep mold of the right size and a pretty shape. The apples look best when they stand up on the serving platter in a fairly high narrow mound. Flatten a bit of aluminum foil on the bottom of the mold for later ease in unmolding. When the apples are slightly thickened, taste for sweetness and, if necessary, add a bit more sugar or stir in a little lemon juice. When cool enough to handle, strain them through a hand food mill and pack them fairly tightly into the mold. When it is down to room temperature, set in the refrigerator overnight.

On the Day

Purée the ice-cold raspberries, either in an electric blender (which is best) or in any other way. Keep the purée cold. Carefully unmold the apples onto a handsome cold platter. They should by now be quite firm. Pour the red fruit purée over the bright green mound of apples in such a way that the red runs down in irregular trickles, leaving some of the green to show through. More of the red can be dribbled around the base. If the children want snow on top of the mountain, use confectioners' sugar at the last moment.

A Christmas Dinner

MENU

WINES

ERNEST HEMINGWAY'S
GAZPACHO

A light and dry Spanish white Rioja from the valley of the Ebro River

---

ROAST OF VENISON WITH
CHOCOLATE SAUCE

with

Brussels Sprouts with Italian
Chestnuts

A great red Burgundy

and

Celeriac Mashed Potatoes

REGAL ENGLISH PLUM PUDDING

A fine French Champagne

with

Sweet Egg Custard

and

Cognac Hard Sauce

Demitasse

A superb French Cognac

Christmas at Home

We will usually have prepared our Christmas pudding in October to give it at least 2 months to mature (page 648), and the various glacé fruits remaining from that operation will have been carefully stored away to be used in the chocolate sauce for today's venison. Regardless of the purists, we often enjoy starting a party dinner, even in winter, with an ice-cold soup. Especially in this menu, with the richness of venison and plum pudding to follow, the ideal prologue is the refreshing lightness of the *gazpacho,* which has been called "a liquid salad," served with ice cubes in the bowls (see page 233). Venison is a word that has had various meanings at different periods of gastronomic history. In ancient Roman times, it referred to all animals killed in the hunt, but in modern usage it means only the meat of the deer and its family cousins, the caribou, the elk, and the moose. Of these, we consider the deer as outstanding in flavor and texture, and it also has the advantage of being available in fancy butchers or of being reasonably easy to order.※ However, this recipe would work equally well with other large cuts, say, a standing roast of brown bear or a saddle of mutton. The chocolate sauce is not as fantastic as it may seem at first thought. It is closely related to the Mexican *mole.* Only a small quantity of bitter chocolate is used and the delicately sweet-sour flavor, magnified by the glacé fruits, is the perfect foil for the firm and almost Spartan texture of the venison.

Planning and Timing

This menu presents no special problems beyond the single fact that all game meats must be carefully prepared in advance and closely watched in cooking. They do not have the layers of fat, as in prime beef, so there is always the danger of drying out unless they are larded, marinated, and thoroughly basted. The final result is one of the great adventures of gastronomy. The *gazpacho* is prepared the day before, leaving only a few bread croutons to be fried and served with it. Both the Brussels sprouts with chestnuts and the potatoes mashed with celeriac can be completed before sitting down to table and then kept warm. The plum pudding, tightly enclosed in its waterproof mold, of course, simmers in its steam bath until the last moment. The hard sauce can be made days ahead and even the smoothest egg custard can be kept warm in a double boiler. Since the joyous concentration on the venison seems to create an irresistible desire to stretch the legs afterwards, we usually invite our guests to join in the ceremonial unmolding of the plum pudding, in its decoration with holly and in its flaming parade to the table.

ERNEST HEMINGWAY'S GAZPACHO

See recipe on page 233.

ROAST OF VENISON WITH CHOCOLATE SAUCE

For a party of 8 to 10

Marinating the meat for 3 days is essential to the success of this dish. This involves no more than 1 hour's work on the first day, plus a couple of minutes 3 times a day to turn the meat over. We used to put our children in charge of this and it was part of the build-up toward the feast.

Check Staples:

Salt butter (½ lb.)
Corn-belly salt pork, piece about 10 inches long, to be cut into lengths for larding (about 2 lbs.)
Aromatics: crystal salt, freshly ground black pepper, whole bay leaves, whole cloves, garlic (4 cloves), thyme
Carrots (7 medium)
Green Pascal celery (1 head with leaves)
Yellow onions (7 medium)
Parsley (small bunch)
Ground arrowroot (a few tsp.)
White granulated sugar (2 Tbs.)
Spanish Sherry vinegar or a good white wine vinegar (about ½ cup)

Shopping List:

A fine roast of aged venison (about 10 lbs.) (The leg is the best cut, but a whole leg can weigh from 10-20 lbs., so if the beast is very large, a half leg is in order, properly trimmed to a good shape.)
Unsweetened cooking chocolate (about 4 oz.)
Pine nuts, pignolas (2-oz. jar)
The following fruits (which may have been left over from the advance preparation of the Christmas pudding, page 648: candied citron (2 oz.), candied orange peel (2 oz.), dried currants (¼ cup), seedless white raisins (¼ cup)
Medium-priced red wine, say a Beaujolais (2 bottles)
Dark rum (about 1 cup)

3 Days Before—Larding and Marinating the Meat

Many fancy butchers will do the advance larding of the venison, but we rather enjoy the semi-skilled operation of a larding needle.* Also, there is a substantial flavor bonus in first soaking the salt-pork "lardoons" in rum. Cut the salt pork lengthwise into ⅜-inch-thick slices, then cut these into long square strips. Marinate in some of the rum for about 4 hours. Meanwhile in an open bowl large enough to hold the meat, assemble the aromatic vegetables: 4 of the onions, peeled and chopped; 4 of the carrots, scraped and sliced; the celery leaves, finely chopped; 5 of the celery stalks, washed and chopped; the 4 cloves of garlic, peeled and sliced; plus 4 whole bay leaves, about a dozen whole cloves, a small handful of parsley, finely chopped; about 1 teaspoon thyme; then pour in 1 bottle of the red wine, stir, and hold. Wipe the meat clean with a damp cloth and, when lardoons are ready, thread each in turn into the larding needle and draw into the meat, working with the grain. Finally, there should be lardoons throughout the meat, each about 1 inch apart. Now pound into the surface of the meat, using the heel of the hand, plenty of crystal salt and some freshly ground pepper. Stir marinade and gently lower meat into it, turning around several times to moisten thoroughly on all sides. Now carefully pour in as much red wine from the second bottle as is needed to fill the bowl. If meat can be completely covered with wine, so much the better, but this is seldom possible. Cover bowl with foil and refrigerate for 3 days or store in a cold place, turning meat 3 times each day.

Early on the Morning of the Day

Bring venison out of refrigerator and, still soaking in its marinade, let it slowly come to room temperature.

About 3 Hours Before Serving

The marinated venison can now be cooked and served as if it were a roast of beef, but since venison is much drier, it is roasted only to 130 degrees on the internal meat thermometer. We use our "high-heat method" of oven-roasting, as described for the turkey on page 529, with the remaining carrots, celery and onions placed in the roasting pan at the halfway time. Turn on oven to 350 degrees. Lift venison out of marinade, pat dry, weigh it, then place on a rack to hold it about 1½ inches above the roasting pan. Insert meat thermometer, making sure that it does not touch any internal bone. Oven time will be about 15 minutes per pound, but the thermometer is "the boss."

About 2½ Hours Before Serving—for a 10-Pound Roast

Set venison in center of oven and do not open oven door for first 30 minutes. Meanwhile strain marinade into a saucepan and bring to a boil. As it heats up, chunk into it the ½ pound of butter. Let it boil fairly hard for a few minutes, to reduce and concentrate flavors, then hold hot, just under boiling, and use for basting venison every 20 minutes during the rest of the oven time. Remember to turn up oven temperature in two steps to 400 degrees, as described for turkey on page 530. When all of marinade has been used up, continue basting with increasingly rich pan juices.

While Roasting Is in Progress—Advance Preparations for the Sauce

Soak the 1/4 cup of currants for about half an hour in a little more of the rum. Dice the candied fruits, assemble together in a mixing bowl, and hold. Lightly brown the 2 ounces of pine nuts by shaking for a minute or two in a hot, dry frypan, over fairly high heat, then add to candied fruits, with the 1/4 cup of white raisins. If the unsweetened chocolate is in squares, grate enough to fill 1/3 cup.

About 30 Minutes Before Serving—the Chocolate Sauce

It is best prepared in an old-fashioned cast-iron pan of about 1 1/2- to 2-quarts' capacity, to allow room for vigorous stirring. Put into it the 2 tablespoons granulated sugar and place on fairly high heat to melt and brown the dry sugar, stirring continuously with a wooden spoon, as for a caramel. When sugar is liquid and brown but not black, turn off heat and cool for a couple of minutes, then carefully blend in 1/2 cup of the vinegar. Heat up to gentle simmering, then add the candied fruits, nuts, and raisins, plus the currants, first drained from the rum. Stir well and keep simmering gently, uncovered. Using a bulb baster, draw off about 1 1/2 cups of the winey meat gravies from the roasting pan and strain into a jug. Stand jug and small bowl of grated chocolate next to saucepan. Blend 3/4 cup of gravy into sauce. Sprinkle 1 tablespoon of chocolate into sauce and carefully stir, then add 1 more tablespoon of gravy. Keep adding, alternately, until sauce is quite thick and creamy and there is a slight taste, but only slight, of chocolate. Usually, about 6 tablespoons of chocolate will be enough, but a little more may be added if needed. If sauce becomes too thick, add more gravy. If it becomes too thin and one does not want to add more chocolate, first turn off the heat, then carefully blend in 1 or 2 teaspoons of arrowroot, first liquefied with a dash or two of the gravy. Finally, taste and make sure that overall flavor is distinctly sweet-sour. If sweetness predominates, add a drop or two more vinegar.

Serving at Table

Since venison and chocolate sauce need to be served absolutely piping hot, we usually place an electric hot plate next to the board on which venison is carved. The carver does not wait for the various serving plates, but carves as quickly as possible, placing the slices on a platter on the hot plate. The chocolate sauce is served from a small brightly polished copper saucepan, also standing on the hot plate.

BRUSSELS SPROUTS WITH ITALIAN CHESTNUTS

See recipe on page 157, doubling amounts of all ingredients.

CELERIAC MASHED POTATOES

For a party of 8 to 10

Celeriac (also called celery root and celery knob) usually comes into the market with other root vegetables in the Fall. It adds a delicate flavor of celery to the fluffy potatoes.

Check Staples:

Clear chicken bouillon (1 to 2 cups)
Lemon (1)
Aromatics: crystal salt,☧ freshly ground black pepper☧

Shopping List:

Celeriac (4 to 5 knobs, according to size)
Potatoes, fluffy, for mashing, *see* list, page 515 (about 4 lbs.)
Heavy cream (up to ½ cup)

About 35 Minutes Before Serving

We use an electric blender for this operation, but it can also be well done with a food mill or hand masher. Boil or steam potatoes with some salt (we think steaming them in their jackets holds more of their flavor). Cut away all dangling roots from celeriac, peel, coarsely chunk, and gently boil in salted water until fork-tender, usually in 15 to 20 minutes. Do not cook celeriac in same pan with potatoes, as potatoes tend to suck away celery flavor. In a saucepan heat up the 2 cups of chicken bouillon to just below boiling. When celery root is done, drain and put into jar of blender. Turn on to lowest speed, adding only enough chicken broth to ensure proper circulation and continuing only until just puréed, with small lumps still evident, usually 10 to 15 seconds. Turn on oven to 200 degrees and warm a covered serving dish. Now peel and mash the potatoes in any preferred way and lightly blend, in mixing bowl, with celery root, adding, at the same time, a few squeezes of lemon juice, plus salt and pepper to taste. Lightly pile mash into hot serving dish and reheat, briefly, in oven. Finally, at the last moment before serving, whip cream and lightly fold into mash only enough to make a smooth and rich texture. With experience, one learns exactly how much whipped cream one likes. Reheat briefly before bringing it to the table.

REGAL ENGLISH PLUM PUDDING

For a party of 8 to 10, with some left over

It is not really satisfactory to try to make a true plum pudding within a few days of Christmas. For the slow development of the "regal" flavor, it must, like a rich fruit cake, rest and mature for at least two months. We usually make ours at the end of September or the beginning of October, according to the basic recipe on page 648. In the instructions which follow, it is assumed that a mature plum pudding is at hand, either previously homemade in a watertight tin mold or a store-bought one in an old-fashioned pudding basin with a reasonably waterproof cloth cover.

Check Staples:

Superfine grind white sugar (a few Tbs.)

Shopping List:

Pre-cooked plum pudding (about 4 lbs.)
Dark Jamaica rum, 80-proof or more, for flaming (1/3 cup)
Holly sprigs, for decoration

About 3 Hours Before Serving

Stand plum pudding in its mold, lid upward, on a rack in a large pan with enough surrounding space for a gallon or more of boiling water. The larger quantity maintains a hotter head of steam and also prevents too-rapid evaporation. Pour in enough boiling water to bring the level up to within about 3/4 of an inch below top of mold. The objective is to keep as much as possible submerged, while avoiding the risk of water bubbling into the top. Adjust heat for a merry bubbling, enough to maintain plenty of steam, cover, and continue for at least 2 hours or more. Two hours is the minimum for proper caramelization, but a longer time does no harm. Check every hour and add more boling water if needed. Meanwhile prepare the sweet egg custard sauce (see recipe following), then hold warm in a double boiler. By the time pudding is to be unmolded, have warmed and ready a handsome serving platter.

Bringing It to Table

Unmold pudding onto platter and decorate to taste. Sprinkle sugar over pudding, arrange holly sprigs around base, quickly heat up the 1/3 cup of rum only to slightly above blood heat (if it gets too hot, the alcohol evaporates and it will not burn), pour over pudding, dim the lights around the dining table, then carry in the pudding wreathed in purple-blue flames. By the time it reaches the table, the holly will probably be on fire, but what is fun without danger! As soon as flames die down, pour enough custard over pudding to cover top and run irregularly down sides, like the snows on Mount Fuji. Stick the best remaining sprig of holly into the top and begin serving. More custard sauce is ladled over each portion and homemade cognac hard sauce (page 545) is placed alongside.

SWEET EGG CUSTARD FOR PLUM PUDDING

About 1 pint

Check Staples:

Eggs (4 large)
Aromatic: table salt
Dark-brown sugar (2 cups, fairly tightly packed)

Shopping List:

Light cream (2/3 cup)
Good dry Spanish Fino Sherry (about 1/2 cup)

Up to 1 Hour Before Dinner—Preparation in About 15 Minutes

Use a double boiler and have water in bottom half gently simmering. Separate the 4 eggs and put the yolks into a small mixing bowl reserving whites for some other purpose. With small wire whisk lightly beat yolks with 1/4 teaspoon salt. Put into top of double boiler the 2/3 cup of light cream and the 2 cups of sugar. Set directly onto heat (the double-boiler operation comes later) and stir continuously until sugar melts and is liquefied into cream, usually in about 2 minutes. Turn off heat before it gets too hot. Now, while vigorously beating yolks, very slowly pour in sugar-cream—do not stop beating for even a fraction of a second. As soon as mixture is thoroughly blended, pour back into top of double boiler and set into simmering water. Stir continuously until sauce thickens to consistency of very heavy cream. Turn down heat, so that water is well below boiling (about 175 degrees), cover top, then hold warm until serving time.

Just Before Serving

Stir sauce and check consistency. It should now be slightly thicker and this is balanced out by addition of Sherry. At the very last moment, slowly blend in enough sherry to bring sauce to perfect consistency, usually about 1/2 cup. Bring to table in a hot sauceboat with a pretty serving ladle.

COGNAC HARD SAUCE FOR PLUM PUDDING

About 3 cups

It can be made up to 3 days in advance and stored, tightly covered, in the coldest part of the refrigerator. We like to mold it into amusing Christmas shapes with a cookie press and various cutters.

Check Staples:

Sweet butter (1/4 lb.)
Aromatics: table salt, pure vanilla extract (2 tsp.)
Confectioners' sugar (2 cups)

Shopping List:

Heavy cream (1/2 cup)
Medium-priced French Cognac (2 Tbs.)

Up to 3 Days Beforehand—Preparation in About 15 Minutes

Soften the 1/4 pound of butter, then cream with the 2 cups of sugar and 1/4 teaspoon salt. This may be done by hand or, slightly more quickly, with an electric beater. Next, work in the 2 teaspoons of vanilla and the 2 tablespoons of Cognac. Finally, whip the 1/2 cup of cream and lightly work in to make a frothy and fluffy sauce. Refrigerate, tightly covered, for about 4 hours. It will then be stiff enough to mold into fancy Christmas shapes, or it can be served simply as a pile of fluff to be spooned out. Remember that it is extremely rich and individual portions should be quite small.

An Alternative Main Dish for the Christmas Dinner

ROAST WHOLE SUCKLING PIG

For a party of 8 to 10

This is surely one of the most magnificent dishes in all of gastronomy: the nearest that modern man can come to the ancient feasts of history, when whole animals were brought in and laid on the festive board. The piglet rests on its haunches, front paws forward, a bright red apple in its mouth, a garland of red and green around its neck and a neat curl in its tail. However we disagree violently with the standard recipes. By the time the piglet has been eviscerated and cleaned, it is not much more than a thin shell of crackling skin and delicate white meat, with a very large central cavity. Standard recipes call for this to be stuffed with a combination of ground meats, including several pounds of mature pork, all rather highly seasoned. The result of this ridiculous method is a twofold disaster. First, by the time this huge central core of old ground meat is thoroughly baked through, the thin outer shell of piglet is ruinously overcooked. Second, the baked piglet then becomes nothing more than a huge sausage, with the central stuffing entirely overpowering and dominating the delicate and lovely flavors of the piglet. We believe that the ingredients of the stuffing should be so delicate, and need so little baking, that they serve only to support and magnify the piglet itself. Thus, our stuffing is mainly of fruit and nuts and, when the side of the piglet is cut open at the table, there is a puff of steam and the internal "goodies" fall out as from a cornucopia. Also, when we know that a piglet is coming, we begin a day or two beforehand by preparing batches of our whole-wheat kasha and our basic applesauce. The size of the piglet is controlled by the size of the available oven, from the smaller, at about 10 pounds, to the larger, at about 20 pounds. The amounts for the stuffing in the following recipe are for a middle-of-the-road piglet of about 15 pounds.

It is better to have too much stuffing than too little, so that the piglet's belly can be nicely rounded out. Finally, it is the repeated rubbing of the skin with olive oil that produces the marvelously crisp crackling that is one of the supreme joys of this dish.

Check Staples:

Corn-belly salt pork (1 lb.)
Eggs (2 large)
Aromatics: crystal salt, freshly ground black pepper, MSG, ground cinnamon, whole nutmeg
Indian chick-pea flour, or all-purpose flour, or the sauce (a few Tbs.)
Olive oil (about 1 cup)

Shopping List:

Whole suckling pig, cleaned and oven-ready, with hooves trimmed (about 15 lbs.)
Pork liver, sliced (3/4 lb.)
Tart cooking apples, fairly small, for stuffing, *see* list, page 508 (about 1 1/2 lbs.)
Bright red apple, for piglet to hold in its mouth (1 small)
Chestnuts (1 1/2 lbs.)
Button mushrooms (3/4 lb.)
White boiler onions (1 1/2 lbs.)
Yellow onions (1 1/2 lbs.)
Pistachio nuts, shelled (1/2 lb.)
Seedless white raisins (1 1/2 cups)
Sweet wine, perhaps a California Muscat de Frontignan (about 2 cups)
Optional—brightly colored vegetables, for garnish around piglet's neck:
- **small bright red peppers (about 4)**
- **bright green watercress (a few sprigs)**

Optional accompaniments:
- **our homemade applesauce, page 174**
- **our whole-wheat kasha, page 167**

Choosing the Piglet

We usually pick out our piglet at the fancy butcher's a few days in advance, but insist that delivery be made at a convenient hour on Christmas Eve. The animal should not be slimy and all orifices should be perfectly clean. The butcher should clean the head, cut out the eyes, and trim the hooves. We also arrange with the local iceman to deliver, at the time when the piglet is due to come, 2 medium-sized blocks of ice and 20 pounds of ice cubes.

The Day Before—Preparing the Stuffing in About 1 1/2 Hours

Bake, peel, and skin the 1 1/2 pounds of chestnuts, according to our BASIC RULE (page 158). While chestnuts are baking, prepare other ingredients and hold them. Set the 1½ cups of raisins to soak in 1 cup of the sweet wine. Grind the pound of corn belly and put it in a fair-sized mixing bowl. Drop the ¾ pound of sliced liver into boiling salted water, leave until just stiff enough to handle easily, usually in about 3 to 4 minutes, then chop and add to corn belly. Wash and core but leave whole and unpeeled the 1½ pounds of tart apples. Wipe clean (never wash) the ¾ pound of mushrooms and slice thickly lengthwise into hammer shapes. Peel the 1½ pounds of white onions, leaving them whole, then parboil them in boiling salted water for 15 minutes. Peel and coarsely chop the 1½ pounds of yellow onions. Then we take out our largest mixing bowl and work the ingredients together, in order (there are no better tools for this operation than a pair of clean hands): the ½ pound of shelled pistachio nuts, the chopped yellow onions, the corn belly and liver, the sliced mushrooms, the soaked raisins (drained, but with sweet wine held in reserve), 1½ teaspoons ground cinnamon, 1 teaspoon freshly ground nutmeg, plus salt, pepper, and MSG to taste. Now bind all this into a lightly firm stuffing, by blending in alternately large handfuls of the baked chestnuts, coarsely crumbled, plus the 2 whole eggs, 1 at a time, and as much as needed of the wine in which raisins were soaked. When the stuffing seems perfect, cover it tightly and refrigerate overnight. Also refrigerate the whole cored apples and the parboiled white onions.

The Evening Before—When Piglet and Ice Are Delivered

Wash piglet thoroughly inside and out, then lay it in a bathtub, with a block of ice at its head and tail. Now fill the belly with ice cubes and cover the outside with remaining ice cubes, then run in cold water just to cover. Leave soaking overnight. This is not an alternative to refrigeration; it is an essential process to freshen and whiten the meat.

At Any Time on the Day—Stuffing and Trussing the Piglet in About 30 Minutes

This is simply a physical problem. The piglet must be given a nice fat round belly, so there must be plenty of stuffing inside; the corners can conveniently be filled with the whole apples and whole white onions. More apples and onions can be pushed into the center of the stuffing. Finally, with a sharp instrument (an ice pick or a larding needle are good), punch rows of holes about 1 inch apart along both sides of the belly flaps, then tightly lace up the belly with thick string, just as one laces a shoe. Now comes the important matter of setting the piglet in a handsome, reclining position on the baking pan. It should be just like a dog resting on its haunches. Tuck the hind legs neatly in on either side of the belly and hold them in this position by tying them together with string. Make the essential curl in the tail and hold it in position with Scotch tape or a bit of string. See that the front legs are straight forward and place the head low between them. We stick a pair of blue marbles into the eye sockets. Now the piglet can be left at room temperature, but in the coolest possible place, until roasting is to begin. Any remaining stuffing can be put into a separate baking pan.

About 4 Hours Before Serving

Preheat oven to 450 degrees and set shelf so that piglet will be in exact center of oven. Thoroughly rub every square inch of piglet's skin, including of course head, legs, and even tail, with olive oil. Place in hot oven and sear for 15 minutes. Turn oven down to 325 degrees. Take out piglet and again rub everywhere with olive oil, then pour ½ cup of remaining wine into roasting pan to provide steam, cover ears and tail with foil to prevent premature browning, hold mouth open with a small block of wood, then return to oven. We always calculate total oven time at 15 minutes per pound of piglet's unstuffed weight, or 3 hours 45 minutes for our piglet. One must remember that piglet's meat is mostly a thin shell near the surface, and therefore cooks more quickly than a solid roast. The one absolutely fixed rule is that piglet's skin *must* be rubbed with olive oil without fail every 20 minutes during entire oven time. The last of these coatings must be 5 minutes before piglet finally comes out of oven.

About 2 Hours Before Serving

If there is any extra stuffing being held in a baking pan, place it in oven with pig.

About 20 Minutes Before End of Oven Time

Remove foil caps from piglet's ears and tail, so that they will brown to a nice color. Polish up the apple, ready for its mouth. Make a necklace by stringing together with cotton thread sprigs of the watercress and the small whole red peppers (or whatever other bright vegetables have been chosen).

When Piglet Comes Out of Oven—the Sauce and the Decoration

With enormous care (remember that piglet is now quite brittle and could even break in half!) slide, do not lift, piglet onto largest serving platter or carving board. Set back in turned-off oven to rest until sauce is prepared. Place roasting pan over 1 or 2 burners on top of stove and skim off fat. Bring remaining gravy to a boil and scrape off succulent bits from roasting pan. Liquefy some of the chick-pea (or alternative) flour with a little more of the wine, then turn down heat under pan until bubbling stops, stir in liquefied flour, 1 tablespoon at a time, and work around until gravy is thickened to taste. Adjust seasonings as needed. Keep warm until piglet is ready to go to the table. Now decorate piglet: put the apple neatly in its mouth, the bright garland around its neck, and remove the burnt Scotch tape, or string, from its

tail. We like to surround it with a bed of whole-grain kasha (page 167), wetted down with a good deal of the gravy. The remaining gravy comes to the table in a hot sauceboat. We think that homemade applesauce (page 174) is another essential accompaniment. We drink one of the rich white wines of Burgundy with the meal, say, a Chevalier-Montrachet.

Welcome to the New Year

Many years ago, while visiting in Germany, we learned to make *Berliner Pfannkuchen,* which are traditionally served during the first moments of the New Year. *Berliner Pfannkuchen* are neither especially from Berlin, nor are they true pancakes, since they are deep-fat fried. They are so good that they stimulate the excitement of any New Year's party. According to the state of the weather, they may be served with hot spiced wine (page 632) or a cold eggnog. After years of practice, we have the timing shaved to the nearest minute. Perhaps, at the first try, one should allow a few extra minutes for possible fumbling!

BERLINER PFANNKUCHEN—GERMAN NEW YEAR PANCAKES

About 24 individual pancakes

Check Staples:

Sweet butter (4 Tbs.)
Eggs (3 large)
Milk (about ⅔ cup)
Dried powdered yeast (1 envelope)
Aromatic: table salt
Granulated instantized flour (about 4¼ cups)
Superfine-grind sugar or vanilla sugar (a few Tbs.)
Plus oil for deep-fat frying

Shopping List:

Good, tart jam for the fillings, say, a Swiss mountain plum or alternative (1-lb. jar)

At 8:00 p.m.—Working the Yeast in 15 Minutes

Warm the ⅔ cup of milk to just a little above blood heat, then turn off heat, sprinkle yeast on the surface and leave undisturbed to work and dissolve for about 10 minutes. Break 2 of the eggs into a small bowl and beat lightly. Separate the third egg, putting away yolk for some other use, then hold the white, with a pastry brush alongside. Put 1 cup of the flour into a medium-sized mixing bowl, then when yeast-milk is ready, add to flour and work together thoroughly with a wooden spoon. Cover bowl with waxed paper. Turn on oven to 500 degrees for exactly 60 seconds, then turn off heat, set bowl in center of oven, shut oven door and leave yeast to rise for 45 minutes. Meanwhile go back to the New Year's Eve party.

At Exactly 9:10—Mixing the Dough in 15 Minutes

Take bowl out of oven and work yeast-flour vigorously with a wooden spoon to punch dough down. Just melt the 4 tablespoons of butter. Now work into the dough: the melted butter, the 2 eggs, ¼ teaspoon salt, and 3 more cups of flour. Beat vigorously with a wooden fork or an electric beater until the mixture is a smooth, soft batter-dough, but stiff enough to be rolled out. As needed, work in either 1 or 2 tablespoons of extra flour or 1 or 2 tablespoons of extra milk until the proper consistency is achieved. Cover bowl with waxed paper. Turn on oven to 500 degrees for exactly 60 seconds, then turn off heat, set bowl in center of oven, shut oven door, and leave dough to rise for 35 minutes. Meanwhile, back to the party. . . .

At Exactly 10 p.m.—Rolling Out the Pancakes in 25 Minutes

Take bowl out of oven. Set out pastry board and rolling pin and lightly flour both. Work dough with fingers for a few seconds, roll into a ball, and set at one corner of pastry board. Pull off pieces, each a little larger than a walnut, and quickly roll out into a round cookie shape about 3/8 inch thick and 2 inches across. When first two have been rolled and trimmed, put about 2 teaspoons of jam in center of first one, paint about 1/2 inch all around edge with egg white, lay second pancake on top of first and press edges firmly together all around. Lay aside on a platter. Repeat process until all dough is used up, when there will be about 24 double-sided filled pancakes. Separate layers of pancakes on platter with waxed paper. Set platter in warmest part of kitchen to encourage pancakes to rise further. Set out deep-fat fryer, but do not yet heat it up. Set out absorbent paper for draining pancakes. Have ready a sprinkler of superfine-grind sugar. It is now 25 minutes after 10. Go back to the party.

At Precisely 11:30 p.m.

In our house, two people work together in a smooth production-line operation. Turn on deep-fryer to 375 degrees. Preheat oven to keep-warm temperature (about 150 degrees), then set in it a large flat serving platter.

At Precisely 11:40 p.m.

We slide the first pancake into the deep fat. Exactly 15 second later, the second goes in. Exactly 15 seconds later, the third. Exactly 15 seconds later, the fourth. This is as many as our fryer will hold. After 1 1/2 minutes, the first pancake is turned over to brown on the second side. Fifteen seconds later, the second is turned over. And so on. . . . After 3 minutes, the first pancake comes out, is set on the absorbent paper, and is instantly replaced by the fifth, and so on. . . . When each pancake is dry, it is sprinkled on both sides with sugar and set on the platter in the oven to keep warm. An elementary calculation shows that we complete 4 pancakes every 3 minutes, which means that 24 pancakes will be completed in 18 minutes. Therefore . . .

At Precisely 11:58 p.m.

The platter is lifted out of the oven and begins a slow and dignified progress toward the living-room door.

On the First Stroke of Midnight

The platter comes in and the *Berliner Pfannkuchen* are served.

Informal Party Menus

Apart from the great holiday feasts, which are the climax of the gastronomic year, the fall, for us, seems to be a time for simple, informal parties, involving no more than a reasonable effort in planning, shopping, and preparation. For example, we might build an excellent party on any one of the following menus.

FALL PARTY LUNCH I:
- Clear Vegetable Bouillon, page 111
- Brandade de Morue, page 559
- Turkish Potato Köftesi, page 606
- Bowls of Salted Watercress
- French Poires Bon-Chrétien, page 618

FALL PARTY LUNCH II:
- Tomatoes Stuffed with Anchovies, page 605
- French Lambs' Kidneys in Champagne, page 336
- Green Salad with Fall Dressing, page 612
- Cheese and Fruit, page 173

FALL PARTY LUNCH III:
- Billi-Bi, page 429
- Cheese Soufflé, page 147
- Cold Green Beans Athenian Style, page 156
- Ruedi's Chestnut and Raspberry Müsli, page 614

FALL PARTY BUFFET SUPPER I:
- French Marinated Mushrooms, page 107
- New Orleans Jambalaya aux Chorices, page 572
- Green Salad
- Cold Pseudo-Soufflé of Raspberries, page 480

FALL PARTY BUFFET SUPPER II (for Algerian Independence Day, November 1):
- Hunkar Begendi, page 258
- Samak Bi Taheeni, page 594
- Couscous, page 578
- Honey Pastries
- Turkish Coffee, page 261

FALL PARTY DINNER I:
- Cream of Inebriated Mushrooms, page 113
- Grenadine-Glazed Roast Pork, page 124
- Brussels Sprouts Purée, page 309
- Whole-Grain Kasha, page 167
- Old English Applesauce, page 174

FALL PARTY DINNER II:
- Cold Roasted Red Pimiento Cream, page 565
- French Pot-au-Feu, page 115
- Amaretti in Rum Chocolate, page 620

FALL PARTY DINNER III:

Vitello Tonnato, page 423
Cotriade Bretonne, page 143
Green Salad
Bananas Flamed with Rum, page 618

FALL PARTY DINNER IV (for Saint Andrew's Day, November 30):

Scotch Woodcock, page 264
Non-Intestinal Haggis, page 642
White Turnips in Maple-Mustard Sauce, page 163
Our Simplified Creamed Potatoes, page 470
Tipsy Laird, page 624

FALL LAZY SUNDAY BREAKFAST I:

Fresh Squeezed Orange Juice
Royal Court English Breakfast Trifle, page 626
Toast with Homemade Bitter-Orange Marmalade, page 183
Coffee

FALL LAZY SUNDAY BREAKFAST II (for Swedish Saint Lucia Day, December 13):

Vouvray Fruit Cup, page 178
Swedish Omelette with Lingonberries, page 627
Filbert Soufflé Cake, page 629
Coffee

THE FAMILY MEALS OF THE FALL
Day-to-Day Recipes

This is the time of year for sharply varied menu patterns. During October and the first part of November, we are often involved in last-minute informal parties for old friends arriving unexpectedly in town. When our girls were at home, they would suddenly fill the house for the weekend with hungry young friends. This called for solid, expansive meals adapted to the weather. If the hail was beating on the windows, the accent was on velvety cream soups, on filling stews, and flaming desserts. Then, after mid-November, comes the concentration on Thanksgiving and Christmas, when all families turn homeward and draw together, each within its own circle. As the December shopping pressure rises, our concern is more and more on saving time with one-dish meals (page 572) and on foods which can be ready in the refrigerator to be converted in 3 or 4 minutes into a quick lunch or late supper (page 566). In the Fall holiday season gastronomic luxury often rubs shoulders with extreme simplicity.

¶ *Prologues (Appetizers)—Shellfish Hors d'Oeuvres · Smoked Salmon Canapés · Pork on Toothpicks · All-Purpose Pâté*

CELIA'S SHELLFISH MARINARA

For our family of 4

This is a superb opening to a holiday dinner, or, served on a bed of boiled rice, it can be a rich but light main course. There are no particular difficulties in its preparation, but it involves several steps and a certain amount of time. The result is worth it.

Check Staples:

Salt butter (2 Tbs.)
Egg (1 large)
Aromatics: crystal salt, freshly ground black pepper, red cayenne pepper, MSG, basil, whole bay leaves, garlic (2 cloves), oregano
Green Pascal celery, with some leaves (2 to 3 stalks)
Yellow onion (1 small)
Fresh parsley (small bunch)
Ground arrowroot (1/4 tsp.)
Olive oil (1 Tbs.)
Granulated white sugar (1/2 tsp.)
Italian peeled and seeded plum tomatoes (1 cup)
Tarragon white wine vinegar (about 1 cup)
Dry vermouth (1 cup)
Red wine (1/4 cup)
Dry white wine (about 1 cup)

Shopping List:

Bay scallops, *see* page 62 (1 1/4 lbs.)
Jumbo shrimp—for number per pound *see* page 62 (1 lb.)
Anchovies, flat fillets (2-oz. can)
Heavy cream (1/3 cup)
Medium-priced French Cognac (1/4 cup)

The Day Before—Advance Preparation in About 45 Minutes

Set the 2 tablespoons of butter to soften. Wash the 1 pound of shrimp and remove legs, but do not shell. Cook shrimp in a vinegar-wine *court-bouillon* by the Greek method (page 108), using the celery, cayenne pepper, bay leaves, and 1 clove of the garlic. However, since shrimp will receive extra cooking later in the *marinara,* they should be simmered in the *court-bouillon* for only about 2 to 3 minutes, then cooled and marinated in it overnight. While *court-bouillon* is simmering, prepare the anchovy butter, according to our BASIC RULE (page 137), and a simple *marinara* sauce.

BASIC RULE FOR SIMPLE MARINARA SAUCE: Peel and finely mince remaining clove of garlic; peel and chop the onion. In a 1-quart saucepan, preferably tinned copper for instantaneous response to adjustments of temperature, heat up the tablespoon of olive oil, then quickly sauté chopped onion until just beginning to gild. Add the drained flesh of the tomatoes, holding back liquid juice. Stir around, crushing tomatoes, then add: the 1/4 cup of red wine, the minced garlic, the 1/2 teaspoon of sugar, 1 teaspoon basil, and 1/2 teaspoon oregano. Stir thoroughly and adjust heat so that sauce bubbles gently. Now melt in 1 tablespoon of the anchovy butter and add black pepper and MSG, to taste. Saltiness is controlled by adding a little more anchovy butter, if needed. Continue gentle bubbling, uncovered, stirring occasionally, until sauce reduces and thickens to consistency of heavy cream, usually in 15 to 20 minutes. Finally, stir in 1 tablespoon of chopped parsley, taste and adjust seasonings if necessary, then cool and refrigerate overnight in a tightly screw-topped jar to blend and mature flavors.

About 1 Hour Before Serving

Let shrimp (still soaking in *court-bouillon*) and *marinara* sauce come to room temperature. Wash and dry the 1¼ pounds of bay scallops, then put into a 1½-quart saucepan and pour over them the cup of vermouth. Set over moderate heat and bring slowly to a boil. As soon as liquid bubbles, stir with a wooden spoon, turn off heat at once, and strain the hot vermouth into a saucepan. Hold scallops covered. Bring vermouth back to gentle simmering, then add *marinara* sauce and continue simmering. Pour the ¼ cup of Cognac into a very small ½-cup saucepan and warm up to just above blood heat, then set alight and burn off alcohol until flames subside before adding brandy to vermouth and *marinara*. Continue to gently simmer, uncovered, to reduce and thicken slightly, for about 30 minutes. Meanwhile, drain shrimp, shell, devein, and hold with scallops. Separate the egg, putting away white for some other use, dropping yolk into a small 1-pint saucepan and with a small wire whisk beating in first the ¼ teaspoon of arrowroot, then the ⅓ cup of cream. Hold until vermouth-*marinara* is ready.

About 20 Minutes Before Serving

Place yolk-cream over very gentle heat and, beating continuously, warm it until it feels just hot to the fingertip. Turn off heat under vermouth-*marinara* and gradually beat in the yolk-cream. Turn heat back on, but very low, to avoid any danger of boiling. Continue beating until sauce thickens to the consistency of heavy cream. Add shrimp and scallops and stir well. Turn up heat slightly, but keep below boiling, cover, then leave for shellfish to heat through, usually in about 10 minutes. Do not let shellfish overcook. Finally, taste sauce, and adjust seasonings, if necessary. Serve on very hot small plates.

CANAPÉ SMOKED SALMON ROLLS

For about 2 dozen canapés

If the "jelly rolls" are prepared about 5 hours before serving and allowed to become quite firm in the refrigerator, the cutting and assembling are easy. Otherwise, the rolls tend to squish.

Check Staples:

Lemon (1)
Aromatics: crystal salt,☆ Indian *garam-massala* curry spice mixture☆
Shallots☆ (2 cloves)
Watercress (small bunch)
Toast triangles, or melba toast rounds (about 2 dozen)

Shopping List:

Nova Scotia smoked salmon, cut thin (4 large slices)
Cream cheese (3-oz. package)
Heavy cream (1/3 cup)
Cucumber (1 medium)
Green pitted olives (about 1 dozen)

About 5½ Hours Before Serving—Advance Preparation in About 15 Minutes

Assemble in a fairly large mixing bowl: the 3 ounces of cream cheese the 2 cloves of shallot, peeled and finely minced, plus ¼ cup of finely chopped watercress leaves. Cream these together with a wooden spoon, gradually working in about 3 tablespoons of the cream, at the same time sprinkling on 1 teaspoon of the *garam-massala* and about ½ teaspoon salt, more or less, according to saltiness of smoked salmon. When all ingredients are thoroughly blended, adjust consistency to a fairly thick, yet easily spreadable, smooth paste by adding, as needed, a few more dashes of cream. At same time, taste and adjust seasoning, if necessary. Flatten out the 4 slices of smoked salmon on a cutting board and spread each all the way to the edge all around with the aromatic cheese; the cheese should be divided equally between the 4 slices. Then carefully roll up into 4 separate jelly rolls, place in a flat, covered dish, and refrigerate for about 5 hours to stiffen and set.

About 15 Minutes Before Serving

Wipe cucumber clean; do not peel, but score lengthwise with a fork. Now assemble canapés. On each piece of toast, place a thin slice of cucumber, then a ¼-inch-thick slice of smoked salmon roll, then a green ring sliced from an olive and topped with a minute sprig of watercress. Repeat until all ingredients are used up. Until they are served, keep canapés in refrigerator. At the last moment, squeeze on a few drops of lemon juice.

KOREAN BROILED PORK ON TOOTHPICKS

For our family of 4

This should be prepared the day before so that the pork cubes can absorb the sauce overnight in the refrigerator.

Check Staples:

Aromatics: crystal salt,☆ freshly ground black pepper,☆ MSG,▣

Shopping List:

Pork, lean fillet, cut into ½-inch cubes (1 lb.)

Check Staples (continued):
garlic (2 cloves), Indian ground ginger, whole sesame seed, Chinese soy sauce (½ cup), Tabasco
Green scallions (small bunch)
Olive oil (1 Tbs.)
Granulated white sugar (1½ Tbs.)

The Day Before—Preparing the Marinating Sauce in About 15 Minutes

In a covered refrigerator dish large enough to hold the meat, mix the sauce: the ½ cup of soy sauce; the tablespoon of olive oil; enough of the green scallion tops, finely chopped, to fill ⅓ cup; 6 of the scallion bulbs, finely minced; the 1½ tablespoons of sugar; the 2 cloves of garlic, peeled and finely minced; 1 teaspoon ginger, 2 teaspoons sesame seed, a few drops of Tabasco, plus salt, pepper, and MSG to taste. Season rather strongly. Mix thoroughly, then put in pork cubes and work around until each is thoroughly coated with sauce. Refrigerate, covered, overnight.

On the Day—About 4 Hours Before Serving

Bring dish out of refrigerator, stir pork cubes again thoroughly, to recoat with sauce, then continue marinating at room temperature for about 4 hours.

About 15 Minutes Before Serving

Preheat broiler, arranging height of pan so that pork cubes will rest about 2 inches below heat. Remove pork cubes from sauce and grill until brown on first side, with our broiler usually in about 3½ minutes. Then turn over and brown the second side; usually it takes about 2½ minutes. Meanwhile pour sauce remaining in dish into a small saucepan and bring rapidly to a boil. Also put a serving platter in the oven to get warm. When pork cubes are done, set on platter and dribble hot sauce over them. Impale each on a toothpick and serve immediately.

OUR QUICK VERSION OF FRENCH BRANDADE DE MORUE—A PÂTÉ OF SALT COD

A supply for several meals

This great specialty of southern France used to involve so much hard work that two cooks shared the steady stirring and a third pounded for an hour or so. We use the electric meat grinder and blender to do the work in hardly more than 15 minutes. Salt cod is one of the oldest of preserved foods. It was a staple on the long voyages of sailing ships. It is still a staple of many fine dishes of France, where it is called *morue;* of Spain, where it is *bacalao;* and Italy, where it is *baccalà.* In the United States, we get an extremely good quality of salt cod,⚜ caught by Canadian fishermen off Nova Scotia and salted and dried by the French Canadians of Quebec. *Brandade* keeps for many days in the refrigerator and is a highly flexible basic preparation: used as an appetizer or dip, or as a luncheon or supper main dish, or as a mayonnaise over vegetables, or a midnight snack. It is solid, strong in texture, and so good that it is habit-forming.

Check Staples:

Aromatics: freshly ground black pepper,⚜ red cayenne pepper, MSG,⚜ garlic (any amount from 2 to 12 cloves, according to taste)

Olive oil⚜ (almost 1 pt.)

Fine rice flour,⚜ or, second best, cake flour, only used in an emergency separation (1 to 2 Tbs.)

Shopping List:

Best quality salt cod, all skin and bones removed (2 lbs.)

Heavy whipping cream (1/2 pt.)

Soaking out Salt in 3 to 12 Hours

Salt cod varies tremendously in quality. Some appears to be years old and is as hard as a wooden board. (One of the early morning sounds in Venice is of the hard salt cod, the *baccalà,* being softened by being slapped against the stone mooring posts of the gondolas along the canals.) If it is encrusted with salt, it will need to be scrubbed under running water, then soaked for 12 hours, with several changes of water. Our Canadian salt cod needs no scrubbing and hardly more soaking than 3 hours. Incidentally, salt cod must never be soaked or cooked in bare metal pans, or it will darken. We use china, earthenware, or enameled cast-iron.

Cooking in About 10 Minutes

Rinse the now-softened fish under cold running water, pick off all final bits of skin and bone, cut into 2-inch squares, and place in suitable pan (above), and just cover with cold water. Bring gently up to boiling and, the moment the first bubbles appear, turn off heat and leave soaking for about 5 minutes. (If salt cod is boiled hard it becomes as tough as leather.)

Grinding and Mixing in About 15 Minutes

We pass drained pieces of salt cod through the fine cutter of a meat grinder.* This produces a light and fluffy pile. In a large enameled cast-iron cocotte,* over fairly high heat, we warm 3/4 cup of the olive oil up to the point where it just starts smoking. Arming ourselves with a heavy wooden spoon and a strong wooden pestle, we shake the salt cod, all at once, into the hot oil and immediately start the most vigorous pounding and stirring. Within 2 or 3 seconds, there is a miracle! All that large quantity of oil is suddenly and instantly absorbed, the salt cod is now a paste and the bottom of the cocotte is dry. At once turn heat down to simmering, while continuing vigorously to pound and mash the salt cod into a smoother and smoother paste. Crush as many cloves of garlic as desired through a press and work into the salt cod paste.

Two other small saucepans must now be kept just warm on the stove. In one, heat up another 3/4 cup of olive oil to blood heat and keep it at that temperature. In the second small pan, do exactly the same with the 1/2 pint of heavy cream. Now, alternately, tablespoon by tablespoon, blend oil and cream into the ever-thickening and expanding salt-cod paste. It seems to have a virtually unlimited capacity to absorb the liquids, becoming more and more like a rough textured mayonnaise. (If, at any time, it acts like a rebellious mayonnaise and separates, it can be whipped back into line by the addition of 1 or 2 Tablespoons of the rice flour, vigorously worked in.) When about half the oil and cream have been added, we transfer the paste a cupful at a time into an electric blender and switch it on for just a few seconds at low speed. Switching off and on, we work the paste back down around the cutters, until there is another miraculous transformation. The salt-cod paste has now become a true *brandade,* a light and smooth fluff. This goes back into the warm cocotte and the process of working in more oil and cream is restarted. When to stop adding liquids must be a matter of judgment by eye and taste. The final consistency should be that of mashed potato. Then the seasoning is adjusted with a little black and cayenne pepper, and it all goes into a covered dish in the refrigerator, where it remains good for several days.

Many Ways of Serving

Brandade is always served just warm, usually with little triangular croutons of bread, on which it is spread. Or it can be used as a dip with slices of carrot, chunks of tomato, wedges of green pepper, slices of cucumber, etc. It is excellent as a supper dish with hot boiled potatoes or tossed in with hot spaghetti. . . . The longer one has it around, the more excellent ways one finds of using it.

¶ *Prologues (Soups)—Hot Cream · Iced Cream*

CREAM OF CHESTNUT SOUP

For our family of 4

This is a velvet restorative for a day of icy wind and rain, one of the most luxurious of all soups. It is so rich and filling that it must be followed by a light course and fluffy dessert.

Check Staples:

Salt butter (4 Tbs.)
Aromatics: crystal salt, freshly ground black pepper, MSG, whole cloves
Carrots (3 medium)
Green Pascal celery, with leaves (1 head)
Yellow onions (3 medium)
Parsley (small bunch)
Olive oil, for shelling chestnuts (2 to 3 Tbs.)
Dry white wine (2 cups)

Shopping List:

Fresh chestnuts (1½ lbs.)
Knuckle of veal cut in half, with some lean meat attached (1)
Leeks (3 medium)
Heavy cream (½ pt.)
Italian Parmesan cheese (¼ lb.)
French Calvados apple brandy (about ¼ cup)

On Any Convenient Day—Preparing Stock and Chestnuts in About 2 Hours

Most recipes for this famous soup call simply for "some stock." We consider it essential to the success of the dish to prepare our own enriched veal stock with a particular balance of flavors.

BASIC RULE FOR BUTTERED VEAL STOCK: Trim off and discard green leaves and roots from white parts of 3 leeks, then make crosswise cuts most of the way down and carefully wash under cold running water to get out every last grain of sand. Then soak in cold water until needed. In large soup pot, assemble the aromatic vegetables: the 3 carrots, scraped and sliced; the 3 onions, peeled and chopped; the celery leaves, finely chopped; the center heart of the green celery, washed and chopped; the parsley stalks and a few of the leaves, finely chopped; plus the drained white leeks, now chunked. Set pot over medium frying heat, drop in the 4 tablespoons of butter, and stir around with wooden spoon until butter begins to sizzle. Then turn down heat so that vegetables simmer rather than sauté, stirring occasionally, until they are fairly soft, usually in about 10 minutes. Meanwhile wash veal knuckle and, when vegetables are soft, lay knuckle halves on top, cut sides down. Add the 2 cups of white wine, freshly drawn cold water just to cover, plus salt and MSG to taste. Turn heat up full and bring rapidly to a boil, carefully skimming, until it starts bubbling. Then turn heat down to simmering and continue cooking, covered, for about 1½ hours.

Meanwhile bake, shell, and skin the 1½ pounds of chestnuts, according to our BASIC RULE (page 158). Then hold, covered, in refrigerator, until needed. When stock is ready, stir well, taste, and add a little more salt if needed; allow to cool and hold in refrigerator.

Perhaps the Next Day, if Convenient—Cooking and Puréeing Chestnuts in About 15 Minutes, Plus 30 Minutes Unsupervised Simmering

We cook the chestnuts in a thick-bottomed enameled cast-iron cocotte,* which minimizes the slight tendency of the chestnuts to burn. Bring chestnuts out of refrigerator and put them into cocotte. Take veal stock out of refrigerator and carefully skin off fat. With a slotted spoon, lift out all mush of vegetables from bottom of stock and add to chestnuts, then ladle over just enough veal stock to cover, taking care not to add any veal meat. Then bring chestnuts gently up to boiling, meanwhile adding: a small handful of parsley, finely chopped, about 6 whole cloves, plus a few good grinds of pepper. Adjust heat to gentle simmering and continue cooking, covered, until chestnuts are soft enough for puréeing, usually in 25 to 35 minutes. Then taste and adjust seasoning if necessary. Pick out about 8 well-shaped whole chestnuts and hold for garnishing. Now put entire contents of pot through a food mill. The result is a thick concentrate that can be stored in the refrigerator for several days.

About 2½ Hours Before Serving

Take chestnut purée, remaining veal stock, and whole chestnuts out of refrigerator and let come to room temperature.

About 25 Minutes Before Serving

Gently heat the chestnut purée, stirring continuously at first, to avoid any danger of burning. At the same time, work in enough extra veal stock to achieve consistency of a cream soup. Then work in ¼ cup of the cream. Make soup very hot, but do not under any circumstances allow it to boil. Finally, grate Parmesan cheese.

Serving at Table

Soup bowls should be very hot. Stir into each serving 1 more tablespoon of cream and 1 tablespoon of Calvados, which seems to sharpen and frame the chestnut flavor. Place 1 whole chestnut in center of each bowl and sprinkle on Parmesan. The total effect is exhilarating!

CREAM OF CARROT SOUP

For our family of 4

There are two versions of this comforting cold-weather soup: "family style," with the solid bits left in; or, "party style," with the soup strained to a smooth, pastel-colored cream. We think the first way has the more character.

Check Staples:

Salt butter (3 Tbs.)
Floured butter for thickening—*beurre manié,* *see* page 12 (about ½ cup)
Clear chicken bouillon (3 cups)
Milk (3 cups)
Aromatics: crystal salt,* freshly ground black pepper,* MSG,* mace chips*
Yellow onion (1)
Fresh parsley (small bunch)
Shallots* (about 4 cloves)
Granulated instantized flour* (2 Tbs.)
Dry white wine* (¼ cup)

Shopping List:

Carrots (1 bunch, about 8 medium)
Heavy cream (¼ cup)

About 1¼ Hours Before Serving—Including About 45 Minutes of Unsupervised Simmering

We usually prepare this in a 3-quart enameled cast-iron cocotte* with a tightly fitting lid. Put in the 3 tablespoons of butter and gently melt it over low heat. Meanwhile scrape and grate or finely shred the carrots, then add to cocotte. Stir around and turn up heat to gentle simmering (do not, under any circumstances, fry or brown) for about 7 or 8 minutes, uncovered, stirring occasionally. Peel and chop together the onion and 4 cloves of shallot, then hold, covered. When carrots are ready, stir in onion and shallot and continue simmering for not more than 1 minute longer. Then absorb butter and juices in bottom of cocotte by sprinkling on and blending in just enough of the flour to make a light paste. Now turn up heat to high and immediately start working in, gradually at first, the three cups of chicken bouillon. Keep stirring vigorously to avoid lumping. As liquid in cocotte starts bubbling, keep turning down heat, bit by bit, to maintain no more than gentle simmering. When all bouillon is in, start adding the 3 cups of milk, adjusting heat to bring back to gentle simmering as quickly as possible. At same time, add the aromatics: the ¼ cup of wine, about 4 whole sprigs of parsley, about ½ teaspoon of freshly grated mace, plus salt, pepper, and MSG to taste. Adjust heat for very gentle simmering, cover, then keep simmering, stirring occasionally, for about 40 to 45 minutes.

About 15 Minutes Before Serving—Less, If Not To Be Strained

Finely chop about 1/4 cup of remaining parsley and hold for garnishing. If soup is to be strained, it should be done at this point. Otherwise, all that is necessary is to fish out and discard the whole sprigs of parsley. Now re-heat soup to just below simmering and thicken to the consistency of light cream by working in lump after lump of the floured butter, according to the BASIC RULE (page 12). Simmer for about 5 minutes.

Serving at Table

Float about 1 tablespoon of the heavy cream on top of each serving and sprinkle liberally with parsley. The bright green makes a handsome contrast to the delicate yellow of the soup.

COLD ROASTED RED PIMIENTO CREAM

For our family of 4

Of course our main interest in cold soups is during hot spring and summer weather, but sometimes we also like to start a solid winter dinner with a light liquid, refreshingly iced (see also Hemingway's *gazpacho,* page 233). The brilliant red of this soup adds pomp to any holiday table. The pimientos must be the bright red Spanish roasted type that come in 4-ounce or 8-ounce jars.

Check Staples:

Clear beef bouillon (1 cup)
Aromatics: crystal salt,☧ freshly ground black pepper,☧ MSG,⛁ dried basil, dried dillweed, dried rosemary (only if fresh unavailable)

Shopping List:

Roasted red pimiento (two 8-oz. jars)
Tomato juice (1 cup)
Small bunch of each of the following fresh herbs, if available: basil, dill, rosemary
Small green pepper, for garnish (1)

1 or More Days Ahead—Advance Preparation in About 15 Minutes

Mash 1 jar of the pimientos in a mortar, then pass through a food mill. The objective is to crush it, not cream it, so it cannot be done in an electric blender. Put the red mash into a 1-quart saucepan and hold. With kitchen scissors, finely snip enough of the available fresh herbs to fill 1/4 cup, then add to saucepan (if fresh herbs are not available use 1 teaspoon each of the dried). Add 3/4 cup of the beef bouillon and 3/4 cup of the tomato juice, plus 1/2 teaspoon salt, a few grinds of pepper, and ½ teaspoon MSG. Now taste and balance the flavors. The slight smokiness of the pimiento must remain dominant, supported by the beef. If necessary, add a dash more bouillon or tomato juice, plus more seasonings. Gently heat soup, stirring occasionally, until it just comes to the boil. Turn off heat and let cool. Meanwhile finely chop or thinly slice remaining pimiento and put into bottom of covered dish in which soup will be refrigerated. When soup is cool enough, pour into dish, stir again thoroughly, then refrigerate for at least 12 hours, or up to several days.

A Few Hours Before Serving

Dip the green pepper for a few seconds into rapidly boiling water, remove skin and seeds, then finely slice into covered jar and refrigerate. Take soup out of refrigerator, stir thoroughly, then taste again and restore flavor balance, if necessary, with another dash of bouillon, or tomato juice, plus more seasonings. Cover again and refrigerate until moment of serving.

Serving At Table

Soup bowls should be chilled in the freezer or over a large bowl filled with ice. Decorate each serving of the bright red soup with a sprinkling of bright green pepper. Its crispness is the final element in the texture pattern.

¶ *Main Dishes (Meat)—Beef · Pork · Ham · Liver · Four Great One-Dish Meals*

The following recipes reflect our general pattern of living during the busy holiday season. Several of the dishes are extremely simple and quick to prepare. On the other hand, the one-dish meals may take more time (the first from New Orleans, the second from France, the third from North Africa, and the fourth from Israel), but they are made in substantial quantities and each will last, giving continuing pleasure for several days.

4-MINUTE CLUB STEAKS FLAMED IN A SAUTÉ PAN

For our family of 4

This is a famous French way with small, individual steaks.

Check Staples:

Salt butter (about 4 Tbs.)
Aromatics: crystal salt, whole black peppercorns, garlic (1 clove), Chinese soy sauce (¼ cup)

Shopping List:

Individual club steaks, or filets mignon (4, usually about 2 lbs.)
Medium-priced brandy, possibly a good Californian (¼ cup)

About 4 Minutes of Preparation

Peel the clove of garlic and crush through a press, then mix with about ¼ cup of the soy sauce in a fairly flat, open bowl, so that steaks can eventually be dipped in. Coarsely crack about 2 teaspoons of the whole peppercorns in a small mortar, then, with the heel of the hand, pound this pepper, plus desired amount of coarse crystal salt, into both sides of each steak. Then dip each side into garlic-flavored soy sauce, which will color steaks to a handsome brown and, during the frying, burn to a crisp salty crust.

About 4 Minutes Before Serving

Work fast and use a sauté pan just large enough to hold the 4 steaks to minimize overheating. Rapidly melt 2 tablespoons of the butter in a sauté pan over fairly high frying heat, until butter just begins to turn brown, then slip in 4 steaks and fry vigorously for about 1½ minutes on each side. Continuing to work fast, melt in the 2 remaining tablespoons of butter, then drench steaks with the ¼ cup of brandy and flame. If frying becomes too fierce at any point, turn down heat slightly. As soon as flames subside, serve on a very hot platter, with the brandy-butter sauce poured over steaks.

BELGIAN CARBONNADE FLAMANDE—BEEF IN BEER

For our family of 4

This is a classic dish of the Flemish part of Belgium. The slight bitterness of the beer seems to heighten and sharpen the natural flavor of the beef. It is a fairly solid main dish, excellent served on a bed of rice. It can be prepared the day before and seems to improve with reheating.

Check Staples:

Salt butter (2 Tbs.)
Floured butter for thickening—*see* page 12 (about ½ cup)
Aromatics: crystal salt, freshly ground black pepper, MSG, garlic (1 or 2 cloves, to taste), mace chips, crumbled sage leaf
Yellow onions (5 medium)
Olive oil (2 Tbs.)
Granulated white sugar (2 tsp.)
Red wine (½ cup)

Shopping List:

Lean beef, top round, in 1½-inch cubes (about 2 lbs.)
India Pale Ale or other full bodied beer (2 pts.)

About 1½ Hours Before Serving—or at Any Time Beforehand

Peel and chop the 5 onions and hold. We usually prepare this dish in a 4-quart enameled cast-iron cocotte,* which can be used first as a sauté pan. Place it over medium-high frying heat and melt the 2 tablespoons of butter and 2 tablespoons of olive oil, making sure that butter does not brown. Quickly brown on all sides the cubes of beef, a few at a time, and set aside. When last pieces are removed, sauté chopped onions until lightly gilded. Return meat and wet down with the ½ cup of red wine, then pour in enough of the beer just to cover. While heating up to simmering, add the aromatics: the 1 or 2 cloves of garlic, peeled and finely minced, a few grinds of mace chips (from a nutmeg grater), the 2 teaspoons of sugar, 1 teaspoon sage, plus salt, pepper and MSG, to taste. Stir thoroughly, adjust heat to very gentle simmering, "just smiling," cover, then keep simmering for about 1 hour.

About 15 Minutes Before Serving

Preheat oven to keep-warm temperature (150 degrees) and put in a deep serving bowl to warm up. When meat is tender but still firm, remove all cubes with a slotted spoon and keep warm in serving bowl in oven. Turn up heat under cocotte and boil beer sauce hard for 4 or 5 minutes to reduce and concentrate flavor. Then turn down heat to just below simmering and thicken sauce by working in, lump by lump, the floured butter, according to the BASIC RULE (page 12). Use only enough of the floured butter to achieve the thickness of heavy cream. Taste and adjust seasonings as needed. Put back beef to be thoroughly impregnated with sauce and reheated for 2 or 3 minutes—or the dish may be allowed to cool and reheated later.

PORK CHOPS WITH APPLES AND APRICOTS

For our family of 4

We like winter dishes in ceramic casseroles, where there is a warm glow from the hot pot as it is placed on the table and a puff of aromatic steam as the lid is lifted. This is a medium-light main course, which might be preceded by a cream soup and followed by a flaming dessert.

Check Staples:

Clear chicken bouillon (about ¾ cup)
Aromatics: crystal salt,* freshly ground black pepper,* MSG, ground cinnamon, Indian ground ginger, oregano, Chinese soy sauce
Yellow onions (3 medium)
Olive oil (about 3 Tbs.)
Dark-brown sugar (about ⅓ cup, fairly loosely packed)
Dry white wine (¼ cup)

Shopping List:

Loin pork chops, about 1 inch thick
Tart stewing apples, preferably Greening when available, or alternative, *see* list of foods in season, page 508 (3 medium)
Dried apricots (about 6 oz., or half the usual 11-oz. box)
Dried figs or canned Kadota figs (about 6 oz.)

At Any Time Beforehand—Browning the Chops and Assembling the Casserole in About 10 Minutes

In a dry sauté or fry pan over medium frying heat lightly brown the chops on both sides; usually it takes about 4 minutes. There is almost always enough fat on the chops to lubricate the pan, but if they show signs of sticking, a few drops of olive oil may be added. For the oven-baking, we use a low covered earthenware casserole large enough to hold the 4 chops, into which we first assemble the spiced fruit garnish: the 3 onions, peeled and finely chopped; the ⅓ cup of brown sugar; the 3 apples, peeled, cored, and chopped; the 6 ounces each of dried apricots and figs (drained, if canned), both coarsely chopped; 1 teaspoon ground cinnamon, ½ teaspoon ground ginger, ½ teaspoon oregano, plus salt, pepper and MSG, to taste. Mix thoroughly, then press in the browned chops so that they rest on a thin layer of the fruit mixture and are surrounded and partly covered by the remainder. Cover casserole and hold until cooking time. If only 2 or 3 hours, it may remain at room temperature. If longer, refrigerate, but return to room temperature before baking.

About 1 Hour Before Serving

Preheat oven to 350 degrees. Lightly pour over chops ⅓ cup of the bouillon and the ¼ cup of white wine. Cover tightly and set in center of oven to steam for 30 minutes. Meanwhile in small mixing bowl combine 2 tablespoons each of the soy sauce and olive oil, then hold. Have a pastry brush available.

About 30 Minutes Before Serving

Check casserole to see whether there is enough liquid in bottom to continue to provide plenty of steam. If not, add more bouillon. Re-cover tightly and set back in oven for 25 minutes longer.

About 10 Minutes Before Serving

Take casserole out of oven and turn broiler on high, setting grill shelf so that pork chops in casserole will be about 3 inches from heat. While broiler is heating up, scrape fruit from top of pork chops and arrange it neatly around and between them. Liberally paint bare surfaces of chops with olive oil–soy sauce mixture. In 1 or 2 minutes under the grill they will glaze to a shiny brown. Paint with more olive oil–soy sauce and glaze for a couple of minutes longer. Replace lid and speed casserole to the table.

HAM STEAK WITH SELF-MADE APPLE-MUSTARD GARNISH

For our family of 4

Check Staples:

Aromatics: Dijon mustard (about 1 Tbs.), Chinese soy sauce⊜ (1 Tbs.)
Olive oil⊜ (1 Tbs.)
Dark-brown sugar (about 2 Tbs.)

Shopping List:

Ham steak, either 1 or 1½ inches thick, according to luxury of occasion (1½ to 2¼ lbs.)
Tart stewing apples, *see* list, page 508 (3 medium)

About 2 Hours Before Serving

Mix the tablespoon of olive oil and the tablespoon of the soy sauce, then thoroughly rub ham steak on both sides and leave to marinate at room temperature for 1 hour. Meanwhile peel and core the 3 apples, then slice about ¼ inch thick and hold.

About 1 Hour Before Serving

Rub ham steak once more with olive oil–soy sauce mixture, then place in an open au gratin dish in which the ham just fits. Preheat oven to 350 degrees. Spread top of ham with 1 tablespoon of the mustard, a little more or less according to taste, then place a neat layer of overlapping slices of apple on top of ham, using up all the apples. Sprinkle with brown sugar, the amount controlled by the tartness of the apple, from about 1 tablespoon up to 2 or more. Place ham in center of oven and bake until it is done through and apples are quite soft, usually in about 50 minutes for a thin steak, slightly more for a thicker one. This is excellent with a purée of Brussels sprouts (page 309) and celeriac mashed potatoes (page 543).

BASIC METHOD FOR LIVER IN AROMATIC WINE

For our family of 4

We choose our liver according to the state of our pocketbook, and this recipe works equally well with economy beef, medium-priced pork, or luxurious calf's, *provided* that the butcher can be persuaded to slice it not more than ¼ inch thick. The trouble with liver served in most restaurants and many homes is that it is desperately overcooked. Whether it has the texture of soft leather or hard leather, depends on the degree of overcooking! By our method, one might say that the liver hardly touches the pan and the result is liver that is moist, butter-soft, and with its flavors sharpened and magnified.

Check Staples:
Salt butter (4 Tbs.)
Lemon (1)
Aromatics: crystal salt,☆ freshly ground black pepper,☆ dried dillweed, savory, tarragon
Chives, fresh or frozen (enough for 2 Tbs., chopped)
Parsley (enough for 2 Tbs., chopped)
Granulated instantized flour (about 1/4 cup)
Dry white wine (1/2 cup)

Shopping List:
Liver, *see* above, cut into even 1/4-inch slices (about 1 1/2 lbs.)

About 15 Minutes Before Serving

Mix together the 1/4 cup of flour, 1/2 teaspoon dillweed, 1/4 teaspoon each of savory and tarragon, plus salt and pepper to taste, then spread on a plate, ready to coat liver slices. Cut liver into roughly 2-inch squares and lightly coat on both sides with seasoned flour. Chop about 2 tablespoons each of chives and parsley and hold. Preheat oven to 150 degrees and put in a serving platter to get warm. In a frypan over medium-high frying temperature make the 4 tablespoons of butter quite hot, but do not let brown. We now arm ourselves with a wooden spoon in each hand and prepare to work fast for about 5 minutes. We never use forks for this operation, since they would puncture the liver and release its internal juices. Lift liver squares one by one and place in a neat circle around the pan. The instant circle is complete, go back to first square and turn it over. Immediately turn over second square and continue around the pan. When circle is again completed and we are back to first square, lift it out and place on warm platter. Lift out remaining squares in turn around the circle. Return platter to oven and start a second circle of liver squares, continuing same sequence until all liver squares are cooked and are safely on platter in oven. Pour the 1/2 cup of wine into frypan and turn up heat so that it boils hard, to reduce and concentrate flavors. At the same time scrape bottom of pan so as to dislodge any flavorful bits of crust. The moment wine begins to thicken and glaze, stir in chopped chives and parsley, plus a few squeezes of lemon juice and any extra salt and pepper that may be needed. Pour over liver and serve.

VARIATIONS: This is exactly the way we like our liver done. Naturally, the degree of doneness depends on the speed of the whole operation. However, there is an easy way of slightly adjusting the degree of doneness to suit personal taste. Instead of setting oven to 150 degrees, set it to 200 degrees, or even 225 degrees. Then the liver will continue cooking slightly while waiting for the sauce and the first pieces will be better done for those who prefer it.

Four Great One-Dish Meals

ONE-DISH MEAL FROM NEW ORLEANS—JAMBALAYA AUX CHORICES

2 or 3 meals for our family of 4

This is one of the greatest of authentic American Creole dishes, appropriately a blending of three gastronomic cultures: the French, the Spanish, and the Choctaw Indian. It is a worthy brother to the other great rice dishes of the world: the *paella* of Spain (page 234), the pilau of India (page 99), the pilaf of the Arab world (page 166), and the *risotto* of Italy (page 190). We usually make enough for two or three meals, since it keeps perfectly for several days, reheats without loss of quality and is even excellent cold. The small hot *chorice* sausage is probably obtainable only in Louisiana,✲ but in New York we replace it with the hot Spanish *chorizo,*✲ or a hot Italian *peperone*. This is a magnificent and solid main dish, to be accompanied by a salad and preceded and followed by light courses.

Check Staples:

Bacon or ham fat (about 3 Tbs.)
Lemon (1)
Aromatics: crystal salt,✲ freshly ground black pepper,✲ red cayenne pepper, MSG,✲ whole bay leaves, garlic (4 cloves), dried thyme (if fresh not available)
Green Pascal celery, with leaves (1 head)
Yellow onions (6 medium)
Parsley (1 bunch)
Long-grain white rice (1 lb.—about 2¼ cups)
Italian peeled and seeded plum tomatoes (2 lb. 3 oz. can)
Italian tomato paste (6-oz. can)

Shopping List:

Louisiana hot *chorice* sausage, or Spanish *chorizo,* or Italian *peperone* (1 lb.)
Lean cooked ham (1 lb.)
Deep-sea scallops (1½ lbs.)
Fresh jumbo shrimp, in shells (2 lbs.)
Green peppers (3 medium)
Tomatoes (4 medium)
Fresh thyme, if available; if not use dried (small bunch)
French Muscadet dry white wine or alternative✲ (1 bottle)

The Day Before—Advance Preparation of Shrimp in About 30 Minutes

The gastronomic excitement of this dish comes largely from the wine flavor of the shrimp, and this is achieved by first boiling and marinating them in their shells in a strong, dry white wine, such as a Muscadet of the Loire Valley, or a California Pinot Chardonnay from the Livermore or Napa valleys. The flavor seems to concentrate inside the shells as the shrimp soak overnight and the process cannot be hurried. Pour the bottle of wine into a 1-quart jug, make it a full quart by adding freshly drawn cold water, then pour into a 2½-quart saucepan and bring quickly to the boil. While it is heating up, add: the lemon, sliced; 2 cloves garlic, peeled and slivered; 2 whole bay leaves; a small handful of celery leaves, finely chopped; plus 2 teaspoons salt, a few grinds of black pepper, a small shake of red cayenne, and 1 teaspoon MSG. When it boils, turn heat down, cover, then simmer to bring out and mingle flavors for as long as it takes to prepare shrimp, usually about 15 minutes. Wash shrimp thoroughly under cold running water and pull off legs, but do not remove shells. When all are ready, slide them, more or less all at once, into boiling wine. Turn heat up full, to bring back to a boil as quickly as possible. All shrimp must be covered by liquid. If they are not, add a little more hot water. When first bubbles reappear, set timer to exactly 4½ minutes, and turn heat down slightly so that shrimp bubble gently for that time. Then turn off heat, let shrimp and marinade cool, then turn entire contents of pan into a covered dish and refrigerate for about 24 hours.

On the Morning of the Day—Preparing Sauce in About 20 Minutes, then Unsupervised Simmering for 2 Hours

We use a large enameled cast-iron cocotte* with a tightly fitting lid. Before turning on heat, put into it: the 3 tablespoons of fat; the 1 pound of ham, cut into bite-size cubes; the 6 onions, peeled and chopped; the 2 remaining cloves of garlic, finely minced; then turn on heat to medium frying temperature and sauté, stirring continuously, until onions are just wilted, usually hardly more than 1 minute. Stop the frying by adding the can of plum tomatoes with all the juices. Stir, bring quickly to a boil, and keep bubbling fairly strongly, leaving cocotte uncovered so that excess water will evaporate, while adding the pound of hot sausage, cut up into bite-size chunks; the 3 green peppers, coarsely chunked; the 4 fresh tomatoes, cut in wedges; 3 or 4 sprigs of fresh thyme, finely snipped (or about 1 teaspoon dried) ; a handful each of celery leaves and parsley, both chopped; 3 whole bay leaves, plus salt, pepper, and MSG to taste. Finally work in with a wooden spoon the entire 6 ounce can of tomato paste. Mix thoroughly, then simmer, tightly covered, for about 2 hours. This is the same process of slowly blending and concentrating the flavors as in the making of a fine Italian tomato sauce. After the 2 hours, the heat can be turned off and everything held until the final preparation.

About 40 Minutes Before Serving

Remove shrimp from marinade, shell and devein, then leave in open bowl at room temperature. Briefly wash scallops under cold running water and add to shrimp. Strain and hold marinade, squeezing out solids before throwing them away. Blend the pound of rice into the now-fairly-thick sauce in the main cocotte, then add the marinade. Place cocotte over high heat and bring quickly to a boil, then turn down to simmer, cover tightly, and do not lift lid for exactly 15 minutes. By this time, rice will have expanded and absorbed most of the liquid but will still be just firm enough so that it can be stirred without mushing. Using light folding strokes with a wooden spoon or spatula, fold in shrimp and scallops, so that they are evenly distributed throughout rice. Put back lid and continue simmering for about 5 minutes more. Meanwhile chop parsley for garnish at the table. The dish is ready to serve when the rice is soft, shellfish are hot, and there is no more liquid in bottom of cocotte. If it is necessary to evaporate a small amount of remaining liquid, boil hard for a minute or so with lid off. Serve at once in hot gumbo bowls with chopped parsley sprinkled over each serving. Make sure that each diner gets a fair proportion of shrimp, scallops, *chorices,* and ham.

ONE-DISH MEAT AND VEGETABLE STEW FROM FRANCE—LA GARBURE

Several meals for our family of 4

This is our modified version of a famous peasant dish from the Pyrenees of the southwest. It is simple to prepare and is economical and flexible in its ingredients. It is usually said that the ladle should stand upright in the thick stew. We say that it is then too thick. We have lightened our *garbure,* but have kept the one ingredient that is essential to the flavor balance, the salted goose, the famous *confit d'oie,* of southwestern France. As to the other meats, there is wide flexibility: smoked or salt pork, a shank of ham, garlic or other spiced sausages, a chunk of cooked meat from a roast. The final touch is always the inclusion of a handful or two of shelled and skinned baked chestnuts. The first step comes a few days ahead. . . .

BASIC RULE FOR SALTING A GOOSE: Before the use of refrigeration, this was the French farmwife's way of preserving the geese which had to be killed off at the coming of winter. The cured pieces were placed in large stone crocks in the cellar and hot fat was poured around them. When the fat solidified, it provided an airtight seal under which the goose would keep almost indefinitely. When a piece was taken out of the crock, with some of the fat adhering to it, the remaining fat was smoothed back to reseal the crock. It is this luscious fat, as much as the goose itself, which provides the exceptional flavor to the dishes in which it is used. When we have a supply of salted goose in our refrigerator, we find the fat wonderful for frying potatoes, slices of bread, and for making croutons.

Pieces of the goose added to a soup or stew contribute a rich flavor, or they can be fried in their own fat and served as a luncheon dish with mashed potatoes or lentils or split peas. An excellent quick stew can be made by first slightly browning the pieces of goose in their own fat, then simmering them in chicken bouillon with vegetables and pre-soaked haricot beans. Salted goose is a marvelous staple to have on hand all year round.

Check Staples:

Aromatic: coarse crystal salt☧ (about 1/4 lb.)

Shopping List:

Fat young goose, cut into 6 to 8 pieces (5 to 7 lbs.)
White beef fat (about 1/2 lb.)
Pure pork lard (about 1/2 lb.)

3 Days Before the Goose Is To Be Cooked

Cut away all visible fat from the pieces of goose and set aside to be rendered later. Rub each piece all over with as much crystal salt as can be worked into it. Set the pieces in a covered dish in the refrigerator for 3 days.

On the Day of the Cooking

Under cold running water wash the excess salt off the pieces of goose. In a large, thick pan or Dutch oven render the goose fat and add equal quantities of pork lard and beef fat to make sufficient liquid fat to cover the goose. Put the pieces of goose into this hot fat, making sure that all are covered. Keep it at simmering temperature, covered, for about 3 hours. Test the goose for doneness by taking out one of the legs and pricking it with a skewer. It is ready when juice runs pink. Let pan cool slightly, then lift out pieces of goose and pack tightly into a deep, covered refrigerator dish. Allow liquid fat to cool almost to room temperature, strain and pour enough over goose to cover. In this form the goose will keep in the refrigerator a year!

Preparing la Garbure

Check Staples:

Salted goose with plenty of adherent fat, *see* above (2 or 3 pieces)
Dark smoked bacon, in one piece (1/2 lb.)
Aromatics: coarse crystal salt,☧

Shopping List:

The meats for this dish are flexible and one should begin with anything left in the refrigerator:
A ham bone with some ham left on it

Check Staples (continued):
- freshly ground black pepper,
- dried hot red chili peppers,
- MSG, garlic (several cloves), marjoram, thyme
- Carrots (2 medium)
- Parsley (1 bunch)
- Olive oil, for the chestnuts (2 to 3 Tbs.)

Shopping List (continued):
- Any solid piece of roasted meat
- The remains of a smoked pork butt, or a tongue, or one can buy garlic sausages, or Hungarian *Kolbasz,* or Polish *Kielbasa* or German *Kasseler Rippchen* (smoked pork chops), etc.
- Also, any good bones or pieces of bacon rind will add flavor to the broth
- Green beans (1 lb.)
- Chestnuts, shelled, peeled, and roasted (1 lb.)
- Leeks, white part (2)
- White boiling potatoes (1 lb.)
- Green peas (1 frozen package)
- Green peppers (2 medium)
- White turnips (2 medium)
- Good red Beaujolais wine (1 bottle)

A Few Hours Beforehand—Advance Preparation of Chestnuts in About 45 Minutes

Bake, shell, and peel the pound of chestnuts, according to our BASIC RULE (page 158).

About 2¼ Hours Before Serving

On its home ground in a farmhouse of southwestern France, *la garbure* would be cooked in a large earthenware casserole, or *toupin.* However, we find it more convenient to prepare it in a large iron soup pot with a capacity of about 10 quarts, which can be placed over high heat on top of the stove for the preliminary frying and has a tightly fitting lid. Then, at the last moment, we transfer the entire dish to our toupin, which has been preheated with boiling water to avoid cracking, and we serve from this at the table.

We set the iron pot over medium-high frying heat, put into it the ½-pound slab of bacon, then slightly fry it on all sides until it is lightly browned and the bottom of the pot is nicely oiled, usually in 3 to 4 minutes. Then hiss in 2 cups of the red wine, letting it bubble fiercely for a couple of minutes. Now add freshly drawn cold water until pot is slightly more than half full and bring it up to a boil. Meanwhile, prepare and assemble together the main vegetables: the pound of potatoes, peeled and halved; the 2 leeks, split, carefully washed under strongly running cold water, and cut into 1-inch lengths; the 2 turnips, peeled and quartered; plus the 2 carrots, scraped and chunked. When water boils, put in vegetables, bring back again to boiling as rapidly as possible, then at once reduce heat to gentlest simmering, "just smiling." The secret of the rich texture of a *garbure* is always to bring it back to boil as quickly as possible, but never to let it go on bubbling for more than a few seconds or everything will disintegrate. Check occasionally throughout entire cooking to see that the pot never really boils. As soon as it is safely simmering now, stir in the aromatics: about 2 teaspoons each of marjoram and thyme, the 2 or 3 cloves of garlic, put in whole and unpeeled, as they will melt away, plus salt, a very few grinds of black pepper, and MSG to taste. Very gently simmer, covered, for about 30 minutes. Meanwhile prepare the variety of cooked and raw meats that are essential to a *garbure,* keeping them in fairly large chunks and assembling them together in a bowl with the 2 or 3 pieces of salted goose, with plenty of their aromatic fat adhering to them. It is another secret of the *garbure* that the goose fat flavors and enriches the vegetables. Also assemble together any bones, chicken carcasses, pieces of rind, etc., which will go in primarily to flavor the bouillon, then wrap and tie these in a double thickness of cheesecloth, with 1 small dried hot chili pepper.

About 1½ Hours Before Serving

Add bag of bones, meats, and the goose to the pot, return as rapidly as possible to the boil, then again adjust heat to gentlest possible simmering, taste and, if necessary, adjust seasoning, and continue to simmer covered for 1 hour longer. Meanwhile assemble garnish vegetables: the package of frozen peas; the pound of green beans, trimmed but left whole; the 2 green peppers, seeded and quartered; the chestnuts, and a small handful of chopped parsley.

About 25 Minutes Before Serving

We place our large toupin in the center of the oven and turn it on to 250 degrees. Put the garnish vegetables into the iron pot, again bring bouillon rapidly back to boiling, then readjust heat to gentle simmering and continue cooking, covered, for 15 minutes longer.

About 10 Minutes Before Serving

Transfer contents of iron pot to hot toupin, at the same time removing the cheesecloth bag, then at once cover toupin and put back in oven, turning heat up to 325 degrees, so that dish will come to the table boiling hot. Meanwhile, if we are in an economical mood, we open up cheesecloth bag, pick out any useful bits of meat, cut up any edible bacon rinds, then add these to toupin, throwing away remaining bones, etc. If serving of *garbure* is for any reason to be delayed, oven temperature may be turned down to 225 degrees and dish held for half an hour or so. Then heat is turned up again just before serving. Finally, skim off any stray fat, and readjust seasoning.

Serving at Table

We set a large wooden board on the table, ready to receive both the hot toupin and a hot oval serving platter on which pieces of meat are placed and neatly sliced as they are dug out of toupin. Each diner is served in a deep, wide soup plate into which is first poured about 2 tablespoons of the remaining red wine, then the meats and vegetables are served, and finally the aromatic bouillon is ladled over. Make sure that each diner gets a quota of chestnuts. *La garbure* improves with keeping and reheating.

ONE-DISH MEAL FROM NORTH AFRICA—MOORISH COUSCOUS

Several meals for our family of 4

There are many theories as to the ancient origins of the fantastic name "couscous." We go along with those who say that it simply represents the sound of the bubbling, hissing steamer (appropriately called a *couscoussière*) in which both lamb, or mutton stew, and the whole-grain wheat are often cooked. Authentic *couscoussières* are available in some specialty shops,✲ but our method (below), in which the couscous wheat is wrapped in cheesecloth, allows it to be cooked in any kind of steamer, or even in a colander fitted into the top of a pot of boiling broth. To achieve the true character of this dish, the first essential is to use a good quality of hard-grain wheat. The real couscous wheat from Algeria, Morocco, or Tunisia is now being imported into the United States and is available by mail order.✲ Or one can use one of the whole- or cracked-grain wheats discussed under "kasha" (page 167). The essential cooking trick is to avoid the wheat mashing into a pudding. Each cooked grain must be separate and dry, with a texture like brown rice. This is a wonderfully dramatic and satisfying one-dish meal.

Check Staples:

Eggs (4 large)
Aromatics: crystal salt,✲ freshly ground black pepper,✲ red cayenne pepper, dried flakes of hot red chili peppers✲ (if available, otherwise use more cayenne), MSG,✲ basil, whole bay leaves,

Shopping List:

Lean neck of lamb or alternative, for stock (3 to 4 lbs.)
Lean lamb, preferably from leg, to be cubed (about 4 lbs.)
Meat bones, for stock, cut up by butcher (3 to 4 lbs.)
Stewing hen (5 to 6 lbs.)

Check Staples (continued):

whole caraway seed, whole cloves, whole coriander, whole cumin seed, garlic (4 or 5 cloves, to taste), marjoram, thyme
Carrots (6 to 8, according to size)
Green Pascal celery (1 head)
Yellow onions (8 or 9 medium)
Parsley (small bunch)
Granulated instantized flour⛁ (a few Tbs.)
Olive oil⛁ (a few Tbs.)
Italian peeled and seeded plum tomatoes (2 lb. 3 oz. can)
Italian tomato paste (6-oz. can)
Dry white wine⛁ (2 cups)

Shopping List (continued):

Couscous whole-grain wheat,✠ or alternative, *see* above (1 lb.)
Dried chick peas (1-lb. box)
Green cabbage (1 head, smallest possible)
Leeks (3 or 4 according to size)
Small white boiler onions (about 6)
Green peppers (3 medium)
Small white turnips (about 6)
Zucchini (2 or 3, according to size)

2 or 3 Days Ahead—the Lamb Stock

Preheat oven to 400 degrees. Wash the soup bones, rub them lightly with olive oil and dab with flour. Set them in an open roasting pan in the oven and brown to a dark tan—usually in 10 to 15 minutes. Then put the bones in the bottom of a very large soup pot and loosely pack down among them: the neck of lamb, cut up, plus 4 or 5 yellow onions, peeled and quartered. Remembering that there will be 3 or 4 quarts of liquid, sprinkle suitable amounts of salt, black pepper, MSG, as well as basil, marjoram, and thyme. Wet down with the 2 cups of wine and add freshly drawn cold water to cover—usually it takes about 3 or 4 quarts. Bring to a boil and skim off scum or foam. Gently simmer, covered, 3 to 4 hours. Cool, strain, and refrigerate, then remove fat. (Although the soup meat is pretty well boiled out, a thrifty North African housewife would pick out the pieces carefully, and sharpen them in a vinaigrette marinade for later use as body in salads.) The clear aromatic stock is kept refrigerated.

Starting About 3 Hours Before Serving—the Stew

Put 1 quart of the lamb stock into a saucepan, bring to a rolling boil, and dribble into it through the fingers the pound of chick peas. Boil hard for 4 minutes, then turn off heat and leave soaking. Next we set out on the stove our largest stew pot and a copper sauté pan. Cut the lamb from the leg into 1-inch cubes and the stewing hen into serving pieces. Heat up 2 tablespoons of the olive oil in the sauté pan and lightly brown lamb and chicken pieces, transferring them when done to the big stewing pot. Sprinkle with salt, black pepper, and MSG. Peel and chop remaining 4 or 5 yellow onions and lightly brown them in the sauté pan, adding more olive oil if needed. Then blend in enough of the tomato paste to absorb any surplus oil and spoon this now thickish mixture into the big pot. Pour in enough lamb stock to cover, and, while bringing it up to simmering, add: the 4 or 5 cloves of garlic, finely minced; 1 or 2 teaspoons of the caraway seed; a pinch or two of flaked hot chili pepper (or a shake or two of red cayenne) ; 1 teaspoon of cumin; the entire contents of the can of plum tomatoes; the 3 or 4 leeks, carefully washed and chunked; 3 or 4 inner stalks of the celery, diced; plus 2 or 3 whole bay leaves. Now keep the pot gently simmering, "just smiling," covered, for about 1 hour. Meanwhile start steaming the couscous wheat.

1¾ Hours Before Serving—Cooking the Couscous Wheat

We usually serve our couscous at the table on a china platter about 30 inches in diameter, like a large round tray. It also serves a vital purpose in the preparation of the couscous wheat. First we spread the dry couscous on the platter, sprinkle it liberally with cold water, loosening it with a wooden spoon, until all the grains are wet. We also have ready a steamer and a 4-ply piece of cheesecloth large enough to cover the platter. The wheat is now to be cooked in aromatic steam. Put about 3 cups of the broth from the main pot into the bottom of a steamer and bring to a rolling boil. The top of the steamer is lined with the cheesecloth and the wet couscous is spooned into it. The four corners of the cloth are brought together, completely enclosing the couscous. Put on lid and steam vigorously for 20 minutes. Open the cheesecloth and prod couscous with a wooden spoon, to break up any lumps. Cover again with cheesecloth, put back lid, and continue steaming 20 minutes longer. Meanwhile put the large platter to warm in a 200-degree oven. When timer rings, lift out cheesecloth and pour wheat onto warm platter. Dribble 1 or 2 cups of the aromatic liquid from the steamer over the grain, spreading it around with a wooden spoon while the hot liquid is being absorbed. Add a little more hot liquid, then cover the swollen grains with the damp cheesecloth and put it all back in the 200-degree oven for 6 or 7 minutes. Then dribble on more liquid, stir again—and after more absorption and swelling, the wheat is ready to be served. Cover again with cheesecloth and set back in oven to keep warm.

40 Minutes Before Serving

Add chick peas and the stock in which they were soaked to the stew. Set sauté pan going again over frying heat, with a little more olive oil, and slightly brown before adding to the big pot: the 6 turnips, peeled and chunked; the 6 or so white boiler onions, peeled (2 of them stuck with 4 cloves each); and the 6 to 8 carrots, scraped and chunked. Continue gently simmering.

25 Minutes Before Serving

More ingredients are now added to the big pot, after being lightly browned in the sauté pan: the 2 or 3 unpeeled zucchini, thickly sliced; half the cabbage, cut in wedges; plus the 3 green peppers, chunked. Continue the gentle simmering. Hard-boil the 4 eggs, then shell and slice lengthwise.

About 15 Minutes Before Serving—the Hot Pepper Sauce

We ladle about 1 cup of the broth from the big stewpot into a small shiny copper saucepan (which will come to the table), and heat to gentle bubbling. Put into a small mortar: 1 tablespoon each of whole coriander and cumin, then coarsely grind together. Now add to the small saucepan, ¼ teaspoon at a time: black pepper, red cayenne, and the mixture from the mortar, stirring and tasting after each round of additions. The object is to produce a pepper sauce—(as powerful in its way as a Mexican hot sauce)—so hot that only a few drops need be sprinkled over each serving of the couscous. When enough of the spices have been blended in, the sauce is reduced over high heat for about 5 minutes, with continuous stirring to mature the flavors. We bring the pan to the table with a decorative small ladle.

Final Adjustments, Decorations, and Service at Table

Check that the meat, chicken, and vegetables are perfectly done. Finally, balance the seasonings. Take the platter with the wheat out of the oven and remove its cheesecloth cover. With a large wooden spoon, scrape the grains toward the center of the platter and pile into a tall pyramid. With a large slotted spoon, lift out the meat, chicken, and vegetables from the big stewpot, letting them drain, and set them on the platter around the base of the pyramid. Decorate the pyramid with the egg slices, add a few touches of green here and there with parsley, and bring the platter to the table. Each guest has the choice of sprinkling onto his plate a little or a lot of the hot pepper sauce.

ONE-DISH MEAL FROM ISRAEL—CHOLENT OF BEEF IN BAKED BARLEY AND BEANS

Several meals for our family of 4

In Israel, the *cholent* recipe varies from family to family, but it is, of course, related to the famous *cassoulet* of France and to all the other great bean pots of the world. It gains its special character from being cooked extremely slowly, for a minimum of 5 hours, but preferably overnight, or even for 24 hours, virtually without attention. Obviously, there is no problem when guests are late!

Check Staples:

Chicken fat, or alternative (4 Tbs.)
Aromatics: crystal salt,* freshly ground black pepper,* MSG,* Hungarian medium-hot paprika*
Granulated instantized flour* (4 Tbs.)
Red wine* (2 cups)

Shopping List:

Beef brisket, not corned, preferably from the "front section," or, as a compromise alternative, chuck, or bottom round, a lean, solid, rectangular chunk (about 4 lbs.)
Medium barley (1 cup)
Large lima beans, dried (½ lb.)
Navy or pea beans, dried (½ lb.)
Yellow onions (2 lbs.)
Boiling potatoes, *see* list of foods in season, page 515 (2½ lbs.)

A Few Hours in Advance—About 10 Minutes to Scald Beans and Set to Soak

Put about 2 quarts of freshly drawn cold water into a 4-quart saucepan and place over high heat to bring rapidly to a rolling boil. Meanwhile mix together in a colander the ½ pound each of lima and navy beans, pick them over, then wash thoroughly under strongly running cold water. When hot water in pan is at a rolling boil, dribble in beans through fingers, but not so fast as to take water off boil. When all beans are in, keep boiling hard for exactly 4 minutes, then turn off heat and leave beans to soak in hot water. They must soak for at least 3 hours, but may, with some advantage, be left for as long as 12 hours. They should remain at room temperature.

Assembling the Bean Pot in About 15 Minutes

We usually prepare this dish in a large iron pot of about 10 quarts' capacity, which can be used for frying on top of the stove, or in the oven, and has a heavy, well-fitting lid. Put into the pot the 4 tablespoons of fat and set over very gentle heat, just to melt. Meanwhile peel and slice the 2 pounds of onions, put into pot, stir around to coat with fat, and leave to soften while preparing potatoes. Peel and quarter the 2½ pounds of potatoes and add to pot. Now turn up heat to medium frying temperature and lightly sauté potatoes and onions, until latter has just gilded slightly. Then turn off heat. Now place the piece of beef on this potato-onion bed, exactly in the center of the pot and put in the drained limas and navy beans, plus the cup of barley, setting them around and over the meat and adding, between the layers, salt, pepper, and MSG to taste. Put a kettle on to boil with about 4 quarts of freshly drawn cold water, and meanwhile, in a small bowl, mix together the 4 tablespoons of flour with 4 teaspoons of paprika, then sprinkle on top of beans in pot. Now soak everything with the 2 cups of red wine and add enough of the boiling water just to cover. Turn on fairly high heat under pot, still uncovered, and bring liquid up to gentle simmering. Now decide on the method of cooking in relation to the time when the dish is to be ready. If it is needed in 5 hours, leave pot where it is on top burner, turning down heat slightly so that liquid is *just below* simmering (it must not even "smile"), cover tightly, then leave undisturbed for 5 hours. However, occasionally during the first hour, as pot slowly heats through, check to see that there is no bubbling. If this dish is allowed to boil, the result is a disastrous mash. Also, at the 2½-hour, halfway mark, check to see whether more hot water is needed to return level to top. On the other hand, if there is more time for the cooking, it is much better to place covered pot in the center of an oven set at 250 degrees and leave undisturbed for 12 hours. Now there is no danger of boiling and no need to add more hot water. Or, even better, if there is time, the oven can be set as low as 225 degrees and the pot left undisturbed for from 18 to 24 hours. The longer the cooking the better the flavor.

Serving at Table

We like to wheel the huge pot in on a small wagon. Once the beans and vegetables have been dug away from around the meat, it can be carved into neat slices. If the cooking has been slow enough, the meat will still be perfectly firm, but perfectly done and its juices will have permeated the entire dish. *Cholent* is also excellent cold and can be reheated again and again.

¶ *Main Dishes (Birds)—Chicken · Guinea Hen · Wild Goose*

FRENCH COQ AU VIN BEAUJOLAIS—CHICKEN IN RED WINE

For our family of 4

This is another of those classic dishes of which it can truthfully be said that there are as many versions as there are cooks in France. Ours is a simple one, and its success depends largely upon the quality of the wine. This is not to say that one should use a great and expensive wine, but it would be disastrous to use an ultra-cheap so-called "cooking wine." We use a light red Beaujolais, preferably one bottled in the town of Fleurie, which gives an ideal balance to the dish. It is fun, also, to experiment with other red wines from other regions. The dish is excellent cold, when the wine sauce will have jelled.

Check Staples:

Salt butter (2 Tbs.)
Corn-belly salt pork (¼ lb.)
Aromatics: crystal salt, freshly ground black pepper, MSG, whole bay leaves, garlic (2 cloves), thyme
Yellow onions (2 medium)
Parsley (1 bunch)
Ground arrowroot (1½ Tbs.)
Meat glaze, which the French call *glace de viande* (1 Tbs.)

Shopping List:

Roasting chicken, preferably a capon, cut-up (about 4 lbs.)
Mushrooms, preferably small button (1 lb.)
Small white boiler onions (1 lb.)
French red Beaujolais, preferably from Fleurie (up to 2 bottles)
French Martinique rhum or some alternative light rum (1 oz.)

About 1¾ Hours Before Serving—Including 1¼ Hours of Unsupervised Simmering

We prepare this on top of the stove in a fairly large enameled cast-iron cocotte* with a tightly fitting lid, which is good-looking enough to be brought to the table. Set it over medium-high frying heat and melt in it 1 tablespoon of the butter and a piece of fat from the chicken about the size of a large cherry. Make sure that the butter does not get so hot as to brown. Now quickly sauté the chicken, adding a little more butter if needed, until the pieces are just flecked with brown on all sides. As each piece is done, take it out and hold it. Peel and chop the 2 yellow onions. When all chicken is out of cocotte, lightly sauté onions in remaining fat until just transparent, then put back chicken, packing pieces down fairly solidly. In a ½-cup butter-melting pan, over fairly gentle heat, carefully warm up the 1 ounce of rhum until it is just hot to the finger, but no hotter or alcohol will evaporate. Pour over chicken and flame. Reserve ½ cup of the red wine, then pour in enough of the remainder to cover chicken by about ½ inch. Sometimes 1 bottle is enough, but generally part of the second bottle is needed as well. Heat up rapidly to the boiling point, adding, before it boils, the aromatics: 2 whole bay leaves, 2 cloves garlic, finely minced, ½ teaspoon thyme, 4 or 5 whole sprigs of parsley and the 1 tablespoon of meat glaze. Liquefy the 1½ tablespoons of arrowroot with the reserved ½ cup of wine. As soon as liquid in cocotte begins to bubble, turn off heat and, when bubbling subsides, quickly and vigorously stir in the liquefied arrowroot, making sure that no lumps form and that the arrowroot is thoroughly dispersed throughout liquid. Turn on heat, bring back to gentle simmering, "just smiling," cover, then keep simmering until chicken is almost, but not quite, done, usually in about 1¼ hours. Meanwhile prepare and hold remaining ingredients. Cube the ¼ pound of salt pork into large dice. Wipe clean (never wash) the pound of mushrooms, trim off and discard dry ends of stalks, and then pull out remaining stalks, leaving caps whole. Peel, but leave whole, the pound of white onions.

About 25 Minutes Before Serving

In a sauté or fry pan over medium-high frying heat quickly sauté the salt-pork dice until they have given off enough fat to lubricate bottom of pan. Put in white onions and sauté until lightly flecked with brown, then remove with slotted spoon and hold. Put mushroom caps and stalks into pan and sauté until just beginning to soften, usually in not more than 3 to 4 minutes. Remove with a slotted spoon and hold with white onions. Finally, also with slotted spoon, remove the now-crisp salt-pork dice and hold separately.

About 15 Minutes Before Serving

Add mushrooms and onions to cocotte and continue simmering gently until white onions are just soft, but still slightly crisp, usually in about 10 to 12 minutes.

Just Before Serving

Add salt-pork dice to the cocotte, plus salt, pepper, and MSG to taste. Remember that some salt from the salt pork will have penetrated mushrooms and onions and then will have been absorbed into chicken and sauce. The essential trick of this dish is to time it so that chicken is done to perfection at the precise moment when mushrooms and onions are just cooked but not overcooked. Before bringing the cocotte to the table, skim off any floating fat, but there is usually very little. After serving, there is always plenty of wine sauce left over. It jells in the refrigerator and can be used as garnish for the cold chicken, or the sauce may be reheated and served over rice or vegetables.

HUNGARIAN PAPRIKÁSCSIRKE—CHICKEN IN PAPRIKA CREAM

For our family of 4

This dish is never worth preparing without a first-class grade of Hungarian medium-hot paprika. The stuff that comes in small cartons or cellophane bags or tins that cannot be properly resealed after opening has about as much character as brick dust. Good Hungarian paprika, properly packed, is now available from many fancy-food stores, or can be ordered by mail from Hungarian specialty shops in New York City.* It gives a subtle fruitiness as well as warmth to the authentic version of this famous dish, of which there are so many pale imitations. We always serve it with Hungarian *tarhonya* (page 611).

Check Staples:

Chicken fat or goose fat or, as a compromise, sweet butter (3 Tbs.)
Lemon (1)
Aromatics: crystal salt,* MSG,* Hungarian medium-hot red paprika*
Yellow onions (3 medium)

Shopping List:

Broiler-fryer chicken or young capon, cut up (about 3½ lbs.)
Sour cream (¾ pt.)

About 1 Hour Before Serving

Peel and chop the 3 onions and hold. Rub the pieces of chicken with the cut side of half the lemon. We prepare this dish in one of our enameled cast-iron cocottes* with a tightly fitting lid. We set the cocotte over medium-high frying heat and melt the 3 tablespoons of fat, then lightly sauté the chopped onion until just gilded. Now turn off heat and blend in the paprika, the exact amount depending on its quality—1 tablespoon is enough if it is strong and fresh; otherwise the amount may have to be substantially increased until the onions are bright red and they taste fairly strongly peppery. Now put in the pieces of chicken, one by one, making sure that each piece is well coated with aromatic fat and lightly sprinkling each with salt and MSG. When all chicken is loosely packed in, turn on heat to medium boiling temperature and cover cocotte tightly. (It is entirely wrong either to fry chicken or to add any liquid. The basic Hungarian trick is to steam chicken in its own juices.) Do not open lid for the next 30 minutes. As cocotte heats up, temperature should be adjusted by listening close to the pot and judging sound coming from inside. There must be a gentle sizzling, no more, no less. After the first 30 minutes, check chicken and continue steaming until it is just tender, usually in about 5 to 10 minutes longer. Then remove chicken pieces to a bowl and quickly stir into sauce in cocotte about three quarters of a pint of sour cream, at the same time turning up heat to bring cream as quickly as possible almost to boiling. Put back chicken and see that each piece is thoroughly coated with cream. Adjust heat so that cream stays just below boiling, replace lid then leave for about 15 minutes longer. When chicken is thoroughly reheated and impregnated with sauce, finally recheck seasoning, adding both salt and paprika if needed.

OUR MODIFIED INDONESIAN GLAZED CHICKEN

For our family of 4

There are subtle variations to this dish according to the extent to which the marinade is allowed to "infiltrate" the chicken. By marinating for a longer or shorter time, and especially by controlling the amount of marinade spooned over during the steaming and glazing, one can experiment until one's taste is satisfied. The shiny dark mahogany color adds a fine appearance to a light main course.

Check Staples:
Salt butter (¼ lb.)
Limes (2)
Aromatics: crystal salt,✗ freshly ground black pepper,✗ MSG,☺ garlic (1 to 3 cloves, to taste), Indian ground ginger,✗ Hungarian sweet red paprika,✗ Chinese soy sauce☺ (¼ cup), plus dried herbs, only if fresh not available: basil, dillweed, tarragon
Ground arrowroot☺ (2 tsp.)
Pure maple syrup☺ (about ¼ cup)
Olive oil☺ (½ cup)
Dry vermouth (3 Tbs.)

Shopping List:
Frying chicken, cut up into serving pieces (3 to 4 lbs.)
If available, a few sprigs each of 2 or 3 fresh herbs, chosen from: basil, chive, dill, parsley, tarragon

The Evening Before—Preparing the Marinade in About 10 Minutes

Just wipe the chicken with absorbent paper, rub with the cut side of half a lime, and then pound in with the heel of the hand, crystal salt, black pepper, and paprika. Over a low flame just melt 4 tablespoons of the butter. In a covered dish large enough eventually to hold chicken as well, mix the marinade: the melted butter, ¼ cup of the maple syrup, 1/4 cup of the olive oil, the 1/4 cup of soy sauce, the 3 tablespoons of vermouth, garlic to taste, crushed through a press, 1 teaspoon Indian ginger, 2 teaspoons arrowroot, plus salt, pepper, and about 1 teaspoon MSG to taste. Now squeeze in the juice of the lime, 1/2 at a time, possibly also adding a dash or two more maple syrup, until a slightly sweet-sour taste is achieved. Stir well, then swish chicken pieces around in it and leave them soaking overnight, covered and refrigerated.

About 2 Hours Before Serving

Bring chicken in marinade out of refrigerator and let come to room temperature.

About 1 Hour Before Serving

Finely snip with kitchen scissors the available fresh green herbs, mixing them together and allowing about 2 tablespoons per person; hold in screw-top jar in refrigerator. (If fresh herbs not available, sprinkle 1 teaspoon each of dried herbs over chicken in marinade.) For cooking chicken, we use a tin-lined copper sauté pan with a tightly fitting lid, one just large enough to take all chicken pieces without stacking them. Before putting in chicken, heat pan over medium-high frying temperature with 4 tablespoons of the butter and 2 tablespoons of the olive oil, being careful not to let butter brown. Take out chicken pieces, shake off excess marinade, and brown quickly on all sides in sauté pan. They will color to dark mahogany in 2 or 3 minutes. Turn heat down to gentle bubbling, put on lid, and let chicken steam for 15 minutes. At this point it can be held over low keep-warm heat for a few minutes, if necessary.

About 30 Minutes Before Serving

Turn chicken pieces over and spoon onto each a little of the marinade, more or less according to taste, put lid back on, and readjust heat to gentle bubbling, simmering until chicken is just done, usually in about 20 minutes more.

About 15 Minutes Before Serving

Turn on broiler and give it time to heat up to maximum temperature. Take chicken pieces from sauté pan and lay neatly side by side, close together, in shallow pan to go under broiler. Pour all juices from sauté pan into the marinade and stir well. Spoon plenty of marinade over chicken, even if pools form in botton of broiling pan. Set pan about 2 inches below heat for about 2 minutes. Then spoon more marinade over. This routine can be repeated every minute or so, two or three times more, until glaze is thick and shiny. Serve at once, with the fresh green herbs sprinkled over; it is also very good cold.

GUINEA HEN WITH LENTILS AS THEY DO IT IN ARGENTINA

For our family of 4

For a note on the guinea hen (see page 60) and sources of supply (see page 709).

Check Staples:

Salt butter (1/4 lb.)
Lemon (1)
Corn-belly salt pork (enough for 6 slices)
Aromatics: crystal salt, freshly ground black pepper, MSG, whole juniper berries

Shopping List:

Young guinea hens (2)
French sweet Sauternes wine (1/4 cup)
Plus ingredients for jumbo lentils Argentine style, page 609

About 1 1/4 Hours Before Serving—the Lentils

Prepare a dish of jumbo lentils Argentine style (page 609), but do not yet start the cooking.

About 1 Hour Before Serving—the Guinea Hens

Cut salt-pork slices about 1/4 inch thick. Put 2 tablespoons of the juniper berries into a mortar and coarsely grind. Preheat oven to 350 degrees. Do not wash guinea hens, but wipe clean with absorbent paper, rub thoroughly, inside and out, with cut side of half a lemon, and sprinkle about 1/2 teaspoon MSG inside each. Using small skewers, pin slices of pork onto breasts, completely covering them, then pin down legs and wings. Place birds on rack, breast upward, in roasting pan.

40 Minutes Before Serving

Place guinea hens in center of oven and do not open oven door for first 20 minutes. Meanwhile in a small saucepan mix the basting sauce: melt the 1/4 pound of butter, stir in the ground juniper berries, and add the 1/4 cup of sweet sauterne. Heat up to just below boiling, then hold, hot.

35 Minutes Before Serving

Bring lentils up to simmering on top of stove and continue, covered, until lentils are soft but not mushy. Each seed should be separate, like rice, and this usually requires about 20 to 30 minutes.

20 Minutes Before Serving

Turn oven temperature up to 375 degrees. Take out guinea hens and thoroughly baste with sweet juniper butter, opening oven door as little as possible and quickly putting birds back into oven.

10 Minutes Before Serving

Turn oven temperature up to 400 degrees. Again, baste guinea hens thoroughly, spooning plenty of juniper butter inside, then remove salt pork from breasts and put birds back in oven as quickly as possible. Crumble salt pork and hold. When lentils are done, pour off remaining bouillon from their dish and leave uncovered on very low flame for lentils to dry out slightly. Warm up a large serving platter to hold guinea hens and lentils. To check exact moment when guinea hens are perfectly done, release one leg and wiggle it. At right moment, joint will be very loose and leg meat quite soft. Turn off and place guinea hens on serving platter. Place dish of lentils in oven, uncovered, for a couple of minutes, to complete drying out. Pour juices from roasting pan back into saucepan with remaining juniper butter and heat up once more almost to boiling, at the same time adding salt and pepper to taste. Spoon lentils onto serving platter around guinea hens, then pour juniper butter over both birds and lentils. Finally, sprinkle on the crisp salt pork which was removed from breasts. Each diner is served half a guinea hen.

ROAST WILD CANADA GOOSE

Several meals for our family of 4

When the "great honkers" fly south for the winter, what every gourmet needs is a hunter friend to bring a gift of one of these great birds. Failing that, a Canada goose can be ordered by mail✲ and it comes oven-ready, chilled with dry ice. It makes magnificent eating; the flesh is slightly dark, with a faint flavor of venison. It is one of the truly wild game birds and one must always remember that its flesh is lean and muscular, with very little fat so it must be well larded and steadily basted. Some birds weigh up to 12 pounds, but we think that a 7-pound gosling is better. When we know that one of these is on the way, we prepare for it by making a batch of our own sausage meat for the stuffing. As to the temperature and timing in the oven, we follow exactly the high-heat method described for the Thanksgiving turkey (page 529).

Check Staples:

Our homemade pork sausage meat, page 178 (1 lb.)
Bacon drippings (a few Tbs.)
Clear chicken bouillon (1 cup)
Corn-belly salt pork,🥫 in one piece (½ lb.)
Lemons (2)

Shopping List:

Young Canada goose (about 7 lbs.)
Heavy cream (½ pt.)
Cooking apples, fairly tart, *see* list of foods in season, page 508 (3)
Chestnuts (1 lb.)
Button mushrooms (½ lb.)
Black olives, pitted (½ cup)

Check Staples (continued):

Aromatics: crystal salt, freshly ground black pepper, MSG, garlic (2 cloves), rosemary, sage, tarragon, thyme
Green Pascal celery, with leaves (4 good stalks)
Yellow onions (4 medium)
Parsley (small bunch)
Arrowroot (a few tsp.)
Olive oil, for the chestnuts (2 to 3 Tbs.)
Dry Madeira (1 cup)
Dry white wine (1 cup)

Shopping List (continued):

Walnuts, shelled (1/4 lb.)
Oloroso Sherry (3/4 cup)

On the Morning of the Day—Preparing the Stuffing in About 1½ Hours

Bake, shell, and peel the pound of chestnuts, according to the BASIC RULE (page 158). While they are baking, begin assembling stuffing. Wipe clean (never wash) the ½ pound of mushrooms, slice lengthwise into the hammer shapes, and hold. Slice the 4 stalks of celery about ¼ inch thick, finely chop the leaves, and add both to mushrooms. Peel and finely mince the 2 cloves of garlic and hold, covered. Set a sauté pan over medium frying heat and put in the pound of sausage meat. As it begins to soften and fry, break it up with a wooden fork. As soon as sausage is lightly brown, add mushrooms and celery, stirring around for not more than 2 minutes for vegetables to absorb aromatic fat. Then add ½ cup of the chicken bouillon and ½ cup of the Madeira and adjust heat for gentle simmering. Also add: the minced garlic, ½ teaspoon rosemary, ¼ teaspoon sage, 1 teaspoon tarragon, 1 teaspoon thyme, plus salt, pepper, and MSG to taste. Stir well, then continue gently simmering, uncovered, to reduce liquid and develop flavors while remaining ingredients are assembled. Put into a large mixing bowl: the baked chestnuts, mashed; the ½ cup of olives, coarsely chopped; the ¼ pound of shelled walnuts, coarsely chopped; plus a small handful of parsley, chopped. Mix lightly, then add the contents of the sauté pan and start working everything together to achieve the texture of a firm stuffing. Add equal parts of bouillon and Madeira as needed until the proper final consistency is reached. If stuffing is to be held longer than 2 hours, refrigerate, covered, but return to room temperature before stuffing the goose.

About 2½ Hours Before Serving—Time Varies According to Size of Bird

Slice the ½ pound of corn belly lengthwise into ¼-inch-thick strips and hold. Peel the 4 onions and leave whole. Quarter the 3 apples, leaving skin on, but cut out cores. Thoroughly rub the Canada goose inside and out first with the cut side of half a lemon, then with some of the Sherry. Next, working carefully with the fingers and starting from the back end, loosen the skin above the breasts (preferably without breaking skin) and slide under 2 slices of the corn belly, resting 1 directly above each breast. Now weigh the bird and work out the oven timing according to the BASIC RULE for high-heat oven-roasting (page 529). Then stuff the goose, leaving just enough space above the stuffing to push in the apple quarters. They should rest just below the breast. Also follow the general instructions on page 529 for skewering and trussing the bird, for laying the slices of corn belly across breasts and on legs, and for fitting aluminum foil caps over breasts and legs. Preheat oven to 350 degrees. Finally, thoroughly rub all remaining exposed skin of bird with the bacon fat.

About 2 Hours Before Serving

Place goose, breast upward, on a raised rack set in a roasting pan and place it in exact center of oven. Meticulously follow instructions on page 529 for step-by-step raising of oven temperature and for repeated basting of bird. As soon as goose is in oven, prepare the special basting sauce: mix in a 1-quart saucepan the remaining ½ cup of Sherry, the cup of white wine, plus 2 tablespoons of lemon juice, then heat up to just below simmering and keep hot as long as needed for basting goose. Do not forget, at the halfway point of the total oven time, to place the 4 whole onions in the roasting pan underneath the goose, to provide steam. Also follow instructions for removing aluminum foil caps at the proper time for the final browning of the skin.

About 15 Minutes Before Serving—Completing the Pan Gravy

Follow instructions on page 530 for removing bird from roasting pan and letting it rest in turned-off oven, for removing fat from pan gravy, and for crumbling corn belly and mashing onions. Then, for the Canada goose, proceed as follows. Add a few tablespoons of aromatic liquid made up of any remaining bouillon, Madeira, and Sherry. While these liquids are bubbling in pan on top burner, scrape off all bits of succulent crust from bottom of pan. Now boil gravy hard to reduce liquid and concentrate flavors, until it shows first signs of glazing and thickening. Turn down heat to gentle simmering and begin gradually working in ½ cup of the heavy cream. Taste and adjust seasonings as needed, then work in as much more of the cream as is required to make a smooth and rich sauce. It may finally be thickened with a few teaspoons of arrowroot, liquefied with a little more cream and worked in according to the BASIC RULE (page 14). Do not be afraid to make a rich sauce. Remember that Canada goose has lean, dry flesh, with none of the fat of domesticated goose. When the big bird comes magnificently to the table, with the gravy served in a hot sauceboat, it is worth accompanying it with one of the great red wines of Bordeaux.

¶ *Main Dishes (Fish, Shellfish)—Chowder · Fish Platter · Shrimp · Fish in Red Wine*

OUR QUICK AND SIMPLE FISH CHOWDER

For our family of 4

The basic trick to this chowder is to adjust the amount of water and the heat under the pot so that all the liquid is absorbed at the precise moment when fish and potatoes are exactly done. Then the bottom layer begins to fry and brown slightly, and it is this browning that gives the interesting and unusual flavor. After the first and second tries, one can usually do it perfectly every time.

Check Staples:

Salt butter (6 Tbs.)
Corn-belly salt pork, in one piece (about 6 oz.)
Milk (about 1 pt.)
Aromatics: crystal salt, freshly ground black pepper, MSG, Hungarian medium-hot red paprika
Yellow onions (5 medium)

Shopping List:

Boneless fillets of one fish or a mixed assortment—possibly bass, bluefish, cod, or other fish in season, page 509—all cut into 2-inch squares (about 2 lbs.)
Light cream (1 pt.)
Starchy boiling potatoes, *see* list of vegetables in season, page 515 (6 medium)

About 45 Minutes Before Serving

We prepare this in an enameled cast-iron cocotte,* which can be used for both the frying and the simmering, has a tight-fitting lid, and is handsome enough to be brought to the table. Coarsely dice the 6 ounces of salt pork and spread them across bottom of cold cocotte. Peel the 5 onions, slice them about 1/4 inch thick, and hold. Peel the 6 potatoes, slice 1/4 inch thick, and hold. Wash and dry the fish and pull off any stray bones or unwanted bits of skin. Set cocotte over medium-frying heat and sauté corn-belly dice only until they have released enough liquid fat to coat bottom of cocotte, then turn off heat. While sautéing is in progress, bring about 1 quart of freshly drawn cold water to a boil. When heat is off under cocotte, put a layer of fish on top of corn-belly cubes and lightly season with salt, pepper, and MSG. Then put in a layer of onion slices, followed by a layer of potatoes, with more seasoning as needed. Repeat this procedure with fish, onions, and potatoes until all are used up. Now pour into cocottes only enough boiling water to come up to ½ inch *below* the top layer of the solid ingredients. (The critical decision is the exact amount of water, and this is slightly adjusted as one gains experience in preparing the dish.) Turn on heat under cocotte and adjust so that water is gently bubbling, to produce a small amount of steam; cover cocotte and leave bubbling, without opening lid, for at least 20 minutes. Then check whether fish is just flaky, potatoes are tender, and water is all absorbed. If not, replace the lid and continue bubbling for 5 or 10 minutes longer. Meanwhile in a 1½-quart saucepan mix the pint each of milk and light cream and heat mixture to just below the boiling point. When fish and potatoes are finally done, turn up heat under cocotte for 2 or 3 minutes, to boil off remaining water, until sizzling noise signals that bottom layer is beginning to fry and brown. Let this continue for about 1 minute. Then turn off heat under chowder and pour in hot milk-cream. Turn on heat under cocotte and, being careful not to let milk-cream boil, bring everything up to just below simmering and let flavors blend for about 5 minutes, uncovered, before serving. The chowder bowls should be very hot and each portion should be dotted with bits of yellow butter and sprinkled with bright red paprika.

LEBANESE SAMAK BI TAHEENI—RED SNAPPER UNDER A BLANKET OF SESAME

One hot meal, one cold, for our family of 4

Since the magnificent red snapper from Gulf and Caribbean waters is now in season in most parts of the country, this is the time to frame its flavor with the aromatic oil of sesame. The tiny sesame nut contains so much oil that it grinds to a creamy paste, the famous *Taheeni* of Arab cookery. Canned sesame paste, or *Taheeni,* is increasingly available in fancy-food stores, or by mail.♔ This dish may be served hot or cold, and is excellent for a buffet supper.

Check Staples:

Lemons (3)
Aromatics: crystal salt,♔ MSG▣
Yellow onions (3 medium)
Olive oil▣ (a few Tbs.)
Dry white wine♙ (about 1 cup)

Shopping List:

Whole red snapper, head on (about 4 lbs.)
***Taheeni* sesame paste♔ (8-oz. can)**
Decorative bits: green pepper, carrots, watercress, tomato wedges, etc.

On the Morning of the Day

Our Italian fishmonger cleans and scales the snapper, leaving the head on, and neatly clipping the fins and tail. We rinse it under cold water, dry it, rub with crystal salt, and cool in the refrigerator for at least 4 hours; then return to room temperature before the final preparation begins.

About 1¼ Hours Before Serving

Preheat oven to 400 degrees. Rub snapper all over with olive oil and set on a well-oiled open baking dish. Bake until the flesh is just opaque and slightly flaky when gently opened up with a fork, about 25 to 35 minutes according to the size and thickness of the fish.

Meanwhile peel and finely mince the 3 onions, sauté in a little olive oil until barely golden, and hold. Squeeze juice from the 3 lemons. Spoon about ¾ of the can of *Taheeni* into a medium mixing bowl and begin to work into it with a wooden spoon, alternately by tablespoons, the lemon juice and the white wine. At first the *Taheeni* is very thick, but soon it is possible to switch to a small wire whisk to beat in air, until creamy. When we have achieved the right texture and flavor (with lemon strongly predominating), we whip in the sautéed onions.

About 30 Minutes Before Serving

Bring fish out of oven and reduce temperature to 350 degrees. Using a small sharp knife, neatly remove the top skin. Carefully spread the *Taheeni* mix all over the exposed flesh, then return fish to oven for about 20 minutes more. During this period, the sesame oil, lemon, and wine are absorbed into the flesh, leaving the onions as a browned crust on top.

Just Before Serving

Carefully transfer the fish to an oval platter, which may be decorated with the green of watercress, the red of tomato wedges, the yellow of carrot strips, etc.

SICILIAN GRILLED SHRIMP WITH AROMATIC BUTTER

For our family of 4

For more than twenty years this has been without question the family's favorite way of preparing shrimp. Its attraction, especially for our daughters, seems always to have been a combination of the picnic atmosphere of being able to pick up the shrimp by the tail, plus the extreme simplicity and speed of preparation. This is a fairly light main course and goes excellently with whole-wheat kasha (page 167), which absorbs the sauce and adds a nutty flavor and contrasting texture.

Check Staples:

Salt butter (8 Tbs.)
Lemon (1)
Aromatics: crystal salt,* freshly ground black pepper,* garlic (3 cloves, or more to taste)
Parsley (enough to fill 1/4 cup, chopped)
Granulated instantized flour (6 Tbs.)
Olive oil (1/4 cup)
Dry Madeira (1/4 cup)

Shopping List:

Jumbo shrimp, in shells—for number per pound *see* page 62 (about 1 1/2 lbs.)
Clam juice (8-oz. bottle)

About 25 Minutes Before Serving

Turn on broiler to medium temperature and set height of shelf so that shrimp in their dish will be about 3 inches from heat. Pull legs off shrimp and remove shells, but leave tails firmly attached. Devein, wash, and dry. Spread 4 tablespoons of the flour on a plate and mix with it 1 teaspoon of salt. For the broiling we use an enameled cast-iron au gratin dish 10 inches across, but a pie pan will also do. Put in 4 tablespoons of the butter and the 1/4 cup of olive oil, then set under grill to get hot, but watch to make sure that butter does not brown or burn.

Meanwhile lightly flour shrimp. Take out au gratin dish from under broiler and neatly arrange shrimp in hot fat, making sure that each is well coated all around. Put back under grill and broil until shrimp are beautifully pink and the flesh just opaque. Under our broiler it takes exactly 8 minutes, but the first time it is well to taste one of the shrimp. While shrimp are broiling, prepare the sauce. With practice we find we can do it in the 8 minutes; but when the shrimp are done, they can be taken out from under broiler and held for a couple of minutes if necessary. So there is no need to feel pressured while making the sauce.

Peel the 3 cloves of garlic and have ready a garlic press. Do not be troubled by the amount of garlic, most of it evaporates under the broiler. Chop enough parsley to fill 1/4 cup. Pour the 8 ounces of clam juice and the 1/4 cup of Madeira into a small 1-pint saucepan and gently heat up but do not let boil. In a 1-quart saucepan melt 2 more tablespoons of the butter, then make a *roux* by smoothly working in the remaining 2 tablespoons of flour. Now start working in the clam juice-Madeira, dash by dash, using only enough to make a smooth, creamy sauce slightly thicker than heavy cream. Adjust heat so that it gently simmers. Add, squeeze by squeeze, enough lemon juice to give sauce a fairly strong lemon flavor, usually about 1 tablespoon. Also add salt and pepper to taste. Let sauce gently simmer until shrimp are almost ready. At the last moment, stir into sauce the remaining 2 tablespoons of butter, the garlic, mashed through the press, plus the chopped parsley. Taste and adjust seasonings, including a few more drops of lemon juice if needed. Take shrimp out from under grill, turn up broiler to high temperature, and raise shelf so that shrimp will be about 2 inches from heat. Finally stir sauce and pour over shrimp, making sure that all are covered by sauce. Put back under grill for only about 2 or 3 minutes, until sauce is bubbling and shrimp are just lightly flecked with brown. Be careful not to overcook shrimp. Serve at once on very hot plates. The shrimp may be picked up by their tails.

BURGUNDIAN MEURETTE—FISH STEWED IN RED WINE

Several meals for our family of 4

This is the classic French dish which proves that red wine and fish do sometimes go together. The secret is that the Burgundians use the rich, oily-fleshed fish from their rivers and lakes to balance their rich red wine. In our saltier part of the world, we find that we can strike a good balance with about 1/3 freshwater fish, about 1/3 oily-fleshed saltwater fish, and 1/3 shellfish, always with some eel as an essential basic ingredient. At this time of year, a good combination with the eel might be chosen from buffalo fish, sauger, sheepshead, whitefish, halibut, and crab. At other times of the year, see the lists of fish in season. The wine should always be a red Burgundy, which includes, of course, Beaujolais.

Check Staples:

Salt butter (1/4 lb.)
Lemon (1)
Aromatics: crystal salt, freshly ground black pepper, MSG, whole bay leaf, whole cloves, garlic (5 cloves, essential), mace chips, thyme
Carrots (3 medium)
Green Pascal celery, with leaves (3 stalks)
Parsley (small bunch)

Shopping List:

A balanced mixture of freshwater, saltwater, and shell fish, *see* above, always with some eel, all skinned and boned (total about 4 lbs.)
Fish heads and bones (about 2 lbs.)
Leeks, white part only (3)
Bermuda or Spanish onion (1 large)
Long loaf of French bread (1)
Red Burgundy wine, say a medium-priced Côte de Beaune-Villages (1 bottle)
Burgundy marc brandy (1/4 cup)

About 1 Hour Before Serving—Preparing the Wine Bouillon

We use an enameled cast-iron cocotte,* with a tightly fitting lid. Pour into it the bottle of red wine and gently heat it up, but do not let it boil. As it is warming up add: the fish heads and bones, washed; the large onion, peeled and chunked; the 3 carrots, scraped and sliced; the 3 leeks, slit open, carefully de-sanded under fast-running cold water, and chunked; 1 of the cloves of garlic, peeled and finely minced; 1 whole bay leaf; 4 whole cloves; 1/4 teaspoon of mace chips; 1/2 teaspoon thyme; the 3 stalks of celery, chunked, the leaves chopped; 4 whole sprigs of the parsley, plus salt, pepper, and MSG to taste. Stir around and bring up to gentle bubbling, then cover and leave for 30 minutes. Meanwhile wash and trim the pieces of fish, divide into large chunks, and hold. Prepare the garlic bread, according to the BASIC RULE (page 497), using butter, lemon juice, parsley, and the remaining garlic. Wrap bread in foil, but do not put into the oven yet.

About 20 Minutes Before Serving

Turn off heat under the now richly aromatic wine bouillon, strain out all solids and discard them. Rinse out cocotte and return wine bouillon to it, bringing liquid back to gentle bubbling. Stir in the 1/4 cup of marc brandy, then at once add fish and keep gently bubbling, uncovered, until fish is just opaque and flaky, usually in 15 minutes. Meanwhile, turn on oven and put in garlic bread. Make sure that fish keeps bubbling merrily, to distribute flavors and reduce liquid slightly. Chop enough parsley to fill 1/4 cup.

Serving at Table

Meurette is served in the same magnificent manner as the *cacciucco* of page 494. When the lid of the cocotte is lifted, there is an excitement in the variety of colors, smells, and shapes. The bread comes to table on a board, still wrapped in its foil. A chunk is broken off and placed in the bottom of each hot gumbo bowl, a variety of fish is piled on top of it, and the red bouillon ladled over. Finally, it is all sprinkled with bright green parsley.

AN ENCORE VARIATION: *Meurette* is excellent cold, or can easily be gently reheated. We perfer, however, to "encore" it as a molded aspic. When cold, separate bouillon and fish by straining. Clarify bouillon and convert to an aspic, according to the basic method (page 135). While aspic is cooling, flake the fish, stir back into aspic, and set in a handsomely shaped mold. The red color is most attractive.

¶ *Main Dishes (Cheese, Eggs)*

ENGLISH CHESHIRE CHEESE WITH OKRA AND TOMATOES

For our family of 4

In our house, recipes come and go. As we try new ones and adopt the best into our repertoire, many an old recipe dies away, from lack of being remembered. This recipe has stayed with us for more than thirty years. Why? Because it involves only ten minutes' work with ingredients that are always easily available. Even more important, because the Cheshire cheese (a lemon-yellow and more aromatic version of Cheddar), when melted down with the vegetable juices and intermingled with the firm okra pods and soft tomato flesh, produces a most unusual balance of contrasting flavors and textures. This is a fine light luncheon or supper dish. We often precede it with the cream of chestnut soup (page 560), and this combination is good enough for a small dinner party.

Check Staples:

Salt butter (about 1 Tbs.)
Aromatics: crystal salt, freshly ground black pepper, MSG
Green scallions (1/2 bunch)

Shopping List:

Imported English Cheshire cheese (1 lb.)
Whole okra pods, fresh in season, *see* list, page 515, or frozen (1 lb.)
Tomatoes (4 medium)

About 50 Minutes Before Serving

Cube the pound of cheese into large dice. Wash, then top and tail the pound of okra and cut extra-large pods in half. Chunk the 4 tomatoes. Coarsely chop the scallion tops. Using a sharp knife, mince the scallion bulbs. Choose a fairly deep 2-quart casserole with a lid and liberally butter the inside. Preheat oven to 350 degrees. Cover bottom of casserole with a layer of 1/3 of the tomato chunks. Cover with 1/3 of the okra. Sprinkle with 1/3 of the chopped scallion tops, plus salt, pepper, and MSG to taste. Cover with 1/3 of the cheese dice. Repeat these layers twice more. Sprinkle the top layer of cheese with the minced scallion bulbs.

Exactly 40 Minutes Before Serving

Set covered casserole in center of oven and forget for 40 minutes. We like to serve this dish on a bed of simple pilaf of rice (page 166).

ANDROUET'S SWISS CHEESE "STEACKS"

For our family of 4

The famous Paris cheese shop Androuet has a small restaurant upstairs where every dish on the menu from soup to dessert is made with cheese.

Since American tourists are always asking for steaks, Androuet developed this recipe with Swiss Gruyère or Emmenthaler, which we have slightly modified over the years. Warning: this method of cooking works only with the imported Swiss Gruyère or Emmenthaler, which soften under the heat without actually melting and running. This is a quite solid main course.

Check Staples:

Salt butter (about 1¼ sticks—10 Tbs.)
Eggs (9 large)
Milk, for batter (about ½ cup)
Aromatics: crystal salt, freshly ground black pepper, MSG, garlic (1 clove)
Parsley (small bunch)
White bread (4 thick slices)
Granulated instantized flour, for batter (1 cup)
Granulated white sugar, for the batter (¼ tsp.)
Olive oil, for batter (3 Tbs.)
Dry white wine (about ⅓ cup)
Oil for the deep-frying

Shopping List:

Imported Swiss Gruyère, or Emmenthaler cheese (about 1 lb.)
Fresh button mushrooms (½ lb.)

About 2 Hours in Advance—Preparing the Frying Batter in About 5 Minutes

Prepare a batch of our ultra-light frying batter according to the BASIC RULE (page 140). Let it stand, uncovered, to mature for about 2 hours.

About 45 Minutes Before Serving

Break 8 eggs into a bowl, add salt, pepper, and MSG to taste, then beat lightly with a few strokes of a fork, and hold. Peel and finely mince the clove of garlic and hold, covered. Choose a fairly large, open au gratin dish, preferably of enameled cast-iron because it heats up slowly, then holds the heat, and is good-looking enough to be brought to the table; however a shallow, open ceramic dish will also do. Liberally butter it, lay the 4 slices of bread in the dish, sprinkle enough of the white wine onto them so that they are pretty well soaked, then hold. Cut the pound of Swiss cheese into ½-inch slices, then cut into large triangles, preferably 1 per person; or several smaller triangles. Wipe clean (never wash) the ½ pound of mushrooms, then pull out stems from caps, and hold. Set a sauté pan on medium-high frying heat and melt 9 tablespoons of the butter. As soon as it is liquid, spoon out 4 tablespoons and sprinkle over the bread. Add to remaining butter in sauté pan, the minced garlic, the mushroom caps and stems, sprinkle on plenty of MSG, plus salt and pepper to taste, then sauté fairly strongly, stirring continuously, for mushrooms to absorb flavors in about 3 or 4 minutes. Turn down heat to simmering, cover, then steam for about 10 minutes. Meanwhile turn on deep-fat fryer* to 375 degrees. Complete the batter (BASIC RULE, page 140) by beating remaining egg white and lightly folding into flour mixture. Batter should be quite thick.

About 25 Minutes Before Serving

Now, working fast, dip each cheese triangle into batter, making sure that it is thickly coated all around. Slide into deep-fat and brown to a good color on one side, then turn over and brown the other side; usually it takes about 2 minutes per side. Several triangles can usually be fried at same time. When each is well browned, lift out and drain on absorbent paper, then lay neatly on bread. Now turn on oven to 375 degrees. When all cheese triangles are neatly in place in dish, fill spaces between and around them with mushrooms, pouring on all buttery juices from sauté pan, then give the eggs a few more strokes and pour over cheese and mushrooms.

About 15 Minutes Before Serving

Set au gratin dish in center of oven and bake until eggs have souffléed up slightly and are very lightly browned on top, usually in about 10 to 15 minutes. Meanwhile finely chop parsley for garnish. When dish comes out of oven, sprinkle top with parsley, bring at once to the table, and serve on very hot plates. Each cheese triangle will have kept its shape, but will be so soft that it can be cut with a fork.

CHINESE FOO YOONG DAAHN—CRAB OMELETTE

For our family of 4

The Chinese omelette is prepared differently from its Western counterpart and is not so demanding as to timing. Separate omelettes, 1 per person, are brought to table piled one above the other, as if they were pancakes.

Check Staples:

Salt butter (3 Tbs.)
Eggs (6 large)
Aromatics: crystal salt,⁑ freshly ground black pepper,⁑ MSG,▣ fresh ginger root⁑ (1 tsp., grated)
Parsley (small bunch)
Green scallions (4)
Olive oil▣ (about 2 Tbs.)

Shopping List:

Flaked crab meat (½ lb.)
Dark smoked ham, in one slice (2 oz.)
Chinese pea sprouts⁂ (½ lb.)
White celery (enough to fill ¼ cup, diced)
Fresh mushrooms (¼ lb.)

A Few Hours Beforehand—Advance Preparation in About 30 Minutes

Prepare and hold the ingredients. Pick over the ½ pound of crab meat and put into a fairly large mixing bowl. In a second fairly large mixing bowl assemble: the 2 ounces of ham, diced; the ¼ cup of celery, diced; the ½ pound of pea sprouts, washed and coarsely chopped; the 4 scallions, including the peeled bulbs, finely chopped; and the ¼ pound of mushrooms, wiped clean (never washed), sliced. Into a small jar grate enough of the ginger root to fill 1 teaspoon, then cover. Finely chop plenty of parsley for garnishing. All these may now be held at room temperature for about 1 hour. If it will be longer, they should be refrigerated, but should be returned to room temperature for final preparation.

About 30 Minutes Before Serving

Break and lightly beat the 6 eggs and add them to crab meat. In a fairly large sauté or fry pan or Chinese wok,* heat the 2 tablespoons of olive oil to medium-high frying temperature, add ginger and sauté for not more than 5 seconds. Then add, all at once, the ham and vegetables, plus salt, pepper, and MSG to taste. Stir around and fry briskly for not more than 1 minute. Turn off heat, lift with slotted spoon, draining each spoonful, then add to eggs and crabmeat. The final frying of the omelettes requires a large frypan or a top-burner griddle, perfectly smooth and bright, on which several omelettes can be cooked simultaneously. Bring pan to medium-high frying heat and sizzle on enough butter just to grease entire surface, adding more later, as needed. With a fairly large ladle, give egg mixture a final gentle stir, then pour enough onto hot surface to form a round about 3 inches across. It is cooked slightly harder than a French omelette and is turned until both sides are lightly browned and texture is slightly crispy; usually this takes 1 to 2 minutes. Have ready a warm platter and as each omelette is done place it on top of the previous one, making a single pile. Bring platter to the table at once and serve each omelette with plenty of parsley sprinkled on top.

¶ *Vegetables*

FRESH FAVA BEANS WITH SPINACH

For our family of 4

This is a solid dish and one usually does not need a starch foundation with it. At seasons of the year when fresh favas are not available, we might use the dried (see end of recipe).

Check Staples:

Salt butter (5 Tbs.)
Lemon (1)
Aromatics: crystal salt, freshly ground black pepper, MSG, dried dillweed

Shopping List:

Fresh fava beans, still in pods (about 2 lbs., giving about 2 cups, shucked), or frozen or dried, *see* end of recipe
Fresh spinach, pulled and washed (2-lb. cellophane bag)
Heavy cream (about 2 Tbs.)
Italian sweet red onion (1 medium)

About 50 Minutes Before Serving

Put the shucked favas into a saucepan with about 1 inch of slightly salted water, 1 tablespoon of the butter, and about ½ teaspoon of MSG. Gently bubble them, uncovered, for 15 minutes. Then sprinkle on ½ teaspoon dillweed and continue simmering, now covered, until favas are just tender but still slightly crisp, usually in about 15 to 20 minutes longer. Meanwhile peel and mince the onion. Wash the spinach under fast-running cold water, then throw it by handfulls into a pot over high heat, salting it heavily and pressing it down with a wooden spoon. Cook spinach for about 4 or 5 minutes, then turn off heat and let it cool until it can be handled. The spinach is then squeezed until juice runs out. Now put spinach on a chopping block and finely cut with a large chef's knife. Then blend into spinach, while still fairly hot, the remaining 4 tablespoons of butter, the minced onion, plus salt and pepper to taste. Turn on oven to 200 degrees and put a covered serving dish in to get warm. As soon as favas are ready, drain them and fold them into spinach. Put into the serving dish and set it back in oven, covered, for a few minutes to reheat.

Using Dried Fava Beans—Start the Day Before

Use about 1 cup of dried favas, since they usually expand more than 2 to 1. Wash them, scald them for 2 minutes in boiling water, then leave them soaking for about 12 hours. At the end of this time, drain and rinse them, cover them with freshly drawn cold water, float a couple of tablespoons of butter on top to avoid foaming, then gently simmer, covered, until favas are very soft, usually in 2 to 3 hours, according to the age of the favas. Then fold them into the prepared spinach, as above.

FRESH FENNEL KNOBS BRAISED IN SHERRY

For our family of 4

This is a translation into our own kitchen of the classic French way for *fenouil au Xérès.*

Check Staples:

Salt butter (1 Tbs.)
Floured butter—*beurre manié, see* page 12 (a few tsp.)
Aromatics: crystal salt, freshly ground black pepper, MSG
Yellow onion (1 small)
Olive oil (2 Tbs.)
Dry Sherry (⅔ cup)

Shopping List:

Fresh fennel (2 large heads)

About 45 Minutes Before Serving

Trim off green fronds from heads of fennel and save (they are wonderful for flavoring all sorts of dishes). Trim off tops of stalks, almost down to knobs (stalks, too, are excellent in soups, stews, etc.). Cut knobs into quarters, wash under cold running water, place in saucepan, cover with hot water, add some salt and simmer for 12 minutes. Meanwhile peel and finely chop the onion and hold. In an enameled cast-iron cocotte* with a tightly fitting lid, melt the tablespoon of butter over medium frying heat. Add the chopped onion and sauté, stirring intermittently until just soft, usually hardly more than 2 minutes. Then add the 2 tablespoons of olive oil and the ⅔ cup of Sherry. Stir, adjust heat to gentle simmering, cover, and cook until fennel quarters are ready; drain them by holding them until all water runs out. Turn up heat slightly so that sauce bubbles merrily and provides plenty of steam, then cover tightly and continue steaming until fennel is quite tender, usually in 20 to 25 minutes.

About 10 Minutes Before Serving

Turn on oven to 225 degrees and put an open serving platter in to warm.

About 5 Minutes Before Serving—When Fennel Is Ready

Carefully lift fennel quarters with slotted spoon, holding them so that sauce runs back into cocotte, then arrange neatly on hot platter and put back in oven to dry out slightly while sauce is being finished. Turn up heat under cocotte so that sauce boils hard for a couple of minutes to reduce liquid, then turn heat down to just below simmering and thicken sauce with just enough of the floured butter, worked in lump by lump, to reach the consistency of heavy cream. When sauce is rich and smooth, pour over fennel and serve.

TOMATOES STUFFED WITH ANCHOVIES AS THEY DO IT IN MONACO

For our family of 4

Check Staples:

Salt butter (4 Tbs.)
Aromatic: freshly ground black pepper
Yellow onion (1 medium)
Parsley (small bunch)
Packaged spiced bread crumbs, often called "Herb Stuffing" (about ½ cup)
Italian Marsala wine (a few dashes)

Shopping List:

Ripe tomatoes (4 fairly large)
Flat anchovy fillets (2-oz. can)
Capers (1½ Tbs.)

About 35 Minutes Before Serving

Stand the 4 tomatoes firmly on their stem ends on the chopping board, cut off a ¼-inch slice from each top, then, using a sharp-edged spoon, scoop out insides, leaving walls about ⅜ inch thick. Turn tomatoes upside down on rack to drain. Chop insides and tops, then hold. Peel and chop the onion. Fairly coarsely chop about a dozen of the anchovy fillets. Finely chop a small handful of the parsley. In a small frypan over medium heat melt 2 tablespoons of the butter and lightly sauté chopped onion. Then add chopped anchovies, oil from anchovy tin, and ¼ cup of the bread crumbs. Sauté for a couple of minutes more to crisp bread crumbs. Then add: the chopped tomato, the chopped parsley, the 1½ tablespoons of capers, drained, plus a few grinds of pepper. The anchovies provide sufficient salt, so none need be added. Continue sautéing for 2 or 3 more minutes to blend flavors. Meanwhile preheat oven to 350 degrees. Now moisten stuffing mixture in frypan with a dash or two of the Marsala. If it becomes too soft, add more bread crumbs. Turn off heat under fry pan and stuff tomatoes. Set empty frypan back over medium-heat, melt remaining 2 tablespoons of butter, add another ¼ cup of the bread crumbs, stir around for a minute, then spread on top of tomatoes. Stand tomatoes in a baking dish and pour around them enough hot water to be about ½ inch deep.

About 20 Minutes Before Serving

Set baking dish with tomatoes in center of oven and bake until bread-crumb topping is lightly brown, usually in about 20 minutes. Serve as a light lunch dish or as a separate course.

¶ *Foundations—Potatoes · Chestnuts · Yorkshire Pudding · Lentils · Black-Eyed Peas · Tarhonya*

TURKISH KÖFTESI—SAVORY POTATO RISSOLES

For our family of 4

This is an ideal way of using up cold mashed potatoes, but we like it so much that we are quite prepared to start from scratch with raw potatoes, as in this recipe.

Check Staples:

Salt butter (2 Tbs.)
Eggs (2 large)
Aromatics: crystal salt,⁑ freshly ground black pepper,⁑ MSG🅱
Fresh parsley (enough for 2 Tbs., chopped)
Scallions (6)
Dry bread crumbs (about 1 cup)
Granulated instantized flour🅱 (about ½ cup)
Olive oil🅱 (a few Tbs.)
Italian peeled and seeded plum tomatoes, well drained (½ cup)

Shopping List:

Starchy boiling potatoes, *see* list, page 515 (about 2 lbs.)
Cottage cheese (½ cup)

At Any Time Beforehand—Boiling and Mashing Potatoes

We would steam the potatoes in their jackets, but they could also be boiled, with a slight loss of flavor. Then peel and mash them.

About 35 Minutes Before Serving

Separate the 2 eggs, holding yolks in a small mixing bowl and putting away whites for some other use. Chop the tops of the 6 scallions; peel and mince the bulbs. Chop the 2 tablespoons of parsley. In a small bowl, mash the ½ cup of drained tomatoes and hold. Preheat oven to 400 degrees. Just melt the 2 tablespoons of butter in a small pan. Place mashed potatoes in a large mixing bowl and work into them, in sequence: the melted butter, the chopped parsley, the chopped scallion tops and bulbs, the mashed tomatoes, the ½ cup of cottage cheese, and the egg yolks. Mix well with a wooden spoon, then work in only enough of the flour to make a smooth and firm dough, at the same time adding salt, pepper and MSG to taste. Put pieces onto a floured pastry board and press into hamburger-shaped patties. Lightly paint with olive oil, place on a cookie sheet and bake until golden-brown, in our oven usually in about 15 to 20 minutes. They should end up slightly crisp on the outside, but soft and juicy inside.

ITALIAN CASTAGNE IN BRODO—CHESTNUTS IN PLACE OF POTATOES

For our family of 4

In addition to their many uses, in soup (page 560), in stuffing (page 531), or as a dessert (page 614), chestnuts also can make what is surely the most luxurious of all "starch-filler" accompaniments to a festive main dish. Here we use the pre-shelled, dried chestnuts, which, while being a little less than perfect in flavor and texture, do save the time and trouble of shelling. However fresh chestnuts can be substituted by first baking and shelling them by the BASIC RULE (page 158). Then they would go straight into the turtle broth.

Check Staples:

Aromatics: crystal salt,☧ freshly ground black pepper,☧ MSG,⛁
Dry Sherry♁ (1 cup)

Shopping List:

Italian dried shelled chestnuts, or fresh chestnuts, *see* above (1½ lbs.)
Clear turtle soup (12-oz. can)

On the Morning of the Day—Advance Preparation in 10 Minutes; Unsupervised Soaking for 6 Hours

Boil and soak the 1½ pounds of chestnuts by the BASIC RULE (page 159).

About 1¼ Hours Before Serving—Simmering in Broth, Almost Entirely Unsupervised

Drain and rinse chestnuts under cold running water. Put them into a 2½- to 3-quart pan and pour over them the can of turtle soup and the cup of sherry, plus enough freshly drawn cold water just to cover. Stir around, taste liquid, and add salt, pepper, and MSG as needed. Bring up to a boil and simmer very gently, covered, moving chestnuts around occasionally and adding more water if needed until they are *al dente,* soft, but still slightly chewy, usually in about 1 hour. We like to serve them whole, exactly as if they were boiled potatoes. Save the broth, which is excellent for stock.

NOTE: As a variation, chestnuts also make a wonderfully fluffy mash. Simmering must then be extended until they are quite soft, usually an extra 15 minutes. Mash in the usual way, with butter, cream, and a pinch or two of ground cinnamon.

YORKSHIRE PUDDING AS THEY DO IT IN YORKSHIRE

For our family of 4

We learned this recipe about thirty-five years ago from the best of our premarital landladies in the Yorkshire city of Leeds. She never served it cut up into squares with the meat, but always as a separate course before the meat, in saucer-shaped rounds (each about 6 inches across), covered with plenty of meat gravy, and one to each person. We still prepare it in this way and keep a set of 6-inch pie pans for the purpose. We have modernized the recipe only to the extent of doing some of the beating in an electric blender.

Check Staples:

Beef dripping, or a compromise alternative which will not burn at a very high heat (about 3 Tbs.)
Eggs (2 large)
Milk (1 cup)
Aromatics: crystal salt, freshly ground black pepper
Granulated instantized flour (1 cup)

About 50 Minutes Before Serving—Including About 40 Minutes of Unsupervised Baking

Preheat oven to 450 degrees. Put 2 teaspoons of the beef dripping into each of the four 6-inch pie pans and set them in oven to get very hot. We break the 2 eggs into the container of our electric blender, add the cup of milk, and switch on motor to slowest speed. Add 1 teaspoon salt and a few grinds of pepper. Then begin adding the cup of flour, tablespoon by tablespoon, sprinkling it in, until smoothly blended. Then cover container, switch motor to highest speed, and run for a full two minutes. (Of course all this *can* be done by hand, but it involves about 15 minutes of steady beating.) Now pour batter into a copper beating bowl and beat air into it furiously with a balloon wire whisk, until large bubbles begin to rise to surface, usually after about 3 minutes of steady beating. For the next steps, work very fast. Take the 4 pie plates out of the oven, but be careful, since their fat will be almost smoking. Pour hot fat from first pan into batter and beat hard for 5 seconds. Repeat with fat from second pan, then with third and fourth, beating hard each time. Then at once pour batter into pans, dividing it equally between them, and instantly put them back into oven. Door of oven must now remain tightly shut for next 30 minutes. Keep oven at 450 degrees for the first 20 minutes, then, without opening door, turn temperature down to 350 degrees and hold for 10 minutes longer.

Then gently open oven door and check. Yorkshire puddings should be light brown and puffy almost like soufflés. If not quite done, close oven door gently (slamming it may make them fall) and continue baking for about 5 minutes longer. Serve 1 round to each person, on a very hot plate, with saucer-like center filled with gravy.

JUMBO LENTILS ARGENTINE STYLE

For our family of 4

Packaged lentils are usually pre-softened and require no advance soaking. However, we check the label and, if required, soak for the proper time before beginning this recipe.

Check Staples:

Thick-sliced dark smoked bacon⊜ (6 slices)
Clear chicken bouillon (2¼ cups)
Corn-belly salt pork⊜ (3 fairly thick slices)
Aromatics: crystal salt,☧ freshly ground black pepper,☧ MSG,⊜ whole cloves, whole coriander seed, garlic (1 clove), savory, thyme
Yellow onion (1 medium)
Parsley (small bunch)

Shopping List:

Jumbo lentils (1½ cups, about 10 ozs.)

About 40 Minutes Before Serving

We prepare this dish in a 1½-quart enameled cast-iron cocotte* with a tightly fitting lid. The pot should be ¾ full when all ingredients are in. Put the 1½ cups of lentils into a strainer and thoroughly wash under fairly fast-running cold water, then put them into cocotte. Peel the onion and stick with 4 whole cloves, then bury in center of lentils. Cut the 3 slices of salt pork into small cubes and the 6 bacon rashers into 1-inch squares, then quickly sauté together until slightly brown and crisp; lift pieces out with a slotted spoon and bury them among the lentils. Put 2 teaspoons of coriander into a mortar, grind coarsely, and add to lentils together with: the clove of garlic, finely minced; a small handful of the parsley, finely chopped; ½ teaspoon each of savory and thyme, plus 1 teaspoon salt, 1 teaspoon MSG, and pepper to taste. Now pour on the 2¼ cups of chicken bouillon.

About 30 Minutes Before Serving

On a top burner quickly bring liquid in cocotte (uncovered) to boiling, then turn down heat to gentle simmering and cover—or, if more convenient, place covered cocotte in 350-degree oven. Continue simmering until lentils are tender but not mushy. Each seed should be separate and chewy, like well-cooked rice. This usually takes from 20 to 30 minutes, depending on the type of lentil. Then pour off any remaining liquid and leave lentils uncovered, either in a slightly warm oven or over low heat on a top burner, so that they dry out.

NOTE: This dish is excellent served with roasted guinea hen (page 589).

BLACK-EYED PEAS BAKED IN BUCKWHEAT HONEY

For our family of 4

See the notes on the various honeys (page 521).

Check Staples:

Thick-sliced dark smoked bacon (8 slices)
Salt butter (about 1 Tbs.)
Aromatics: crystal salt, freshly ground black pepper, MSG, whole caraway seed, dried dillweed, English dry mustard, oregano
Yellow onion (1 medium)

Shopping List:

Black-eyed peas (1-lb. box)
Buckwheat honey (1 cup)
Crystallized ginger (1/4 lb.)
Indian sweet chutney (1/4 cup)
Fresh green fennel fronds, optional, but excellent if available (a handful)

On the Morning of the Day

Follow the BASIC RULE for black-eyed peas (page 316).

About 2 Hours Before Serving

Put the black-eyed peas into a well-buttered bean pot, with a tightly fitting lid. Peel and chop the onion, then hold. Coarsely chop the 1/4 pound of crystallized ginger, mix with the 1/4 cup of chutney, and hold. Cut the 8 slices of bacon into 1-inch squares and quickly sauté over fairly high frying heat, then, as soon as there is liquid fat in the bottom of the pan, add the chopped onions and continue sautéing until just golden. Turn off heat, pour off excess fat, then blend in: the ginger and chutney, 2 teaspoons dry mustard, plus 1 teaspoon salt, 1 teaspoon MSG, and pepper to taste. Preheat oven to 325 degrees. Working gently, with a rubber spatula or wooden spoon, blend bacon mixture into black-eyed peas. Pour in the cup of honey without working it in.

About 1½ Hours Before Serving

Set bean pot, covered, in center of oven and bake for 1 hour.

About 30 Minutes Before Serving

Take out bean pot, very gently stir contents, then put back in oven, uncovered, for last half hour. Finally black-eyed peas should be almost dry. We bring the bean pot to the table.

HUNGARIAN TARHONYA—NOODLES SHAPED LIKE PEARL BARLEY

For our family of 4

This Central European type of *pasta asciutta* is different, both in appearance and texture, from any of the Italian forms. When properly cooked it remains attractively "chewy," and we would never think of serving anything else with our paprika chicken (page 586). Boxes of imported Hungarian *tarhonya* are now available in many fancy-food stores, or can be ordered by mail from Hungarian specialty shops in New York.※

Check Staples:

Salt butter or any aromatic fat (6 Tbs.)
Clear beef or chicken bouillon (4 cups)
Aromatics: crystal salt,※ Hungarian medium-hot red paprika※
Yellow onion (1 medium)
Fresh parsley (1 bunch)
Dry white wine※ (1 cup)

Shopping List:

Hungarian *tarhonya, see* above (1½ cups, or about ½ lb.)

About 25 Minutes Before Serving

Put the 4 cups of bouillon and the cup of wine into a saucepan and heat up to just below boiling. Peel and chop the onion and hold. Finely chop enough parsley to fill 2 tablespoons. We prepare *tarhonya* in a 2½-quart enameled cast-iron saucepan with a tightly fitting lid. Set over medium frying heat and melt the 6 tablespoons of fat, then add the chopped onion and sauté until just gilded. Then add the 1½ cups of *tarhonya* and stir around until well coated with fat. Pour in the hot bouillon-wine mixture and adjust heat for gentle simmering. Stir in 2 teaspoons of paprika, plus salt to taste, depending on saltiness of bouillon. Cover and simmer gently until *tarhonya* are soft but still quite "chewy," usually in about 20 minutes. *Tarhonya* will expand about 3 times in volume and should absorb all the liquid. The trick is to measure liquid and time it so that *tarhonya* are just done when pan becomes dry and sizzling noises begin on bottom of pan. Then add the chopped parsley, stir around once more to recoat *tarhonya* with fat, then serve very hot. They are also excellent cold with an oil and vinegar dressing, or as an expander in a salad.

¶ *Salads*

As the first fall frosts spread across the land and the delicate summer greens are replaced by the more robust winter varieties, we turn back to our more dominant dressings (page 612). For the best salad ingredients of the fall holidays see the list of foods in season (page 514).

FALL SALAD DRESSING

For our family of 4

Check Staples:

Aromatics: crystal salt,☧ freshly ground black pepper,☧ garlic (½ clove), plus dried herbs, only when fresh not available: basil, rosemary, thyme
Parsley (enough for 1 Tbs., finely chopped)
Green scallion tops (enough for 2 Tbs., finely chopped)
Green virgin olive oil🗎 (4½ Tbs.)
Tarragon white wine vinegar🗎 (1½ Tbs.)

Shopping List:

Any of the following herbs, home-grown or hothouse, if available (enough for 1 tsp. each, finely chopped): basil, rosemary, thyme

Before the Salad Goes into the Bowl

Precise details of each operation are given in our BASIC RULE (page 93). Run the inside of the bowl with the cut side of half a clove of garlic. Wash, completely dry, and assemble the salad, then freshen and crisp it.

We Prepare the Dressing at Table

Put ½ teaspoon of the salt into the mortar, grind it a few times, then add enough pepper to speckle salt, plus ¼ teaspoon each of any of the dried herbs used in place of the unavailable fresh. Grind again to bring out oils, then add the 1½ tablespoons of vinegar and the 4½ tablespoons of oil. Stir well and hold. In small mixing bowl assemble the fresh aromatic herbs: the 2 tablespoons of chopped scallion tops, the tablespoon of parsley, and, as available, 1 teaspoon each of the basil, rosemary, and thyme.

Just Before Serving

Stir up dressing in mortar. Add chopped fresh herbs and stir again. Spoon dressing over salad. Toss thoroughly and serve instantly.

FRENCH SALADE LA BELLE VAUGHAN

For our family of 4

This is what French cooks call a *salade composée* in which the ingredients are not tossed haphazardly, but are "composed" into a design to bring form and color, as well as taste, to the table. There are dozens of such salads in classic French cookery and each is usually given the name of a girl. This one represents a daisy in bloom. Since it includes potatoes, it is a solid course. It is one of the few salads which we think can be satisfactorily prepared with frozen vegetables, when the fresh are out of season.

Check Staples:

Our homemade mayonnaise, page 423 (1 cup)
Salt butter (3 Tbs.)
Eggs (6 large)
Aromatic: crystal salt☧
Fresh parsley (enough for 1 Tbs., chopped)

Shopping List:

Asparagus tips (1 frozen package)
Fresh cauliflower (1 medium)
Fresh green beans, if available (1 lb.) or frozen, crosscut (1 package)
Waxy boiling potatoes, *see* list, page 515 (1 lb.)

Several Hours Before Serving—Cooking the Vegetables in About 30 Minutes

This is one salad which will not wilt if stored in the refrigerator for several hours. All the ingredients can be prepared in advance, refrigerated, then assembled later. Each of the vegetables must be cooked separately until just tender. We might steam 3 of them at once in the 3 compartments of our multiple steamer.* The potatoes will take the longest time, so put them on first to boil, or steam, in their jackets. Break the fresh cauliflower into its flowerets and cook until just tender but still crisp. Crosscut the fresh beans and cook until just tender. Very lightly cook the asparagus tips. Hard-boil the 6 eggs. While all this is in progress, make the mayonnaise, according to our BASIC RULE (page 423). Then, if necessary, refrigerate all these ingredients in separate containers until time for assembly of the salad.

1 or 2 Hours Before Serving—Assembling the Salad in About 20 Minutes

Let the 3 tablespoons of butter come to room temperature. Cut 4 of the hard-boiled eggs lengthwise into 6 segments each. Remove yolk from each segment and put yolks together in a mixing bowl. Hold white segments separately. Mash yolks with enough of the butter, plus a little salt to taste, to make a smoothly firm paste, which will become the central button of the daisy. Cut the remaining 2 eggs crosswise into ¼-inch-thick slices, leaving yolks in centers. Finely mince enough

parsley leaf to fill 1 tablespoon and hold. Peel the potatoes and cut into ½-inch cubes. In a large mixing bowl, lightly mix the vegetables, being careful not to crush them: the asparagus tips, the green beans, the cauliflowerets, and the potato cubes. Now begin assembling the salad in a wide, low salad bowl, not more than 2½ to 3 inches deep. Place the vegetable mixture in the center of the bowl and, using the back of a large wooden spoon, mold them into a neat, low dome. Next, entirely cover this dome with a smooth coating of mayonnaise. In a complete circle around the center of this dome, like the petals of the daisy radiating outwards, set the 24 segments of egg white, round-side up. Leave a ½-inch circle at the center and cover this with the buttered egg yolk, using a small spatula to mold the yolk paste into the shape of the central button of a daisy, and spreading it out to cover the inner tips of the petals; score it with criss-crossing lines, thus completing the central daisy. Next, decorate the base of the yellow dome with a complete circle of remaining egg slices. This leaves a central band of undecorated mayonnaise, which should be lightly and carefully sprinkled with green specks of chopped parsley. If the salad is not to be served at once, lightly cover the bowl with waxed paper and refrigerate up to an hour or so.

¶ *Desserts*

RUEDI'S CHESTNUT AND RASPBERRY MÜSLI

For our family of 4

This is another dish prepared by our Swiss friend Ruedi, an athletic young man who seems to like an inch of whipped cream on everything he eats. This dessert is the finest thing ever invented by the Swiss.

Check Staples:

Vanilla sugar🅢 (enough to sweeten raspberries)

Shopping List:

Fresh chestnuts (1½ lbs.)
California winter raspberries (about 1 qt.)
Heavy whipping cream (½ pt.)

On the Morning of the Day—Baking and Shelling the Chestnuts in About 1 Hour

Bake the 1½ pounds of chestnuts until very soft, then shell and skin them by the BASIC RULE (page 158). Refrigerate, covered, until needed.

About 1 Hour Before Serving

Set a handsome serving bowl to chill.

About 30 Minutes Before Serving

Pass chestnuts through a grinder with the fine cutter in position or through a food mill. They will come out as a light fluff and the essential trick is to hold the lightness by handling the fluff as little as possible, by keeping it refrigerated until the last moment before serving, and by doing everything possible to avoid it settling of its own weight. Therefore it is best to place the chilled serving bowl directly under the grinder, letting the chestnut fluff build up into a pile. Do not try to spread it. Place immediately in refrigerator.

About 10 Minutes Before Serving

Whip the cream. Lightly place the raspberries around and over the fluffy chestnuts. Sprinkle on vanilla sugar to taste. Crown with whipped cream. Bring the dish to the table at once, before it has time to subside.

BASIC METHOD FOR STUFFED BAKED APPLES

For our family of 4

This is a favorite dessert during the fall and winter months and many variations are possible. We usually bake them a dozen at a time, since they are so good cold. They are never worth making, however, except with the proper type of baking apple, which holds its shape and texture in the oven. At this time of year, the Rome Beauty is supreme; for other first-class bakers at other times of the year, see the lists of foods in season.

Check Staples:

Sweet butter (7 Tbs.)
Bitter-orange marmalade, preferably

Shopping List:

Large baking apples, *see* above (4)

Check Staples (*continued*):
our own homemade, page 183, or one of the well-known English brands (about 3 Tbs.)
Pure maple syrup⊜ (about 1/4 cup)
Dark-brown sugar (6 Tbs.)
Whole-wheat bread, to be cut into rounds as bases for the apples (4 slices)

Preparation in About 10 Minutes, Plus 40 Minutes in the Oven

Set out the butter to soften. Core the 4 apples, starting at the top and carving out a fair-sized hole, but only about 3/4 of the way through the apple. The hole must *not* go right through. Pare off the skin around the top of the hole, in a circle, for about 3/4 of an inch, but no more. Trim the 4 bread slices into rounds. Cream together 6 tablespoons of the butter and the 6 tablespoons of brown sugar. Turn on the oven to 350 degrees. Put 1 tablespoon of the sugared butter into each apple. Butter one side of each bread round and place, buttered side down, in an open oven-baking or au gratin dish, then place an apple on top of each round. This "bread base" is an excellent trick, since the bread absorbs any juices which run down, thus avoiding hard crusts on the pan and providing a crisp, taffy-like bonus when the diner has finished eating his apple. Set the apples in the center of the oven and bake, uncovered, until quite soft, usually in about 40 minutes. Baste every 10 minutes without fail with the maple syrup, which adds a brilliant glaze around the hole. At the 20-minute, halfway mark, drop the remaining 1/2 tablespoon of sugared butter into the hole of each apple. Continue basting every 10 minutes during the second half of the baking. When apples are done, bread will be very crisp and must be carefully scraped off pan with a spatula. If pan contains any liquid juice, it should be poured over apples. Loosely fill holes with marmalade and serve each apple on its bread base.

VARIATIONS: Different glazing and taste effects can be achieved by substituting for the maple syrup one or other of the many types and colors of honey (page 521). The marmalade can be replaced by any one of many kinds of jams and jellies, but they should always be slightly tart, as a foil to the sweet apple.

VIENNESE APPLE SCHMARREN

For our family of 4

This is one of the quickest of all apple desserts. From start to serving, it generally takes less than 15 minutes.

Check Staples:
Sweet butter (5 Tbs.)
Whole-wheat bread (6 slices)
Dark-brown sugar (2 to 3 Tbs.)

Shopping List:
Tart stewing apples, preferably Greenings or alternative, *see* list, page 508 (4 medium)

About 15 Minutes Before Serving

Coarsely dice the 6 slices of bread. Peel, core, and coarsely dice the 4 apples. Set a sauté pan over medium-high frying heat, then quickly melt in it the 5 tablespoons of butter. Do not let it brown. Put in the bread cubes and sauté until brown and crisp, usually in hardly more than 2 minutes. Shake cubes around every few seconds. Then add apple dice and continue sautéing fairly hard for 2 or 3 minutes longer, until apples are pleasantly mushy, but not too mushy. Stir every few seconds with a wooden spoon. Finally, lightly blend in brown sugar to taste, according to tartness of apples. Serve very hot on hot plates.

OUR QUICK APPLE DUMPLINGS IN A FRYPAN

For our family of 4

This has been one of our most-often-repeated apple desserts for more than twenty years. Although it is not precisely the classic form of apple dumpling (with the pastry surrounding the apple), the effect, when it is tasted, is about the same: a balance of soft and aromatic apple, with light and crumbly pastry. The advantage of our method is its simplicity and speed. The frypan must be fairly deep, with a domed lid so that the pastry can rise.

Check Staples:
Sweet butter (2 Tbs.)
Lemon (1)
Aromatic: ground cinnamon
Dark-brown sugar (½ to ¾ cup)

Shopping List:
Tart stewing apples, preferably Greenings, or alternative, *see* list, page 508 (2 lbs.)
Ready-to-bake buttermilk biscuits (1 tube, usually about 6 to 8 biscuits)
Sweet apple cider, or sweet wine (½ cup)

Preparation in About 10 Minutes, Plus Unsupervised Frying for About 35 Minutes

Peel, core, and thinly slice the 2 pounds of apples and spread slices in a cold frypan. Taste apple and judge amount of sugar, from ½ to ¾ cup, according to tartness of apple. Thoroughly blend sugar, in a mixing bowl, with ½ teaspoon of the cinnamon. Set frypan over medium-low frying heat and let apples "sweat" for 2 minutes. Then sprinkle over apples, in turn: the cinnamon-sugar, 1½ tablespoons of lemon juice, the ½ cup of cider or wine, then, finally, dot with the 2 tablespoons of butter. Turn up heat and bring liquid quickly to a boil, then turn down heat to gentle bubbling. Carefully place buttermilk biscuits on top, keeping them well apart, then immediately cover and keep gently simmering until biscuits have puffed to slightly brown dumplings and apples have mushed to a thick, golden brown sauce, usually in 25 to 35 minutes.

Serving at Table

Place a dumpling in center of each hot plate, then cover with the apple sauce. More sugar and lemon juice may be sprinkled over the pile, to personal taste.

BANANAS FLAMED WITH RUM

For our family of 4

This is one of Nature's basic marriages. The banana, a tropical fruit, blends brilliantly with rum, a tropical spirit. For the perfect result, we use one of the fine brandy-like rums (see page 654). This is an extremely festive dish and should always be brought in flaming.

Check Staples:

Sweet butter (4 Tbs.)
Lemon (1)
Dark-brown sugar (about ⅓ cup)

Shopping List:

Large ripe bananas (6)
One of the great rums (½ cup)

About 25 Minutes Before Serving

Preheat oven to 450 degrees. Peel and crosscut bananas into ½-inch chunks. Choose an open, low heatproof dish, handsome enough to come to the table. Put into it the 4 tablespoons of butter and set in the oven for 2 or 3 minutes for the butter just to melt. Put in the banana chunks, gently working them around, until each is thoroughly coated with butter. Put back in oven and bake until banana is quite soft, usually in 15 minutes. Then sprinkle bananas with the brown sugar and a few squeezes of lemon juice to taste, and put back into oven until sugar is melted, usually in 3 to 4 minutes longer. Pour in the ½ cup of rum (no need to heat it in such a hot dish), set it alight and rush, flaming, to the table.

FRENCH POIRES BON-CHRÉTIEN—GOOD CHRISTIAN PEARS

For our family of 4

Some friends have said that the superb sweet Sauternes wine of Château d'Yquem is much too good ever to be used for cooking, but we think it is worth the luxury, for it gives a flavor to the pears that is ambrosial. If the mood is not so luxurious, one can substitute a sweet Malmsey Madeira or a sweet Muscat de Frontignan from California.

Check Staples:

Lemon (1)
Aromatics: whole stick cinnamon, whole cloves, mace chips
Dark-brown sugar (about 6 Tbs.)

Shopping List:

Winter pears, fat and unblemished, a type chosen from the list of foods in season on page 512 (4)
Pineapple juice (about 1/4 cup)
Sweet dessert wine, preferably French Château d'Yquem, or alternative, Muscat de Frontignan from California (1/2 to 3/4 cup)

At Any Time—Advance Preparation in About 15 Minutes

Squeeze juice from the lemon. Use about 1 tablespoon to acidulate enough cold water in a bowl to cover pears—after they are peeled—to prevent them from browning. Thinly peel pears, but do not core. It is traditional in France to leave on the small stem. If necessary, trim the bottom so that pear will stand up straight. Drop at once into acidulated water. Choose a saucepan large enough to hold pears (lying on their sides) and with a little extra room in which to maneuver them. Into it put 1/2 cup of the wine, the 1/4 cup of pineapple juice, 1 tablespoon of lemon juice, the 6 tablespoons of sugar, plus 3 or 4 mace chips, a 2-inch stick of cinnamon, and 6 whole cloves. Bring mixture to a boil and bubble rapidly for 2 or 3 minutes, stirring, to bring up flavors and produce a poaching syrup. Then turn heat down to simmering and put in pears, on their sides. As soon as liquid returns to gentle bubbling, turn pears around, using 2 wooden spoons, so that aromatic syrup impregnates surfaces on all sides. When pears are slightly colored and surface of flesh is just soft, transfer them to a covered casserole deep enough to take them standing up, and turn on oven to 325 degrees. Turn up heat under sauce and boil hard for 2 or 3 minutes longer, adding a little more wine and sugar if necessary, until sauce glazes and begins just to thicken. Remove cinnamon, cloves, and mace chips, then pour sauce carefully over pears, so that they are glazed with it, and excess runs down.

Oven-Baking for About 45 Minutes, Largely Unsupervised

Cover casserole, place in center of oven, and bake until pears are fork-soft, usually in about 45 minutes. Baste roughly every 15 minutes with syrup in bottom of casserole. Watch carefully that pears do not overcook and become mushy. If they begin to lean drunkenly, they are no longer good Christians. When done, they may be served at once hot, with syrup spooned over them, but we prefer them refrigerated and served cold, but not ice-cold. They keep excellently, refrigerated, for several days.

FRANCO-ITALIAN AMARETTI IN RUM CHOCOLATE

For our family of 4

This is one of the most splendid of all desserts, from the Franco-Italian border country around Nice on the Mediterranean Riviera. It combines the tiny Italian almond-vanilla macaroons called *Amaretti di Saronno* with one of the best grades of French bitter chocolate and a fine brandy-like rum (see page 654). The dramatic effect is the contrast between the smooth elegance of the chocolate cream and the rummy crispness of the macaroons. For perfection, one must use the imported ingredients and these are now available at most fancy-food stores or can be ordered by mail.⚜ With substitutes (especially with mushy macaroons), this dish is a pale imitation of itself.

Check Staples:

Sweet butter (¼ lb.)
Eggs (2 large)
Milk (about ¾ cup)
Aromatic: pure vanilla extract (1 tsp.)
Pure maple syrup⛁ (¼ cup)
Vanilla sugar⛁ (½ cup)

Shopping List:

Imported Italian *Amaretti di Saronno*⚜ (1 lb. 2 oz. tin)
French bitter *Chocolat Meunier*⚜ (½-lb. slab)
One of the fine rums⚱ (about ⅓ cup)

The Day Before—Total Preparation in About 20 Minutes, Then Refrigerated Overnight

BASIC RULE FOR OUR CHOCOLATE CREAM SAUCE: Soften the ¼ pound of butter at room temperature. Separate 1 of the eggs, putting away white for some other use and holding yolk in a medium-sized mixing bowl. Scald ½ cup of the milk, then let cool. Cream the now softened butter with the ½ cup of sugar. When milk has cooled to about blood heat, beat it into the yolk. Coarsely grate the ½ pound of chocolate and put into a 1-quart saucepan (preferably tin-lined copper, for instant response to heat adjustments). Add the ¼ cup of maple syrup to chocolate, and heat gently, stirring continuously with a wooden spoon, until chocolate is melted. Turn off heat, give egg-milk a final beat and gradually work into chocolate. Reheat slowly, stirring continuously. When it is hot, but still well below boiling, begin blending in, tablespoon by tablespoon, the butter-sugar. It must now be worked into a rich and thick sauce. If it becomes too thick, dribble in a little more milk; if it does not get thick enough, separate the second egg, beat yolk into remaining milk, then turn off heat and blend gradually into sauce. When sauce is perfect, hold it hot, covered, over a very low keep-warm temperature or half-submerged in a bowl of hot water.

Assembling the Amaretti in About 10 Minutes

The *amaretti* must be assembled in a flat-bottomed serving dish of about 2 quarts capacity. We use a round Mexican casserole, but a china soufflé dish will also do. Cover the bottom with a single layer of *amaretti,* all touching each other. With the rum in a cup and using a ¼-teaspoon measuring spoon, dribble just a drop or two of rum on top of each of the *amaretti.* No rum should fall in between. Too much rum on any one macaroon will sog it and this is to be avoided. Take chocolate sauce off heat and stir into it 1 teaspoon of vanilla extract. Then, using a small ladle, dribble some of the chocolate sauce over the rum-soaked *amaretti.* Do not fill air spaces between. At once make a second layer of *amaretti,* pressing them lightly down over spaces in first layer. Again dribble with rum and ladle on chocolate. Continue this sequence, layer upon layer, until dish is full almost to its brim. Pour over any remaining chocolate sauce. Top with final layer of *amaretti* without rum or chocolate. Cover entire dish tightly with foil and refrigerate overnight.

Serving at Table

Serve at room temperature, using a large, flattish serving spoon, digging it straight down, so that each diner gets a balanced portion of the bottom and the top *amaretti,* which will have remained crisp and crunchy, imbedded in the rich chocolate.

LONA'S BERLINER ROTE GRÜTZE WITH FROZEN FRUITS

For our family of 4

This is of course a first cousin to the Scandinavian *rødgrøt* and the Russian *kissel* (page 479). Yet this a most unusual family recipe from Germany. It is one dessert that, we think, can be satisfactorily prepared with canned and frozen fruits. However, in the summer, fresh fruits can be substituted and then one should add 1 pound of fresh red currants, not available in the fall.

Check Staples:

Ground arrowroot⛁ (a few Tbs.)
Pure maple syrup⛁ (¼ cup)

Shopping List:

Sour cherries, often called "pie cherries" (1-lb. can)
Raspberries (2 frozen packages)
Strawberries (2 frozen packages)
Imported German *Himbeersaft,* raspberry syrup,✠ or other sweet fruit syrup (about ½ cup)

The Day Before—Total Preparation in About 15 Minutes

Put into a fairly large 3-quart saucepan, the cherries, drained, the raspberries, and the strawberries, then heat up gently, thawing out frozen fruits, adding the 1/4 cup of maple syrup and a dash of the fruit syrup, until everything comes gently to a boil. Stir carefully with a wooden spoon, to avoid crushing fruit, and let gently bubble for not more than 1 minute. Taste and, if more fruit syrup seems desirable, add another good dash or two. Turn off heat and carefully drain all juice into a measuring jug, then, after noting amount, pour into a second saucepan and reheat to gentle simmering. For each 1 cup of juice, measure into a small mixing bowl 2 1/2 teaspoons of the arrowroot, then liquefy it with just enough of the fruit syrup. Turn down heat under fruit juice, then thicken with the arrowroot mixture, teaspoon by teaspoon, according to the BASIC RULE (page 14), using only enough to achieve the consistency of light cream. As it thickens stir continuously, scraping sides and bottom of pan. If necessary, liquefy and work in a little more arrowroot. Put fruits into a handsome glass serving dish, gently stir in the thickened juice, cover, then set in refrigerator overnight. Serve cold.

FLAMING SOUFFLÉ OMELETTE

For our family of 4

This is a classic French everyday dessert. Since it is also a nourishing egg-filled dish, it can round out an otherwise light meal.

Check Staples:

Sweet butter (1 Tbs.)
Eggs (4 large)
Aromatic: Pure vanilla extract (1/2 tsp.)
Vanilla sugar◘ (about 3 Tbs.)

Shopping List:

One of the fine rums◘ (3 oz.)

About 35 Minutes Before Serving—Advance Preparation in About 10 Minutes

Separate the 4 eggs, placing yolks in a mixing bowl and whites in the copper beating bowl (see BASIC RULE, page 74). Turn on the oven to 325 degrees. Put 2 tablespoons of the vanilla sugar into the yolks and beat with a wire whisk until lemon-colored. For the baking, we use an open enameled cast-iron au gratin dish, about 9 inches in diameter, but a pie pan will also do. Lightly butter it and sprinkle about 2 teaspoons of vanilla sugar across the bottom. Lightly beat into the yolks the 1/2 teaspoon of vanilla extract, then quickly beat the whites and, preferably with a rubber spatula, lightly fold yolks into whites. At once pour fluffy mixture into au gratin dish, and place on lower shelf about 3 inches above floor of oven. Set upper shelf about 3 inches above omelette with an inverted cake pan to reflect heat down onto omelette. Close oven door gently and do not re-open for next 25 minutes.

A Couple of Minutes Before Omelette Is Ready

Pour the 3 ounces of rum into a small 1-cup saucepan and gently heat until just hot to the touch (see BASIC RULE for flaming, page 44). At the same time, warm up a serving platter. When omelette is ready, slide in onto the platter, sprinkle over about 1 more tablespoon of vanilla sugar, pour on warm rum, set on fire and rush, flaming, to the table.

JEFF'S IROQUOIS INDIAN PUDDING

For our family of 4

Surely this is still one of the best of all native American desserts. It may not be *exactly* what the Iroquois cooked up on the shores of Lake Cayuga, but it is comfortingly solid for a cold and hungry evening. It should be preceded by a light prologue and main course.

Check Staples:

Sweet butter (3 Tbs.)
Milk (about 2½ cups)
Aromatics: crystal salt,⁑ ground cinnamon, ground ginger, whole nutmeg
Vanilla sugar⁂ (¼ cup)

Shopping List:

Yellow cornmeal, coarse water-ground (½ cup)
Dark molasses, unsulfured (6 Tbs.)
White raisins, seedless (1 cup)
Shelled pecans (½ cup)
Optional accompaniments: heavy cream for whipping, or vanilla ice cream, or our hard sauce (page 545)

About 5¼ Hours Before Serving—Advance Preparation in About 15 Minutes

Coarsely chop the ½ cup of pecans and hold. Put 1½ cups of the milk into a 1½-quart saucepan and heat up almost to boiling, then put in the cup of raisins, stir around for about 1 minute and turn off heat. Mix ½ cup of remaining cold milk with the ½ cup of cornmeal, then stir into the hot milk and raisins. Now gradually heat up mixture, stirring continuously and carefully scraping sides and bottom of pan, until cornmeal absorbs liquid, expands, and thickens, usually in about 10 minutes. Meanwhile turn on oven to 275 degrees. As corn thickens, add, in turn: the chopped pecans, the ¼ cup of vanilla sugar, the 6 tablespoons of molasses, 1 teaspoon ground cinnamon, ½ teaspoon ground ginger, about 5 grinds of nutmeg, plus ½ teaspoon of salt. Melt in 2 tablespoons of the butter, taste and add more of any of these aromatic ingredients, as desired. Finally, adjust thickness if necessary by adding a dash, or two, of more milk. Mixture should be quite thick but still capable of being poured into baking pan. When taste is perfect, turn off heat. We bake our Indian pudding in a rectangular baking pan of about 1-quart capacity, but any 1-quart baking dish of any shape will do. Butter it liberally, then pour in the pudding and smooth it out. Dig a hole in the center and pour into this hole the remaining ⅓ cup of the milk. Do not stir milk in.

About 5 Hours Before Serving—Unsupervised Baking for 3 Hours

Set a large pan, with cold water about ½-inch deep, in the center of the oven. Stand the pudding pan in this water and bake, uncovered, for 3 hours. Meanwhile, we would prepare our hard sauce (page 545), but this is optional.

About 2 Hours Before Serving—The Process of Cooling and Maturing

Let Indian pudding cool in its pan at room temperature for 2 hours. Then it is ready to serve at once, or it may be refrigerated, covered, to be held for another day. However, it should always be served slightly warmer than room temperature, with any of the traditional accompaniments mentioned above.

TIPSY LAIRD

For our family of 4

This is basically an English custard trifle, transmuted by the force of the Scottish character into something as powerful and untamed as a Highland moor. We might serve it on November 30 for Saint Andrew's Day.

Check Staples:

Eggs (2 large)
Milk (1½ cups)
Aromatics: table salt, whole vanilla bean, pure vanilla extract
Vanilla sugar⊜ (about ½ cup)

Shopping List:

Sponge cake (½-lb. loaf)
Small crisp macaroons, either imported Italian *amaretti*,✠ or locally baked *ratafias* (about 1½ dozen)
Good Scottish Seville orange marmalade (about ½ cup)
Almonds, either in shells or preshelled or blanched (½ lb. in shells, ¼ lb. shelled)
Sweet Malmsey Madeira♁ (¾ cup)
French Cognac, medium-priced♁ (¼ cup)
Triple Sec orange curaçao♁ (¼ cup)

The Day Before—Preparation in About 15 Minutes

BASIC RULE FOR EGG POURING-CUSTARD: Put the 1½ cups of milk into a 1- to 1½-quart saucepan, preferably copper for instant response to adjustments of temperature, then stir in 3 tablespoons of the sugar. Cut a 3-inch length of the vanilla bean in half lengthwise, then, using the point of a small sharp knife, scrape out the central seeds from each half and drop them into the milk. Cut remaining two halves into ½-inch lengths and also drop into milk. Place pan over fairly gentle heat and bring up slowly, stirring fairly regularly, almost to boiling, but do not let it actually boil. Then turn off heat and let it cool. Meanwhile over second burner arrange a double boiler and adjust heat so that water in lower half is only just simmering. Contrary to usual practice, we use whole eggs in making custard. Break the 2 eggs into a bowl and beat very hard with a wire whisk, at the same time incorporating ¼ teaspoon salt. While still beating, incorporate 2 tablespoons of the hot vanilla milk. Next, still beating, slowly pour in remainder of hot milk. Strain mixture into top of double boiler, getting rid of bits of vanilla bean, which have now completed their job. While mixture is heating up in double boiler, stir continuously, until it thickens and coats a metal spoon, usually in about 5 minutes. At once remove top from double boiler and dip it into a basin of cold water, to cool custard. Taste and if necessary add a little more sugar and a few drops of pure vanilla extract. Cut a circle of waxed paper and press it very lightly onto surface of custard to prevent skin from forming. Hold at room temperature until needed.

Assembling the Laird in About 15 Minutes

Mix the "tipsy" in a bowl: the ¾ cup of Madeira, the ¼ cup of Cognac, the ¼ cup of curaçao, plus 2 tablespoons of sugar, then hold. Choose a handsome serving bowl and line bottom with a sparse layer of the macaroons. Dribble a few drops of the tipsy onto each. They should be slightly wetted, but not soggy. Cut ½-inch slices from the sponge loaf, spread each on one side with the marmalade and lay slices neatly in serving bowl. As each slice fits into place, dribble a little tipsy onto it. Continue with more macaroons and more sponge cake, fitting them in neatly until all are used up and all tipsy has been dribbled on. Pour on custard, making sure that it runs into every crevice, finally putting a solid layer on top about 1 inch thick. The peculiarly Scottish quality of this arrangement is that the custard hermetically seals in the flavor and power of the liquor! Loosely cover bowl with waxed paper and set in refrigerator to cool for at least 24 hours.

Shortly Before Serving

If the almonds are not already blanched, blanch them now according to the BASIC RULE (page 253). Cut each almond in half lengthwise and stick halfway into custard in a decorative pattern. Serve cold, but not ice-cold.

¶ *Family Specialties—Sunday Lazy Breakfast · Halloween Cakes and Drinks*

ROYAL COURT ENGLISH BREAKFAST TRIFLE

For our family of 4

This dish is from the breakfast menu of the quiet old Royal Court Hotel on Sloane Square in London, where we often stay, to be near our friends in Chelsea.

Check Staples:

Sweet butter (1/4 lb.)
Eggs (3 large)
Milk (1 1/2 cups)
Aromatics: table salt, whole vanilla bean, pure vanilla extract
Confectioners' sugar (2 to 3 Tbs.)
Granulated white sugar (1/4 cup)

Shopping List:

Light cream (1 1/2 cups)
Fruits, according to season, *see* list, page 512: strawberries, raspberries, peaches, plums, etc., or frozen equivalents (enough to make 1 cup mashed)
Long French bread (1 loaf)
French Calvados apple brandy♁ (about 1/3 cup)

The Night Before—Advance Preparation in About 15 Minutes

We remove skins, stones, pits, stalks, etc., from the fruits and mash the flesh into a coarse purée with a fork, or we run the fruits in the electric blender for just a second or two. Hold purée, covered, in refrigerator.

About 45 Minutes Before Serving

Prepare a vanilla egg custard by the BASIC RULE in the previous recipe. When custard is thick and cool, blend in the fruit purée. Cut the French bread on a slant into thick slices. In a mixing bowl beat the remaining egg with: the 1 1/2 cups of light cream, 1 tablespoon of the confectioners' sugar, the 1/3 cup of Calvados, and 1/4 teaspoon salt. Set a sauté pan on medium frying heat and melt just enough butter to lubricate the bottom. Each slice of bread is now dipped into the egg-cream batter and fried on both sides until brown. Melt in more butter as needed. Turn on oven to 400 degrees. Butter an open heatproof dish, which can be brought to the table, and arrange the browned pieces of bread in it. Pour over them the custard and sprinkle on confectioners' sugar. Then bake in oven until the top is lightly browned, usually in about 15 minutes.

SWEDISH BREAKFAST OMELETTE WITH LINGONBERRIES

For our family of 4

We might celebrate the Swedish national holiday of Saint Lucia on December 13 with the Party Breakfast menu on page 554, including this omelette as the main course. Fresh lingonberries imported from Sweden are briefly available at this time of year from Scandinavian shops,✽ or canned the year-round. If neither is available, cranberries can be the second choice.

Check Staples:

Dark smoked ham, in one piece (½ lb.)
Salt butter (3 Tbs.)
Eggs (8 large)
Milk (2 cups)
Aromatics: crystal salt,✽ freshly ground black pepper,✽ MSG✽
Granulated instantized flour✽ (5 Tbs.)
Olive oil✽ (about 1 Tbs.)
Superfine-grind white sugar, for lingonberries (enough to sprinkle over)

Shopping List:

Light cream (1 cup)
Imported Swedish lingonberries, fresh or canned, *see* above (1 lb.)
Sweet cider, only if fresh lingonberries are used (½ cup)

About 1 Hour Before Serving

We prepare this in a shallow enameled cast-iron baking dish, which can first be used for frying on a top burner, then can go into the oven, and is good-looking enough to be brought to the table. First cut the ½ pound of ham into large dice. Set the baking dish on a top burner over medium frying heat and spread in just enough olive oil to lubricate bottom, then put in ham dice and let slowly brown, stirring occasionally. Meanwhile separate the 8 eggs, putting whites into a copper beating bowl (see BASIC RULE, page 74) and the yolks into a large mixing bowl in which batter is now assembled. Beat yolks with a wire whisk until they ribbon. Gradually beat the 5 tablespoons of flour into the yolks. Then gradually beat in the 2 cups of milk and the cup of cream, until the mixture is light and frothy. Taste and add salt, pepper, and MSG as needed, remembering that some salt will come from the ham and butter. Turn on oven to 375 degrees.

About 30 Minutes Before Serving

Beat egg whites until stiff, then, using a rubber spatula or wooden spoon, lightly fold them into batter. Quickly melt the 3 tablespoons of butter around the ham, and, as soon as hot, pour in batter, set baking dish in center of oven, and bake until it has souffléed and lightly browned, usually in 25 minutes. Meanwhile, prepare lingonberries. If fresh fruit is being used, it should be simmered in the ½ cup of sweet cider until berries are just soft, usually in about 5 to 10 minutes. A little sugar may be added to taste. Drain off excess juice just before serving. Canned lingonberries are usually pre-cooked and sweetened and need only be slightly re-heated in their own juice. When omelette is ready, bring at once to table and serve with lingonberries, slightly sugared if they are too tart.

OUR CORN-BELLY WHITE SAUCE

Makes about 2 cups

This simple, rough-and-ready sauce was taught us many years ago by Southern friends. It is so succulent and aromatic (and at the same time so solid) that it can make a light supper out of a dish of potatoes and vegetables. It is the perfect "dressing up" for many reheated "encore" foods.

Check Staples:

Corn-belly salt pork (½-lb. slab)
Milk (1 pt.)
Aromatics: freshly ground black pepper, MSG
Granulated instantized flours (about 5 Tbs.)

About 20 Minutes Before Serving

Cut the ½ pound of corn belly into fairly small dice. Set a sauté, or fry pan, over medium frying heat and, when it is hot, put in corn-belly dice. At first they will stick and need to be scraped off the bottom. Continue gentle frying until dice are very crisp, usually in about 5 minutes. Meanwhile gently heat up the pint of milk, but do not let it boil. When dice are crisp, turn off heat, remove dice with a slotted spoon and spread on absorbent paper to drain. Measure exactly 4 tablespoons of the liquid fat from the frypan into a small 1-quart saucepan, then heat up gently and blend in enough of the flour just to absorb the fat and make a smooth *roux,* usually between 4 and 5 tablespoons. Also stir in a few grinds of pepper and about 1 teaspoon of MSG. There is enough salt in the fat. Now begin smoothly working in the hot milk, until sauce is somewhat thicker than the thickest cream. Sometimes, all the milk is not needed. Simmer, stirring occasionally, to cook flour, for about 5 minutes. At the last moment before serving, stir in the crisp dice.

OUR SPARKLING VOUVRAY SAUCE FOR FISH

Makes almost 3 cups

This is better than any Champagne sauce we know and can be substituted in any recipe for fish, whether baked, broiled, or boiled. The making of this sauce involves a small amount of skill and one should not expect absolute perfection the first time. After the second or third time, it will be easy.

Check Staples:

Sweet butter, best available (6 oz.)
Fish *fumet,* if available, page 70 or clam juice (3 Tbs.)
Aromatics: crystal salt,* freshly ground black pepper*
Shallots* (6 cloves)

Shopping List:

French sparkling Vouvray (⅔ cup)
Heavy cream (2 Tbs.)

About 20 Minutes the First Time, About 15 Minutes After a Little Practice

Peel and finely mince the 6 shallot cloves and hold. Put the ⅔ cup of wine into a small 1-quart saucepan (preferably tin-lined copper for instant response to heat adjustments), then add the chopped shallot and the 3 tablespoons of fish *fumet* or clam juice. Bring rapidly up to boiling and bubble hard to reduce and concentrate flavors, until only about 3 tablespoons of liquid remain in bottom of pan. This usually takes about 4 to 5 minutes, depending on shape and type of pan. Now, using a small wire whisk and while liquid is still bubbling, begin beating in, bit by bit, the 6 ounces of softened butter. Then, turn down heat so that bubbling stops and beat in the 2 tablespoons of cream. (Once cream is in, there can be no more boiling, or cream will curdle and one will have to start over.) Adjust heat so that sauce remains close to boiling and continue beating hard for several minutes, so that butter froths and cream is virtually beaten stiff in the sauce. Do not stop beating for even a second. Finally, just before serving, beat in a very little salt and pepper to taste. This sauce cannot be held, or the fluff will subside. The beating must continue until the very second that sauce is poured over fish. The final effect is magnificent.

FILBERT SOUFFLÉ CAKE

About 8 servings

This is the simple "first recipe" tried by each of our daughters on her seventh birthday (page 414) and still is a favorite dessert. It is made entirely without flour and rises without benefit of baking powder or yeast.

Check Staples:

Sweet butter (1 Tbs.)
Eggs (10 large)
Vanilla sugar® (2 cups for cake, plus extra for dusting pan)

Shopping List:

Filbert nuts (1 lb. shelled)
Optional garnish for cake: heavy cream for whipping (1 pt.)

Total Preparation in About 1¼ Hours—Including 50 Minutes of Unsupervised Baking

Using the finest blade of the grinder, finely grind the pound of filberts and hold. Separate the 10 eggs, placing the yolks in a large mixing bowl and whites in a copper beating bowl. Beat the yolks for only a few seconds until mixed, then gradually beat in the 2 cups of vanilla sugar until mixture is bright yellow. Then beat in the ground filberts. Turn on oven to 300 degrees. For this cake we use our largest ring pan with a removable bottom. Lightly grease the pan with butter and sprinkle a little sugar on the bottom and sides. Beat the egg whites by our BASIC RULE (page 74), lightly fold into yolk mixture, pour into pan and set in center of oven. It takes a little longer than the average soufflé, usually about 50 minutes, and the oven door should remain shut for the first 40 minutes. Then, when a bright knife comes out dry, the cake is done. It is essential to let it cool completely before taking out of pan, and best to let it set for 24 hours before serving. We fill the central hole with whipped cream, but this is optional.

OUR HALLOWEEN CHOCOLATE-MARSHMALLOW GINGERBREAD

For about 12 people

After we have scooped out the jack-o'-lanterns, we save the pumpkin meat and use it up with the encore recipes beginning on page 633. Then we bake this festive version of gingerbread and, at the last moment, prepare the hot and cold drinks (recipes follow).

Check Staples:

Sweet butter (about 9 oz.—2 sticks plus 2 Tbs.)
Eggs (2 large)
Aromatics: table salt, ground allspice, ground cinnamon, ground clove, ground Jamaica ginger,⚘ ground mace, freshly ground nutmeg, pure vanilla extract (2 tsp.)
Granulated instantized flour® (4¾ cups)
Baking soda (1½ tsp.)
Dark-brown sugar (2 to 3 Tbs.)
Strong black coffee (about ½ cup)

Shopping List:

Tart cooking apples, *see* list of foods in season, page 508 (3 or 4)
Sour cream (1 pt.)
Semisweet chocolate bits (½ cup)
Miniature marshmallows (1 cup)
Unsulfured dark molasses (1 pt.)

Preparation in About 30 Minutes—Plus 40 Minutes for Baking

Mix in a 2-quart saucepan: the 2 cups of molasses, the 9 ounces of butter, chunked, ¼ cup of the coffee, and heat quickly just to boiling, stirring continuously. As soon as it bubbles, turn off heat and let cool. Meanwhile mix dry ingredients in a fairly large bowl: the 4¾ cups of flour, ½ teaspoon salt, 1 teaspoon ground allspice, 4 teaspoons ground cinnamon, 1 teaspoon ground clove, 4 teaspoons ground ginger, 2 teaspoons ground mace, 2 teaspoons freshly ground nutmeg, and the 1½ teaspoons of baking soda. We use a 2-inch deep square, open baking pan, 13 inches long and 9 inches wide, but this can be varied somewhat. Lightly butter the pan. Peel and core the 3 or 4 apples, slice them ¼ inch thick, and cover entire bottom of baking pan with them, overlapping slightly in neat rows. Sprinkle lightly with the brown sugar, using more or less according to tartness of apples. By now the molasses mixture in saucepan should be cool enough. Blend in the pint of sour cream, then smoothly combine with dry ingredients. Break the 2 eggs into a small bowl, lightly beat, then also blend in. Add the ½ cup of chocolate bits, the cup of miniature marshmallows, and the 2 teaspoons of vanilla extract, and blend in lightly so as not to crush marshmallows. Turn on oven to 350 degrees. Finally, check texture of dough; it should be fairly thick, but still just pourable. If not, lightly work in a little more of the coffee. Now carefully pour dough into baking pan, making sure that the rows of apples are not pushed out of place. Smooth top with spatula. Set pan in center of oven and bake until a silver knife inserted comes out dry, usually in about 40 minutes. Let cool in the pan, then cut into 2-inch squares and turn over so that apples are on top.

OUR HALLOWEEN HOT SPICED WINE

For 12 people

In our experience the older members of the party, after standing around supervising the children on a cold evening, like something hot to drink. The younger children prefer to slake their energy in something cold and fruity, yet they want to feel they are sharing the wine. So we prepare these two drinks, both from the same Spanish Rioja, perhaps a Clarete from the vineyards of the Marqués de Riscal.

Check Staples:

Lemons (3)
Aromatics: whole cassia buds, whole cinnamon sticks, whole cloves
Vanilla sugar (3¾ cups)

Shopping List:

Spanish red Rioja wine, *see* above (4 bottles)

Hardly 10 Minutes Before Serving

Wipe lemons clean and cut into ⅜-inch slices. Into a gallon pot (preferably enameled, tinned copper, or stainless steel to avoid interaction with the wine) put: the 3¾ cups of sugar, four 2-inch sticks of cinnamon, 6 teaspoons whole cassia buds, and 4 teaspoons whole cloves. Then pour in the 4 bottles of wine and quickly bring just to the boiling point, stirring occasionally. As soon as wine begins to bubble, drain out aromatics. (If they are left in longer, we think wine becomes too spicy, but this is a matter of taste.) Bring drained wine back to just below boiling. We serve it in ceramic mugs, with a slice of lemon floating on top and a tall spoon with which to crush the lemon. (Cinnamon sticks, after drying out, can be used again.)

OUR HALLOWEEN SPANISH SANGRÍA—A COLD WINE PUNCH

For 12 children

Although this is a tradition for Halloween in our home, it is also a fine thirst-quencher on any hot spring or summer day, and the fruits can be varied according to the season. It is especially good with the soft berries, but there should always be at least a few slices of citrus. For a note on the wine, see the previous recipe.

Check Staples:

Vanilla sugar (1 cup or more, to taste)

Shopping List:

Spanish dry red Rioja wine, say a Marqués de Riscal (2 bottles)
Lemons (8)
Juice oranges (6)
Fruit to float in punch, according to season, say: apples, bananas, pears, pineapple, etc.
Soda water (about 2 qts., according to dilution required for youngest children)

Preparation in About 15 Minutes—Chill for About 3 Hours Before Serving

This is best ladled from a large punch bowl resting on a bed of ice. As each ingredient is prepared, it can be put straight into the bowl. Begin by putting in the juice of 6 of the lemons. Wipe the remaining 2 lemons clean and slice them into bowl. Then add the juice from 2 of the oranges. The remaining 4 oranges are wiped clean and cut into bowl in neat wedges, including skin. Add 1 cup of the sugar, and more later if desired. Now pour in the 2 bottles of wine and stir well. Peel, core, and chunk other fruits as required, then float them in the wine.

After chilling, just before serving, taste for sweetness. Ladle into tall glasses, putting at least one chunk of fruit in each. Dilute each glass with soda water according to the age of the imbiber.

The Budget Pull-Back and Encore Dishes of the Fall

The Aftermath of Halloween

We hate waste and for years we resented throwing away the good pumpkin meat scooped out of the Halloween jack-o'-lanterns. One October, when we were staying in an apartment with a lovely view of Lake Michigan, there was a glut of pumpkins in Chicago and we began experimenting. After many pumpkins and much tasting we filed several recipes good enough to keep in our repertoire. One of the best is cream of pumpkin soup (page 527). Others are . . .

ENCORE PUMPKIN AS A VEGETABLE RING

For our family of 4

Check Staples:

Chunked pumpkin meat, remaining from Halloween (1½ to 2 lbs.)
Salt butter (¼ lb.—1 stick)
Eggs (3 large)
Milk (about ½ cup)
Aromatics: crystal salt, freshly ground black pepper, MSG, whole allspice, ground clove, ground Jamaica ginger, whole nutmeg
Yellow onion (1 small)
Dry spiced bread crumbs or packaged "Herb Stuffing" (½ cup)
Dry Sherry (a few Tbs.)
Red wine (1 cup)

About 1¼ Hours Before Serving

Put the chunks of pumpkin into a saucepan and wet them down with the cup of red wine, add boiling water just to cover and some salt, then simmer until pumpkin is very soft, usually in about 20 minutes. Meanwhile melt 2 tablespoons of the butter in a frypan and sauté the ½ cup of bread crumbs, adding more butter if needed, until crumbs are slightly browned. In a small saucepan melt 4 more tablespoons of the butter and hold, just warm. Peel and finely chop the onion. Beat the 3 eggs in a separate bowl. Coarsely grind in a small mortar 1 teaspoon allspice. When the pumpkin is soft, drain and pass through a food mill (do not use an electric blender, which will swirl it into a paste) and begin making something lovely out of the orange purée by blending into it: the melted butter, the beaten eggs, half the buttered bread crumbs, the chopped onion, the ground allspice, 1 teaspoon ginger, ½ teaspoon ground clove, a few grinds of nutmeg, plus salt, pepper, and MSG to taste. Finally, work in a couple of tablespoons of the sherry and ¼ cup or a little more of the milk, until the purée will just hold its shape on the spatula. If it gets too thin, add more bread crumbs. Taste and adjust seasonings. Turn on oven to 350 degrees. Butter a 1-quart ring mold and spoon pumpkin into it.

About 45 Minutes Before Serving

Set ring mold in a shallow pan of hot water in the oven to bake until set. A bright silver knife plunged in usually comes out dry after about 45 minutes. Turn the pumpkin out onto a hot serving dish. We often fill the center with a second vegetable of a contrasting color.

ENCORE BAKED PUMPKIN DESSERT WITH CRYSTALLIZED GINGER

For our family of 4

Check Staples:

Chunked pumpkin meat, remaining from Halloween (1½ to 2 lbs—3 to 4 cups)
Sweet butter (6 Tbs.)
Aromatics: crystal salt,☆ freshly ground black pepper☆
Dark-brown sugar (½ cup)
Pure maple syrup☆ (¼ cup)

Shopping List:

Crystallized ginger (¼ lb.)
Dark buckwheat honey☆ (¼ cup)
English bitter Seville orange marmalade (a few Tbs.)

About 1¼ Hours Before Serving

Cut pumpkin meat into large dice. Butter a shallow open baking dish and put in pumpkin dice, making a single layer about 1 inch thick. Dot with good dollops of the marmalade. Coarsely chop the ¼ pound of ginger and sprinkle over pumpkin. Turn on oven to 350 degrees. In a heavy cast-iron saucepan melt together: the 6 tablespoons of butter, the ½ cup of sugar, the ¼ cup of buckwheat honey, the ¼ cup of maple syrup, plus a sprinkling of salt and a couple of grinds of pepper. Keep simmering and stirring until sugar is completely dissolved, then spoon onto pumpkin, making sure that every bit is covered. Hold back some of the sugar mixture for later use.

About 45 Minutes Before Serving

Set dish in center of oven and bake until pumpkin is quite soft, usually in about 45 minutes. Baste with more syrup every 15 minutes. This dish may be served hot or cold.

The Aftermath of Thanksgiving

After exhausting the possibilities with cold sliced turkey, we have always looked for encore ways which would return some moisture to the drying-out meat and add some variety to the narrow repetition of flavor. We have found the following worth repeating many times.

ENCORE TURKEY SOUFFLÉ PUFFS

For our family of 4

Check Staples:

Cold roast turkey meat (enough, when ground, to fill 2 cups)
Freshly mashed potatoes (2 cups)
Salt butter (4 Tbs.)
Eggs (2 large)
Aromatics: crystal salt,☧ freshly ground black pepper,☧ MSG,▣ Indian *kala-massala* curry blend,☧ French Dijon mustard, tarragon

Shopping List:

Heavy cream (¼ to ½ cup)

About 1½ Hours Before Serving

Cook and mash enough potatoes to fill 2 cups. Cut off and coarsely grind enough light and dark turkey meat to fill 2 cups. Hold both, covered.

About 1 Hour Before Serving—Including 30 Minutes of Unsupervised Baking

Soften 3 tablespoons of the butter and cream with 2 tablespoons of the mustard. We separate the 2 eggs, and hold the whites in our round-bottomed copper beating bowl. The yolks go into a small mixing bowl and are immediately beaten until frothy. In large mixing bowl, preferably using a rubber spatula or wooden spoon, quickly and lightly work together the ground turkey, the mashed potatoes, the egg yolks, the butter-mustard, 1 teaspoon of the Indian *kala-massala,* 1 teaspoon tarragon, 1 teaspoon MSG, plus salt and pepper to taste. Finally, blend in enough of the cream to make a soft paste that will just hold its shape. Turn on oven to 350 degrees. Butter a large open baking pan or cookie sheet. Beat whites until they just hold a peak, then fold lightly and rapidly into mix, as for a soufflé (BASIC RULE, page 74). Immediately spoon this fluff onto baking sheet in 8 separate piles, each about the size of a doughnut. Do not try to smooth or shape them, as this forces out air. Set at once in center of oven and do not reopen oven door for first 20 minutes. Puffs are done when they have souffléed up and are lightly golden, usually in about 30 minutes. Serve at once, preferably with a green salad or a light green vegetable.

ENCORE TURKEY WITH CHEESE, ITALIAN-SWISS STYLE

For our family of 4

Check Staples:

Cold roast turkey meat (enough fairly thick slices for 4)
Dark smoked thick-sliced bacon (8 slices)
Salt butter (about 1/4 lb.)
Egg (1 large)
Milk (2 Tbs.)
Aromatics: crystal salt, freshly ground black pepper, MSG, oregano, rosemary
Dry spiced bread crumbs or packaged "Herb Stuffing" (a few Tbs.)
Indian chick-pea flour or all-purpose flour (a few Tbs.)
Olive oil (a few Tbs.)
Imported Italian peeled and seeded plum tomatoes (1 lb. 1 oz. can)

Shopping List:

Imported Swiss natural Gruyère cheese (1/2 lb.)
Green peppers (2 medium)

About 1 Hour Before Serving—Including 25 Minutes Unsupervised Baking

Put the 8 bacon slices in a cold sauté pan and fry gently until crisp. Meanwhile set out 3 plates with a few tablespoons of the flour sifted onto the first; the egg, lightly beaten with 2 tablespoons of the milk, on the second; and a few tablespoons of the finely ground bread crumbs on the third. Chunk the 2 green peppers and hold. Thinly slice the 1/2 pound of cheese and hold. Choose an open oven-proof casserole (of roughly 2 quarts' capacity and about 3 inches deep) and liberally butter it. When bacon is crisp, drain on absorbent paper and pour off bacon fat from pan. Put in 2 tablespoons each of the butter and olive oil, heat up, then quickly sauté green pepper chunks, lift out with slotted spoon and place in the bottom of the casserole. Coat each slice of turkey, first with flour, then with egg, then with bread crumbs, pressing them on firmly, then quickly brown on both sides in hot fat. As fat is absorbed, add more butter and olive oil in equal proportions. As each turkey slice is browned, place it on green peppers in casserole. When half the turkey is in, cover with a layer of half the crisp bacon, then a layer of half the cheese slices, with a sprinkling of salt and MSG, plus a few grinds of pepper. Repeat with second layers of turkey, bacon, cheese, and seasonings. Turn on oven to 400 degrees. When last piece of turkey is out of sauté pan, pour into pan the can of tomatoes, bring quickly to boiling, adding at the same time 1 teaspoon each of oregano and rosemary, then bubble hard for a few minutes, stirring and breaking up tomatoes, to evaporate excess water. As soon as tomatoes show first signs of thickening, pour them over the contents of the casserole.

About 25 Minutes Before Serving

Set casserole in center of oven and bake, uncovered, for only as long as required to melt cheese, usually in 20 to 25 minutes. Serve at once on very hot plates.

The Aftermath of Christmas

If there is venison for the feast (page 540), we know of no better way of reheating it than by this classic Indian *kari*. In fact, any cold roast or boiled meat takes on a new glamour with the almost magical tricks of Indian aromatic spices. This is among the best and most generally useful of all our encore recipes.

ENCORE INDIAN CURRY OF COLD ROAST VENISON

For our family of 4

For general notes on preparing and serving Indian curries, see the Indian party menu on page 93. One of the best possible accompaniments to this dish is the pumpkin vegetable ring (page 633), which seems to balance the dramatic flavor pattern of the curry with a creamy smoothness. This method of preparation, eliminating the curry powder and adding each spice separately, allows the curry to be made either "gentle" or "hot," according to one's personal taste.

Check Staples:

Cold roast venison remaining from Christmas dinner, or other meat (2 lbs.)
Salt butter (¼ lb.)
Aromatics: crystal salt,☧ chili

Shopping List:

Green pepper (1)
Tomatoes (3 medium)
Plain yogurt (1 pt.)
Coconut flakes, the Hawaiian toasted are the best (1 small can)

Check Staples (continued):

powder,⁑ fenugreek seed,⁑ North Indian *garam-massala,*⁑ garlic (4 cloves), frozen ginger root,⁑ South Indian *kala-massala,*⁑ ground turmeric
Yellow onions (2 medium)
Watercress (1 bunch)

Shopping List (continued):

Crystallized ginger, if ginger root not available (about 3 oz.)

About 2¼ Hours Before Serving—Advance Preparation in About 15 Minutes—Unsupervised Marination for 1½ Hours

Cut the 2 pounds of meat into bite-size cubes and marinate in the pint of yogurt for 1 hour, stirring occasionally to keep pieces well coated. Then transfer meat and yogurt into a saucepan, add about 1½ teaspoons of salt and simmer, covered, until a good part of yogurt is absorbed, usually in about 30 minutes. Then remove lid, turn up heat slightly and bubble away remaining liquid yogurt, until meat is almost dry.

About 30 Minutes Before Serving—Blending the Curry

Prepare and mix together: the 4 cloves of garlic, peeled and finely minced; enough of the frozen ginger root, grated to fill 1 tablespoon, see the BASIC RULE on page 25 (or the crystallized ginger, coarsely chopped); plus the green pepper, diced. Peel and slice the 2 onions and hold separately. In a large sauté pan, melt 3 or 4 tablespoons of the salt butter, then lightly fry onions until just transparent. Stir in half of the ginger mixture and begin coloring the curry by blending in turmeric, ¼ teaspoon at a time, until a deep brown is achieved, usually with about 1½ to 2 teaspoons of turmeric. It tends to absorb the butter, so an extra tablespoon or two may have to be added. Also blend in: about 1 teaspoon salt, 1 teaspoon of the *garam-massala,* 1 teaspoon of the *kala-massala,* ½ teaspoon of the chili powder, ½ teaspoon fenugreek seed, plus ¼ cup of the coconut. Blend and stir for about 2 minutes. Turn heat down to simmering and coarsely chunk or slice the tomatoes into the pan. Let them simmer, blending and mashing them in, until they have cooked down, usually in 3 or 4 minutes. Add the meat; remembering that it is already cooked and is now only being warmed and impregnated with the aromatics. Also, add a handful of the watercress leaves, coarsely chopped. Now begins the fun of balancing the separate qualities of the curry. To increase the pungency, add more of the ginger mix; to sharpen the contrasts, add more fenugreek; to enrich the color, more turmeric; for an over-all increase of aromatic strength, more of the *massalas;* for a more chewy texture, more coconut. When the curry balance is exactly to taste, simmer, covered, for about 5 minutes longer, then uncover and turn up heat to boil away any remaining liquid, stirring gently, until curry is almost dry. Serve of course with rice in one form or another.

OUR SIMPLE MINESTRONE

For our family of 4

Although, of course, this is technically a soup, it is so solid and interesting in texture and flavor that, served with plenty of grated cheese, it makes a satisfying main supper or luncheon dish. Sometimes we use it at dinner, to expand a light main course into a hearty meal.

Check Staples:

Salt butter (4 Tbs.)
Aromatics: crystal salt,* freshly ground black pepper,* MSG,* garlic (1 clove) savory
Green Pascal celery, with leaves (4 good stalks)
Yellow onion (1 medium)
Fresh parsley (enough for 2 Tbs., chopped)
Imported Italian peeled and seeded plum tomatoes* (1 lb. 1 oz. can)

Shopping List:

Dried navy or pea beans (1 cup)
Elbow macaroni (1 cup)
Parmesan, or other hard grating cheese* (¼ lb.)
Young cabbage (smallest possible head)

The Day Before—Preparing Dried Beans for Soaking in About 10 Minutes

In a fairly large saucepan, bring about 1 quart of freshly drawn cold water rapidly up to a rolling boil. Meanwhile put the cup of dried beans into a collander, pick over, and wash under strongly running cold water. When water in pan is bubbling hard, dribble in beans through the fingers slowly enough so that water does not go off boil. After all beans are in, continue bubbling hard for 4 minutes, then turn off heat and leave to soak at room temperature overnight.

On the Morning of the Day—Unsupervised Simmering of Beans for 1½ to 2 Hours

Beans will by now have expanded to about 2½ cups and have absorbed a good deal of the soaking water. Add more freshly drawn cold water just to cover, plus 1 teaspoon of savory, then bring up to gentle simmering and continue cooking, covered, until beans are quite soft, usually in 1½ to 2 hours.

About 45 Minutes Before Serving—Including about 30 Minutes of Unsupervised Simmering

We usually assemble the *minestrone* in a 4-quart enameled cast-iron cocotte* with a tightly fitting lid. Put into it the beans with their liquor and bring up to boiling, then adjust heat for gentle simmering. Meanwhile peel and chop the onion. Set a sauté pan over medium-high heat, melt the 2 tablespoons of butter, then lightly sauté the chopped onion until just gilded and add with all juices to beans. Also add, as each is prepared: the clove of garlic, peeled and minced; the 4 stalks of celery, washed and sliced 1/4 inch thick, the leaves chopped; 2 tablespoons of chopped parsley, the can of tomatoes, plus salt, pepper, and MSG to taste. Discard the outer leaves of the cabbage, then shred enough to fill 1 cup and add to cocotte. Continue gently simmering, covered, for 30 minutes. Meanwhile grate the 1/4 pound of cheese and put into a small serving dish, which will be brought to the table. Also, cook the cup of elbow macaroni in the usual way in boiling salted water, until it is *al dente,* still chewy, usually in about 12 minutes. Then drain and hold, warm.

About 5 Minutes Before Serving

Stir macaroni into *minestrone,* reheat for a minute or two, then serve with plenty of grated cheese sprinkled on top. This dish is so good reheated that we often prepare it in larger quantities, incorporating the macaroni only into the part that is being served and cooking fresh macaroni for each reheating.

LEMON-CREAM SPAGHETTI WITH FISH STUFFING

For our family of 4

One of our simplest and most often-repeated pull-back dishes. The fish filling is flexible: canned tuna, as in this version, or canned or frozen crab, lobster, salmon, or lightly cooked fresh fish. It is especially good with salmon or swordfish steaks, fried, then coarsely flaked. It is excellent cold, although not much usually remains.

Check Staples:

Salt butter (1/4 lb.)
Lemons (2)
Aromatics: crystal salt,☧ freshly ground black pepper,☧ MSG▣

Shopping List:

Thin spaghetti (3/4–1 lb., according to appetite)
Tuna fish (three 7-oz. cans) or other fish, *see* above (about 3 cups)
Sour cream (1 pt.)

About 45 Minutes Before Serving

Cook the spaghetti in the usual way in about 4 quarts of highly salted, rapidly boiling water. When a single strand twisted around a wooden fork tastes *al dente,* firmly chewy, drain and rinse away excess starch with hot water. Meanwhile coarsely flake or chunk the fish and make the sauce. Mix in a bowl: the pint of sour cream, the juice of the 2 lemons, the 1/4 pound of butter, melted, with salt, pepper, and MSG to taste. Turn on oven to 400 degree. Butter a fairly shallow, open casserole and put about 2/3 of the drained spaghetti into it, lifting with a wooden fork to make sure that it does not pack down. On top put the fish as a single layer. Cover loosely with the rest of the spaghetti. Pour sour cream sauce over the spaghetti and, with a wooden fork, but without disturbing the layer of fish, lift it slightly here and there to encourage sauce to run down. Set the casserole, uncovered, in the center of the oven and bake just long enough to get everything piping hot and bubbly, usually in about 20 minutes. We bring the casserole to the table and plunge the serving spoon straight down, so that each person gets the proper proportion of spaghetti, fish, and sauce.

BASIC METHOD FOR HEARTS IN AROMATIC CREAM

For our family of 4

The choice of our hearts depends on the state of our pocketbook. Small veal hearts, 1 for each person, are very nice and tender, but much more expensive than a single beef heart, which serves 4 people. We prefer a smaller beef heart of about 3 pounds to the very large 5- or 6-pounders, which tend to be tough. The basic trick of this recipe is the marination in buttermilk and the cooking in Madeira and sour cream, which combine to tenderize the meat and give it an interesting flavor.

Check Staples:

Salt butter (4 Tbs.)
Aromatics: crystal salt,☆ freshly ground black pepper,☆ MSG,▣ rosemary
Shallots☆ (4 cloves)
Watercress (1 bunch)
Olive oil▣ (2 Tbs.)
Dry Madeira♁ (1/2 cup)

Shopping List:

Beef heart, small (about 3 lbs.), or, for greater luxury, veal hearts (4)
Buttermilk for marinating (1 qt.)
Sour cream for cooking (1 qt.)
Mushrooms (1/2 lb.)
Good boiling potatoes, *see* list, page 515 (4 medium)

The Day Before—Advance Preparation for Marination in About 10 Minutes

Cut the heart lengthwise into slices about 3/8 inch thick. Trim off all fat and pipes, then wash under cold running water and pat dry. Place slices in a lidded refrigerator dish, pour in enough of the buttermilk to cover, then refrigerate overnight.

About 2 Hours Before Serving

Let heart slices come to room temperature, still in buttermilk marinade. Also take sour cream out of refrigerator.

About 1 Hour Before Serving

Peel and slice the 4 potatoes about 1/4 inch thick, then steam until just tender, usually in 12 to 15 minutes. (If preferred, potatoes may first be boiled whole, then sliced, but this involves some loss of flavor and requires more time.) Meanwhile wipe clean (never wash) the 1/2 pound of mushrooms, cut off and discard any dry ends of stems, then slice mushrooms lengthwise into hammer shapes and hold. Remove heart slices from marinade, rinse and pat dry. In a sauté pan over medium-high frying heat, melt the 4 tablespoons of butter, then lightly sauté mushroom slices for not more than a minute or two, remove with slotted spoon and hold. Add the 2 tablespoons of olive oil to sauté pan, allow to heat up, then quickly sauté heart slices until lightly browned on both sides. We finally assemble this dish in an enameled cast-iron cocotte* with a tightly fitting lid. As each heart slice is browned, lay it in bottom of cocotte. When all heart slices are in, turn on oven to 350 degrees. Place sautéed mushrooms around and between the heart slices and sprinkle on salt, pepper, and MSG to taste. Mix together in a bowl the quart of sour cream and the 1/2 cup of dry Madeira, then pour half over heart slices. Place sliced potatoes as a layer on top, again sprinkle with seasonings, then pour over remaining sour-cream–Madeira sauce. Cover, place in center of oven, then bake until a tasted piece of the heart is quite tender, usually in 40 to 45 minutes. The acid in the wine will partially clot the sour cream, giving an attractively firm texture to the sauce.

OUR MODIFIED "NON-INTESTINAL" SCOTTISH HAGGIS

For our family of 4

Haggis is not a Scots joke in our house; in this modified form we find it excellent and serve it regularly, especially in honor of Saint Andrew's Day on November 30. Since, however, we neither cook nor serve it stuffed in a skin, we call ours "non-intestinal." This is a solid main course and, since there is oatmeal in it, only a vegetable is needed as an accompaniment. In Scotland this would be white turnip (page 163). We might precede it with a Scotch woodcock (page 264) and follow it with a tipsy laird (page 624).

Check Staples:

Clear beef bouillon (about 3 cups)
Aromatics: crystal salt,* freshly ground black pepper,*
Yellow onions (2 medium)

Shopping List:

Beef liver, sliced 3/8 inch thick (1 lb.)
White beef suet 1/4 (lb.)
Whole-grain Scottish oatmeal (1/2 cup)
Scottish Rowan jelly,* as garnish, optional (1 lb. can)

At Any Time Beforehand—the Flavor Improves with Keeping

Peel and chop the 2 onions and hold. Shred the 1/4 pound of the beef suet and hold. Ease the slices of liver into boiling water and simmer until just firm, usually in about 5 to 10 minutes. At once remove from water. When cool enough to handle, dice on a chopping block with a chef's knife (grinding would squeeze out juice). We then put the diced liver into a 3-quart enameled cast-iron cocotte* with a tightly fitting lid. Add the 1/2 cup of oatmeal, the shredded beef suet, the chopped onions and plenty of pepper. Mix thoroughly, adding enough bouillon to be about 1/4 inch deep on bottom of cocotte. Place cocotte over fairly high heat and bring quickly to a boil, then turn down heat to gentle bubbling, cover tightly, then leave to steam for 2 to 2 1/2 hours. However, every 15 minutes during the first hour and punctually every 30 minutes for the remaining cooking time, it must be checked, gently stirred, and more bouillon added, as the grains of oatmeal swell and absorb liquid. There must always be a little bouillon on bottom to provide steam, but grains must never be swimming. When oatmeal is soft but still slightly chewy, turn off heat, cool, then, if it is to be left much longer than 3 hours, refrigerate.

About 2 1/2 Hours Before Serving

Let *haggis* come to room temperature.

About 30 Minutes Before Serving

Moisten *haggis* with 1/2 cup more bouillon, bring up to boiling, then turn down to gentle bubbling and continue, covered, until liquid is again absorbed, usually in 30 minutes, add salt to taste. When *haggis* comes to table, it must be dry and very hot.

We accompany our *haggis* with dollops of canned Rowan jelly.

MONSTER CHICKEN POT WITH FALL HERBS AND VEGETABLES

Will serve 12, but also keeps well

This is one of our favorite ways with a large and economical stewing hen, and there is an extra saving in cost and time by preparing this substantial quantity. The vegetables can be varied, but each must be dropped into the stew at exactly the right moment, to be "done to a turn" just as the stew is served. It is a solid one-dish meal, to be teamed with a light first course and dessert.

Check Staples:

The rind of a country ham, page 369, or about 1/2 dozen strips of

Shopping List:

Large stewing hen, *see* shopping notes, page 520 (6 to 8 lbs.)

Check Staples (continued):

thick-sliced dark smoked bacon, or the same amount of corn-belly salt pork
Lemon (1)
Aromatics: crystal salt, whole black peppercorns, MSG, whole allspice, whole bay leaves, whole cloves, dillweed, garlic (3 cloves), marjoram, oregano, Hungarian sweet red paprika, dried rosemary (if fresh not available), savory
Carrots (4 medium)
Green Pascal celery (4 good stalks, with leaves)
Yellow onions (5 medium)
Parsley (1 bunch)
Imported Italian peeled and seeded plum tomatoes (2 lb. 3 oz. can)
Dry red wine (1½ cups)
Dry white wine (2 cups)

Shopping List (continued):

Pearl barley (½ cup)
Dried red kidney beans (1 cup, just under ½ lb.)
Cauliflower (smallest possible)
White celery (2 hearts)
Small button mushrooms (about 1 dozen)
White boiler onions (½ lb.)
Green peas (1 package frozen)
Green pepper (1 medium)
Boiling potatoes, small (2 lbs.)
Spinach (large handful)
Fresh rosemary, if available (small bunch)

The Day Before

Drop the kidney beans into a large pot of boiling water and leave soaking overnight.

On the Morning of the Day—About 1 Unsupervised Hour to Cook the Kidney Beans

Drain the kidney beans, saving the soaking water. Put them in the covered pot in which they are to be simmered and add: the 1½ cups of red wine, enough of the soaking water just to cover, 1 of the onions stuck with 4 cloves, ½ teaspoon each of dillweed, oregano, and savory, plus salt, pepper, and MSG to taste. Then very gently simmer for 1 hour and leave to cool in broth until needed. Their cooking will be completed in chicken pot.

About 2¼ Hours Before Serving

We use our largest soup kettle and place on its bottom, as a carpet for chicken, the rind which we have saved from our country ham (or one of the alternatives). Pour in the 2 cups of white wine and bring slowly to a boil. Meanwhile, rub the hen, inside and out, with the cut side of half a lemon, then dab lightly all over with paprika and lay to rest in the simmering wine. If the giblets are available, place them around.

Cover pot and let hen steam in wine while preparing vegetables. Peel the 4 remaining onions and the 3 cloves of garlic and drop in whole alongside hen. Chunk the 4 stalks of green celery and coarsely cut the leaves with kitchen scissors, then add to pot. Also a small handful of parsley sprigs and salt to taste, usually about 1 tablespoon. Now pour in enough freshly drawn cold water just to cover, bring quickly back to boiling, then gently simmer, "just smiling" (page 117), covered, for 30 minutes.

Meanwhile prepare the next batch of vegetables, assembling them together in a large bowl. Coarsely chop the 2 white celery hearts. Pick over, wash well, and coarsely tear up the spinach leaves.

1½ Hours Before Serving

Add the white celery and spinach to the pot. Also add: the ½ cup of barley, the red kidney beans, including their broth, the can of tomatoes, 3 whole bay leaves, 6 whole black peppercorns, 3 whole cloves, 8 whole allspice, 1 teaspoon marjoram, and either a sprig or two of fresh rosemary or 1 teaspoon of the dried. Bed all these down, add more freshly drawn cold water, if needed, just to cover, bring back quickly to the boiling point, then continue gently simmering, covered, for 1 hour.

Meanwhile prepare next batch of vegetables, assembling them together in a large bowl. Peel the 2 pounds of potatoes and the ½ pound of white boiler onions. Remove the outer leaves from the cauliflower and break center into flowerets. Remove central seed pod from the green peppers and cut into quarters. Scrape and chunk the 4 carrots.

30 Minutes Before Serving

With two large carving forks, carefully lift hen, holding over pot to drain, then place on cutting board. Add latest batch of prepared vegetables to pot, bed down, bring back to boiling, then continue simmering, covered. Quickly cut all meat off hen and chunk into bite-size pieces. Put these back into the pot. Meanwhile prepare final batch of vegetables, again assembling together in bowl. Break block of frozen peas into chunks. Wipe the ½ pound of mushrooms clean (never wash), trim off dried bits of stalks, then cut off stalks level with caps.

10 Minutes Before Serving

Add peas, mushroom caps and stalks, stirring everything carefully around, and tasting for possible adjustment of seasonings. Bring the dish to the table in a piping-hot tureen.

RED CABBAGE WITH SMOKED PORK AND KNACKWURST AS THEY DO IT IN GERMANY

For our family of 4

We think red cabbage has such a dominant personality that it is better as the star of its own main dish than simply as a supporting vegetable. The smoked pork chops are available at many fancy butchers or in German food markets, where they are known as *Kasseler Rippchen.*

Check Staples:

Corn belly salt pork (about 6 oz.)
Yellow onions (6 medium, or 1 lb.)
Orange, for peel (1)
Aromatics: crystal salt, freshly ground black pepper, MSG, ground clove, mace chips, oregano, thyme
Dark-brown sugar (6 Tbs.)
Red wine vinegar (½ cup)
Red wine (½ cup)

Shopping List:

Red cabbage, medium size (about 3 lbs.)
Smoked pork chops, about ¾ inch thick (4)
All-beef knackwurst (4)
Tart cooking apples, *see* list of foods in season, page 508 (3 or 4)
Green peppers (2 medium)

Preparation in About 15 Minutes—Cooking, Almost Completely Unsupervised, in 4 Hours

We prepare this in an enameled cast-iron cocotte* with a tightly fitting lid, and good-looking enough to come to the table. Prepare ingredients and hold each separately. Wash cabbage, remove and discard tough outer leaves and hard parts of stalk. With large heavy knife, cut entire cabbage into slices about ½ inch thick; cut each slice in half from stem to top. Slice salt pork. Peel, core, and slice apples about ¼ inch thick. Peel and slice onions. Cut seed pods out of peppers and chunk. Coarsely grate yellow outer rind of the orange. Turn on oven to 300 degrees. Now assemble ingredients in cocotte: on the bottom, a layer of cabbage; cover it with a layer of onion slices, then apple slices, then 2 or 3 slices of the salt pork; sprinkle in turn with salt, pepper, MSG, about 2 tablespoons of the brown sugar, about ¼ teaspoon ground clove, some grated orange rind, about ½ teaspoon mace chips, about ½ teaspoon oregano, and about ½ teaspoon thyme. Put some chunks of green pepper on top. Then repeat this sequence exactly with more layers until all cabbage is in the cocotte and all apples, onions, sugar, green pepper, and orange rind are used up. Finally, add the ½ cup of vinegar and the ½ cup of red wine. Cover cocotte tightly, put in oven and forget for 3 hours. Meanwhile let pork chops and knackwurst come to room temperature. Then lightly brown chops by sautéing for about 5 minutes on each side. Usually their own fat is sufficient to lubricate the pan.

1 Hour Before Serving

Open up the cocotte and be prepared for a magnificent aroma. Using a wooden fork, lightly lift top layers of cabbage and bury pork chops right in the center. Replace lid tightly and put back in oven.

30 Minutes Before Serving

With the same light touch, bury knackwurst in center of cabbage. Replace cover tightly and put back into oven for final half hour. This dish calls for a robust red wine from a sunny Southern vineyard, say a Châteauneuf-du-Pape or a Côte Rôtie, both from the valley of the Rhône.

Christmas Is English Plum Pudding

Many years ago, when we lived in London, we learned that even Frenchmen have a high regard for "Le Plimpe Puddink"—at least according to the testimony of Alin Laubreaux, the great French gourmet. . . .

There was once in France a fat country priest who was a fabulous gourmand and his love of good food grew so strong that he thought less and less of anything else. He gabbled his sermons and listened with only half an ear to the problems of his parishioners. The crisis came when he stopped off at the pastry shop on his way to attend a dying woman. There was a public scandal and he was called before his bishop.

At the bishop's palace, there were important visitors in the office, so the bishop saw the priest in the dining hall. On his knees, the gluttonous curé confessed his sins and vowed to mend his ways. The bishop was moved by this repentance and pardoned him. As the relieved priest rose to leave the dining room, his glance turned to a huge golden platter on a side table, on which was mounted a magnificently rounded loaf of *pâté de foie gras*. His nostrils dilated. His breathing accelerated. His lips became moist.

"Oh, Monseigneur," he breathed, "how *good* that smells!"

There was a fearful silence. As the priest opened his trembling lips to speak, the bishop stopped him with an imperious gesture.

"I will give you one last chance," he said. "The dean of our school in England has written asking me to appoint a chaplain. You will go——"

The priest broke into a cold sweat. This was the middle of November. Christmas was only six weeks away. He thought of the annual round of feasts in the homes of his parishioners: the turkeys bulging with chestnuts, the geese decorated with glacé cherries and strips of orange, the silken sweetness of the Château d'Yquem. "To England?" he sobbed.

"Yes, to the land of oatmeal porridge, of cast-iron meat, of sauces swimming in grease. After a few years of English cooking you will return to France cured of your appalling greed."

Within two weeks the glutton had relinquished his parish to an ascetic young priest and was on his way to England.

This was in the first week of December. For the next three weeks My Lord the Bishop heard not a word from England. Then, two days after Christmas, there was a message:

> . . . On my knees I beg Monseigneur to recall me immediately. Christmas night was fatal to my soul. I fear damnation from this English Plum Pudding.

REGAL ENGLISH PLUM PUDDING

For a party of 8 to 10, with some left over

During our time in London, we had a cook who had a sister who had a friend who had a brother-in-law who was alleged to be a chef in one of the royal Palace kitchens, and who claimed to have sneaked out some of the royal recipes. From this highly questionable source comes our method.

We prepare a large pudding, since the mixing and steaming times hardly vary with size. We use a 2-quart tin melon mold* with a watertight lid, and for the steaming it stands on a rack in a large covered pot of boiling water.

Check Staples:

Sweet butter (about 1 Tb.)
Eggs (6 large)
Milk (1 cup)

Shopping List:

Tart Greening apples (2 medium)
Candied citron (1/4 lb.)
Currants (1/2 lb.)

Check Staples (continued):

Aromatics: crystal salt,☆ ground cinnamon, ground clove, whole nutmeg
Dry white bread crumbs, fairly coarse (3 cups)
Dark-brown sugar (about 1/2 lb.)

Shopping List (continued):

Pitted dates (1/4 lb.)
Candied lemon peel (1/4 lb.)
Candied orange peel (1/4 lb.)
Seedless white raisins (1 lb.)
White beef suet, preferably from around a kidney (6 oz.)
Sweet cider (2 Tbs.)
French Cognac, medium-priced (2 Tbs.)
French light Martinique rhum (2 Tbs.)

About 3 Months Beforehand—Many Helpers Make Light of the Advance Preparation

This is an orderly mixing operation involving several bowls of different sizes. Save the largest of all for the final assembly. The second largest will hold the fruits as they are prepared. First finely grind the 6 ounces of beef suet and hold in refrigerator. Now prepare and assemble the fruits in the second largest bowl: 1/4 cup each, coarsely diced, of the citron, candied orange peel, candied lemon peel, and pitted dates; about 3/4 cup of coarsely diced tart apple, first cored, but with skin left on; the 1 1/2 cups of seedless raisins, and the cup of currants. Everything can now be held for awhile or we can proceed at once to the . . .

Final Assembly

Break the 6 eggs into a medium bowl and beat with a wire whisk until frothy, then blend in the ground beef suet, breaking up lumps with a wooden spoon. Now begin the work in the largest mixing bowl. Make a layer on the bottom with the 3 cups of bread crumbs. Sprinkle over them in turn: 1 teaspoon ground cinnamon, 1/2 teaspoon ground clove, 1 teaspoon salt, then grind on nutmeg until 1/4 of the nut is used up, and over the top shake 3/4 cup, tightly packed, of the brown sugar. Mix thoroughly with a wooden spoon. Quickly scald the cup of milk and work enough into the mixture to make it moist and soft but not the least bit runny. It usually absorbs about 3/4 cup of milk. Give a final stir to the eggs and suet, then blend into mixture. Now pile in all fruits, but do not mix for the moment. Give the final blessing by sprinkling on 2 tablespoons each of the cider, Cognac, and rhum. Wash hands, roll up sleeves, and plunge into the final blending. No kitchen tool in existence is half as effective for this operation as a set of sensitive fingers. Feel around for lumps of sticky fruit and break them up. Keep it all as light as possible by lifting rather than bearing down.

Feel for dry spots and make sure that liquids are evenly distributed. Meanwhile, someone else can lightly butter the 2-quart mold. We think it best to fill mold by hand, so that pudding can be very loosely packed in, yet without air spaces. In our experience, if mold is properly packed, all ingredients will just fit. Lightly smooth top, cover with piece of aluminum foil, and tightly press on waterproof lid.

Steaming for 6 Hours, Almost Completely Unsupervised

Stand mold, lid upward, on a rack in a very large pot, with plenty of room around for a gallon or more of boiling water. This helps to maintain an even head of steam. Pour in enough boiling water so that surface will be about 3/4 inch below top of mold. Keep water bubbling merrily, covered, to maintain plenty of steam. Continue for 6 hours, checking roughly every hour and adding more boiling water, as needed, to maintain original level. After 6 hours, turn off heat, remove mold from water, and let cool slowly. Curb the natural desire to peek inside. Do not open. Finally, wipe mold clean and dry, then store away somewhere in an obscure closet, at room temperature, until Christmas.

Instructions for final reheating on Christmas Day are on page 543. Incidentally, any of the candied fruits that remain unused should be stored away, tightly covered, for the chocolate sauce for the Christmas vension (page 540).

HOLIDAY THOUGHTS ON AFTER-DINNER WINES AND SPIRITS

WE are not much attracted to sweet drinks after dinner. When one has dined well, the syrupy sweetness of many liqueurs, cream Sherries, and sweet Madeiras, etc., brings an uncomfortable feeling of oversaturation. We prefer the sharp warmth of the dry spirits, and the following notes concentrate chiefly on these. However, if the ladies demand something slightly sweet and there is a fine aged cheese at the end of the menu, we often turn to the great fortified wine that was once the most popular of all after-dinner drinks . . .

The True Port from Portugal

Again, we take the firm stand, already discussed in relation to other wines, that the name has a strictly geographic significance and can be applied only to a fortified wine produced on the slopes of the hills along the upper valley of the Douro River in Portugal, and then blended and matured in the port city of Oporto. There are many excellent sweet fortified wines produced in other places, but none of these has the character, nor can ever achieve the perfection of balance, of a great Port. True Port is "fortified" by the addition of a brandy to the fermenting trough soon after the grapes have been pressed. The new wine is then shipped in flat-bottomed barges down the rapids of the Douro River to Oporto. Here in the vast cool cellars of famous firms the young wine is destined to become one of the three types of Port. If the weather in the vineyards and the vintage have been almost perfect (an event which happens about once every 5 years), the wine may be declared to be "vintage," and only wines of that year will be blended together. After about 2 years in the wooden casks, this wine is bottled and left to mature slowly, often for 20 years or more. This is "vintage Port," the greatest and most expensive. Young wines from other than vintage years may be left much longer in the wooden casks, where they mature more rapidly and are ready for bottling and sale at lower prices within a comparatively few years. However, during their longer contact with the wood, they lose some of their strength and their color changes from the original deep red to a dark shade of brown, which is why they are sold as "tawny Port." Between these two types there is a third, a compromise (and, perhaps for that reason, less interesting). This is called "ruby Port," made from wines which are left longer in the cask than "vintage" but not as long as "tawny." However, the wine does not have the quality to continue maturing in the bottle, and it is sold when still fairly young.

For guests who insist on sweet liqueurs, there are dozens of types from which to choose. It is easy to combine a distilled spirit with sugar or honey, and new liqueurs with fancy names seem to be announced almost every month. Some are merely "conversation pieces" with bits of decorative flotsam and jetsam floating around inside the bottle. However, there are a few sweet liqueurs that have been highly regarded for hundreds of years and we accept this fact as reasonable proof of their quality (page 695). There are other sweet wines which many of our friends enjoy, including the *oloroso* cream Sherries, the sweet Madeiras called *boal* or *malmsey,* white Port, the Greek Mavrodaphne, and the better grades of Sicilian Marsala.

Cognacs, Calvados, and Other Brandies and Distilled Eaux-de-Vie

Although the discovery was probably first made accidentally by an Arabian, it was Arnauld de Villeneuve, a professor of medicine and philosophy at the University of Montpellier in southwestern France toward the end of the thirteenth century, who first scientifically established the fact that wine contained more than grape juice and water. While bringing some wine to the boil, he noticed that even before the wine was actually boiling, it started gently bubbling and giving off a vapor that was certainly not steam. He cooled this vapor and produced, drop by drop, a clear, colorless, tasteless liquid which had such an immediate and remarkable effect on the body and mind of anyone who drank it that it was named "water of life." He had discovered the principle of the distillation of alcohol, which is the source of

every modern form of spirits. Today the name *eau-de-vie* is used, not so much for the pure alcohol, as for the various strong drinks distilled from many fruits, vegetables, and other plants, including even wood pulp. If all these distilled drinks, from brandy to whiskey, could be made absolutely pure, they would be exactly alike, as clear and tasteless and odorless as water. It is the tiny amounts of the impurities, the aldehydes and acid salts, among other things, which are responsible for the enormous differences in the bouquet, taste, color, and quality of the various brandies, gins, rums, whiskeys, etc. (Every gourmet should be aware of the importance of the impurities in his drinks and in his food.)

The word "brandy" (which comes from the Dutch *brandewijn,* burnt wine) is one term that has no geographic significance. It can be properly applied to any spirit distilled from grapes anywhere in the world. However no brandy may be called "Cognac" unless it is made from grapes grown around the small French town of Cognac on the river La Charente where, without question, the best brandies in the world (and some quite inferior ones) are produced. Since Cognacs are always blended, and since each of the famous producers tries to keep his particular brand exactly the same in quality and character year after year, the only way to buy Cognac is to experiment until one finds which labels provide the drinks that are most acceptable to one's personal taste, at prices also acceptable to one's pocket. However one must always remember that the best-known brand names (i.e., the ones most extensively publicized) by no means always represent the best values. Firms of great repute (hence with high promotion costs) are nowadays putting out expensive Cognacs of a general sameness that is downright depressing. Some producers try to add glamour to their labels by decorating them with fancy stars and initials. One star is said to mean that the Cognac is not less than 3 years old; two stars, that it is at least 4 years old, and three stars that it is at least 5 years old. Sometimes the stars are replaced by crowns and 4 or 5 are included, without any definition of their meaning. The initials "V.S.O." are said to mean "Very Special Old"; the initials "V.S.O.P.," "Very Special Old Pale"; and the initials "V.V.S.O.P.," "Very, Very Special Old Pale." We prefer to choose Cognacs that have impressed us by their bouquet and taste rather than by the glamour of their advertising and the cabalistic signs on their labels.

Cognac is by no means the only good distilled spirit from France. There is the famous apple brandy of Normandy, Calvados. When it is young it is so strong that it assaults the stomach, boring its way through the contents. This is the basis of the famous Normandy expression *le trou normand* ("the Norman hole"). However when Calvados is properly aged,

often for as long as 15 years, it is an after-dinner drink second only to Cognac. There is the brandy which takes its name from the town where it is produced, Armagnac, and which at its best can be much better than an inferior Cognac or Calvados. In other wine areas of France, a brandy is often distilled from the "must," (or mash) of the grapes after the wine has been pressed, and these are called "marcs" (pages 695–7).

As to the multitude of other brandies and *eaux-de-vie* produced from fruits and other plants in many parts of the world, the list is enormous, but our personal taste is narrow. Among those which we find most joyous are the spirits distilled from the sloe berry, Prunelle, and from the brown Williams pear, the deliciously overpowering Williamine, or *Guillaumin* (page 697). We include among these one gin so strong in character and personality that it can never be used as a mixer but is best drunk as an after-dinner *eau-de-vie,* the Holland Genever, which comes in tall ceramic crocks (page 697).

Rum, the Eau-de-Vie of Sugar

Rum (the name comes from the Latin for sugar, *saccharum*) was discovered by the men working in the cane fields in the West Indies who found that the cane juice could be fermented and slowly distilled in earthenware pots over wood fires. This was a wasteful process and most modern rums are mass produced from molasses, the byproduct of sugar production, and are generally used simply as mixers. However there are a few very fine rums, some of them still made directly from cane juice, others from molasses, but fined and aged often for as long as 10 to 15 years. We think that some of these are good enough to drink after dinner as if they were brandies, sometimes straight, often diluted with a little water. Some are extremely strong yet smooth and silky (page 697).

The Great Whiskeys of Scotland

The word "whiskey" comes from the Gaelic *usquebaugh,* which is simply a translation of *eau-de-vie.* The term has no geographic significance and may properly be used anywhere in the world for a spirit distilled from cereal grains. The process involves first allowing the grain to germinate and ferment into a "mash," then distilling off the alcohol. Again it is the impurities, transferred from the grains to the alcohol, which control the enormous differences between various whiskeys.

Scotch whiskey is of course distilled in Scotland and only from barley. Its character and strength are dependent on the quality of the barley, on the skill of the distillers, on the time and care given to the maturing, and on the ultimate judgment of the blender. When the whiskey comes from the Highland distillery, it is "straight malt" and up to about the year 1850, no other type of Scotch whiskey was available. Then, a whiskey shipper in Glasgow had the idea of in effect "watering down" the straight malt whiskey by blending it with comparatively cheap, mass-produced plain alcohol. Thus was born the "light blended" Scotch whiskey, which today, in hundreds of types, under dozens of different labels, is sold all over the world. Nevertheless true connoisseurs of Scotch whiskey continue to regard the "straight malt" as the "great vintage" whiskeys of Scotland, with a dominant character and superb smoothness and power. The proud names among these whiskeys are those of the areas where they are produced: Glenlivet and Speyside, these generally being the best; then also Moray and Campbeltown, the latter producing a smoky whiskey, while from the island of Islay comes the most powerful and pungent of all (see page 698). Any drinker who develops an appreciation of these "straight malts" will not willingly return to the comparatively bland simplicity of the blended whiskeys.

Epilogue

Appendices
and
Indices

On Being A Gourmet

We began this book by defining a gourmet as a perfectionist—in the market, in the kitchen, and at the table. The essence of the gourmet's attitude is expressed by two basic qualities of living: respect and integrity. When friends enter the circle of our hospitality, the care we take in preparing the food is a measure of our respect for our guests. To achieve the final perfection at the table, we must begin with respect for the gift of Nature's raw materials. Respect demands that good meat, for example, shall not be spoiled in the oven; that it shall be brought to table at the proper temperature; that it shall be carefully carved to preserve its texture and served in such a way as to enhance its natural flavors. In the market, the gourmet has a right to demand integrity in the growing and distribution of food, whether it be the farmer cultivating his peaches for flavor rather than size, or the butcher cutting his carcasses for maximum quality rather than maximum profit, or the grocer taking care to store his eggs at the right temperature. When fresh fruits and vegetables are allowed to deteriorate through incompetent handling, when the contents of a can fail to fulfill the promise of the label, when a package is deliberately designed to mislead the shopper, these are all reflections of that lack of respect for the customer which is implicit in the phrase "the public won't know the difference."

We believe it to be the responsibility of the gourmet to demonstrate in every possible way that the public *does* know the difference and to demand respect for the good taste and intelligence of the consumer. It should never be too much trouble to write a letter to the president of a manufacturing company demanding the replacement of a poor-quality product. If the first taste of a bottle of wine shows it to be inferior, the bottle should be re-corked at once and returned to the wine merchant with a demand for a refund. Above all, the gourmet makes demands upon himself: he must continually raise his own standards and resist the multitude of compromises that are constantly offered to tempt him.

It is perhaps a strange twist that it was an Englishman, not a Frenchman, who expressed the ultimate definition of the attitude of the gourmet. It was Dr. Samuel Johnson who said: "He who does not mind his belly will hardly mind anything else."

Appendices

OUR DIRECTORY OF CHEESES

Finding the Best Cheeses

THERE HAS BEEN a revolution in the world of cheese and it is now much harder to find the great and good cheeses in the swamping flood of the mediocre. What has happened can best be seen through the experiences of a typical French farm family in the village of, shall we call it, Beaulieu. On their land Jean and Marie François kept a large herd of goats and, for as long as anyone could remember, late every summer there was a glut of goats' milk. Then Mme François would bring out the cheese forms and begin making a small, unpretentious, soft and creamy little dessert cheese, which, for more than a hundred years, had been called "Chèvre Beaulieu." By October the little cheeses were ripe and they had a deliciously fresh taste and a strong character, which came, basically, from the minerals in that particular soil, which affected the grasses which fed the goats. There was just enough cheese for the needs of the François family, plus a small supply for the neighbors and some for a few stores in the village, which quickly sold out to passing tourists. By the end of November all the Chèvre Beaulieu had gone for another year.

The first step in the revolution came with the development of the refrigerated truck. A Paris cheese merchant offered to carry some of the Chèvre Beaulieu to the big city and sell it on his cheese stall in Les Halles, the great Paris wholesale food market. Thus a few specialty shops began to stock the cheese and it was bought at first mainly by people who had come to Paris from the Beaulieu region. Also, two or three bistros, which specialized in the food of that region, served the cheese to their customers, from about the first week in October to the end of November. However, the Paris trade was very profitable for the Françoises and they were tempted to enlarge their production. They turned a barn over to cheese-making and bought some machinery that would produce the cheeses much faster. Next they had to find a larger supply of goats' milk, and they arranged for deliveries from several farms in the next valley. That was a larger step than anyone at the time realized. The soil in the next valley was different, the grass was different, the milk did not have precisely the same properties. The cheese lost its individual character. It was no longer "Chèvre Beaulieu," but "Chèvre Régionale."

Then one day a big black limousine brought an American who introduced himself as the representative of one of the great cheese importers of New York. He said that there was a "cheese explosion" in the United States; that Americans were now collecting cheeses as they used to collect stamps. Would the François family be interested in helping to supply this enormous market? The first requirement of the proposed contract would have to be, of course, that the production of cheese must continue steadily throughout the year. Naturally, American capital would be available. . . .

So a concrete factory building went up on the Françoises' land and the most modern electric automated machinery was installed and the cheeses began rolling off the production line. A chemical consultant showed the François family how to add preservatives that would keep the cheese in good condition during its travels across the Atlantic. To cover up the taste of the preservatives, it was easy to add certain artificial flavoring essences, supplied from a chemical factory. The cheeses were made a little firmer and pressed a little harder, so that a larger number would fit into each standard packing case. Meanwhile, on Madison Avenue, a famous firm of marketing consultants was designing a new box for the cheese, printed in six colors. Finally, after a number of "Consumer Preference Surveys," it was decided to drop the name "Chèvre Beaulieu" in favor of "La Belle France." So it was launched on the American market and a famous New York cheese shop, which until then had been advertising that it had a stock of 700 different cheeses, was now able to advertise that it had 701.

"La Belle France" would, of course, never appear on our cheese shopping list, nor do many of the hundreds of other small local cheeses which should never have left home. After a good many years of careful tasting, we have prepared a master list of the great and fine cheeses which travel well and have been reasonably easy to find in many parts of the country. However, even a list of names does not entirely solve the problem; for the same name is used for the good and the bad product, for the authentic cheese and the phony imitation. Although Gruyère is a town in Switzerland and Cheddar is a village in England, anyone in any part of the world has the legal right to make cheeses and call them by these names. Also, cheese, like wine, even after it has been well and truly made, must be carefully stored and properly aged. Therefore the buyer must know enough about the cheese to be able to separate the good from the bad. The following practical notes are designed to help. We divide the cheeses into four broad types, according to use, and try always to keep at least one of each type on hand.

1. The Firm General-Purpose Cheeses

American Red Cheddar, or American Cheddar, or American Cheese

This is *the* universal cheese in the refrigerators of supermarkets and delicatessens across the land, in dozens of types under dozens of labels and generally rindless, precut, and prepackaged. This is what one is likely to get if one simply and foolishly asks for "half a pound of cheese, please." As to the quality, it may be anything from wonderfully good to absolutely dreadful. There are four sad facts about AMERICAN CHEESE:

SAD FACT 1: Out of every 3 pounds of cheese sold in the United States, 2 pounds are of this one kind. What a pity that more Americans do not try to get to know at least a few of the 400 or so authentic cheeses of the world!

SAD FACT 2: Huge quantities of American cheese are still being sold in "processed" form. No one has ever more accurately defined this factory method of mass-producing cheese than the essayist and cheese-lover Clifton Fadiman: "The best I can say for it is that it is nonpoisonous. . . . In the preparation of this solidified floor wax—often the product of . . . steaming and blending odd lots of cheese, of paralyzing whatever germs might result either in loss of profit or gain of flavor—every problem but one is solved: packaging, keeping, distribution, slicing, cost. One problem alone is not solved: that of making cheese."

SAD FACT 3: Increasing amounts of what might be called "artificially naturalized" American cheese are being offered for sale in an effort to meet the growing public distaste for "processed" cheese. Good cheese must have time to mature and develop in flavor. The mass-production cheese industry is in a hurry. American cheese is now being offered for sale labeled "natural sharp," which has not been sharpened by age but by being treated with chemicals: for example, sodium citrate (an artificial form of lemon juice), sodium phosphate, or Rochelle salts.

SAD FACT 4: While American cheddar is actually an imitation of one of the most famous of English cheeses, originated in the small town of Cheddar in the county of Somerset, and while English farmhouse Cheddar is still the creamiest and most magnificent member of the vast family, not a single ounce of authentic English Cheddar is legally permitted to enter the United States. This shocking fact highlights the fantastic anti-gourmet policy of the U. S. government in regard to foreign cheeses, a policy which we believe to be about a hundred years out of date. Several of the authentic, great cheeses of the world, which are consumed every day by millions of people in Europe and elsewhere, are entirely banned from entry into the United States on the grounds that they are sanitarily unfit for human consumption. The United States Department of Agriculture adopts the somewhat arrogant point of view that "foreigners" who make cheese are likely to have dirt under their fingernails and probably work with unwashed equipment in dank cellars. Also, the government seems to think that the American cheese industry needs protection from foreign competition. This may have been true a few decades ago, but today the best of American cheese is good enough to meet any free competition in any open market. It is only the "processed junk" that needs protection! Even with foreign cheeses that are legally permitted entry into the U.S., the importers are continually hamstrung by the haphazard day-to-day administration of the law by Agriculture Department inspectors. A shipment of a particular cheese may be passed through the port of entry on Monday, while on Tuesday a second shipment of the same cheese may be seized and destroyed. Recently, one of the well-known Swiss cheeses was arbitrarily banned because a single grain of sand was found imbedded in a single cheese in a shipment of several hundred. All this means that American gourmets are denied by their government their freedom of choice in the world of cheese.

Basic Rule for Buying American Cheddar: Unless compelled to order by mail or telephone, always go to the store, inspect, select, and taste before ordering. The best American cheddar is never prepackaged, is always cut from a fairly large wheel, and should have been aged for a minimum of 60 days, but is much better if aged for 12 months, and better still if aged for 2 or 3 years. The color of properly aged cheese varies from light yellow to almost orange; the texture should be dry to the point of being slightly crumbly; the flavor is partly a matter of taste, from fairly bland to quite sharp, but there should never be a bitter or lemon-flavored aftertaste, which indicates that cheese has been "artificially naturalized." We have tasted excellent American cheddar from Herkimer County in New York State and from Vermont, but several states have their own names for fine cheddar variations: California Monterey Jack, Colorado Mountain Blackie, Oregon Tillamook, Wisconsin Longhorn, as well as the famous Canadian Black Diamond.

Appenzeller from Switzerland

Character: Properly aged APPENZELLER has the heavily accented flavor of Gruyère with a wonderfully nutty texture. Often hard to find. It is least known of the three great Swiss-cheeses-with-holes: the others being Emmenthaler and Gruyère. Appenzeller is strongest of the three, since it is cured in spiced wine; the holes, or "eyes," spotted through the cheese are the size of pinheads, often too small to be easily seen. Its name means "from Appenzell," a northeastern Swiss canton near the Austrian border. **Basic Rule for Buying:** First make sure that cheese is authentic Swiss, then taste for degree of aging to suit personal preference.

Asiago from Italy

Character: Extraordinary cheese with, when fairly young, a distant honeyed sweetness from a type of sweet clover eaten by cows on the Asiago Plateau in the province of Vicenza and around the cities of Padua, Venice, and Verona. When the cheese is thoroughly aged, its sweetness disappears under a smooth sharpness, and when dry and hard is excellent for grating. **Basic Rule for Buying:** Look for light yellow color; taste for slight sweetness; since imitations are made in several other places, make reasonably sure that cheese comes from the above-mentioned areas.

Cacio a Cavallo from Italy

Character: CACIO A CAVALLO is an unusually shaped version of provolone, sold in round balls about 5 pounds each; it is made from cows' milk, but has an attractive saltiness reminiscent of ewes' milk. Its name, which means, literally, "horse cheese," is said to have come from the traditional method of aging by stringing two cheeses together and hanging them from a wooden workhorse as if they were saddlebags. **Basic Rule for Buying:** Make certain that cheese is an authentic Italian import and not a pale imitation from some other part of Europe or from a domestic source.

Cheshire from England

Character: One of the world's great cheeses, with a magnificently individual flavor and texture that comes from the salty marsh grass eaten by Cheshire cows. CHESHIRE CHEESE has never been successfully imitated anywhere else, and hence is one of the safest of all cheeses to buy. **Basic Rule for Buying:** Color varies according to type, from lemon-yellow to pale orange. When the cheese is too young, its texture is creamy; when properly aged, it is dry to the point of being slightly crumbly. Look for the "three-C" mark stenciled on the outer rind, which the Cheshire Cheese Council allows only to be put on cheeses from the best districts.

Dunlop from Scotland

Character: Creamy-textured cheese with, when properly aged (for about 4 months), an unusually clean sharpness; one of best of all cheeses for grilling or toasting, since it softens and browns without melting. DUNLOP originated in the small town of that name in the county of Ayr. **Basic Rule for Buying:** Its color should be between cream and butter, and its rind should be thin. Properly aged specimen shows smooth, velvety surface when cut. Sample for slightly sharp aftertaste.

Edammer from Holland

Character: The famous "red cannonball" of which at least 95 per cent is sold much too young and dully bland; however, properly aged EDAMMER (sometimes matured for 3 years or more) can be outstanding. It is hard to find, but always worth watching for. This cheese was named for the small town between Amsterdam and Vollendam. **Basic Rule for Buying:** After noting authentic color of red rind, check on label that cheese is produced in Holland. Except from an entirely trustworthy merchant, never buy a whole cheese without first cutting and tasting it. When comparing two cheeses, the older one is always darker yellow; when too young, the texture is creamy, and when properly aged it is dry and crumbly. We often order aged Edammer by mail* from authentic Dutch sources in the U.S., or even direct from Holland.

Emmenthaler from Switzerland

Of all cheeses in the world, EMMENTHALER is probably the most abused, most imitated, and most misunderstood. It is the best known of the three famous Swiss-cheeses-with-holes, and it is what one should get if one is foolish enough to ask simply for "half a pound of Swiss cheese, please." However, there is no copyright on the word "Swiss," hence there are thousands of pale imitations all over the world. In fact, in our opinion, the authentic Swiss producers seem to have lost heart and are sending only their blander and less interesting Emmenthalers to the United States. In Switzerland, it can be extremely good; at home, we usually replace it by Gruyère. However, we often suggest to friends that they taste the three principal Swiss cheeses (Appenzeller, Emmenthaler, and Gruyère) side by side, then decide which they prefer. **Basic Rule for Buying:** Never ask for "Swiss cheese," always specify by name; at least be fair to Emmenthaler and get an authentic Swiss one by looking for the word "Switzerland" stenciled all over the outer rind.

Feta from Greece

Character: A most unusual goat's-milk cheese which, in the authentic Greek version, is sold from a wooden tub where it is kept soaking in a mixture of milk and brine; at home, it should be stored tightly sealed to keep moist. FETA has an outstanding and unusual goats' milk flavor; it is excellent for eating as is or for grilling or melting in various Greek dishes (see Index) . **Basic Rule for Buying:** Purchase feta from a Greek store if possible, and always ask for the "imported sharp type"; the "mild type" is usually a very bland version made in Wisconsin and sold, not from a wet tub but dry from the refrigerator. Authentic Greek feta is white.

Gloucester and Double-Gloucester from England

Character: These are in fact two cheeses, and it is vital to understand the differences between them—the "Double" means, very roughly, double in size, but it also means cheese aged for about double the length of time. GLOUCESTER is sold while still young and creamy and is comparatively uninteresting; DOUBLE-GLOUCESTER on the other hand, when properly aged, is one of the most magnificently pungent of all British cheeses. The name refers not so much to the county as to the Gloucester breed of cow. **Basic Rule for Buying:** Make sure, first, that cheese is authentic English import, aged from 6 to 12 months, and not a pale imitation from elsewhere; the color of an authentic cheese should be carroty-yellow, and the outside rind should be either reddish-yellow or straw-colored. The finest Double-Gloucester is hard to find, but it can be ordered direct from England.⌘

Gouda from Holland

Character: This famous cheese is almost always sold much too young, when it is quite bland and interesting only for the richness and creaminess of its texture. In Holland, however, farmhouse-made GOUDA, properly aged, can be a magnificent cheese. It is named for the commune of Gouda near Rotterdam. **Basic Rule for Buying:** It comes in many sizes, from "babies" of about ½ pound (almost always the worst quality), through flattened balls of about 1 to 2 pounds, to large wheels. Except from an entirely trustworthy merchant, never buy a whole Gouda uncut. The relative ages of two cheeses can be roughly judged by the color of a fresh-made cut—straw-yellow when very young, growing darker with age. In the finest cheeses the paste is dotted with tiny, often irregularly shaped holes; the best cheeses are farmhouse-made and have the words *Boerenkaas Holland* (farmer cheese) stenciled in gray ink on the outside of the rind.

Gruyère from Switzerland

Character: One of the truly great and unique cheeses of the world, by far the finest, we think, of the three Swiss-cheeses-with-holes—we mean, of course, the authentic natural cheese cut from a large wheel and NOT the dreadful processed stuff that comes in small foil-wrapped triangles in flat round cardboard boxes! Gruyère is the name of a Swiss district, but authentic GRUYÈRE is made all over Switzerland and also in French Alpine districts just across the Swiss border; hundreds of worthless imitations are made all around the world. True Gruyère, when properly aged, has an extraordinary dry and nutty texture, with an entirely unique, slightly salty flavor. We think it should be used wherever "Swiss cheese" is called for in a recipe or on a menu. **Basic Rule for Buying:** While Appenzeller is dotted with pinhole eyes and Emmenthaler has eyes roughly the size of cherries, Gruyère has eyes about the size of peas; mature cheese is ivory to pale yellow in color and each eye is wet inside with very salty fluid. Authentic Swiss-made cheese is stenciled all over the outer rind with the word "Switzerland," but remember that this is only a guarantee of origin and not necessarily of properly aged cheese. The French version has no rind markings and should be bought only from a trustworthy merchant.

Kasseri from Greece

Character: KASSERI is an excellent ewe's'-milk cheese with a strongly individual, slightly winy flavor and somewhat grainy texture, faintly like a very young Parmesan. It is generally hard to find, but worth watching for. **Basic Rule for Buying:** Choose only an authentic imported Greek version—try Greek neighborhood stores, or if there is no other way (and only in cool weather), order it by mail.*

Münster from Alsace

Character: MÜNSTER is the great creamy-textured cheese made in farmhouses in the high valleys of the Vosges Mountains and in small factories in cities from Colmar to Strasbourg. It should NEVER be confused with the bland and uninteresting "American Munster" of the supermarkets or with equally pale imitations from countries other than France or Germany. Authentic, well-ripened Münster has a powerful personality and dominant boquet. It is a safe cheese to buy. **Basic Rule for Buying:** First, make sure it is of the true Alsatian type, with a brick-red outer rind and bright yellow paste (never with caraway seeds), which comes in wheels from about ½ pound to about 3 pounds. Never buy a small whole cheese prepackaged, except from an entirely reliable merchant; it is better to buy a wedge cut from a larger wheel, and ask the cheese-man to cut off a thin slice for tasting, then watch whether the slice bends away from the knife or stands up straight like a stiff board—in the first instance, it will be milder and creamier; in the second, drier and stronger. It is best to buy Münster only from November to April.

Provolone from Italy

Character: PROVOLONE might be called the standard "cheddar" of southern Italy; it is usually strung from the ceiling in neighborhood Italian groceries. *Provo* means "oval" and refers to the usual shape of the whole cheese, banded with thick and greasy string, but the cheese may also be sausage-shaped, pear-shaped, or round (see cacio a cavallo) and comes in every size, from very small (5 pounds) to enormous (200 pounds). Nowadays it is usually made from cows' milk, but it still has a sharp salty sting reminiscent of ewes' milk. **Basic Rule for Buying:** The large size is called "Provolone," the small, "Provolette." First make sure that cheese is authentic Italian, since imitations are worthless, then taste and choose one of two types: *dolce* ("soft"—but had better be defined as "very strong"!) or *piccante* ("sharp"—but best defined as "knockout sharp"!). When the cheese is too young, its texture is soft and waxy; when properly aged, it is dry and crumbly, and mature cheese should be honey-colored. Buy cheese preferably from a neighborhood Italian grocer and look for deep grooves on the outside rind where the string has bitten-in from long hanging.

Queso Manchego from Spain

Character: A most unusual and charmingly unsophisticated (yet with strong personality) farmhouse-made ewe's-milk cheese from Don Quixote's province of La Mancha. Since authentic cheeses are virtually all made by farm families and there are apparently no factories, there is considerable variety in taste and texture; however, the sense of responsibility of the Spanish farmers is such that we have never found a bad one. QUESO MANCHEGO is a rare type, but well worth the trouble of getting. **Basic Rule for Buying:** We know of one authentic source in New York City, which will also ship by mail.* However, since the cheese is quite creamy, this should be attempted only during cold weather.

Sage from Vermont

Character: SAGE is one of the best American country-style cheeses; basically, it is a simple cheddar paste mixed with coarsely ground dried sage leaf, which gives it a delightfully fresh flavor and slightly crunchy texture. **Basic Rule for Buying:** Sage can be found at some cheese merchants, but it is seldom as good as it should be; it is far better to order a whole cheese of about 5 pounds direct from a Vermont farmer-producer.*

"Swiss Cheese"

This ubiquitous title should, we think, be entirely eliminated from the vocabulary of cheese. Literally, of course, it means any cheese made in Switzerland, but by long tradition it has come to be used, first, only for the blandest and dullest types of Swiss cheeses-with-large-holes and, second (and far worse), for any cheese-with-holes made anywhere else in the world. The quality of these imitations varies from just edible to tasteless soap! Instead of asking for "Swiss cheese," one should know the names of the authentic types from Switzerland: Appenzeller, Emmenthaler, or Gruyère (see under these names).

Wensleydale from England

Character: One of the greatest, but least known, of British farmhouse cheeses from the gloriously beautiful and unspoiled valley in the Pennine Mountains in the county of Yorkshire. It has a unique and magnificent flavor, with crumbly and grainy texture when properly aged. WENSLEYDALE has been made in the valley for more than 1,000 years; some is also made in local factories, but it is noticeably less good. Farmhouse Wensleydale is very rarely available through U. S. cheese merchants. **Basic Rule for Buying:** It is best to order the cheeses direct from England,* specifying "farm-made," but do not attempt this except during cold weather. (See also entry on Blue Wensleydale.)

2. *The Natural Blue-Veined Cheeses*

In the early days of cheese-making, a blue-veined cheese was an accident of nature. There is the famous story of the French shepherd boy on the high plateaux of the Cévennes Mountains near the village of Roquefort, who, one hot day, decided to keep his bread-and-cheese lunch cool by placing it on a rock ledge in a cave on the slope of a nearby hill. A few minutes later, his herd was attacked by a wolf and in the excitement he forgot his lunch. Next day, he was assigned to a different herd on the other side of the village. He did not remember his missed lunch until about three months later and idly climbed up to the cave. He was not surprised to find the bread moldy and inedible, but the piece of cheese was interestingly shot through with jagged blue lines. It had been attacked by a penicillin-type mold floating in the air of the cave. Courageously, the shepherd boy tasted it, and—Roquefort cheese was born.

For many decades all blue-veined cheeses were produced by this natural, selective process. Then scientists isolated the various molds, so that they could be injected into the cheese through copper needles. Yet it was still a natural process, with time allowed for the normal development of the molds.

Today, however, vast quantities of so-called "blue cheese" are artificially produced at high speed with a kind of "ready-mix" of pre-prepared blue mold forced into the cheeses at high pressure. We find an unpleasant artificiality in the flavor of such cheeses and none of them (not even the world-famous ones) are included in the following list.

Blue Cheshire from England

Character: Perhaps the rarest, most magnificent, and most luxurious of all cheeses. It is produced entirely by natural selection—a very few 50-pound wheels of Cheshire cheese, kept long enough at the right temperature and humidity, develop the internal blue mold; the chances are about 1 in 1,000, hence BLUE CHESHIRE is a collector's item. It is never available through U. S. cheese merchants. **Basic Rule for Buying:** Disregard the expense and have a piece flown over by refrigerated air freight from authentic sources in England*; this should only be attempted in cold weather and special arrangements must be made for fast pick-up from the airport, as any lengthy period at warm temperature will cause the cheese to overripen and lose its extraordinary delicacy.

Blue Wensleydale from England

Character: Originally it was made exactly as Blue Cheshire, but now, there is limited production in small local factories of BLUE WENSLEYDALE; the internal mold is "induced" by injection. After proper aging, it is a magnificent cheese, always rivaling and often surpassing the famous Stilton. Blue Wensleydale is never available through U. S. cheese merchants. **Basic Rule for Buying:** Order it by mail from England.* Blue Wensleydale is much less perishable than Blue Cheshire and can be sent by fast refrigerated ocean freight; the English shippers will advise about the exact requirements.

Gorgonzola from Italy

Character: Magnificently creamy, buttery-yellow, with green rather than blue veins, GORGONZOLA is so soft at room temperature as to be almost spreadable. We place it second only to Roquefort, among the greatest of all "blues." Gorgonzola originated in the village of that name near Milan and is now one of that town's major industries. **Basic Rule for Buying:** First make sure that the cheese is authentic Italian—one test is that the green veins should be in jagged lines, more truly like "veins" than the mottled formation of other blues. Italian Gorgonzola is one of the safest cheeses to buy, since the export association maintains tight quality control; however, local merchants can ruin cheese by improper storage, so it is best to buy from a neighborhood Italian grocery.

Norwegian Blue from Norway

Character: NORWEGIAN BLUE CHEESE is of outstanding quality, now being fairly widely distributed in the United States. Extremely tight quality controls are maintained by Norway's export board in order to build the reputation of the cheese. Generally two types are available: the best is farmhouse-made, with blue veins developing naturally during storage; the less expensive is factory-made, with veins "induced" by injection. If demand develops and distribution widens, it may become one of the best of the easily available fine blue cheeses. **Basic Rule for Buying:** First make sure that the cheese is an authentic Norwegian import, then check whether it is farm- or factory-made. It is a safe cheese to buy.

Roquefort from France

Character: The greatest of the "blue" cheeses, perhaps of all cheeses, is ROQUEFORT. Its extraordinary gastronomic impact comes, we think, from the sharp contrast between the almost austere, crumbly simplicity and saltiness of this white ewe's-milk cheese and its rich, soft, luxurious layers of mottled blue mold. It is still made in caves around the town of Roquefort but now on a vast scale with extra miles of space tunneled out of the rock. The production quality is tightly controlled by a huge cooperative association; one entire subdivision is devoted to making slightly milder cheeses considered most popular in American markets. **Basic Rule for Buying:** Look first for the "Red Sheep" seal on the foil wrapping, then for the name of the particular "cave group" where the cheese was made—our favorite is "Société B," dramatized on English labels as "Society Bee" with a picture of a bee. Do not buy Roquefort in small foil-wrapped segments, too small to continue ripening, but in cuts from a larger wheel (judge its age by taste and by the degree of mottling); best of all, buy a whole cheese, about 5½ pounds, place it in a handsome round covered casserole, raise it off the bottom about ⅜ inch so that brine can collect underneath, then dig it out as needed from the top with a silver spoon, being careful to use up whiter, outer cheese equally with mottled center. Properly handled in this way, it *would* keep for months if it were not so habit-forming!

Stilton from England

Character: We place STILTON third among the "great blues"; it is a cheese with a very strong individuality—it is dry, where Roquefort is moist; firm, where Gorgonzola is soft; a sparse and muscular cheese, rather than a rich and indolent one. None is ever made in the British parish of Stilton, but many magnificent specimens are still farmhouse- or factory-made (in small local plants under tight quality controls), hence Stilton is a safe cheese to buy. **Basic Rule for Buying:** First make sure that the cheese is authentic English, then check degree of aging—it should be dry and crumbly; the brown rind should be "crinkly"; and its color should be yellowed ivory darkening around the edge toward amber. Choose a cheese with mellow flavor. Some British producers now make small cheeses of 3 to 5 pounds, called "minors," and this is the ideal way to buy. Store and "dig down" as described for Roquefort (see above). Stilton "minors" can be ordered direct from England.✲

3. The Soft After-Dinner Cheeses

An American gourmet who has never tasted Brie or Camembert in Paris or London or anywhere else in Europe must face the fact that he has never really tasted Brie or Camembert. The true versions of these superb cheeses are forbidden entry into the United States by federal law. The theory behind this nonsensical policy is that the so-called "soft, freshly ripened" cheeses are not sanitarily safe enough to be passed through cosseted American mouths, unless the milk from which they are made is first pasteurized. This is murder to cheese which depends for its life on benign bacteria. In Paris when one brings home a Camembert, it continues to develop day by day and one controls its ripening exactly to one's taste, just as one controls the ripening of a banana or a peach. In New York when one buys a French Camembert, pasteurized for export to the U.S., the cheese is often chalky-white in the center, and absolutely nothing can be done about it because the cheese is dead. This must be remembered when buying many of the cheeses listed below.

Brie from France

Character: At its best, BRIE is the greatest of all soft cheeses; it is never worth eating until it is "quite runny," then there are three ways of eating it, according to taste: for strongest flavor, eat the center with the rind and the outside fluffy white mold; for less strength, first scrape off and discard mold; for sissies, eat only the center, discarding all rind. **Basic Rule for Buying:** Choose only authentic French imports cut from large rounds about 10 to 12 inches across; never buy it in small round Camembert-size boxes; never buy it without cutting it open first and making sure that the cheese is soft all the way through. Buy Brie only from October to April.

Camembert from France

Character: CAMEMBERT is the second greatest of the soft cheeses; it has the same general points as Brie (see above). **Basis Rule for Buying:** Look for the square seal on the box label marked "Veritable Camembert de Normandie" and always choose a single round in the box, never the foil-wrapped triangular portions. Since the cheese should not be cut open in advance, learn to judge by appearance, feel, and smell—open the inner paper wrapping and see that the crust is golden, with patches of fluffy white mold; if the cheese has shrunk in the box, it is too old and has dried out; press center: it should be soft and resilient; if it smells of ammonia, it has begun to go bad. Buy Camembert only from October to June, the best months being January to April.

Hablé Crème Chantilly from Sweden

Character: HABLÉ CRÈME CHANTILLY is an outstanding cheese with a silky texture and a flavor faintly like sautéed truffles and walnuts; it comes in triangular chipboard boxes. **Basic Rule for Buying:** The authentic cheese is labeled "Old Walla." When properly ripened it should feel slightly soft. Buy it only during cool months.

Le Banon from France

Character: One of the best of a large family of small goat's-milk cheeses, a slightly smaller round than an authentic Camembert, LE BANON comes wrapped in chestnut leaves, always alleged to have been dipped in brandy. It has a simple, unsophisticated flavor, not outstanding, but with refreshing country-picnic quality. **Basic Rule for Buying:** The true French version is always labeled as shipped through Marseilles. Also, a very fair Canadian imitation is made in Iberville, Quebec.

Liederkranz from the United States

Character: One of the best of native mass-produced cheeses, its name is actually a copyrighted trademark, owned by a large dairy company. As LIEDERKRANZ ages, it can become very strong and smelly. **Basic Rule for Buying:** Each cheese is marked with an "expiration" date—the closer one comes to this date, the more one is likely to "expire" from an overwhelming odor. Buy, according to taste, by dateline!

Liptauer, or Liptai, or Liptoi, from Hungary

Character: A simple farmhouse-made, cottage-type, milk-curd cheese from the agricultural districts of the Hortobagy plain from cows', ewes', or goats' milk, or a combination of them. It has a refreshingly sharp sour-milk flavor but is seldom eaten by itself without first being blended with aromatics to make an appetizer cheese spread (see recipe following). **Basic Rule for Buying:** Make sure, first, it is made of authentic Hungarian cheese, which comes in a large wooden tub and is dug out with a small wooden scoop. It is available from Hungarian specialty stores.* Also it is sometimes sold ready-spiced, but it is far better to buy the fresh cheese and do one's own blending. . . .

BASIC METHOD FOR MAKING AROMATIC LIPTAUER CHEESE SPREAD

For our family of 4

Check Staples:
Salt butter (1 Tbs.)
Aromatics: dill salt, Hungarian medium-hot paprika*
Parsley (enough for about 2 Tbs., chopped)
Green scallion tops (4 to 5 stalks)

Shopping List:
Hungarian Liptauer cheese (½ lb.)
Sour cream (2 to 3 Tbs.)

A Few Hours Before Serving—Allow Time for Flavors to Blend and Mature

Put cheese into a medium-sized mixing bowl, then break it up, preferably with a wooden fork. Now begin lightly blending in the aromatics for flavor, the softened butter and sour cream for spreadable texture, and the paprika for pale-orange color. We use up to 1 tablespoon of paprika, with enough finely chopped parsley and scallion to give a heavy speckling of green, plus plenty of dill salt. (With experience, these amounts are adjusted to personal taste.) Then we spoon the spread lightly into an earthenware crock, cover and refrigerate it for several hours. Then bring it back to room temperature and serve on triangles of dark pumpernickel bread. Not much usually remains, but it keeps almost indefinitely, tightly covered and refrigerated.

True Mozzarella Italian Style

Character: When this simple ball of rubbery cheese is made fresh every morning by an old Italian cheese-maker, it is a charming cheese to slice and eat fresh—well salted and peppered—quite apart from its universal use in pizzas. However, MOZZARELLA cannot travel or be mass-produced. **Basic Rule for Buying:** First, find your Italian cheese-man—he will take the mozzarella out of a tub and it will still be wet when he wraps it. Heave a sigh of regret that it is no longer made from buffalo milk. Avoid the labeled stuff in cellophane bags, except for cooking.

Petit Suisse, or Petit Gervais, from France

Character: In France, this is the most universal of all simple double-crème cheeses; it is eaten either savory-style, salted and peppered, or dessert-style, with sugar worked in. Now it is being increasingly imported into the U.S., but of course in a pasteurized version. It was first named in honor of the Swiss cheesemaker who invented it while employed on a French farm; Gervais is the name of the original Paris cheese merchant who introduced it and made a fortune from it. **Basic Rule for Buying:** Make sure that the cheese is an authentic import, packaged either in the original French waxed-paper rolls or in special export square foil-wrapped packages, designed to compete with domestic cream cheese.

Reblochon from France

Character: REBLOCHON might be called the Camembert of the Alpine district of southeastern France; it also comes in a round chipboard box, but is usually larger, 8 to 9 inches across. It has the same general characteristics as Camembert (see). **Basic Rule for Buying:** Make sure that cheese is an authentic French import. The rind varies in color from reddish-brown to deep orange; even when ripe, it never feels quite as soft as Camembert. The inside wrapping paper must not be sticky, and there should never be any strong smell.

Taleggio from Italy

Character: A magnificently flavored cheese naturally aged in the caves on the northern plains of Lombardy. TALEGGIO is one of the finest of all soft cheeses, with a full and nutty taste and richly creamy texture inside its thickly waxed rind; outstanding for melting in fondues, etc. **Basic Rule for Buying:** An authentic Italian import has the words "Taleggio Italia" stenciled on the outer rind. Sniff close to a freshly cut surface—it should smell pleasantly mild; if the odor is strong, the cheese is already overripe and delicacy will be lost. When tasting, remember that it increases fairly rapidly in strength, even in refrigerated storage.

Triple-Crèmes Parfait from France

Character: One of the best of the comparatively new family of cheeses which are 75 per cent pure cream; perhaps the TRIPLE-CRÈMES symbolize modern "affluent society," which can produce such an extravagant excess of cream and can also provide enough people able to afford their extravagant price. We occasionally enjoy wallowing in their voluptuous texture, but have to admit to ourselves that their flavor is comparatively bland and uninteresting. Other cheeses in this family are "Boursin," "Brillat-Savarin," "Gourmandise," "Fromage Monsieur Fromage," etc. All come in small round chipboard or cardboard boxes thicker but smaller than Camembert. **Basic Rule for Buying:** Make sure the cheeses have authentic French labels; they are usually not imitated because the names are copyrighted. Judge the age by smell—it should be pleasant and mild. Remember that all become overripe within a few days, so buy only enough for virtually immediate use. Avoid accepting the first cheese the merchant picks out, since he may be trying to get rid of rapidly overaging specimens. The inside wrapping paper must appear fresh; if it is dark and sticky, beware.

4. The Hard Grating Cheeses

Parmesan, or Parmigiano-Reggiano from Italy

Character: It is certainly the greatest of hard cheeses and among the three or four greatest of all cheeses, since, when young and soft, it also makes superb eating from the after-dinner cheese board. PARMESAN is the leading member of the large family of *grana,* cheeses made up of millions of tiny crystals suspended in the paste; these can be clearly seen on close inspection of a fresh cut of Parmesan and they give it a wonderful grainy texture. The cheese is named for the fortress city of Parma. None is exported from Italy until it is at least 2 years old. Parmesan is unduplicated anywhere in the world, and hence is one of the safest of all cheeses to buy. **Basic Rule for Buying:** Authentic Italian cheeses have the words *Parmigiano-Reggiano* stenciled on the outer rind. Buy preferably from a good Italian neighborhood grocery, where finicky Italian housewife customers see to it that properly aged and dried Parmesan is available. Remember that even after 2 years it is still quite soft (very pleasant to eat chunked) and needs another year or two to dry out and harden. Well-aged cheese is pale yellow; younger cheese, whitish—but there are some white patches even on old cheese, where grains have been crushed during previous cutting. If the surface is rough with spotty spores, the cheese is too old.

Pecorino Romano from Italy

Character: PECORINO is the family name of a group of cheeses made from ewes' milk; it is much saltier than Parmesan and not as fine in flavor. The cheese is usually made by shepherds in their huts on upland pastures behind Rome; several other pecorinos are made in other parts of Italy—all are interesting variations. **Basic Rule for Buying:** Authentic pecorino cheese has a yellow crust, and a fresh cut should be straw-colored; make sure that cheese is hard and dry.

Pecorino Pepato from Sicily

Character: It is a spiced form of pecorino, with the paste dotted with whole black peppercorns. PECORINO PEPATO is a useful occasional variation. **Basic Rule for Buying:** Same as for pecorino Romano (see).

Sapsago from Switzerland

Character: SAPSAGO is a strangely shaped little cheese, like a truncated cone about 2 to 3 inches long, called *stockli,* filled with finely ground aromatic clover; it has a pungent, earthy flavor and a scent of hay. It is very hard and should be used for grating only; it is good worked into butter as a sandwich spread. **Basic Rule for Buying:** It presents no special problem, since the cheese has never been imitated. Each small cone comes individually wrapped in paper marked "Genuine Swiss Green Cheese"; the packaging itself also gives sound advice—do not use too much, since sapsago is powerful.

Sardo from Sardinia

Character: Very hard and pungently salty, SARDO is the famous member of the pecorino family, which comes in round black cannonballs, each weighing about 5 pounds. However, it seems that less and less is being made and authentic sardo is becoming quite rare. Fortunately, a fairly good imitation is made in Argentina; it comes in normal 5- to 7-pound wheels. **Basic Rule for Buying:** Check that the cheese is authentic: note the black rind. It should be too hard to cut and is broken off in irregular pieces with steel wedge and hammer.

Sbrinz, Saanen, or Spalen from Switzerland

Character: These are comparatively little-known hard cheeses now being increasingly exported from Switzerland under tight quality controls; none are released for sale until they are at least 3 years old. They might be defined as grating forms of Gruyère, with the usual eyes. Some of these cheeses have been proved to remain edible up to 100 years; many connoisseurs consider them almost as majestically great as Parmesan. **Basic Rule for Buying:** Make sure they are of authentic Swiss origin; these cheeses can hardly be imitated.

OUR DIRECTORY OF WINES FOR THE TABLE

THIS IS A personal list of the wines and spirits we have enjoyed. For more than twenty years we have noted our ratings on small colored cards—red cards for red wines, pink for *rosés,* etc. All are from reliable producers and shippers and they represent fair value at every price level. We have deliberately avoided suggesting particular vintage years, since each wine merchant carries a different range and it is best to discuss with him the available choices. Every one of the following labels may not always be on hand, but most of them are in stock in warehouses in major cities and can usually be obtained within a few days. The order of the directory is as follows:

Spanish Sherry and Sherry-Type Wines

The Famous Brands—**Basic Rule for Buying:** The easiest, though relatively expensive way is to look for the brands of famous companies (often with English names of original founders) from the usually heavily promoted, hence high-priced Spanish Sherry capital, Jerez-de-la-Frontera, or from London or Bristol. The two principal before-dinner types are the Finos and Amontillados.

FINOS

Character: light and dry, each carefully blended to the same flavor year after year. **Our choice:**

LA INA, shipped by Pedro Domecq of Jerez
OLIVAR, shipped by Wisdom & Warter of Jerez
PALE DRY, shipped by Rolson & Brown of London
PANDO, shipped by Williams & Humbert of Jerez
PINTA, shipped by Duff Gordon of Jerez
SAN PATRICIO, shipped by Garvey of Jerez
TIO PEPE, shipped by Gonzalez, Byass, of Jerez (The name means "Uncle Joe," in honor of an uncle of one of the original owners who as a hobby in his retirement developed this famous Sherry.)
VICTORIA, shipped by Bobadilla of Jerez

AMONTILLADOS

Character: fuller-bodied and softer; also blended. **Our choice:**

CECILIA, shipped by Findlater of London
DON FEDERICO, shipped by Croft of London
DRY SACK, shipped by Williams & Humbert of Jerez (Sack was the term for Sherry in Shakespeare's time, because the casks came wrapped in sacks, as do the modern Dry Sack bottles.)
SHOOTING, shipped by Harvey of Bristol

The Lesser-Known Types—**Basic Rule for Buying:** Exploring unusual wines from districts other than Jerez is a more venturesome and less expensive way of buying Sherry; one pays virtually nothing for promotion, everything for the wine, hence prices are often half of those of famous brands. Make sure that district name is on label. **Our choice:**

MONTILLAS

Character: Sherry-type wines from the Montilla-Moriles district, refreshingly light, yet with power and an almost sharp dryness, ideal for raising the appetite. **Our choice:**

MONTILLA MUNDA
MONTILLA SOLERA FINA

MANZANILLAS

Character: faintly salty Sherries from the seacoast of Sanlúcar de Barrameda, in our opinion, second only to the Montillas as ideal before-dinner appetizers. **Our choice:**

MANZANILLA LA GUITA ("The String," with a string attached to the neck of the bottle near the cork.)

MANZANILLA LA GITANA ("The Gypsy Girl")

MANZANILLA LA LUNA

Other Aperitifs—Madeira and Vermouths

THE FORTIFIED WINES OF MADEIRA

Character: delicately flavored, yet full-bodied and powerful wines from the Portuguese island of that name, ranging from dry to very sweet, the latter better for after dinner. **Basic Rule for Buying:** Choose first by general name of dry types: Sercial or Rainwater (sweet types are Boal or Malmsey). **Our choice:**

BELLOWS RAINWATER

BLANDYS "DUKE OF SUSSEX" SERCIAL

COLUMBUS SERCIAL

LEACOCK'S SERCIAL

NOBREGA LIGHT RAINWATER

VERMOUTHS

Italian Sweet and Light

Character: moderately sweet aperitifs for drinking unmixed. **Our choice:**

GANCIA BIANCO, from Turin

CINZANO BIANCO, from Turin

French Dry

Character: vermouths with strong personalities, better mixed, especially with Cassis, the black-currant syrup of Dijon. **Our choice:**

DRY BOISSIÈRE, from Chambéry

DRY DOLIN, from Chambéry

DRY NOILLY PRAT, from Marseilles

The Great, Dominant Red Wines of Bordeaux

Character: the most magnificent of all red wines, worth the large investment. **Basic Rule for Buying:** Château names absolutely dependable, the district in which each château is located being relatively unimportant with these great names. Ask wine merchant's advice as to prices of various vintage years, remembering that the word "château" is essential part of the identification. **Universal choice:**

CHÂTEAU AUSONE, said to have been first planted with vines by the Roman poet Ausonius in the fourth century and still producing wine of astonishing quality

CHÂTEAU CHEVAL BLANC (White Horse), producing a wine that is often called "incomparable"

CHÂTEAU HAUT-BRION, owned by the American Dillon family and producing a sumptuous wine of rich purple

CHÂTEAU LAFITE, or LAFITE-ROTHSCHILD, often called "the greatest red wine vineyard in the world"

CHÂTEAU LATOUR (The Tower), producing a rich and powerful wine (However, one should not confuse this wine with that produced by the many châteaux having the words "La Tour" as part of their name; the label of the great "Chateau Latour" bears a stylized tower surmounted by a lion.)

CHÂTEAU MARGAUX, producing a wine that feels like velvet and has the distant fragrance of wild violets (However, one must read the label carefully and remember that there are several quite ordinary wines labeled simply "Margaux," produced by small vineyards in the village of that name, but only one great "Château Margaux.")

CHÂTEAU MOUTON-ROTHSCHILD, producing a wine that is often called "the most powerful and robust of all Bordeaux reds"

CHÂTEAU PETRUS, producing a wine that is often described as "clean and crisp"

The Great Red Burgundies

Character: the most powerful and seductive of all red wines, worldwide demand making them the most expensive of all. **Basic Rule for Buying:** Because different vineyards, widely varied in quality, often have virtually the same names, look first for the name of the village, then the *precise* name of the vineyard, remembering that the many great vineyards are broken up among various owners, each more or less making different wines. **Our choice:**

From the Village of Aloxe-Corton

LE CORTON, producing some of the finest red wines of all Burgundy (However, here again one must note the label carefully, for there are several quite ordinary wines simply named "Corton," which are wines from the smaller vineyards of the village, but there is only one great "Le Corton.")

From the Village of Chambolle-Musigny

MUSIGNY, producing some of the most exquisitely delicate wines of Burgundy, especially those under the label of the principal owner, Comte Georges de Vogüé.

From the Village of Flagey-Échézeaux

LES GRANDS ÉCHÉZEAUX

From the Village of Gevrey-Chambertin

LE CHAMBERTIN, producing wines that have been famous for more than a thousand years (The name comes from "Le Champs de Bertin," in honor of a farmer named Bertin who discovered that one corner of one of his fields had perfect soil for growing magnificent wine grapes.)

CHAMBERTIN-CLOS DE BÉZE, the word *clos* meaning a vineyard enclosed by a high stone wall

From the Village of Vosne-Romanée

ROMANÉE-CONTI, producing one of the greatest red wines of the world, a wine which caresses the tongue and has a fragrance of the spice islands of the Orient

LA ROMANÉE, LA TÂCHE } these two producing wines of almost equal magnificence

LE RICHEBOURG, producing a wine which has the same character as the others but is more powerful and of a deeper color

From the Village of Vougeot

LE CLOS VOUGEOT, one of the most famous of all vineyards, originally part of the ancient Cistercian monastery (However, the label must be read carefully, for there are several quite average wines named simply "Vougeot," produced by lesser vineyards in the village, and only the wines with the word "Clos" *in front* of the village name are from the great vineyard.)

The Middle Range of the Fine Red Bordeaux

Character: enormous range of types, from light and delicate to dark and strong, often depending on the year, from more than 4,000 named vineyards. **Basic Rule for Buying:** Choose by the château name; gradually learn to recognize special characteristics shared by wines from each major district shown on labels, until a pattern of preference emerges. **Our choice** (some almost as famous and expensive as "greats," others ranging down to quite modest):

CHÂTEAU BEYCHEVELLE, a wine which often represents an exceptional value

CHÂTEAU CALON-SÉGUR, generally soft and fine

CHÂTEAU CERTAN

CHÂTEAU CHASSE-SPLEEN, a wine that has often "chased away our spleen"

CHÂTEAU LA CLOTTE, delicate and fragrant, should always be opened and allowed to "breathe" for an hour or so before being drunk

CHÂTEAU COS D'ESTOURNEL

COUVENT DES JACOBINS, the ancient convent, still producing wines which are often an excellent value

CHÂTEAU FIGEAC, producing wines so good as to be close to the "greats"

CHÂTEAU LA GRACE DIEU, one of the less well-known vineyards, producing wines often of exceptional value

CHÂTEAU GRUAUD LAROSE, one of the finest vineyards in Bordeaux, producing a delicate and silky wine

CHÂTEAU HAUT-BAILLY, a strong and sturdy wine

CHÂTEAU LASCOMBES, now American-owned

CHÂTEAU LYNCH-BAGES, a robust and powerful wine
CHÂTEAU PALMER, another wine so good as to be almost great
CHÂTEAU TALBOT, another wine among the finest of Bordeaux
CHÂTEAU LA VIEILLE CLOCHE, another less well-known vineyard with wines often of extraordinary value

The Middle Range of Fine Red Burgundies

Character: Again, an enormous range, from wines of famous vineyards almost as magnificent as the "greats" to simple community wines, blended from grapes of many smaller vineyards, their names carrying only the villages or districts where they were grown. **Basic Rule for Buying:** As with the great Burgundies, look first for the name of the village and then the *precise* name of the vineyard, and gradually learn names of owners with greatest wine-making skill. With less expensive wines, especially community and district wines where there are no vineyard names, rely on names of famous shippers. **Our choice:**

From the Town of Beaune

CLOS DES MOUCHES, shipped by Joseph Drouhin

From the Village of Gevrey-Chambertin

CLOS SAINT-JACQUES, a wine so good as to be rated almost with the "greats"

From the Village of Morey-Saint-Denis

CLOS DE TART, another wine among the finest of Burgundy

From the Village of Nuits-Saint-Georges

LES SAINT-GEORGES, again one of the finest wines

From One of the Dependable Vineyards of the Village of Pommard
(The name Pommard itself is no guarantee of quality)

LES ÉPENOTS, a soft, warm wine

From the Neighboring and Rival Village of Volnay

LES CAILLERETS, a wine with gaiety and charm

From the Various Communities and Districts Which Lend Their Names to the Cheaper Blended Wines (And Here the Shipper Is All-Important)

CÔTE DE BEAUNE-VILLAGES, shipped by Joseph Drouhin
CÔTE DE BEAUNE-VILLAGES, shipped by Louis Latour
FIXIN, shipped by Jean de Besse
GEVREY-CHAMBERTIN, shipped by Bouchard
GEVREY-CHAMBERTIN PREMIER CRU, shipped by Louis Latour
SAVIGNY-MARCONNETS, shipped by Jean de Besse

The Fine Red Wines of the Rhône

Character: the most southerly reds of France, "roasted" by hot Mediterranean sunshine, dark and powerful. **Basic Rule for Buying:** Choose first by names of three famous districts—Châteauneuf-du-Pape, Côte Rôtie, L'Hermitage. Remember that district names in themselves offer no guarantee of quality, since each has a few extremely good producers, some very poor ones. Within each district, look for names of vineyards and/or reliable shippers. **Our choice:**

From the District of Châteauneuf-du-Pape

LA BERNARDINE, shipped by Marc Chapoutier
CHÂTEAU FORTIA, one of the best vineyards of the district
SAINT ESPRIT, shipped by Delas Frères
CHÂTEAU DE VAUDIEU, always dependable, sometimes splendid

From the District of the Côte Rôtie

BRUNE ET BLONDE, shipped by Marc Chapoutier

From the District of the Hermitage, Which Produces What Has Been Called "the Manliest of All Wines"

MURE DE LA SIZERANNE, shipped by Marc Chapoutier

The Fine Red Wines of Italy

BAROLO (From Lake Garda)

Character: the best of all Italian reds, often with extraordinary depth and subtlety of taste. **Our choice:**

BAROLO, produced and shipped under the label of the Marchese di Barolo

CHIANTI (From Tuscany)

Character: simple peasant wine, much abused all over the world. **Basic Rule for Buying:** Always buy chianti, not in the straw-covered *fiaschi* bottles but in normal straight-sided, Bordeaux-type bottles, and look for the older vintages in the small area between Florence and Siena known as *Chianti Classico,* which carry the small *Marca di Gallo* (the Black Rooster) label on the shoulder of the bottle. Learn to recognize the famous vineyards and the great chianti-producing families. **Our choice:**

CHIANTI BROLIO, produced and shipped under the label of the Barone Ricasoli

CHIANTI MACHIAVELLI, produced and shipped under the label of the Conte Serristori

CHIANTI MELETO, produced and shipped under the label of the Barone Ricasoli

CHIANTI TENUTA, produced and shipped under the label of the Marchese Antinori

The Reasonably Priced Everyday Red Wines

THE GOOD AMERICAN REDS

Character: the greatest reds, grown from transplanted European grapes, come from northern California, absolutely equal to their similar-priced European leave California, but some excellent ones do have national distribution. Rougher peasant wines, grown from native American grapes, come from Ohio island vineyards on Lake Erie. **Basic Rule for Buying:** Best American wines carry "varietal" labels, in which name of grape defines character of wine. Avoid such misleading phrases as "Burgundy-type" or "claret-type." **Our choice:**

From the Northern Vineyards of California

LIGHT RED CABERNET SAUVIGNON, from the vineyards of Beaulieu in the Napa Valley, reasonably available all over the country

LIGHT RED CABERNET SAUVIGNON, from the vineyards of Concannon in the Livermore Valley, generally available in the West and in major Eastern cities

LIGHT RED CABERNET SAUVIGNON, from the vineyards of Inglenook in the Napa Valley, generally available in the West and to a limited extent in other parts of the country

LIGHT RED CABERNET SAUVIGNON, from the vineyards of Mayacamas in the Napa Valley, available only in California

DARK RED PINOT NOIR, from the vineyards of Beaulieu in the Napa Valley, reasonably available all over the country

DARK RED PINOT NOIR, from the vineyards of Inglenook in the Napa Valley, generally available in the West and to a limited extent in other parts of the country

DARK RED PINOT NOIR, from the vineyards of Louis M. Martini in the Napa Valley, reasonably available all over the country

From the Lake Erie Vineyards of Ohio

OHIO "ISLE ST. GEORGE" MELLOW RED, from the Meier's vineyards, available mainly in the Middle West

The Best Red Wines of Spain

Character: some quite extraordinarily good light reds from the high upland Rioja district of Aragon—usually offered at such low prices that they are among the best values in all red wines. **Basic Rule for Buying:** Lighter, younger wines are labeled *clarete;* more full-bodied and older ones are called *gran reserva.* Famous shippers are the best insurance of quality. **Our choice:**

RIOJA GRAN RESERVA POMAL, shipped by the Bodegas Bilbainas

RIOJA CLARETE, produced and shipped under the label of the Marqués de Murrieta

RIOJA CLARETE, produced and shipped under the label of the Marqués de Riscal

Two Everyday Red Wines from Italy

Character: both Bardolino and Valpolicella from districts around Verona and Lake Garda can be charming and refreshing. **Basic Rule for Buying:** Reliable shippers names are all-important, since both wines are almost always blended. Bardolino so light in color that it is halfway to a *rosé* and in hot weather can be *very* slightly chilled. **Our choice:**

- BARDOLINO, shipped by Bolla from the village of Bardolino on the shore of Lake Garda
- BARDOLINO, shipped by Folonari
- VALPOLICELLA, fragrant and fruity, shipped by Bertani from Verona
- VALPOLICELLA, shipped by Bolla from Verona
- VALPOLICELLA, shipped by one of the cooperative cellars called Cantina Sociale in the village of Negrar

THE YOUNG WINES OF BEAUJOLAIS

Character: enormously variable. **Basic Rule for Buying:** Anyone who buys a wine simply labeled "Beaujolais" has only himself to blame. Beaujolais must be associated with one or other of the famous legally defined village communes or districts, such as Brouilly, Fleurie, Juliénas, and Moulin-à-Vent, where it is required that grapes shall be made and grown on local ground. If listed, the name of an honorable shipper is an added guarantee of quality. **Our choice:**

- BEAUJOLAIS-BROUILLY, an outstanding young wine, shipped by Jean de Besse
- BEAUJOLAIS-BROUILLY "COURONNE D'OR"
- BEAUJOLAIS FLEURIE CHÂTEAU DES LABOURONS, shipped by the Comte de Lescure
- BEAUJOLAIS CHÂTEAU DE JULIÉNAS
- BEAUJOLAIS MOULIN-À-VENT CHÂTEAU DE CHENAS
- BEAUJOLAIS SUPÉRIEUR, shipped by Bouchard Père et Fils
- BEAUJOLAIS SUPÉRIEUR, shipped by Louis Latour

EVERYDAY REGIONAL WINES FROM THE RHÔNE

Basic Rule for Buying: The regional name "Côtes-du-Rhône" offers no guarantee of quality without the added name of a reliable shipper. **Our choice:**

- CÔTE DU RHÔNE, shipped by Marc Chapoutier
- CÔTE DU RHÔNE, shipped by Delas Frères

The Great, Dominant White Wines—Always Expensive

THE SUPREME WHITES OF BURGUNDY

Character: greatest of all white Burgundies come from the southern district of Côte d'Or and are associated with the name "Montrachet"—a name now so valuable that it is used and hyphenated in a dozen different ways covering a range of wines from the very greatest to the relatively ordinary; the greatest, in the best years, are incomparable—liquid and transparent gold, with prices to match. **Basic Rule for Buying:** Follow the usual sequence for Burgundies—look first for name of village, then for *precise* name of vineyard, remembering that even the great "Le Montrachet" vineyard, probably the most valuable 18 acres in the world, is divided among sixteen owners, making in effect sixteen different wines. The following list begins with the supreme wines, then passes down to nearly-as-great wines from other parts of Burgundy.

The Five Great Vineyards in the Twin Villages of Chassagne-Montrachet and Puligny-Montrachet

LE MONTRACHET, the most celebrated dry-white-wine vineyard in the world, the only one legally permitted to use the famous name alone and unhyphenated; in our opinion its most elegant and powerful wines are being produced and shipped under the separate labels of four of its sixteen owners: the Marquis de Laguiche, the Baron Thénard, the Comte de Moucheron, and Bouchard

LE CHEVALIER-MONTRACHET, the second greatest, its rarest and most memorable wines produced and shipped under the separate labels of two of its ten owners: Joseph Déleger-Lagrange and Bouchard

LE BÂTARD-MONTRACHET, the third greatest, with fifteen owners producing wines often undistinguishable from those of the first two

CLOS DU CAILLERET, shipped by Joseph Drouhin

LES PUCELLES, not considered as great as the others, but often producing magnificent wines

From the Village of Aloxe-Corton

CORTON-CHARLEMAGNE, said to have been first planted with grapes by the great emperor himself in the eighth century, its wines still magnificent, produced and shipped under the label of Louis Latour

From the Village of Meursault

LES PERRIÈRES, one of the most delicate and fragrant of all the white wines of Burgundy

From the Village of Vougeot

CLOS BLANC DE VOUGEOT, the only white wine produced among the many great reds of the Clos Vougeot

THE GREATEST OF CHABLIS

Character: a dry white wine, one of the most famous of all. Chablis, named for the district in northern Burgundy, is a wine which the world has almost loved to death. Amidst the flood of often fair, but generally mediocre wines, a few vineyards in a small area continue to produce wines that are among the greatest of France. **Basic Rule for Buying:** Look for the names of those few vineyards that are always marked *grand cru* on the label—for lesser Chablis, see the middle-range section. **Our choice:**

CHABLIS GRAND CRU LES CLOS

CHABLIS GRAND CRU LES GRENOUILLES

CHABLIS GRAND CRU PREUSES
CHABLIS GRAND CRU VALMUR
CHABLIS GRAND CRU VAUDÉSIR

THE GREAT WHITE WINES OF GERMANY

Character: rich and fruity, ranging from light to supremely luscious. Although the most consistently great wines come from only three vineyards in the Rheingau district, they offer a choice, not of three wines but often of twenty, each vineyard producing several types each year, from light dinner wines to superb, sweet dessert wines, literally worth their weight in gold. **Basic Rule for Buying:** Name of vineyard is all-important, because each has only one owner. Remember that the word *Schloss* is often an essential part of the title, since, for example, smaller vineyards of village of Johannisberg may use its name on quite ordinary wine—various wines of each great vineyard are signaled partly by a color-coding system of bottle capsules and partly by definitive words used on labels. **Our choice:**

SCHLOSS JOHANNISBERG, the greatest name in German wines, but not to be confused with wines labeled simply "Johannisberg" (without the "Schloss"). The great wines of the *Schloss* are produced and shipped under the label of Fürst von Metternich. In deciding between one bottle and another on the wine merchant's shelves, one can rely on the following sequence of color-coding of the capsules:

Red capsule—the simplest and least expensive
Green capsule, slightly richer, then continuing through . . .
Pink
Orange
White
Sky-blue
Gold capsule, the best and most expensive

STEINBERG (Stone Mountain), probably the best known German wine all over the world, the vineyard owned by the German state. The various types of wine each year are indicated by the word immediately following the name "Steinberg" on the label, in the following sequence:

Steinberger—the simplest and least expensive
Steinberger Kabinett, slightly richer, then continuing through . . .
Steinberger Spätlese Kabinett
Steinberger Auslese
Steinberger Trockenbeerenauslese, the best and most expensive

SCHLOSS VOLLRADS, producing wines of a magnificent fruitiness. Two bottles of the same year can be judged from the sequence of the following color code of the capsules:

Green, either solid, or striped with silver or gold, for the three grades, in ascending order, of the simplest and least expensive

Red, either solid, or striped with silver or gold, for the three grades of the slightly richer group of wines

Blue, either solid, or striped with silver or gold, for the 3 grades of the richest and most expensive group

The Middle Range of Fine White Wines—At Medium Prices

THE LESS-THAN-GREAT, BUT STILL FINE CHABLIS

Character: the middle range of fine Chablis, with strongly individual characteristics, are far above the general run of the mass-Chablis. **Basic Rule for Buying:** Look for names of vineyards classified on the label as *premier cru.* **Our choice:**

CHABLIS PREMIER CRU MONTÉE DE TONNERRE

CHABLIS PREMIER CRU MONTMAIN

CHABLIS PREMIER CRU MONT-DE-MILIEU

THE OTHER FINE WHITE WINES OF BURGUNDY

Character: wines that vary from the near-great to the simple; blended community and district wines of which some represent an extremely good value. **Basic Rule for Buying:** As with other Burgundies, look for village name first, then exact name of vineyards, coupled with names of outstanding owners and shippers. **Our choice:**

From the Central Wine Town of Beaune

CLOS DES MOUCHES, famous both for red and white wines, but the white are the more distinguished, shipped by Joseph Drouhin

The Fine Vineyard of the Village of Meursault

LES CHARMES, especially the wines produced and shipped under the label of the Comte de Moucheron

And from the Village of Puligny-Montrachet

LES COMBETTES, especially the wines shipped by Jean de Besse, or the Comte de Moucheron

From the Twin Villages of Pouilly and Fuissé

Character: excellent, lighter white wine, generally less expensive than those of the Côte d'Or above. **Basic Rule for Buying:** Since we are now in the general Beaujolais area, basic Beaujolais rules apply; avoid wines simply labeled "Pouilly-Fuissé," and look for guarantee of quality of named vineyard, community, or reliable shipper. **Our choice:**

POUILLY-FUISSÉ LE CLOS

POUILLY-FUISSÉ "COURONNE D'OR"

POUILLY-FUISSÉ CHÂTEAU DE FUISSÉ

POUILLY-FUISSÉ LE PARADIS

POUILLY-FUISSÉ, shipped by Cruse

POUILLY-FUISSÉ, shipped by Joseph Drouhin

POUILLY-FUISSÉ, shipped by Louis Latour

Community and District Wines

And at the lower range of quality and price are the community and district wines, named simply for the places where the grapes were grown from which they were blended. **Our choice:**

MEURSAULT, especially the wines shipped by Joseph Drouhin

PULIGNY-MONTRACHET PREMIER CRU, especially the wines shipped by Leflaive

THE FINE WHITE WINES OF GERMANY

From the Valley of the River Rhine

Character: some of the freshest and fruitiest of all white wines, with an enormous range of types, qualities, and prices, from sharply dry wines, light as a zephyr, to the most magnificent aromatic sweet wines. **Basic Rule for Buying:** With a very few exceptions, the first word of the main title on a label is the name of the town (always with suffix *er* meaning "from") from which the wine comes; then comes name of vineyard within that town; last, one of standard German words describing the type of wine, from dry to very sweet. Avoid world-renowned towns with wines so popular that prices are inflated; learn the names of famous wine families so jealous of their reputations that they maintain impeccable standards of value at every price level, and remember that vintage years are most important in Germany: less sunshine means drier wines; more sunshine, sweeter. Ask wine merchant's advice.

WARNING: The word *Liebfraumilch* in itself is no guarantee of quality; it can be used freely by any irresponsible producer and should be studiously avoided, as it is by the good producers. **Our choice:**

DEIDESHEIMER KALKHOFEN, produced and shipped under the label of the Bürklin-Wolf family

ELTVILLER RHEINBERG, usually an excellent value

ERBACHER SCHLOSS REINHARTSHAUSEN

ERBACHER MARKOBRUNN

FORSTER JESUITENGARTEN, produced and shipped under the label of the Basserman-Jordan family

FORSTER KIRCHENSTÜCK, also from Basserman-Jordan

HATTENHEIMER ENGELMANNSBERG

HOCHHEIMER NEUBERG

RÜDESHEIMER BERG ROTTLAND, usually an excellent value

RÜDESHEIMER KLOSTERKIESEL

From the Valleys of the Rivers Moselle, Ruwer, and Saar

Character: some of the lightest, most refreshing, and fruitiest white wines of the world; in good years, magnificent—in years with too little sunshine, wines almost-sharply dry. **Basic Rule for Buying:** Same as for the Rhine, above. In between the world-famous towns are a few villages and smaller towns not yet popular enough to inflate prices of some superb wines.

WARNING: A wine labeled "Moselblümchen" is to the Moselle what a "Liebfraumilch" is to the Rhine, see preceding entry. **Our choice** (names of towns again appear first):

AYLER BISCHÖFLICHES KONVIKT, a name which reflects church ownership

AYLER BISCHÖFLICHES PRIESTERSEMINAR

EITELSBACHER MARIENHOLZ

LEIWENER LAURENTIUSLAY

WEHLENER SONNENUHR, one of the famous names, which must be included in any Moselle list, on the strength of the extraordinary quality of the wines produced and shipped under the label of the Prüm family

The Refreshing German Steinwein

Character: a charmingly light and clean wine which is one of Germany's simpler wine pleasures—always comes in famous fat flagon called *Bocksbeutel* (goat's neck), the best from city of Würzburg in the province of Franconia. **Our choice:**

FRANCONIAN STEINWEIN IM BOCKSBEUTEL, from the city of Würzburg, one of the best labels with the name "Spital zum Heiligen Geist" (Spittle of the Holy Ghost)

THE DRY WHITE WINES OF BORDEAUX

Character: fine wines of strong individuality—not so dry as to be sharp; faint sweetness never enough to cloy during the meal. Usually called "Graves," which is the name of the district where they are produced. **Basic Rule for Buying:** Choose by names of vineyards—some vintage years are drier than others—ask wine merchant's advice as to what he has in stock. **Our choice:**

CHÂTEAU CARBONNIEUX

CHÂTEAU CHEVALIER

CHÂTEAU OLIVIER

THE DRY WHITE WINES OF THE VALLEY OF THE RIVER LOIRE

Character: the two best white wines of the Loire are called "Pouilly Fumé" and "Sancerre," Pouilly Fumé, in fact, having a slight gunflint smokiness. **Our choice:**

POUILLY FUMÉ CHÂTEAU DU NOZET

POUILLY-BLANC-FUMÉ LES LOGES, produced and shipped under the label of Jacques Mard

SANCERRE, shipped by Bailly

THE FINE WHITE WINES OF ALSACE

Character: beautifully light and refreshing wine, often among best values in fine whites. The finest always have "varietal" labels, name of grape indicating type of wine: Sylvaner, simplest and least-expensive; Riesling, fuller and more luxurious; Traminer and Gewürztraminer. **Basic Rule for Buying:** Since there are virtually no named vineyards in Alsace and almost all wines are blended, names of famous shippers are all-important guarantees of quality. **Our choice:**

SYLVANER: see under "Everyday Wines" on page 692

RIESLING, shipped by Dopff & Irion from Riquewihr

RIESLING, shipped by Hugel from Riquewihr

RIESLING, shipped by Jerome Lorentz of Bergheim

TRAMINER, shipped by Dopff & Irion from Riquewihr

TRAMINER, shipped by Jerome Lorentz of Bergheim

GEWÜRZTRAMINER CLOS DES SORCIÈRES, shipped by Dopff & Irion from Riquewihr

GEWÜRZTRAMINER CUVÉE SPECIALE, shipped by Jerome Lorentz of Bergheim

THE HONEYED WHITE WINES OF THE RHONE VALLEY

Character: extraordinary wines with color of pale gold and distant fragrance of honeysuckle. **Basic Rule for Buying:** General district name, "Hermitage," refers to single steep hill with large number of terraced vineyards, some fine, some poor; reasonable guarantee of quality comes with added name of a particular vineyard or reliable shipper. **Our choice:**

HERMITAGE BLANC "CHANTE-ALOUETTE," shipped by Marc Chapoutier

HERMITAGE BLANC, shipped by Delas

THE ELEGANT WHITE WINE OF SWITZERLAND

Character: famous wine, light and refreshing, from the Canton of Vaud. **Our choice:**

SWISS DÉZALEY, from the wine district of Lavaux, shipped by Chatenay from Neuchâtel

The Reasonably Priced Everyday White Wines

THE GOOD AMERICAN WHITES

Character: many superbly refreshing, the best so much in demand that they are hard to find. Absolutely as good as similar-priced European equivalents. **Basic Rule for Buying:** Best American wines carry "varietal" labels, in which name of grape defines character of wine. In the following list, type of wine is noted first, then grape name as indication of character, and, finally, a note as to availability of wine. Urge wine merchant to order some if not in stock. **Our choice:**

White Wines from California

LIGHT PINOT BLANC, from the vineyards of Inglenook in the Napa Valley, generally available in the West and to a limited extent in major Midwestern and Eastern cities

LIGHT PINOT BLANC, from the Wente vineyards in the Livermore Valley, generally available all over the country

FULL-BODIED PINOT CHARDONNAY, from Inglenook, generally available in the West and to a limited extent in major Midwestern and Eastern cities

FULL-BODIED PINOT CHARDONNAY, from the vineyards of Mayacamas, above the Napa Valley, one of the finest of American wines, but usually available only in California

FULL-BODIED PINOT CHARDONNAY, from the Stony Hill vineyards 6,000 feet above the Napa Valley, the finest American wine we have ever tasted, but usually available only in California

FULL-BODIED PINOT CHARDONNAY, from the Wente vineyards in the Livermore Valley, only a shade below the finest and generally available all over the country, but often in short supply because of the great demand among wine-lovers

LIGHT RIESLING "BEAUCLAIR," from the Beaulieu vineyards in the Napa Valley, generally available all over the country

LIGHT JOHANNISBERG RIESLING, from the vineyards of Louis M. Martini in the Napa Valley, generally available all over the country.

LIGHT SAUVIGNON BLANC, from the Concannon vineyards in the Livermore Valley, generally available in the West and to a limited extent in major Eastern cities

The Native White Wines of New York State

Character: could be called "truly American country wines," slightly earthy and "peasant" in character, but uncomplicated and refreshing. **Basic Rule for Buying:** Choose wines by lilting names of grapes and explore them all until personal preferences emerge. Avoid wines without grape name or with such general titles as "Burgundy-type" or "Vin Rouge," etc. **Our choice** (with type of wine and grape name coming first):

LIGHT DELAWARE, from the Gold Seal vineyards, generally available

LIGHT ELVIRA, from the Widmer vineyards, generally available

LIGHT MOORE'S DIAMOND, from the Great Western vineyards, generally available

LIGHT VERGENNES, from Widmer, usually in somewhat limited supply

FULLER-BODIED AND FAINTLY SWEET NIAGRA, from Widmer, generally available

INEXPENSIVE WHITE WINES FROM EUROPE

Character: many so wonderfully good at such low prices that they represent best values in all wines. **Basic Rule for Buying:** Since almost all are blended, quality can only be guaranteed by names of reliable shippers. Vintage years relatively unimportant, since wines are blended to be about the same every year. **Our choice:**

- FRENCH MUSCADET, shipped by Ackerman Laurance from southern Brittany
- ALSATIAN SYLVANER "DOMAINE VOLTAIRE," shipped by Dopff & Irion from Riquewihr
- ALSATIAN SYLVANER, shipped by Hugel from Riquewihr
- FRENCH SEYSSEL BLANC DE BLANCS, a dry and tingling mountain wine from the village of Seyssel in the Alps, shipped by Varichon & Clerc
- FRENCH BOURGOGNE ALIGOTÉ, the simplest and most charming of small blended wines from Burgundy, especially the label shipped by Jean de Besse
- FRENCH PETIT CHABLIS, the simplest blended wine from the famous district, with many labels from which to discover one's personal taste
- ITALIAN SOAVE, the beautifully light and refreshing wine from the village of Soave near Verona, especially the labels shipped either by Bertani or Bolla
- YUGOSLAV LIGHT CHIPON OF LJUTOMER, shipped by Slovenija Vino from Ljubljana
- YUGOSLAV FULLER-BODIED TRAMINER OF RADGONA, from the same shipper

Champagnes and Other Sparkling Wines

TRUE CHAMPAGNE FROM FRANCE

The Famous Names—**Basic Rule for Buying:** Every Champagne drinker seems to have his own favorites in the basic list of the great producers, each of whom usually puts out both an extremely expensive dated "vintage cuvé" and a moderately expensive undated "non-vintage":

- BOLLINGER
- HEIDSICK DRY MONOPOLE
- KRUG
- MERCIER RÉSERVE DE L'EMPEREUR
- MOËT ET CHANDON DOM PERIGNON
- MUMM CORDON ROUGE
- PERRIER-JOUET
- PIPER-HEIDSIECK
- POL ROGER BRUT SPECIAL
- POMMERY-GRENO
- ROEDERER
- TAITTINGER
- VEUVE CLICQUOT

Less Expensive French Champagnes—**Basic Rule for Buying:** There are strong reasons why it is impossible to suggest individual names of inexpensive shippers. Apart from the great names, there are about 150 small French firms in the Champagne district and the production of each is so small that national distribution in the United States is out of the question. Therefore in different states and different cities there will be different small French Champagnes. Some of the best of these are often sold under the names of the Champagne villages in which the wine was made, for example: Avize, Ay, Cramant, or Mailly. These are usually non-vintage, unblended, and often represent an extremely good value.

SPARKLING VOUVRAY FROM FRANCE

Character: a lively and lovely wine from the Loire Valley, better and more refreshing than many Champagnes. **Basic Rule for Buying:** Look for vineyard and/or shipper's names. **Our choice:**

SPARKLING VOUVRAY CHÂTEAU MONCONTOUR, usually among the finest

SPARKLING VOUVRAY CLOS LE MONT, shipped by Ackerman Laurance

SPARKLING VOUVRAY CHÂTEAU GAUDRELLE

SPARKLING VOUVRAY CLOS PARADIS

SPARKLING VOUVRAY BALZAC, shipped by Baron de Koenigswarter

SPARKLING SEKT FROM GERMANY

Character: one of the most refreshing of German sparkling wines is produced by the owner of the famous Schloss Johannisberg.

GERMAN SPARKLING SEKT SÖHNLEIN RHEINGOLD, shipped by the Fürst von Metternich

AMERICAN SPARKLING WINES

Character: two famous wines from California are every bit as good as majority of French Champagnes; two from New York State are dry and refreshing:

CALIFORNIA KORBEL "NATURE," entirely unsugared and generally considered to be the finest in the U.S.

CALIFORNIA DRY ALMADEN BLANC DE BLANCS, made entirely from Pinot Chardonnay grapes

NEW YORK STATE BRUT, from the Great Western vineyards

NEW YORK STATE BRUT, from the Taylor vineyards

True and False Rosés

Character: the magnificent brown-tinged wines of the Tavel district of the French Rhône Valley have always been and will always be the best of all *rosés*. Next, there are the very few *rosés* of Anjou, Alsace, California, and New York State that have a special character because they are made only from a single type of grape and, finally, a charming small *rosé* from Greece, which seems to be rapidly increasing in favor and distribution. **Our choice:**

TAVEL ROSÉ, shipped by Paul Blanc

TAVEL ROSÉ, shipped by Delas

TAVEL PAVILLON ROSÉ, shipped by Sichel

TAVEL ROSÉ CHÂTEAU DE TRINQUEVEDEL, shipped by Demoulin

TAVEL ROSÉ SAINT FERREOL, shipped by Bellicard

ANJOU ROSÉ DE CABERNET, shipped by Ackerman Laurance

ALSATIAN PINOT ROSÉ "CUVÉE SPECIAL," shipped by Jerome Lorenz

CALIFORNIA GRENACHE ROSÉ, from the Almaden Vineyards

NEW YORK STATE ISABELLA ROSÉ, named for the native grape, from the Great Western vineyards

GREEK RODITIS ROSÉ, shipped by Achaia Clauss from the Greek wine district of Patras

The Natural Sweet Wines for Serving After Dinner

SAUTERNES AND BARSAC FROM FRANCE

Character: most average sweet wines simply have added sugar, but natural sweet wines that draw only upon the sweetness of the grape are in an entirely different class. Among these, one French vineyard stands on a pinnacle entirely beyond competition: the Château d'Yquem, a few miles south of Bordeaux. Our list places it first, followed by some of the other great sweet wine vineyards of France. **Our choice:**

CHÂTEAU D'YQUEM

CHÂTEAU CLIMENS

CHÂTEAU COUTET

CHÂTEAU FILHOT

CHÂTEAU LA TOUR-BLANCHE

NATURAL SWEET WINES FROM CALIFORNIA

CALIFORNIA MUSCAT DE FRONTIGNAN, made from the famous sweet golden grape of the village of Frontignan in the south of France transplanted to the Livermore Valley, a sweet wine that is an exceptionally good value, from the Concannon vineyards

CALIFORNIA PREMIER SEMILLON, a most delicate natural sweet wine, from the Cresta Blanca vineyards

True After-Dinner Port from Portugal

Basic Rule for Buying: In making truly fine Port, time is the overwhelming factor. Therefore the first rule in judging a bottle of Port on the shelves of a wine merchant is to check how old it is. If there is no date on the bottle, it is at once suspect. A fine *ruby* should be from 7 to 10 years old; an outstanding *tawny,* at least 15 years old and a great *vintage,* at least 20 years old and possibly 30, 40, or 50 years. The second insurance of quality is, of course, the name of one of the great Oporto shippers. **Our choice:**

COCKBURN, SMITHES, of Vila Nova de Gaia, across the Douro River from Oporto
CROFT, of Oporto
RICHARD HOOPER, of Vila Nova de Gaia
ROBERTSON BROTHERS, of Oporto

Sweet Liqueurs Only if Guests Insist

From the enormous range of sweet spirits we usually choose one of the three which seem at least to have strongly individual characters and to have gained a certain status from historic and international acceptance:

BASQUE GREEN IZARRA, less sweet than the "yellow"
FRENCH CHARTREUSE "WHITE ELIXIR," the strongest and least sweet of the three types, often hard to find, but very fine as a concentrated essence of Chartreuse
FRENCH GRAND MARNIER "CORDON ROUGE," less sweet than the "Cordon Jaune"

Cognacs, Calvados, and Other Brandies and Distilled Eaux de Vie

COGNACS ONLY FROM COGNAC

The Famous Names—**Basic Rule for Buying:** The first warning about choosing French Cognacs is that one should never judge them by price alone. Some producers seem to pro-rate their prices according to their own estimates of the importance of their reputations! Thus, two Cognacs of precisely equal merit may vary widely in cost. Also, each of the great firms puts out several grades, each under a different trade name, and we find it useful to have a list of the names of the first-grade Cognacs of some of the principal companies. **Our choice:**

BISQUIT-DUBOUCHE "Extra"
COURVOISIER "Napoleon"
HENESSEY "Extra"
HINE "Triomphe"
MARTELL "Cordon Bleu"
MONNET "Anniversaire"
OTARD "V.S.O.P."
POLIGNAC "Réserve"
RÉMY MARTIN "Louis XIII"

The Smaller and More Individualistic Cognac Producers—**Character:** the best Cognacs we have tasted in the last few years have come, not from large and famous companies but from small, individual producers in the villages surrounding the town of Cognac, who gather and press their own grapes from their own vineyards and slowly mature their own unblended Cognacs in their own comparatively small cellars. These Cognacs have a dryness of flavor that is almost austere, a light texture and natural color that makes them quite out of the ordinary. **Basic Rule for Buying:** Unblended Cognacs are hard to find. Learn to know the various delimited Cognac areas as they appear on the labels: the phrase *Grande Champagne,* or *Grande Fine Champagne,* on a label means that the Cognac is made only from grapes grown in the finest area, with the best soil, while *Petite Champagne* on the label means that the grapes were from the second best area, *Borderies* means third, and *Les Bois* means fourth. These are legally enforced definitions and can be entirely trusted. We have found at least one superb small Cognac in New York which might, although supplies are limited, be specially ordered:

COGNAC GRANDE FINE CHAMPAGNE "UNBLENDED RESERVE" M. RAGNAUD "DOMAINE DE LA VOUTE," distilled, aged and bottled by M. Ragnaud from his own grapes in his own cellars in the village of Ambleville

CALVADOS FROM NORMANDY

Basic Rule for Buying: The main requirement for the famous French apple brandy is that it be smooth and fine by being thoroughly aged. **Our choice:**

CALVADOS ARC DE TRIOMPHE, ten years old, shipped by Boulard from the town of Yvetot

CALVADOS BELLOWS "VALLÉE D'AUGE," five years old, shipped by Morin from the village of Ivry-la-Bataille

CALVADOS BUSNEL "PAYS D'AUGE," twelve years old, shipped from Pont l'Eveque

ARMAGNAC FROM ARMAGNAC

Basic Rule for Buying: In the French brandy district of Armagnac, there are also three legally delimited districts representing on the label of any bottle the three grades of quality: first, the district of *Bas-Armagnac* around the small town of Gers for the top grade; second, the district of *Ténarèze,* and, third, the district of *Haut-Armagnac.* The finest producers are small and cannot have wide distribution, so the search for the best labels must be an individual pursuit. **Our choice** of larger producers with fairly wide distribution:

ARMAGNAC MARQUIS DE CAUSSADE, ten years old, shipped from Gers in the Bas-Armagnac

ARMAGNAC SEMPE, thirty years old, shipped by Sabazan

MARC FROM BURGUNDY

Character: *marc* is used to describe a grape brandy distilled from the *must* of wine grapes, and it has a most attractive musty character. Various *marcs* are made in all parts of France. **Basic Rule for Buying:** The best available in the U.S. come from Burgundy. **Our choice:**

MARC DE BOURGOGNE DOMAINE DE LA ROMANÉE-CONTI, a magnificent brandy, shipped by the famous vineyard in Vosne-Romanée

MARC À LA CLOCHE, shipped by Jules Belin in the village of Premeaux in Burgundy

THE FAMOUS FRUIT BRANDIES

Our choice from the enormous range of fruit brandies, or *eaux de vie:*

FRENCH FRAMBOISE, the brandy distilled from raspberries

FRENCH MIRABELLE, from the small golden plums of Alsace

FRENCH PRUNELLE, from the sloe berry

SWISS WILLIAMINE, the superb brandy that completely captures the flavor and fragrance of the Williams pear, shipped by Morand from the village of Martigny. This is often hard to find, but can be ordered. There is also a German version . . .

GERMAN WILLIAMS BIRANNEN BRANTWEIN, shipped by Kammer-Kirsch from Karlsruhe

ONE GIN WITH PERSONALITY

Character: perhaps the one gin left in the world that has not been "purified" to the color and taste of water and retains such an individual and dominant character that it can never be used as a mixer, but can be sipped, we think, as an ice-cold after-dinner *eaux de vie:*

BOLS "GENEVER" GIN, shipped, in tall ceramic crocks, by Lucas Bols of Amsterdam

RUMS AS FINE AS BRANDY

Character: extremely fine rums, still being made in the West Indies and around the Caribbean, should be treated with as much respect as a fine brandy. **Our choice:**

GUYANA DARK DEMARARA, aged for fifteen years until it reaches 151 proof (slightly more than 75 per cent alcohol), making it one of the strongest of all spiritous drinks, shipped by Lemon Hart of London

JAMAICAN "THREE-DAGGERS," the same age and proof, shipped by Wray & Nephew from Kingston, Jamaica

JAMAICAN "FIFTEEN YEARS OLD," 86 proof, shipped by Lemon Hart

JAMAICAN "SPECIAL RESERVE FIFTEEN YEARS OLD," 86 proof, shipped by Wray & Nephew

MARTINIQUE "PLANTATION SAINT JAMES," shipped from Fort-de-France

PUERTO RICAN "RON DEL BARRILITO," shipped by Fernandez Bayamon

The Greatest Whiskeys from Scotland

Character: "Highland straight malts," the truly authentic whiskeys of Scotland, are a very far cry from the normal "blended Scotch" and most connoisseurs are agreed that "The Glenlivet" is the smoothest and silkiest whiskey in the world. Violent controversy, however, always surrounds "Laphroaig" (pronounced Lafroyg), which we, among many afficionados, consider to be a kind of concentrated essence of all Scotch whiskeys, while others consider it undrinkable. The other straight malt whiskeys we recommend are more conservative, but nonetheless fine. **Basic Rule for Buying:** There are three grades of Glenlivet: 1. the famous "The Glenlivet"; 2. distilleries that use the name hyphenated; 3. distilleries that use the name as part of the address. Also get to know the names of famous whiskey-producing families, jealous of their reputations. **Our choice:**

THE GLENLIVET, aged for twelve years, produced and shipped under the label of George Smith of Glenlivet Parish

LAPHROAIG, aged for ten years, distilled on the island of Islay

GLENFARCLAS, aged for ten years, distilled and shipped under the label of the Grant family on Speyside in Banff

GLENFIDDICH, aged for eight years, distilled and shipped under the label of the Grant family from Dufftown

GLEN GRANT, aged for twelve years, also distilled in the Glenlivet valley, shipped from Moray

MACALLAN-GLENLIVET, aged for twelve years

AN INDEX OF MARKETING AND MAIL-ORDER SOURCES

EDITOR'S NOTE: *This index is accurate as it goes to print. Even so, there are bound to be changes—although for the most part these stores are family institutions and should not have strayed far. Many of the ingredients are easier to find because of the proliferation of fancy and unusual foods and ingredients in local markets and specialty shops around the country in recent years. However, this mail-order list should provide a source for almost anything the reader has difficulty in obtaining.*

THE MAIL-ORDER catalogue has been so much a part of American life for so many years that it seems quite natural for gourmets to use the mails to bring them their rare and delicate gastronomic pleasures. In making out any list of domestic and foreign sources of rare delicacies, one can hardly avoid beginning with the shop that is generally considered to be the first fancy-food store of New York City, an international version of an old-fashioned general store. The Trinacria Importing Company, 415 Third Avenue, succeeds in compressing into the space of a small neighborhood shop more activity and a larger stock of exotic foods than would seem possible within the bounds of human ingenuity. It is a greengrocery with fresh fruits and vegetables, a sandwich bar dispensing "heroes" with fantastic homemade fillings, and a cheese shop. There is also a kitchen-equipment department, which literally hangs from the ceiling and includes Moorish *couscoussières* from North Africa and hand-woven bread baskets from Madeira. These departments are linked by aisles so narrow between the tall banks of shelves and storage cabinets that one rubs shoulders with canisters of Chinese mung beans, jars of Banda mace shavings, or Mexican fried hot chiles, or English marrow-ginger jam, or Turkish fava beans, bottles of Syrian flower water, or a pot of Indian vindaloo curry paste. Rounding a corner, one may stumble over a 300-pound provolone cheese, or a sack of Indian Patna rice. Everything is organized according to a master plan known only to the owner, Louise Bono, who can produce the rarest item from an obscure corner of the store, and is meticulous in filling mail orders. Other stores listed below generally specialize in the foods of a particular country or region. Trinacria seems to cover the world.

Here is our list of such exceptional stores and reliable suppliers of the unusual items mentioned in this book:

ABALONE

Available fresh only in California, but shipped canned under reliable "Calsea" label and can be bought in many Chinese food markets:

In New York: Wo Fat, 16 Bowery, New York City

or can be ordered from:

Marine Products, Box 81246, San Diego, California

AMARETTI DI SARONNO

Famous Italian small almond-vanilla macaroons: *see* ITALIAN SPECIALTIES

ARAB AND MIDDLE EAST SPECIALTIES

Most can be shipped by mail from:

The Garden of Delights, 1192 Lexington Avenue, New York City
Mr. Christopher Sotiro, The House of Yemen, 370 Third Avenue, New York City
Mr. Kerope Kalustyan, 123 Lexington Avenue, New York City
The Malko Brothers, 197 Atlantic Avenue, Booklyn, New York
Sahadi's, 187 Atlantic Avenue, Boooklyn, New York

Arab honey pastries cannot normally be sent by mail; one must explore for local sources. We get ours from:

The Damascus Bakery, 195 Atlantic Avenue, Brooklyn, New York

However, one type of Arab honey-nut cake, a solid *baklava,* can be mailed. We order from:

Malko Brothers, 197 Atlantic Avenue, Brooklyn, New York

A more adventurous way is to order Turkish candies (including superb *halvah* and *loukoumi,* said to be made by the secret recipe of the Caliph of Baghdad!) direct from the famous *pastahane* (confectioner):

Haci Bekir pastahane, Atatürk Bulvari, Ankara, Turkey

AROMATICS

Apart from our local specialty shops, we order hard-to-get herbs and spices from:

David Kobos, The Kobos Company, The Water Tower, 5331 S.W. Macadam, Portland, Oregon
H. Roth & Son, Lekvar by the Barrel, 1577 First Avenue, New York City
Mrs. Barbara Boyer, Edibles, 2246 North Clark Street, Chicago, Illinois

For herb plants, *see* HERBS, FRESH

ARROWROOT, GROUND

Available in fancy-food stores, or by mail from:

Trinacria Importing Company, 415 Third Avenue, New York City

BACON, DARK SMOKED, SLAB: *see* HAMS AND BACONS

BAMBOO SHOOTS: *see* CHINESE SPECIALTIES

BATH OLIVER BISCUITS: *see* BISCUITS, ENGLISH

BEANS AND LEGUMES, DRIED

The more unusual types (including Argentinian jumbo lentils), if not available locally, can be ordered by mail from:

H. Roth & Son, Lekvar by the Barrel, 1577 First Avenue, New York City

BESAN, INDIAN CHICK-PEA FLOUR: *see* INDIAN AND INDONESIAN SPECIALTIES

BISCUITS, ENGLISH

Bath Oliver, thin ginger, and wheat malt are among the last handmade biscuits in the world; sometimes they are available in fancy-food stores, or can be shipped in tins direct from the makers:

Fortt and Son, 5 Milsom Street, Bath, Somerset, England.

BOMBAY DUCK: *see* INDIAN AND INDONESIAN SPECIALTIES

BOUILLON CUBES AND CONSOMMÉ MIXES

We find the best labels are Knorr, Liebig, and Telma.

BRANDADE DE MORUE: *see* SALT COD

BREAD, BLACK RYE: *see* RUSSIAN AND EAST EUROPEAN SPECIALTIES

BUCKWHEAT GROATS: *see* RUSSIAN AND EAST EUROPEAN SPECIALTIES

BUTCHERS, FANCY AND FOREIGN, IN NEW YORK

Czechoslovakian:

Bohemian liver sausage

Krakauer sausage

Kurowycky Meat Market, 124 First Avenue, New York City

Franco-Italian: *see also* PÂTÉS

Molinari Brothers, 776 Ninth Avenue, New York City

French:

Bacon, dark smoked slab

Game birds, including guinea hen
Saucissons à l'ail (garlic sausage)
Squab
Venison
Arsène Tingaud, 1070 Second Avenue, New York City
German: *see also* GERMAN SPECIALTIES
Schaller & Weber, 1654 Second Avenue, New York City
Hungarian:
Debrecen *kolbasz* sausage, cooked or uncooked
Paprikás speck (spiced pork)
Jossef Mertl, 1508 Second Avenue, New York City
Italian (including sausages of many types):
Ottomanelli's Meat Market, 281 Bleecker Street, New York City
Polish (many sausages, including):
Kielbasa
Kiszka, meat- and wheat-filled
Krakowska salami
Pork krayana
Smoked *siekana*
Kurowycky Meat Market, 124 First Avenue, New York City

CAKES BY AIR FROM VIENNA

Two famous Viennese pastry houses ship one of their supreme specialties direct to U.S.—*Sacher Torte,* apricot-filled, chocolate-covered layer cake named for its inventor, Franz Sacher, chef to Prince von Metternich. Two bakeries have been fighting each other for years in the courts over which owns rights to the original recipe; both accept airmail orders. In our experience, the rich and delicate cake arrived beautifully packed and in perfect condition:

Charles Demel and Sons, Kohlmarkt 14, Vienna, Austria.
Confiserie Sacher, Philharmoniker Strasse 4, Vienna, Austria.

CAMARONES SECOS: *see* SPANISH AND LATIN AMERICAN SPECIALTIES

CANADA GOOSE: *see* GAME BIRDS AND OTHER ANIMALS

CHEESES

Buying cheese is really a local and personal business; one must inspect the cheese and taste it. Get to know your own stores. In New York City visit:

Ed Edelman, The Ideal Cheese Shop, 1205 Second Avenue, New York City

During the colder months it is possible to order cheese by mail direct from England and France:

English cheeses:

The Export Manager, Fortnum and Mason's, 181 Picadilly, London, England

The Export Manager, Paxton and Whitfield's, 93 Jermyn Street, London, England

French cheeses—the best-known cheese merchant will send lists and advise which cheeses are forbidden entry into the U.S.:

M. Pierre H. Androuët, Le Fromager Androuët, 41 Rue d'Amsterdam, Paris, France

Greek cheeses:

Feta and kasseri: *see* GREEK SPECIALTIES

Hungarian cheese:

Liptauer: *see* HUNGARIAN SPECIALTIES

Spanish cheese:

Queso Manchego (a rare ewe's-milk cheese) from:

Mr. Jesus Moneo, Casa Moneo, 210 West Fourteenth Street, New York City

CHICK-PEA FLOUR, BESAN: *see* INDIAN SPECIALTIES

CHILE PEPPERS, MEXICAN: *see* SPANISH AND LATIN AMERICAN SPECIALTIES

CHINESE SPECIALTIES

We order from these stores in New York:

Kam Man Chinese Supermarket, 200 Canal Street, New York City
Little Mandarin Foods, 133 West Thirteenth Street, New York City
Wing Fat, 35 Mott Street, New York City
Wo Fat, 16 Bowery, New York City
Yuit Hing Grocery, 23 Pell Street, New York City

CHOCOLATE, MEXICAN: *see* SPANISH AND LATIN AMERICAN SPECIALTIES

CHOCOLAT MEUNIER

French bitter chocolate; available from fancy-food stores

CHORICES: *see* NEW ORLEANS SPECIALTIES

CHORIZO: *see* SPANISH AND LATIN AMERICAN SPECIALTIES

CHRISTSTOLLEN: *see* GERMAN SPECIALTIES

COCONUT CHIPS, TOASTED: *see* INDIAN AND INDONESIAN SPECIALTIES

COCONUT WITH PEANUTS, SPICED: *see* INDIAN AND INDONESIAN SPECIALTIES

COFFEE BEANS, BLENDED AND ROASTED TO ORDER

The following merchants will send lists and can indefinitely repeat a personal blend once established:

Empire Coffee Mills, 486 Ninth Avenue, New York City

The House of Yemen, 370 Third Avenue, New York City

McNulty's Tea and Coffee Shop, 109 Christopher Street, New York City

Schapira's Coffee Company, 117 West Tenth Street, New York City

Mrs. Barbara Boyer, Edibles, 2246 North Clark Street, Chicago, Illinois

CORN-BELLY SALT PORK

In New York: Arsène Tingaud, 1070 Second Avenue

CORNICHONS, FRENCH

Baby sour pickles bottled by Dessaux Fils of Orléans; available from fancy-food stores

CORNMEAL, COARSE WATER-GROUND: *see* GRAINS

CORN SCRAPER

Called "Lee's Corn Cutter and Creamer," by mail from: **Lee Manufacturing Company, P.O. Box 20222, Dallas, Texas**

COUSCOUS: *see* ARAB AND MIDDLE EAST SPECIALTIES

CRAB BOIL, NEW ORLEANS: *see* NEW ORLEANS SPECIALTIES

CRACKED WHEAT: *see* GRAINS

CRAWFISH, LOUISIANA BAYOU

Shipped frozen by air express, from:

Don's Crawfish, 301 East Vermilion, Lafayette, Louisiana

CRAYFISH, WISCONSIN:

Shipped live by refrigerated air or rail express from:

The Wisconsin Fishing Co., Green Bay, Wisconsin

See also SCANDINAVIAN SPECIALTIES

CREOLE MUSTARD: *see* NEW ORLEANS SPECIALTIES

CRYSTAL SALT

Coarse crystal salt, or sea salt, or, in French recipes, *gros sel,* comes in best quality from salt marshes of England or France. It is widely available but can be ordered from one of the reliable London specialist shops:

Fortnum and Mason, 181 Piccadilly, London, England

Or *gros sel* from the famous Paris fancy-food store:

Maison Hédiard, 21 Place de la Madeleine, Paris, France

DOW SEE: *see* CHINESE SPECIALTIES

DÜSSELDORFER SENF MUSTARD: *see* GERMAN SPECIALTIES

DUTCH SPECIALTIES

We order from:

The Dutch Cupboard, 273 North Eighth Street, Prospect Park, New Jersey

EMPING MELINDJO: *see* INDIAN AND INDONESIAN SPECIALTIES

FENUGREEK: *see* INDIAN AND INDONESIAN SPECIALTIES

GAME BIRDS AND OTHER ANIMALS

We order game (including Canada goose and venison) from one of the most reliable of the mail-order firms, which will send a printed list and is experienced in shipping to all parts of the country:

Mr. Rudy Czimer, Czimer Foods, R.R. #1, P.O. Box 285, Lockport, Illinois

Locally in New York, limited supplies of farm-bred game birds are available from:

Morganbesser Brothers, 109–25 Forty-sixth Avenue, Corona, Queens, New York

The Village Live Poultry Market, 205 Thompson Street, New York City

GARAM-MASSALA: *see* INDIAN AND INDONESIAN SPECIALTIES

GERMAN SPECIALTIES

Available by mail from the fine stores in New York's Yorkville district:

The Bremen House, 218 East Eighty-sixth Street, New York City

The Karl Ehmer Store, 230 East Eighty-sixth Street, New York City

Schaller & Weber, 1654 Second Avenue, New York City

and in Chicago:

Kuhn's, 3053 North Lincoln, Chicago, Illinois

Some of the finest German cakes can be ordered by mail from the famous Munich bakery formerly in Dresden; they send lists and ship by air freight:

Mr. Fritz Kreutzkamm, The Kreutzkamm Bakery, Maffeistrasse 4, Munich, West Germany

GINGER ROOT, FRESH: *see* CHINESE SPECIALTIES

GLACE DE VIANDE

A concentrate of meat gravy used in many French recipes; if unavailable, we use a bottled meat concentrate. *See* MEAT GLAZE, MEAT EXTRACT

GOOSE FAT, WHITE: *see* GERMAN SPECIALTIES

GRAINS

Apart from local specialist and health-food shops, the best grains can be obtained from:

Foods for Life, 2231 North Lincoln, Chicago, Illinois
Old Grain Mill, 1494 Third Avenue, New York City
Pete's Spice & Everything Nice, 174 First Avenue, New York City

GREEK SPECIALTIES

In New York, we shop at:

Kassos Brothers, 570 Ninth Avenue, New York City

Also, *see* ARAB AND MIDDLE EASTERN SPECIALTIES

GUMBO FILÉ: *see* NEW ORLEANS SPECIALTIES

HALVAH: *see* ARAB AND MIDDLE EAST SPECIALTIES

HAMS AND BACONS, DARK SMOKED AND AGED

Some reliable mail-order sources for sound country hams and fine pieces of dark smoked slab bacon:

Jim Kite's Hams, Wolftown, Virginia
Rose Packing Company, R.R. 3, South Barrington Road, Barrington, Illinois
Winston's, 338 Waughtown Street, Winston-Salem, North Carolina

The following firms produce and ship authentic Smithfield hams and dark smoked bacon:

Gwaltney, Inc., Smithfield, Virginia
The V.W. Joyner Company, Smithfield, Virginia
The Smithfield Packing Co., Smithfield, Virginia

And for nitrate-free hams we order from:

Burger's Smokehouse, R.F.D. 3, California, Missouri

HERBS: *see* AROMATICS

HERBS, FRESH

Fresh herb plants can be ordered from a large herb farm which ships to all parts of the country:

Nichols Garden Nursery, 1190 North Pacific Highway, Albany, Oregon

HIMBEERSAFT: *see* GERMAN SPECIALTIES *and* HUNGARIAN SPECIALTIES

HONEYS AND OTHER NATURAL SWEET SYRUPS

Buckwheat (Ukranian-style, New Jersey), clover (New Jersey), linden (New York State), raspberry (New Jersey), and wildflower (New Jersey) are honeys from the bee-hives of:

Mr. Myron Surmach, The Surma Bookshop, 11 East Seventh Street, New York City

For alfalfa, blueberry, orange blossom, Tupelo (from Georgia), write or visit:

Jack's Honey Farm Store, Asbury-Washington Road, Asbury, New Jersey

Two remarkable honeys, Clover Moorland and Heather Moorland, come by mail from England (although sometimes are available at U.S. fancy-food stores). They are grainy in texture and have a faintly bitter aftertaste. They are made by Benedictine monks and we order from:

Brother Adam, Buckfast Abbey, Buckfastleigh, Devonshire, England

From Vermont come maple sugar cream, maple hard sugar, and maple syrup; we order from:

Mr. Maynard Rogers, Jr., R.F.D. #1, Swanton Road, Swanton, Vermont

Mr. Philip Spooner, Brigham Road, St. Albans, Vermont

HUNGARIAN SPECIALTIES

The two general stores in New York's Hungarian district both send printed catalogues and ship by mail:

H. Roth & Son, 1577 First Avenue, New York City

Mr. and Mrs. Edward Weiss, The Paprikas-Weiss Store, 1546 Second Avenue, New York City

Hungarian butcher for sausages and other meats, in New York:

Jossef Mertl, 1508 Second Avenue, New York City

IKAN TERIE: *see* INDIAN AND INDONESIAN SPECIALTIES

INDIAN AND INDONESIAN SPECIALTIES

This importer in New York sends printed lists and ships by mail:

K. Kalustyan Orient Export Trading Corp., 123 Lexington Avenue, New York City

Chutneys, mango and lime pickles, curry paste and powder, can be ordered direct from this reliable exporter in India:

M. M. Poonjiaji & Company, 42 First Marine Street, Bombay, India

ITALIAN SPECIALTIES

There is one large and efficient store that will send a printed catalogue and ship almost anywhere:

Manganaro Brothers, 488 Ninth Avenue, New York City

Smaller stores are perhaps better for personal shopping. In New York we often visit:

Alleva's, 188 Grand Street, New York City

The Adamita Dominick Salumeria, 1109 First Avenue, New York City

Salumeria Biellese, 362 Eighth Avenue, New York City

Modica's Latticini, 6319 Eighteenth Avenue, Brooklyn, New York

In Chicago there is a superbly-stocked store that accepts mail orders from anywhere:

Il Conte di Savoia, 555 West Roosevelt, Chicago, Illinois

KALA-MASSALA: *see* INDIAN AND INDONESIAN SPECIALTIES

KASHA: *see* RUSSIAN SPECIALTIES

KASSELER RIPPCHEN: *see* GERMAN SPECIALTIES

KITCHEN EQUIPMENT

Apart from local shops in every corner of the U.S., one can always order esoteric items from the most famous kitchen shop in the world. It is, quite properly, in Paris—old, established, and reliable—and will send a comprehensive catalogue and ship anywhere:

E. Dehillerin & Cie., 18–20 Rue Coquillière, Paris, France

KOLBASZ SAUSAGE: *see* HUNGARIAN SPECIALTIES

KRUPUK: *see* INDIAN AND INDONESIAN SPECIALTIES

KUMQUATS, CANNED IN SYRUP: *see* CHINESE SPECIALTIES

LAVASH BREAD, ARMENIAN: *see* ARAB AND MIDDLE EAST SPECIALTIES

LEMON PICKLE, INDIAN HOT: *see* INDIAN AND INDONESIAN SPECIALTIES

LENTILS: *see* BEANS AND LEGUMES, DRIED

LINGONBERRIES, SWEDISH FRESH: *see* SCANDINAVIAN SPECIALTIES

LIPTAUER CHEESE: *see* HUNGARIAN SPECIALTIES

LOBSTERS AND CLAMS
Freshly caught; shipped by refrigerated air freight from:
Saltwater Farm, York Harbor, Maine

LOUKOUMI: *see* ARAB AND MIDDLE EAST SPECIALTIES

MANDARIN ORANGES: *see* CHINESE SPECIALTIES

MANGO CHUTNEY, INDIAN SWEET: *see* INDIAN AND INDONESIAN SPECIALTIES

MANGOES, ALPHONSE: *see* INDIAN AND INDONESIAN SPECIALTIES

MAPLE SYRUP, PURE: *see* HONEYS AND SYRUPS

MARMALADE, ENGLISH BITTER SEVILLE ORANGE
The famous name in England is Cooper's "Oxford," universally distributed in the U.S.

MASSOOR DALL: *see* INDIAN AND INDONESIAN SPECIALTIES

MEAT GLAZE, MEAT EXTRACT
If concentrate of meat gravy not available, we substitute a British bottled meat extract called "Bovril." Available from fancy-food stores.

MEATS, FANCY AND FOREIGN: *see* BUTCHERS, FANCY OR FOREIGN, IN NEW YORK

MEMBRILLO, PASTA DE: *see* SPANISH SPECIALTIES

MOSTARDA DI FRUTTA: *see* ITALIAN SPECIALTIES

MUSHROOMS, DRIED WILD
They come in small cellophane packages, imported from France or Italy, available from fancy-food stores. *See also* CHINESE SPECIALTIES

MUSHROOMS, DRIED WILD BLACK, FROM NORTH AFRICA
We order from:
Maison Hédiard, 21 Place de la Madeleine, Paris, France

MUSTARD, CREOLE: *see* NEW ORLEANS SPECIALTIES

NEW ORLEANS SPECIALTIES
We order from:

The Central Grocery, 923 Decatur Street, New Orleans, Louisiana
Creole Delicacies, P.O. Box 1042, New Orleans, Louisiana

OATMEAL, IRISH WHOLE-GRAIN AND SCOTTISH ROLLED: *see* GRAINS

OILS—OLIVE, WALNUT, ETC.

For everyday use, representing very fair value, we prefer the Greek "Minerva" olive oil—*see* GREEK SPECIALTIES

Magnificently luxurious virgin olive, walnut, and other oils can be ordered directly from France:

Maison Hédiard, 21 Place de la Madeleine, Paris, France

OLIVES, FRESH, SOLD LOOSE: *see respectively under:* GREEK SPECIALTIES, ITALIAN SPECIALTIES, *or* SPANISH SPECIALTIES

ORANGE-BLOSSOM WATER, LEBANESE: *see* ARAB AND MIDDLE EAST SPECIALTIES

OYSTERS, OLYMPIA

Tiny, delicate oysters about the size of a quarter; a great specialty of the Northwest, now being refrigerated and shipped to many parts of the country. They have a limited season and are quite expensive by air express. We write to:

The Olympia Oyster Company, Route 1, Box 500, Shellton, Washington

PAPPADUMS: *see* INDIAN AND INDONESIAN SPECIALTIES

PAPRIKA, FRESH: *see* HUNGARIAN SPECIALTIES

PASTA DE MEMBRILLO: *see* SPANISH SPECIALTIES

PÂTÉS, TERRINES, APPETIZER SAUSAGES, ETC.

We often shop at an authentic French-Niçois *charcuterie,* with its own kitchen producing many appetizer meat products—garlic sausage in pastry crust; Niçois sausage, hot; *pâté maison; rillettes de porc* (pork *pâté*); *rillon de foie* (aromatic goose and pork liver loaf):

Molinari Brothers, 776 Ninth Avenue, New York City

PEA SPROUTS: *see* CHINESE SPECIALTIES

PEDA BREAD, ARMENIAN: *see* ARAB AND MIDDLE EAST SPECIALTIES

PELMENY, SIBERIAN: *see* RUSSIAN SPECIALTIES

RICE FLOUR: *see* INDIAN AND INDONESIAN SPECIALTIES

RICE, VARIOUS TYPES

Patna long-grain: *see* INDIAN AND INDONESIAN SPECIALTIES
Persian long-grain: *see* ARAB AND MIDDLE EAST SPECIALTIES
Risotto short-grain: *see* ITALIAN SPECIALTIES

RILLETTES DE PORC: *see* PÂTÉS, ETC.

ROWAN JELLY, IMPORTED: *see* SCOTTISH SPECIALTIES

RUSSIAN AND EAST EUROPEAN SPECIALTIES

On the east side of Manhattan, there is a small Polish and Ukrainian neighborhood with several fascinating stores stocked with products that are American-made but in the old-Russian style and of very high quality:

Surma Bookshop, 11 East Seventh Street, New York City

For Polish sausages:

Kurowycky Meats, 124 First Avenue, New York City

Also for Slavic delicatessen specialties such as caviar, smoked fish, etc:

Mr. Arthur Cutler, Murray's Sturgeon Shop, 2429 Broadway, New York City

Russ and Daughters, 179 East Houston Street, New York City

SAFFRON FILAMENTS, SPANISH: *see* AROMATICS

SALT COD

The best quality in U.S. comes from Canada—found in Greek stores (where it is called *bakaliaro*), Italian (where it is *bacalà*), or Spanish (*bacalao*). In New York we order from:

The Kassos Brothers, 570 Ninth Avenue, New York City

SALT PORK, CORN-BELLY

In New York, we order from Tingaud: *see* BUTCHERS, FANCY AND FOREIGN, IN NEW YORK (FRENCH)

SAMBALS: *see* INDIAN AND INDONESIAN SPECIALTIES

SAUERKRAUT, IMPORTED GERMAN, WINE-BOILED, CANNED: *see* GERMAN SPECIALTIES

SCANDINAVIAN SPECIALTIES

We order from the long-established and reliable New York store:

Nyborg & Nelson, 937 Second Avenue, New York City

And specialized items from:

TARHONYA: *see* HUNGARIAN SPECIALTIES

TEA MERCHANTS

After almost 200 years of domination of the world tea market by famous English shippers of Mincing Lane of London, one is proud to report the appearance of at least one American company devoted to importing and blending finest tea grades; they send lists and ship by mail:

Mr. Frank Cho, The Grace Tea Company, 799 Broadway, New York City

Other reliable domestic and foreign tea merchants who ship by mail:

Simpson & Vail, 53 Park Place, New York City

Mrs. Barbara Boyer, Edibles, 2246 North Clark Street, Chicago, Illinois

Mr. H. Adrian Kramers, The Tea Planters & Importers Company, 55–56 Aldgate High Street, London, England

Also, *see* COFFEE BEANS

TELLICHERRY BLACK PEPPER (whole corns)

We think this is the best of all peppers. It can be ordered from:

White Flower Farms, Litchfield, Connecticut

TOHEROA—NEW ZEALAND GIANT CLAMS

There are severe problems in obtaining this "rarest food in the world"—call the local New Zealand consul or write to the only firm permitted to export surplus canned toheroas when available, direct from the beach where they are dug:

Meredith Brothers, Tikinui, Tekopuru, Northern Wairoa, North Auckland, New Zealand

TURKISH COFFEE: *see* COFFEE BEANS

TURMERIC, GROUND: *see* INDIAN AND INDONESIAN SPECIALTIES

TURRÓN: *see* SPANISH SPECIALTIES

TURTLE MEAT, CANNED AND FRESH

Sometimes available fresh locally; it is shipped everywhere canned from:

Mr. Andrew Paretti, Moore & Company, 166 Abington Avenue, Newark, New Jersey

VANILLA BEANS, WHOLE

Vanilla beans can be ordered directly from French importers from Madagascar:

Mr. Bernard P. Champon, L. A. Champon Company, 70 Hudson Street, Hoboken, New Jersey

VINEGARS, WINE

French *vinaigre d'Orléans* is among the best in the world: French red wine vinegar and French tarragon white wine vinegar are bottled by Dessaux Fils of Orléans.

Our most luxurious sherry vinegar is Spanish "Juan Santa Maria," bottled in Jerez de la Frontera. We order French or Spanish vinegars from:

Bloomingdale's Gourmet Shop, 1000 Third Avenue, New York City
Maison Glass, 52 East Fifty-eighth Street, New York City
Mr. Jesus Moneo, Casa Moneo, 210 West Fourteenth Street, New York City
William Poll, 1051 Lexington Avenue, New York City
S. Wagner Imports, 505 East Eighty-second Street, New York City

WALNUT OIL: *see* OILS

WHEAT: *see* GRAINS

WOODRUFF (WALDMEISTER): *see* HUNGARIAN SPECIALTIES

GENERAL INDEX

G

H

Q

T

U

V

W

Y

Z

MENU-PLANNING INDEX

REGIONAL INDEX

A NOTE ABOUT THE AUTHOR

Roy Andries de Groot was born in London and educated at St. Paul's school there and at Oxford University. In the early part of his career he worked as a news and feature writer as well as a film writer and director. When war broke out, he joined the British Ministry of Information; he suffered several eye injuries in the London blitz, which caused total blindness twenty years later. Mr. de Groot has lived in the United States since 1941 and has been an American citizen since 1948. In the forties he inherited, as the last member of an old Dutch family, an obscure title, and he is known among friends, particularly in gourmet circles, as "the Baron." He has worked for Time Inc., the State Department, and *The New York Times,* and he has lived in New York, Chicago, San Francisco, and New Orleans. A house on Bleecker Street in New York's Greenwich Village was the home of Mr. de Groot and his wife, the actress Katherine Hynes, for many years: it was there that their daughters grew up. Mr. de Groot and his wife now work together in a tower studio high above the Hudson River. Mr. de Groot is president of the International Gourmet Society, a contributing editor for food and wine for *Esquire,* and a contributing editor for *Vintage.* His latest book is *The Auberge of the Flowering Hearth.* Mr. de Groot is now completing a book about the new wave in French cooking.